FROM LONDON TO LINCOLN VIA BAGHDAD

FROM LONDON TO LINCOLN VIA BAGHDAD

The Life of Bishop Colin Dunlop
1897–1968

based on his journals, articles and letters

Francis Dunlop

AESOP Publications
Oxford

AESOP Publications
Martin Noble Editorial / AESOP
28A Abberbury Road, Oxford OX4 4ES, UK
www.aesopbooks.com

First edition published by AESOP Publications
Copyright (c) 2019 The Estate of Francis Dunlop

A catalogue record of this book is
available from the British Library.

First edition 2019

ISBN: 978-1-910301-76-0

Bishop Colin Dunlop in cope and mitre
at service in Lincoln Cathedral, c. 1960

CONTENTS

LIST OF PHOTOGRAPHS

PREFACE

OR THE LAST five or six years I have been doing research for, and then writing, a biography of my father, Bishop Colin Dunlop. The main basis of this is the collection of very interesting personal journals he kept at various points in his life, a good many family letters to my mother and her guardian, and later to me, official correspondence in the Lambeth Palace Library, and articles he published in various church papers, parish and diocesan magazines, etc. My chief aim is to try to give a rounded portrait of him as a man, but also to show what the life and work of a clergyman and dignitary involved, against the background of the early to mid twentieth century. I hope also to be able to include illustrations.

In one of his published letters, Bishop Hensley Henson writes about Colin, who had visited him in his retirement home, to Dean Alington of Durham, as follows (my italics): 'We were charmed with the Bishop of Jarrow, and would have been pleased if we could have seen more of him. *What an unusually interesting career he has had! That he should have emerged from it with such admirable balance and good sense, discloses qualities of a high order*, and he has a taking aspect and manner to provide a suitable "shop-window" for the goods beneath the counter!'

Colin's own writings are always well written, and I make extensive use of them.

Outline of life and career

Born 31 July 1897 into the family of a London merchant, trading with Burma and the Far East. Colin was the fourth child, with two brothers and two sisters. They lived in Hampstead and later in Beckenham.

When the Great War began Colin was at Radley College, but left in December 1914 to be trained as an accountant. After passing his exams with distinction he was articled in a City firm in the summer of 1916, but left almost at once to follow his two brothers and enlist in the army. He was commissioned in the East Kent Regiment (The Buffs), and then seconded to the Royal Engineers for Signals training. He was then sent out to the Somme in December 1916, and later had a spell in Flanders, being twice mentioned in despatches, once on each front. After demobilisation in January 1919 he studied History and then Theology at New College and St Stephen's House, both in Oxford.

A summary timeline from 1922 follows:

1922–27	Ordination and curacy at St Mary's, Primrose Hill, under Duncan-Jones (nearly always known as 'D-J').
1927–28	There followed short summer 'curacies' in Paris and St Moritz, before starting as domestic chaplain to Bishop Winnington-Ingram, of London. Resigned after 15 months because of the Bishop's 'soft' attitude to 'Romanising' priests.
1929	Embassy chaplain at Stockholm.
1929–32	Domestic chaplain to Bishop George Bell, of Chichester.
1932	Became engaged to Mary Geraldine O'Malley
1932–34	Civil chaplain in Baghdad
1934–36	Vicar of St Thomas's, Hove, Sussex
1935	Marriage to Mary O'Malley
1936–40	Vicar of Henfield, Sussex
1937	Appointed Wyckamical Prebend of Chichester
	Note: Between 1937 and 1946, he and Mary had four sons, of whom I am the oldest.
1940–44	Provost of St Mary's Cathedral, Edinburgh
1942	Appointed by the Air Ministry on the recommendation of the Archbishops of Canterbury and York to 1 year's special duty with the RAF as from Jan 1943.
1944–49	Bishop of Jarrow, Residentiary Canon of Durham and Archdeacon of Auckland.
1949–64	Dean of Lincoln.
1964	Retired to Henfield.
1968	Died at Chichester on 23 February from arteriosclerosis.

Colin was also the first Chairman of the Church of England Liturgical Commission, and at various times chaired the English Hymnal and other committees and advisory councils, mostly in the fields of liturgy and church ornaments, and nearly all stemming from the work of Percy Dearmer.

Note: Words and short explanations in square brackets may be found scattered throughout the text. They are inserted in material quoted from my various sources to make things clearer to the reader.

Francis Dunlop
2017

1

ANTECEDENTS

COLIN'S FATHER, David Jugurtha Dunlop, was born in Leith in 1852, the fourth of seven children. We know quite a lot about him, thanks to the journal he kept throughout his life, even though it is mainly confined to his mercantile doings. His father, James Usher Dunlop (1817–1871), was an Edinburgh wine and spirit merchant, like his grandfather, William Dunlop (1777–1839). David Jugurtha writes of James Usher that he was 'a tremendous favourite with all who knew him and a very handsome looking man'. In 1846 he married Annie Thomson, daughter of David Jugurtha Thomson, after whom Colin's father was named.

He, Colin's father, had a good education at Edinburgh High School, and then the Edinburgh Collegiate School, and in 1869 left to start work in the National Bank of Scotland in Leith. But in 1871 his father died in Algiers, where he had doubtless gone for a good supply of the alcoholically weak wines of Algeria, which it was standard practice to mix with the much stronger wines of France in order to meet the requirements of most wine-drinkers in the British Isles. His body was shipped back home to be buried in the family grave plot, bought by William Dunlop, in the Greyfriars cemetery in the heart of the old town of Edinburgh.

Annie, Colin's grandmother, was now faced with providing a free home for the three youngest of her seven children (now 15, 12 and 10) and probably David Jugurtha's two older sisters on about £350 per annum. This is what David Jugurtha says about her:

> She was adored by her childen and beloved by all who knew her – a very highly educated and intellectual woman – singularly elegant in body and refined in mind and of a beautiful, simple faith in Christ. The keynote of her life was Duty... (She) devoted herself to (her children) with such untiring unselfishness and sound judgement as won her the admiration of all friends. She never spared herself if she could help them – surely she was an angel if ever there was one on earth!

David Jugurtha now did his bit to eke out the family finances by coaching two boys in the evenings after his work at the bank. The result was overwork and pleurisy. Probably to aid his full recovery he was given:

a free trip in the Anchor Line S.S. Olympia to Alexandria touching at 'Gib', Malta, Algiers and Tunis. In February 1872, I stayed at Ramleh (near Alexandria) and Cairo for 2 months and returned via Palermo, Naples, Bologna, Turin and Mont Cenis Tunnel to Paris and so home to Leith, April 1872.

No doubt much of this was the gift of one of his mother's many relations and friends in Edinburgh.

It seems clear that David Jugurtha did not really see his future in banking, and so, in January 1873, he 'went to Knudson & Moller, grain factors, as general clerk at a salary of £60, in Nantes, France'. After a little over a year, he writes:

I came to London and got a stool in the office of Archibald Stewart, accountant [husband of one one of his father's sisters]. I lived with them at 11 Norfolk Terrace, Bayswater, and received £100 p.a. and free board and lodging. Uncle got softening of the brain and went a trip to Australia, and I then went to rooms at 8 Lismore Circus, Gospel Oak, NW (Mrs Eldridge), Jan 1875, where my brother Jim (James Bourne Dunlop) joined me, as he had come up to the (Old) Oriental Bank Corporation, London. Several of our Edinburgh friends lived next door and near us and we spent a very happy time in 'Ye Den' where Mother and one of our sisters paid us several visits.

At the beginning of 1877, he 'started in a firm of rice millers in the City'. In June they asked him to go out to their Rangoon office, but he felt his health wouldn't stand it, so stayed with them in London until 1882, when, having risen to £295 p.a., he joined the well-known firm of Russell & Co. of China and went out to their Hong Kong office, where he 'had a very good time ... and enjoyed good health'. But at the end of 1887 he started for home, as his mother was very ill, but arrived too late to see her before she died.

David Jugurtha now felt well enough established in the world of export and import merchants to get married and start a family. On 25 July 1888 he married Laura Frances Beddard. His journal entry is well worth giving here:

I met Laura at Grand Hotel, London, at the invitation of Mrs Arthur Holme, with whom and her husband (my 2nd cousin and also Laura's) I had been staying in Liverpool. I saw her photo in their house and told them that I meant to marry that beautiful creature! I then arranged with Mrs Holme and my sister Annie to take rooms at Westgate and invite Laura thither, and on 22nd May I proposed to and was accepted by her. So much for a photo. Rather smart piece of work! We spent a week's honeymoon at the Grand Hotel, Eastbourne, and then I hurried back to begin a partnership with Henry Lifton Wynne as Hide and Leather factors at 45 Bermondsey St, SE, under the style of Wynne & Dunlop. 10th Aug 1888.

He and Laura began their married life in Westcombe Park, Blackheath. Whether he had met Laura before seeing her photograph in Liverpool, he doesn't say.

Almost all the information I have about Laura's family was found on the Internet and in county Archives, since I grew up knowing almost nothing about them.[1] She had one brother, Frank Evers Beddard, who became a well-known zoologist. He was educated at Harrow and New College, Oxford, where there is a memorial wall tablet in the cloisters with the fine legend:

> To the Memory of Frank Evers Beddard, F.R.S., 1858-1925, Linnaean Medallist and Prosector of the Zoological Society, an ardent and distinguished student of Nature, and in this College, of which he was sometime a Commoner, a Pioneer of Scientific Studies.

He was taken on as a young student to record the zoological findings of the Challenger Expedition; the Linnaean Medal was awarded for his study of Oligochaetes, a group of worms, one aquatic species of which was discovered and named by him 'Bothrioneurum Iris Beddard', the name of his daughter.

Laura's father, John, was an Iron Merchant who lived in Dudley, the son of a local farmer, Samuel Beddard. John's first marriage, in 1852, to Sarah Neve Cresswell, whose father and uncle jointly ran the Tipton Ironworks, only lasted two and a half years, when his wife died of TB, six months after the death of their son, who had died very soon after birth.

In 1857 John married Emma Jones, whose father is recorded on the marriage certificate as a 'gentleman', living at Caverswall Castle, but in what capacity – owner, tenant or factor – I do not know. At this time John lived in Springfield House, in Dixon's Green, on a ridge just to the south of the old town of Dudley with a fine view of the castle on a hill to the north. It was a large house, standing in its own tree-girt grounds, its site now occupied by blocks of flats.

1857 also saw John elected Mayor of Dudley, in which capacity he seems have to acquitted himself well. However, in 1859 he was admiitted as a patient to Droitwich private Lunatic Asylum. Laura can hardly have known her father when he died in 1862. His death certificate says he had been suffering from *morbus cerebri* (brain disease!) for three years, and had had three attacks of paralysis, the third of which lasted for eight days. All this may account for why, according to the 1861 census, Laura and Frank were living with their mother in Handsworth, Birmingham, and also for the fact that John does not appear on official lists of Dudley's mayors. Most of John's fellow patients were recorded in the census as gentlemen or gentlewomen; one was a fellow of King's College, Cambridge.

After his death, Emma commemorated him with a large stained glass window in their former Parish Church, St John's, Kate's Hill, which was

---

[1] When I sent the results of my own research to Chris Smith, who was writing a second collection of *Tales from a Churchyard* to raise money for the reopening and restoration of St John's, Kate's Hill, Dudley, he found out quite a lot more about John Beddard, and I am therefore much indebted to him.

opened in 1840, and where Frank and Laura were baptised. Some time after John's death, probably before Laura became a pupil at Minshull House girls' boarding school in Beckenham, which was between Croydon and Bromley, Emma moved to London. Later, she became senile herself, and Frank's family and the Dunlops took turns to look after her in their homes.

We must now return to the Dunlops. In May 1889, they moved to 117 Alexandra Road, South Hampstead, which is almost in St John's Wood. David Jugurtha's next journal entry runs:

> 1st Apr 1891. I found Wynne (his partner of ten months) such a difficult man to work with – so jealous and irritable – that I suggested a dissolution of partnership after 2½ years of great unhappiness and arranged to become a partner for 5 years in Milne & Co, 123 Bishopsgate St, Within, EC [they are listed in a contemporary P.O. Directory as East India Merchants], and Finlay Fleming of Rangoon, Import Merchants, contributing £10,000 as my share of capital.

The entry for 1 January 1896 runs: 'Started on my own account as D.J. Dunlop & Co, 15 Great St Helen's, EC, and Dunlop & Co, Rangoon, as importers into Burma of soft goods, hardware, etc.' In 1897 he took his brother Jim into the firm and a year later David, Laura and family moved to a larger house, 50 Belsize Avenue, Hampstead. Later in the year they moved the business into larger premises in Bishopsgate itself, instead of what was the maze of little alleys that made up Great St Helen's (whose plan and constituent buildings have entirely disappeared now, except for St Helen's Church and its immediate surrounds), while in Rangoon 'we steadily worked up a very important and remunerative trade'.

In October 1900 he felt relaxed enough to go on a bicycle tour with Laura (who had now had all her five children) to Oxford, Stratford on Avon, Dudley and Kenilworth. In November he went out to Rangoon for four months and, on the way home next year holidayed again with Laura, this time on the French Riviera. They got home in time 'to take the bairns to Swanage for Easter holidays' and again in the summer holidays. In the autumn he 'went to Rodono, St Mary's Loch, Selkirkshire, and had a fortnight's rough shooting' with his youngest sister (Jemima Jane Algeria Paterson) and her husband.

In 1902, having admitted William Cotterell in Rangoon as his partner in the firm, the idyll was abruptly broken, and he:

> had to hurry back to London as business in Rangoon was terribly bad – our overdraft to the national Bank of India was increasingly large – and they were beginning to get alarmed and to reduce our facilities. My fatal error was in allowing Cotterell to start the Burma ironworks in 1901, as we could not afford to finance these as well as our own business at such a critical time, and despite my instructions that we were not to finance them, and Cotterell's assurances that he would not do so, the blackguard involved us to such an extent that he fell ill (haemoplagia on the left side of the brain), had to return home, and my brother

Jim ... had to go to Rangoon in July to take charge and look into affairs. He found out so many disgraceful irregularities on the part of Cotterell that we kicked him out of the firm in Jan 1903, as the bank said they would close our account if he were allowed to go back to Rangoon again as partner. ... By agreement – in view of his having had a stroke of paralysis – we remitted his indebtedness to the firm (£3-4000) and agreed not to prosecute him for his irregularities, and assigned him a certain amount p.a. for the rest of the partnership term, and he on his part bound himself to have no further business with Rangoon, and especially with our dealers.

But David Jugurtha had now made another costly mistake.

As it was evident that we must get rid of the Burma Ironworks, and Cotterell asseverated that he could dispose of them to Lim Soo Hean or some other big dealer, we arranged that he should go to Rangoon for that purpose only and then return. However, as soon as the scoundrel got to Rangoon, he suborned our manager (Marshall) to leave us and to form a company among our best dealers, and alarmed the agent of the National Bank of India to such an extent that he sent the most hysterical cable to his London office and Jim and I were forced to go out to Rangoon to practically wind up our business. Apr 1903. (However) By lucky sales of the Ironworks and our office properties, we saved the situation and wound up with about £6000 to the good – as against some £25,000 shown in our previous balance sheet!

David Jugurtha now

arranged to amalgamate with (Fred) Norman & (John Gay) Clarke as Norman, Clarke, Dunlop & Co Ltd, Feb 1904, they looking after their indent business with India, while I worked up again my Rangoon connection.

Unfortunately he was not able to take Jim into the firm with him, though the firm later took him on and sent him out to trouble-shoot in Shanghai, where they profited greatly from his advice to sever connections with another 'thorough scamp'. This period saw David Jugurtha's health becoming much weaker, and he continually suffered from attacks of severe bronchial catarrh, malarial fever, persistent diarrhoea, and other things, and made several journeys as far as Japan, on one occasion returning home via Canada, and taking ship across the Atlantic from Quebec. He also mentions a great number of the people he meets and those he befriends in the far-flung commercial centres of the Far East merchant trade and on board the liners, whose names and captains he usually records. For example, here is part of his entry for 1910:

18 Mar: Left Marseilles for Hong Kong per SS Moltau (Capt Sweeny) and met on board Mr Littledale (a great hunter and traveller who had got nearer to Lhasa even than Sven Hedyn) and Lord & Lady Poulett. Transhipped to SS Delta at Colombo. Stayed the night at Singapore with JS Baker, manager of the H Kong and Shanghai bank. Met HH The Gaikwar of Baroda and his Maharani and daughter on SS Delta.

Back at home the family took their usual holiday at Felixstowe Ferry, and he and Laura often met relations at Gullane, near Edinburgh, for golf. In 1907 they moved to a new house in Beckenham, named Dudley House after Laura's birthplace, and near her old school, where living was cheaper.

Next year he had influenza, pleurisy and sciatica and:

> My partner John Gay Clarke (was) declared a bankrupt, June 1909, having squandered in about 18 years £60,000 left him by his father, so de facto he ceased to be a director of Norman, Clarke & Dunlop, and Norman retired on a pension of £300 from the firm. I then arranged with my three managers – Fred W. Pow (London), Geo W. Watson & A.C.O.K. McEwen (Rangoon) to put in £5000 and become life directors, while I was appointed Managing Director for life – a most excellent arrangement for me as it bound them to the firm for life and put an end to the periodical demands for new terms of remuneration and attendant friction.

But this did not make him any less active. In 1910 he went out to the Far East again, stopping off at Colombo, Singapore, Hong Kong and Shanghai, and so once more to Japan (Kobe and Yokohama), where he also fitted in a lot of sightseeing. In 1913 he made a very similar trip (visiting Kyoto in Japan), again meeting many interesting travellers and business people and staying in various places either at institutions all referred to as 'The Club', or with friends (Bob Shewan of Hong Kong is frequently mentioned). On the way home the P&O special train from Marseille only just escaped a terrible accident. He arrived home three days before Christmas, 'unspeakably glad to be there again and find my dear ones well and happy'.

This was the last of his journeys to the East, but the respite was not enough to allow his body to recover fully, especially as, in 1915, he 'strained his heart' doing one of Sandow's exercises, and then, in 1918 added appalling dental problems to his list of dire afflictions. He was told that he must now lead a really tranquil life if he wanted to live a few more years. This didn't stop him and Laura having a five-month 'tour' of Algeria and Tunisia, which greatly aggravated his bowel problem. Then in 1921 the world economic situation became so bad that his firm went into voluntary liquidation and he personally retired. There followed kidney pain, and a more gentle holiday with Laura in the Hydro at Falmouth in 1922. They returned home in April, but in June he:

> had become gradually so weak through constant diarrhoea and inability to eat enough to maintain (his) strength that he went to Gullane, but still went down hill. Was thoroughly examined by Prof Meaken in his [Nursing] home, who said he was in such a precarious state of health that he must at once return to Beckenham on July 17th, where, despite much devoted care by (his family and a nurse), he steadily continued to lose strength.

David Jugurtha died on 14 October, and was buried very near Laura's mother in Shirley churchyard, just south of Beckenham.

2

LIFE IN THE DUNLOP FAMILY

COLIN WAS HIMSELF the fourth child of David Jugurtha and Laura. The oldest was Jim, born in 1890, followed by Walter, born in 1892. Then came Sibyl, who was born in 1894, Colin arrived in 1897, and finally Evelyn in 1898. The chief source for the nature, indeed the flavour, of Colin's family background, in its early stages, is his elder sister Sibyl's short memoir, *Nana: 'A Genuine Sort of Person'*. This privately printed memorial is a memento of the 'noble and unselfish' nursemaid who virtually took on the duties of both parents, and became Sibyl's beloved companion until her death in November 1951.

It can be supplemented, of course, by the information in David Jugurtha's own journal extensively drawn on in the last chapter and, indirectly, by *Pug*, a family magazine which the children composed, with their parent's encouragement, from 1904 to 1908. In addition, Colin sometimes refers to his childhood in diaries and letters, and even sermons, and of course in family conversations when my brothers and I were growing up. David Jugurtha and Laura moved from Blackheath to Alexandra Road, South Hampstead, in 1889, then, in 1898, to 50 Belsize Avenue, to make extra room for Evelyn's arrival, and in 1907, after the dishonest dealings of William Cotterell in Rangoon, to the relative cheapness of Dudley House, Beckenham.

Nursery life, under Nana's supervision, was close and intimate. Laura herself featured very little in it. In Sibyl's words:

> My mother, like many other Victorians, left the children very much to their nursery life, coming in from time to time looking gloriously beautiful, and having us down in the drawing room for half an hour before dinner for which we were washed and brushed, and carefully arrayed.

My cousin Ian was told by his father Walter that the children were more likely to see Laura for a brief moment as she looked round the nursery door, and Colin himself said that what Laura really enjoyed was receiving visitors in her drawing room while reclining on her sofa. In her memoir Sibyl goes on: 'My Father was devoted to us and spent most of his spare time with us and this was not much as he was a very busy man...' As we have seen, his business took him away to the Far East for months at a time, but, despite that and the anxieties brought on by Cotterell's conduct and its results, it is clear that he meant far more to Colin and his brothers and sisters than his mother (who, of course, never really knew her own father). Colin wrote in 1951 (in the manuscript of a Memorial sermon on one of his heroes, General Gordon, which he gave in Khartoum cathedral), 'When my father beat me he did so, not because he hated me, or was indifferent to me, but because he loved me.'

Nana came to the Dunlops at the age of 20, shortly after Jim's birth.

> She had been for a year under a famous head nurse in one of our well-known families and this was her first place in sole charge. The family to whom she had been under-nurse was connected with her native village in Buckinghamshire.

The village was Hambleden, and the family the one that produced Sir Stafford Cripps and lived at Parmoor House, a few miles north of Hambleden. So she must have been well trained, besides having imbibed a great fund of common sense and practical skill from her own very humble family – the 1871 census classified her father as an agricultural labourer. So, Sibyl goes on, she 'stood for most things that children need in the way of care and love and understanding, law and order and above all security'. She comes across as one who could be both strict and kind, with a very developed sense of justice, founded on a strong religious sense.

'All our early Religious education came from Nana – not as something to be taught and learned – but as part of herself which she gave to us in her convincing and simple way.' So she read the children Charlotte Young's *Stories of Bible History*, never shrank from telling them individually when they had done wrong or acted carelessly, yet was equally ready to tell them how pleased she was at their especially good behaviour.

Sibyl also mentions her powers of creating something special out of what might seem quite commonplace, by revealing the magical aspects of everyday life.

> Although we were the children of the 'idle rich' [writes Sibyl] it was small things made great, virtually pumpkins into coaches that she created by some means. She was able to make a glow and a wonder, and a transformation of a 'candle tea', which simply amounted to a small Christmas tree candle of a different colour by each plate on the tea table and one or two flanking the tea tray. Then the lights were put out, and the blinds being already down the effect was unearthly, beautiful and romantic.

She was also a consummate needlewoman, making most of the children's clothes, and had an innate sense of good design. She abhorred sentimentality and 'gushing' – 'I don't believe in kissing', 'I prefer deeds to words' – and was utterly direct and straightforward, to the point of appearing 'hard and grim to strangers'. But she was devoted to the family, for when David Jugurtha was facing apparent ruin in 1903, she came to him and said she would never leave him as long as she was needed for the children, and would not only take no wages but even pressed him to accept all her savings to help tide him over the difficult time. (He was so overwhelmed by this selfless offer that he burst into tears, much to Sibyl's consternation when she came to see him very shortly afterwards.)

This picture of Nana is, of course, seen through the eyes of Sibyl, and no doubt could have been modified a little by any of the other children, but, although the boys were able to laugh at her by ironically calling her 'The Bard' behind her back because she had never been known to sing a note, there is no reason to think that any of them would have greatly disagreed with it. Walter, who took over the editorship of *Pug*, the short-lived magazine the Dunlop children produced during the Christmas holidays between 1904 and 1908, pays tribute to her in this context by calling Nana the 'sower' in his 'Legion of Honour', which lists all those concerned in various ways in its origins and production. Sibyl recalls what a good story-teller Nana was, and she undoubtedly created the group spirit that kept the venture afloat for four years and made them all contribute regularly. When Colin left the family house in the summer of 1915 to join the army he could hardly hold back his tears after saying goodbye to her.

Pug (or *Pugg*) ran through nine issues between 1904 and 1908, and was at first edited by Iris and Jim. Iris, born in 1891, was actually christened 'Doris', and was the first of Uncle Frank's two children, and thus first cousin to the young Dunlops (it was she after whom the new species of water-worm was named!). As the Beddards then lived in Hampstead, the two families may well have seen a lot of each other, though relations between Frank and David Jugurtha cannot always have been cordial, as Colin more than once referred to an occasion when his father ordered Laura's brother out of the house in no uncertain terms ('never darken my doors again!', or something to that effect).

The joint editorship only lasted for three issues, after which Jim and Walter both edited volumes, but it isn't always clear which. Usually everything is hand-written, but later quite a lot is typed, and there was only one copy of each issue. The stories, puzzles and poems give us a few insights into the capacities of the five children. Of the compositions, the best are undoubtedly Walter's, who is extremely versatile in rhyming, and really much the most original and inventive of them all. Jim, by comparison, is conventional, and rarely very interesting in his stories. Sibyl's stories come nowhere near foreshadowing her fine aesthetic achievements in the design of silver and jewelry.

Colin matures quite a lot over the five years; but even at this very juvenile stage of his life it is clear that his real gift – abundantly shown in his later letters and diaries – is for conveying the feel and sound of things experienced in reality, rather than for literary invention. Evelyn's weakness in logical or connected thinking is already apparent here. Laura's adult contributions are sometimes good, though probably derivative rather than creative. By and large the 'stories' told in these pages are heavily influenced by the fairy and folk tales Nana told the children, and rarely based on searching observation, though as the magazine goes on there is more of this (though a certain tedium also sets in). 'The Domestic Column' in volume 7 of 1906, gives us some interesting information about how the editor saw the various members of the family. It is probably by Walter, as he is the only person not mentioned in it. I shall return briefly to this below.

It is time now to refer to the important theme of the family's public worship. David Jugurtha was clearly very attached to the Presbyterianism of his Scottish upbringing, and all the children were baptised in St John's Wood Presbyterian Church, the three oldest being also confirmed as Presbyterians. Laura, however, had a Church of England background, and Colin and Evelyn were both confirmed as Anglicans, Colin at his public school, Radley, and Evelyn at Bromley Parish Church, no doubt under the auspices of Bromley High School, which she and Sibyl attended. The resulting uncertainties for the family were seized on by Walter, in his Christmas 1906 *Pug* article 'The Domestic Column', as follows:

> Dada by the way has budded forth into a poet, not only a poet but a quick composer. While staying in Gullane this summer the rumour goes that early in the morning on Sunday he suddenly began to sing this:

> *Will ye gang to the Kirk, Laury Beddard,*
> *Will ye gang to the free Kirk wi' me,*
> *Or do ye prefer the established,*
> *The English, or else the U.P.?*

'The Kirk' is the established Presbyterian Church of Scotland, 'the English' the Episcopalian, and the 'U.P.' the United Presbyterian, which combined two former Presbyterian sects. One or both of these would be 'the Free Kirk', which 'Dada' seems to have favoured, according to Walter. That this was so is supported by something Colin mentioned *en passant* in his Vicar's letter in the Henfield Parish Magazine in 1938: 'In my Presbyterian home we never observed Christmas Day or Good Friday in a religious way', adding that this was in keeping with the early work of the Reformers, though things were changing when he wrote. But sometimes the difference in religious allegiance between his parents may have resulted in one of the 'rows' described in a letter from Colin to Evelyn in December 1915 as fairly frequent occurrences:

> What a wretched time you seem to have been having with this ridiculous row between Mother and Dada. Poor baby, I do pity you, for I remember well how perfectly miserable they used to make me. You may be sure that I will be praying for you and that the row may stop. It always seems to be at this time of year that rows occur. Don't you remember that awful Christmas Day (1912) when there was a row and when we were all missing Jim and Sibyl who were abroad. ... I can't think, though, how Dada, who is such a religious and God-fearing man can possibly keep up his anger for long, because anger is one of the worst sins there is, especially when it concerns a lot of people.

It is also tempting to relate the 'rows' to the dismissal of 'Uncle Frank', who may (this is only speculation) have brought an unwelcome, perhaps even agnostic or atheist ethos into the house. But the one clear fact is the irritableness of David Jugurtha. ('Can't you *see* we're a family party?', he once blurted out when a single traveller once attempted to take the last free seat in the railway compartment on the journey to Felixstowe.) In one of her fragmentary diaries Evelyn once reminded herself of Colin's own irritableness: 'he has a mighty reserve of inherited temper which he has valiantly to curb. I worked through this at a tenderer age'. It is clear that their father was the source of this inheritance. It seems also to be reflected in another letter from Colin (September 1915), who was about to enter the army next day:

> At supper on Sunday evening it was terribly martial. There was only a very little butter left and you can just imagine what a state Dada got into – dividing it up into square millimetres and apportioning one to each of us – and then if you please he insisted on making the sandwiches for their journey before we had supper so as to see how much tongue there would be left for supper and breakfast!'

David Jugurtha, then, was undoubtedly a God-fearing man, but Colin at least (followed later by the rest of the family) found something lacking in the hard religion of Calvin and Knox, the fathers of Scottish Presbyterianism. He said in a sermon he preached in All Saints, Margaret Street in 1959:

> I had been brought up in a strict and godly home, but I had reached the age of 17 without two very important factors in true religion having come home to me. My religion was without much joy and without much penitence.

We may relate this to two other facts about Colin's childhood: Sibyl, in *Nana*, recalls him blurting out to Nana that he was scared to go to Heaven, because he might meet King Herod there (the instigator of 'the massacre of the innocents' in Matthew's Gospel, ch. 2); at the same time a favourite theme of Colin's contributions to *Pug* is that of the young protagonist coming to some cruel or terrible end. Perhaps Nana herself somehow reinforced this harsh aspect of at least the outward appearance of David Jugurtha's faith, though Sibyl also portrays her as always ready to comfort her after a horrible dream.

Here are two other Calvinist glimpses of Colin's early life and its influence; in another of his sermons, this time on the prophet Elijah, he recalls: 'Some of us were brought up to be suspicious of Jezebel because it is said that when Jehu arrived at the palace she painted her face.' Writing in the early 1930s to Ida O'Malley, my great aunt who brought up my mother,[2] he says that, until he left the army in 1919 and went to Oxford, he used to think sexual desire was in itself evil.

As for Colin's relations with his siblings, his closest family tie was always with Evelyn, or 'Baby' (the two were, by age, a somewhat separate group among

---

[2] See below, p. 97.

the five children), and in later life she twice lived in a self-contained flat under our roof, and at others lived in close proximity to us. She and Colin shared a lot of memories and private jokes preserved from their childhood. His relations with Sibyl also remained very good, and in adult life he loved staying at Felixstowe in the remote cottage on the edge of the marshes where Sibyl and Nana then lived, holidays which also enabled him to relive once more some of the magic of the family holidays they had always taken at Felixstowe Ferry. But he found Sibyl's inability to bear Evelyn's proximity for long hard to take, and Evelyn found her frequent attempts in later life to be accepted by Sibyl constantly and even brutally rejected, despite Colin's efforts to bring them together.

Perhaps Sibyl, who was for a short time the only girl among three brothers, never got over the fact that Evelyn was prettier, and much more good-natured and relaxed, than she was, and could not exercise her talent for design without the practical and emotional support of Nana. As for Walter, the cleverest of the five, Colin told me more than once that he used to bully him. On one occasion, he said, Walter had been playing football and came home ravenous; he seized on the first 'eatable' he could find in the children's quarters – some treasured rice-paper pictures that David Jugurtha had brought back from the Far East as a present for Colin. On another occasion he told Bede that Walter had tied his hands to the handlebars of his bicycle and launched him down hill. But none of Colin's four siblings had anything but good to say of Jim, who died of complications from a wound he received in the 1st Battle of Messines (near Ypres), a very early battle of the Great War. After he had been invalided home much later from the Mediterranean as beyond medical help and died in much pain at Dudley House in 1917, his superior officer wrote to David Jugurtha in glowing terms about the great affection and admiration he had inspired among officers, NCOs and men of his regiment.

Here are two other glimpses of Dunlop family life at Beckenham. Among the many letters of condolence my mother received after Colin's death there was one from Esther (May Melville) Dunlop, who was one of the children of James Bourne Dunlop, David Jugurtha's younger brother and several times business partner. She said that, although she had seen very little of Colin as a grown-up, except on occasions like family funerals:

> up to the time that we grew up Colin and all the Beckenham crowd, Dunlops and Baynes, were so much part of our family's life that we knew each other terribly well, and I shall always remember him as the school boy who came to us for holidays in Hampshire or as a member of the crowd of us in the garden at the house in Wickham Road [the location of Dudley House].

Colin himself also had good memories of that garden. On Whitsunday, 1943, he wrote in his diary: 'In my mind Whitsunday recalls the garden at Beckenham with its scent of wild parsley and early summer flowers, and the taste of lemonade in my silver Christening cup with the flavour of roast meat and vegetables.' The house and garden have now, alas, been replaced by a group of small and not very good-looking houses or flats, but the christening cup, a fine piece of Victorian work, has survived. As for relations with the wider family, Colin's own general attitude to this found expression in a letter to Ida O'Malley (who brought up my mother) in December 1933, in which he compares his own family with hers: 'Our relations were always a source of friction and disharmony among us; it is nice to see instances where this is not so and where you appear to like each other'. Whether this view was shared by his brothers and sisters, and whether it extended beyond the relations between David Jugurtha and 'Cousin Frank' I do not know.

3

SCHOOLING AND ACCOUNTANCY

OLIN HIMSELF says nothing about his life at either of the two prep schools he attended. The first was a day school called Heddon Court, in Hampstead, owned by W. Stallard, to which both Jim and Walter had gone before him. He was there from 1904 until the move to Beckenham in 1907. At Christmas, 1906, the editor of *Pug* reported in 'The Domestic Column' that 'Colin ... is climbing up Heddon Court like Sibyl, I mean a monkey, up a fir tree.'

Colin does once remark in his diary for the Middle East tour he made with the RAF in October 1945, that a fellow-traveller on the plane to Malta (almost certainly an officer in the Armed Services), where they stopped before going on to Cairo, was one de Ferranti, who had brothers who were at school with him there. A Google search also revealed the fact that the painter Ben Nicholson was also at the school during some of the time when Colin was a pupil.

In April 1907, soon after the move to Beckenham, he became a day boy at The Abbey School, Beckenham, whose grounds were on the opposite side of the road from those of Minshull House Girls' School, which his mother had attended. This well known boys' school, which later sent many boys on to Eton, Winchester and Harrow, evolved from a room over a baker's shop, where The Revd Thomas Lloyd Phillips, who had come as a curate at the Parish Church, St George's, himself started to teach a small group of boys in 1866. Later he 'designed (a) group of Victorian Gothic-style buildings ... to look like an old abbey', whence the Abbey School got its name.

The buildings, in a spacious park, were completed in the 1880s. To a later pupil at Minshull House, 'It always seemed to be the epitome of the perfect private school.'[3] By the time Colin went there it was owned by three men, one of whom was a Church of England archdeacon. From the start its boarders, like those of Radley, Colin's public school, slept in private cubicles within the dormitories. Colin started to board there from September 1911. Its academic standards were also good, and Colin did well there. In June 1911 he won a £30 scholarship to Malvern, but his father must have felt that he could do better

---

[3] Mary McInally, *Minshull House, Beckenham,* privately printed, n.d., but after 1966, and available from Bromley Archive.

than this, so he turned it down. The gamble paid off and in the following month Colin won a £40 scholarship to Radley, which was accepted.

In September 1911, then, he went to Radley, which stands in a park a few miles south of Oxford, and was enrolled in F.J. Barmby's House, now bureaucratically known as 'C Social'. Unfortunately, none of the House records spanning Colin's time at the school survive, though Mr Barmby certified on Colin's application form (MT 393) for a Temporary Commission for the duration of the First World War that he was of 'good moral character' and had 'attained a good standard of education'.

There are also very few references to him in the school magazine, *The Radleian*, though his name crops up in the reports of the Debating Society; in a debate during his last term on the motion: 'This House believes that the English Public School Education is the best obtainable', he is reported as having said from the floor that boys ought to be trained to love art. He seems to imply that Radley was deficient in this respect when he was there (though the fine chapel had, and still has, a beautiful medieval altarpiece) and that he was against the motion.

In 1932 he also told Ida O'Malley in a letter that he wouldn't send his children to public schools (though he later changed his mind) since his Radley experience taught him that public schools educated their alumni merely to be good members of the middle classes. But the point about teaching boys to love art might also have been made with the philistine atmosphere of 'Bloodery' in mind, which seems to have pervaded Radley at the time according to Christopher Hibbert, who wrote *No Ordinary Place: Radley College and the English Public School System 1947–1997* (John Murray, 1997).

Although *The Radleian* reveals that Colin rowed well enough to represent his house in the Junior Division of the Coxed fours in 1914 – the standard of rowing in Division II was said to be 'low' – there is no record of his having distinguished himself in other games, such as cricket and rugby football, which 'the Bloods' would have set much more store by. Unlike The Abbey School, Colin told me, there was almost no interest in politics at Radley; this reinforces the suspicion that the cultural and intellectual atmosphere of the school was not of a kind which would have acted as a great stimulus to him.

Christopher Hibbert also says that during the wardenship of Field, who was replaced a year before Colin left, the school had declined to a rather low general moral standard, which may account for his remark, in a letter to my mother before they were married, that 'he underwent much unrelieved suffering in adolescence' at Radley. This certainly involved bullying, as he once told my brother Charles, and some of this was almost certainly of a sexual nature, since Colin was a strikingly good-, even girlish-, looking boy. For a boy of his upbringing and sensitivity this would certainly have made him suffer, which may have made him feel something of an outsider.

The paucity of references to him in *The Radleian* also suggests that he rather 'kept his head down' when at the school. However, he did make some firm friends there. One of them was Douglas Chandor, who also fought in the

Great War, and became a wealthy portrait painter, based in the USA, and whose subjects included Churchill, Roosevelt and Queen Elizabeth II amongst other celebrities. Another was Jack Finch, who was godfather to my brother Bede. He had a career in the Foreign Office, and, as we shall see later, the two met up in Iraq when Colin was there as Civil Chaplain in Baghdad. Another Radleian Colin met in Iraq was Bob Sturges, who was Political Secretary in the British High Commission during the first part of Colin's short chaplaincy, where they saw a good deal of one another.

Later in life he met up again in 1949 at Bückeburg in Germany with T.A. Langford-Sainsbury, a parson's son, who had become an Air Vice Marshall in the RAF. He asked Colin to dine with him, and the latter records in his diary: 'he has turned out a boisterous but shrewd man, with some real charm and goodness lurking behind his tiny little eyes'. The frequency of such reunions in Colin's life is not perhaps remarkable in one who attended one of the top public schools, but Colin's inclusion of them in letters and diaries is an indicator of the high value he put on friendship. Another Radleian he met in later life was Geoffrey Carlisle, who was vicar of Buxton when I was at a prep school in the town. Carlisle had been 'clerk' of the Radley Debating Society.

Four picture postcards sent by Colin during his first term at the school survive, two to Evelyn, one to Jim and one to Nana. The one to Jim reveals that Colin had joined the school (Army) Officer Training Corps (OTC). As Jim was at this time in the 'London Scottish' Territorials, before going out to Argentina, Colin writes: 'We had great fun at our field day. We have another next week at Abingdon. Our uniform is a very nice one only we have to clean our buttons every week. Love from Colin.'

David Jugurtha's journal, which meticulously records illnesses in the family, even mild ones like chicken pox, tells us that Colin was twice ill during his time there. In May 1912, he 'had nasal growth removed', and in the following March he was 'laid up with pains in his feet', two months before his confirmation. Colin's health was not very good when a young man, but it is not always easy to say what caused his periods 'off sick' during the twenties and thirties. However, it is not difficult to surmise that the poison gas which lingered in the trenches during the war and to which he would sometimes have been exposed may have had something to do with it.

David Jugurtha's last entry concerning Colin's school days reads as follows: '1914, 18 Dec, left Radley and did not return there.' The wording suggests that this was a rather unexpected decision, and this is confirmed by the fact that there is no mention of Colin in the usual termly 'Valete' list in *The Radleian*, where all the term's leavers would normally be mentioned. Colin's father must have told the school after the lists had been compiled.

The reason for this is suggested by what follows in David Jugurtha's own list of important events in Colin's life. On 26 January 1915, Colin 'went to Mr Jno Gilson, Chancery lane, to be coached for Accountants' exam'. The Institute of Chartered Accountants exams were at the beginning of June. Colin, his father writes, 'passed out 3rd in honours out of 200 men'.

Then, on 30 July, he was 'articled to ... Whittem Hawkins' (DJD leaves a blank for his first name) in the firm of 'Geo A Touche & Co for 5 years, fee £300 + £15 stamps'; 9 August, '1st day at Touche's office. There till 18th'; 22 August, 'heard he had been appointed from Aug 26th 2nd Lt in 3rd E Kent Regt (The Buffs) and ordered to go to Worcester College, Oxford, for Officer training with Oxford Univ Contingent OTC'. 4 October, 'Joined 3rd Buffs at Dover'.

It looks from this record as though Colin left, or was withdrawn from, Radley, in time for him to train for the accountancy exams before joining up in the army at the minimum age of 18, which he attained on 31 July. Although the First World War had begun on 4 August 1914, there was no shortage of recruits for well over a year, and no conscription until 1916, but both Jim and Walter had joined up in 1914 (Jim setting sail from Buenos Aires almost as soon as war was declared), and Colin would not have wanted to hang back. It was perhaps David Jugurtha who persuaded Colin to put off a little his application for a Temporary Commission so that he might get a taste of an accountant's work in practice before disappearing into service life.

The payment of the £300 fee was certainly an act of faith on his part, since Colin's practical acquaintance with accountancy was only to last a week! It was probably also through his father's initiative that Colin, who had not yet finished his military training, was invited to a large civic lunch at the Mansion House in July 1916, on the occasion of the unveiling of the Kitchener Memorial in St Botolph's churchyard, while George Touche was Lord Mayor.

The Touches were in fact Dunlop family friends from Edinburgh days. George Touche, somewhat younger than David Jugurtha, came to London after 1883, and soon acquired a great reputation for saving failing businesses. He founded his own firm in 1899, and co-founded Touche & Niven in New York in 1900. Deloitte Touche has now an important Japanese offshoot. Back in 1915 David Jugurtha clearly thought that a foothold in George Touche & Co would be a sound financial investment for Colin's career when the war was over. I have seen nothing to suggest that he thought Colin would take a university degree, let alone get ordained.

But the first decisive step that led to his eventual rejection of accountancy as a career had already been taken. It seems to have begun with a chance visit to All Saints, Margaret Street, in the West End. This meant so much to Colin that, on 2 June 1959, he recalled it in a sermon he preached there:

> Some time between 5 and 5.30 p.m. on an early Spring evening in 1915 chance or providence directed my footsteps along a street I had never passed through before. I found myself stopping at the gate which leads into the courtyard of this church. I had never heard of it before, but the lights were shining through the coloured glass window, and the bell was ringing, so I walked in. In a minute or two the choristers entered in the very characteristic way they still do, and then Evensong began. I had been brought up in a strict and godly home, but I had reached the age of 17 without two very important factors in true religion having come home to me. My religion was without much joy and without much

penitence. I took to dropping in at Evensong at All Saints on my way home. Then I got to know Roscow Shedden (the Vicar), and after a while I made my first confession and then later on I became an occasional server. The life and worship at All Saints began to reveal to me a new vision of the splendour and glory of God and that meant joy and penitence. ... I had now a religion of my own which didn't depend on outward circumstances. Now when I say that All Saints did this for me, I don't mean that the building or the memory of the services did it, though probably they helped. It was the people of All Saints and their clergy and their life together through which God spoke.

Colin's Cuttings Book contains two very tattered picture postcards, which he carried about in his 'pocket case in France 1916–18'. One of them is of the interior of All Saints, a view looking east from about half way down the nave. The other is a similar picture of St Alban's, Holborn, on which Colin wrote in ink '2.viii.16. 12m'. If '12m' is his shorthand for midday, it sounds as though Colin had attended the daily midday Communion at St Alban's, which gave a chance to those who worked nearby but perhaps lived in other parts of London to communicate.

The first 'perpetual curate' of the parish had been Father Mackonochie, who was not only almost always involved in defending himself against prosecutions initiated by the Church Association, dedicated to stamping out 'Ritualism', but was also by many called a martyr for a non-Roman but Catholic understanding of the meaning of the Christian faith as proclaimed by the Oxford Movement. Colin had clearly been much impressed by what he stood for, which included all kinds of social work and practical demonstrations of love for his fellow men and women in addition to high church ritual, a ministry continued after Father Mackonochie's death.

The presence of this card alongside that of All Saints makes one wonder how significant St Alban's was in his life. The other London church which became very significant to him from 1916 is, of course, St Mary's, Primrose Hill, which I shall write about in a later chapter.

4

THE GREAT WAR

THERE IS a very rough outline of Colin's army career in his father's journal, which gives some valuable details of dates and places, but his sister Evelyn kept some letters which he wrote to her during the period 1915 to 1917, which tell us not only quite a lot about his life as a soldier, but also about his religious concerns at this time; what he writes under the latter category, which forms a significant part of the whole content of these letters, makes it seem very natural that he should eventually go on to study at Oxford and then train for the ministry. Useful material has also been gleaned from official records, from the web, from histories of the war, and from his own memories and diary entries.

Colin did his initial officer training at Oxford. This was not because he was already a member of the university, but because he had been in the OTC at Radley, and therefore had a start over all those who had no experience at all of service life. On his application form for a Temporary Commission in the Regular Army he asked to serve in a 'Southern Unit' of the Infantry. He also declared that he had 'never suffered from any serious illness or injury', and that he needed 'glasses for reading and writing only, as my right eye is weaker than the left'.

When the time came for him to be called up (22 August 1915) he was told he would be in the 3rd East Kent Regiment, 'The Buffs', and that on the 30th he should report first to Worcester College, Oxford, where he would be 'assigned rooms', and where he was to leave the considerable amount of kit he had been told to bring, and then go to the OTC HQ in Alfred Street. The heart of the five-week course would be 'instruction in the Administrative and Field Duties of a Platoon Commander'.

Here is most of the text of Colin's long letter to Evelyn from Oxford, dated Monday, 4 September, interspersed with my comments:

Ever so many thanks for your lovely letter which I got a few days ago. I will now give you an account of all that I've done since you went on Saturday morning. I went back from the station and packed up till about 11 o'clock. Then I took the train to Penge and fetched Walter's motor bike, but unfortunately something happened to it down by Howard's stores and I had to push it all the way through the village and up Manor Road in the boiling sun, and, as the bike is frightfully heavy, it was no joke. In the afternoon Walter arrived and he and I and Nana walked to Bromley and then took a fly and drove out to Downe where we had tea. ... After tea we walked about and Walter took a photo of Nana who didn't mind in the least. ... We drove back via Green Street Green and Farnboro. On Sunday morning I took him up to town but the train didn't get in till 5 to 11 and so, as I was too late for All Saints [Margaret St], I contented myself with Westminster Cathedral. But don't tell Dada or Mother as they think I went to the former and if they knew they might think I was too late on purpose but as you know I would never miss All Saints through any fault of my own.

It seems from this passage and other things that Colin's parents were by this time rather alarmed by his High Church leanings and ready to think he might even – *horribile dictu!* – be about to become a Roman Catholic, since Westminster Cathedral, very different from Westminster Abbey, is Roman Catholic. All Saints was a good deal higher in its Anglican churchmanship than Beckenham Parish Church, which is mentioned in the next part of the letter. His parents were by this time prepared to go there for Evensong, but not for Communion.

He goes on:

In the afternoon I continued packing up and putting away my things. I put my playbox under your bed with the crucifix in it. In the evening of course I went to the parish [church] with Mother and Dada ... and said goodbye to Canon Arnott [the Rector] and dear old Mints [a clergyman whose real name is never mentioned, though he is quite often referred to by this name] who seemed quite sorry – also to Williams and some of the choir men and choir boys. Incidentally the Lay Reader said goodbye too. On Monday morning Dada and mother went off by the 8.30 and I by the 9.10. It was too awful saying goodbye to Nana and I almost cried as I went down the drive – it seemed so terrible. Poor old Manny seemed so unhappy too and had his tail down all the time. ...I met Porter at Oxford and we had lunch together.

Will Stevens Porter was a close friend of Colin's, and a little older than him. Colin may possibly have met him first at either All Saints, or even St Alban's, Holborn (or he may just have given Colin his postcard of it – they were both keen on church-crawling). He got a First in English at Oriel College, Oxford, in 1914, then taught in a school in Newport, Monmouthshire, during which time he decided to get ordained, and went to Cuddesden in 1917.

After serving his title and a second curacy, he became Rector of Papworth Everard in 1926. He appears to have died in the 1940s but was at one time at the Community of the Resurrection. There can hardly be any doubt that he encouraged Colin in his later decision to get ordained, and was regarded by him at this time as something of a religious expert, though it is interesting that in April 1917 he could write that Will's helping the Vicar of the little mission church in Newport by taking weekday evensong, extra services and Sunday schools while he was on vacation from Cuddesden, is something which 'a year or two ago he and most of his friends would absolutely have despised'.

The letter continues with an account of his officer training.

We are worked pretty hard here. ... We get up at about 6.30. Parade at 7.15. Breakfast at 8.15. We have lovely meals here and at breakfast you can have as much toast as you like, nice coffee, eggs and bacon or sausages or ham or scrambled eggs etc. Then parade again at 9.30 and nothing but hard work till 1, such as trench digging, musketry, drill, map-reading and every other thing that the army goes in for. Lunch at 1 and after that the same routine as the morning till 4. We are free from 4 till 7 when there is dinner but of course there is such a lot to read up and not much time for writing letters. After dinner at 7 there is a lecture at 8.30 till 9 and then I'm usually so tired that I clear straight off to bed. I have a nice sitting room with a bedroom leading out of it.

Colin successfully completed his officer training on 2 October, passed through Beckenham for a short weekend and then, in his father's words 'joined the 3rd Buffs at Dover' on 4 October.

The next letter to Evelyn is headed 'No. 3 Officers' Training Company, Connaught Barracks, Dover. 27th October, Wednesday, 1915'. Clearly his officer training is not yet finished, but now he is with his own regiment with, to some extent, its own way of doing things. The letter itself has nothing about the army, but is a response to Evelyn's confession that her faith in God is very weak and sometimes non-existent. Colin confesses that he too has sometimes doubted everything, and has been tempted to throw the whole thing over, but his faith always returns after a while.

He then tries to argue her back into faith by pointing out how much of a non-religious kind we all take on trust in our everyday lives, and appealing to the conviction brought by the benefits of prayer, worship and Communion which she has experienced for herself, and by the testimony of the bible and martyrs of the Church.

There is no *proof* in any of this; rather we believe on the authority of those whom we trust, who carry conviction. The next letter was written on All Saints Day. In it Colin shows his interest in all the details of worship at Beckenham Parish Church, where he thinks Evelyn and Nana, and perhaps Sibyl will be, and says how much he is looking forward to the next Sunday, when All Saints Margaret Street celebrates with great splendour its own patronal festival, and when he will be serving at the choral Eucharist – a very great honour. He commiserates with Evelyn, who, he believes, will then be with her parents at Shortlands (an old postcard reproduced on the web shows a very uninspiring interior) for Matins, where the churchmanship is very low.

In the next letter, dated 7 December, he talks about the 'rows' between his parents (see above), and describes his recent visit to Radley, which he much enjoyed, though bewails the fact that, now he has gone out into the world more, he finds he can't relate to his old friends as he used to do. He ends by asking Evelyn, who has asked him about 'C' (for Confession, a warning to her not to read out this part of his letter at home), whether he should write to 'Mints' on her behalf, since Garnier, then a curate at All Saints and probably Colin's own confessor, lives so far off.

After spending Christmas at home (which he did every year while the war was still being fought) he was transferred to Dunstable for a Signals Course, and had digs with a Mrs Gravestock at Houghton Regis. His first letter is dated 5 January 1916, and starts by discussing dates when they could meet. Evelyn was staying at Felixstowe Ferry, where Nana now lived; she had left the family to marry the recently widowed Mr Frost, in whose house the Dunlops had so often stayed *en famille* as children.

There are many details about ceremonies and members of the staff of St George's whom he had met again while he was at home on leave. He ends: 'This signalling course is very interesting and I'm in very good billets. So far I have seen no sign of straw hats in Dunstable or Luton. Do you remember the picture on the Counties of England card?' He was back at Dover for a time in February, and visited Canterbury Cathedral with an unnamed companion. 'We had a very good time at Canterbury last weekend', he writes.

> The cathedral was however very disappointing. The actual architectural structure was wonderful but the ornamentation of it was dreadful. The service and music was even worse; so lifeless and inartistic in every possible way. All the clergy too were doddering old fools of about 90. No wonder England's religion is dead when its cathedrals are so dreary and lifeless; and its dignitaries so old and decrepit. It made me feel ill. The school was very picturesque and old world looking from the outside, but the inside was mean and squalid and a very sorry contrast to the clean and spacious interior of Radley buildings.

The scornful remark about the doddering old fools, especially its wording, is not in character, and is probably a sign of the army influence he bewails elsewhere. He ends: 'I wonder when my transfer into the Royal Engineers is coming off – it will mean higher pay, more interesting work and a horse for me. I hope it comes soon.' All army signalling was in fact within the remit of the RE at that time.

The transfer didn't take place until 25 May, on which date, David Jugurtha records, he 'passed all his exams at Fenny Stratford and was seconded to the Royal Engineers' (possibly at Haynes Park, a few miles south of Bedford, where he was for a time). One memory of Dunstable is worth quoting. In 1943 Colin was visiting the RAF station in Peterhead, Scotland, and wrote in his diary: 'I was sitting reading in the Mess after supper ... when the wireless gave us "If You Were the Only Girl in the World"' (I more than once heard this myself at school in the early 1950s).

> Of all songs I know this is the fullest of vivid memories. It inevitably conjures up a series of scenes and impressions all lit by an idyllic glow of mellow sunlight – 1916 summer at the Signals Depôt at Dunstable, my delight in boarding the train for weekend leave proud of my first pair of field boots and my riding whip, the faces and personalities of fellow-officers: Hamilton-Baines, tall and pasty-faced and a little pimply, but congenial; Cornwall McAliece, shrew-faced and malicious, always running after girls; Manson in his Glengarry,

serious and without ceremony; fussy, academic little Kingsford; tall, easy-going, paternal Captain Howard with protruding eyes and ceaseless smile.

'Then', the passage goes on – I am here running slightly ahead in time – it recalls:

> the journey to the Front, breakfast of bacon and eggs in the YMCA on a sunny September morning in le Havre; arrival at Couin, in the Pas de Calais, my billet in a ruinous old farmyard and the ceaseless cries of Madame to Henri and Marie Louise, the noise of the rats at night; my first experience of shellfire at Euston Dump, Colincamps [about 4 miles from Couin and 2 from the front]; going into Doullens and buying a 7lb box of biscuits at Felix Potin; going into rest at the same town, the faces and mannerisms of Colonel Danielsen, Carey-Thomas, Hussey, Smithy and Prosser – and so on, an endless procession of faces and voices and significant or trivial experiences – all buried in the past yet called into a wonderful life by this absurd sentimental refrain. I can recall the glittering taste of the Pommey and Crémo champagne at the Quatre Fils d'Ayman, the look of anger on the French interpreter's face when I protested that I had been charged too much for a bottle of red wine at the estaminet next to our mess at Acheux. 'There would be such wonderful things to do' – even though I consciously despised the trashy words at the time, they were yet a vehicle of aspiration and wistful longing.

Only two letters written by Colin to his mother survive, and both cover this momentous journey to the Somme valley to join up with the 52nd (Northern) Division, who had garrisoned the Somme section of the Allied front since April 1915. The Battle of the Somme had begun on 1 July 1916, a day when, as John Keegan puts it, 'the greatest loss of life in military history' took place: 20,000 of the British were killed, and another 40,000 were wounded; the German dead were about a tenth of the British total. How much Colin knew about this at the time we don't know. The first letter, dated 3 September from Southampton, reads as follows:

> My Dear Mother, we are here for a few brief hours before crossing to Rouen via Havre on a dreadful tiny little boat called the Duchess of Argyll. I don't know how long we will remain in Rouen but probably not for long as we are apparently quite urgently needed. There are about 80 officers altogether going, so there is no chance of feeling lonely. We sail at 6.30 pm and, judging from the look of the sea, we will not have a particularly smooth crossing.

His premonition was right. On the 5th, writing from The British Officers' Club, APO No. 1, BEF, he tells her:

> We arrived here after an exceedingly rough passage over the Channel on the tiniest little steamer you ever saw – smaller even than the Belle steamers at Felixstowe we used to go on. I managed not to be sick, but wasn't at all comfortable, and we had to sleep on our luggage. Everything over here seems so strange – the shops, the people, the streets etc, but I find I remember my French

pretty well. The most confusing thing is the money – I simply get muddled every time, and people in shops never try and help you out of your trouble. This Club is very nice, for you can get nice food etc at reasonable prices, without the danger of being hopelessly swindled. I don't know how long we are going to be here, probably not long. Incidentally, I am not allowed to tell you where we are, but I can assure you it is not yet the trenches. The sun is shining quite brightly, which is pleasant after the rain of yesterday, and it is warmer too. ... With love to all, I remain, your very affectionate son, Colin.[4]

Colin's first letter to Evelyn from France, dated 22 September, was probably from Couin (see above). The Battle of the Somme was still going on, but no longer with much hope of a great break-through. Instead, it was a matter of relatively small but frequent attacks, to keep the Germans on their toes and prevent too great a transfer of troops to the war on the Eastern Front against Russia. Up until 18 November, when the campaign was broken off, the furthest line of advance was only 7 miles, and total losses were possibly 600,000 Germans and 419,654 British. The chalky surface of the area was now glutinous slime.

Colin first thanks Evelyn for her 'numerous letters which have cheered me up a lot' (many of his letters to Evelyn begin in this vein). He seems to have his horse at hand, as 'this afternoon I went for a lovely ride all over the place'. 'The village', he goes on, is 'awfully pretty and on the side of a hill and surrounded by lovely tall trees'. He is taking much comfort also from daily attendance at Mass in the village church (though of course, being Anglican, he is unable to take Communion), and also from saying the offices of 'Prime, Vespers and Compline nearly every day'.

At the entrance to the village is a huge tall crucifix and opposite a shrine of Our Lady – the religion out here is all so simple and picturesque. Altogether I like the place very much. I have left my tent for a billet now and am writing this in my room ... – a large room with a large window at each end. It is very bare, of course, as bar my camp bed, a chair and a table it is devoid of furniture. The wallpaper is very pretty. The only drawback is the rats which make an appalling noise at night and even drown the shells!

But another good thing is the presence of 'Mr Walker', who was perhaps someone from Beckenham whom Evelyn also knew. He finishes with a piece of what they called 'Spot Rot': short dialogues making gentle fun of two Beckenham characters, an elderly priest attached to St George's, whose initials are 'P.W.', who often preaches at evensong but is not the rector, and a Mr Allan, probably someone in the congregation. 'P.W.' may possible be 'Mints', already mentioned above, with whom Colin corresponded. There are several examples of this kind of thing in the letters. This sample is all that is needed to

---

[4] I have, wherever possible, used entries from his father's journal and his own later addition to his letters of place names, to remind himself where they were written from.

fill out our picture of Colin and the private world of infantile humour he shared with Evelyn for the rest of their lives:

P.W: Dunlop seems to be quite safe – miles behind the line.
Mr A: Really, man!
P.W: I expect, you know, they think he's too young to be in the trenches.
Mr A: Yes, man!
P.W: I wonder if he will keep up his churchmanship now he's away from all his home influences. I know some people seem to let it all slip away when they go abroad.
Mr A: Indeed, man?
P.W: Dunlop's rather a queer chap too – I shouldn't be at all surprised if he gave up the Church.
Mr A: Really, man?

On 13 October he addresses his letter '0. Signal Coy, B.E.F.', though, once in England, he added the name of Acheux, which is about 5 miles south of Couin. In this letter he first answers his mother's question about what his work is all about. 'Well it is chiefly burying cables, or repairing cables or testing lines which have broken. It sounds easy but all the above jobs are most arduous and tiring.' 'You would laugh', he goes on,

to see me in a shrapnel helmet, sitting on the floor of a deep dugout with a chunk of bread in one hand and a hunk of cheese in the other. You never saw such a wreck – all covered with mud and with black hands and face. As a matter of fact I rather like the work there and during the intervals I go into an Artillery Observation Post and watch our shells knocking the Boche lines to pieces',

an end rather less often attained than was known at the time, as the German trenches in the Somme valley were dug in places over 30 feet deep, and in hard, dry, ground.

It is a fine sight. Our aeroplanes too are splendid. They fly right down onto the Boche trenches and pepper their occupants with machine guns and then fly up and loop the loop over them. Of course the Boche never sends up any of his planes as ours are always on the spot to bring them down. The 'Tanks' too are a fine sight although I have not seen them in action. They walked past my billet last night and are too ridiculous for words, but very formidable.

Tanks were a British invention first used on the Somme on 15 September. The letter has an urgent 'P.S.' at the start: 'Don't read out the part underlined'. It contains the news that Will Porter is definitely going to be ordained, and is going to Theological College quite soon. Colin adds 'I enclose a rule for religious life which Porter drew up and which I think is very good'. It's not, of course, a rule for 'religious' in the monastic sense, but for laymen. Colin hopes Evelyn will keep as much of it as she can, but thinks she'd better not try Confession yet.

When Colin wrote from Acheux a month later (17 November) there had just been an especially big attack by the Allies. Wikipedia tells us: 'The final act of the Battle of the Somme was played out between 13 and 18 November, 1916, along the Ancre River (a tributary of the Somme), north of Thiepval. ... the 51st (Highland) Division took Beaumont Hamel', which is about 5 miles east from Acheux.

> I am awfully sick at present [he writes] at not having been up in the trenches during the recent attack – I feel so useless being back here in warm and comfort while all the infantry are in bad quarters and in continual danger up in the line. Of course, don't tell anyone else about this because they will think I'm trying to appear brave when really I don't want to be there – but I know you will believe what I say. As a matter of fact I shall be up there probably every day as soon as the attack is finished, repairing or laying new cables, but it is not the same – I want to be in the attack, not after it.

He was no doubt thinking of all those he knew who had taken part; among whom was his brother Walter, now in the Machine Gun Corps, who had come through at least physically unscathed and whom he had invited for dinner on the next Saturday. He himself says he had been greatly helped by using the psalms in his prayers, and tells his mother to remember that they are 'the Church's prayers'; he goes on to show her that they can be used to express a Christian's devotion and thanksgiving:

> When you find words such as 'enemy persecuteth my soul' etc, think of the enemy as being your besetting sin. And again when they speak of the Lord giving you victory or smiting the enemy on the cheekbone it means that you praise God for giving you strength to overcome sin.

He encloses with his letter a little silver medal of the Virgin Mary which he hopes she will wear, explaining that she can talk to her 'and tell your troubles to her and ask her to pray to her son for you' but can't ask her directly for 'gifts or virtues, for these come from God alone'.

He then returns to military matters:

> There are rumours that, when the attack is finished and we have consolidated, our corps is going into rest right behind the line for two months. I do hope it is true as I'm getting sick of the sound of the guns here and the continual rush and bustle. The place to which I hear we are going has a lovely big church too – a really magnificent one which will be a help. The town I mean is the place where I bought your medal. By the way, you remember the P.C. I sent you the other day of a huge church tower? It has been shelled dreadfully and the statue of the B.V.M. and child on top is left hanging on by the feet and yet has not fallen. [This was the small town of Albert, on the Ancre, also very near.] You have probably seen it in the papers. By the way please put all P.C.s I send you into my album. ... We are still very busy in the telegraph office and for the last two days we have had over 3000 telegrams. The operators have to be on duty for

about 24 hours in two nights, and are on duty all night every other day. I have only been on night duty once and it was pretty awful.

After Christmas leave at home he wrote from Acheux again, on 13 January 1917:

Well we are back again up the line now for work, and the mud and cold are awful especially the former – the horses are always muddy up to their thighs and it is impossible to get them cleaned up. I miss the comfort and warmth of the last place we were in very much, but I expect we shall soon get accustomed to this place and after all we are exceedingly lucky to have as good a place as we have got – the infantry don't get half such good quarters, or even machine gun corps. I have the same billet here as we had before we went into rest and the people were really quite pleased to see me.

When he wrote on the 30th, he was at Mailly-Maillet (between Acheux and the Ancre). 'You will have heard by now' [presumably from a letter to Laura]:

that I am living in a dugout – it is really awfully comfortable and you can get such a lovely fug up in the evenings. Also you can be quite free about getting up time or meals – I am in fact getting very slack having breakfast at 9.30 on ordinary days and when I have been out on a night party don't get called even until ten.

This letter also implies that Evelyn had written to him asking him whether it was, or would be, right for her, an Anglican since late 1914, to take Communion from Dr Gibson, who was the Presbyterian minister at the church in St John's Wood which the family used to attend. Colin is sure it isn't right, but hasn't got time to go into the reasons at present. However, he will write to Will Porter and ask him to tell her.

His letter of 6 February, also from Mailly-Maillet, is entirely concerned with religious and ecclesiastical matters. It is as though Colin needed totally to forget the war and his part in it. He passes from a copy of Challoner's Meditations which he had sent Evelyn (it was promoted by the Society of Saints Peter and Paul, an extremely High Church group, whose shop their father sometimes called 'the Idolatrous Booth'), to Father Baker, a young bachelor priest, with whom Colin had corresponded, and who talked about the 'great fun' to be had from saying the church offices in Latin – though, Colin hastily adds, 'I'm sure he's really sincere and not merely what one would call a "spike"'. He then mentions his correspondence with 'Spot', and confesses that his last letter, which ended with 'Spot Rot', 'was very futile'; 'but I felt slack and silly at the time and wrote any nonsense that came into my head'. Next he asks how

old St George's is getting on? Any more fiascos? Or High Masses with Rector, Woodward and Courtney officiating and the Bleating Ba Lamb in choir; with the knowledge that Spot is preaching for certain in the evening but that you have to go to Shortlands? Poor Evelyn, I pity you. When I come back after the war I shall always go to All Saints for Sunday High Mass to serve once a month and probably one early Mass in each week up there. St George's I shall always go to on Sunday mornings. We must strike out a line for ourselves.

He then returns to Confession, which Colin is anxious that Evelyn should adopt soon. Finally, he bewails his inability to get to Communion at Corps Headquarters the previous Sunday, as his work started at 7. 'It makes one feel all the more the value and privilege of the Church's Treasures and Sacraments.'

Between this letter and the next, Colin was granted ten days compassionate leave to see Jim, who was dying at home in Beckenham. Jim had arrived there from Argentina on 8 September 1914, to re-enlist in the London Scottish (a Territorial Regiment) as a private. A week later his unit had been shipped out to France, where new troops were then urgently needed. On 31 October Jim had received a bad shrapnel wound in the arm at the first Battle of Messines, on the 'Ypres Salient', when 394 out of 700 officers and men of the London Scottish had died. He was brought back to England and sent to Westminster Hospital. Either his wound was even more serious than first thought, or else it was very badly treated, because it seems to have led, over the course of the next two years, to cancer of the spine.

He was discharged from hospital on 29 November and given two months sick-leave, though his arm had to be treated in Beckenham Hospital as he could not straighten it, and (as David Jugurtha says) 'he was in a very bad state'. However, at the end of March 1915, he was sent for officer training, and commissioned in the Black Watch at Tain, near Inverness, in June. Quite soon, however, he was home again for a little over seven weeks with (probably stress-induced) eczema, and then returned to the Black Watch as Assistant Adjutant of the 11th.

In November he was transferred to the Royal Irish and sent out to Salonika (or Thessalonica), in northern Greece, with the Regiment. In July 1916 he was promoted to full Lieutenant in the 5th Royal Irish, but in August he was hospitalised again because of 'severe indigestion and acute pain while walking'. He was then operated on in Malta on 27 October, where the surgeon, Col. Ballance 'found an inoperable retro-peritoneal sarcoma'. Then, David Jugurtha's journal continues, 'November 16th, left Malta for Netley via Mudros' (which is about 40 miles across the Aegean from Gallipoli, on the Greek island of Lemnos), and, on 30 December 1916, brought home to Beckenham as one who had been pronounced beyond medical help.

Jim's death on 5 March 1917 was so horrible, with convulsions and appalling pain, that it was never directly referred to in Colin's letters from the front, whether out of consideration for Evelyn, who helped to nurse him during his last two months, or because Colin himself could not bear to refer to it directly. Indeed, although he must have seen countless harrowing sights in and around the trenches, where his work lay – and he himself was never far from the front, either in the area of the Somme or near Ypres, in Flanders, except while 'resting', or on days off – he never refers to them either.

However, a month later he does mention 'the awful things that were happening all round us' during his last leave, and encourages Evelyn with the thought that a life based on trust in God can never be completely dominated by sadness. It is possible that Colin's phobia of blood (even 'blood oranges' were – jokingly – referred to in our family as 'wine oranges'), which was very familiar to me as a child and youth, was a result of the bloody scenes he witnessed so often during his time as a soldier.

Colin's next letter to Evelyn is dated Passion Sunday, 25 March 1917, and sent from Ervillers, near Bapaulme and about equidistant from Arras and Albert. He tells her that he had had no letters from home since he came back from leave (about the 12th), but adds:

> I expect it is the mails, because transport is very difficult just now owing to the advance. I have a splendid job now with the cavalry, as perhaps you know already, but the food and mails are not of course as regular as when with the infantry. But in spite of the interesting work etc I long for this ghastly war to be over so that I can come and enjoy home life and a civil occupation again. ... I do wish I could be at home now – it would be so glorious compared with the vile life here, for the worst part is that there is no-one to talk to – i.e. about the really interesting things.

(The mention of the 'civil occupation' seems to imply that he is still thinking of a career in accountancy.) 'The advance' he mentions was a result of a German decision to surrender some territory in this area and retreat to prepared positions they would find more suitable (Keegan). Gilbert Laithwaite (see below) later (early March 1918) refers to the 'utter ruin and desolation' of the village of Hermies: 'I have seen few villages more thoroughly destroyed.' Much of the destruction 'was wanton and not the result of shell fire', clearly the result of a scorched earth policy by the Germans when they had retreated the year before.

From his next letter to Evelyn, dated Monday in Holy Week, 2 April 1917, it is clear that he had already told someone, probably his mother, that he was now in hospital himself (near Mailly-Maillet). He does not say what was wrong with him (though it may have been TB), but that he is enjoying the rest and the chance to 'spend Holy Week properly', which would otherwise have been impossible. There are references to other private jokes, and the usual requests for detailed accounts of the Holy Week services at St George's.

A very short letter dated 5 April implies that he is now well again. He has 'no news' to give her, 'but our doings have been graphically and quite accurately described in the papers'. But the thought of his own death is not far from him, since he asks her, 'should anything ever happen to me', that she should let Will Porter know at once. It is worth adding here that, about 16 years later, he answered Mary O'Malley's question: 'were you afraid in the war?' with the answer that, although he was 'often terribly frightened, terribly', he never believed he'd be wounded or killed.

The following incident may be a case of this. In recalling it to Bede, he said that he and a brother officer were once strolling unarmed (one imagines the relative peace and quiet of an evening) along a road sunk between high banks which made it almost impossible to leave it. They then became aware that the two officers approaching them were armed and German. They rapidly decided that the only thing they could do without exciting these enemy officers to shoot or take them prisoner was to walk straight on and past them as though this were a perfectly normal situation of civilian life. They did so unscathed, possibly greeting them into the bargain (though Bede can't recall), and this sounds perfectly credible in the light of other records of an underlying civility among many officers and men to their enemy counterparts.

The event may well have taken place during the great German break-through of March 1918, possibly near the temporary HQ of Colin and his friend. In the letter to Evelyn dated 5 April he goes on to say he is sad that he has not been able to take Communion on Easter Day, because of his work schedule, but adds 'my thoughts are so full of battle that there is very little thought of God in me, I'm afraid. Still, my religion has kept me cheerful and optimistic and I thank God for it.'

On the 9th he writes at greater length, thinking that his inability to take Communion had been perhaps providential, as he had not had time to prepare himself properly, and enlarges on the importance of such preparation. But he is able to pray and meditate easily now, since he has a little wood and canvas collapsible hut to himself, which the 'section carpenter' has fitted up with shelves and a table, and he has a chair 'looted' from a house blown up by the 'Boche' before their retreat. There is here too a paragraph on plainsong, in which his life-long love of it, with its 'freeness and smoothness' of rhythm and its adaptability to 'the beauty of the words of the liturgy', is already clearly expressed. He singles out especially the great Passiontide Hymns: 'The Royal Banners Forward Go' and 'Thirty Years Among Us Dwelling', which he had obviously been singing and hearing in imagination.

In his next letter, of 21 May, from Bihoucourt, very near Ervillers, he tells Evelyn that he is sending her 'a rather nice statue of St Joseph and the Holy Child which I found on the floor of a much shelled and evacuated house near here', talks about possible Reservation at St George's ('it would make all the difference to the church') and mentions Rogation Processions, of which one at Newport, according to Will Porter, had been joined by Wesleyan Methodists just emerging from church as it passed. His letter of 6 June is largely devoted to a lyrical description of a late-evening visit to what he later wrote on the letter was the cathedral at Amiens, culminating in a service of Benediction. He sums it all up as follows:

I can never fully describe the wonderful dignity and yet simplicity of this beautiful service – the darkening cathedral – the incense rising up before the brilliantly lit altar – the priest praying with real faith to God and the voices of the children singing their praise to Him in the Blessed Sacrament. And then the priest gave them the Benediction and all heads were bowed low before the host and all was silent except the big deep bell right up in the cathedral, which rang three times very slowly and solemnly. It was a very happy and peaceful relief to get to this scene of devotion after the busy bustle of life out here up the line.

Colin was clearly very moved by the occasion and the devotion of the worshippers. To what extent he actually entered into the spirit of this very un-Anglican worship is not clear, but the earlier remark that Reservation (of some of the bread and wine consecrated in the Communion service) would 'make all the difference' to St George's suggests that he did. However, in the last letter we have from Colin's time in the army, dated 29 November, he does carefully distinguish the English Church (i.e. the still Catholic Church which is, or tries to be, in continuity with the medieval church in England) from 'Dissenters and Roman Catholics (who) are wrong' and have departed from the early church of the great Councils, which first laid down the fundamentals of Christian Doctrine. The Dissenters 'have denied many of the doctrines drawn up by these councils'; the Roman Catholics 'have added to them', whereas [we] Anglicans have done neither, 'but still take them as our authority' – hence the saying 'The Church to teach; the Bible to prove'. Benediction, he might have said, distorts the doctrine of the Eucharist, in so far as it presupposes that the host (the wafer) still remains identical with 'the Body of Christ' quite apart from the essentially social act of Holy Communion, in which the events of Christ's Passion, especially the Last Supper, are remembered and somehow made present, and the congregation then approach the altar together to share in the bread and wine, instead of remaining in their places for essentially private devotion. He had, perhaps, yet to attain the insight he later emphasised, that liturgy and ceremonial must be the expression of doctrine. I shall come back to these matters in the chapter on St Mary's, Primrose Hill.

This last letter, headed simply 'Flanders 29.xi.17', which lacks his usual addition of a local place-name, is the only one from Flanders among those sent to Evelyn. But he seems to have been there, with the 17th (Northern) Division, for much of the second half of 1917. Elsewhere there are some other valuable clues to what he did and where. In a letter to me he once wrote: 'I spent my 20th b'day (31 July 1917) in the trenches near Ypres and contrived to enjoy it'. This was also the day on which the 3rd Battle of Ypres began, after two weeks' continuous bombardment, with the battle of Pilkem Ridge.

'Over 5000 men were killed and wounded here on that day, the most murderous of the entire war in the Ypres salient, when along the entire front in Flanders more than 6000 died'; this comes from the website 'BBC History: Boesinghe – The Forgotten Battlefield', the place being hardly more than a mile from Pilkem Ridge. David Jugurtha then records him as having arrived home from Boesinghe for 10 days' leave on 27 August. He had paid a brief visit to Oxford first, where he was very likely visiting Will Porter, and perhaps also putting out feelers for studying there after the war. On 20 September, the second phase of '3rd Ypres' began with the battle of the Menen Road Ridge, and on the 27th, his father wrote, he was 'promoted to 1st Lt and very highly mentioned (in despatches) for splendid work under arduous and hazardous conditions'.

The conditions in much of the Ypres salient at that time were indeed almost unbelievable – 'a porridge of mud'. Apart from the few modest ridges the ground was extremely low-lying; there had been an almost unprecedented quantity of rain that late summer and autumn, so as to produce, under the two weeks of high explosive shelling, that landscape of continuous and slimy overlapping crater holes, almost full of water and crossed or bordered by slippery duck-boards, which characterises so many pictures of the First World War. Many soldiers and animals died by missing their footing and drowning, quite apart from the more usual ways involving gas, high explosive shells, rifle and machine gun fire, and so on. The communication wires, the main concern of Signallers, had to be strung up on metal posts screwed into the ground, and were constantly severed.

On 9 October, his father continues his record, he was put in charge of the Signals in the 52nd Infantry Brigade of his division. Three days later the First Battle of Passchendaele began, in which the Division took part; it also took part in the Second Battle of Passchendaele, between 26 October and 10 November. On 29 November comes the letter mentioned above, where the only reference to soldiering is this:

> I can always write much better when I am in the line – somehow I feel more energetic and not so flabby in mind – it is the long dull days of waiting till you get into the line that take it out of you so much and dull the faculties. In those kind of days I can't even summon sufficient energy to read, but loll about smoking all day.

There cannot be any doubt about the general nature of the thoughts and images that must have battered on the doors of his mind on those days. Between July and November the British gained 7 miles. There were 265,423 casualties among the British, 206,000 among the Germans.

Colin managed to get home for Christmas, and, some time after the Third Battle of Ypres was over, his brigade was sent back again south-east, to the higher ground west of Cambrai and those parts of the Somme battlefield which he had known during his first nine months in France. In March 1918, the Germans began there 'the largest, most violent and most decisive campaign of the war', which came near to driving the English back to the Channel.[5] This long-planned German onslaught, so different from the usual indecisive

---

[5] Correlli Barnett in A.J.P. Taylor (ed.), *History of World War I.*

engagements of this area, which had in any case had very limited objectives, was occasioned by the threat presented to the Germans by the ever-growing numbers of American troops on French soil, food-shortages at home almost approaching famine as a result of the Allied blockade, and the German victory on the Russian front, which made possible a great transfer of some of their best forces to the West. (The United States had actually declared war on 6 April 1917, though it was a very long time before they were in a position to put battle-ready troops into the trenches.) The German High Command knew that, if they were to win the war, it had to be done soon.

A small, privately printed, book by Sir Gilbert Laithwaite, entitled *The 21st March, 1918: Memories of an Infantry Officer*, sheds some light on this campaign, with its vivid descriptions of the rapid English retreat over ground so long contested yard by yard in trench warfare. Whether his and Colin's acquaintance and friendship began before the war I don't know, but he had been part of the same brigade as Colin from April 1917, was sent back to Dunstable for a Signals Course, and returned in February 1918 to be a battalion Signals officer. After the war he joined the India Office and eventually became Principal Private Secretary to the Viceroy, the Marquess of Linlithgow. The website of the Lancashire Fusiliers, which he joined on entering the army, says: 'He deserves to share with Linlithgow the credit for ensuring India's vital role as supply centre for the war effort' – in, of course, the Second World War. Colin and he were clearly kindred spirits, Laithwaite being a devout Christian (a Roman Catholic) and 'a lover of fine artefacts'. Colin once told Mary in a letter from Iraq that he and Gilbert Laithwaite used to meet in his club, where they always drank Liebfraumilch. His name was often mentioned at home in our family. Laithwaite's memoir starts by telling how his batallion, the 10th, was taking over a section of the front from a batallion of Sherwood Foresters.

> It contained a magnificent Boche dugout: You went down a long stair with three turnings and a handrail: at the foot on the right was a pantry, on the left a kitchen; straight ahead a room with bunks for men. A passage to the left led to the Officers' Quarters – first came a large mess with a central supporting pillar, two good mirrors, chairs, tables and cupboards. From this one passed on into a passage from which there opened out three bedrooms for officers, all with beds, chairs, mirrors, and doors on hinges. ... From the Officers' Quarters ran a passage leading into an elaborately equipped signal office, from which in turn there ran a separate staircase giving exit on to the road running north from Havrincourt to the Bapaume-Cambrai Road.

In view of this it is not surprising that the English shelling of the German lines often had very little of its intended effect back in the autumn of 1916.

Laithwaite describes the beginning of the expected German attack like this:

> In a thick mist, at 5 a.m. on the morning of March 21st, 1918, the storm broke. Front and support systems were deluged with thousands of gas shells, mixed with high explosive: communication trenches and junctions were barraged, all

avenues of approach for reinforcing troops blocked by a chain of fire. Simultaneously, all rear Headquarters transport lines, and heavy guns of which the positions were known, were subjected to a heavy bombardment from long range high velocity guns. Corps (HQ) was shelled into its dugouts at Villers au Flos; Division (HQ) into its cellars in Bertincourt: in the banks of the Canal du Nord the deep dugouts of 52nd Brigade Headquarters were blown in, and their locality so thoroughly dealt with that no message by a Brigade Runner reached us in front all day. Dumps were fired by mapshooting as far back as Haplincourt and Villers. Brigade Transport lines and the Quartermaster's Stores in Velu Wood were shelled with high velocities, and amidst great confusion started to apply the defence scheme and move backwards across the open to pre-arranged stations.

'Within an hour from the opening of the barrage', he goes on,

the units holding the forward area were isolated from their brigades: by 6 a.m. there was no longer any communication backward – cable trenches were blown in, air lines cut, ordinary cross-country wires smashed as soon as mended, while the mist rendered visual signalling impossible, and pigeons uncertain.

One consequence of this was that forward battalions 'had to fight their own battle, make their own decisions, and carry out the policy which seemed advisable by arrangement with one another', perhaps with the help of runners. Amidst all this chaos, Laithwaite was able to write: 'The noise was so great, and the whole thing so immense, that one's nerves steadied automatically.' Others, however, have written that, after about three hours of continuous shelling, a man was driven almost into a state of torpor.

The order to retreat came on the evening of 22 March. The 17th Division had not yet fully recovered from the battles of Paschendaele, and were numerically the weakest of Haig's four armies, and yet the 52nd Brigade were able to respond to their Brigade major's heartening assurance that they were 'the only Division which had held its own on an eighty mile front'. John Keegan, writing 80 years later gives what must be a more objective summing up of the situation, at least as regards the British:

Along a front of 19 miles the whole forward position had been lost, except in two places held heroically by the South African Brigade and a brigade formed of three batallions of the Leicestershire regiment, and much of the main position had been penetrated also.

But the 52nd Brigade had not gone to pieces, as many units had, and Laithwaite mentions a sergeant of the pre-war army weeping as he retreated with the rest, not because of shell-shock but because he so strongly felt the dishonour of what he saw as an ignominious rout. They set off on the morning of the 23rd, with all the others; some resistance might still have been possible, but because the Germans were trying to cut the British forces in two, only by retreating so as to keep together with the rest of the Corps could they avoid inevitable defeat in the end. Somehow, burdened with many essential items of equipment, the units of the brigade managed to keep fairly well in touch, though moving in individual companies, as 'a continual stream of men, wounded and unwounded, from the various divisions of the Corps', marched, and often staggered, along the muddy and shell-pocked roads and tracks to the West. Near Le Transloy Laithwaite met Colin at the temporary HQ of their Brigade:

> I talked for a while with Dunlop, and got a little news. ... Dunlop, who always disliked the noisy side of war, made no secret of his disgust at the state of things. 'As for you', he said, 'up in the front with a battalion – I simply can't understand how you can all be so cheerful. I should go mad.' He grinned and went off.

On the 24th, Laithwaite, viewing the country to the rear against the evening sky noted 'black streams of men and limbers', 'half a dozen tanks puffing along' with 'wounded on top of them'. Another tank was burning, four new motor lorries being destroyed as there was no petrol to drive them away.

> All around was evidence of the most utter confusion and surprise. For the first time since the beginning, one's heart sank and one began to fear that morale might be giving and that we might be getting a harder knock than we could withstand.

He found great piles of batallion records dating back to 1914 by the side of the track, including secret papers, which no-one had tried to destroy.

> All along the track were masses of clothing – sets of silk pierrot suits from some divisional concert troupe; music; a dump of damaged boots; old khaki tunics; socks; equipment – littered for half a mile. When he and his company saw this they could not help saying 'whatever will the Boche think when he sees this – he'll think he has us on the run and has broken us'.

All this time they were afraid the Germans might appear on their left in the attempt to cut them off, so, when they made out the enormous quantity of crawling traffic ahead, they bore to the right across country, and, after half an hour got to the Albert–Cambrai road through long grass and thistles. Shortly afterwards 'Marsden and Dunlop rode up on bicycles – Brigade Intelligence and Signals respectively; they could give us no news as to the position of other units, but confirmed our orders to go to Le Sars.' Cyril Marsden was by now a friend of Colin's and attended one of the 21st Birthday dinners given in his honour later that year. They had some contact after the war but, as far as I know, he was never as close to him as Gilbert Laithwaite. Eventually, on 26 March, they reached Hénencourt, where the Brigade had established headquarters in the chateau, and gradually the other units arrived and joined the batallion camps now organised on the edge of the village. Slowly the pressure on the retreating troops eased, and they stayed in Hénencourt until 2 April, when they 'marched behind the line to rest'. Despite the chaos and harrowing scenes he had witnessed, Laithwaite ends his account of the retreat thus:

> In retrospect, the excellent spirit and good morale of the men, their capacity for endurance, the good temper, forbearance, give and take of everyone, officers and men alike, in conditions of great strain, will be an abiding memory.

Colin, who as Brigade Signals Officer was never quite so directly exposed to front line danger, nevertheless received another glowing mention in despatches, this time by P.R. Robertson, Commanding Officer of the 17th Division, for 'conspicuous gallantry and devotion to duty in the unceasing energy displayed in keeping open communications, 21st March to 2nd April'.

There are several reasons why the German attack failed of its purpose in the end. Keegan first points to the ultimate concentration on only part of the front attacked, with the object of separating the French from the English forces, and thus inevitably relieving the pressure on other parts, which enabled the British there to recover. Secondly,

> the nearer they approached Amiens, the more deeply did they become entangled in the obstacles of the old Somme battlefield, a wilderness of abandoned trenches, broken roads and shell-crater fields left behind by the movement of the front a year earlier. ... Moreover, the British rear areas, stuffed with the luxuries enjoyed by the army of a nation which had escaped the years of blockade that in Germany had made the simplest necessities of life rare and expensive commodities, time and again tempted the advancing Germans to stop, plunder and satiate themselves. The German officer, Colonel Albrecht von Thaer, recorded that 'entire divisions totally gorged themselves on food and liquor' and had failed to 'press the vital attack forward'.

After their rest, the 52nd Brigade seem to have moved back to Hénencourt, as, on 30 July (actually a day early) Officers of the Headquarters gave a 21st birthday dinner in honour of Colin at the Chateau. The 'roneoed' menu for the lavish meal, 'Hors D'oeuvres Variés, Crême de Tomate, Homard á Dunlop, Boeuf Rôti, Pommes de Terre, Choux, Omelette Épatant, Sardines Corses and Dessert', under a drawing of a gnome-like figure with thumbs up and the name 'Billikin', seemingly Colin's nickname, survives with a selection of signatures. Next day, his birthday proper, the 17th Division Signals Company gave a similar dinner at nearby Toutencourt, this time with the menu in English and, instead of the 'Billikin' figure, the badge and supporting griffins of the Royal Engineers.

The Division now took part in a huge Allied counter-attack, beginning at Amiens on 8 August. Within four days, Keegan writes, most of the old Somme battlefield had been retaken, and by the end of August they were at the outworks of the Hindenburg Line, from where they had been so rudely thrust back in March. At the end of September Colin went home on leave from Léchelle, not far from the line, and, according to David Jugurtha, returned on

15 October to Caudry, which is some way beyond it. Then came the Armistice, signed on 11 November, when the Division was withdrawn to a position west of Le Cateau. On 6 December, it moved back behind Amiens and went into billets round Hallencourt, south of Abbeville.

For the first time Colin spent Christmas away from home, and another 'roneoed' menu survives of the dinner given to officers of the Division Signals by the Senior NCOs during the festival. A traditional Christmas dinner menu is here followed with the words 'God save the King'. Colin wrote to me, on my spending Christmas in Germany on National Service in 1956, that, 'as the war had just ended and my fellow officers were friends of several years standing it wasn't too bad'. On 17 January, his father records, he was 'home on leave from France and demobilized a few days later'. The official record gives his occupation in civil life as Student and his medical category as A1. On the 20th, David Jugurtha writes, he 'went to Oxford and was enrolled at New College (Dean Spooner)'.

5

OXFORD

APART FROM one or two 'business' letters, I have seen none written by Colin to friends or relations while he was at Oxford, so these four years, which include his ordination course, are not well documented. However, the main outlines of his Oxford career are reasonably clear from David Jugurtha's journal, one or two official letters and documents, and Colin's own memories, as written in letters and diaries and recounted to his family in later years.

Having 'enrolled' at New College on 20 January 1919, and found himself somewhere to live, Colin went home for nearly three weeks to catch up with civilian and family life. He then returned to Oxford on 10 February and moved in to lodgings at 9 St John's Street, which he shared with Tom Staveley.

Tom, who was at Trinity College, had fought at Gallipoli, perhaps the least successful allied campaign in the war, mounted in response to Russia's repeated requests to Britain and France to take some of the pressure off their southern front with Austria, so that she would be better equipped to meet the German and Austrian attacks through Poland.

A series of landings were accordingly made at the end of the long peninsula projecting westwards on the north side of the Dardanelles, the channel that connects the Aegean and the Black Sea. The strategic objective was to take Istanbul from the Turks, Germany and Austria's ally in the south-east of the European war zone, but came nowhere near to realisation. Tom Staveley became one of Colin's closest friends, and was one of my godfathers. After Colin's death his sister, in her letter of condolence to my mother, recalled how 'just after the 14–18 war ... he came to stay with us on the Quantocks. Tom truly loved him', she goes on, 'and could always draw strength and inspiration from him. This was specially so after his stroke'.

This affliction, which came on Tom in the middle of a bicycle tour in Ireland, left him completely paralysed on his left side. By then he had retired from teaching at Tonbridge School, where he was Head of English and Housemaster of Judd's. I used to visit him on my own bicycle quite a lot in the late 1950s and early '60s, and can entirely endorse the sentiments expressed by Colin in a letter to me in 1960 just before Tom died: 'How wonderfully he copes with his catastrophic suffering. ... One goes to him hoping to give sympathy and gets more than one gives.'

I also remember his wonderful collection of records, through which he introduced me to, among others, his 'beloved Carl' (Nielsen), who was very little known in England at the time. Colin and he had much in common. Jack Finch, Colin's Radley friend, was also at Trinity College and shared lodgings with A.L.P. Norrington, with whom Colin also became a lifelong friend. After a career in the Oxford University Press, he became President of Trinity, and was knighted as 'Sir Arthur Norrington', though he was always known by friends and others as 'Thomas'. This new friendship probably also led to his getting to know another Trinity man, John Christie, who was an uncle of my wife, Anna. John became Principal of Jesus College, Oxford, after two spells as a public school headmaster, the first at Repton (as a young successor of Geoffrey Fisher, who went on to be Archbishop of Canterbury) and the second at Westminster. After Colin's death he wrote in a letter of condolence to my mother:

> My memories of Colin are all so good and so bright – from Oxford just after the First War, to glimpses at Henfield, and Lincoln and Oxford. What gifts he had, and what charm!, and much more than that, as the Times Obituary rightly said.

Colin's first studies were in History, though he later told me in a letter that he rather wished he'd 'had the discipline of Greats [Latin, Greek, Philosophy and Ancient History] like many of his Oxford friends'. He got his BA in January 1921, under the special arrangements made by the universities for ex-servicemen returned from the war. Colin was very lucky in his New College Tutor, Sir Ernest Barker, who was a devout Christian as well as a first class historian, and 'used to talk about God even when criticising my history essays'. Sir Maurice Bowra, an exact contemporary of Colin at New College and a friend of his, mentions Ernest Barker in his memoirs as a distinguished don who, 'unfortunately for his pupils, left New College at the end of Summer 1920'.

He adds that he was educated at Manchester Grammar School and frequently spoke with a Lancashire accent, which some said (in fact, erroneously) was 'assumed'. Bowra himself became an eminent scholar, the author of numerous books and Warden of his college, Wadham. He confesses in the memoirs that, as a student, he wilfully broke the New College rule that undergraduates should attend chapel every Sunday. He also describes the effect of the war on himself, and those of his contemporaries who had fought, in these terms:

> it had broken into our lives and so upset our balance that we had real difficulty in regaining it; ... in the army I developed a mocking, cynical way of treating events because it prevented them from being too painful. I had formed such a habit of this that I kept it even at Oxford when it was no longer necessary.

We may compare this with a passage from one of the many letters Colin wrote to his future wife, Mary O'Malley, from Baghdad in February 1934. After a general lament over his own spiritual state when at New College he goes on:

the Oxford of which I found myself a part was so blasé, sceptical and cynical, and I became too much of it. It is taking me a long time to get out of the errors of faith and feeling that I adopted when I was there, largely out of vanity and out of a desire to have a reputation for 'enlightened' and 'cultivated' Christianity.

My brother Bede also recalls Colin telling him that, when he was first up at Oxford, he got into a circle of friends who gambled, and that he was gradually drawn in to this circle to such an extent that he had to ask his father to settle his debts. In a sermon entitled 'Why Judas Fell' Colin also says, probably with Oxford in mind, 'I know that in my own life at an earlier period, there was a time when I allowed my mind to see the force of all the arguments against Christianity – allowed it with keen approval'.

But it was not only Colin – always highly sensitive and impressionable – and his New College friends who allowed this; Hastings tells us, in his monumental *History of English Christianity 1920–2000* (p. 221) that during the 1920s the 'principle intellectual orthodoxy of England' was 'confident agnosticism'. It is not hard, therefore, to understand how important must have been the counter-influence of Ernest Barker in such matters.

After leaving New College, he became Principal of King's College, London, was approached by more than one person about becoming Warden of New College (his refusal to encourage this idea was partly based on a feeling that his working-class roots would be against him), took up a Rockefeller Professorship at Cambridge, and was awarded many other academic and civil honours (including, of course, his knighthood); on the basis of his deep study of Plato and Aristotle, he developed a political and social philosophy which was very influential in his lifetime, and is now enjoying a renaissance in our own day. He became a firm friend of Colin's, who wrote to Mary when staying at Felixstowe in 1947 that it was 'Lovely having tea with Ernest Barker and family', and said that they 'may visit us at Hintlesham' during our family holiday. He also recalls how Sir Ernest wrote and congratulated him warmly on his brief study of Cranmer, 'the First Great Figure in Anglicanism', delivered as a University Sermon in St Mary's Church in 1956.

At some time, possibly January 1920, Colin moved to lodgings in 94, High Street ('The High'), which is now a hotel. This would have helped him to start freeing himself from the effects of the prevailing agnosticism in college. A photograph of his living room shows on one of the walls his Arundel Print of Van Eyck's triptych *The Adoration of the Lamb*, and numerous other pictures, and there is a cushion on the sofa with the arms of New College sewn onto it (see Photo 9). Photo 8 shows him as stroke of the New College War Veterans' Eight – Colin told me that 'he used to do a lot of rowing at New College'. He also took up Morris Dancing, which he continued to practice for many years. In 1953 he records how, at a Folk Dancing Festival at Lincoln, he 'was charmed to meet again old Kimber who still presides over the Headington Morris Men' – though by that time he had ceased to participate himself. There are one or two photographs of Morris Dancing at the Bishop's Palace in Chichester and elsewhere in Sussex.

It was probably during this second year of history studies that Colin finally decided to offer himself for ordination, though, since he later told Ida O'Malley in a letter that 'Ordination somehow was inevitable, though it meant giving up another plan for my life, but it seemed much more a following of inclination and taste', it doesn't sound as though this was the culmination of a great internal struggle. No doubt he discussed this with Ernest Barker, who left New College after the Trinity term of 1920.

Among papers he kept are two short notes written to him by the Warden of New College, who was the famous Spooner, after whom the linguistic solecism of the 'spoonerism' is – some say misleadingly – named. The first is dated 21 December 1920, and must have come at the end of his history studies. The Warden says he is glad Colin is 'going to do Professor Headlam's course'. Professor Headlam, who been Professor of Dogmatic Theology at King's College, London, was now Regius Professor of Divinity at Oxford, and had made radical changes to the study of theology there, as well as planning and organising the special Oxford Ordination Course for ex-servicemen. Accordingly, Colin had applied to live at Pusey House for a time, where there was (and still is) an extensive theological library and a small religious community of high church Anglican clergy. Colin seems to have been concerned about the implications for his continuing membership of the college if he lived there. Spooner puts his mind at rest: he can continue to attend chapel and dine in hall as much as he likes, and hopes that the chapel visits in particular will be continued, as this is 'a matter in which people need a good example to be set them.' Two days later he tells Colin he has 'written a recommendation to Dr Headlam', and repeats much of what he said in the previous note, but also advises Colin to get tuition outside the college if he wants to avoid paying what would presumably be higher tuition fees. Each letter ends with good wishes for Christmas and the New Year.

Colin took up residence in Pusey House in St Giles Street on January 14th, 1921. When I lived there in 1961–2 there were 14 undergraduates in residence. However, Colin told me that when he was there he was one of only two 'permanent' residents, with a Principal and three Librarians (as opposed to Principal, Librarian and Chaplain in 1960). In his letter he adds that the Principal, Dr Darwell Stone, a theologian who gradually took over the leadership of the Anglo-Catholic Movement in the Church of England (*Oxford Dictionary of the Christian Church*, 1958), 'hardly ever opened his mouth except to ask for the salt'.

His tutor for the Oxford Ordination Course was The Revd G.A. Michell. Colin must have worked hard – indeed, he used to go to Theological lectures in the Chapter House at Christ Church three times a week during this year – and on 22 October E.A. Berrisford, of Queen's College, the chief theology examiner, wrote to him to let him know that he had passed the three papers of the first exam 'pretty well'. Whether he was examined on any other topics is not clear, but his three papers were Old Testament Theology, awarded what looks from his letter like β+, Church History to 800AD β+, and an α- for Doctrine (Church and Sacraments in the Hilary Term and Eschatology in the Trinity Term), with Headlam's comment 'Very thoughtful and Mature'.

Other lecture courses he attended in these terms were on The Apostolic Age, Ethical Teaching of the New Testament and the Christian Doctrine of Sin. There were also lectures on Voice Production and Religious Education. After the long vacation he paid what seems to have been an extensive visit to Cologne and Bonn, taking up the whole of the Michaelmas Term. The purpose of this visit was, according to David Jugurtha's journal, 'to keep Walter company'. When sending his exam marks Berrisford wished him 'a good time' but exhorted him 'not to get stabbed in the back by Junkers'.

Walter, Colin's brother, had suffered much more from the war than Colin. As an officer in the Machine Gun Corps, he must have directed the fire which killed, or 'mowed down', hundreds, even thousands, of men advancing from enemy trenches. After his demob in January 1919 he had worked hard for the Civil Service exam, which he passed with a Class 1, before returning to Christ Church in April (where he had already spent the year of 1913–14 before joining the army in October 1914). Appointed to the Indian Civil Service in August 1919, he went down from Christ Church and sailed for India in December. But his memories of the war (possibly aggravated by the number of Indians condemned to death by his fellows in the legal department) were so oppressive that he could not stand the strain. In David Jugurtha's words, he was invalided home 'in a very nervous state – very discontented and miserable'.

However, not long after his arrival at home his father began his last struggle against his many ailments and died on 14 October. A few days before, Walter had left for Cologne 'with Duncan Jones' (quite likely Austin, the eldest son of 'D-J.', see next chapter), a fellow classicist and future Professor of Philosophy at Birmingham), to be joined on the 15th by Colin and Evelyn, where the three of them (Duncan-Jones having presumably gone on) lived in a hotel. Colin later told me that life was still absurdly cheap there for those with a foreign currency to exchange, and that he frequently went to the opera. He and Evelyn also spent Christmas there, where, he later wrote to Mary, he had been 'thrilled' by reading the words '*Stille nacht, heilige nacht*' [Silent Night, Holy Night] on a Christmas Card. Evelyn outlined the programme for this Christmas Day, possibly her 'happiest ever', as follows: it started:

> with a 5.30 Mass in the Dom, a huge breakfast in the Ewige Lampe in the Domplatz, which I fear is no more; then a bright evangelical service for any British folk in a large hall, and a gigantic lunch complete with a Schwedische Platte and Schnapps.

Colin returned to Oxford in January 1922 for the Hilary and Trinity terms, and lived in St Stephen's House, a proper theological college, to do the second part of the Ordination Course. In the final exam in June he certainly sat papers on Liturgies and Prayer Book, and two on the New Testament, testing his knowledge of Greek, Biblical Criticism and New Testament Theology. Lecture courses attended included Philosophy of Religion, the Study of Religion and the Theology of St Paul; he was also given experience in practical teaching of children in south Oxford schools. No record of his exam marks survives in the family, but he certainly passed the course with much credit. In September he took the first part of The Bishop's Exam at Fulham Palace, the residence of the Bishop of London.

Other glimpses of Colin's Oxford life are few, but it is surprising how many of his friends and acquaintances he met in after years. Among them were at least one member of the Roman Catholic Elwes family. Gervase Elwes was a celebrated tenor of an earlier generation whose singing he much admired, and it may have been one of his sons whom he had in mind when he wrote to thank me for the gift of an LP of Vaughan Williams's *Songs of Travel*: 'I had a very great friend at Oxford who used to sing them very beautifully'. Perhaps he was Valentine (Val), whom he was glad to meet again in the Orkneys in 1943 at Scapa Flow, as an RC chaplain.

But three more of his life-long friends deserve special mention. The first was Philip Usher, who read History and then was a contemporary of Colin's at St Stephen's House. Usher was a brilliant young man who became an expert on contemporary Greece, and could converse easily with Greeks from any region or social class. He was very prominent in the Church of England's efforts towards reunion with the Orthodox Church and other continental churches. He and Colin both attended a conference on doctrine in Norway with a small number of members of all the Scandinavian Lutheran churches (see below).

Usher had much to do with Professor Headlam, acting for some years as his chaplain when he became Bishop of Gloucester, editing a periodical owned by him, *The Church Quarterly Review*, and assisting him on the Church of England Council for Foreign Affairs, of which Headlam was chairman. Colin invited him to preach when he was an incumbent in Sussex and he became a godfather to my brother Philip. After the German invasion of Greece in the Second World War he became an RAF chaplain and was sent to Palestine, but was killed in a motor accident on the very night of his arrival, 6 June 1941. Colin was able to visit his tomb in Ramleh War Cemetery in 1945 (see www.cwgc.org for details) and pick a sprig of rosemary, which grew profusely around, to send to Usher's sister after his return to England.

Two other great friends survived Colin's death and wrote to Mary when he died. Martin Browne, who read theology at Oxford before working for the British Drama League and the Adult Education Movement, became a very important figure in religious drama, and married Henzie Raeburn, an actress. 'Colin was a very special person in our lives', he wrote:

> for me at Oxford, in the days when we worked for George Bell at Chichester, in the war days at Edinburgh when you were both so good to the Pilgrim visitors

[Martin Browne directed the Pilgrim Players; he and his wife stayed with us], and of St Mary's (Primrose Hill) he was one of the special people too: that congregation will feel a deep sense of loss. He has shed light and comfort and joy on so many lives.

Thanks to George Bell, Martin Browne began a long association with T.S. Eliot, and produced his religious plays, beginning with *Murder in the Cathedral* in 1935. The other friend was J.S. MacArthur, who also studied theology when Colin was at Oxford, and was Episcopalian Provost of the Cathedral of the Isles at Millport, on Great Cumbrae Island in the Firth of Clyde. 'Colin helped one', he wrote, 'to go on believing in goodness':

I wish I could focus more clearly my memories of him in those Oxford days of more than forty five years ago ... It is only in the 1940s at Cumbrae, Edinburgh, Durham, and then Lincoln that I get the clear recollection of his unfailing kindness and patience, his faculty of listening in such a way that one began to imagine that one was saying something worth while.

In later years Colin would look back on his time at Oxford with nostalgic pleasure. His favourite term, he told me, was the Michaelmas, the sights and smells of autumn itself, associated with 'seeing what the freshers were like', though autumn came to remind him more strongly of his first confession in the autumn of 1915 and his ordination in 1922. But summer always filled him with melancholy, especially at Oxford, where he 'used to wander disconsolately about on the long summer evenings longing for something and quite unhappy without it, though I never could fit anything in as the aim of my longing.' Nevertheless, he always had some 'golden memories' of Oxford in the summer, and 'really did enjoy Oxford more than anything previous in life, though, oddly enough, I enjoyed being on active service in France almost as much.'

Photo 1: Dunlop family, 1899. *Back row*: Sibyl, Jim.
Front row: Walter, Laura Frances (with Evelyn on knee);
David Jugurtha (with Colin on knee).

Photo 2: Colin, c. 1901.

Photo 3: Colin and siblings, 1904.
Back row: Walter, Jim, Sibyl.
Front row: Evelyn, Colin.

Photo 4: Colin at Radley College, c. 1912.

Photos 5 and **6**: Colin in army uniform. *Top*: during training in the UK, 1915. *Bottom*: at Abbeville near the Somme front, 1916,

Photo 7: Colin at New College, Oxford, 1919.

Photo 8: Colin in New College War Veterans Eight, 1919.
Colin is rowing in 'stroke' position.

Photo 9: Colin's room at 94 High Street, Oxford, 1920. This is in the building on the corner of Magpie Lane, which is now part of the Old Bank Hotel.

Photo 10: Colin soon after his ordination, c. 1922.

Photo 11: Colin with servers at St Mary the Virgin, Primrose Hill, 1927.

6

ST MARY THE VIRGIN, PRIMROSE HILL

C OLIN WAS ordained deacon in St Mary the Virgin, Primrose Hill on 29
October 1922, by William Wilcox, Bishop of Willesden, one of the
Bishop of London's suffragan, or assistant, bishops. The diocese paid
him £200 p.a. The Vicar, Arthur Stewart Duncan-Jones, who was always
known in our house – and indeed to a great many people – as D-J, had asked
the Bishop of London (Winnington-Ingram) to allow this rather unusual
procedure – unusual because deacons were and are normally ordained among a
crowd of other ordinands by the Diocesan Bishop in his Cathedral. This is
perhaps why *The Church Times* gave such a detailed account of the service,
whose carefully rehearsed ceremonial was carried out with the richness and
precision that St Mary's did so well. Colin's reading of the Gospel, in the
Eucharist that followed the ordination, was decribed as follows:

> the candidate, by this time in alb and amice, was vested by the assistant
> ministers in stole and maniple, and, attended by the deacon of the Mass, he read
> the Gospel in a clear voice which made every word heard throughout the
> building. It was all very dignified and yet so simple, so direct, so personal, so
> intelligible, that it was plainly a religious act, the deep significance of which
> must have been grasped by the youngest worshipper in the church, and it was
> good to see how many young people were present.

As noted above, Colin had first visited St Mary's in 1916, and much later
recalled the occasion as follows: 'I can still, after 43 years, feel the thrill which
my first Sunday morning visit to St Mary's, Primrose Hill, gave me, with
Dearmer at the altar and Martin Shaw at the organ.' This was, of course, not
very long after he first became acquainted with All Saints, Margaret St, and
became for a time committed to this West End church as an altar server, and
was so proud of being asked to serve at the Patronal Festival service in 1915.

But Roscow Shedden, the Vicar of All Saints during the war, who had
heard Colin's first Confession, left in 1919 to be Bishop of Nassau, in the
Bahamas. D-J had succeeded Dearmer as vicar of St Mary's quite soon after
Colin's first visit there, and he was clearly drawn back because of D-J's
incumbency. He must have repeated his visit and got to know D-J well, since,
in a letter he wrote to Mary in 1933, he says of D-J that they had been

'tremendous friends ever since 1916' and had 'lived in each others' pockets'. D-J had become to him 'half father and half brother'; he was to D-J 'half brother, half son'.

Percy Dearmer, whose conduct of the service which Colin witnessed at his first visit had so enthralled him, was the 3rd Vicar of St Mary's, and took up office in 1901. Two years before, while curate of St Mark's, Marylebone Road, he, in the words of the excellent recent Guide to St Mary's: *The Parish Church of St Mary the Virgin Primrose Hill: History and Guide,* compiled by John Hawes, Christopher Kitching and Bryan Almond, 'published *The Parson's Handbook,* a small book which was to revolutionise worship in the Church of England'. It was, in Dearmer's own words, an attempt 'to help, in however humble a way, towards remedying the lamentable confusion, lawlessness and vulgarity that are conspicuous at this time'. The Guide continues:

> Many churches still followed an extreme Protestant form of liturgical practice, whilst many more adopted a mild form of ceremonial with the priest facing East at an altar which had two lighted candles. At the catholic end of the spectrum, a small number of parishes followed mediaeval English practices, generally of Sarum origin, and another small faction followed Tridentine Roman usage more or less accurately. Most Anglo-Catholic churches mixed the two styles of ceremonial, sometimes with strange results, and many incumbents added a few 'simple' ceremonies of their own.

Dearmer himself was an advocate of the revival of medieval English practices. 'But Dearmer's little book', the Guide goes on:

> was totally unlike anything that had gone before, being well written, with occasional evidence of humour, and was soundly practical rather than antiquarian. It gave authority for the practices recommended, all of which were strictly within the letter of the law. This was an important point in view of the then still strong possibility of a demonstration or lawsuit from ... the Protestant Truth Society. [Dearmer was, then,] quite clear that the Book of Common Prayer was the only liturgy sanctioned in the Church of England, and although susceptible of improvement was to be used without addition or deviation.

When Colin, a great admirer of Dearmer, was asked in 1959 by George Timms, a later Vicar, to consider the wording of a memorial to him in St Mary's, he rather tentatively suggested:

Remember with thanksgiving
Percy Dearmer
Master of Arts, Doctor of Divinity
Vicar of this church from 1901-1916
who made St Mary's Primrose Hill
a centre of church life
which has influenced the worship of
the whole Anglican Communion.

He adds a biblical quotation, Psalm XLVIII, verse 2, and goes on to explain in his letter that it was 'no good trying to go into details', since it would be extremely difficult to do so 'simply and worthily'. He was thinking here of the many aspects of Dearmer's conception of Christian worship apparent in *The Parsons' Handbook* and other achievements. For example, in his little book on Dearmer, Donald Gray summarises his 'aims and concerns' as follows:

> Liturgical reform (for that is what it was) using art and artists to bring colour and inspiration into the church; finding strong and suitable songs for the people of God to sing; affirming the unity of the ministry of both men and women in the priesthood, ministering to bodies as well as minds and spirits; confronting those who saw Christian faith and belief as only to do with personal morality and nothing to do with the needs of society as a whole. (Donald Gray, *Percy Dearmer*, Norwich: Canterbury Press, 2000, p. 4)

We may well recall here the aims of Father Mackonochie of St Alban's, Holborn.

The Dictionary of National Biography strongly emphasises Donald Gray's first point: 'At heart (Dearmer) was an artist; his most creative work revealed this, and his permanent contribution both to the church and to national life is to be found in his profound understanding of the true relation between religion, particularly worship, and art.' Dearmer's attempt to kindle a new understanding of the beauty of worship found practical expression not only in the services and ambience of St Mary's, but also in two other lasting projects: *The English Hymnal*, founded and co-edited by Dearmer, with Vaughan Williams as the musical sub-editor, and, in conjunction with Mowbrays, the initiation of The Warham Guild, which began as a means of supplying the church with vestments consonant with the principles set out in *The Parson's Handbook*, but developed under its advisory committee to become a channel of supply for all kinds of church furnishings and ornaments of 'outstanding design, high-quality-workmanship and good taste'. As a result of all this, St Mary's became:

> a mecca for artists, who found there a satisfaction they could find nowhere else, and he did successfully impress upon the clergy as a whole that half the secret of worship that is alive lies in a scrupulous, tireless attention to small details. (Roger Lloyd, *The Church of England 1900-1965*, SCM, 1966, p. 155)

As noted above, Dearmer was succeeded by D-J in 1916. After his ordination in 1904, D-J became, first, Chaplain, and then Fellow and Dean of Gonville and Gaius College, Cambridge. He married Caroline Roberts, the Master's daughter, in 1907, and in 1912 accepted the college living at Blofield, near Norwich, where 'he did much good and lasting work' (S.C. Carpenter, *Duncan-Jones of Chichester*, Mowbray's, 1956, p. 28). Then, after a very short period as incumbent of Louth, in Lincolnshire, 'was unable to resist the attractions of a call to become Vicar (or actually Perpetual Curate) of St

Mary's, Primrose Hill,' (op.cit., p. 29) where, although he 'inherited a tradition with which few would dare to tamper' (St Mary's Guide), he in fact considerably enriched the liturgical regime. He made, for example, Anglican adaptations of the English medieval ceremonies for Candlemas and Holy Week, special days uncatered for in the Book of Common Prayer, in a way with which few bishops would have problems. They were published by the Alcuin Club in its *Directory of Ceremonial.* 'But he made no changes whatsoever to the basic tradition left by Dearmer' (St Mary's website) and, when he became Dean of Chichester in 1929, he 'put the principles of the English Use into practice in a cathedral setting' (St Mary's Guide) – in a way still more or less carried on by all English cathedrals and many other churches in the Anglican Communion today.

Colin is among those whose 'valuable help' is acknowledged by S.C. Carpenter in his short biography of D-J (op.cit.). Here are four longish passages about him in a letter Colin wrote in response to Carpenter's appeal. The first is on the relation between D-J and his congregation:

> Congregations in flourishing town churches are often drawn together by a personal devotion and liking for the incumbent. Though D-J was greatly beloved by many of his flock, it was yet his teaching and leadership rather than his personality which brought the people together. Quite a number of the firmest adherents of St M's were extremely critical of their Vicar, and a few were antagonistic to him, but it did not occur to them to go elsewhere (so easy in London), for it was D-J's teaching and leadership that they valued. I have always thought this was a great tribute to his powers as a teacher and a seer. His powers of leadership were great, and he had the gift of infecting very varied types of people with his enthusiasms. He did not try to entice, or cajole, or persuade. He marched, and others followed, even if at first a little unwillingly (p. 45).

Here is Colin on D-J's verger, Mr P.H. Bradbury, and the relations between the two:

> No one dared take liberties with him, not even D-J. Bradbury's attitude to his Vicar was a blend of bewilderment and intense loyalty. He could never thoroughly understand him, but he instinctively trusted him, and secretly admired him. At the giving of an order or the inauguration of some change in the way things were to be done, Bradbury would apparently bristle with opposition, but in a week's time any critic of the innovation could receive very short shrift from (him) ... (p. 46)

Since the stipend of St Mary's was very small, and D-J had a wife and, eventually, seven children to support, it was generally understood that he had to earn money in other ways too. Here is Colin's comment on this situation:

> Although outside activities, as they are called, did reduce the amount of time he could spend in his parish, they undoubtedly enhanced the quality of his work

both as a preacher and as a future ecclesiastical statesman, and this was generally understood by his parishioners. But the outside work never engulfed him or diminished his pastoral energies. There are many today [the '50s] who look back to D-J's ministry to them in the nineteen-twenties as a golden age, who owe to it, humanly speaking, the very foundation of their faith in God and of their initiation into the life of a Churchman. Though his interests and his scholarly mind made him of peculiar value to the more educated and cultivated parishioners, yet his straightforward nature, the clarity of his thought, and his fund of deep affection made him the much-prized pastor of many plain folk whom impulse or choice or Providence brought to St Mary's (p. 46).

Here, finally, is what Colin thought of D-J's preaching when at Primrose Hill:

He brought to the work of preaching the trained mind of a Cambridge don, together with a Celtic sensibility.To these must be added his very wide sympathies with ordinary people of all ages and classes. During his twelve years at St Mary's he nearly always occupied the pulpit himself at the Solemn Eucharist on Sundays. Here, to a congregation of about 400 – a very mixed bag, socially and intellectually – he expounded the truths of the Gospel as the Church of England has received them with a force and clarity not often heard. His sermons were topical in the sense that they were illustrated by, or brought to bear upon, current events and trends of thought, but they were always dominated by the message of the Gospel and the teaching of the Church, and always disciplined by his devotion to and familiarity with Holy Scripture. Nearly always his text came from the Epistle or Gospel for the day. (p. 123)

D-J gave Colin a handsome welcome in the Parish Magazine for April 1922:

In October I hope we shall be joined by Mr Colin Dunlop, who is already known to some of St Mary's people... It may be asked why I choose a Deacon in a church where there must be many celebrations. I reply that it is peculiarly important that we should have the right man. I believe that we have got him, and that he is worth waiting for, and having as a Deacon.

In the November number he added:

He will be living at Rothwell House, Regent's Park Road [he moved to 19 Fellows Road in 1925] and will be in charge of the Little Catechism (the confirmation class for under-13s, with 80 members in January 1923) and the Junior Guild. It is satisfactory to know that had he been ordained at the general Ordination at S. Paul's, he would have been Gospeller, an honour which is given to the candidate who comes out top in the Examination.

The Guild, dedicated to St George, 'ha(d) for its object to bind together the boys of S. Mary's for the purposes of perseverance in their religion and for instruction and social fellowship'. The juniors were under 14 and met on Saturdays in the Church Room. Colin was also in charge of the Missionary Union.

I have seen no letters of a personal kind written to or by Colin when he was at St Mary's, but the following two diary fragments of his, two pages from a small notebook inserted in a continuous journal he kept while chaplain at Stockholm in 1929, tell us something very important about his personal struggles as an ordained clergyman of the Church of England, and also shed light on the nature of his work and extra-parochial life. They were written in 1923, his first full year at St Mary's:

4 June: I suppose it is the reaction after holidays in Italy which makes me feel so frequently depressed just now. ... But it is my ridiculous sensitiveness which really makes me unhappy, I suppose. If a boy or two is away from Catechism, if the guild is not a successful evening, if some friction occurs with any member of the congregation – at once I am plunged into the abyss of despondency. I feel inefficient, unloving, ungenerous, lazy and at times wonder if I have a vocation. This evening as I returned from evensong I dreaded lest there should be any boys waiting to come up to my room for I felt I could not cope with them. But now that no one has come I am depressed feeling that none of them want to come. I hoped all this would be cured by a holiday, but it is just the same. What is the use of it all? What have I done since I have been here? A sermon or two may have pleased some old women, a lesson in the catechism may have momentarily arrested the children's attention; but the guild has steadily declined in numbers and the boys seem to be more and more disappointed in me. My visiting has been a tame, half-baked sort of proceeding.

But this can all be remedied in time. I firmly believe that this depression is only temporary and that God will give me more and more love so that I may do his will. I can never forget the joy he has given me; the feeling of his love and help. All that Whit Sunday in Lucca and in Bagni di Lucca [where he had spent his summer holiday] I felt the greatness and nobleness of life. Seldom have I felt so keenly and vividly that life is divine and that God is all round us and in us. ...

30 June: Saturday: I write in a peculiarly happy frame of mind. Last night there was Die Meistersinger – with Phil, Sibyl and Laurence Bayard. It was curious to meet Phil, Eddie Sackville-West and Maurice Bowra all in evening dress and opera hats (except for Eddie who characteristically wore a rather large brimmed felt) eating refreshments in the 'Lyons' opposite Covent Garden: Cedric Glover was of course at the performance. The overture was very disappointing – one could hardly hear the strings – the bass tuba and other brass being far too prominent. The voices were all rather disappointing too. But the orchestra got better and all through the lovely 2nd act things were quite perfect. The impression of the whole opera is one of great gaiety – as Cedric Glover said – it makes one so very happy.

Then this morning there was the cricket match between the Guild (with others) and York House school. I don't quite know why I enjoyed it so. A combination perhaps of the sunshine, the smell of the grass, the excitement as to our destiny in the game and the pleasure of knowing that the boys were happy. Peter Pettit played for us – he seems a delightful boy. Very serious-minded. Unfortunately Bernard Hull couldn't play as he was playing for William Ellis 1st XI. After the match (in which we lost) I took eight of them to the Finchley Road Baths. It was very nice. I picked up Dick Patient and threw him in, to the immense delight of the others. 'Get Mr Dunlop to throw you in' was then the theme of their conversation.

Tonight I go with the Guild to play 'rounders' on Primrose Hill. For about the first time since I have been here the Guild has no terrors for me.

Of the people mentioned in the entry of 30 June, 'Sibyl' is, of course, Colin's sister, who had opened her shop-cum-workshop for designing and making jewellery at 68 Church Street, Kensington, in 1920. At Easter 1924 she presented a jewelled morse (the fastening of a cope) to St Mary's, which is still there (in 1925 Colin and D-J together presented a green chasuble for daily use made by the Warham Guild). The first 'Phil' is probably Philip Ritchie, who introduced Colin to the Glovers on the day after his ordination. The Glover family lived in the parish, and, although Cedric wrote to Mary after Colin's death that they had been 'intimate friends for some forty five years', he felt constrained to add that their friendship 'was of course completely secular and founded, I like to think, on mutual respect' – and certainly also on their love of music.

Colin often stayed at their house in after years, when Cedric would frequently take him to Covent Garden for the opera, which Colin could not then have afforded himself. His daughter, Rowena, remembers Colin when she was taken to St Mary's as a child. 'He charmed us children', she recalls, and although 'he twinkled at us, ... he boosted our egos by taking us seriously'. When older, she goes on, we loved listening to 'an argument between Colin and my father, ... who is inclined to bait people in the interests of a good discussion'. Cedric was also a friend of the composer Vaughan Williams, and used to take him to the opera too. I don't know what he did for a living. He may well have known Maurice Bowra's companion, Eddy Sackville-West, who himself became well known as a music critic and reviewer of gramophone records.

In the short passage I quoted above in which Colin recalls his first thrilling visit to St Mary's, music, represented by 'Martin Shaw on the organ', plays a prominent part. Martin Shaw had left for St Martin-in-the-Fields by the time Colin was ordained, though his brother Geoffrey, who had already been singing bass in the choir, had become organist in his place. Martin, and his wife Joan, became life-long friends of Colin, and I recall our visiting them during the early 1950s in Blythborough, when we had family holidays in Suffolk. I found it very hard to avoid staring at his face, since a huge strawberry mark covered almost all of its left side, and he used always to exhibit his right profile if he knew he was going to be photographed.

The occasion of Colin's reminiscence was a short obituary he wrote for a periodical relating to organs and organists. He recalls too 'the (to me) wholly new ability of English boys to sing English vowels properly', thanks to Martin's training, and laments the fact that even in 1955, when he died, the music he himself had composed – uplifting and un-sentimental – was rarely used in 'churches or cathedrals in spite of its excellence and strong liturgical character', not to mention the fact that both Vaughan Williams and Holst thought highly of it. Colin attributes this to the resentment of the 'older generation of organists' at 'Martin's gay and slightly reckless condemnation of some of the stuffy bequest of the nineteenth century in the realm of church music', and also 'his championship of plainsong'.

Geoffrey Shaw's deputy at St Mary's was J.H. Arnold, known as Jack, who became an important authority on plainsong and its use in the liturgy. He too became a life-long friend of Colin's, and Jack asked him to be the godfather of his youngest child, who was named after him. When Colin went out to Baghdad to be chaplain of the British Community Jack and Olive (Mrs Arnold) gave him a chasuble, 'a lovely thing of plain white spun silk, reaching almost to my feet and hanging in rich classical folds – so austere and so pure'. Colin would wear this when celebrating Holy Communion. There were many meetings in London over the years, and the Arnolds both stayed with us at Henfield, and then at Lincoln, Jack coming twice by himself after Olive's death, and, in later years Colin would sometimes stay with them at Stanmore when paying a business visit to London.

When Jack died in 1955, Colin sang the Solemn Requiem at St Mary's. He had a fine voice, especially when a young man, and a member of the congregation, Miss Pulling, wrote in a letter of sympathy to Mary after his death: 'One of my most vivid memories of the Primrose Hill days is the veneration of the Cross on Good Friday with Colin's [tenor] voice just behind me in the repeated chorus of 'Faithful Cross' – so uplifting to the devotions of the congregation.' Another man whom Colin got to know at St Mary's was the Honorary Assistant Parish Clerk, Dr F.C. Eeles, whom Percy Dearmer had especially befriended and encouraged. He became a member of the Warham Guild Advisory Committee and later was 'of the greatest possible significance for the care, protection and conservation of the churches of England' (Donald Gray, *Percy Dearmer*, Norwich: Canterbury Press, 2000, p. 80). He was the first secretary of the Council for the Care of Churches, an advisory body set up after the 1914 Government report on 'Ancient Monuments (Churches)'. He stayed with us twice in Durham.

A few pages back I mentioned The Alcuin Club. This played a great part in Colin's life, as also in the lives of others at St Mary's, notably D-J, Jack Arnold, Francis Eeles and Vivian King, who was Senior Guild Master when Colin arrived, and also responsible for the servers and everything connected with the ceremonial of the church services. The Club was named after Alcuin of York, the great eighth-century educator and inspirer of the revival of art and learning in Western Europe under Charlemagne. It was founded two years before Dearmer published his *Parson's Handbook*, and we can say that the handbook and the club had very similar concerns.

The original object of the Alcuin Club was 'promoting the study of the History and Use of the Book of Common Prayer' (BCP), but this was fairly soon enlarged to 'the practical study of ceremonial, and the arrangement of churches, their furniture and ornaments, in accordance with the rubrics [directions or rules of procedure] of the BCP, strict obedience to which is the guiding principle of the work of the Club'. Its many publications included 'leaflets', 'pamphlets', 'tracts' and long scholarly works on topics related to its aims.

It seems very probable that Colin, under the influence of D-J, was already very interested in the Club before his ordination, and possibly even during the war (see, e.g., letter to Evelyn, 21 May 1917). In his Cuttings Book there are two of a series of three letters from *The Church Times* dated July 1922. One is Colin's reply to a correspondent who called himself 'Sexagenarian Priest', who had insisted that the BCP was not really a Catholic book, in the sense of a book which maintained the historic continuity of the Church of England after the Reformation, as Dearmer and the Alcuin Club took for granted. Colin defends the BCP from this charge, on the grounds that the possible doctrinal ambiguities in the text and rubrics of the Communion Service do not themselves make it uncatholic, since it is not the task of a liturgy (as opposed to a creed) to avoid all possible ambiguity in doctrine, but only to ensure that nothing is clearly implied or affirmed that is *contrary* to the faith.

Throughout his ministry Colin never doubted the catholicity and authority of the BCP, which was at the heart of the Alcuin Club in its early days. Michael Manktelow, who retired as Bishop of Basingstoke, told me that, in a discussion of the BCP he overheard Colin conducting with D-J, Colin had said that, in his opinion, 'Cranmer got it just right' – that is, his 1549 prayer book, which was slightly altered to be known as '1662', proved in the end acceptable both to those who wanted continuity with the English (largely Sarum) style of worship in the late Middle Ages and to those who wanted their liturgies to draw much nearer to those of the leading Reformers in Germany, France and Switzerland.

At a meeting of the Club on 1 February 1923, D-J, then the Hon Sec, anounced that he felt constrained to retire from this post because of his increasing involvement with *The Guardian*, an Anglo-Catholic weekly which rejected the Romanising tendencies of the *Church Times* of that period. He considerably softened the blow to his colleagues by proposing that his place be taken by Colin, a young man who, he could assure them, was willing and able to do this. As the first step he was elected as a club member. Then, at another meeting on the 16th, he was elected to the committee and then at once as Hon Sec. His proposer was Dr Frere, one of the most widely respected liturgists in England at the time, who had become Bishop of Truro the previous year. Frere was Chairman of the Publications Sub-committee, and wrote to Colin on 21 April to let him know that he found his 'Prayer Book Pamphlet' entitled *What Is the English Use?* excellent; it only needed a few small changes, but, when these were done, he wanted to get it published as soon as possible.

By 4 July it was announced in committee that it had appeared and already sold 499 copies in paperback and 70 in hardback. Colin's 35-page pamphlet (a summary of contemporary thought about the liturgy in Alcuin Club circles) is worth spending a little time on, since it adds to our picture of what Colin and his ministry stood for within the wider Church under the influence of D-J, who was himself continuing what Colin later called the tradition of St Mary's, which Dearmer had founded. (In an article in the Parish paper D-J writes of it as 'tracing its history through the writings of Dr Gore and Dr Scott Holland back to those of Dr Pusey and Mr Keble and behind them to William Law, Cosin, Andrewes, Laud and Hooker' – the 'Caroline Divines'.)

Colin's pamphlet still reads very well, but as Peter Jagger, author of *The Alcuin Club and its Publications 1897–1987*, has written, 'The work reflects very much the times in which it was written.' Much had happened in the Church of England since the Oxford Movement in the middle of the nineteenth century. At the heart of this call to renewal was a conviction of the 'Catholic' nature of the Church of England – as a church with a continuous tradition of faith and practice going back to New Testament times despite its reformation – and a revitalisation of worship and the administration of the sacraments, especially the Eucharist, or Holy Communion. There had always been some clergy who valued these things, notably the 'Caroline Divines' around the time of Charles II's restoration, but as the nineteenth century advanced, the feeling became much more general. One result of this was the revival of rich ceremonial, including the reintroduction of practices and forms of worship dating back to pre-Reformation times.

Since much of this was commonly thought to go against the Book of Common Prayer, which every ordained clergyman of the Church of England had to swear to uphold and to take as the prime authority for the conduct of worship, there was among many people a strong reaction against it. There were riots in some churches, especially in London and other large cities, and, with the approval of some of the bishops, clergy were tried and some actually imprisoned. A climax came with the impeachment of Edward King, Bishop of Lincoln, in 1888. Two years later he was tried in the court of the Archbishop of Canterbury, E.W. Benson, and acquitted with the proviso that he must cease from employing or sanctioning certain specific forms of ceremonial (including those which Archbishop Lang was to 'canonise' in the 1930s – Hastings' *History*, p. 197ff). His funerary monument, with a larger-than-life-size bronze statue of the man seated and leaning forward in a chair in the act of blessing his people – the very picture of a saintly father in God – stands in the south transept of Lincoln Cathedral, and has been admired by countless visitors to the building.

Although by the 1920s 'ritual protests' were still regularly being made from the Protestant wing of the Church (and still occasionally are), the principles championed by the Oxford Movement had been much more widely accepted in the C of E, and the church authorities themselves, the Bishops in Convocation, though far from united among themselves as to the ceremonial aspects of worship, were no longer inclined to deal drastically with 'ritual offences'.

The big question at the beginning of the twentieth century was, granted that a more elaborate ceremonial was now widely accepted, was it to be according to the English or Sarum Use, or the 'Western' or Roman? Colin's pamphlet, wholly eirenic and free from the caricature and scorn so often to be met with in the secular and even church press, and in more scholarly publications, was an attempt to persuade the ordinary incumbent that the English Use, or form of worship and its accompanying ceremonial, was not just a matter of personal preference, or High Church faddishness, but the proper form for the Church of England as such. The question, he emphasises, is one of Liturgical Authority, and his answer is based on the latest liturgical research available at the time.

He accepts that the 'Romanisers' among the clergy had never been primarily out to defy the authorities of the Church of England, but acted in ignorance of this research, lack of understanding of the Book of Common Prayer (the BCP), or, in some cases, because they had become disillusioned with the bishops and the Church of England itself because of the Ritual prosecutions. For in many cases, he stresses, clergy were persecuted for being, as they thought, loyal – or at least not disloyal – to the BCP.

Colin takes it for granted that ceremonial and the 'ornaments' of worship are not just a matter of 'externals', or 'frills', since ceremonial acts and the material surroundings of liturgy have a meaning (as, we might say, the gestures and facial expressions of any speaker do). Ceremonial is the outward expression of liturgy. How then, can the BCP be our guide in such matters when it gives so few detailed pronouncements on these things? It was this paucity of detailed directions which had led many zealous clergy of the Church of England to imitate contemporary Roman ceremonial. Here, at least, they thought, was something both expressive and regulated, and surely – it was sometimes argued with a singular lack of prescience – must encourage reunion between the churches.

Colin makes various points in answer. In the first place he calls attention to the references to 'ancient custom' and the like scattered (thinly) about the BCP, and especially in the introductory material. The fourth section of this is entitled 'Concerning Ceremonies: why some be abolished and some retained'. The very title presupposes both reform and continuity with late medieval customs obtaining in England in the public worship of the Church. If we ask for a rule or set of laws about how we are to make this distinction, Colin argues, we are asking for something that did not exist in the Middle Ages, where custom was, in most matters, so much more important than law. Detailed rules or laws in the sphere of liturgy and ceremonial are in fact an innovation of the Church of Rome under the influence of the Renaissance, with its preference for law over custom, a tradition quite foreign to the BCP. But custom itself is never a matter of 'One size fits all', as law must aim to be, but varies according to particular circumstances.

Where custom prevails it is appropriate to talk about its *spirit*, or the *principle* it embodies. But it is absurd to lift particular items from one tradition with its own spirit and combine them with those of another tradition and another spirit, as the 'Romanisers' do. They must either accept the Roman liturgical code as a whole, and, in effect, become Roman Catholics, or leave it alone, seeking to enrich the Anglican liturgy either from the traditions of worship established in this country before the Reformation and left alone by the reformers – they are mostly but not exclusively according to the Use of Sarum – or by painstaking development of this tradition through immersion in its spirit, as the best liturgical scholars seek to do.

Promoters of such change should ask: is this fitting, or suitable?, having in mind both the practice of the early and pre-reformation Church, in so far as we have knowledge of it, and of our own particular tradition and circumstances; Roman Catholics, on the other hand, must ask: is this correct?, and the answer will be the same for all, wherever they are situated. The BCP tradition thus gives scope for ceremonial variations according to churchmanship, or local preference and resources (or lack of them), for more or less elaborate ornaments and ceremony. What must not vary is the words of the liturgy itself, though even here changed circumstances may license omissions, as in the case of the long exhortations in the BCP about attendance at Communion, which presuppose a situation where hardly anyone but the priest usually communicates.

Two things are worth noting here about the position Colin himself had now reached on these matters. In *The English Use* he gives it as his opinion that 'enrichment and scientific development' of the ceremonial tradition 'is very desirable'. The other matter concerns the differences in ceremonial between St Mary's and All Saints, Margaret Street. The postcard he carried about in France during the Great War shows six candlesticks on the altar, whereas the English Use (and indeed other traditions in the Middle Ages) required two. I well recall how indignant Colin could be in the 1950s and '60s at any Anglican clergy whose churches had six (we did many 'church crawls' together), and the same can be said of flower vases on the altar, and of 'gradines' or stepped platforms as a basis for the cross; the English Use was and is a cross and two candlesticks on a 'fair linen cloth'. All Saints, Margaret Street certainly has two today, thus conforming to the general tendency for 'The English Use' to become more and more the norm in the Church of England, especially in cathedrals.

Dearmer's ceremonial borrowings from medieval liturgical sources were in fact not all as exclusively 'English', as the term *The English Use* suggests; what they did achieve, however, was the purging of Anglican worship, in so far as the bishops' agreed rules were obeyed, from all elements of the Catholic liturgies of Northern Europe which had been added since the Reformation. As for the musical ideals of the tradition he founded, when Colin recorded in his 1951 diary a pastoral tour with the RAF in November 1951, he was able to write of a Church Parade at the former RAF airfield at Habbaniyah, near Baghdad:

> We sang 'Guide me O thou great redeemer' to [the tune called] Cwm Rhondda and 'Jesu lover of my soul' to Aberystwyth and 'City of God' to Richmond. It is so interesting to notice how the lead of St Mary's Primrose Hill has 'gone out

into all lands' and the ideals set up there are now taken for granted (some of them) even in Church Parades in the Forces.

I have gone into Colin's pamplet and the issues which gave rise to it at such length because of their importance in Colin's ministry. Colin remained the Alcuin Club's Hon. Sec. until he left St Mary's in the summer of 1927, when Dearmer, who naturally took an active interest in the Club took over temporarily – he was now Professor of Ecclesiastical Art at King's College, London. Colin seems to have remained on the Committee for much longer – though the club records and procedures (members were elected for three years, but could be re-elected at the same meeting in which they resigned) do not make it easy to be sure. His name continually recurs as a committee member until the last meeting he attended, in July 1966, two years after his retirement from Lincoln.

But it is high time we returned to St Mary's, Primrose Hill itself, and Colin's curacy there. He preached his first sermon at Evensong on 12 November, a fortnight after his ordination. Colin became much in demand as a preacher in his later years, and, although D-J normally preached the main Sunday service himself, he also asked many fine preachers to take his place, so Colin heard many excellent exemplars apart from D-J during his time at St Mary's, some of whom he got to know very well. On the Sunday after his ordination there was an inspiring sermon by Logie Danson, the Bishop of Labuan in the East Indies, on the Church's missionary task in non-Christian countries.

Other preachers included Dr Frere, the liturgist who had fully approved Colin's Alcuin Club pamphlet, and later became Bishop of Truro; Winnington-Ingram, Bishop of London, who ordained Colin priest in St Paul's on 7 October 1923, and asked Colin to be his chaplain, an offer Colin then declined because he felt he needed to get more parochial experience; Bishop Roscow Shedden of Nassau in the Bahamas, who had been his first confessor when Vicar of All Saints, Margaret St; Kenneth Kirk, whose tutorial class on the Study of Religion Colin had attended at Oxford, and who later became Bishop of Oxford; William Temple, who became Archbishop of Canterbury in 1942 and had the makings of a great one, though he died towards the end of the war; Henry de Candole, a prominent liturgist, who became Bishop of Knaresborough; the Revd Herbert Fleming, an important figure in Toc H, the Christian Fellowship network which developed after the First World War from the war-time work of 'Tubby' Clayton at Talbot House; and Basil Jellicoe, whom Colin had known at St Stephen's House, and who became a great pioneer of Housing Aid Societies in London.

His visit seems to have inspired Colin to investigate some poor housing in St Mary's parish, and he was later able to report to the Parish Church Council (PCC) that the residents were satisfied with the recent repairs. I have kept until last Bishop Charles Gore, first Bishop of Birmingham and one of the most prominent members of the Oxford Movement in the late nineteenth and early twentieth centuries. Colin had got to know and quite often consulted him while he was studying theology at Oxford, after Gore had retired from the see of Oxford and living at 6 Margaret Street helping out with the work of All Saints. In a letter he wrote to Ida O'Malley in November 1932 Colin says: 'I never forget the way he used to embrace me when I left his room after a talk. He would give me a great hug and one really felt 'virtue' proceed out of him into oneself. Barnes [Bishop of Birmingham] can say what he likes about science, but there *is* something magical about grace!'

Colin used nearly always to write his sermons out in full. The only one he preached at St Mary's to survive was preserved by Evelyn. It was preached on the evening of St Bartholomew's Day on 11 June 1924, to the text from Acts XIV 22: 'We must through much tribulation enter into the Kingdom of God.' He begins with the observation that being a Christian doesn't seem a very costly affair today – we are, on the whole, very much at our ease with the world around us. But Our Lord constantly warns his disciples of something rather different. So we should all ask ourselves, if we feel very much at ease with the world, whether we are not straying too far from the Christian path. This is a good and mature sermon, earnest, direct and simple, and Colin does not make the mistake (very common among beginners) of trying to bring too much in. Colin was also getting used to addressing children and young people. During his first Lent it was his job to take a weekly children's service on Wednesdays, with an address.

Colin's work with boys and young men obviously meant a lot to him, as is clear from the autobiographical passages I inserted above. Among the photographs he kept from this time, there are two with six of the St Mary's servers in all, five of them in a group centred on him. When D-J went to the USA to study at the Berkeley Divinity School in Connecticut at the beginning of 1926, and Colin was in charge of the parish, at his request with the help of a retired priest, for three months, he organised a team of young people to whitewash the choir vestry.

After the Second World War, when he was Bishop of Jarrow, he was commissioned as an Assistant Regimental Chaplain of the Church Lads' Brigade, and was said by the *Yorkshire Post* to be a 'forthright' speaker to them, as he was also to Rotary Clubs and The British Legion. Although there were many gifted people in the congregation of St Mary's, Colin also found himself helping at the children's Christmas pageant and similar productions. When, in 1933, he heard that D-J's successor was neglecting his ministry to the young, he was immensely upset, especially as he had letters from servers and others pointing all this out (see also below on this).

Colin's faith in the ability of young people not only to become full members of the congregation (apart from serving, singing in the choir, etc), is reflected in a series of short articles he wrote in a series 'Five Minute Talks to Councillors', in the church paper *The Guardian*. Here, he argues the case for having under-25s on the Parish Church Council, and to look at the benefits not only to the Council itself, but also to young people, and to the important business of getting the parish as a whole interested in church matters as they affect individual worshippers. It is based on the practice at St Mary's, and there is much practical advice as to how younger people can be secured for the Council and what sort of contribution they can be expected to make. There may be something a little utopian in these short articles, but this was in keeping with Colin's youthful left-leaning enthusiasm.

But his appeal to history, experience and Christian principles together is very persuasive. Colin's defence of the very young comes out in another liturgical 'controversy' in *The Guardian*. Against the idea that children should be given some substitute for the prayers of the Communion service, which are too difficult for them, he links this practice with the almost total disregard of the public liturgy apparent among lay persons in so many continental churches, especially in parts of Spain. Better, he argues, to find ways gradually to teach children 'the art' of joining in public prayer.

Colin also contributed articles to the Parish Magazine, in which he draws on his various interests. His increasing involvement in liturgy is reflected in short pieces on the Early Church's very close link between baptism and confirmation, the emergence of an agreed date for Christmas, the Catechism, passages in English literature (including cookery books!) which refer to the keeping of Lent, the history of the cope (a church vestment). There is also a longish (by parish magazine standards) article in two parts about St Mary's 'fifty years ago', based on a run of the Parish Magazine during the period 1875–79 which a printer had discovered among a pile of old junk and conveyed to the Vicar. There is a great deal of interesting detail here, especially about Bishop Jackson's prohibition of various things which were then a normal part of St Mary's public worship. Colin singles out a poem from one number,

> presumably from the pen of a worshipper at St Mary's, entitled The Present Distress. In this poem is reflected the bitter grief which many endured to see their priests hailed before Lord Penzance's court and consigned to the common prison and how heroically they bore the sentence of outlawry which was meted out by the authorities to churches where a dignified and beautiful worship was appreciated.

Colin also reviewed D-J's book on Archbishop Laud, recommending it strongly to his readers. One paragraph is very well worth quoting, since it is not only interesting about the subject of the book, but also clearly illustrates a very important politico-social-religious principle which D-J and Colin both approved:

> The book shows that Laud's death (he was executed on Tower Hill) has a wider significance than at first appears. He died not merely for the Catholic conception of the Church, not merely for the Church of England, but for England itself. His enemies were not laymen who resented too much clerical domination; they were those who resented what has always been characteristic

of England both in secular and church affairs – an ordered liberty. As the author once said, 'If Laud was intolerant, it was in order to win the principle of toleration.'

Colin also had time as curate of St Mary's to publish elsewhere, especially in *The Guardian*, which D-J helped to edit. Apart from his short pieces on young people and the Parish Church Council, he also wrote reviews and articles for it. D-J commissioned him to describe and comment on the 'Liturgical Three Hours' service conducted at St Mary's on Good Friday, whose primary purpose is to bring home to the imaginations of the congregation the events of Our Lord's Passion.

In another number he reviews a pamplet on *The Good Friday Liturgy* by Nevil Truman, in which the writer also pleads for the revival of old liturgical services for Good Friday. Colin heartily approves the principle behind this, but does suggest some specific things to take the place of the 'Mass of the Presanctified'. The most generally attractive of these *Guardian* articles are two pieces recording what he saw on successive summer holidays.

In 1925, he visited northern Spain with Sibyl and Evelyn, and spent some time in Galicia. The article describes Santiago de Compostella, with special attention to the Fiesta of St James. This is a most lively piece, with excellent word pictures of the cathedral and the great ceremony of the *Botafumeiro* – a vast incense vessel which is swung in a great arc from one transept to the other spewing forth smoke and even flames (I was immensely impressed, indeed, thrilled, at this sight when I visited the cathedral many years later). Its original purpose was to fumigate the church against the many pilgrims who had come hundreds of miles mostly on foot to worship at St James's tomb. Colin's article contains much detail, too, concerning the cathedral worship, where between 30 and 40 clergy might attend ordinary weekday services of the status of our evensong and mattins. He is quite critical of clergy behaviour in the choir, whose casual and at times almost irreverent nature he contrasts strongly with the attentive demeanour of the cathedral congregations.

The next year he holidayed in Sicily with Evelyn. His article is entitled 'A Uniat Village in Sicily', and it describes a drive south from Palermo to visit Piana dei Greci, one of two old Albanian colonies in the island. It is full of vivid descriptions of scenery and the religious life of the place. Unfortunately, the churches (three are described) disappoint him very much as buildings, with their drab interiors, but the survival in Sicily of these islands of orthodox liturgy – he dwells enthusiastically on the 'Russian flavour' of the music – in congregations owing allegiance to the Pope ('it was strange to see the Sacred Heart on an ikonostasis'), makes up for it. Evelyn, who was with him on this summer holiday (1926) also wrote a brief account of the visit, especially of a wedding which they witnessed in one of the churches. She emphasises the look on the bride's face, which she interpreted as one of blank despair.

Colin also published two other articles elsewhere while at St Mary's. One was also the fruit of the Spanish holiday, entitled 'Folk Dances in Galicia', which appeared in the *English Folk Dance Society News*. Colin's own experience of Morris and country dancing enabled him to describe the Galician *Jota* very vividly, and also the liturgical dances performed in the cathedral. But he was also very attentive to the music sung in the streets at the time of the Fiesta:

> Some of the peasants sang what I took to be folk-songs. They were very strange and wild, often just melodies without words. They had a sort of savage ferocity about them. Beginning usually with a reckless animation and sung in harsh and nasal accents they died away in a sustained melancholy wail. It would be difficult adequately to describe the fascination of this music. Judged as pure melody it would not rank very high. But there was a sort of straining after the unearthly and the other-worldly which would fully justify its inclusion in the category of art.

The other article, on Prayer Book revision, was written for two numbers of *The Sign* in June 1925 and describes new proposals for liturgical revision, similar to those which were to be debated in the House of Commons in 1927, and again, after some alterations, in 1928, as 'permissive variations' to the BCP, and decisively rejected each time, though the 1928 Prayer Book was almost at once widely used in the Church of England with the permission of the Bishops and Archbishops. Colin's approach to Prayer Book revision here is, I think, slightly more 'revolutionary' than that of his much later book, *Anglican Public Worship*, or at least of its first edition.

There is another article on Prayer Book revision in his Cuttings Book whose position is very similar to that he sets out in *The Sign*. However, it was published in *The Observer* and merely signed 'By a Church Correspondent'. I think it could be by Colin, but it seems to me unlikely that a curate would be able to publish such an article in a secular organ without some previous connection with it or *entrée* to it. It appeared very shortly before the 1927 book was discussed in the Commons, and very clearly outlines the purpose of the revised book.

Colin also took his 1923 holiday abroad, this time in Central Italy. He left no personal record of this, but D-J's extract in his Parish Notes from a letter of Colin's from Lucca are worth quoting:

> last Sunday I heard Mass at an amazing little mountain chapel up above the village. What interested me was that the servers wore albes and a boy sang the Epistle. The music was congregational throughout.

'The music in the more imposing Italian churches,' D-J adds, 'seems to have filled him with that desire to fly from the building which all who know italy will recollect.'

Colin preached his final sermon at St Mary's on 8 May 1927, and left some time during the next few days. Here is his farewell letter in the magazine:

> My dear friends, I want to thank you again – particularly those who were not at the presentation – for your tremendously generous gift. I feel it was hopelessly

undeserved and anyhow your kindness to me during the past four years was a sufficient mark of gratitude for anything I may have been able to do for you. But this special act of generosity has made it easier for me to leave S. Mary's and to go assured over and over again of your good wishes. I shall always regard S. Mary's as my home in a way which no other parish can ever be – for it was you who trained me to be a priest of God. Yours affectionately, Colin Dunlop

And here is D-J's valedictory piece in the same number:

I have already through the Church Council expressed my gratitude to Mr. Dunlop for the loyal comradeship of these last four years. We are such old friends that the parting will be particularly severe. And there are many who, though they have not known him as long as I have, will have very much the same sense of personal loss. We can assure him that he will always have friends at S. Mary's, as long as there are any that remember his ministry here, and dozens of the young people will always think of him as a great friend and the first priest they knew intimately. We know that to him the departure from the Church of his Ordination will also be a wrench, and that he will always treasure many of the things that he has learnt here. He goes to important and difficult work, followed by the good wishes of everybody, and not least by those of the person who has most reason to feel grateful. During May and June Mr. Dunlop will be helping at that wonderful church in the Rue Vacquerie, S. George's Paris. After that he will be chaplain at S. Moritz for two months, and we shall all hope that the wonderful air and the peace of the mountains will send him back invigorated for his responsible task at Fulham in October.

The two brief chaplaincies D-J mentions here were 'fill-ups' of the time before he could take up his post as Resident Chaplain with the Bishop of London, who had renewed his request for Colin's assistance now that he had had time to become more familiar with the work of a priest. In doing so Colin had also turned down a chance of, 'if not an incumbency' (as the Archdeacon of Middlesex put it), yet still a vacancy at Chelsea Old Church which would give him 'a very free hand' in organising the work of this well-known place of worship.

We may also add here that Colin's connection with St Mary's did indeed become almost a permanency in his life. I shall come back later to letters written by former St Mary's people to Mary after Colin's death. But here, to end this chapter, are some moving words from a letter written by Miss Maud E. Collins of Haverstock Hill on the day of his last sermon. She had only encountered Colin once, when making her confession at St Mary's, but had clearly been much affected by his kindness and sympathy. She was an unmarried mother with a little boy whom she was bringing up. 'We can never forget you, who have worked so faithfully among us. You will always be thought of as the very great friend and help to all at St Mary's.' As one who hardly knows him she feels maybe she should not have written, 'but I just wanted you to know how strangers do appreciate you'.

7

THE O'MALLEYS

A LTHOUGH the chapter about St Mary's, Primrose Hill, above, contains
information about quite a number of people Colin got to know there,
some of whom became his friends, I have so far omitted to say
anything about Ida O'Malley, who took over responsibility for the upbringing
of her two nieces Mary O'Malley and Honor, her sister. But Mary played such
an important part, not only as wife and mother of his children, but also as an
assistant in Colin's ministry, especially during his time of parish incumbency
and his last days, that it is worth devoting a complete chapter to outlining the
important points of her background and early life.

Ida, Mary's aunt, was born in 1873, the only daughter of George Hunter
O'Malley and Mary Frances, née Younghusband, known in the family as
Minnie. Unlike most people called 'O'Malley', Ida's family pronounced it to
rhyme with 'bailey', not 'rally'. They traced their descent from the 'Pirate
Chieftain' Grace, who once sailed to Greenwich in her own ship in order to ask
Queen Elizabeth I in person, though at considerable risk of imprisonment, for
various favours, which the Queen granted her.

The O'Malleys were from County Mayo, in the west of Ireland, and ceased
to be Roman Catholics around of the turn of the seventeenth century into the
eighteenth. Ida's grandfather, Peter Frederick O'Malley, born in 1804, took his
degree at Trinity College, Dublin, and, because his brother Charles was already
a practising barrister in Ireland, decided to be called to the English, rather than
the Irish, bar, and moved to London. In his early days there he earned his daily
bread as a journalist and contributor to magazines such as *Blackwood's*, while
climbing the preliminary steps of a legal career. Eventually he was called to the
bar and became a successful barrister on the Eastern Circuit.

In 1867, not long after his appointment as a QC, he became Recorder of
Norwich. Some time before that he had a serious illness and underwent a
Damascus-like conversion, becoming very strict in his evangelical religious
views. He married Emily Rodwell, from a Suffolk brewing family, in 1839,
and they had ten children, six of whom died in infancy. The two older boys,
Edward Loughlin and Ida's father George Hunter, had an extremely close
relationship, in which a strong ingredient was Edward's continual anxiety
about George, especially in money matters. Some of this was recorded by
Edward in a memoir he wrote after his younger brother died in 1909.

Edward followed his father Peter into the law, and became a colonial judge, but George himself chose a career in the army, going to the Artillery School at Woolwich on leaving Rugby, and serving as an officer in the Royal Horse Artillery, retiring with the rank of full Colonel. He met his future wife Minnie in the course of his army life. The Younghusbands were very much of an Army family, but Minnie's own father, Ida's maternal grandfather, was a scientist as well as a soldier, and retired as a Lieutenant General after a highly distinguished career in the Royal Artillery. Minnie Younghusband was a writer and intellectual, and had much influence on her daughter.

Apart from a boy, Rupert, who died in infancy, George and Minnie had two children, of whom Ida, born in 1873, was the older by 9 years. Much of her childhood was spent abroad with one or both of her parents. Letters from Minnie to her own mother show that, as a child, Ida could be extremely wilful and difficult to manage. In 1881, when George was stationed at Halifax, Nova Scotia, Ida nearly died of diphtheria, a by-product of the faulty plumbing of an up-country hotel. Her father had it too, and Minnie told her mother in a letter that she herself never took her clothes off for 10 days (except for baths), since she had to administer their medicine every hour, and Ida would only take it from her.

'Poor little pet', she wrote, 'she has developed an astonishing talent for invective, and calls us all, doctor, nurse and me, by various bad names whenever it is a question of medicine, wine, etc ("cruel old beast", "ugly old bat", "horrid old rat" ... "I hate you"'..)', yet, 'in between whiles she is as sweet as ever', and, on the worst night of all, she said 'Go to bed dear Mother, you will be ill yourself.' When she was about 15, she was sent to St Leonard's School at St Andrews, in Scotland, and then, in 1893, to Lady Margaret Hall, at Oxford, where she read history. Here she made friends with several people who became prominent in the law-abiding campaign of the Suffragists, who used rational and non-violent means to secure votes for women, and the abolition of other legal handicaps.

Ida did much voluntary work for women's suffrage, but, as her obituary in *The Times* was later to put it: 'she was chiefly interested in the women's movement from the educational point of view'. This approach was doubtless encouraged by her mother, who had a similar interest, and also by the Jones family of Jesmond Dene, near Newcastle on Tyne, who were her cousins. Ida was more like a sister than a cousin to the older girls, but, like them, a person of wide cultural and historical outlook. The literary fruit of this was *Women in Subjection* 'which showed how women had suffered from the prevalent doctrine that they were to be considered not as ends in themselves but as means to the development of men', an anonymous correspondent wrote in *The Times* in a supplementary obituary. Such a topic might have led her to produce a mere pamphlet, this appreciative correspondent goes on, had not 'her keen interest in literature, in history, and in general ideas, added to her great literary gift, enabled her to write the most stimulating book published by any modern writer on the subject.'

Her other big book was a life of Florence Nightingale, which she was asked to write by the Nightingale family to redress the imbalance of Lytton Strachey's *Eminent Victorians* and the play *Lady of the Lamp*; in *Florence Nightingale, 1820–1856* 'she attempted to give an impression of what might have been in an autobiography if such had existed, and to show Florence Nightingale's early years as they might have appeared to herself' (official *Times* obituary). The first volume (she was never able to complete the second) breaks off at the end of the Crimean War. It and *Women in Subjection* are still most readable today. Apart from them she wrote many journal articles and book reviews, and, indeed, when her financial position became precarious as a result of the collapse in value of the shares she largely lived on after her nieces, Mary and Honor, became permanent members of her household, she was forced to take on a good deal of work she would not otherwise have chosen. Like her two major works, *Great Englishwomen*, a series of 13 short 'lives' written to encourage young ladies to develop their gifts in life, it is also very readable.

In one important matter Ida definitely went against her mother's example. Both her parents were very interested in the ideas of Darwin and Huxley, and complete agnostics, and several of her suffragist friends lived decidedly Bohemian lives, yet when, after her mother's death, she went to live with her father in Oxford, she was converted to the Christian faith at the age of 33 by one of the Cowley Fathers. It was during that period of her life that she became a close friend of Maude Royden, the well-known and forceful preacher, and passionate champion of women's ordination, and used to go on holiday with Maude and Maude's father. When she moved to Steele's Road, Hampstead, after her own father's death, Ida attended St Alban's, Holborn, for a time, but also went to St Mary's, Primrose Hill occasionally, and is very likely the 'Miss O'Malley' elected to the PCC while Colin was D-J's curate. But, as Mary later recorded, she did not set much store by church-going as such, though in other respects tried to live an essentially Christian life, with a strong belief in the importance of self-sacrificial love – which, after all, is an absolutely fundamental component of it.

Ida's brother, Charles Arthur Gerald, was born in 1882. This was Mary's father, who grew up to be a very different kind of person from his sister. He followed his father to Rugby and then to the Royal Artillery School at Woolwich, and was commissioned in the early 1900s. Charles's battery was sent to Nowshera, then part of India, about fifty miles from the Khyber Pass and the Afghan frontier. However, despite his excellent Artillery connections, he bought himself out of the army at the age of 27, about a year after the death of his father. He was hoping – ignoring his sister's advice – to make money in a business career. In his letter to Ida of 31/08/09 he declared 'I am sick of soldiering and that's a fact. It bores me stiff.' He went on to say that he had £7,000 capital and had asked a friend about prospects in South America, though he'd sooner work in England. He planned to come home for about a week, en route for Buenos Aires, to pick up letters of introduction. Then after 'looking around' for several months in Argentina and Patagonia he would return to train in the Special Reserve. That would stand him in good stead if there was a war. But, he stresses again, he hates the life in 'this beastly country', hates the natives, and finds nothing to interest him there.

Six months later, Ida was astonished to receive the following letter from him, sent from Lima, Peru:

> I am engaged to be married, at least not regularly engaged but Lisa and I are pretty well agreed and I am to stay here about a month and if she is quite certain at the end of it we shall be allowed to announce it. You see we only met on board the Oronsa at Punta Areñas, so she has not known me 3 weeks yet.
>
> She is a Miss Lisa Carroll and her father, who is dead, was a Carroll from Galway and in business first in B. Aires and then here, where I think he died. Mrs Carroll is a charming old lady and has been awfully kind to me. She and Lisa had been staying with relations in Buenos Aires and Mrs C came back about a month ago, leaving Lisa there with a sister in law; so she came home alone in charge of the Captain and we met when I boarded the ship at Punta Areñas. By the time we got to Valparaiso I knew I must come on up to Lima, so I did and here I am ... I cannot describe Lisa to you in the least, and I am longing for you to meet each other. Mrs Carroll's father was Irish and her mother English so, as Mrs Carroll was Irish, Lisa is quite Irish. She was born at Kingston on Thames, is 25, has one sister married, and has 3 brothers and 1 sister, is dark with the most darling brown eyes in the world, and is, I suppose, about 5'5', a good height for a girl. We differ on all sorts of subjects, and Lisa has been brought up on awful sheltered life inferior sex lines, but I shouldn't be surprised if she doesn't modify her views when she knows more of things.
>
> Anyway we argued about suffrage and she told me she liked my views about women. She is awfully good and religious and was rather worried when I told her about the things I cannot believe (I am sure there's nobody wishes more than me that I could), but I think I am going to be able to make her happy as we get happiness here.
>
> I am not going to say anything more about her now except that she is altogether adorable and I cannot think how I can have got so much more than I deserve.
>
> Of course as I am going to stay here a month it will mean coming home later probably not till the end of May. I must cable for an extension of leave which I don't suppose there will be much difficulty about. It means getting to the Argentine much later than I intended, but I must use my letters there as that seems to be going to be my adopted country. I suppose we shall have to wait about 18 months or at least a year before we can get married, till I can get settled work and I hope by working like a nigger to have a fairly decent knowledge of the language and generally my way about then, anyway if I can't work with such an object I'm not worth much.
>
> Lisa's youngest brother [Leo] is in Duncan Fox & Co here and her sister's husband [John Reid] is also one of their managers so that is why Mrs Carroll is living here. The eldest brother [John Carroll] has been in Buenos Aires owner of the Phoenix Hotel where all the camp people always stay, but is just going home for good so as to get his boys educated.

The second brother [brother in law, John Reid] is a mining engineer down the coast here on one of the copper mines. ...

Isn't it strange how things happen? I never thought of going round to Valparaiso till I got to Punta Areñas, and Lisa nearly went home (to England) with her brother [John] and sister in law [Emelita] from Buenos Aires instead of coming back here. Oh my dear how I wish you were here with me and could meet her now. We have discussed no plans yet and anyway it is too early, and she hasn't seen half enough of me to be bound in any way, but if all goes well I want to try and get her sent home to her sister in law some time this year and then she can see my relations.

You will sympathise if this letter is somewhat incoherent.

Much love

Your loving brother

CAGO'M.

PS: Use your discretion in telling my news; it is confidential at present.

PPS: Since I wrote this I have seen Mr Gallagher Mrs Carroll's brother [presumably the older, John] who stands in l.p. to Lisa and as he naturally wanted to know who I am etc and I am anxious to give references I gave the names of Uncle Edward, Shaldforth, and Cox's as my bankers. Mr G thinks I ought not to stay longer than till the next steamer and I agree so I am leaving by the Oronsa on the 19th. I am so happy and I think L is too. Much love, CAGO'M

In the event, they were married early in the following year (1911), and began their married life at Clare Cottage in Radlett, Herts, where Charles had found work as a motor salesman. Mary was born the same year on 13 December. A little over 15 months later another girl, Honor Lisa, was born. Ten days later (13 April) her mother died of a pulmonary embolism. Charles himself never really recovered from this shattering event.

He first arranged to take Mary and Honor, and the nurse, to the Kensington apartment of Lisa's elder brother, Edward John, and his wife Emelita. However, after a few months Ida offered to share her house with her brother, as there would be plenty of room for all of them at 6 Steeles Road. Mary continued to be looked after by the nanny Ida had taken on, and became very attached to her, while Honor was still in the care of the 'monthly nurse'. When war broke out, Charles was called up as a reservist. Next year (1915), the German Zeppelin bombing raids on London began, and, in July, Ida took the children and Annie Drane, the nanny, down to Saunton Sands, an idyllic hamlet on the north Devon coast, where several of her cousins with children were already staying. She herself paid frequent visits from London during that summer.

Meanwhile Charles had decided to marry again. His new wife was called Cicely Franks, 'a country girl from March from a working class background, who had risen socially to become a secretary in London', as Mary described her much later in life. In October Annie and the children returned to London, at Cicely's request, and there were some extremely sad partings at Paddington –

Annie, who had for some time taken the part of her mother in Mary's affections, was dismissed by Cicely, and, in Mary's words 'walked out of her life', never to be forgotten, and the children were introduced by Ida to their 'new mother', who at once took them off to a small furnished cottage at Loudwater, near High Wycombe, to live with her, while Ida returned to Hampstead by herself. 'It is *miserable* not having (the children) here, but it will be better for them to be out of London', she wrote in her occasional diary.

The exact chronology of Mary's early life can only be made out approximately, since the chief sources are Mary's own memories after a great many years had passed, supplemented by occasional diary entries by Ida, and a few letters and inadequately labelled snapshots from the family archives; however, I think the following account is true in all essentials. Some time in the Spring of 1916 Mary was with Ida for quite a long time, while Honor was with Cicely, who had been given the use of a flat in Great Portland Street by Oscar Cox, a South American business friend of Charles's. Charles himself was now training with his battery in Ireland, near Cork, and he wanted Cicely to bring the children out to join him there. However, this was not only the time of the Easter Rebellion in Ireland, but the Germans were torpedoing passenger ships in the Irish Sea, so Ida protested against their going, perhaps supported by Cicely. In the event, Ida surmised, Charles came to England himself and took his wife and children out with him.

During the winter of 1916–17 Cicely and the children returned to England, and, as before, there was a period when Mary lived with Ida, and Honor and Cicely stayed in the Great Portland Street flat, though after that all three were at Steele's Road. During that summer (and later) they spent some time at March (making occasional seaside trips to Hunstanton) with Cicely's parents, whose outlook and way of life presented a very great contrast to Ida's. Mary was sent to the local school for a brief time, though derived very little of lasting benefit from it. The next 'home' was at Slough, where she felt rather more settled than she had before, and where they were living when the war came to an end. After Charles was demobbed, probably in early 1919, they all moved to 17 Willow Road, Hampstead, a road which borders part of the Heath. In her memoir Mary says it was not so nice a house as 2 Upton Park Road, Slough; the park was, to Mary, much more attractive than the Heath, which she found rather frightening. I quote now from Mary's memoir:

> We went on at Willow Road until 1920. My father, like many others who came out of the army after the First World War, found it difficult to get a job. I believe he worked as a motor car salesman for some time, but he was quite unused to any kind of economy about money, being rashly generous by temperament and having been brought up by fairly well-off parents to think that he and his family ought to have what they wanted to have. Cicely, I think, was a very industrious housewife and certainly a good economical manager, but she was struggling against the stream. These financial troubles were not the only ones between them and some time in 1920 or 1921 the breaking point came .

My father decided to emigrate to Australia. She refused to stay with him any longer and they split up.

Mary later discovered the existence of another very serious issue between them, the fact that Charles had contracted syphilis when a young soldier in India, but never told Cicely (or, I presume, Lisa) about this at the outset of their relationship. When Mary and Honor were later tested for traces of the disease, Mary was found to be completely in the clear, but Honor was not. This could well have accounted for Honor's deafness, which became very severe in time, and for other physical and character traits which put her at a grave disadvantage in finding any kind of permanent work. After Charles and Cicely parted, the children went back to Ida, possibly, Mary surmised, as a temporary arrangement, and the Carrolls and the O'Malleys discussed whether they should get them made wards in chancery in case Charles should try and take them to Australia with him. But, in the event, they remained with their aunt at 6 Steele's Road, and, though Ida never formally adopted them, they became to all intents and purposes her children, and, after a few years, were calling Ida 'Mother'.

In a letter of 16/9/24 to Leo Carroll, Lisa's youngest brother, Ida expresses the hope that Leo wasn't shocked by this; she explains that they were not taught to do so, but that after Mary had read Tennyson's poem 'Oenone', in which the abandoned Oenone frequently invokes 'Mother Ida', she began to call her Aunt 'Mother Ida', since 'Auntie' didn't express all she felt for her. Honor then copied this and soon dropped 'Ida'. Ida herself demurred but couldn't stop her. 'There seems a natural instinct to call someone 'mother', she writes, so that perhaps she didn't try hard enough to stop it. But I do *feel* so like a mother to them', she concludes.

Mary came to feel enormous admiration for Ida, and, as she emphasises in more than one place, loved her very much. For one thing, she felt that Ida really *understood* her, and could enter her imaginative world, whereas Cicely could not, although she did her best for her according to her lights, and was, for a time, her main 'symbol of security'. Ida also fully accepted Cicely as a member of the family. She and her new sister-in-law, Mary later said in a recorded interview,

> were about as far apart as they could be, but ... she had a tremendous family loyalty, and she would always...have bent over backwards to try and be on good terms with anybody who was related... if she possibly could... She had no illusions about my stepmother. My stepmother was a most terrible liar... She was a very attractive woman, but ... nobody could ever believe a word she said ....Nobody ever really knew the story about her past.

She refers obliquely here to the enormous contrast between the social and educational environment of Cicely's native home in March (where, towards the end of his life, her father would frequently get drunk and beat her mother on his arrival home from the pub), and that of the circles in which she now felt at home in London. Mary came to think in later life that Ida's loyalty – fostered, no doubt, by several generations of soldiers in her family – was extreme, and sometimes led to a rather naive overestimation of people.

It was, of course, family loyalty which inspired Ida's eventual acceptance of full responsibility for Mary and Honor, since it meant a big change in her life. Letters and messages she received from keen suffragists when she first took in the children in 1913, show how much her suffrage work meant to others. In a letter addressed to 'O'Malley' *tout court,* Millicent Fawcett, for example, expresses the hope that her action won't take her from her suffrage work, and Kathleen Courtney lets her know that she hopes she will keep on the Literary Committee Secretaryship, and feels that Ida won't want to give up 'direct suffrage work such as canvassing' which she does for the London Branch. Her cousin Lilian Jones writes that 'the Committee' feels very helpless without her and Maude [Royden] – who had also ceased to work for it – and Lilian's sister Hilda says: 'The Cause cannot spare you altogether'. But as the children grew up and no longer needed to be looked after all the time by nurse or nanny, but sought the loving stimulus of their aunt, it was the production of works involving scholarly research that suffered most. Helen Phillips, a life-long friend of Mary's from their school days, during which she often visited the house, recalled that, even when the children reached their teens, Ida still sometimes seemed unconsciously to resent being taken so often away from her more literary composition.

As regards non-literary work, to which she gave herself without reserve during the first years of her adult life, Mary says of Ida in the written text of an interview she gave to Brian Harrison, who was writing about the suffragists:

> She did all the committee-work and so on, but I don't think she...really liked it very much: I don't think she was really cut out for that sort of public life... She had two really strong inclinations: one was towards personal relationships with individuals, which she was very good at, and another was towards...history...as a scholarly discipline. Committees and fund-raising for feminist causes weren't really her cup of tea.

Mary also surmises that 'she had a very strong maternal instinct, but was not at all prepared to marry...This applied to quite a lot of the people she lived among.' The result of this desire for children, but rejection of marriage because they thought the marriage relationship as it then was was rather degrading to women, was the adoption of children by several of her suffragist friends and colleagues. But Ida's adoption of Mary and Honor was more successful than most of theirs, probably because of the genetic link between Ida and the children. Apart from the inroads made on her precious time, with which any writer will sympathise, there was also a big financial burden for Ida – leading to the necessity of producing the 'hack-work' mentioned above, and greatly exacerbated by the collapse of Armstrong Whitney, where most of her inherited money was invested, and the fact that Charles did nothing to support his daughters financially himself. Fortunately Lisa's brothers, especially Leo, who was unmarried, contributed very handsomely to make up for this.

I should also mention at this point what Mary calls 'the one adverse effect on my life' of Ida's bringing them up at the cost of having very little time for serious research and writing, namely Ida's strong hope that 'I was going to do all the things that she hadn't been able to do.' 'The relationship was a bit of a strain, because ...having terribly high expectations of me, which I was always having to live up to, I grew up with a fairly hefty sense of guilt...', though Mary did not feel for a moment that Ida was clearly aware of these effects on her.

Mary had begun to attend Frognal School in Hampstead when still with her father and stepmother, but didn't remember much about it. It seems to have provided quite a good preparatory education, but the tensions produced in her – now a highly sensitive and intelligent 13-year-old – by family life in Willow Road prevented her from being happy there. But in the summer of 1925, about 5 years after Ida had taken full charge of her and her sister, she entered St Paul's School, and from then on enjoyed her education:

> I was very happy on the whole at St Paul's. I had been in the dumps at my preparatory school in Hampstead, and got across all the staff, and was feeling terribly frustrated. St Paul's seemed to me a new world. I loved the school buildings, enjoyed the higher standard of teaching, and above all the musical opportunities. The very first time I entered the school was when I attended for the entrance exam. It was All Saints day, and Mr [Gustav] Holst was playing the organ for Prayers himself. We sang 'For All the Saints' to Vaughan Williams' tune, and when it came to the last verse 'Gussy' let fly and the whole school sang mightily. I was absolutely thrilled and felt that I simply must go to that school at all costs!

Eventually she won a school scholarship, which meant free schooling, and, later still, won an Exhibition to Lady Margaret Hall, Oxford, to read 'Mods and Greats', which meant Greek and Latin language and literature, history and philosophy.

I mentioned above that 'Miss O'Malley' was probably, while Colin was curate there, a member of the PCC at St Mary's Primrose Hill. It seems very likely that Colin, once he had got to know Ida as a regular worshipper at the church, would have persuaded her to stand for election to the PCC, in view of her great gifts. Although Mary later said that they first met when she was 17 (hence at the end of 1928 or in 1929), by which time Colin was chaplain to the Bishop of London, she had certainly had her aunt's attention drawn to him by 1924, since her scrapbook contains a ticket for the service in which he was ordained priest in St Paul's.

A photograph in the same album also contains a picture of the St Mary's Sunday School pupils, in which she appears. But, more revealing than either of these is a letter from Colin in Baghdad, to Mary as an undergraduate at Oxford, when they had been engaged for half a year but still had some time to go before they could marry. The immediate context is the question of family planning, which Mary and Colin had already discussed and found that they agreed on. This leads Colin on to D-J and his wife, the latter of whom, he suspected (they had seven children), took a different view from that of her husband, which might have accounted for a sense Colin had that his very close friendship with D-J had been rather disturbed by his and Mary's engagement. He had noticed that D-J no longer encouraged him to talk about Mary as his future wife, as though when he and Mary married he would 'have less to give him' and that he, Colin, would 'depend far less on him'. On the other hand, when Colin

> very urgently asked his opinion or advice in our connection he has always very nobly pulled himself together and viewed us dispassionately and given me good and right advice. It was he in fact who first encouraged me to think of you as one I might love (even if I didn't already at the time). When I was at Primrose Hill I several times had infatuations and imagined myself in love with the most unsuitable girls. I used to tell D-J. about these and he was always most scathing and used to prove that I was not really in love at all. One day, before I left Primrose Hill we were talking over my past infatuations (there were only two) and I said suddenly to D-J 'I believe in the end I shall fall in love with Mary O'Malley' and he said 'Ah, that's more like it.'

So by 'met' Mary probably means 'got to know well', or something similar, since she must have been aware of him, both in the parish, and as a very welcome, indeed, much loved visitor at the house where she lived, some time before the first significant 'meeting'. Ida's letters to Colin, from 1929 onwards, might almost make a reader think that she herself was in love with Colin – though the language is in fact quite compatible with a strong 'maternalistic' affection – and, in any case, Ida 'was very attracted towards young men and women, because she was a *very* good listener, very sympathetic, ... (and) had great powers of empathy with people' (BH interview).

But the position of Colin as a potential suitor for Mary was rather different from that of the young people she met abroad, who were perhaps rather lonely or in need of practical advice. What she really wanted was to give Mary time to begin a career as a don or learned writer after leaving Oxford – which, in view of Colin's age (he was about 14 years older than her), might effectively rule out marriage for them. So, for some time after it became quite clear that Colin and Mary were strongly attracted to each other, she tried to convey her conviction that any open acknowledgement of this might prevent Mary from developing the self she had it in her to be ('she has it in her to be great'). Her formative years should therefore be as free as possible from 'emotional excitements'.

However, this over-cautious view could not stand up against Ida's desire to do justice to Colin as well. During his time with George Bell the Colin–Ida correspondence shows the gradual emergence of a different view, in response to the clearly emerging determination of the two to marry each other. In June

1929, Ida is 'not absolutely certain that he and Mary ought to marry' – this in response to Colin's eagerness to meet Mary on his return from the Stockholm chaplaincy. In any case, Mary was working hard for her forthcoming exams and other school activities. By the middle of July Colin had clearly agreed not to see Mary 'too much'; Ida acknowledges his unselfishness and hopes he's really all right, but also tells him that Mary 'very much wants to see you before you go to Chichester, as do I and Honor'.

Ida's worries about their marrying each other are expressed partly as a concern for Mary to have time to begin the literary or academic career she envisaged for her, reinforced by the idea that Mary might feel she ought to pay back her uncles for the money they had given towards her education, and additionally strengthened by the obvious possibility that she might well meet someone younger and apparently more suitable while at Oxford. Her worries were strengthened by Colin's telling her that he can't envisage any continuation of his work as a priest without Mary to make him a more complete person, but she is relieved when he tells her that he wasn't thinking of Mary as his partner in the sense of a '2-i-c' in the parish, or anything similar, but (rather vaguely) as his spiritual partner, and acknowledges that he ought to try and develop his ministry without leaning on Mary (though he is also haunted by the fear that Mary may marry him without previously discovering all his shortcomings).

After a time she is brought by Colin to see that his inhibition when with Mary about talking of the future imposes a very artificial barrier between them, and comes round to admitting the absurdity of his never even raising the *possibility* of their eventually marrying. Inevitably, under the circumstances, both Colin and Mary felt that this was really tantamount to an engagement. When the inevitable did come to pass in the summer of 1932 and they became officially engaged, Ida found that she too was immensely glad – chiefly because of her own great love and affection for them as a couple.

It was soon after his return to England in July after a brief return visit to Stockholm to stand in for the present chaplain on holiday (see next chapter). Colin had accepted the invitation partly so that he could say Goodbye to his sister Evelyn, who was then teaching English in the city. Appropriately enough 'the word' was finally 'spoken' and accepted in the garden of the Bishop's palace at Chichester. In her reply to the news, Ida wrote to thank him for his 'lovely letter. I too feel as if something new and wonderful has happened to us, and brought us all nearer together.' She certainly wanted Mary to marry him, but occasionally felt that noone was good enough for her and dreaded the inevitable separation; but Colin's unpossessiveness had inspired her efforts to feel the same.

8

CHAPLAINCIES I

Paris, St Moritz, as Residential Chaplain to Arthur Foley Winnington-Ingram of London, and at Stockholm

A S ALREADY RECORDED in Chapter 6, Colin was asked by the Bishop of London, Arthur Foley Winnington-Ingram, to be his chaplain as early as 1923, before or very soon after his ordination as priest. Colin had excused himself on the ground that he wanted to get more parish experience. The offer had later been repeated, and, now that he had been at St Mary's, Primrose Hill, for five years, Colin obviously felt that this was a request he could not now refuse, and agreed to come. The post would, therefore, be open to him in the autumn of 1927. Before saying a little about the significance of the Bishop's invitation, and Winnington-Ingram's character and style of ministry, I shall briefly add something about what he did in the interim between leaving St Mary's and going to Fulham Palace, where successive bishops of London had lived for centuries.

D-J's brief announcement in the Parish Magazine gives the bare bones of it: 'During May and June Mr. Dunlop will be helping at that wonderful church in the Rue Vacquerie, S. George's Paris. After that he will be chaplain at S. Moritz for two months' – his official licence gives the dates as 17 July to 11 September 1927 – 'and we shall all hope that the wonderful air and the peace of the mountains will send him back invigorated for his responsible task at Fulham in October'. In his 'Chaplain's letter' for May and June 1927, The Revd F. Anstruther Cardew said farewell to his temporary assistant in the following words:

> In the few weeks that Father Dunlop has been with us he has found his way into our hearts. For myself, I have found in him a loyal, earnest, whole-hearted colleague, and I only wish that we could keep him at St George's. Unfortunately, before he knew of the vacancy here, he had accepted the appointment as Chaplain to the Bishop of London. No one could have thrown himself more whole-heartedly into the work of our Church, and no one could have been a greater help and comfort to me than he has been. I know that he loves the church and the work, and I trust that we shall often see him here in the

days that are to come. We wish him every happiness in his new sphere of dignity.

Colin himself wrote an account of his work in a letter to D-J, part of which was published in the St Mary's Parish Magazine:

I thought I had come for a fairly easy time but I now find myself almost as busy as I was in Lent. There is an immense amount to do here – really even the assistant chaplaincy is a grand field of work for an able bodied person. One's days pass in a whirl of activities; confessions to hear, people to advise, visits to the Hospital, Boy Scouts, the British Legion – and many other things. Daily Mass is at the de luxe hour of 8.30; once a week it is at 7.30 and considered very early – a young man's job.

Cardew is a most wonderful person – a great power in Paris. He does wonders with chorus girls and the like. He has started a club for English actresses and ballet girls in Paris. As he has suddenly had to go home for the weekend, I had to go up today to this club and hold a short service in the lounge. I have never been so terrified in my life – think of it, preaching a sermon in a lounge filled with bobbed hair, powder, paint and short skirts. But they are perfect dears and made me feel quite at home. In fact, here one gets so used to powder, paint and short skirts. If one goes into the Vestry on the mornings when the brass is cleaned, one finds the place filled with fashionable young ladies dressed up to the nines – but all really working. They almost wept in sympathy when I told them how difficult we found it to get brass cleaners.

The Hospital here is very interesting – one meets anyone in it from a music hall star to a stable boy from the race courses – all English nominally – but in fact some of them can't speak English or are Maltese or Bermuda niggers. But they really look forward to the Sunday service and join in the hymns and listen like anything to the address. They are so pleased when one visits them and are eager to talk about religion. Being in a foreign land does seem to make them care about these things. The British Legion too makes one very welcome when one turns up of an evening. I have joined it so that when I go to Fulham I shall still have some link with the world of ordinary human beings – there is a branch at Fulham. The Scouts too – though attached to no Church – are delighted when a priest turns up. I had not been there half an hour before I was asked to go to their Whitsun Camp and say mass for them. All this just shows how strong the C. of E. really is in the minds and hearts of ordinary English people. Directly they get away from their home they immediately see that religion means something to them.

But I shall never get over the strangeness of actually working in Paris – a place one associates merely with holidays and jollification. It is strange to go scooting down the Avenue des Champs Elysées in a taxi taking the Sacrament to a sick person, or to walk actually under the Eiffel Tower on the way to the Scouts. But it is nice after holding forth in the Hospital wards to be able to fortify oneself with an ice cold 'Bock' at a café before going on to Evensong at S. George's, and nobody thinks it a bit odd.

Colin also wrote an article for *The Guardian* (Summer 1927) on the work of St George's and its predecessors, beginning with the very 'Romantic origin' of the first English church in Paris in 1824 when 'Mr Lewis Way, a member of the "Clapham Sect", received a legacy of £300,000 from a man of the same name who was neither known nor related to him' and 'purchased the Hotel Marboeuf not far from the Champs Elysées, and converted its large picture gallery into an English church'. It was soon recognised as the Embassy Chapel, but had to be abandoned when building alterations in the area made this necessary. The same happened with a successor church in the nearby Rue Marboeuf. But the present St George's, a fine building, writes Colin, in the Rue Vacquerie, still retains 'the original plate, furniture and registers, together with the Royal Arms, of the Marboeuf Chapel', though there is no longer an Embassy Chapel in Paris, but three English churches. But the present church 'does not end by being beautiful to look at. There is a homeliness about it' which 'suggests the meeting place of a family' – a characteristic seldom found in English churches abroad.

Colin is also full of praise here for Mr Cardew's work, especially for his foundation of the Theatre Girls' Hostel in Montmartre for American and English chorus girls. Colin may not himself have known, or perhaps tactfully omitted here, the highly 'romantic' precursors of Mr Cardew's vocation, which came to him after an emigration to Canada in 1884, in which he volunteered to fight Red Indians, and followed it up with a spell as an American cowboy [from an article in *Time* magazine of 1942, now on the web].

Colin's passport seems to show that he entered Switzerland to take up his locumtenency at St Moritz on 13 July. In an article published in *The Guardian* entitled 'Some Americans abroad' he begins with a few remarks about

> [the] drawbacks of a four months' exile on the Continent as an English chaplain. It is irksome to be away from one's friends and one's books for so long a time; life in hotels and pensions is apt to produce leanness of soul (though not necessarily leanness of body) and one misses the general background and environment of one's normal round of work and relaxation. But the gains far outweigh these discomforts. ... I only wish now to speak of one. I refer to the contact with members of the Episcopal Church of America which most European chaplaincies brings about.

He goes on to comment on the churchmanship of the Americans he ministered to under three heads. First, there is the markedly Anglican mentality they manifest, which 'leads one to the conclusion that Anglicanism is more than a merely national religion, but is a 'version of Catholicism' of permanent and extra-racial value'. Secondly, he is struck by their 'great reverence ... for religious duty', shown in their very regular and determined participation in worship, despite the 'unfamiliarities of the English Prayer-book'. Thirdly, they have the ability 'to rise above mere nationalism', so that 'the average mental and spirtual horizon of episcopalians is apt to be wider than that of non-churchgoing Americans'. Colin admits that two months in Paris and two in St Moritz might well be thought an insufficent basis for his praise, yet, he is sure that Anglicans at home have a lot to learn from them.

Four further articles by Colin survive in his Cuttings Book dating from this summer, which give some idea of his concerns during this time. The first is entitled 'The Sacristan of Auxerre: an impression', which drew forth an appreciative letter from a reader in a subsequent issue. It is based on Colin's visit to the cathedral of Auxerre (deprived of its own bishop and chapter after the French Revolution) for Mass, and I quote here the last paragraph to give an idea of its main theme (he has been describing the sacristan's singing):

> That is what is so wonderful about Plainsong. Sung even by one person who really understands it, it has a dignity and unearthliness of which nothing can rob it. It sums up in itself all the aspiration of longing of the church below, all the prophetic vision of the Temple worship at Jerusalem, and some of the triumphant song of the Church above. The traveller to Auxerre will forget the cheap furniture, the false candles, the decaying woodwork, the unsightly vestments, the casual ceremony, but along with the splendid arches of the nave, the glory of the glass and the splendour of the carved stonework, he will remember the voice of the old [sacristan] as he sang:
> Tu nos pasce, nos tuere/Tu nos bona fac videre/In terra viventium.
> (Feed us, guard us and help us to see thy good things in the land of the living)

The second of these articles is entitled 'The Cathedral of Meaux: a pilgrimage to the home of Bossuet'. Colin had a great admiration for this seventeenth century preacher and writer, and I remember seeing his name on the spines of books in his study. Bossuet became Bishop of Meaux, and the article describes in some detail the architecture of the cathedral (Colin was 'sharply ordered off' from his inspection of the stalls), and the garden of the old Bishop's palace (the house was, 'of course', closed that day). I shall again quote the concluding parapraph:

> Above the garden at the north end is a beautiful terrace, laid out on a fragment of the old town ramparts. It is planted with larches and yews and scented shrubs and trees. There are shady, twisting little paths, and seats in secluded, peaceful corners. It was here that Bossuet, we are told, delighted to walk and think. It was here, too, that the celebrated conversion of the Prince of Condé took place. In the middle of it all is a severe little seventeenth century pavilion of great charm and simplicity. In this little retreat Bossuet composed his Oraisons Funèbres (funeral orations); and here, I felt, the goal of my pilgrimage had been reached.

His third paper is called 'An Engadine Church: a vision of reconciliation'. It was clearly written after a walk along the valley from St Moritz to Silvaplana shortly before the first conference of the Ecumenical Movement of 'Faith and Order' at Lausanne, and he has pasted into the cuttings book a picture of a simple little protestant church in that village, cut out from some other publication. As usual, he gives a detailed description of the building, spending some time on a curious old mural high on the north wall of the interior which either dates from the days before the Reformation had taken hold of the

Engadine or is a deliberate throw-back to them. 'Apart from this fresco', he writes:

> the church is not at all baffling. Its bare walls, its severe furnishings, its deliberate exclusion of nearly every definite appeal to the eye, are all typical of Continental Protestantism. And yet in spite of this self-immolation, the building is very lovely and beautiful and uplifting,... there is a purity and unearthliness lurking upon every stick and stone that makes up the whole. The church ... is eloquent of supernatural truth and experience. It is, one might say, saturated with the spirit of the Epistle to the Galatians ... Here one is helped to understand, so vividly and so forcibly, that religious experience that took as its watchword 'Justification by Faith only'. ...

Unlike, say, St Peter's, Rome, 'It is not preoccupied with itself, it conceives its only function to be to point higher. If it has anything to say about itself it is "I will tell you what the Lord hath done for my soul".' And yet, 'beautiful and noble as is the appeal of the little church, there are gaps and weaknesses'. The provision for the sacraments of baptism and the Eucharist is hardly inviting; and would one not have already to feel oneself one of the elect to worship here? The Catholic church nearby, with its font at the door, its confessional and altar seems to speak more eloquently of 'a God Who takes delight in "lifting the poor out of the mire"'. But we do not have to be either Catholic or Protestant, each utterly rejecting the other, today. 'If the religion which this church enshrines is

> at all representative of modern Protestants, then we who boast of our Catholicism have much to learn from them. Here is something which we must have if we are to be real Catholics. If the Lausanne Conference does anything to bring this about, it may come to be an event to which all Christians will look back in gratitude.

The fourth article is entitled 'Catholicism, Puritanism and Pantheism: an impression of Munich'. Colin uses the word 'gaiety' (akin to merriment, and *joie de vivre*) to set against the restrictive mood that inspires Puritanism, and seeks to show that there is a specifically Catholic kind of gaiety, as opposed to the 'pagan' and non-moral gaiety of Naples, Palermo and Rio de Janeiro, all Latin cities. This Catholic *joie de vivre*, he finds, is especially characteristic of Munich, as opposed, say, to Berlin and Dresden, which are also centres of art and culture, yet unmistakably Protestant in their outlook. He then passes to a fascinating comparison of Wagner and Mozart, occasioned by his having spent a whole week in Munich attending operas by the two composers, turn and turn about. Wagner undoubtedly wishes to 'grind a moral axe' in some of his operas, and, as a result, there is an air of unreality about his often wonderfully beautiful creations, which betrays his essentially pantheist world view. Mozart, by contrast, never preaches, and the human life of his operas is, no doubt unconsciously, conceived 'against the background of eternity', and the whole is perfectly expressed in the music. It is these works which best express the Catholic gaiety not only of Munich but of all time.

Some time in September or October 1927, Colin took up his duties as residential chaplain to Bishop Winnington-Ingram, almost 40 years older than himself. By the end of November 1928, he had resigned. Colin does briefly mention this event in the (unfinished) diary he kept of his Stockholm chaplaincy in the first half of 1929, but also refers to it in a letter to George Bell before his consecration as Bishop of Chichester. Bell had written to Colin in April 1929, asking him to be his domestic chaplain. Colin at first replied that he would not be able to leave Stockholm by the time Bell wanted him, but the bishop elect said he would be content to wait. So on 27 April Colin accepted, writing that he was 'deeply touched by your confidence in me. The only cloud on the horizon', he goes on:

> is the pain which my action will give to the Bishop of London. It is the third time on which I have hurt his feelings – the first when I refused his first offer (in 1923) to be his chaplain, the second when I resigned last November, and now the fact of my resignation will be all the more emphasised by my acceptance of another domestic chaplaincy. One cannot lightly wound the feelings of a man of his character and sensitiveness ...

In the diary record he also asks himself, without attempting any answer: 'Is the pain that has been brought about by my relation with London just one of the inevitable tragedies of life or ought I to have refused the offer to go to Fulham in the first place?'

A chaplaincy with one of the senior bishops in the Church of England was often followed by the holder's attaining to high office later on. In reading the biographies of important ecclesiastics one finds again and again that the man concerned has been at some time a chaplain of the Archbishop of Canterbury or of York, or the Bishop of London, Durham or Winchester, or some other prominent bishop. Colin certainly saw such appointments as the best way of becoming thoroughly familiar with church administration, and, more generally, with how things of importance get done in the church. It thus seems clear enough that a young priest, conscious both of his considerable gifts and also of his lack of experience should welcome a call from a bishop to bring him into such an advantageous position.

In the case of this particular bishop, however, Colin was by no means as pleased to be asked as he might have been by others, and, of course, was later by George Bell. Winnington-Ingram was certainly at this time one of the best known of Anglican bishops, but it is also true to say that his fame amounted to notoriety with many clergy and lay people. Colin certainly shared many of his more boyish traits, and must have been attracted by aspects of his personality and the evangelical and pastoral gifts which stemmed effortlessly from it, but, at the same time, he deeply disapproved of his pastoral oversight of the London clergy, and perhaps also his failure to manifest the statesmanlike qualities required by the head of a diocese like London, in which all social problems are at their most complex and severe.

S.C. Carpenter, Dean of Exeter, who seems to have known him at Oxford, and to have had a lot to do with him in later life, wrote a very readable biography of his friend (*Winnington-Ingram*, Hodder & Stoughton, 1949). In it he attaches great importance to a literary tribute by the bishop's friend Henry Scott-Holland, entitled *Arthur of London*, and written when he and Winnington-Ingram were approaching old age. It begins with a little poem:

God, who created me
Nimble and light of limb
In three elements free
To run, to ride, to swim:
Not when the sense is dim,
But now from the heart of joy
I would remember Him:
Take the thanks of a boy.

Scott-Holland goes on to say:

he has retained the heart of a boy. No weary years can stifle it: no burden break it. He is a boy still: keen, generous, cheery, hopeful. He flings himself into his work with the spirit that revels in the joy of a football scrum. He faces difficulties as a boy riding at first fences. Nothing daunts: nothing can defeat him. He goes forward with a cheer against impossible obstacles; he is convinced that he will tumble over somehow. The one thing is, never to look back. It is bound to be right, if only you go straight on.

In his preface to the biography, Carpenter names The Bishop of Jarrow (this must have been Colin, from the date) as one of four chaplains from whom he had much help in the matter of reminicences and general observations. Their individual contributions are not distinguished in the text, but it seems quite likely that the 'very musical chaplain' who had never played the organ, yet who was made, under protest, to accompany palace prayers on the organ, in accordance with the palace custom that this was the chaplain's job, was Colin. Carpenter adds that though some of the domestics giggled, 'the Bishop would not yield, and said: "That's all right, old boy. Rome wasn't built in a day."'

But the following reminiscence is not only very characteristic of the kind of thing Colin would recall, but also of the way he would describe it: 'A vivid little picture of him will always remain in my mind of an occasion or two when he had been "caught out" in some mistake – he would look at you with a half guilty, half mischievous look of a small boy discovered in the act.' It is also mentioned in the text that the Bishop played squash, and I remember well my father saying he used sometimes to play that game with him. Otherwise I cannot recall Colin saying anything at all about his time at Fulham.

The notoriety mentioned above was especially rife in church circles, and almost any historian of the Church of England in the first half of the twentieth century or biographer of an ecclesiastical statesman is likely to allude to it. In his biography of Archbishop Fisher, who succeeded Winnington-Ingram, Edward Carpenter puts it thus:

> Many were the clergy and laymen who complained that there was a lack of order and general discipline in the [London] parishes; that the Prayer Book was being ignored and that many a church was becoming an 'island refuge' for a bewildering variety of liturgical exiles. The Times wrote of the London Diocese that 'every party organisation had its headquarters in London and nowhere else were the evils of party spirit in Church affairs so evident'.

As far as the 'Romanisation', and, in particular, the use of Perpetual Reservation and Benediction went, the Bishop's justification can be found in this reference to him in Adrian Hastings' *A History of Christianity in England, 1920–2001* (SCM, 2001):

> The episcopal Trojan Horse of Anglo-Catholicism felt that the solace of prayer before the reserved sacrament could not be refused to 'the tide of human grief and anxiety ... (and) the longing to get as near as possible to the Sacramental presence of our Lord'.

Owen Chadwick records Bishop Hensley Henson's attitude to his fellow-bishop thus in connection with the rejection of the 1927–1928 Prayer Book (Hensley Henson, OUP, 1983, p. 198): One of Henson's 'personal diagnoses' was that the extreme Protestants abhorred 'the encouragement which a few bishops gave to ritualists – Winnington-Ingram because he encouraged all good work and had the charitable illusion that everybody did good work'. We must end this paragraph with a delightfully meiotic, yet balanced, quotation from S.C. Carpenter's biography: 'Ingram's affection for the Anglo-Catholic clergy, and his light-hearted way of considering that a friendly interview, a prayer and a blessing had settled a question for ever, did not promote the discipline which were being demanded in many quarters, which he himself really desired to see.'

Much of Colin's time at Fulham was inevitably taken up with attending the Bishop in many of his engagements. The Cuttings book contains press photographs of the Armistice Day ceremony at the Cenotaph, with Colin just visible at the edge of the picture holding the Bishop's Pastoral Staff; he is there again behind the Bishop as he blesses the new colours presented to the London Division of the Church Lads' Brigade; he stands behind the Bishop's chair as the Chairman of Lloyd's reads the Corporation's address to the King; he attends him as he gives a Blessing in the slum area of Somer's Town, and, carrying his Staff, precedes the Bishop in a long procession at Whiteland's training college for women teachers at Chelsea, and in another photograph precedes him towards the door of St-Martin-in-the-Fields Church for 'the private 'Prayer Book Synod' of 1400 clergy, the first held in the Diocese since the Reformation'.

Colin always appears in these pictures wearing his MA hood in the medieval fashion, that is, *as* a hood which, when not worn on the head, covers the shoulders and upper arms, not just as a piece of material hung round the wearer's neck and allowed to hang down the centre of the back. In this he followed the lead of Percy Dearmer and 'the Warham Guild tradition'. There are also two splendid photographs (probably reproductions of press photos) in his sister Evelyn's scrap book of Colin and the Bishop. In one, Colin is elegantly dressed in what looks like ecclesiastical formal morning dress; he is all in black, with gleaming topper, waistcoat, long, square-cut frock coat, and narrow trousers, with his white dog-collar above his black stock and the gloves in his left hand the only departures from sable; with his right hand he holds a black umbrella over the bishop, who is putting on what seems like a cloak above his cassock, held by a man who is probably his chauffeur.

In another photo from this source Colin heads a small procession with the bishop in cope and mitre, supported either side by clergy in dalmatics and birettas, while what looks like the incumbent of a church walks in cassock, surplice and stole, also wearing a biretta; the occasion may well have been a somewhat 'Romanising' church service in a dockland, or industrial, area, since they walk on a narrow footpath beside a very neglected railway line. In the background is a policeman who has perhaps been keeping away protesters. In neither of these photographs does Colin look at his ease.

The Cuttings Book also contains 'the substance of' a fine sermon preached by Colin at St Paul's on 25 November 1927. His text is 'The fear of the Lord is the beginning of wisdom'. This is a straightforward piece of analysis and exposition of the Christian virtue of reverence, of reverence for the world and what it contains, for all God's creatures and especially our fellow human beings, for God's truth and for God's nature as revealed in his acts. It seems to me a mature sermon, very clear and well developed, such that anyone who heard it would be inspired to do something about its content. Apart from this material there are two descriptions of walks in Switzerland, one from the *Alpine Post* and one from *The Engadine Express*, which reflect his summer holiday in 1928. However, I have seen nothing at all arising from a New Year trip to Czechoslovakia, which he took at the beginning of January 1928, except three passport stamps, which show he travelled by way of Aachen and then entered and left through Cheb, in the extreme north-west of the country.

As I have already implied, we cannot tell now what straw it was that broke the camel's back of Colin's apparent readiness to put the best possible interpretation on his Bishop's failure to apply effective discipline to those incumbents who continued wilfully to disregard the BCP, and also the 1928 'deposited' Prayer Book, in the matters of Reservation, Benediction and other 'Romanising' practices which threatened the coherence of the Church of England (the two convocations didn't actually 'lay down the law' about this until July 1929 – though it made little difference to the Bishop of London).

Nevertheless, a few months later there was an encouraging announcement in 'The London Diocesan Leaflet', which included the words: 'The good wishes of his many friends will go with the Reverend David Colin Dunlop, who has been appointed Residential Chaplain to the Bishop of Chichester. Mr Dunlop began his work at Saint Mary's Primrose Hill; after a time as Chaplain in Paris he became Residential Chaplain to the Bishop of London. Since then he has been for a short period Embassy Chaplain in Stockholm.'

As Colin was now living, with Evelyn, in his mother's house in Fellow's Road, which is just outside the parish boundary, he was able to help out regularly at St Mary's during December and January. It looks as though Laura had identified herself with St Mary's while she had been living there since returning to Hampstead from Beckenham shortly after David Jugurtha's death, but her own health was now giving cause for alarm.

*

Colin left London for Harwich on the evening of 6 February, had 'a calm crossing in bright sunlight' to Esbjerg, and took the 'luxurious' sleeping car to Copenhagen, where he had a day's sightseeing on the 8th. Here are his impressions:

> I carry two pictures in my mind. The first, of the scene in the Amalienborg square during the changing of the palace guard – the bright sunlight, the superb baroque palaces, the soldiers in their dark blue coats and fantastic bear-skin helmets; the second, of the courtyard of the Christianborg Palace in the twilight, covered with snow – suddenly there canters in bare-back a fair-haired youth gaily laughing – so reckless, so elemental. I made also an adventurous excursion in a tram out to a suburb to see the much spoken-of Grundtvigskirken [completed 1921] with its daring, bizarre, organ-pipe façade in creamy yellow brick. Something quite new, but assuredly appropriate and grand. And then of course there was the Marmorkirken surrounded by a quiet square of sombre rococo mansions. A city to see again and again and enjoy.

Apart from his diary, maintained for eleven and a half weeks, Colin also wrote a short article for the *Anglican Church Magazine* at the instance of the Bishop of Fulham, who visited the English congregation while Colin was ministering to them, and also saw Archbishop Söderblom. This was reported in the *Svenska Dagbladet* some time in June, and illustrated by a press photo of the Bishop and the chaplain standing on a station platform. Colin's article is entitled 'Four months in a Swedish chaplaincy'. He explains here that the British Chaplain in Stockholm is only Honorary Legation Chaplain; his prime task is to 'be of service to the British community, to preach the Gospel and to administer the sacraments' in the Anglican Church of St Peter and St Sigfrid.

Since the Church of England, he emphasises, is still a National Church, the services tend to attract worshippers of all varieties of churchmanship, and a variety of nonconformist bodies who may have no access to their own places of worship; they are also often attended by members of the Swedish church, which in fact has, Colin wrote, closer relations with the Anglican Church than any other Continental church. 'The Crown Prince and Princess of Sweden', he writes, 'are seat-holders in the Church and take a real interest in the affairs of the British Congregation', supporting it financially and in other ways. All this means, he concludes, that the chaplain must stick to the Book of Common Prayer, and keep a decent mean between extremes of Churchmanship. This need not produce a 'colourless' style of worship:

> The Prayer Book used as directed, suitable hymns, simple music of a congregational character, a reverent conduct of the service by the Chaplain, appropriate additional prayers drawn from the many sources now available and permissible, sermons which deal with the more important things in religion and life – such principles applied with care and sympathy will never produce a colourless worship.

He also stresses the importance of the social side of a Chaplain's work. In a small community like Stockholm (150–200 persons) this means he should encourage existing 'secular' organisations rather than 'Church organisations for Church people', and above all 'provide in his own flat or house an English home in which the many unattached or lonely people ... may find welcome and company'.

After another comfortable night in a sleeper Colin was met at the station in Stockholm on 10 February by 'a clerk from the British Legation', who saw him on his way to his lodgings at 10 Fredrickshofsgatan, after relaying an invitation to lunch tête á tête with the British Minister, Sir Tudor Vaughan. Colin describes him as 'an impressive yet approachable individual, very irreproachably dressed (Colin was glad he had brought his frock coat), ready to talk of all manner of things: the Bishop of London – prayer book revision – Anglo-Catholicism – the state of the English church in Stockholm, etc.'. Before lunch he had been visited by Herr Gustav Petré, his Church-Warden, and Hansson the verger, who showed him the church. The vestry was 'occupied by two spinsters of the orthodox vestal-viper type – brass-cleaning'. Next day, Sunday, he noted 'two ladies at the 9am celebration and about 50 at Mattins – plenty of men – a small ladies choir and one choirman. An easy church to speak in. The minister and Consul both present'. After lunch he had a 'good walk round Stockholm ... but the cold is so intense that I can scarcely bear the pain of it on my ears. Have bought a fur cap'.

Here is his entry for the 12th:

> One great blessing about Sweden is that one does not have the meagre continental breakfast. Porridge, eggs, cold ham and sausage – this is what one starts the day with. To-day my first experience on skis. The nice Finn who lives in the next room provides the skis while his talkative son of 9 years of age takes me out under his wing. Many falls today but I think I shall like it... In the afternoon, tea with Fru Löf, Mrs Howard Glover's friend. Seldom have I met

such an indefatigable talker, but then she has plenty to talk about. Plump and vivacious she pours forth her words, her experiences in England, books, music, people she knows. I have never been out to tea tête á tête and spoken so little. A dear person. Still feel a little diffident in the public rooms of this pension. Ought one to bow and speak to the Swedish people one does not know? The maids here are nice and hard working; a pleasant blend of familiarity and diffidence in their attentions. One of them presented me with a case to keep my table napkin in, magnificently labelled 'Herr Legationskaplan Dunlop'.

And so it goes on, with two or three entries a week, nearly all including something worth quoting; there was a fine orchestral concert on Ash Wednesday evening and a meeting with 'Kammerherr von Heidenstam, the grand old man of the English Church in Stockholm', looking like 'Clemenceau himself, with his white imperial and bulging forehead'. On the 15th comes 'A skiing expedition in the morning with two English ladies and the little Anglo-Finn boy staying in the Pension'. He's definitely improving. They enjoyed 'a cup of hot wine in a little country café before a vast blazing open fire.' He has another lunch at the Legation, the party including Dodds, first secretary of the legation, and the Finnish representative on the League of Nations. He has 'a very thorough and scientific haircutting', but is 'appalled at a bill of 3.15 Kr for cut and shampoo'. He finds something 'very touching' about the English wife of the Finn next door; she takes her enormous anxieties and insecurities arising from her husband's 'nerves' and poor prospects so calmly and bravely. That evening he hears rather bad news about Laura. On Saturday, 16th there is more skiing, but Colin rides on horseback with Mr Nordin 'dragging people behind on skis'; that evening there is a 'British colony dance at the Hotel Atlantic.' The British 'as represented did not thrill me much, but they are all friendly.' Next day, Sunday, there is no one at the 9am Mass but a fair congregation at 11. He preached the first address of a Lenten course 'Pictures of Christ in the New Testament'. Afterwards there was lunch with the Legation secretary and his family.

> Mrs Dodds is one of those beautiful stately good women whom it is a pleasure to watch but with whom it is not easy to converse on matters of real interest. Infinitely genuine and in a way really holy, they must have such a strong and gracious influence everywhere they go.

Next day, the 18th, Colin heard from Evelyn that their mother, Laura, had died early on the previous Wednesday. There were also letters of condolence from Ida and Mary, and from Jack and Olive Arnold. On the Friday there was to have been a Requiem at St Mary's, followed by burial at Shirley Cemetery, Surrey, where Laura's mother Emma Beddard had been buried, and, in the adjoining double plot, David Jugurtha and Jim. The Requiem was taken by Hubert William Harcourt, who succeeded D-J. No preacher, communicants or collection were recorded in the Register of Services.

Two days later there is another entry:

I am leading an aimless life at the moment, finding it hard to pray, hard to study, hard to throw myself into the work here. Suffering from a sort of all-round inhibition. How is a mortal to set about getting an object in life? Directly one object appears upon the horizon and the pursuit of it begins, a second seemingly better and more suitable one appears. Direction being changed accordingly, a third object appears and so on. Nothing is more curious than the ease with which we can be deluded. I was at a loose end during my two months at home after leaving Fulham. But all the time I said 'things will be different at Stockholm'. Yet they are not different. How little effect space or time has upon the mind or the soul.

Two days later he writes 'it is colder than ever', though there was 'a fair congregation at Mattins – the Crown Princess present. A Swede named Barker sang in the choir. He is so fond of England that he has taken an English name, he wears a metal Union Jack pinned on to his tie, and his woollen scarf is red, white and blue. A zealous and enthusiastic person.' There was more skiing, and a visit to *Don Giovanni*, 'Elizabeth Schumann magnificent'. But 'how difficult it is to take in mother's death, not having actually been there and seen her dead. Even now it seems a fact quite improbable and if true quite external to myself.'

On 26 February he records the 'First confirmation interview with Britt Carter, a dark-eyed girl of 16, her mother, a widow, Swedish. Intelligent and pretty, but why does she smile all the time?' In a letter to Ida of 7 May he sums up his difficulties with such interviews:

to teach girls who cannot speak English very well and whose lives have had an entirely different background and setting from those I have been accustomed to teach in the past ... means a great strain – or rather an added strain to what is even in the most favourable times a great demand on one's resources.

The observation he makes in connection with another candidate, that 'confirmation among the upper class girls is regarded as their 'coming out'' may well have exacerbated this difficulty. The remorseless social life continues: dinner 'last night with the Consul, tonight with the Windetts. Tonight's party as charming as yesterday's was distasteful'. One of the two guests 'was a Swedish girl of 21, of tantalizing beauty. But of course just as we were getting on nicely it transpired that she is engaged! When, when am I going to meet my bride?'

On 3 March they had the first choral Eucharist at 11 since he had been there, but, alas, 'Merbecke murdered. Had Barker ... to lunch. He tells me that what first attracted him to the Anglican church was people really kneeling in the service. He has promised to present a verger's mace.' That evening Mrs Lindman took him to an enjoyable musical evening.

On the 6th 'Evelyn arrived ... accompanied as usual by a male escort. We are now comfortably housed in 3 rooms in the Pension.' The next day he goes with Evelyn to an evening of Swedish folk dancing, when the different parts of Sweden were identifiable by their dress.

The dances are more vigorous and, so it seems at first sight, more elaborate and difficult than ours. The physical relations of the male to the female partner are less restrained than in our decorous country dances; girls are lifted up, or whirled round and round held tight by the waist, etc. There is far more of the flavour of the soil about them – even more than in our Morris dances.

The next day he 'obeys a written command' of the Crown Princess 'to present myself before (her). She received me simply and pleasantly'.

The day after, he moans: 'There never seems to be enough time to get anything done here... there is a perpetual sense of there being no time to 'settle' to anything' – a complaint echoed in the letter to Ida of 7 May. A few days later he says he and Evelyn:

> seem to be living in a whirl of fashionable tea parties and dinners – and cocktails and charming middle aged women in smart clothes and bewitching girls in still smarter ones and young men in smart suits who are 'good fellows'. Sometimes I find myself deliberately trying to be the 'broad-minded human parson'. Oh how difficult it is to behave naturally in the presence of God, how easy to assume masks or to adopt attitudes, or to be always wondering what other people are thinking of me. If I drink cocktails I think 'now they will see I am a human parson' or I think 'ought I to have a second one?' It is so hard to drink one's cocktail in the presence of God just because it is pleasant to do so.

This leads him to ask himself 'what ought I to aim at in this mixed society here?', and to pick holes in all the answers that present themselves to him.

One of the character-traits which comes over strongly in Colin's diaries is his ability to put impressions into, almost always, strongly evaluative terms. After a performance of *Boris Godunov*: 'An opera ... full of dignity and unearthly beauty'; after being taken to the modern church of Högalid:

> The decoration of the interior, if inclined to an ultra modernity, is most effective. Everywhere the eye rests upon severe clean lines, and gay cool colours sparingly used. A beautiful black cloth altar frontal with a cross and stars worked upon it.

After a performance of *Parsifal* with Fru Löf: 'I do not know that I can say sincerely more than that I like it very much in parts.'

Two encounters with members of the Swedish Church can be put together at this point. On neither of them is he, in general, complimentary. The first was a dinner with the Pastor Primarius of Stockholm:

> On entering the salon my eyes were greeted with the most odd and unexpected assemblage of gentlemen. They looked like shrewd and capable men of business, but it appeared they were all pastors. While the absence of any professional stamp of countenance was refreshing in one sense, one missed something in their faces and manner – but what precisely I cannot say. The P-P himself is a short plump little man lacking, so it appeared, both in dignity and

intelligence. Except for two (one of whom was Pastor Sandegren) the guests had little about them to commend them to the stranger. I was never less impressed with a number of new acquaintances before. Pastor Sandegren ... alone, with one other, struck me as having much spiritual and intellectual horizon. It was plain he had a strong pastoral sense and a real longing for reunion and the deepening of the spiritual life of the Church as a whole.

This dinner was in Holy Week, and he also wondered whether the 'almost luxurious' spread was quite appropriate to the season, though, as it was held in his honour, he felt he could not refrain from doing it justice. Then, on 10 April he 'went to the Blasieholms Kyrka to see a meeting of the Kyrkliga Mötet which I presume corresponds to the Church Assembly'. He found it extremely depressing, especially the unimaginative composition of 'so-called Morning Prayers', which contained 'a long speech from the pulpit', then a paper on 'Uplift' read in an exceptionally monotonous voice and taking a whole hour in the reading. At this point he 'escaped', but

> saw Archbishop Söderblom for the first time. Having heard such adverse estimation of his personality from Bishop Gore and Dodds and others (he) was prepared for a personage of much less attraction and even grace than the individual with the gold cross and the black coat who sauntered into the church as soon as prayers were over. He looks full of vitality...

Perhaps this paragraph can be rounded off by what what Colin records of a visit from Nordin. a young Swedish medical student who came to consult Colin about his religious difficulties. He himself seemed 'a most beautiful character with an alert sensitive soul and a sense of responsibility for his fellow students. He appear(ed) dissatisfied with the Swedish church and its lack of insistence upon the "Numinous" in its worship.'

On Palm Sunday at SS Peter and Sigfrid, he 'missed the solemn palm ceremonies of S. Mary's and the rugged plainsong and the severe yet beautiful hangings of the English rite very much', though consoled himself with his judgement that the BCP service is 'most moving at this season'. However, he could not escape feeling that:

> There is not much of the familiar Holy Week atmosphere this year. I do not know whether this is a good or a bad sign. A great deal of personal vanity was bound up in my delight in the children's week-day services at St Mary's and in the solemn ceremonial observances there at this season. Possibly what I am missing this year is just these unworthy yet consoling sensations. Perhaps this apparent absence here of any spiritual experience is just my normal spiritual condition now not reinforced by the purely emotional and accidental attributes of past days.

Nevertheless, his introduction of a Liturgical Three Hours on Good Friday 'seems to have been a success', even with champions of the old regime, and Easter Day 'was full of joy and brightness', with a 'very acceptable' Easter

Offering. About two weeks later he opines that 'his new children's service had gone well. The joy of teaching them Martin's tune to Loving Shepherd! The rows of round faces with wide-open saucer-like eyes! One told her mother about "such a lovely *party!*"'

It will hardly need saying by now that Colin's diary of his Stockholm chaplaincy is the expression of a man undergoing a great many conflicting but powerful emotions. Obviously the death of his mother, coming so soon after his decision, which must have been a very difficult one, to resign his chaplaincy to Bishop Winnington-Ingram, had upset him considerably, despite what his sister Sibyl says of their mother's neglect of her children. The Swedish Chaplaincy was probably applied for and accepted as a convenient solution of his loss of a salary, but it is clear that this post, with its endless 'social whirl' and liturgical-pastoral undemandingness was not really what he was best fitted for.

But there was another and deeper emotional need, which, of course, comes out in what he says about the tantalisingly beautiful nubile women he kept meeting, and in other places too. He was at this time seriously considering whether he ought not to ask Mary O'Malley to marry him – a matter into which I shall look more fully in the next chapter. Meanwhile he had met the half-English Elsa Frick, a former school friend of Evelyn's, 'sparkling with life and humour and beauty', who, he writes, 'thrills me deeply'. He met her on other occasions, too, though it is clear that he fairly soon began to have second thoughts about her. Evelyn and he went to dinner with Elsa and her mother one evening, and he wrote in his diary that she attracted him a great deal, 'but what is she really like? Is she really a person, or just a collection of qualities and a bundle of tastes and appetites? And have I anything to give her which is worth while?' Mary herself was able to tell Ida, in a letter dated 1 September 1936, when she and Colin had been married just over a year and were holidaying in Sweden:

> We had dinner with the Skagerlinds. Mrs is an Englishwoman married to a Swede but now divorced from him [presumably reverting to her maiden name]. She has 3 children – a boy whom we did not see, a student – and two charming daughters. The younger, who was destined once for Colin (but there is no ill-feeling about it!) is quiet and very agreeable but faintly dull. She works in a bank.

The diary ends on 24 April. The relief at George Bell's invitation to him to be his chaplain and, what is more, at a slightly later date than he really wanted him to begin, seems to have driven out of his head any need to keep it up. I have no record of any meeting between Colin and Bell before Colin returned to England (though the way he writes about him to Ida – see below – suggests that they had at least met), but Bell was clearly sure that Colin would be a good chaplain, and may have been helped in his choice by D-J, who went to be Dean of Chichester in 1929, and probably knew Bell already in any case. D-J had in fact prepared Colin for Bell's invitation, and he wrote in this last entry: 'It is important work, he (D-J) thinks I can do it, and there is no reason why I should stay here. Also to be asked to share the labours of a bishop such as he (George Bell) will certainly be is too attractive a prospect to reject.' This entry also records that he and Evelyn

> lunched in state at the Grand Hotel as the guests of Lord Ebbisham who is visiting Stockholm. ... In the afternoon we had tea with Princess Ingrid's 'lady's maid' at the Palace, and the Princess herself came in, looking so demure and sweet – she shook hands with us and talked for a few minutes. So gracious and uplifting. What a fine thing 'royalty' is.

On 5 May Colin wrote to Ida as follows:

> I have recently decided to leave here. In spite of my vivid illusions there is not really enough to occupy the full time of someone of my age here. There is scope for the development of the work here, but a more experienced man and a settled man is needed for that particular kind of development of which I am thinking. So when George Bell who is to be the new Bishop of Chichester wrote and asked me to be his chaplain (or chief of staff as he was kind enough to put it) I decided after ten days reflection to accept. He is only some ten years older than I and a very vigorous industrious person with a real vision of what the C of E can be. He seems to think I can be of use to him ... I decided I would be more useful there than here. ...
> I shall be sorry in a way to leave here. It is such a beautiful place. Also I have been able to be of some use here – one can say these things to friends – and I shall be sorry to go and leave the people. I have just started a children's service too – and other things like that. All the same I don't think I ought to stay, I know I should go to pieces with too little to do....Tell Mary I shall be writing soon.

Colin was, in the end, able to leave Stockholm in June. Before his final leave-taking he made a one-day visit to Turku in Finland, for which he obtained a diplomatic visa, finally saying goodbye to Sweden on the 19th. Meanwhile George Bell had been consecrated Bishop at Canterbury on the 11th. Colin arrived back in England a day or two before the new Bishop was enthroned in Chichester Cathedral, making it possible to serve as his chaplain on the occasion.

9

CHAPLAINCIES II

George Bell's First Residential Chaplain

COLIN LEFT NO DIARIES during his three years as Domestic Chaplain and Secretary to Bishop George Bell (late June 1929 to late June 1932), and even his letters to Ida O'Malley, some of which have survived, give little detail about what exactly he did. This may well be a result of the fact that, in the Bishop's words as quoted by Colin, '... a chaplain's first duty is to be a slave to his bishop'. The Bishop was, in fact, referring to his own relation to Archbishop Davidson, whose chaplain he had been for almost ten years during the First World War and its aftermath, and to the fact that he had had to be prepared at all times to be available to help the Archbishop should he be needed, even when he had made arrangements to go out with his wife on a Saturday afternoon.

But even Bell himself, who was something of a workaholic, had begun and kept up a daily journal during those years, and, in any case, Davidson had been Primate of All England long enough to have developed an established routine for his relations with his chaplains, whereas George Bell, being new to the episcopate, had not had a chaplain before. In another letter to Ida of October 1929 Colin writes: 'I get nowadays so little time off that I can hardly think at all about things outside my work. I am practically never free of it – or if I am it is because I have to be hanging about for the bishop in places where one can't read and can't be quiet'. (He had, in fact, no regular day off each week.)

Even when the Bishop was away without him, his absence 'means less rush, but more actual work and more responsibility ...' In his biography of Bell, Ronald Jasper provides a telling detail of the chaplain-cum-secretary's work: 'Normally (Bell) began his day by saying Mattins in chapel at eight o'clock. Then came family prayers, followed by breakfast, at which he expected to be given the more important of the morning's letters already sorted'.

Nevertheless, on 26 August 1929, Colin was able to tell Ida in a letter: 'on the whole I am glad to be doing some work again and to work with George Cicester: it is an experience with an almost continual thrill. He and his delightful wife came home last Wednesday but they are away again now, so I sit once more in the palace in rather lonely ecclesiastical state.' One compensation he mentions for the lack of spare time is that he can say Mass (probably at the Bishop Otter Teacher Training College) two or three times a week. But another must undoubtedly have been the consequence of the Bishop's comparative youth. The Bishop of London had been forty years older than Colin, and was no doubt rather set in his ways; Bishop Bell was a mere ten years older, and thus his offer to Colin to be his 'Chief of Staff' was compatible with many opportunities for him to be a good deal more than a mere 'slave' to the Bishop, however kindly he was treated, and for there to have been a good deal of give and take between the two.

George Bell and William Temple are now generally considered, by historians of the Church, to be two of the most outstanding figures in the Church of England of the first half of the twentieth century. When Temple died in 1944, after his short time as Archbishop of Canterbury during the Second World War, many people, among whom were newspaper editors and columnists, thought that there could be no doubt that Bell should succeed him. It is often said that Winston Churchill, Prime Minister at the time, would not consent to this because of Bell's outspoken criticisms of the conduct of the war.

He continued to argue that the allied war-aim of 'Unconditional Surrender' was a tragic mistake, and was based on the false assumption that there was no real difference between Nazis and ordinary, rather unpolitical, Germans who, in their hearts, disapproved of Hitler and his henchmen but felt that the Nazi grasp of power had become inescapable. Two of the most glaring manifestations of this, for Bell, were the obliteration bombing of cities, including non-industrial areas, and the absolute refusal to respond to unofficial peace overtures made to Bell and to one or two others, usually through intermediaries in Sweden, by members of the small undergound anti-Nazi resistance movements.

In his biography of Bishop Bell, Ronald Jasper raises the question why Temple, who was also widely known on the Continent of Europe and also never ceased to argue that Christianity could not and should not be kept out of politics, since the fundamentals of Christian belief had implications for human behaviour in all spheres of life, yet still achieved the Primacy, whereas Bell was denied it. As a man, Bell was well-liked and much admired, even by those who held completely different views:

> But in those places in England where impressions counted for so much – in the House of Lords, in Convocation, and in the Church Assembly, he had not that kind of mastery which was Temple's ... He was pertinacious: but his pertinacity could grow to a point at which his influence on others suffered – he could appear to be just obstinate or harbouring bees in his bonnet. The question would then be asked, 'Is it really wise to have such a man at Lambeth? Again, he was not always persuasive; he had a tendency to lecture; and a lighter touch might well have helped him. (Ronald C.D. Jasper, *George Bell – Bishop of Chichester*, p. 285)

Jasper drives home this point with quotations from two other people, one from Charles Smyth's biography of Cyril Garbett, Archbishop of York at this time, in which the author says that Bell 'was by nature a protagonist, and seemed to make every subject controversial when he spoke on it', whereas Garbett 'could tackle a notoriously difficult and controversial question ... and somehow take the controversy out of it; his speech was just an honest expression of opinion'. The other is from an appreciation of Bell by Lord Longford, broadcast on the BBC in 1959. Here he tries to explain why those who:

> differed from so saintly a man found him so tremendously irritating, and so acutely provocative in public, although for the most part they had an enormous admiration for him in his private life. It was partly perhaps his manner. It was a mild manner, and yet immensely assured with none of the mock diffidence with which the professional parliamentarian commends himself.

It was also the case, he goes on, that 'expediency, and reasons of state, ... seemed to play no part whatever in the Bishop's philosophy'.

Lord Longford's claim that Bell rejected 'expediency' cannot help but remind Christians that, in his long account of Jesus's Passion and Execution, the author of the Gospel according to John emphasises, in the words of the Authorised Version, that it was Caiaphas, the High Priest, who had considered it 'expedient that one man should die for the people'. Modern versions of this passage tend to substitute the word 'better' for 'expedient', but, whichever translation is preferred, the comparison must be between expediency and justice.

Many Christians believe, and have believed, that there are circumstances in life when a choice between evils is forced on almost everyone. In such situations the better, or less evil alternative is almost bound to be one where knowledge of the facts of the case, and of the likely outcome of each alternative, plays an extremely important part in the decision. There is thus always a strong temptation to think one really *knows* the answer to such questions and make one's choice in accordance with one's own subjective preference.

It is clear now, perhaps, that the political alternatives George Bell defended with 'obstinacy' were sometimes justified by superior knowledge of facts and probabilities, but such knowledge can never be certain, and it may be that his attitude to political controversy brought out his worst side, especially when he felt himself to be in the minority, or up against powerful men like Winston Churchill. It is, perhaps, worth remembering here that even William Temple refused to condemn the obliteration bombing of cities (Adrian Hastings, *A History of English Christianity, 1920–2000*, pp. 378–9).

This brief picture of Bell's public persona must be offset by a look at the impression he gave in situations not themselves inherently controversial, where we find a very different Bell. Long before he became Bishop of Chichester, Bell had become the best-known Anglican worker for the reunion of the churches, and had, in the process, made many friends abroad, especially among

Scandinavian and German Lutherans. This is how Archbishop Nathan Söderblom of Uppsala summed up Bell's demeanour at ecumenical meetings:

> He hardly said anything except when he was asked. Then, after consideration, he gave a thoughtful answer which always proved to be reliable. The face is dominated by two large, round eyes which shine with the life and soul behind and indicate a rich inner life. In my opinion, no man means more for the ecumenical awakening than this silent Bell. This bell never rings unnecessarily. But when it sounds, the tone is silvery clear. It is heard, It penetrates more than many boisterous voices. He does not speak without having something to say. The strong spirituality of his personality marks everything he does.

Here too is Colin's own account of how Bell won over the Rural Deans of Chichester Diocese at his first meeting with them:

> At first there was an indefinable air – not at all of opposition, but rather of aloofness. You felt that the rural deans had come intending to observe and not to commit themselves too far. But before the meeting was over Bell had won their confidence and drawn them out, inspiring quite a degree of enthusiasm for certain proposals he tentatively made. One could not help feeling that the results of this meeting of the representative clergy were far-reaching and that a definite wave of confidence and sympathy was initiated. (quoted in Jasper).

Bishop Bell and his wife Hetty were also extremely hospitable (Jaspers, p. 82ff):

> The succession of visitors, diverse in their creeds, interests and nationalities, was endless. The week-end parties, which he tried to arrange once a month, and at which he entertained men of letters, artists, actors and politicians, could produce conversation which was brilliant and stimulating; while some guests provided him with experiences which were quite unique – as, for example, Mr Gandhi's visit in October 1931.

Jaspers emphasises the fact that, in the early years at Chichester before the war, he lost 'his old Chief, Archbishop Davidson' and also his father, 'two Powerful influences in the shaping of his life' (p. 84). But despite this,

> that spirit of youthful gaiety and experiment which Bell had displayed [as Dean] at Canterbury ... was still much in evidence at Chichester ... matched by a great love of the brethren and a great humility ... The young administrator and statesman, described at his appointment as 'one of the few first-class brains in the C of E', had revealed himself unmistakably as a true pastor and father-in-God.

These quotations should make it very clear what Colin meant when he wrote to condole with Mrs Bell when the Bishop died in 1958. After expressions of sorrow and thankfulness, Colin goes on:

How much I owe to you both. The early days of Chichester were really golden days and life at the palace was full of happenings and of an atmosphere both of which are still vivid in their joyfulness ... How much I learned from one who had so much to teach me!

One very significant fact about Colin's three years in the palace at Chichester was the coolness, or antipathy, which existed between the Bishop and the Dean, Arthur Stuart Duncan-Jones (D-J), who took up his duties in the Cathedral about four months after Colin began as Bishop's Chaplain. It is difficult to gauge precisely what this meant in practice, but I have heard (from Bishop Michael Manktelow) that D-J would not allow Bell to preach, or even – he thought – to visit the cathedral officially more than once a year (though it ought to be said that many Deans have jealously guarded this prerogative: the Diocesan Bishop is in no sense 'in charge' of the cathedral in which he has his throne). This coolness was the result both of character and of particular views. Jasper quotes the words of The Revd A. Rouse, who was a student at Chichester Theological College when war [WW2] was declared:

> The Dean in booming tones, with somewhat belligerent flavour, announced the outbreak of war. The contrast was quite extraordinary when Dr Bell, quite on his own, walked from his throne and for a few minutes reminded the congregation that they were to be Christians, to have pity on their enemies, to have compassion, and throughout the war to have forgiveness in their hearts. (Jasper, p. 86)

It is worth quoting here also Adrian Hastings's words on the Church's reception of Prime Minister Chamberlain's announcement of 'Peace in our time' after his talk with Hitler at Munich a few months earler, when the Germans had just invaded Czechoslovakia. Against the almost universal praise and relief at Munich, he says:

> there was hardly any important church dissent except Duncan-Jones, who at once wired both Archbishops about 'the most shameful betrayal in English history'. Temple, Bell and Hinsley [the Roman Catholic Archbishop of Westminster] agreed with Archbishop Lang's 'unctuous and almost blasphemous' expression of gratitude to 'God and the Prime Minister. (*A History of English Christianity: 1920–2000*, p. 348)

Francis Steer, in his short memoir on Bell in the Volume *Chichester 900*, reports a 'sparring match' between the two about nuclear armaments in the Church Assembly rooms, during which they were unable to agree on any point. Steer also says that D-J would sign his letters to his Bishop 'Decanus' ['the Dean']. It is worth adding here that, soon after Colin had left England for Iraq, Bell told him in a letter that D-J was introducing incense into the Cathedral for regular processional use on Sundays before the celebration. 'I have told him I regret it very much. And I do.' This coolness between the two men, both of whom meant a great deal to Colin, cannot always have been easy for him to cope with, and may account for what my mother told the Dean of York after Colin and D-J had died. She wrote to me that the Dean (Addleshaw) asked her what Colin had thought of Bishop Bell. So she re-read the letters he had sent her from Chichester (none of which, alas, have survived). He began, she told me, by being 'very enthusiastic' about him, but later 'began to see the other side' – which 'always happened with him'. But he did admire Bell very much at first and was partly influenced later by D-J.

But the Bishop's Chaplain was certainly allowed by his Bishop to influence what happened in the Cathedral. In one of his letters to Ida, dated 4 January 1931, Colin makes this clear. 'Tomorrow', he writes,

> we have got our music and Epiphany procession in the Cathedral. I feel very proud of it because the whole idea of it, with most of the details, has come out of my own mind – also I have made most of the practical arrangements or directly inspired the Dean to make them. So I hope it is going to be a success. Almost everyone in the County seems to be coming and the Archbishop of York [William Temple, who was not yet at Canterbury] is travelling down from Bishopsthorpe especially for it. I feel a childish gratification in having been responsible for it all and no one guessing it, not even the Dean who always imagines that my ideas are his! (just as I imagine that his ideas on other matters are mine!).

In an article in *The Church Times,* Colin ('Our Special Correspondent') describes what took place in this attempt to 'manifest Christ to the Gentiles', which is 'the Church's duty, as well as its privilege'. The proceedings began with a recital of music from the fourteenth to the eighteenth century, including Christmas and Epiphany carols, performed by Rudolph and Millicent Dolmetch and other musicians gathered by them for the occasion. This was followed by a voluntary collection, while the organist played music by Bach, and Dubois's 'March of the Magi Kings'. As soon as this had ended, the procession of the Three Kings could be heard at the east end of the building, accompanied by recorders, with cross and torch bearers, the Dean and Chapter 'magnificently vested', and then Scouts and Guides and a large number of school children all carrying candles and singing the refrain of 'We Three Kings of Orient'.

By this time a tableau representing the Nativity had grouped itself before the High Altar, at which the procession arrived and the 'gold-bearing' King set down the offerings of the people. After a short offering of prayer, the Ceremony ended with the Bishop's Blessing. The Children's Epiphany Procession certainly took place the following year (1932); on that occasion Colin also reported to Ida on 6 January 'yesterday the Bishop had the children's party for the Clergy's children – masses of them came and we were all fatuously happy'. The procession may have continued up to the war.

The spiritual and evangelistic power of Art and beauty to draw men to God was one thing both Bishop and Dean strongly believed in, and it is likely that one reason Bell had for asking Colin to be his Chaplain (as also for his recommendation to Archbishop Lang that D-J should be Dean of Chichester) was his reputation as a knowledgable lover of the arts. He also had lay friends or connections who could help the Bishop put this belief into practice in his own Diocese. Bell had in fact already got to know Gustav Holst at Canterbury, when he persuaded the Chapter to commission John Masefield to write a play for performance in the Cathedral, with music specially composed for it by Holst. When *The Coming of Christ* was (very successfully) performed, Holst also brought a choir with him to take the part of The Heavenly Host, who sang from the organ loft. The Bishop now asked Holst and his singers (who had become generally known as 'The Heavenly Host') to come and sing in his garden and in the Cathedral on Whit Monday in 1930.

'With some diffidence', Jasper writes (p. 83), 'Holst accepted, for he felt that his amateurs, enthusiastic and versatile though they might be, could do nothing that the cathedral choir could not do better. Their visit, however, was an unqualified success, and the singers also danced with the West Sussex Folk Dancers.' The *Church Times* described this festival of music in detail, pointing out that the singers and players numbered 240, including a large contingent from Bishop Otter College, and emphasising 'the perfect meeting together of fine music and liturgy'. The *Sussex Daily News* was also enthusiastic, and their reporter added, a propos of the dancing, 'among the skilled exponents of folk dancing was the Bishop of Chichester's Domestic Chaplain and Secretary, the Rev David Colin Dunlop'.

Holst's initial reluctance might well have been overcome by Colin's connection with Mary O'Malley, who sang in the 'Heavenly Host' when a senior girl at St Paul's School. The Festival itself became an annual event, and was resumed after the war. There were similar Whitsuntide festivities at Bosham, not far from Chichester, in 1931.

Bell's decision to appoint a diocesan Director of Religious Drama might well have been predicted from his promotion of religious drama in Canterbury Cathedral when he was its Dean. But his choice of E. Martin Browne, Colin's fellow theology student and friend at Oxford, who was in 1930 working in the USA, was no doubt encouraged by Colin. This was the first such post in the Church of England, and much frowned upon by its still considerable puritan cohort. Browne, interviewed during his summer break in England, was at once captivated by this 'incredibly young', and withal 'youthful', bishop, with his 'boyish glee' and soft handshake – under which could nevertheless be felt 'the pressure which denoted his secret strength and his tremendous warmth of heart'. But above all he was won by Bell's vision of drama as 'once more the valued servant of the church', and his belief that 'the standards set for (it) ... should be worthy of the subjects it was to portray'. Browne accepted the three-year post, 'and so began a happy, fruitful and lasting friendship'. (His account of their first meeting, from which I have quoted, is in Jasper, pp. 121–2.)

Another aspect of Bell's episcopate that Colin must have been very happy about, especially in view of his experience of Bishop Winnington-Ingram, was his firm attitude to the exceptionally large 'romanising' Anglo-Catholic element among the clergy of the diocese. Bell was by no means hostile to Anglo-Catholics as such; indeed, the first three appointments he recommended or made in his diocese, The Ven. H.M. Hordern to be Bishop of Lewes, D-J to be Dean and Colin to be chaplain, were all High Churchmen. But he had made it clear in his enthronement sermon that, in the Church of England, 'there is large room for variations of ceremony ... and diversities in the manner of public worship ... provided services [are] conducted with reverence and dignity'.

On the other hand, 'he did have a deep concern for order', and for authority, and, though he had not been a 'leading protagonist for the 1928 Prayer Book', he was 'loyal to the arrangements which were made for permitted deviations from the 1662 Order' (Jasper, p. 165). The problems he encountered in the diocese were indeed great. About one-eighth of its parishes practised permanent Reservation, whilst corporate Devotions, or services of Benediction, 'had been in use in several churches for a very long time, in some cases for over thirty years' (Jasper, p. 166). Soon after Colin left for Baghdad, Bell wrote to him mentioning that he had 'a permanent row with Cochrane [of Winchelsea] over permanent Reservation, and had 'just discovered that Roe of Buxted ... (says) the Latin mass in English always'. In dealing with all this Bell had to balance 'the pastoral difficulty in the sudden prohibition of something which had been winked at for years' (Jasper, p. 166) and the exercise of regulated episcopal authority.

After many meetings with Anglo-Catholic clergy in the diocese and consultations with liturgical experts Bell issued his regulations in 1931; the leading Catholic priests promised to obey them, and the Evangelicals supported him. But the pastoral problem had led Bell to allow the continuation of Benediction (though on no account its introduction) *in certain cases permitted by him* 'pending final canonical settlement of the revision of the Book of Common Prayer'. Since this event was pushed further and further into the future, the 'provisional' permission in certain parishes looked more and like a permanent one, and the situation in the diocese was never fully resolved under Bell's incumbency. It may well have been that Colin, who also knew Oliver Quick, one of the 'liturgical experts' Bell consulted, who felt that Bell's provisional toleration of Benediction applied approval of something with 'an uncertain theological foundation', could not wholeheartedly agree with Bell's provisional solution of the problem in the diocese, and that this is why his admiration for his Bishop began to lose some of its fervour, as Mary wrote to Ida on 16 August 1938.

Another sphere in which Colin's talents and interests were of special assistance to Bell was that of the *Chichester Diocesan Gazette*, of which the Bishop himself became editor in March 1930. When, four years later, the *Sussex Daily News* announced Colin's appointment to St Thomas's, Hove, it recalled that his 'literary ability (had) enabled the *Chichester Diocesan Gazette* to be produced in the popular style now so familiar to Sussex Churchpeople'.

The author is perhaps referring here to such things as the series of articles: *Lay Views of Ecclesiastical Persons*. They include 'If I were a Bishop', by Colin's old Oxford history tutor Ernest Barker, 'If I were a Verger', by Vice-Dean Dwelly of Liverpool, 'If I were a Dean', by Albert Mansbridge, a leading figure in the Workers' Educational Movement, and another with the same title by T.S. Eliot.

In 1932 the 'Bishop's Easter Competition' announced a prize for the best essay on 'Church Attendance in Country Parishes' for which 414 entries were received. Colin's own articles in 1929 (November) include a review of a book of apologetics, *Doubts and Difficulties*, by a future Dean of Durham, Cyril Alington, then Headmaster of Eton. Colin lays much emphasis on the fact that the holder of such an exalted position was addressing himself to the 'ordinary man', though adds that, under Bishop Winnington-Ingram's influence, the episcopate was becoming more aware of this need. He feels, however, that the humorous approach of the introductory part of the book is 'strained', and the jokes 'meagre and conventional'.

People may 'distrust solemnity', but perhaps many more are suspicious of 'heartiness'. But he warmly commends the later part, which he is sure could be used with profit by preachers or study groups. Among highlights he commends the 'peculiar freshness' with which the author presents 'the mystery of goodness', while not shirking the problem of evil. Under Bell's editorship in 1930 Colin reviewed *The Ways of Yesterday*, about Lewis Way, of Stansted Park, an extraordinary but holy man who was left a completely unexpected fortune, with which he championed the Christian cause all over Europe and combatted anti-Semitism. It was he who bought the Hotel Marboeuf in Paris, whose picture gallery he made into the first English church in the city (see also Chaplaincies I above). He also favourably reviewed *The Confirmation School*, by A.R. Browne-Wilkinson. Later he informs readers about some of the findings published in the August 1931 'Book of the Month': the obviously rather pedestrian preliminary report of the 1931 census.

Colin's Cuttings Book contains the texts of various other literary or journalistic pieces published by him during the period. But first I must say something about a very interesting sermon, whose text was published in *The Guardian*, which he preached in August 1929 at St Paul's, Knightsbridge, where D-J was the incumbent after leaving St Mary's, Primrose Hill and before going to Chichester Cathedral. It is entitled 'Creation through Travail', and starts from the text 'A woman when she is in travail hath sorrow because her hour is come, but as soon as she is delivered of the child, she remembereth no more the anguish for joy that a man is born into the world'.

He considers first the labour, discipline and suffering which precedes the completion of a work of art, and goes on to the 'hard work, long hours or strain on their constitution' which social and political reformers undergo before the new thing they are striving for is brought into the world. But, Colin goes on, the travail which leads to creation means more than this. 'The travail of soul through which the creator must pass, the opposition with which he must struggle – is a spiritual thing, it is an inward invisible principle of opposition, it is a spiritual obstruction, an inner inhibition of the creative faculty', like the 'spiritual wickedness in high places' with which St Paul tells us we must struggle.

Colin goes on to show how the call to exercise responsibility, as in parenthood and education is really a call to create a new being, as is any choice of good over evil, through which the chooser gradually creates the 'self' God intends him to be, and thus accepts his share in God's creative work in the world. This leads Colin to the question of why creation should involve travail or suffering, and ends with the challenge to identify ourselves with Christ's suffering and eventual glory. This is a long and dense sermon, which could only be preached to an educated congregation, but it is full of material both profound and heartening.

Several published articles deal in one way or another with liturgy, as we might expect. The first, in the July 1930 number of *The Guardian*, records his comments as a 'Correspondent' on the Lambeth Conference Service in St Paul's Cathedral, which he attended as chaplain to Bishop Bell – the Episcopal Secretary to the conference. He begins: 'It was impossible not to be impressed by two things, namely the excellent singing of the lovely setting of the Litany by Tallis, and the immense grace and dignity which the occupant of the Chair of St Augustine conveyed to the procession by his quiet, recollected bearing as he led his brother bishops to the altar.' (Colin many years later recalled the Archbishop's – Randall Davidson's – 'true courtesy' in a sermon on this virtue; he had been received by him at Lambeth when a mere curate of eighteen months' standing, and was made to feel he really counted for something in the Primate's eyes.)

Unfortunately, he goes on in the article, the music of the liturgy itself left much to be desired. It had neither the light, gay, extravagant and theatrical style of the rococo (as in Mozart, Schubert, Rossini, even Gounod) which has something in common with the architecture of St Paul's itself, nor the serious, intense religious power and vision of the great dramatic composers of the classic Anglican school (e.g. Taverner, Byrd, Vaughan-Williams, Charles Wood). These are the only two practical alternatives, he says, once a congregational setting of the service is rejected. But 'Macpherson in E flat' belongs in neither camp, and was 'meagre' fare to provide for such an occasion in such a place. 'What can one say for the liturgical sense of a composer who will employ trumpets in the musical setting of the responses to the Ten Commandments?'

Again in *The Guardian*, in November and December 1930, there is a four-part exchange on a reform of Eucharistic ceremonial (the manual acts and bodily movements which outwardly express the words of the liturgy) between Colin and Horace Spence, of York Minster. Spence suggests a new pattern of liturgical movements for the Communion service based on 'common sense' rather than the 'use' of any particular church party. Colin replies with praise for the aim, but claiming that some of the ceremonies mentioned by Spence are not consonant with it. Spence counters with the cavil that Colin's points are those of an over-meticulous expert, while Colin in reply points out that Spence appears to advocate certain things simply because they are used by clergy of a particular church party, the Anglo-Catholics. He ends his second reply thus:

> It may be thought that these observations are at bottom based on a prejudice against an elaborate ceremonial. Far from it. There is a legitimate place in the Church of England for services of a most ornate type, and the personal preference of the writer inclines to that type, circumstances being favourable. But no ceremony should be retained for which a good reason does not exist, and it is not a good reason to say of a particular ceremony that it is the custom in most Anglo-Catholic churches or that it has come to stay. Something much more reasonable is necessary, and this something Mr Spence has himself supplied in his article.

In another article on ceremonial, 'Easter in Liverpool Cathedral' (*The Guardian*, 10 April, 1931), Colin shows himself more than just a watch-dog for the Dearmer-Alcuin-Club-Primrose Hill style of worship. Here he tries to show the wonderful results that can be achieved by it. The building of Liverpool Cathedral was begun in 1904, but, by 1931, there was ample space for ceremonial on a grand scale. D.W. Dwelly had just become Dean, having previously been a Residential Canon. His liturgical flair had been known to a few both in the diocese and out of it, and, when still a parish priest in Southport, he was asked to put together a service for the Consecration of the Cathedral in 1924 which made him widely known. Soon afterwards he moved to the cathedral as a Residentiary Canon, became Vice-Dean and then, in 1931, Dean. He had long been a friend of Dearmer, and of George Bell, also of Martin Shaw and others whom Colin knew, and a member of the Alcuin Club. It is, therefore, likely that Colin had been at least acquainted with him for some time before his visit to Liverpool over Easter in 1931, when he enjoyed his hospitality and preached in the cathedral – the first of eight or nine such visits over the next 25 years.

However, Dwelly was still regarded in some church quarters as 'an erratic genius' and something of a 'maverick', partly because of a wilful and slightly autocratic streak in his character – despite his personal attractiveness and great gift for friendship – and partly because of his liturgical innovations, which some people found hard to take. Colin had a great admiration for him, though was quite capable of making specific criticisms of the liturgy and ceremonial at Liverpool, as he did in a letter after his visit at Whitsun 1932, and also of suggesting things that might make things even better.

The purpose of his article is not just to add to the general approval of Dwelly and his work, but to draw attention to its great significance for Cathedral worship, which he thought was still not adequately appreciated, and to convey his own strong impression, recalled from his Easter visit, that the 'principles governing the rites and ceremonies' at Liverpool have now all but become established as the Liverpool 'tradition'. Not only that, Colin insists; his novelties never come over as 'stunts', however striking; 'they are a legitimate development; continuity with the main stream of Catholic liturgy is immediately perceived; they are rooted in Holy Scripture and the old service books'. The same is true of the ceremonial:

> though here again its details were unfamiliar. The obvious practical intent of all the comings and goings within the choir and presbytery, and the absence of ceremony for the sake of ceremony, could not be missed. That the most practical ceremonial is also the most beautiful was strikingly proved by these two great festival services on Easter Day.

Colin goes on here to suggest that, though it is true that some ceremonial is distracting, this depends greatly on its aim and spirit. Some ceremonial, 'even though unfamiliar, can have a quite opposite effect and positively deepen one's sense of recollection and make the heart ready for prayer'. So, when the choir sang 'let not him who seeks cease until he finds, finding he shall wonder, wondering he shall enter the kingdom and having entered the kingdom he shall rest' to accompany the bishop's entry and kneeling before the High Altar, those of us who were present were 'enabled by all that was going on to go through that very experience'.

This 'repose of spirit' was greatly assisted by the harmonious colours of the ministers' vestments. Again, all this was reinforced by the superb conducting and singing of great music by the first-class director of music and choir. The article ends with a final 'picture which will long remain vivid in the mind.' .... 'The service is over and the whole concourse within the sanctuary moves forth down the choir, led by the bishop who, crozier in hand, strides out at their head. Never was the true function of the episcopate more dramatically set forth.'

We may compare the last part of 'Easter in Liverpool Cathedral' with what Colin published in the *Church Times* of 5 June 1931, under the heading of 'Ordination at Chichester: an impression'. After describing the arrival of the Bishop of Chichester at the west door of the Cathedral, and the sermon preached by the Rev. Percy Maryon-Wilson ('It would not be easy to preach a more appropriate sermon for an ordination'), he turns to the text of the service, in which 'the Book of Common Prayer rises to its sublimest heights of noble rhetoric and true Catholic piety'. ....

> How admirably these blended elements of sobriety and exultation, of warning and calm assurance, found their counterpart in the grave, collected demeanour of the Bishop, in the ceremonial throughout the service, so splendid and yet so reticent, and in the austere music of Henry Ley, whose Mass in E minor draws one up into the pure air of spiritual reality!

Colin also wrote a 'tract' for the Alcuin Club, *Processions*, which was published at the beginning of 1932. After reiterating what he had frequently said in various publications, that the worship of the Church of England needed revitalisation, he stated the aim of his new publication as follows:

> to discover briefly the motives which lie behind the Procession as an act of worship, to note what historically have been its main features; and then to try, with the help of the principles thus collected, to reconstruct the Procession as a liturgical means of leading modern congregations into a more ready understanding of the Christian faith, and of expressing less remotely some of their religious aspirations.

Colin reminds the reader that a procession as part of worship cannot be a mere 'circumambulation' of the church or anywhere else. It must involve 'going somewhere *to do something*'. It must involve a 'station', that is, a halt during which there are prayers, readings, homilies, whose general intention, it emerges from the book, is to underline the religious importance of the place halted at (e.g. the font, or children's corner), or the time or season when the procession is made. Anyone who has attended a clerical induction will remember the impression made on the congregation when the archdeacon actually takes the new incumbent to the font, the lectern and the altar. The book is a highly practical manual, whose last section outlines possible processions throughout the Christian year, suggesting readings, versicles and responses, hymns and ceremonial acts.

The little book shows something of what he had learnt from his visit to Liverpool. It was well reviewed in the April *Diocesan Gazette* by Martin Browne, and next year in the *Calcutta Diocesan Record* by 'W.H.G.H.', and no doubt elsewhere too, and became a popular manual in many parishes. In his little book, *The Alcuin Club and its Publications 1897–1987*, Peter Jagger wrote: 'Historic practice and sound liturgical principles, tinged with common sense, lay behind the suggestions made as to the use and development of processions today.'

I have already quoted from the correspondence between Colin and Ida above. Once he had left London, and Mary was preparing to go up to Oxford, Ida asked him to write to her regularly, and a good number of letters survive from his time with George Bell, from which one can get a good idea of some of the things that chiefly concerned him at this time. Foremost among these was, of course, his relationship to Mary, as I have already shown. Here are some other matters of interest.

As I have already pointed out, Ida didn't think church-going very important in itself, and it seems also that she sometimes went to worship at Roman Catholic churches and probably Westminster Cathedral. In his letter of 3 March 1930, it is apparent that Colin and Ida often had arguments when they met. Ida had expressed her concern at this in the letter to which Colin replies. Colin tells her not to take his argumentativeness so seriously. He uses argument to test his ideas, but admits he enjoys it – and will try to meet her wishes in the matter.

It seems they had been arguing about the Roman Catholic Church, which Colin had opposed with great bitterness. The letter gives his main reason: the dangers of 'submission to an external, defined and precisely articulated authority', resulting in the refusal to encourage personal responsibility over faith and morals, and a truly corporate life (though he admits that he sometimes defends it against Protestants!). Colin's *Guardian* article of 13 June 1930, points to a symptom of the non-corporate nature of RC worship at the time. It is entitled 'Eclipse of the Mass: A Sunday in Cologne', and recounts his attendance at three different services: a first Communion in a parish church, then both the High Mass and the *Volksmesse* (People's Mass) in the Cathedral. In all three of these there was an almost complete absence of any attempt to get the congregation to participate in the Mass itself. 'We might as well have been present at a Quaker meeting, or a university sermon or a hymn service.'

Four letters give us some idea of his social-political attitudes at this time. In his letter of 3 September 1931, he is responding to a worry of Ida's that he and Mary would find it hard to make ends meet if they married each other. She feels that, economically as well as politically, hard times are coming. Colin accepts this, but observes that this can be good for religion and faith; the standard for clergy salaries can't be 'gentlemanly middle-class comfort', which must surely make it hard to help the poor spiritually.

On 22 March 1932, he is again responding to Ida on the question of whether he and Mary could afford to marry. He cheerfully admits that they would never be rich, and would have to lower their standards; 'class distinctions are undoubtedly going to disappear. ... privilege (which we've both enjoyed) is bound to go; ... Christians should welcome, not resist this.' And then again he observes that Radley taught him to be a good member of the middle class; so he definitely would not want his children to go to public schools, and adds that government day schools are as good as public schools, appealing to the successful transfer of D-J's two daughters from Frances Holland School in London to the Girls' High School in Chichester.

On 11 November 1931, he first tells Ida about how painful he found it preaching an armistice sermon in a village church. The war, he goes on, 'has brought us nothing but new problems', but 'the *great* thing was the emergence of the Conscientious Objector, and what we learnt from him. I wish I had had the courage, but I thought them wicked at the time!' However, for all her radicalism in some respects, Ida would have none of this. In her reply of 1 December, she argues that 'as we were then we *had* to fight'; nor is the Peace Movement born of conscientious objection, but *of the spirit of self-sacrifice*. This is what we need to foster, she affirms, and what we had in the women's movement. But both Ida and Colin were keen supporters of the League of Nations.

In a letter of 7 February 1932 Colin writes about how 'thrilling' he found 'the Disarmament meeting' (probably in the Albert Hall). 'I eventually got to a seat right up at the top of the organ. Hardly anyone in our block seemed over

30! I heard splendidly but it became so hot that I went out early. The chief purpose of *witness* had been done.'

As the previous chapter has made it clear, Colin had become increasingly confident during his years at Chichester that he and Mary would eventually marry, but that this could not be until she had earned her MA at Oxford in 1935. He and Bishop Bell, it appeared, had also agreed that he would stay at Chichester for three years, leaving in the summer of 1932. There would, therefore, be three years during which Colin needed to be doing something that would keep him fully occupied in a place where he and Mary could not easily distract each other.

I have already mentioned that Colin had been greatly impressed by a sermon preached at St Mary's, Primrose Hill, by Bishop Danson, a bishop in the Far East, stressing the importance of clergy spending some time in the Missionary Field. By the time he came to Chichester he had in fact already had two invitations to work as chaplains to colonial bishops – while he was at Primrose Hill. They were both from clergy he had got to know well at All Saints Margaret Street.

In a letter of 27 April 1924, the former Vicar of All Saints, Roscoe Shedden, who had since become Bishop of Nassau in the Bahamas, reminds Colin about their conversation in the previous year, when he was briefly in England, in which Colin told him that he was thinking of 'doing a turn in the Mission Field', and 'suggested the possibility of coming to Nassau' (Bahamas) after he had served his title at St Mary's. The Bishop had told him that he would 'love to have (him)' as his chaplain there, but that he thought he ought to stay at Primrose Hill a little longer. Then Bishop Shedden's former curate, Mark Carpenter-Garnier, who was curate at All Saints from 1908 to 1921, then Librarian of Pusey House for three years, was appointed Bishop of Colombo, Sri Lanka (then Ceylon). Here is the beginning of his letter:

> My dear Colin, you may have heard that my friends at All Saints are raising some money to enable me to take out a chaplain, who would help me through the difficult first three years of my time. I want to find someone who wants to be a student, and who would help me on the intellectual side (for you can have no idea what a dunce I am!), who would help me socially; and who would really be more of a Keeper than a Chaplain! For some time my thoughts have been turned towards you in this connection, for there is no one I would rather take; but I dared not write to you about it, as I thought you were more or less pledged to Nassau. However I have seen the Bishop, and he says he would not wish to stand in your way or mine if you thought it right to come to Ceylon. So now I feel free to ask you. Will you come?

Carpenter-Garnier went on to list the good things Colin would receive if he accepted, including regular retreats to the (cooler) hills (Ceylon's average temperature was 82° F) and much travel about the island, and returned more than once to the pleasure it would give him if he accepted. The Bishop of Nassau, in the letter from which I quoted above, very much encouraged Colin to accept this new offer; he would not only be 'of very great value to Mark', but he would get a much wider experience of the Mission Field, 'and there is a very important pioneer work to be done there'. 'Of course Duncan-Jones won't like your going, but I very much hope you won't refuse in a hurry. Mark has talked it over with Mackay, and the latter thinks you are just the man.' In the event Colin did decide to accept the offer to go to Colombo, but was not passed medically fit for Ceylon, so had to refuse it.

All that was nearly seven years earlier. He now had to find something to do after leaving George Bell. Colin's letter to Ida of 10 December 1931 mentions his particular desire to see her over his Christmas break in London as he has 'something to talk to you about'. This was clearly work in the Mission Field, and in his letter of 6 January 1932, he writes: 'I feel more and more happy about Africa (or possibly India) and less and less uncertain about my vocation to go there', though (after reverting to the effect of the Danson sermon) he adds 'I have dreaded and shrunk from it, hoping the call would not come.' But it had, and he now felt that, in contrast to his call to ordination as such, to which he had had an inclination in any case, 'this ... seems to be an overcoming of a natural *dis*inclination and a turning of it into a desire'. He had talked to a man called Leonard Browne, whom Ida seems to have known, and who was lecturing in Lahore, and he had approved Colin's offering himself. In a letter of two days later he reassures Ida, who seems to have been thinking that, if they married, Mary might have to go out too, that he does not expect to be abroad for more than three years.

During January his thoughts seem to have turned more persistently to Asia, as a letter of 2 February reports on an interview with the SPG, in which two possible positions were 'put before him', the need for a young man at the Cathedral in Singapore, and a vacant position in Delhi. But he must wait until March to be 'overhauled medically'. Having fully launched himself on a path that would be utterly different from what he had experienced before, he confessed to Ida on 3 March: 'The more God really seems to come into my life, the less easy I find it to preach. I have felt my addresses to the students at Bishop Otter College unusually vapid and empty lately.' Colin often found it difficult to confine his unusually developed imagination to the task already in hand.

It so happened that Archbishop Lang was at that time having trouble about finding a new Civil Chaplain in Baghdad, where they needed a mature priest, 'not too young and inexperienced, if possible between 32 and 40, healthy, able to get on with people in Government circles, intelligent and interested in the position of English Christianity vis à vis the Assyrians, etc.' The post was for two years in the first instance, with a maximum of three. On 3 February the Archbishop was able to tell Hylton I.B. Smith, the current Chaplain at Baghdad, that Colin's name had been mentioned, that he had followed this up and found him very suitable.

'He is a very attractive and of course a thoroughly intelligent person. He is looking in other directions as well and does not want at this stage to commit himself in any way.' When Colin wrote to Ida on 7 February, after his presence had been requested at Lambeth, where the Archbishop's Chaplain had tried to persuade him to go, he said: 'I don't see any point in going there – merely Sussex in an oven!' But it is probable that when the current Chaplain wrote to Colin personally to tell him what the post involved, and included the information that: 'The chaplain ... inherits the oversight of an interesting Arab-Evangelical group on whose future may depend the future of Christianity in Iraq', he rather regretted his comment, especially when he recalled George Bell's article in the Diocesan Magazine the previous October, where the Bishop had explained the very vulnerable position of the Assyrian Christians in Iraq, and the anxiety its fate was causing to those who cared about them.

But Colin was still awaiting his medical for India and Singapore, and, when the Archbishop's secretary wrote again, although he could now say he found the idea attractive, what he really wanted, he said, was 'closer contact with a non-Christian race', which he doubted the Baghdad chaplaincy would provide. The Archbishop was clearly disappointed, and, when Colin wrote to Ida on 3 March, telling her of this refusal, he told her he was more and more convinced that India was right for him, though by the 13th, when he wrote again, he admitted he was feeling 'a twinge of regret'. Then came the medical on the 16th, and there is silence for a few weeks. But on 19 May he told her that 'Delhi does not want a man of my experience and seniority for a short term', so he had applied for a post at Calcutta Theological College, where he was the only candidate. He wouldn't know for another month whether he had been accepted.

In the same letter he told Ida that he had preached again at Liverpool Cathedral, where both the Bishop and a young businessman expressed gratitude for his sermon, whose topic he had discussed with Ida beforehand, and now the Dean was asking him to consider becoming his 'right hand man' there! He loved the liturgy at Liverpool and had a 'golden weekend ... the kindness of the Dean and his staff was overwhelming. The beauty of the services there is a rare and wonderful thing.' 'D-J. thinks I ought seriously to consider it.' Yet he felt he couldn't turn Calcutta down if they wanted him. But when the results of Colin's medical for the Far East came through he found he could not be accepted for India (there was no further mention of Singapore), so on 23 July he wrote to A.S. Sargent, the Archbishop's Secretary, asking whether, if the Baghdad post was still vacant, he could have first refusal. It was almost too late, as they now thought at Lambeth that they had found their man (Eton and Trinity Cambridge, and hunted on his day off!), albeit he was their highly praised 'second string'. But the hunting man had then been found found to have TB, and so, in the end, Lambeth were glad to be able to offer the chaplaincy to Colin.

On 10 August Sargent wrote to the Secretary of the Bishop in Jerusalem telling him about Colin's definite acceptance. He has 'considerable ability and distinction', he added, as well as 'experience of the central workings of the church', and could 'report on the complex of problems of Iraq'. On the same day he wrote to Mr Dillon, secretary of St George's Church Council in Baghdad, telling him that Colin had been passed fit and assuring him that he would deal 'faithfully and wisely' with the wide mixture of churchmanship represented by the English community. One surprising fact about Colin's medical is that traces were found in his lungs which revealed that he had at one time contracted TB himself (very likely during his war service), but had been completely cured.

By this time Colin's work with George Bell had come to an end. The *Sussex Daily News* carried a short paragraph headed 'Loss to Chichester Diocese', and went on as follows:

> The announcement in this column yesterday that the Rev. Colin Dunlop is going to Baghdad as Civil Chaplain will cause a good deal of regret in Sussex. This may be rather selfish; one cannot say, but it is certain that Mr. Dunlop will be very much missed. Many churchpeople and others have come in personal contact with him as resident chaplain to the Bishop of Chichester, and it would not seem to be possible to meet Mr. Dunlop without feeling indebted to him and liking him personally. He was distinguished for patient courtesy, sympathy with all who have asked his help or advice, and for ability not common in one so young.

Another paper (probably *The Guardian* or *The Church Times*) included the sentence: 'Mr Dunlop is an extremely able young man, who, among other things, has done valuable service for the Alcuin Club.' A Swedish paper, doubtless at least in part because of Colin's service with George Bell, announced:

> The distinguished young English pastor Revd. D.C. Dunlop, who served as English minister in Stockholm for the first 6 months of 1929, but was called home to be secretary to the Bishop of Chichester (Dr Bell) is now visiting Stockholm and coming to perform the services in the English church here on Sundays the 21st and 28th of this month.

While he was in Baghdad Mary wrote and told him of a meeting she had had with Bishop Bell at Oxford. In his reply, Colin wrote:

> How delightful your encounter with Bones [their private nick-name for him] sounds, and how nice of him to talk as he did. ... I quite agree about Bones's good point being that he is always real and never exaggerates or flatters. That is why even his crumbs of praise are so valuable. I am sure he will always be a good friend to us.

10

CHAPLAINCIES III

Baghdad

S INCE THE WRITTEN SOURCES for this short but important phase of Colin's life are exceptionally rich – especially the letters to Mary and Ida – this chapter may well seem at first to devote too much time to what is only a space of two years. But, apart from his work as chaplain in a 'professional' (cure of souls) sense, there is also the very important series of events involving the Assyrian Christians. Colin's practical concern about these events, together with his work at St George's, the Anglican church in Baghdad, the capital city of Iraq, tells us a lot about him, and should justify the much greater length of this chapter than that of any other dealing with so short a time. Because of the political situation in Iraq at this time, I shall have to say quite a lot by way of historical background.

The historian in Colin could not help but be awed by the scene of his new labours in Mesopotamia, an area which used often to be called 'The Cradle of Mankind'. Here is a passage from his article in *Church Assembly News*, for March 1934:

> The modern post-war state of Iraq is modern only in the political sense of the word. ... Civilisation after civilisation has arisen, flourished and perished in Iraq. Dynasty after dynasty has grown great and become the wonder of the world, only to be submerged by some later uprising which in turn has drawn the world's attention to itself. Cassite, Babylonian, Assyrian, Median, Greek, Roman, Parthian, Sassanid, Arab, Mongol and Turk have all held sway and flourished in Mesopotamia, and have all, to a greater or less extent, left traces of their day of power.

Shortly after the beginning of the Great War, the vast and unwieldy empire of the Ottoman Turks, which had been disintegrating for well over a hundred years and struggling under its ruler, the Sultan, to modernise, allied itself to Germany, and thus became an enemy of Britain, France, Italy and Russia, who were joined by the USA in 1917. Meanwhile, allied armies lost very large numbers of men in their attempts to drive the Turks back out of Persia (where the oil fields were of great importance to us) into Asia Minor.

145

Like Syria, Jordan, Palestine (later Israel), and Lebanon, which were all, like Iraq, new states carved out of the defeated Ottoman Empire, the League of Nations (set up after the war, and predecessor of the United Nations) had undertaken to ensure that peace and order were so maintained in these territories as to fit them to become independent member-nations of the League in due course. This task was 'mandated' to Great Britain and France, and the initial steps towards building the future nation of Iraq was entrusted to Britain. From all this difficult work resulting from the war, the United States had rapidly withdrawn when the fighting came to an end, leaving behind it the influential 'Fourteen Points' of President Wilson, mostly on the self-determination of the hitherto subject peoples of the Habsburg and Ottoman empires.

Russia, totally involved with its own Revolution, was not in a position to cooperate any more with the Western powers, and Italy had no close links with this part of the world. France and Great Britain were therefore left alone to nurse to maturity five new-born states, on territories where the great majority of people had for centuries been Muslim (though with significant Christian populations) and which had never existed as independent territorially defined political units before. The task would have been hard enough at any time, but after the national traumas of the war, with its hitherto unimaginable expense of material resources and human lives, it was difficult for politicians to give it a very high place on their agenda. It took the League of Nations five years even to give serious thought to the matter of defining the frontiers of Iraq.

The Assyrian Christians are described by the *Oxford Dictionary of the Christian Church* (1957) as 'A small group of Nestorians who have survived to modern times in the confines of Asia Minor and Persia. ... They derive from the Nestorian Church which came into being after the Council of Ephesus (in 431 A.D.).' That Council was called to resolve the question whether Nestorius's teaching was heretical or not, and decided against him. Today it is generally held that the difference between him and those bishops whose teaching was eventually summarised in the Nicene Creed (still a standard of orthodoxy) was more a verbal matter than a genuine difference of belief. In any case, the condemnation of Nestorius and the fact that the Assyrian Church, or 'Church of the East', has never been a state church was largely responsible for its isolation from the West and its tenacious conservatism, even though, during periods of relative political stability and religious tolerance in Asia, it engaged successfully in astonishingly extensive evangelism and survived, despite having, from the seventh century onwards, always to contend with an Islam either actively persecuting, or at least making life very difficult for it.

After over three hundred years as third or fourth class citizens of their Turkish rulers, it had become reduced to two small groups within the borders of what are now Turkey and Iran. In 1886 the Anglican Archbishop Benson had founded the Archbishop of Canterbury's Mission to the Assyrian Christians, 'for purely educational and religious purposes, and especially "the education of those youths who will hereafter become bishops, priests and leaders of the people'" (Bell's *Randall Davidson*, p. 1179).

Not long before the Great War broke out and engulfed this part of the world, the Assyrians had received overtures from Russia, which promised them material, as well as spiritual and educational aid, and so the British church connection became fainter, and had in any case to be brought to an end once the war had started. But the Assyrian contacts with Russia, which led to their fighting as a unit in the Russian army in Persia, made them even more the object of Turkish hostility, and by the end of 1915 they were in great distress, and, as the Russian army lost ground to the Turks, began to fasten their hopes for a better future on Great Britain again.

When the Russians collapsed altogether as a result of the Revolution of 1917, their position became even more precarious, and, by the end of the war, most of the survivors found themselves (thanks to our own forces) collected together in a huge, but not very salubrious, refugee camp in northern Mesopotamia where 'money and care were lavished on them' by the British ('The Assyrians in the Mosul Vilayet', Col. R.S. Stafford, *Journal of the Central Asian Society*, April 1934). Both during the last year of the war and in the fifteen years or so before Colin reached Baghdad, the British had made considerable use of the Assyrians both to fight the Turks, and, later, to put down Arab and Kurdish uprisings against the government of the new state of Iraq. Their Patriarch, the Mar Shimun (Lord Simon), was still waiting for the British to ensure them a secure future as an independent people, and constantly reminding them of the as yet unfulfilled promise the Assyrians believed had been made to them to this effect near the end of the war.

When Colin reached Baghdad on 19 October 1932 in a vast trans-desert bus from Damascus (a largely tedious journey of 534 miles), he was invited to stay with General Rowan-Robinson, Inspector of the Iraq army, until he could find a place of his own. The British had only just surrendered their mandate to govern Iraq, several years before the deadline set for this by the League of Nations, because the Government, encouraged by the Ambassador, now felt that it was capable of governing itself. So, although it was now an independent nation, there were still many British 'advisers' to assist the administrative officials of the new constitutional monarchy.

The General had invited some of the leading supporters of the English church to an outdoor tea-party to meet their new Chaplain. Colin recorded that It was 'hot, but not unpleasant'. Later they had drinks on the terrace overlooking the Tigris, and he enjoyed the 'wonderful but short twilight'. Next morning he had a look at the church building and expressed himself delighted with its 'chaste, cool simplicity'. It had been an old Turkish guard house of the south gate of the city. There was 'nothing to offend, much to please. The verger, an Assyrian, reverently kissed my hand as did also his wife and grandson.' He attended choir practice for a few minutes and called on various other Army officers. That evening, he records, there were 'several delightful

Air Force officers to dinner'. This early contact with the RAF was the first of many throughout Colin's later ministry.

The Baghdad chaplaincy had been set up when the mandate had been awarded to Britain and British civilians had begn to arrive in the ancient seat of the Caliph and other places in the new country. It was the descendant of the regular Chaplaincy run by Army and Air Force 'padres' soon after Baghdad was occupied during the war. Though it now had no official military connections, many members of the armed forces attended services and took a very active part in church life. It was entirely financed by the congregation, who had their own Church Council and held an AGM just like an English Parish Church (Colin wrote to Mary of his satisfaction at getting an Indian elected to it at their 1933 meeting).

During the years after the mandate had been surrendered, when the contracts of the British advisers were gradually fulfilled (a slow process which the more anti-Colonialist elements of the Iraq Press saw largely in terms of a recovery of freedom from their new oppressors), the English presence in Iraq continually shrank. At the same time the Archbishop of Canterbury, who was the spiritual head (the 'ordinary') of the chaplaincy, delegated this responsibility to the Anglican Bishop in Jerusalem. Apart from members of the Army and Royal Air Force, and the various advisers in the departments of public life, there was a very large community of British railwaymen to run the Iraq Railways, and workers and administrators of the oil wells, a continuing interest in which had, not unnaturally, been a strong incentive to the British to accept the Mandate.

Most of this last group was based in the oilfields some way north and east of Baghdad, and it was the chaplain's duty to minister to them, and also to others in centres of administration in the north, while the chaplain at Basra served the south of the country. As Colin had found in Stockholm, the English church proved a very acceptable place of worship for 'a congregation consisting of Christians ranging from Russian Orthodox to Dutch Reformed' (letter to Ida).

After his first full week, Colin wrote in his diary:

> October 29th: During this week I have spent my time in study, visiting, & in anxieties over a place to live in & a car. The latter is really necessary owing (a) to long distances which have to be traversed (b) the short period of the day at which people are at home, i.e. only from 4-7. At present I find I can study with more or less concentration and I am finding it possible to pray and keep my rule about prayer. I am wondering in what ways I can best fulfil my 'ministry' here, and whether I ought always to give a lead in conversation to religious topics. Have met Abdul Karim the chemist who is the leader of the Protestant C.M.S. group of converts in Baghdad who want me to celebrate for them once a month; I propose to do so.

The problem of where to live was eventually solved by his moving into a spacious top floor room in the Alwiyah Club, whose manager was a deacon of the Chaldaean Church, but which catered for the British. During the summer months of 1933 he was able to share a house with the Ambassador's legal Secretary, a Mr Nihill, 'as mad as a hatter', while his family were in England, and later still, when Evelyn came to Baghdad in the autumn for about nine months, they both shared William Allard's spacious house. After Evelyn and then Mr Allard had gone at the end of June 1934, Colin shared with Bill Bailey (one of his deputy organists and the British Hunt's Master of Hounds) until he returned to England at the end of September.

To resume the account of his very early days in Iraq: on 2 November Colin records that he had

> engaged Ibrahim as servant as from today at 50 rupees a month. He is a native of Mysore and has served here with Sir Hubert Young who speaks well of him. Have also today bought a Morris Cowley 2-seater (1927) for £25. Nothing very grand but it just suits my purpose. Coloured blue.[6]

On 12 November Colin wrote:

> I retired to bed last Monday with a throat, a chill and 'internal disorders'. Rather glad of a few days' rest. Monday a terrible day – a dust storm. What an affliction they are (in a later letter he suggested that Psalm 137 – 'By the waters of Babylon' – '*must* have been written during' one). I have done so many different things that I can't recall them all here ... The marriage of a German chargé d'affaires on Monday to a Dutch bride, using the English prayer book, was a delightful occasion though I could hardly speak, my throat was so bad. Last Sunday I preached to the Arab congregation at 9 am – a rather dejected looking crew they seemed and their church is a grim place. Still, it was nice having a common worship with people of a different race. The Ambassador and Lady Humphrys are now here. I met them on Armistice day and lunch with them tomorrow.

Here is Colin's record of this meal:

> Lunched at the Embassy with the Humphrys. Sir Francis talked almost entirely of the Assyrians. He spoke very warmly and energetically of the support which he on behalf of the Government had always given them, he ridiculed all the arguments on the other side of our having let them down. He has a poor opinion of Mar Shimun the Patriarch whom he considers hopelessly ungrateful and as having displayed throughout the attitude of a spoilt child. He denied that the British Government had ever made any promises to them which they have not kept and thinks that both Turkish and Iraq Govts are not at all anti-Assyrian, though they might well be. He said that Mar Shimun is paid 300 rupees a month by the Iraq government and the payment is made by the Secret Service Dept whose funds are not audited, because, were it known he received such a large subsidy, many of the Moslem clergy, who are paid far less, would be furious. He seemed to think there may be some chance of settling the Assyrians in

---

[6] Sir Hubert had been High Commissioner of Iraq.

Hakkariah, their old hill-country, which is still in Turkey. In view of contrary statements by very reliable and credible people I feel unable to discover the true situation. I only feel that desire to get Iraq into the League – and so off our hands – may influence Sir Francis to the extent of blinding him to the other side. His intense eagerness to convince me struck me as evidence of this, i.e. of a scruple unconsciously suppressed which results in an almost emotional desire to justify himself. He was most kind to me.

Colin's perplexity about the Assyrians was eventually resolved in their favour after much thought and consultation of many others – though he had come out to Baghdad as one already holding much the same view as the Ambassador. The main issue concerned the 'promises' which the Assyrians thought the British had not kept in return for the military service they had undoubtedly rendered during the First World War and were still to render for many years after the Second. It is clear that there were never any *written* undertakings by the British, so the issue turned on the nature of the evidence there was for verbal promises. Archbishop Davidson, a true statesman of the church with an exceptional range of friends and acquaintances among leading politicians and other important men in public life, was fully persuaded that promises had been made. The Revd W.A. Wigram, who had worked in the Assyrian Mission before 1918, and had an intimate knowledge of the Assyrian leaders, had no doubt that, towards the end of the war, a Captain Gracey came to the Assyrian community in Persia as an emissary of General Offley Shore and asked them to help the British against the Turks, promising that the British would do what they could to further their interests and to protect them when the war was over. The terms of the request made it crystal clear, said Wigram, that they were 'definitely recognized as an ally of Great Britain'.

Colin's relations with Sir Francis, the Ambassador, who was always trying to convert (or re-convert) him to the 'official' view, were thus very difficult. Although Sir Francis continued to treat him with great kindness, was most complimentary about his work as the English chaplain and although Colin found his conversation interesting and entertaining in many ways, there was always that barrier between them. In a letter to Ida he talks of the strain of dining with the ambassador and having to disagree 'with almost all he says'. When there was a massacre of the Assyrians in the summer of 1934, and Sir Francis discovered that Colin had written an outspoken letter to the Archbishop about it and the subsequent conduct of the Iraq Government, he actually started to complain widely to others about his attitude, but when Colin asked for an interview to have it out with him, the ambassador used all his charm and diplomatic skill to evade any personal confrontation.

Colin's tense relationship with the ambassador was at first, to some extent, paralleled by his relations with George Francis, Bishop in Jerusalem, his ordinary, especially after he emerged as a staunch supporter of the Ambassador's view of the Assyrians. Before this Colin's irritation partly arose because his new-found freedom as the priest in charge of St George's became periodically subject to the kind of bishop-chaplain relationship he had just experienced under George Bell, but with a man of a very different stamp. Hence his allusion to 'the archbishop trail' mentioned in a letter to Mary where he had to go round visiting with the bishop and 'hang about' or do what the bishop required of him. On 5 December 1932 he wrote in his diary:

> The Bishop in Jerusalem is here. I don't like him at all – he gets on my nerves, everything he says or does. I dislike his mincing way of talking and moving, his absurd and unnecessary attempts at self-effacement, his ideas when he begins to speak seem conventional and rather hollow and – I must confess it – I abominate what seems like a self-conscious and rather oily piety.

The Bishop then went off to Mosul for a few days with the Revd J. Panfil of the Assyrian Mission, and, on returning to Baghdad, preached at St George's and had a long talk with Colin before going on to Jerusalem. Next day Colin wrote in his diary:

> I feel somewhat ashamed of my rash judgement of the Bishop. I had a long talk with him yesterday and saw great depths of wisdom and goodness in him. We were speaking of the need for visiting, pastorally, in the right spirit. 'It all depends, he said, on the attitude in which we come to our people. I always make a point when I knock at a door of lifting up my heart to God. Also when I hear a knock at my door I lift up my heart and make the sign of the cross.' At evensong last night he preached a sermon which seemed to grip the very large congregation very hard.

When the Bishop came again in June Colin wrote: 'I like him but he does get on my nerves so', though, a few days later, 'I wish I could manage not to dislike him so much.' Whatever the bishop himself *felt* about Colin, he *judged* that Colin was the man to take the Ordination Retreat in Jerusalem at the beginning of 1934.

Colin had intended to start for this on 25 January by desert bus to Damascus and then go by car to Jerusalem. He had promised his loyal and considerate Assyrian servant Yussuf to take him along with him, but the plan was scuppered by torrential rain – a regular occurrence in Mesopotamia – which made driving across the desert impossible for two days. So he had to get a very expensive air ticket to Damascus, and was only just in time for the retreat at Jerusalem, and poor Yussuf had to stay behind.

Colin gave five addresses to the ordinands, who were deacons about to be 'priested', and preached the sermon in the Cathedral during the ordination service. After the retreat he stayed for three days with the Reeds, friends made in Baghdad but lately posted to Jerusalem. 'Jerusalem was wonderful', he wrote to Ida, 'it seemed to me such a place of promise and hope. It was the country round Jerusalem I liked best, the "hills standing about Jerusalem", Bethany, Emmaus, the Kidron Valley, Bethlehem – the view of the hills of Moab across the Dead Sea'. It was also wonderful to 'see the Jews starting life afresh there', especially under the aegis of a Christian nation. He described the 'beauty and interest of the crowds in the streets' – especially 'the Polish Jews in their fifteenth century hats of velvet trimmed with fur and the Abyssinian monks and clergy in their tall hats and purple cloaks'.

On the morning he left, George Reed took him to the Capitular Mass at the German-Austrian Benedictine monastery, where he was ravished by the beauty of the ceremonial in which 'the rise and fall of the even, consecrated, voices and the glory of the Mass plainsong were like balm to me'. On the other hand, the return motor journey to Damascus took up much more time than he expected because of the actions of a 'pious mullah', who insisted on the driver stopping at every holy place so that he could get out, enter it, and say his prayers, thus making it impossible for Colin to see something of the city in daylight. The bus journey was again tedious, and Colin got home on 3 February in a dust storm.

Soon after, Colin wrote to Ida that he had thought that his addresses were 'very inadequate', but that 'two of the Arab clergy thanked me for them and said they had helped.' Even the Bishop, he added, 'said that some of the clergy from the lonely out-stations "had gone on their way rejoicing" (and wrote to the Archbishop saying much the same) – so my very feeble efforts were used by God'. Indeed, before Colin left, the Bishop asked him if he could publish them in successive issues of his Diocesan Magazine: *Lines of Communication*. 'Thoughts on the Christian Ministry', which Colin sent in under the pseudonym 'Presbyter', still reads very well today.

The addresses are largely based on the Epistles and Gospels, and contain much practical advice and encouragement, as well as setting out simply but clearly what the very early Christians thought about the priestly office. The fifth talk is largely about how to overcome the inadequacies in prayer and pastoral work he was so conscious of in himself, as is especially clear in his letters to Mary. He tells the ordinands: 'We must be ready to respond as S. Paul did: "Most gladly therefore will I rather glory in my infirmities that the power of Christ may rest upon me ... for when I am weak, then am I strong".'

As already implied above, Colin's ministry in Baghdad was generally a matter of taking services and promoting the spiritual life of the community, largely by getting to know people, since there were next to no Church organisations attached to St George's, as there are to Anglican churches at home. Although he was naturally keen to promote a moderately High Church observance, he was well aware that an Anglican congregation in a foreign land has no alternative place of worship, and therefore tried very hard both to hold the balance between High and Low church allegiances in liturgical matters, and to explain publicly any apparent departures from this norm. When preaching, he wrote to Ida, one should always 'appeal to fundamentals of faith and Christian response', and 'never appeal to particular experiences, or devotional or doctrinal emphasis'. 'The "narrowness" of the churches in England', he goes on, 'is at best a means to an end (the universal mission) and not an end in itself'.

All this needs wise regulation, of course; I have always appealed to the Bishop in Jerusalem for advice – nor are there the absolutely constant people (especially women) to fall back on – one must again work out 'the fundamentals of the pastoral care of people'. (5/10/33)

This accounts for his indignation against the RAF chaplain, whom he invited to preach at morning service one Sunday:

Grange-Bennett ..., who is producing 'Outward Bound', preached on the play for me at mattins. I didn't care for his sermon, which was of the scolding, obscurantist type. I can't understand how a preacher of the Gospel can want to scold or how any reasonable man can think he can do any good by scolding from the pulpit.

Colin also believed strongly that, whereas the attempt to to convert Muslims or members of any non-Christian Faith to Christianity was a Christian duty, the attempt to convert from one branch of the Church to another was not:

I have spent the earlier part of this afternoon trying to persuade a group of American missionaries that it is wrong to try and convert native Christians, however unsatisfactory their religion may seem, to the Protestant faith. I begged them, in their dealing with Chaldaeans etc to try to make them better Christians and not to detach them from their allegiance. I don't think I was successful, but we all ended up friends which is something. I was, of course, a little violent. (Letter to Mary 24/7/33)

He often had resort to the *Baghdad Times* when introducing what were probably innovations in the succession of church services at high points in the Christian Year, as when he outlined his reasons for adding a short service of preparation for Christmas Communion, or for daily services during Holy Week. His introduction of children's services was also preceded by an announcement in the paper, as were the Carol Services, which included carols at Advent and Easter. To his Press announcement of midnight Communion he added:

The idea of this service is to enable us to 'live over again' the events of the first Christmas day, to keep 'watch by night' like the shepherds, so that when midnight strikes the earliest moments of Christmas day will find us worshipping the new-born king.

When announcing the Children's Toy Service on 31 December he added: 'At this service children bring presents of toys or warm clothing to be given away to other children.' We may note this, too, from the Christmas announcement:

the collections in church ... will be for three organisations which help destitute children. As in past years, Dr. Barnado's Homes and the Waifs and Strays

Society will each receive a third of the total amount. The remaining third will be given to relieve children of the unemployed in England. Thousands of such children are suffering very terribly this winter, and we ought not to forget them at Christmas. 'The Personal Service League' has been founded to administer such relief, a society of which Her Majesty the Queen has become patron.

This was followed by details about where to send contributions if personal attendance was not possible. Many of the English now remaining in Baghdad were now Iraq government employees, whose day of rest was accordingly Friday, rather than Sunday.

Here is an example of his ministry to outlying groups of expatriate British, as reported to Mary (letter of 27/7/33):

I am just back from Khanaqin (an oil station) where I had an encouraging stay. We had a delightful service out of doors in the twilight – the 10 people there all turned up (2 women, 8 men) and sat in a circle. We sang terribly low-brow hymns: Our blest redeemer e'er he breathed and Abide with me; but I always let them choose. It was really rather lovely singing 'He's that gentle voice we hear, soft as the breath of even' with a cool ghost of a breeze just coming over us from across the Persian mountains. I spoke to them about the Glory of God and life as a continuous aim to glorify God. Yet, darling, I can't tell you what agonies I suffer before preaching to these people in the wilds, how more than ever one feels the necessity and yet the impossibility of speaking to them the Word of God, how conscious one becomes of one's mortality, ignorance and sinfulness. And they are, under a thin veneer of indifference, so eager for something bigger than themselves to take them out of themselves. One can only throw oneself on the mercy of God and hope that through the trite inadequate neat little phrases of one's 'sermon', God will yet somehow speak to their hearts.

Another aspect of his pastoral work in Baghdad was the weekly discussion group he ran during the winter months. This, in fact, took the place of a series of 'religious meetings' run by 'two semi-Oxford Group folk', as he put it in a letter to Mary. From the Press report Colin kept, it sounds as though these two visitors to Baghdad, Capt. J.V. McCormack and Mr Leslie Wright, imparted a rather confessional tone to these meetings on the 'vital issues of life'. Colin's aim was advertised as the encouragement of 'full and frank discussion of Christian teaching and morality'. After a slow start, he reported... :

the Discussion meetings are going very well. About 20 turn up each time and I do get a good chance of saying what Christianity is not, even if I fail to show the people what it is. People talk quite a lot and are no longer shy. They are very interesting to me.... Unfortunately I am always 'let down' by fellow-Christians. There is one rather odious little man from the YMCA who will always queer the pitch by speaking of the Garden of Eden story, for instance, as being literal history. I feel that agnostics get the impression that Christianity is really bound up with that literal interpretation of the Bible. Tomorrow we are going to discuss in what sense Man is made in the image of God.

He may well have treated the YMCA man in the rather 'bellicose' or 'violent' way Ida felt he adopted in the face of determined opposition. But he was also invited by various people to dinner to discuss religious questions, often on a regular basis, like his old Radleian friend Bob Sturges (the Ambassador's Political Secretary) and his wife Gerda, Mr and Mrs Holt of the Iraq Railways, and another Holt, Vivyen (Oriental Secretary to the embassy).

Colin naturally took a special interest in the music and ornaments at St George's. 'We have started rehearsing Easter carols', he told Mary,

My conservative choir seems to like them. Fortunately when you come to Easter carols there are no 'old favourites', so one can have nice ones straight away without 'ousting' anything, or upsetting people. We have also started having descants, which the choir loves too. They do them quite nicely.

When the Carol Service was over Sir Francis and Lady Humphrys told Colin they were delighted with it. He had commissioned Jack Arnold to have a new frontal sent out from England. The church, he wrote, was

looking so lovely with the new red, green and gold frontal ... with the new simple wooden altar ornaments, painted a neutral grey with firm red edging, the new St George's flag on the bell-cot.

The Arnolds had also given him a new chasuble, 'a lovely thing of plain white spun silk, reaching almost to my feet and hanging in rich classical folds – so austere and pure'. A Colonel Dwyer had been in charge of the choir when he arrived in Baghdad, and he was lucky enough to inherit more than one competent organist, one of them a Flight Lieutenant in the RAF, though the gradual exodus of the British from Baghdad began to create problems. Colin told Mary that he could manage at a pinch without an organ; it would at least have the bonus of abandoning Anglican Chant for psalms and canticles, which he hated!

As far as the 'ministry of personal contacts' went, he made a point of losing almost no opportunity for social life. After about six weeks in Baghdad he described the British Community as follows:

I am rather liking Baghdad and ... I am finding the British community here rather interesting. Most people are of the semi-Anglo-Indian type and are very hearty and hunt and shoot and play excessive tennis and golf and drink endless whiskies and sodas and believe in keeping the 'native' in his place, and the 'big stick' and all that. But there are more exceptions than I hoped for and I am finding quite a number of people whom I am on the verge of describing as 'kindred spirits' and several more who while not that are extremely interesting. (Letter to Barbara Strachey)

Colin himself played tennis and squash at times; when he was living in the Club he played pre-breakfast tennis 'with a young Arab boy who is one of the club ball-boys and who plays better than I can ever hope to. He wears a long white robe almost to his feet and a little white straw skull cap; he's called, like so many others, Mohammed.' Near the beginning of his time in Baghdad he took steps towards riding regularly, but, as there was nowhere interesting to ride nearby, had to give it up. Social life was much the same as at home, with invitations to 'drinks', or dinner parties, including a great variety of 'themed' ones (e.g. 'dress up as a criminal'), dances, both informal ones and 'full dress' occasions at the embassy, concerts and plays produced by and from the British in Baghdad (Colin's off-stage part as a radio announcer in *Outward Bound* was much praised by the audience).

During 1934 Colin was asked to form a quartet to sing Tudor music, and the group gave at least one concert of madrigals in the ancient manner, sitting round a table and reading the music by candle light. After some of the singers had left, he started out on a second venture, but found one of the singers made such difficulties for him at rehearsals that he had to resign. But his musical life was shared, as long he was in Baghdad, by Dr Jordan, the German Director of Antiquities in the Museum; he regularly visited his house for private musical evenings, when Jordan accompanied him in lute songs, German *Lieder* or passages from Mozart operas.

As far as parties went, Colin was rarely at his ease when he disliked or did not really know his fellow guests, and told Mary *en passant* that one can only make a fool of oneself among friends. A much favoured way of entertaining when the weather was neither too hot nor too cold (both extremes occurred during the year), and there was no dust storm or torrential rain, which always transformed the sandy ground into deep, glutinous, mud, was a river picnic towards sunset on the Tigris, sometimes with 'surf-boarding', or water-skiing laid on; the centrepiece of these excursions was the catching of a large river fish, which the native cook then roasted on a fire lit for the purpose, and accompanied by a curry sauce.

In general Colin found the city of Baghdad ugly and depressing, but never tired of a trip on the River itself:

> The very varied if human (and squalid) scene upon the banks on either side is endlessly fascinating. Countless boys and youths bathing stark naked, their bright brown bodies glistening in the sun; the mothers in dingy black abbas washing their children on the banks, though prohibited by their inhuman and undivine religion from bathing themselves; the comings and goings on a thousand errands by all and sundry in every sort of garb; the rickety overhanging balconies of the Chi-Khanas, heavy with their loads of unsavoury male humanity; the varied architecture of the houses, mosques and other buildings, all in different stages of decay; the sudden gleams of beauty among all the prevailing squalor, in the shape of a nice contrast of colour, a delicately moulded arch, the swift curve of the high prow of a Tigris sailing boat marooned in the mud; all this provides a scene of interest and fascination which seems to increase with every journey I make. There is one house, the walls of which are picked out in a daringly sickly shade of pale blue which I can never

pass without a thrill of pleasure, though it is nearly always singled out for adverse comment by others in the party. And the surf-boarding is an increasing joy in itself, quite apart from the refreshment of it and the glow of health which possesses one's whole body afterwards. (Diary extract)

He paid many visits to members of his congregation or to non-church-goers who were ill, and, of course, took the funerals of any English people whose next of kin wanted this. These occasions often had a special pathos arising from the environment in which they took place. After about a month in Iraq he recorded in his diary: 'After children's service, a burial at the Civilian Cemetery – wife of an engine-driver who died of small pox. Most of the railway officials [were] there.' It turned out that the dead woman had only been in Baghdad for a fortnight, after failing to be inoculated against it before she came out. In a letter to Ida (30/11/32) he wrote about another funeral:

I had a terribly tragic experience the other day. A Eurasian man came to ask me to bury his little child who had just died that day – aged one and a half – the *third* child who had died young. And then I discovered he was unemployed and in fact 'down and out'. I went to the cemetery at the appointed time and there he was all alone with the coffin – a mere packing case – under his arm. I tried to read the burial service calmly and evenly but it was no good and for most of it we were in floods of tears. But I wish I could do more than cry. I can only give him a little money – I can't get him a job. I can pray with him and urge him to hope and trust. But he knows that afterwards I will go home to a good dinner and economic security and he to his pigsty – even that he may lose.

In a letter to Mary he describes another pastoral visit that specially impressed him:

After lunch I went off into the wilds of Baghdad West suburbs to find the isolation hospital. With great difficulty I found it, driving along roads like ploughed fields, making my way through herds of darkies and Arabs. The matron is an Irish woman and I liked her at once. We had a long talk and she showed me over. There is one ward for men and boys who are prisoners. They lie in bed with great chains round their legs, which are fastened to the beds. Outside are soldiers with loaded rifles. One of the prisoners was a boy of 8 who had burned down a house. He was gasping for breath. Then we saw the lepers – an awful sight – they looked almost like animals. When we got back she made me some tea, and I said a prayer with her before I left. She is a heroic person.

In another letter he wrote:

I am going steadily on with my visiting. It seems rather dull and aimless sometimes but I believe it is worth while. At any rate I am clear it is my duty. The other day I called on an Army officer and his wife. He is Scotch and she is Irish. She called her husband 'Big Boy'!!!

But in one or two places in letters to both Ida and Mary he expresses a worry about the 'shallow' quality of his pastoral care; when visiting, he writes, 'my instinct is not to get into their minds and *see*, but merely to receive and make myself the centre of their interest'. There may have been something in this, but, as I have already implied, it is striking how much self-depreciation Colin put into these letters. There can be no doubt that he suffered greatly from a lack of self-assurance, and hence that he tended to present different aspects of himself to different people. 'At times I scarcely feel a person at all, only a mirror which reflects the prejudices and opinions of others'. When writing to Mary he often reverts to the hideous idea of her waking up one day to find that she has married a very inferior person, so he does his best to expose the whole of himself, warts and all, in advance.

Another aspect of his life as English Chaplain was contact with clergy of quite different branches of Christianity. Most of this was a matter of formal visits, in which visiting cards were left and coffee and cigarettes invariably produced. Cards kept by Colin include the following:

Antonin Drapier O.P., Archevêque de Neo-Cesarée du Pont. Délégué Apostolique de la Mésopotamie. Mossoul (Iraq)
Joseph Ghanima, Èêque de Colybrassus. Auxiliaire de S. B. Le Patriarche Chaldéen. Bagdad (Iraq)
Athanase Behnam Kalian. Syrian Archbishop of Baghdad
Rev. Joseph Cheikho, Chaldean priest. Baghdad, Mesopotamia
Bichop [*sic*] Rouben Manassian. Iraq Representative of His Holiness the Supreme Patriarch & Catholicos of all the Armenians. Baghdad
Jacques Nessimian, Archevêque Arm. Catholique. Bagdad

There is another card in Arabic, probably left by the leader of the Arab Protestants in Baghdad.

This list is another illustration of the extraordinary nature of Iraq under the English mandate as, at least temporarily, a cosmopolitan and secure refuge for so many Christian congregations in the Middle East. The reference to 'le Pont' on the first card is a reminder of the old Kingdom of Pontus on the south-east shore of the Black Sea, which became part of the Roman Empire, was 'Christianised' and was then overrun in the great explosion of Islam in the seventh century. Rather than allow the old episcopal sees in Pontus and other areas where Christians had to lie low to be forgotten, the Western Church kept the names alive in 'titular' sees, where the bishop concerned perhaps never even set foot in the place commemorated. Colybrassus, in the second card, is also a titular see. The list also witnesses to the fact that the old churches of this part of the world often became split in one form or other during centuries of persecution and physical dispersal, and it sometimes became convenient for one part of the old church to join the Roman Catholic Church, not by being completely absorbed but as a 'Uniat' church, keeping nearly all its centuries-old rites and customs (which often included a married clergy), but submitting to the Pope in matters of doctrine and supreme authority.

Thus, cards were left with Colin by the Catholic Armenian archbishop, as well as a representative of the non-Catholic 'Supreme Patriarch and Catholicos of all the Armenians'. The Chaldaean church was another Uniat church, originally part of the Assyrian or Nestorian church, and the 'Syrian' or 'Jacobite' Church, which used the ancient Jacobite liturgy of St James, also had Roman Catholic and Eastern branches. As the first of the two Armenian titles suggests, it was not always easy for all Armenian clergy to have much to do with one another. When mentioning this, Colin emphasises once more the importance of the Anglican Church as a 'bridge' church. The clergy of all churches he came across were friendly to him and interested in Anglicanism, whereas clergy were sometimes unable to speak to each other across the division between Uniat and non-Uniat and other cultural separations.

Colin was naturally very interested in the liturgical and ritual aspects of the public worship of the other churches he visited. In a letter to Mary (10/1/33) he writes:

> The other day I went to a mass at the Chaldaean church. ... The music was the queerest ever. At first it sounded like aimless yodelling, but after a bit I began to get the hang of it and was rather fascinated. No harmony at all, and all quarter tones and outlandish intervals. Sung with fearful gusto by crowds of little urchins. When one remembers all the persecutions of this backwater church ... one couldn't help being filled with pity for its present half-savage state. They have clung on to their faith so nobly , even though they seem a poor lot of rather dirty and dishonest scallywags. I suppose each church has its own characteristic virtues and vices. We have vices enough, so we ought to look for the virtues in others. A tenacious witness, faithful unto death, is undoubtedly the virtue of these Chaldaeans.

On his visit to the patriarchal auxiliary in his 'rather bleak' house on the Tigris opposite the British Embassy, he noted that the bishop wore 'a black douillette', or quilted overcoat, 'over his crimson-piped cassock'. When Colin asked him whether the chalice was given to the laity, as was the practice in the Nestorian church, 'his answer seemed to be "in theory yes, in practice no, for it is so inconvenient"', but that it was given to the deacons. Previous to my visit, he wrote in his diary, I had had a look at the Chaldaean church. Except for the curtain which conceals the sanctuary (drawn aside at the time) there seemed nothing in it to distinguish the church from a Latin one.

Later in the month Colin writes:

> The Chaldaean Bishop Mar Emmanuel paid me a visit yesterday at tea time, with a priest. They sampled Mackie's shortbread and smoked cigarettes (the bishop preferred Gold Flake). Our talk was almost entirely of matters liturgical. The most interesting fact which emerged was that the Chaldaean clergy only say three offices in the twenty four hours, a night office, a morning office and vespers. I gathered (though I find a difficulty in understanding their French) that the night and morning offices are usually said en bloc first thing in the morning, i.e. at about 5am. They were very friendly and pleasant.

The priest, Fr. Cheikho, promised to find him a French teacher, and when Colin asked him a day or two later what success he had had, 'he replied with a triumphant smile "I will teach you myself". But I wonder how much he will charge.' In the event he charged nothing. A different bishop, Mar Joseph, was celebrating when he went again to Mass on

> the last of the three days commemorating the fast of the Ninivites at Jonah's warning. He wore a black cope, with no mitre. He wore deep black silk wristbands and a curious pink veil hung from his right wrist. I had a very prominent seat and prie dieu just inside the veil (which is pulled back for most of the service) and next to the patriarchal throne.

Afterwards he had coffee with Father Cheikho. It turned out that he was Secretary to the Chaldaean Patriarch and 'a sort of Financial Secretary of the Chaldaean Church'. This time he learnt that

> the Chaldaean church practices the Orthodox custom of infant confirmation but the children are specially prepared for and make their first communion at about the age of eight.

Next month he called upon the Syrian Catholic Archbishop, whose Patriarch 'lives at Beyrouth [Beirut] in a grand new house, the cost of which he proudly recited several times'. Here he learnt that 'The special feature of the Ash Wednesday observance among the Syrians is the anointing, not with ashes, but with oil, in conformity with the Evangelical command.' His grace conducted me round the church:

> a very sorry specimen of a purely Latin type with all the essentially Western bad-taste of a church in France or Italy. The enthusiasm of the Vatican for Eastern customs to be maintained seems to restrict itself to the rite and the ceremonies, not to vestments and furniture and general atmosphere ... On the other hand ... (he) seemed more keen on the religious and moral side of his work than is apparent among the other prelates I have met. He spoke of homilies on the Gospel after Mass, of a bi-monthly paper he issues instructing people in faith and morals.

Colin also called on both the Gregorian Armenian Archbishop and the Armenian Catholic one. '(The former) received me with more formality than have the other prelates and sat on a sort of throne in his audience chamber.' They had to converse through an interpreter.

> He wore a long, loose, cassock-like robe lined with violet silk, a butterfly collar and an enamelled picture of Madonna and child round his neck on a chain ... The Katholikos of the Gregorian Armenians has his headquarters in Russian Armenia and is under the Soviets. These did not hinder the election of a new Katholikos which was accomplished last November after a 2-year interregnum.

Both the Turks and the French authorities in Syria forbad their respective subjects from sending representatives to the election.

When being shown round the church Colin especially noted 'the cherubim, mounted on sticks, with bells at the head which are shaken to and fro during the liturgy in token of the ceaseless praise of the angels'. When he called on the Catholic (Uniat) Archbishop he found him more accessible as a man, despite the portraits of his predecessors lining the walls. When he tried to stoop to kiss his ring he wouldn't let him, and they 'conversed amiably about Baghdad and the cold weather. His fifth-century cathedral is at Mardin in Turkey, where the solitary priest who keeps it going is in constant fear of death'. He 'spoke of his hopes for the future reunion of Christendom, and mentioned the Malines conversations and Cardinal Mercier for whom he had a high regard'.

In a sense, these visits were a form of sight-seeing for Colin. But when he describes a baptism he took for the Arab Protestants, he is writing again about his own work. Seven or eight young children were to be baptised,

> mostly about 4 or 5 years old, though some were infants in arms. It was the oddest and rowdiest function I have ever presided at. All ages and all classes and all dresses were represented. People stood about or sat down or squatted just as they pleased. Some talked, some laughed, some prayed. There was a sort of grotesqueness about the whole assemblage which reminded me of a picture by Cruikshank or Hogarth. An Arab in a fez and flowing garments was to read the service in Arabic. He started putting on a cassock! But I prevented him and popped a surplice over his head. His long robes were a cassock in themselves. One gets broken in to noisy baptisms but the caterwauling of two sturdy infants passed all belief and comprehension on this occasion. One mother immediately presented her breast to one of them and this quieted him only for a second or two when the cacophany was renewed. They wore white baptism robes with golden spangles over them. I had to give them all the most outlandish Arabic names which I could barely pronounce, except one very Arabic looking child who was to be called Margaret!

It is easy to imagine that Colin, a highly sensitive man, who believed strongly in the importance of dignity in the conduct of worship, would have found it almost impossible to disguise some negative feelings about all this, and, probably, many other services he took in their church. A passage in a letter to Mary about the Christmas presents he received, written on Boxing Day 1933, after he had been ministering to them for over a year, provides an unspoken comment on this:

> The Arab Protestants gave me a present of silver salt, mustard and pepper pots on a little tray and 3 silver napkin rings ... They are done by the Arab or rather Sabaean workers from Amarra and powdered with little designs done in black (a great trade secret). Not *very* nice , but passable; and absolutely sweet coming from the Arab Prots: who, I thought, hated me. Apparently they were inspired to

do it by my sermon to them on Christmas Eve. They've never taken any interest in my sermons before. As a matter of fact I always feel they don't understand a word, and that saps one's energy and inspiration, but on Christmas Eve I let fly and didn't care whether they understood or not. I now know that's the thing to do!

During the following summer he was able to start an Arab Confirmation Class, which he much enjoyed. Unfortunately the attendance record grew so bad that by the autumn he had had to reduce the numbers to 'two men and a boy'.

Colin's contact with the hierarchy of the Assyrian church began on 7 January 1933, when his diary carries the following account:

In the afternoon went with the Reeds to call on Mar Shimun, the youthful Nestorian Patriarch. He was staying with his father in the camp of the Assyrian levies at Hinaidi. I didn't like the look of him. He has a rather cruel and a rather ruthless expression and cast of features. We exchanged polite observations.

The next meeting seems to have been during a visit to Mosul in early April. He wrote in his diary:

Chaplain visited Mosul. Stayed with the Ashtons. Called on members of British Community, Mar Shimun, the Apostolic Delegate [Antonin Drapier O.P.], the Chaldaean Bishop (in absence of Patriarch), the Jacobite Bishop, and the American Mission. Evensong and address in R.A.F. chapel at 6 pm on Thursday and Holy Communion at 7.30 am on Friday same place (8 am would be a better hour). Flew back in R.A.F. plane on Friday.

This visit and the journey from Baghdad by train and then car opened his eyes to the beauty of northern Iraq. Here is part of his account from a letter to Mary:

I left Kirkuk this morning (after sleeping in the train from Baghdad) and reached here after a seven hours' drive in a car over the most atrocious roads but through the most delightful country. Everything is green; there are no trees of course, but lots of wild flowers and long rolling hills. The special keynote of the day has been storks. They are to be seen everywhere. One small village of about 100 mud hovels had a stork and nest on almost every house. And you see them in the grass and corn looking so clean and dignified. We passed through a number of Kurdish villages; none of them had a trace of anything un-Eastern. No-one in Western dress. ... And there is real beauty here; not merely the picturesque of unfamiliarity, but deliberate wilful beauty such as one never sees in Baghdad. The lovely dark grey marble door-ways, the marble pillars in the courtyards of the houses, the graceful arches – all this is unutterably refreshing. ... In a few moments I am going to visit young Mar Shimun, the Assyrian Patriarch who still calls himself 'Katholikos of the East' and whose predecessors ruled over a church which had bishops in Arabia, Mesopotamia, Persia, India, Tartary and China. Now he rules over a total number of 40,000 scallywags with only 6 bishops, 3 of whom are in rebellion against him.

A few days later he adds to his account:

> Mosul was so interesting and *really* eastern. It was a Mohammedan feast most
> of the time I was there and everybody wore their best clothes: the children in
> brilliant coloured sateen clothes, Kurds in their very picturesque dress and all
> with new clean veils over their heads, mostly of white linen and held down with
> gold or coloured wool cords. It all looked so festive and gay. ... I visited the
> alleged tomb of Jonah in a lovely mosque on a hill outside Mosul – an ancient
> Christian church – on the wall of his tomb hangs the jaw of a small sword-fish
> which the Mullah told me was the jaw of the whale which swallowed the
> prophet! But I can't tell you what a wonderful feeling there was in the mosque.
> It really felt a most holy place. I surveyed the site of Nineveh with all the
> correct emotions (it really was rather moving and I felt rather annoyed that 'Lo
> all our pomp of yesterday / Is one with Nineveh and Tyre' kept running in my
> head!) Then I called on Agatha Christie who is now excavating in the intervals
> of writing detective stories – she showed me some wonderful finds which she
> and her husband have dug up, dating from about 4000 B.C. Vases and bowls
> with quite lovely designs and amusing little amulets. There is no sign that the
> civilization which produced them knew how to write! One of the most
> incredible coincidences exists in Mosul for in this city, opposite the remains of
> Assyrian Nineveh live about 15 English people and one of these has as a
> surname Sargon! There cannot be more than 6 people in the world called that,
> and that he should find himself opposite the city which King Sargon made
> famous is really almost too much of a joke.

Mar Shimun had clearly not yet begun to interest him particularly, as he
says nothing about his visit to him.

It was around this time that Bob Sturges was moved out of Iraq to
Palestine. He had been writing a weekly column of Iraq news for *The
Statesman*, a daily paper published in Calcutta primarily for the English (or
anyone else who might be happy with a paper that advertised British and
American cars and expected its readers to be interested in the Oxford and
Cambridge Boat Race and the new Headmaster of Eton!). Just before he moved
he recommended Colin as the man to take over his column, and the editor
accepted his suggestion. Colin's first article was on 5 April, and published on
the 15th. He soon began to enjoy this weekly labour very much, he told Ida,
though the more he studied the political life of Baghdad the more disillusioned
he grew at Britain's premature surrender of the mandate:

> The public life of this country is appallingly corrupt; politicians seem to have no
> sense of decency or honour or responsibility; they have an impossibly cynical
> view of all kinds of public morality and are crooked to the core. The frequency
> in all walks of life of murder and dishonesty is really dreadful. It's all deeply
> depressing, I can hardly believe Iraq to be ready for self-government; it's the
> poor Christian minorities who will have to pay the price.

One of the first things he had to report to his readers in India was the
reintroduction of public executions; two murderers had been hanged in

Baghdad when 20,000 spectators assembled to see them. Murders were, in fact, very common, and, he reported, often committed for 'the most flippant of motives'. In May 1933, he mentioned the new government's concern for 'public morality'; then, about three weeks later, had to describe two examples of 'flagrant contempt for justice' of people in high places. In his next article he reports on King Faisal's departure on a State Visit to Great Britain, and that there were widespread hopes for the revision of the Anglo-Iraq Treaty, which some of the Press considered 'oppressive and unfair', and 'derogatory to Iraq's honour'.

Spring had seen much anger and discontent among the Kurds, and this was followed by trouble among the Assyrians. I shall return to this below. But Colin's weekly articles are controlled and restrained; he never writes in such an emotion-charged way in his references to the Iraq politicians, and more generally the 'Town Arabs', as he sometimes does in his correspondence. When he came across General Hay's daughter, whom he had first met while chaplain to Bishop Winnington-Ingram, she told him that her father, who had just come from India to succeed General Rowan-Robinson as Advisor to the Iraq army, 'had lately been eagerly reading the weekly "Baghdad Letter"... in anticipation of his coming stay in Iraq'.

Naturally his letters to Mary show what he really felt about Iraq and Islam, as a direct offshoot of his experience of them. He was, of course, keenly aware of the difference between the Sunnis, who were prominent among 'Town Arabs', and the Shiahs, mostly Persian, who formed the majority of the country's Mohammedans. It should also be remembered that Colin gives no sign of having read the Koran. The following incident involves 'Town Arabs', but is then extended to Muslims as such:

> When I came to church this morning, I saw that a sort of refreshment booth had been tacked on the East end of the church, in which several disreputable Arabs were plying a lively trade. I got Vatcha [the verger] to come and interpret for me, and asked them what the blazes they thought they were doing. They said they had a permit from the Amin-al-Asimah, so I asked for it to be shown to me. Of course they had nothing of the sort, so I ordered the whole contraption to be taken down, giving them till this evening to do it in. As a safegard I went along to the office of the municipal inspectors and told them. They say they will enforce my order. One knows that if one so much as leaned for a moment or two against the wall of a mosque, a whole gang of fanatics with beards and tousled turbans would rush out at one demanding one's instant death, yet they put their own sordid booths against our church and seem surprised when politely ordered off. The British have for so long kow-towed to the fanaticism of Islam, supporting it against Christians, that they feel aggrieved if asked to show us a little respect.

This comes from a letter of 16/7/34, nearly a year after the Assyrian Massacre.

Here are some of his his ideas and impressions as they came:

It *is* difficult to be tolerant of Mohammedanism ... They imitate all the worst things in 'Christian' civilization but reject the one thing which is really good and would really help them. (29/3/33)

Here is his response to the discontent of both Kurds and Assyrians:

My sympathies are all with the Kurds and Assyrians: not at all with the loathsome town Arabs who rule the country. Words fail me to describe their nastiness and corruption. I do so thoroughly sympathise with the Crusaders in this Islamic country. Living here makes one almost feel that 'the West' is really Christian. At any rate it is much more Christian than it realizes. What a nightmare Mohammedanism is. (31/5/33)

'These unspeakable Arabs', he wrote:

are only waiting for the moment when they can massacre the Assyrians. Darling, it is awful to hate, but I find a most bitter hatred has grown up in me against the Arabs and everything Islamic. I came out too with the full intention of 'seeing the good in them' and I have always thought I was above racial and religious hatred. I can barely bring myself to speak to an Arab (except the poor people). (2/8/33)

What I really hate is, not individual Arabs, but the whole ethos of Islam which seems to me so diabolical. Especially do I hate the pan-Arab business which seems so hysterical and such an impulse to all the bad things in human nature. (7/12/33)

In fact he draws a big distinction between Shiahs and Sunnis. His first strong impression of the former came when he was invited to witness the fascinating yet repellant Moharram Processions, in which the origins of Shiism are recalled by symbolic re-enactments of the deaths of Hussein and Ali, grandson and cousin respectively of Mohammed, in the battles for the leadership of Islam after the founder's death. Colin also later visited both Khadimain and Nejaf with William Allard, towns with Shiah mosques and large Persian populations, the latter being a highly important place of Shiah pilgrimage, where they were given a police escort. 'You feel (the inhabitants') hate and mistrust as you walk about. There's something fascinating about this primitive die-hard-ism.' But the mosque, he felt, was merely 'pretty', 'I suppose merely the result of puritanism ...; perhaps an inevitable result of the Islamic view of women – just toys for men's amusement in their off-time.' Nevertheless, he goes on, he would rather belong to the die-hard Shiahs than their Sunni counterparts ... 'The latter (sect) seems to have so little religion in it. It's just an antiquated legalism' (12/1/34). Then, again:

The presence of fanaticism fills me with admiration and dread. The absence of care for sanitation or comfort or civilization or Western ideas, and the concentration of the whole city upon the shrine of its martyred hero, even

though it has a terribly seamy side, has yet a certain spiritual distinction about it
which is a joy in these practical progressive this-world-only days. Nejaf might
certainly crucify Christ if he came, but it wouldn't just leave him out in the rain
to die as we would in the West. (8/3/34)

By April 1934, he writes, he has changed his whole idea about giving non-
Christian countries independence:

I can't see how they can get the necessary sense of responsibility apart from
Christianity. Islam does not inculcate it, or indeed any kind of public social
morality (except the duty of murdering your sister if you think she has
committed fornication, willingly or unwillingly). ... These people (the Iraq
politicians) want self-government to get positions of power to feather their own
nests and to play the arbitrary fairy-godmother in the family circle ... None of
the Iraq politicians has any political vision, none of them has any programme
except being anti-British, anti-Christian and anti-Jewish. I don't see how the
country can last as a political unit.

On St George's Day he was invited to the official Embassy dinner:

The speeches actually ridiculed the Disarmament Conference, and then the
German Minister (whom I like very much) got up and rejoiced, he said, to see
the growing decay of internationalism, and the growth of nationalism and racial
pride; he compared the cult of St George to the National Socialists' ideals! Even
our Baghdad Philistines greeted this astonishing observation with roars of
laughter.

Colin now regretted his having refused beforehand to speak, and was
'literally trembling with rage' – though, had he spoken, he 'would probably
have made a fool of (him)self'. But, instead, he responded with his sermon on
the following Sunday, preaching about Nationalism in the light of the emblem
of the cross on St George's shield. In August he told Mary that he was
continuing to enjoy writing his Baghdad Letters for *The Calcutta Statesman*:

I am afraid I am rather ungenerous and critical of Iraq in them but I find it hard
to be any other. It was a very evil day when we gave them independence. It has
made me revise my views about India a good deal, though I am not quite a
diehard yet.

Despite this, his Baghdad Letter for 24 August reported that the Minister of
the Interior had approved the formation of an Iraq Nazi party, who would wear
a uniform of brown shirts. In 1941 there was a putsch by elements of the Iraq
army sympathetic to Nazism and an attack by 15,000 Iraqis on the British base
at Habbaniyah, which the Assyrian levies helped the British to put down.

We must now return to Mar Shimun, whom Colin had rather disliked at
their first meeting. About six weeks after this, the Patriarch had just arrived in
Baghdad at the invitation of the government when the Assyrians, following the

Kurds, were openly venting their discontent at their uncertain position within the newly independent state. On 31 May 1933 Colin wrote as follows to Mary:

> I ... had Mar Shimun, the Assyrian Patriarch, to lunch on Monday. I like him a little better than I did and am immensely sorry for him and ashamed at the way the British Government has treated him.

It should be added here that the Assyrians, who had preserved their faith for nearly two millennia without changing their customs and practices very much, were still an essentially tribal people, like some of the Bedouin Arabs who also inhabited Iraq and periodically erupted at the difficulties arising from the gradual growth of a twentieth century political outlook. At the heart of the Assyrian world-view was the assumption that their spiritual leader must also be their leader in temporal matters too. Colin's letter to Mary just cited also contains the following:

> The conflict between the Arabs and the Assyrians has all the characteristics of pure tragedy; it is difficult on the purely natural plane to 'blame' either side; it seems an inevitable clash between forces far vaster than either of the participants realizes. Any moral blame in the matter seems to lie at our door, for we have both done, and not done, things which have resulted in the present impasse. One thing seems clear at the moment. If the Iraq Government tries to disarm the Assyrians, there is bound to be terrible bloodshed. And the Assyrians have every reason for gravely suspecting the motive for their disarmament, for only last week, in view of the crisis, the Government armed the Kurds, and actually set them at the Assyrians. (Though no actual clash occurred.)

Mar Shimun was now, in fact, a virtual prisoner of the government, since they refused to let him leave Baghdad and return to his people until he had entirely renounced his temporal power, which they said was *ipso facto* an act of disloyalty to the King. After making no progress with the attempt to change Mar Shimun's mind, they banished him from Iraq altogether (perhaps twisting the new constitution to do so) and got the British to accept him in Cyprus, which was still a British colony. Before this happened, Colin had seen a good deal more of him, and had come to have considerable respect for him, as his later Report on the Simel Massacre shows (see Appendix I).

The massacre itself was the culmination of a series of connected events, which began when a large number of Assyrians crossed the Iraqi border with Syria towards the end of July (1933) without permission or warning in order to investigate the possibility of an Assyrian settlement in that country, since the Iraq Government had refused to find enough mountain land for them to settle as a single or very small number of homogeneous groups, which would have been possible had the League of Nations Boundary Commission included their original home, the Hakkiari Mountains, in Iraq rather than Turkey. Instead, the Iraqis told them that they could either leave the country altogether or be settled in a large number of small groups widely scattered across Iraq, which would in fact mean they would always be vulnerable to attacks from the Kurds as well as at the mercy of the Iraqis most hostile to them, among whom were many local officials. The Assyrian men, possibly 1500 of them, who precipately took the second alternative and left the country, were refused permission to settle in Syria, and started back home together to rejoin their families.

At the frontier post they were confronted with the Iraq army, with the demand that they surrender their weapons. There was then some sort of military engagement, and there were casualties on either side. Some of the Assyrians managed to get past the Army and headed off into the mountains. The ensuing disturbances culminated in the massacre of a great many Assyrians in the mountain village of Simel, and the refusal of the Iraq Government to allow any British officials of any kind to enter the mountain area to find out exactly what was happening. As Colin makes clear in his report, it is overwhelmingly likely that the massacre was perpetrated by the Machine Gun corps of the Iraq army. These events were soon followed by the 'triumphal procession' of the Army through Mosul and down to Baghdad, and a huge increase of anti-Assyrian feeling in the press, and the Town Arabs in general. When Colin wrote to Mary on 17 August he told her that they had been expecting a further massacre in Baghdad itself, though mercifully 'the demonstration was called off at the last moment'.

Colin was horrified by this sequence of events and set himself to find out what had really happened. As he knew by now several people who lived or worked in the mountain area, including the Revd J. Panfil, who knew it very well, and Judge Creed of Mosul, he soon discovered that the Iraq Government's version of events was far from true, and that most English newspapers were following the lead of the Foreign Office and largely glossing over it. But he also discovered fairly soon that his own correspondence about it, much of it to the Archbishop of Canterbury, Cosmo Gordon Lang, members of the Church of England Council for Foreign Relations and some newspaper editors, was liable to be opened by Iraq officials, and had to enclose such letters to England, which included his Report to the Council for Foreign Relations, in letters to Mary (addressed to 'M.G. O'Malley, esq'), Ida and other friends.

It was also apparent quite soon that the Ambassador, acting, presumably on Foreign Office orders, was trying to hush things up locally. Judge Creed wrote to the Archbishop in November 1933 telling him that he and his brother both thought that 'the career of Sir Francis Humphrys stands or falls by his ability to gloss over what has happened'. To Colin, the official policy was primarily the result of a naive, or wilful, belief, that whatever was officially decided in the Iraq parliament would necessarily be carried out. His own experience, and that of many others he spoke to, was that the further away from Baghdad they were, the less likely it was that local officials would actually do this, especially when the goverment's decrees challenged long engrained prejudices.

The next time Colin talked to Mar Shimun, the Patriarch was in Nicosia in Cyprus, where he was living in exile with many of his family. For Colin the meeting was possible because he had been determined to see Mary during her long vacation from Oxford, though it had taken a great deal of correspondence, both with Ida and with Mary herself, firstly as to whether she could spare some of her valuable study time (she had not gained her expected First in Classical Mods), then where they should meet (Colin's Jerusalem plan seems to have been scuppered by Ida's mistaken idea that the city was too hot in September), and lastly who should chaperone Mary while she was with Colin. His sister Sibyl at first said she would do this, but, when she backed down because of her fear of travel, Evelyn took her place, which gave Mary the opportunity of getting to know her really well, and becoming attached to her. Evelyn in fact went on to Baghdad with Colin, and stayed with him until the end of June 1934, leaving Mary to travel home from Haifa by herself, which she was happy to do. Her short diary of the holiday only survives in part, but contains a very interesting account of their journey from England: the ship they caught at Brindisi was full of European Jews making for Palestine, and one of their fellow passengers was Gilbert Harding, who later became well known as a bad-tempered radio and TV personality, whom they got to know quite well as they shared a table with him at meals.

Then follows a rapturous description of Cyprus and the particular places they visited. But two short passages from it are worth quoting here. The availability of suitable ships meant that Mary and Evelyn's boat from Brindisi arrived a day before Colin could be in Cyprus himself. But, thanks to his having been put in touch with obliging and highly efficient British contacts on the island, they were met at the port of Larnaca and taken thirty miles over the mountains by car to their very comfortable hotel at Kyrenia. Next morning early there was a car to take Mary back to Larnaca, and she describes how she saw Colin's ship very slowly growing from a dark speck on the south-eastern horizon to a large passenger vessel in full view, and then how those who were disembarking at Larnaca were slowly helped down into the harbour launch, and how she saw Colin gradually approaching until he was at last on the jetty 'wearing shorts and topee and looking like a boy scout of about 18'. The sailors were delighted by their warm embrace on the quayside. Then came the return car journey to the north coast, during which they diverged from the route at Nicosia to visit Mar Shimun and his family. 'He is a young rather shy looking man', Mary wrote,

with an olive skin, long straight nose, flashing white teeth and expressively sad eyes. People think he is unfeeling because he smiles when he talks to you, even about the massacres, but his eyes belie the smile and it is bitter. I liked what I saw of him. I saw his aunt too and his sisters. The eldest is called Rowena and is going to be the patriarchess when Lady Surma (his aunt) dies. Lady Surma is very agreeable. Colin says (she is) a *maîtresse femme*, who is the real leader of the Assyrians. She *looked* like a dumpy little French housewife.

Colin was able to hand over to Mar Shimun various things from Iraq, mostly letters and documents sent by other Assyrian leaders. He already knew quite a lot about Lady Surma, because she had had a good education, thanks to the Assyrian Mission, and spoke excellent English, and had spent some time in England in 1920, doing what she could to encourage the Government to get the Assyrians settled in the Hakkiari Mountains in SW Turkey. She had been invited to stay at Lambeth Palace as the guest of Archbishop Davidson, where she made a great impression on him and became the friend of Mrs Davidson. But though she had put the Assyrian case forcefully to the officials she met, supported by the Archbishop, who wrote many letters to the Colonial Office, the British Government had kept putting off the moment of decision for one reason and another until it was much too late for them to do adequately what the British had promised towards the end of the war.

This was the conclusion at last reluctantly reached by the Archbishop. The British had given their 'debt of honour' far too low a priority in their efforts to solve the great problems raised by the League of Nations mandate, giving far more weight to their own economic interest in the recently discovered Iraq oil fields. In his letter to Ida of 8 September, Colin told her that he was trying to get 'a proper barrister to state (Mar Shimun's) case professionally at Geneva', since he knew that everyone would 'be working against him' in view of 'the larger issues', which 'usually means just selfishness'.

Whether or not he too became resigned to the situation as one which could not now be be solved in a way satisfactory to the Assyrians, he did a lot to help those of them still in the refugee camps, by investigating their amenities, raising the matter to anyone with the power to help, and collecting goods and money from the English community, convinced, perhaps, that even if it *was* too late to make great changes of the kind the Assyrians wanted, some kind of apology, or even a show of sympathy, from representatives of the Government of the UK, would at least prove that foreign relations could never, for Christians, be totally confined to a pursuit of material interests.

Today, the very great majority of Assyrian Christians are in the USA, Australia, and other countries in the 'Western World' (their present Patriarch lives in Chicago), and the tiny minority still almost miraculously hanging on in Iraq may well soon decide they have no future in Mesopotamia, and join their fellow Nestorians elsewhere.

The last few days of the Cyprus holiday were largely dictated by Colin's need to get back to Baghdad for the next Sunday, and by the timetable of the shipping line (which would not allow them to visit Jerusalem). In the event they followed from Larnaca the route of Mary and Evelyn's ship from Brindisi as far as it went, that is, to Beirut, via Port Said. Here, Colin records, he and Mary had a wonderful dinner, and then Colin joined Mary in the first leg of her return journey, to Haifa, where he and Mary climbed Mt Carmel, had their first major quarrel and were reconciled. Finally Colin said good bye to Mary, who probably caught the next boat, and he and Evelyn went north by car to Damascus, where he was in good time to see the Mosque of Omar, and appreciate the 'unstandardised pattern of minarets', the vast area of carpeted space and the building's fine columns, before they caught the Baghdad bus.

Colin felt enormously refreshed by his holiday with Mary, and stimulated by Evelyn's sometimes outrageously unorthodox remarks and the private jokes they had for long shared. At times, however, she irritated him extremely, especially when she said something that seemed at odds with something he held dear, such as the cause of the Assyrians. Evelyn's scrappy diary of the holiday records several occasions when his irritation with her boiled over. She herself soon obtained a part-time job at the American Mission school, teaching English and Geography. Later, in March 1934, she was asked to teach the new King Ghazi's young Queen.

Meanwhile Colin made another journey to the mountains in the north of Iraq in November, 1933, partly to visit his old Radley friend Jack Finch, who was now the English Consul in Diana, Kurdistan, and partly to continue his work of finding out what had really happened to the Assyrians during and after the events of the late summer. He wrote a graphic account of it all in a long, multipart, letter to Mary. He first describes how his chauffeur-servant Yussuf drove him in a car from Kirkuk, with 'two woolly Kurds' on board:

> After two hours we got to Erbil, which is built on a high rock in the middle of a big plain, walled all round. It is the oldest *inhabited* city in the world and was flourishing long before Rome or Athens were thought of. It is the modern Arbela where Alexander the great distinguished himself. We changed passengers here and while the car waited in the khan for the new ones, I walked up the cliff to the town proper, entered its massive gate and strolled through a maze of the narrowest streets I have ever known. Kurds in their outlandish dress everywhere and little Kurdish children with large ear-rings and old little faces and clothes down to their feet. Then we motored on after taking as passengers 3 of the fiercest and most disreputable Kurds I have ever seen: yellow teeth, bloodshot eyes, big knives in their sashes, and rifles. To ingratiate myself I offered them cigarettes continually, which they eagerly accepted.

Gradually the scenery 'got less and less like Iraq, and more green and beautiful'. They gradually climbed

> up the very twisty 'garden-path' road; in the distance snowy mountains appeared. Then we got to a lovely village in a big valley where Mar Yussuf, the Metropolitan of the Assyrians (second in command to Mar Shimun) lives. They told me he had gone for a walk so I went to meet him, and presently I saw a tall white figure coming towards me. He looked most apostolic and beautiful in his coarse white cassock & green Assyrian turban, with his tranquil expression, brown eyes and full black beard. He took me to his 'palace', a small neat little farm house and we had coffee and a long talk. He gave me a bunch of flowers from his very English-looking garden when I left. He took me into his tiny church where a big crowd of children and men had assembled and showed me some of the old Syriac service-books and one new ms. one by his own hand. It was a delightful half hour and I am quite unable in words to convey the charm

of it or of the Metropolitan. I shall never forget the sight of him as he walked back from my car to the church. I don't know why it moved me so, and I wanted to cry and laugh all at once.

They continued climbing until they reached the spectacular Rowanduz gorge:

a magnificent spectacle finer than anything of its kind I have ever seen; great perpendicular rocks towering up with quite a narrow passage between and down below a rushing stream. ... Suddenly we overtook a herd of about 20 camels, untended and unharnessed. They began to trot stupidly down the road ahead of us, then they began to canter and then to gallop. They looked unutterably absurd and I thought my Kurdish fellow travellers would die of laughter. ... Just as we got to the top of the gorge we met an immense tribe of Kurds on trek coming in the opposite direction. ... They had with them all their flocks and herds – cows, donkeys, goats. All the animals had panniers filled with household goods and covered with brilliant coloured carpets. Even the bullocks carried panniers, which looked extremely comic. There was enormous confusion, the animals were terrified of our car and herded towards the edge of the ravine; the men and woman shouted and lunged at them with their shepherd crooks; little boys and girls laughed and yelled or struggled with refractory beasts. ... Finally in the dusk we reached Diana. The Consulate is a rough long low building of mud and wood, rather attractive. It was very nice seeing Jack, very proud and happy in his little kingdom. Huge wood fires (one in my bedroom), oil lamps, a marvellous hot bath in a zinc tub, much pleasant talking and joking.

Some years later Colin referred to this transhumance of the Kurdish tribe in a sermon, to bring before the minds of the congregation the kind of thing involved in the journey of Abraham and Lot from Haran to Canaan mentioned in Genesis. 'Apart from the fact that some of the men had modern rifles there was practically no external difference between the two lots of migrating people.'

The letter is continued next day from Mosul. In the morning Jack and he had gone to a service at the church in Diana, about which he wrote an article for *The Guardian*. While they were there an important group of Assyrians came to pay their respects to the new Consul, but some local police, who had been keeping them under observation, mistakenly thought they had come to see Colin. This was why his correspondence with people in England became liable to be censored. Some time later, when Colin realised what had really been happening he withdrew the article in case it should compromise his friend, and no copy seems to have survived. But – to return to the letter to Mary – it goes on to tell us that when he and Yussuf drove back to Mosul, 'the Kurdish nomads were *still* going through.' He stopped shortly to see Mar Yussuf again, and further on visited a Syrian monastery of great age and much interest and beauty.

I was given ceremonial coffee by the monks and we crawled along an underground passage, stooping, and saw the grave of the saint in whose honour the monastery is built. He is called Mar Behnam and he was a chieftain's son who was martyred under the Sassanian kings.

Since reaching Mosul, he continues,

I have seen some of the sufferings of our friends. It is pitiful and terrible. They are so good to each other. I am seriously thinking of giving no Christmas presents and of giving the money to the needs of the people here. Or at any rate, very small presents. I must try and persuade some Baghdad people to give too. ... Tomorrow I go up to the neighbourhood of Glencoe where I am going to stay with one of the American missionaries. This morning I baptised a little baby after Mass, and this evening we have evensong. I wish I were fit to preach to these people. How humbling it is to be brought face to face with poverty, destitution and the fear of persecution. 'We are like dogs, running from butcher's to butcher's in search of scraps, driven away from each with a kick and a curse' – so one of the priests said to me.

The next part of the letter is dated from Dohuk, where Roger Cumberland and his wife, the American Missionaries, lived. The 'pouring rain and howling wind' meant that they could not reach Glencoe (their code name for Simel) in the available time. Instead, they 'walked round (Dohuk) in the mud and rain and (saw) something of its life':

A queer mixture of people make up its 3000 inhabitants: Kurds, Assyrians, Armenians, Jews, Turcomans. Little cottages of stone or mud brick. A mosque with one low minaret. All built on a series of abrupt hillocks; precipitous little streets, half-cobbled, half mud. Looked very uncomfortable in the damp raw evening.

They called on a weaver of the material the picturesque Kurdish trousers are made of. Other men also also dropped in, and talked to the missionary sitting on their haunches, while Roger Cumberland replied fluently in Kurdish.

We strolled on and the village butcher, a Turcoman, invited us into his house for a talk. A fine looking man with nice gay eyes and a generous expression. His unveiled wife moved silently about her domestic work in the background. He said he felt moved to ask C a question. He is a Moslem and he said that he had been told that according to the Koran a butcher might kill two or three thousand sheep legally, but after that it became a sin. What did C's religion say? C said that according to Christianity if it was not a sin to do it once, no additional number of times could make any difference. He thanked him. Then we called on an influential Kurdish Agha (a sort of squire). We sat in a freezing semi-westernised house and talked. Good coffee and cigarettes.

Back at the Cumberlands' house. they spent the early evening listening to the gramophone, and then Colin sang to Mrs Cumberland's accompaniment.

He had nothing but praise for his host and hostess, and added, 'Mrs C has a vague look of you about her, though it is you with you left out, if you understand me.' Later, Colin drove the thirty-odd miles back to Mosul. His last day in the north was spent in matters relating to the Assyrians. 'In a few minutes', he wrote next day,

> I am going to see the Refugee Camp here and then I want to visit a number of Assyrian houses so as to see the conditions under which they are living. I have found an ally and friend in the British Consul here who fully shares my opinion and fears. He can't do much himself as he is hampered by his official position.
> Tomorrow I leave Mosul in a car at 4 am and am going right through to Baghdad – a long and boring journey. When I get there I shall almost certainly find two letters from you which will fill me with joy. Good bye my beloved dear. I am all yours, Your undeserving and ardent lover.

In 1934, while Colin and Evelyn were both living with William Allard, they made several sight-seeing trips in Allard's car. The first was a New Year's Day trip to the remains of a gigantic ziggurat called the Akerkuf and the Shia Holy City of Khadimaim. A month later they all hired a car to visit Samarra, the fifth holy Shia city, 'where the last of the twelve Imams (reputedly sinless and infallible teachers of the faithful) disappeared' and will 'one day reappear in might and put the world straight'. Unlike Khadimaim Colin found this mosque really beautiful. Outside the walled city they saw the remains of an eleventh century mosque, with a 'half-minaret, half-ziggurat', which they climbed by an ascending spiral slope with no retaining wall. The view from the top was wonderful:

> To the South, Samarra, compact and satisfying in its city wall, dominated by its golden mother. To the West the Tigris straying leisurely and easily over the countryside as far as the eye could reach. And to the North a flattish space full of old ruins for 20 miles ... where one of the later Abassid Caliphs built his new capital. ... Far to the North East is the great mound where the Emperor Julian is supposed to be buried.

But the hair-raising descent to solid ground with a strong wind blowing was no joke!

The next trip was to Kerbela, another Shia Holy City and the totally isolated and 'mysterious Castle of Uchaidr' about which nothing was known in 1934, though It is now praised as a fine example of Abbasid architecture. Then on to a lovely oasis – 'a little village and lots of palm trees and two deep sulphur springs, bright blue. All the inhabitants came out to look at us'. After returning for the night to Kerbela they went south to Nejaf,

> the Rome of the Shiahs, a town of fanaticism, intrigue and every known vice and probably also some of the heights of real religious devotion. ... We passed Babylon and Birs Nimrud and came after 2 hours to Kifl, a charming little Euphrates village where Ezekiel is supposed to be buried. We were conducted

to the mosque, a rare privilege in this country, by about 30 Arabs and shown the tomb. ... The mosque was quaint and beautiful and had fascinating little floral designs painted on the walls. There are Hebrew inscriptions too, for the Jews have certain rights in the mosque.

They crossed the Euphrates at Kufa,

a town of most terrible and poignant associations for the Shiahs, for there Ali, the Prophet's nephew, was murdered while at prayer in the great mosque – the event which started the Shiahs in their schism from the Sunnis.

Then they went on to Nejaf, which stood

within gaunt mud walls and unlike any other town in the South, upon a slight hill. It is surrounded with endless cemeteries and corpses brought here from India and Persia so as to be buried near the tomb of Ali in the great golden shrine; a shrine which possesses a treasury of absolutely fabulous value.

Here they got a police escort, but no-one expressed any hostility that day. 'We walked through the bazaar, all dim and gloomy, till suddenly the brilliant tiled gateway of Ali's shrine burst upon us with its sunlit court beyond.' Colin was deeply thrilled. Evelyn's diary has the detail that, when leaving the town again, they met car after car laden with coffins projecting on either side, and all driving at breakneck speed towards them.

In April they went to Mosul, from where they made two thrilling expeditions. On the first their route took them past the 'lovely little mound-village of Nebi Yunis where Jonah is buried (!)', to visit the remote mountain shrine of Sheikh Adi, 'the Mecca of the Yezidis', popularly known as 'devil worshippers'. The road, 'a mere cart-track, led through lovely green fields of corn with lots of wild anemones and irises – bright red and blue – a sight for eyes sore with the flat brown landscapes round Baghdad', climbed gradually into the hills, amidst shrubs, trees and running water, to 'a real paradise on earth'. They were suddenly confronted with

the white fluted spires of the little nest of shrines, terraced stone buildings, with stone terraces and shady courtyards. ... Smiling men with thick black long bushy beards and white clothing met us with greetings of peace, smoking long wooden pipes. We took off our shoes and walked into the central shrine, an entirely dark church lit only with oil-dips. A clear spring bubbled up in a large stone basin inside. We walked cautiously and were shown the square tomb of Sheikh Adi. All extremely rude and primitive and bare, with no ecclesiastical arts and indeed not much 'religious' atmosphere. It was so homely. ... Impossible to believe that the devil had anything to do with the place. (Letter of 15/4/34)

On the second, Colin wrote to Mary from the goal of the expedition itself:

I am writing this in the school house of this amazing Chaldaean village, Al
Qosh, surrounded by boys and girls in the most ravishing and fantastic native
dresses and turbans. ... This is the native town of the prophet Nahum (the El-
Kosh-ite)... and a more fascinating place it would be hard to imagine. We have
just visited the monastery of Rabban Hormuzd – high up in the rocks on the
edge of a fantastic precipice. We had an amazing lunch of chicken, rice, honey
and lettuce with red wine and sour curds. We were waited on by the prior who
said that in the Gospel Christ said 'Let him that is chief be as him that doth
serve' – so what else did we expect him to do? They were almost massacred last
summer – we felt unfit to lick their boots. (Letter of 12/4/34)

In May Colin and Evelyn took a fortnight's trip to Iran (formerly Persia).
They went by train to Khanaqin on the frontier, about 100 miles NE of
Baghdad, where they were met by a Persian driver, who stayed with them until
their return to the frontier. They had planned to go to Isfahan, but, in the event
there was so much rain in south-west Persia that a crucial bridge had been
washed away and they could not get there. Instead they went via Teheran and
the Elburz mountains to the Caspian coast.

The first part of their journey had been rather depressing. All the towns, let
alone the villages, were deep in mud, and the people seemed desperately poor,
with a great number of hideously mutilated men. The squalor was increased by
the recently promulgated law, according to which all men had to wear western
dress, which Colin found produced 'universal seediness'. On the other hand,
Teheran, he felt, had been far more successful in westernising itself than
Baghdad, however dull it was as a place to visit. But the country beyond the
Elburz was a different matter. He was much struck with the beauty of the local
style of house building: Tudor-style brickwork, with great overhanging eaves
and balconies.

The country was lovely, especially near the Caspian. A warm spring
replaced the wintry weather they had at first experienced (many telegraph poles
were even sprouting!). There was also a very strong Russian cultural influence;
some people in the region could only speak Russian. One evening he was
entranced in his hotel room by the singing, from the next balcony, of two
Russian women, who, it seemed to him, were mourning for their lost
homeland, whose border was about 100 miles off. They both much enjoyed the
local caviar and pale wine. Evelyn returned to England at the end of June, in
order to prepare for another spell of teaching in Sweden.

Colin's appointment at Baghdad had initially been for two years. When he
heard that the first St George's Church in Baghdad, the old Turkish guard
house which he loved but was leased from the city authorities, was going to be
demolished for road-widening during his time there, and a replacement paid for
by the British, he thought it would be right for him to stay on for another year
to oversee the planning and building of the new church, which would be a
memorial to the troops who had died to make the new state possible. But the
events of summer 1933 and their repercussions meant that the Ambassador,
who had gone to England partly to start the business of fund-raising with an

approach to the King, became very heavily engaged in discussing the political crisis in Iraq, and returned without having opened the fund-raising campaign. So Colin reverted to his original idea to go home after his two years were up, and began to consider what he might do.

When the Vicar of St Mary's, Primrose Hill, became very ill in June 1934, it was soon clear that the Trustees of the living would be looking about for a replacement and that he might well be approached. In his letters to Mary he puts forward the pros and cons of accepting the incumbency if it were offered, and decides against it, which Mary completely agreed with. Then he heard that a group of parishioners had sent the Trustees of the living a petition in his favour, so felt bound to write to them himself, telling them that, if he were offered it, he would have to refuse, and suggesting some other names. When he and Evelyn got back from Persia, however, he found waiting for him a letter from 'Bones' (his and Mary's nickname for George Bell), offering him the living of St Thomas's, Davigdor Road, Hove, and adding that D-J and both the Bishop and Archdeacon of Lewes 'agree that it is the place for me'.

After considering the matter and asking Mary to wire either Yes or No (it was Yes), he accepted the offer. He would be starting in November, and his letters became full of instructions and suggestions relating to their future residence in the vicarage.

The series of almost 100 letters Colin wrote to Mary from the Middle East contain a great deal of 'lovey-dovey talk', some remarkably frank, almost always with some remark about his own unworthiness of her, and his fear that one day she will see through him. But another side is revealed in this correspondence – the desire to exercise some control over Mary's own life. There is, for instance, the desire to get them both into the routine of weekly letters (barring occasions when writing was impossible), and of carefully dating each letter. Much irritation gets expressed at breaches of this general rule. There is also a kind of anxious concern that Mary should link up with the people he knew well at Oxford (especially clergy and dons), to get their help with particular difficulties, or simply to gain the advantages of being drawn into their circle. But in other letters he freely admits his faults, especially his irritation, and reminds himself (and her) that calmness 'can only be learned in the Spirit of the Collect for Ascension Day, 'heavenly-mindedness' ('with Him continually dwell').

The letters he wrote arising out of Evelyn's visit are also very revealing. Mary had suggested, as a result of the Cyprus trip, that Colin tended to treat his sister 'as a kind of slave'; Colin admits this, ruefully adding: 'she brings the worst out of me'. Later he tells Mary that he will miss Evelyn terribly, using Sibyl's name for her, 'Bloody Pussy', but confesses that 'something prevents me ever *saying* such a thing to her, though I could write it'.

After a week or two more he says he is depressed at her absence, and this brings out again his general sense of inadequacy as a pastor. 'Just at the moment', he writes, the 'conventionality' of most of his flock 'grates on me terribly' and he resents their finding 'no use for me and the church. ... very petty and wrong. After all, that's what parsons are for – because people don't want the church'. 'But nervously I feel resentment and inferiority complex badly.' Of course, he goes on, most of the people who come to church are good friends, but a lot of them are on leave. The most friendly (and regular) of his congregation are the senior Army and Air Force officers, but, as for 'the young bachelors in the Oil Companies and the Banks, they don't seem to be approachable. I find myself hopelessly self conscious in their company'. He's also having difficulties in the matter of helping Assyrians in distress, and distinguishing between 'genuine and fakes. ... One of the priests has been turned out of his house: I fear he is a rogue. Still it is nice to have money to help here and there.'

Colin's final expedition to the north of Iraq came in July 1934. Jack Finch was now 'doing duty for the summer' in Mosul. Unfortunately, Colin had an attack of tonsillitis there so spent much of his break in bed at the consulate in the baking heat, instead of being in the cool of the mountains near Amadia. When he was well enough, he and Jack went up to the rather primitive rest-house at Sulaf. The last part of the trip was on foot or by mule, since the road was not yet drivable. On the way they called at Simel (alias Glencoe), the site of the worst Assyrian massacre. Colin was amazed at how 'public' the place was, being next to a main road. His photograph of the village was published in *The Guardian* on 3 August. He drove home from Mosul in eight and a half hours, starting at 2.30am and arriving at Baghdad in a dust storm at 11.00. He told Mary that he had been extremely 'nervous of a hold-up', but had dreaded the heat of a later start even more. Around that time the temperature was often at 110 degrees fahrenheit and quite often higher. However, he writes elsewhere, he found the great heat much easier to bear in general than he had expected.

He returned to England in a ship from Port Said, after staying four nights with the Reeds in Jerusalem. He had a good voyage back in the very comfortable P&O liner *Strathnaver*, which took him to Marseille after five nights aboard. From there he went on by train to Lyon, where he spent two days in research into the Lyon Rite, as he was preparing a book on Liturgical changes in seventeenth- and eighteenth-century France (hence the desire to advance his knowledge of French and several requests to Mary to buy for him and send out various background historical works). After a couple of nights in Paris he arrived at Oxford on 17 October. He tells Mary in advance about people he knows well and will try to see there, asking her which of them she would like to see herself. The list reads: 'Thomas [Norrington]; Head of S Stephens House (he *wants* to meet you); Professor Kirk (ditto); R.H. Dundas (senior Censor at the House); M. Bowra (don at Wadham); The Livingstones; Pusey House crowd; A.S. Owen (don at Keble); Tom Armstrong; Bob Meade'. And of course there would be her friends too.

Colin's two years in Baghdad had been an undoubted success. The Archbishop thanked him for them and wrote (3/8/34):

I know from many sources how greatly valued your services have been. I myself have much reason to be grateful to you for the very full and careful reports you have sent to me from time to time about these poor Assyrians, and I am thankful that you were on the spot during the recent painful occurrences.

His successor at St George's, Mr Fortescue-Thomas, incurred some resentment there by his outspokenness and keenness on 'ritual'. It was found very difficult to find a successor to him, and he himself protested, somewhat naively, to the Archbishop's chaplain (15/7/36):

The colour of (the chaplain's) churchmanship doesn't matter in the least. Both Smith and Dunlop were definite Anglo-Catholics, but they were immensely popular and successful, and people all attribute the making of this Chaplaincy to them.

Eventually the Church Council insisted that they themselves be consulted in all future appointments.

Colin's own assessment of his time in Baghdad is, as we might expect, rather self deprecating. But his appreciation of what he has gained and what he will especially miss is worth repeating. In a letter to Ida (30/8/34) he writes that he will very much miss:

The continual contact with people in positions of great responsibility, the opportunities of observing how a country's affairs are run, friendships with local Christian clergy, mixing with Army and Air Force officers, foreign diplomats etc. You know it's nothing snobbish in me, but one will miss it for much more satisfactory reasons. I feel I have made a poor use of my opportunities and responsibilities though. I hope I shall do better at Hove. The community here lives in great difficulties of a spiritual and mental kind. Its priest ought to be a big man and a holy man. I *think* I've done my best — at any rate most of the time.

He also tells Mary on 26/8/34 that he will very much miss writing his weekly *Statesman* articles, and of course we know from the samples I have given above how much there was to interest him in Iraq itself and its endless variety of peoples and cultures. Elsewhere he writes that his time in the Baghdad Chaplaincy has given him more courage and assurance. But the greatest thing of all for him must have been that he would now have much closer contact with his bride-to-be, even though he and Mary could not marry until she had completed her four years at Oxford.

11

HOVE

IN A LETTER from Baghdad to Mary of 5 April 1934, Colin had written: 'There is a living shortly to be vacant in Hove which, humanly speaking, I would love to be offered.'

> It is in the Bishop's gift, but I feel it is so wrong to take *any* steps to get a particular living offered that I could not write to ask him for it or suggest anyone else asking him for me. The church is beautiful and run on St Mary's lines in both music and ceremony and general ethos. ... It has in addition a small modern labour-saving vicarage – just the thing for us. I am very near breaking the 10th commandment [against covetousness], but I have not *yet* broken it, even in spirit.

Then came Bishop Bell's offer of the living, as recorded in the last chapter, with its inducement that other dignitaries in the diocese thought it the very place for him. Colin tells Mary about it in his letter of 2 June, adding that a curate would also be provided, and, after asking her to get Ida to go with her to spy out the land, adds 'the services are a little more Anglo-Catholic than I have been accustomed to, but I don't think I would have to alter anything on conscientious grounds'. This and subsequent letters do seem to me to show that Colin was not *completely* convinced that St Thomas the Apostle, Davigdor Road, was the place for him. The same letter continues:

> The good news of the parish is however terribly damaged by the news of Gussy's [Gustav Holst's] death. It is a really grievous loss to us, let alone the world; I feel he was so much bound up with us and our happiness and even helped us to be more in love than ever. I can never think of our becoming engaged without thinking of him and his happiness and help about it all. ... He was a wonderful example of how possible it is to be really saintly and really nice at once; one of those who can see God because they are pure in heart.

Colin's reservations about St Thomas's take more concrete form in his letter of 7 July:

> I have had a Parish Magazine from St Thomas's. I am rather appalled by the fact that there is a series of Stations of the Cross on the walls. I always think that series overweighs the devotional balance of a church in its relentless

181

emphasis on Our Lord's physical sufferings, and it ends with death and not Resurrection. ... Also they call the Vicar 'Father' which I don't like very much. ... But worst of all there is a troop of 'Sea' Rangers who are 'affiliated' to a battleship and seem to have some connection with the Navy League. What *are* we to do? Also some of the music they do seems to me quite dreadful, though much is lovely.

When he reverted to St Thomas's again on 25 July Mary had told him of her visit to the parish with Ida. He was glad to hear that 'the colour of the unfortunate "Stations" (was) all right ... and (didn't) clash with the general decorative effect'. Nevertheless he rather hoped the parish had never been granted a faculty for them, as he suspected, and that the Bishop might be able to order their removal as *permanent* ornaments. Colin also expressed his agreement with Mary in disliking the Mothers' Union. However, he added, we must try at least to 'steer it on to right lines' if it is of genuine pastoral value, but 'certainly try a branch of L.N.U. or at least in some way get people to feel a responsibility for peace'. This letter is also full of comments, suggestions and reactions to Mary's ideas about furnishing and decorating the vicarage.

On 9 August he wrote that he had turned down Mr Miles's suggestion that he write regularly now for the Parish Magazine. He had in fact had many letters from Mr Miles, who was a prominent member of the congregation and a journalist by profession. It was he who had written the long and extremely commendatory article announcing Colin's appointment to St Thomas's in the *Sussex Daily News* of 16 June, which Colin had told Mary he found rather 'comic'. He also told Colin later that he and his wife had 'yelled' with delight when it was known who was to be their next vicar, since they already knew him a little as George Bell's chaplain and as a special Lenten preacher at St Thomas's. Colin's letter to Mary of 6 September contained the following paragraph:

I got St Thomas's magazine for September – sent by the faithful Mr Miles. You know, darling, the more I read and hear about the parish the more I realise how great our task there will be. It becomes evident that the people there are – in the light of nature only – not at all our sort, either culturally or ecclesiastically. We shall have to be very humble and very persistent in studying the people and understanding them and in transforming prejudice into sympathy. So many of our ideas and aims and ways of looking at things and emotional reactions will seem to the Thomasites most perverse and we shall have to be very tender and gentle. At least that's how it seems to me. Of course one always has to do that in any pastoral work, but the task at St Thomas's appears to be bigger in this respect than I thought. I cannot avoid the impression that at any rate the nucleus of the parish is one that likes to think of its vicar as 'the dear vicar' and all that goes with that. ... It seems rather a drawing room of a parish, don't you think? So we have a big task ahead of us. I am so looking forward to my retreat and feel so much will be given to me then. I do need an immense quantity of grace for this new work.

Mary had clearly been very worried about the music at St Thomas's, so, in a later letter, he is able to assure her that 'they still do have good music, but they mix it with bad ... that's all.' What really worries Colin is 'the starchily conventional "Catholic" clichés and habits which have risen up'.

A few days before his induction, much refreshed by his retreat, which was conducted by Fr Bede Frost at Freeland in Oxfordshire, he told Mary that he had gone over to Hove, seen the church and 'met the churchwardens at tea with the Miles.' He liked them very much and felt that both wardens were 'solid British, really grounded in Christianity' and 'that I can trust them both'.

> I believe we shall get on and have their support in the important things. The congregation seems to consist principally of unmarried middle-aged ladies at present of a rather hot-housey ecclesiastical type; very few men and young people. But the parish outside is full of them so there is a great work to be done.

He goes on to say that he was 'tackled about the Confraternity of the Blessed Sacrament, a very Roman guild. I don't think I *can* join it', since the Mass should unify the parish, not foster 'little societies and groups'. But he feels much more optimistic now and 'itch(es) to get into the houses of those who don't yet come to church'. He has now been to the temporary digs arranged by Mr Miles, and finds them satisfactory, but is putting off his visit to the vicarage until he can share the occasion with Mary.

Colin was overwhelmed by the induction service, so much so that, after it, he even forgot to kiss Mary goodbye when she left to return to Oxford. Next day he wrote to apologise for the powerful distraction that brought this about:

> Till I actually had to be inducted last night I never realised how wonderful a ceremony it is, though I have been professionally present at literally hundreds. And Bones really did give me a send-off, didn't he?

This 'send-off' included the words:

> I had the great happiness of having Colin Dunlop with me as my chaplain for a well- and ever-remembered three years. He was more than a friend, more than a chaplain. He comes to the parish and the congregation of St Thomas's as a vicar of quite unusual experience and gifts – music, art and human understanding. These gifts he offers to God for the service of the Church in your parish.

Colin's letter continues:

> It was specially valuable for I know how carefully he weighs his words (tho' I am not sure what 'more than a chaplain' means!). But I could hardly bear the beauty of the hymn 'The Church of God a kingdom is' – especially the part: 'There pure life-giving streams o'erflow / The Sower's garden-ground' – words which even on ordinary occasions thrill me beyond description almost. ... I can still hardly believe that I am really the vicar. It all seems to have happened

without one noticing it 'as dew in April / that falleth on the grass' – like all great changes.

Next morning he said Mass at the Lady Altar, over which there was 'a lovely statue of our Lady'. 'Dear Mr Miles served. I was furnished with a rigmarole of a missal from which with difficulty I extracted the Prayer Book service.' On examining the vestments he found that:

> some were really lovely – especially the black ones. None are bad. The verger is delightful – he seems a really religious man as well as a good worker. Quite young.

Two days later he wrote in a very brief letter:

> I do agree about the really fine desire of the people here to co-operate and the openly expressed wish not to be afraid of change. ... God bless them for it and you for helping me to realise it more clearly.

After his first Sunday, 'a very happy but tiring day' he wrote:

> I celebrated at 7 and 8 and was deacon at 11 [that is, someone else took the main part in the celebration] and preached. Children at 3 (just like S. Mary's only with far fewer). Solemn Evensong and 39 Articles at 6.30. ... The Mass ceremonies are not what I'm used to and very fussy but I liked the service very much and I felt a pleasant rapport with the people when I preached.

He had been warned by Mr Miles that the children at Catechism were 'unmanageable', but found them

> as docile as lambs and I'm no disciplinarian. I *loved* reading the 39 articles and found I agreed with nearly all of them. ... I love their style; phrases like 'as is blasphemously asserted'. The servers seem very nice; except one whom after 10 minutes I found insufferable. I have abolished the Angelus after Sung Mass (tho' the bell rings it) and restored the Prayer Book rite. One of the ultra-pious women who I thought would disapprove of me most thanked me, almost with tears in her eyes, for reading the Epistle facing the people instead of with my back to them. It's going to be uphill work but well worth while.

To his astonishment he also found that smoking was allowed in the vestry, and quickly put a stop to it.

A few days before Colin's induction, a new incumbent of Holy Trinity, Brighton, had also been inducted to take the place of Colin's friend Horace Fort, who was now temporarily out of a job 'and living rather uncomfortably in an old lady's house near here' with his Swedish wife, Stanny, and their baby. So he began his letter of 16 November by asking Mary whether she would object to letting them live for a few months in St Thomas's vicarage, with himself as their lodger. The Forts' own furniture would fill all but the two rooms he needed for himself, and they would be good company for Colin, who could talk over parish problems with them. When they left, there would still be plenty of time to have the house decorated before they moved in as man and wife in late July. It would also mean that Mary would be able to come and stay at the vicarage adequately chaperoned. Mary agreed that this would be an excellent idea.

The same letter also tells Mary about the busy day he had just had in London. He first saw the Bishop in Jerusalem who wanted him to be on the Council of the Jerusalem and the East Mission. Then there was a committee meeting of the Alcuin Club, at which Colin undertook to produce a Leaflet on Processions (a practical distillation of his tract), and agreed to help the architect Mr Cachemaille-Day produce another on Altars. The Club minutes also record that 'a skeleton of a leaflet on 'What is English Use?' has also been prepared, but pressure of work in the parish seems to have made him unable to finish it. After the meeting he had lunch with Dean Dwelly, of Liverpool, 'who wanted me to come up to Liverpool to harangue the great business magnates on the Assyrians and also preach about them. It's *so* tempting but I felt bound to refuse.' He continues:

Saw Bishop of Gloucester [Headlam] about Assyrians. Apparently Mar Shimun wants me to be sent out to Iraq as a special Commissioner for the Assyrians! It is so interesting to find how all these people – Bishops and others – are now treating me almost as a person of consequence!

Lastly, he dined with Jack Arnold at Victoria [Station], after buying copies of Martin Shaw's Folk Mass which he planned to start (Creed only at first) in Advent with a congregational choir practice. 'Everything is moving, darling.' The letter ends with his reaction to Mary's hope that he will accompany her to 'the Ball' at the Dorchester. He confesses that the prospect would terrify him, as he has 'an innate dislike of dancing in parsons' clothes'. All eyes would be turned on him which would make him miserable. But he'd love to go incognito with her to 'a common or garden Palais de Dance' some time in the Christmas vacation. 'Do let's', he says, and repeats it.

Next week he had to go to Town again, this time for the Archbishop's Council for Foreign Relations, where he much enjoyed the meeting of the Lesser Eastern Churches subcommittee:

I sat next to Lord Hugh [Cecil] and Noel Buxton was opposite. I talked a lot – about the Assyrians – and Lord Hugh said he thought I must go and talk to the Foreign Office. So I am arranging to go and see George Rendel on 4th December if possible. I had tea with Mar Shimun at the Athenaeum after.

In the event he returned to London on 5 December, when he saw and briefed his successor at Baghdad before his meeting with George Rendel at the Foreign Office, where he 'told him about the great decline in British moral prestige in the Middle East because of the Assyrian business'. He also took the chance of seeing Jack Ward, who was on the staff of the Baghdad embassy, and asked them both to lunch with him the following Wednesday. 'I said I would ask you.' After lunching with Gilbert Laithwaite he attended the Alcuin Club AGM 'at which I made a truculent fighting speech which was loudly applauded', though he doesn't say exactly what it was about. Then he dined with D-J and travelled back to Hove. He adds that his lecture on the Assyrians at the Teachers' Training College – his 'first lecture' – went well, with sensible questions from the floor afterwards.

Colin's Congregational practice of the Folk Mass Creed had produced a much better response than he had hoped, and the following Sunday they sang it as part of the service:

> The people are thrilled, not merely at being able to sing, but at being encouraged. It appears that this is something quite new to them. I have also started communicating at the Sung Mass those who can't fast. But it's slow work getting round to know the people. It's difficult to visit more than 4 or 5 a day – sometimes not as much. But I am very encouraged everywhere.

One sign of this comes in a letter to Ida of 21 December, in which he tells her (despite 'deprecating the numbers game') that three times as many people had attended the Patronal Festival service, when D-J preached, than in the previous year.

Colin's letters from Hove are a lot shorter than those from Baghdad. In one of his December letters he excuses himself for this by the fact that he really is 'up to the eyes' in work, as will probably be already apparent to the reader who has taken in all the activities I have mentioned in the last few pages. Somehow it came to the Bishop's ears that he had been overdoing it, and Mary wrote to Ida on 3 February 1935, with the news that 'he has been to a doctor on the Bp's request and is ordered away for a 3 weeks holiday'. Sibyl and he would be going to the hydro at Falmouth for the water cure. It is not clear whether Colin had simply made a mistake about the provision of a curate, or whether there were no curates available, but the fact is, he never did get the help of one at Hove – though there were plenty of clergy there and in Brighton who were able to provide occasional help with taking services. Naturally this worried Mary a lot, and she told Ida in her letter of 11 February that she had been to see him

> because he seemed so dreadfully miserable when I rang up. ... His looks appalled me somewhat, and I feel a bit doubtful as to whether 17 days is really enough – but he is at the moment full of the idea that he *must* be back for Ash Wednesday. ... It is so heartrending to see how he looks when he is worn out. He looks like a very small pinched little child, with dreadful hollow eyes and wrinkled skin all round them like someone who hasn't slept for weeks. I feel full of rage at the bloody Parish for taking it out of him so.

Six days later Mary was able to tell Ida that she had had two 'pretty cheerful' cards from Colin and Sibyl. It had been very sunny in Falmouth had and Colin was 'lapping up Cornish cream'. He was able to stay at St Stephen's House and see Mary again when he passed through Oxford on his way home. He had been rather 'unhappy in his mind' at Falmouth, Mary wrote after a few days, though when she saw him he was 'mentally better but not much so physically – he lunched with the Murrays and Wade-Gearys, and had tea with Robin Collingwood where he discussed his troubles'.

The next glimpse of his progress comes in the PCC minutes for 15 March. They record that Colin 'suggested the formation of a Missionary Committee to look into the objects of the church's charities now and to advise on the future proportion between Home and Foreign missions'. He also proposed 'the removal of 'the old and faded hanging on the screen behind the altar' and at present to leave the plaster wall bare', and 'announced that he had bought 'a verger's gown and verge' from a fund for vestments, etc, handed on by the late vicar'. On the liturgical front he proposed a 'Liturgical Three Hours' on Good Friday. This last was carried unanimously. But, although the parish finances were in not too bad a state, their overdraft was increasing, and various measures (not specified) were voted on to get more offerings from visitors.

When Mary next visited the parish, probably on Friday, 23 March, she found Colin much depressed again 'and looking dreadfully tired and jumpy'. Miss Crookenden had recently announced that 'she had reduced her subscription to St Thomas's because it no longer 'gave her all that she wanted' and that hence she had to go half the time elsewhere'. On the other hand – Mary's letter to Ida next day reveals – the Stations of the Cross were now covered up with 'beautiful Lenten hangings' and that the ceremonial is now simplified, which has shortened the service and 'made it all much more dignified'. In addition, Mary added, 'we've got rid of the Forts' two dreadful servants [the Forts themselves had now left the vicarage] and engaged Mrs Hodges, who is a charming character and seems awfully efficient and quite a decent cook'; she feels she will be able to go home without any worries on Colin's behalf. He did look better and was more cheerful now and had been much cheered by two little girls asking in the church 'Please Sir may we be Guides here?', and coming to church next morning. Mary herself slept at Miss Tatham's, who had been a worshipper at St Mary's, Primrose Hill, when Colin was there.

Next day, Sunday, she wrote to Ida again, telling her that Colin had had to be in church 'from 10 till 12.45, 3.0 to 4.15 and 6.30 to 7.30', but they did manage to walk to St Anne's Well Gardens and enjoy sitting in the sun from 1.30 to 2.45. But Monday was a *most* enjoyable day. It was the Feast of the Annunciation, so there was a sung service at 11.00, and because very few of the choir were able to be there and Mr Gardner was celebrating, she and Colin sang in the choir. 'Then he went out and visited a man and I did a spot of work.' Then came 'the grand excitement of the day: Our CAR'. They had a brief run about in it with the man who delivered it before returning to lunch ('Definitely quite a nice meal'). Then we drove to a Tutorial Class on the Holy Eucharist which Colin had taken over from Horace Fort – it was 'really most interesting'. 'Colin was awfully good, I thought.' Then they picked up the Forts in the car 'and drove to the top of the Devil's Dyke for a farewell tea with them ... Between that and dinner C sandwiched in another visit'!

Afterwards came a visit to the Pavilion for a meeting of the WIL [Women's International League for Peace and Freedom] on the international situation. Colin had been asked to sit on the platform, and Mary was allowed to as well. Mrs Corbett-Ashby made a most excellent speech and Colin proposed a vote of thanks. 'He did it beautifully and I was so proud to hear one C of E clergyman speaking impromptu in public who was neither "unctimonious" nor "facetious!". I was introduced to the Head Mistress of Roedean, who was in the chair. Finally we were able to drive Mrs C-A to the station in time for her train.' Back at the vicarage (which they were now calling 'Didymus') she made Colin a hot drink while he proofread the Parish Magazine! 'And I believe this is not one of his heaviest days!'

> But it does make such a difference all having been so successful and enjoyable. He looked very tired when I left him to go to bed – but not at all worn or dreary – far, far better than when I arrived. He really *needs* to be frightfully overworked in the sense of having too much to do in order to be happy. The thing is for the things to be things which seem worth doing and which he can do well (especially things which we can do together). I have seldom enjoyed a day more – and I do really feel that there is much work here which we shall be able to do together. We have a plan for reading right through S Thomas Aquinas's *Summa contra Gentiles* together – I supplying the philosophical and Colin the historical and ecclesiastical background.

Mary ends her letter by saying that, as it's now after 11 she must get back to Miss Tatham's and sleep; her hostess is so lonely that even having a guest who is out *all* day seems to give her real pleasure: she feels so sorry for her.

Colin's Cuttings Book, which, as we would expect, roughly follows the order of the publication of the items cut out, contains around this point a short passage in Colin's handwriting which long puzzled me. But it clearly reflects what must have been on his mind sometimes in these early Hove days, and I quote it in full:

> Dean Randall used to teach me in his study. I went through the epistles with him. Once he made me kneel down and he placed his hands on my head and said some prayers: and then he said he had consecrated me to carry on his work. I have never told anyone before of this, but I tell you because whenever I have thought to give up and enjoy life: and I could have had quite a different one: I have always somehow felt the feel of his hands and so kept on.

I tried for some time to trace a 'Dean Randall' who was someone who could have taught Colin regularly 'in his study', but in vain, and I have now been persuaded that he was quoting from a published work or a letter by or about some other person with whose position he felt a strong affinity. I think it very likely that Colin was recalling his own meetings with Bishop Charles Gore during the time when he lived in St Margaret's Street after retiring from the see of Oxford. Ida's Christmas present to Colin in 1934 was G.L.Prestige's brief memoir of him. In his thankyou letter Colin writes:

> you know how much he meant to me – his marvellous combination of orthodoxy and radicalism, holiness and approachableness, zeal for faith and zeal for works; rare combinations in one man, especially in so marked a degree of passion.

The *Chichester Diocesan Gazette* for May records (probably through the pen of Mr Miles) that the Liturgical Three Hours on Good Friday at St Thomas's had been a success, and that it 'was much appreciated by a congregation of much larger dimensions than ever before'. In the evening, the account adds, 'the children of the Catechism were given the opportunity of sharing, as their elders had done, in the pilgrimage to the foot of the Cross.' Colin also tells Mary in a letter that he is acting the part of Lovel the Minstrel in the Pageant of Sussex Saints, produced by Mrs Martin Shaw, and performed in late June in the grounds of the Bishop's Palace in Chichester, during which he sings a song about St Richard. His interesting account of the pageant in the *Church Times* says quite a lot about saints in general and the Sussex three in particular, but understandably passes over his own small contribution. Otherwise there is virtually nothing about Colin's work in the diocese between Good Friday and the begining of August, when he and Mary had returned to Hove as a married couple. So this is the place to say something about the wedding.

The wedding invitation card states where and when the marriage would take place (St Mary's Church, Primrose Hill, at 10 a.m. on Saturday, 27 July), but then pointedly adds: 'All their friends will be welcome at the church', adding the words 'Everyday Dress' and a useful sketch map indicating how to reach it. The service followed the 1928 order (in which there is no promise of the wife to *obey* her husband), and ended with Holy Communion (also 1928 order). The music for the service included anthems by Jane Joseph and Holst, and the Creed, Sanctus, Gloria, etc from Martin Shaw's *Folk Mass*, with Purcell's *Trumpet Tune* for the Wedding March. The *Sussex Daily News* printed an account of it, almost certainly by Mr Miles, from which we learn that 'a good number of members of the congregation of the Church of St-Thomas-the-Apostle, Hove, made the journey to London on Saturday and were present at the wedding', that the choir was made up of 'ladies and gentlemen' (i.e. not the regular SMVPH choir), and that D-J officiated at the marriage service and celebrated at the Nuptial Mass, and the Bishop of Chichester gave the Blessing, adding details of Colin's connection with them both. He also adds that the faux-bourdon of the Communion Hymn (*Tantum ergo*) was written by Geoffrey Shaw.

What Ida thought about the influx of people she didn't know from Sussex can be inferred from the letter Mary sent her on 24 March where her references to the wedding are clearly part of a long discussion between them. Ida had wanted the service to be 'entirely private and uncongregational', but, Mary wrote:

> Colin really does feel that (this) would be quite unreal. He agrees with me however that to make it a social function is not at all necessary and although he himself would not mind the seeing and talking to people, he quite understands that I should and how painful it would be for you. It is really the congregation of witnesses that he feels to be such an essential thing and that he can't bear to do without.

It is not absolutely clear why asking people back to the house would be so 'painful' to Ida (a naturally hospitable person) as to amount to 'torment', let alone why she thought (this is implied) that Colin would be 'selfish' to insist on the congregation of witnesses. She knew that he had been very *un*selfish in waiting so long to marry, and had several times written to this effect. Certainly there would be pain at the loss of Mary from her house, but that would be happening anyway. Perhaps there was a lingering feeling in her mind of a much earlier conception of marriage where the woman is 'delivered over' to the man, and didn't want Mary to become a spectacle. We know that she thought the legal position of wives was still demeaning, and many of her dearest friends were women who decided not to marry for this reason. There was also the question of who was to 'give' her in marriage, as the prayer book puts it. Mary herself told Ida that she was determined that Charles should not do this, presumably because in her eyes he had really given up a father's responsibilities, though she also told Ida that he could be invited a few days before the wedding to a private celebratory party at Steele's Road.

The first letter Mary wrote to Ida after the wedding is addressed from the Rose & Crown Hotel, Saffron Walden, and reads as follows:

> Darling. We came here in a leisurely way through Epping Forest and lovely quiet cornfields – quite country. At Bishop's Stortford we met a lot of bell-ringers in the Church and got invited up into the tower to see them doing some change ringing. So we had some wedding bells! This is a nice old inn and a fascinating market town. We watched cricket on the green after tea – so lovely and peaceful. Tomorrow we are going to Thaxted and then on a tour of cathedrals. Both rather tired but very very happy though not quite believing it has all really happened at last.

At Thaxted they spent some time with the vicar, Conrad Noel, whom Colin must have got to know at St Mary's, Primrose Hill, since he had been for some time closely connected to it. Mary, in her letter of 4 August calls him the 'Fanatic', and describes him as 'a wonderful old man like a mediaeval saint' and adds that 'he preached a beautiful sermon all about loving God in all things as well as above all things – which was mostly about being good to animals'. They had a sumptuous lunch with the Noels 'such as, Colin said, you couldn't get anywhere except in the house of a socialist'. They then went on to Ely for a night, where Mary described evensong as 'formal and dull', but loved the town and cathedral.

Next day they saw Peterborough and stayed the night in Stamford, another marvellous town but, being right on the Great North Road, 'the noisiest town I have ever been in, not excepting Florence and Puigcerda'. By the time they got to the White Hart in Lincoln, where they spent two nights and one lovely day of sight-seeing, Mary had heard that, against the expectations of quite a few in Oxford, she had only got a second class in 'Greats'. One wonders whether there was any connection between that result and the tiny little postcard she had sent dated 5 June: 'Sleeping well, eating well, knowing nothing but feeling quite cheerful'! At any rate she was now able to write: 'I feel quite content that all is as it should be', and to express her great happiness over her new status as Colin's husband.

From Lincoln they made their way south via Southwell Minster and Wellingboro', where they were enchanted by Ninian Comper's St Mary's. Mary describes to Ida the window dedicated to Florence Nightingale and Edith Cavell, containing 'in her half ... a darling little Flo' kneeling in a purple dress under the guardianship of a Virgin Saint with Sancta Florentia and the dates of her life'. They spent their last night at Windsor, where Colin knew the organist, Dr Harris, who got them 'seats of extreme distinction in the Garter stalls for the evening service'.

Colin's *Guardian* article: 'Worship in Cathedrals and Elsewhere: a traveller's observations' gives a series of short sketches of some of the services they had attended on their tour. The church at Thaxted comes in for much praise in its sympathetically de-Victorianised state, as does Conrad Noel's pastoral ministry, though the service for the Parish High Mass was 'a purely parochial one and not that of either 1662 or 1928'. The evensongs at Ely and Lincoln are discussed in some detail, but very much from the point of view of the spirit of worship they seemed to express (see the beginning of Chapter 16). The article ends with some general comments about public worship in large and important churches and the friendliness and welcome of their vergers.

Next day they drove down to Hove and were welcomed at a parish party with a cheque for '£45-odd'. They shook hands with all present, and then 'had to get up on a platform (where, Mary wrote) a small child presented me with an enormous bouquet of Pink Carnations as though I were the Duchess of York'. Mr Miles then gave a speech and Mary found that she:

> had made a *terrific* hit in this Parish by getting the *same* degree as the Bishops of both Chichester and London. ... It was all very funny and very embarrassing but I enjoyed it enormously because they all said such lovely things about Colin – and obviously care about him a lot and I think they are beginning to appreciate the sort of man they have got.

However, a week later Mary wrote (11 August) that Colin was 'pretty exhausted' – though it was certainly hot and exhausting weather. But she felt he did need a proper holiday. They had Honor staying with them and now were entertaining Jack Finch, whom Mary described as 'a little tiny man with neat hands and feet and a minute toothbrush moustache with a little pointed nose over it'– 'ridiculously appropriate' for someone with his name. 'He plays the piano well and sings the most absurd songs very very funnily. Most of the time he was here we were all giggling helplessly'. Mary had announced that she would be 'At Home' every Thursday for tea, and she told Ida that the first of these occasions went very well, despite her spilling a jug of milk on the carpet. 'However we all kept quite calm with excellent good breeding!' Two ladies present were 'veteran survivors of the Indian Mutiny', one, a Miss Reason, was really Low Church, but came because Horace Fort 'handed her on' to Colin, whom she regards as something like a saint in the making. She is humble enough not to think that anyone who differs from her must be wrong!

There was also a 'wonderful lively "common" huge, fat woman called Mrs Steer, who is like one of those comic postcards'. She is 'alive – which is more than can be said of the refined ones, some of them'. Mary ends by telling Ida that she has not heard anything more from two schools where she had clearly tried to get regular work or occasional lecturing, and that their excellent cook is leaving because she can't stay longer away from her family. This was the first of a great many 'servant crises' in their life together.

A week or so later Colin wrote to Ida telling her what a great hit Mary had made with the parishioners, who much appreciated the 'style' of her at-homes. 'I feel that the parish and I have got to understanding each other and to value each other'. 'Sundays are hard work, single-handed, and with an unabated succession of services', he added, 'but joy has come to me – quiet, deep and strong'. The same day Mary wrote to tell her what they were doing. There was a visit to Eastbourne for a gathering of mostly young Sunday-school teachers, where Colin gave a talk about Baghdad.

The next day they drove west to lunch with Basil Henriques, a Liberal Jew and friend of Colin's, in his summer camp of 150 boys on Highdown Hill. The boys were from East End clubs run by Basil. Sibyl Dunlop's 'head boy out of the shop' was one of his 'old boys' and was helping to run things. At the end of the meal they 'half-chanted a long Jewish Grace together'. Mary felt that Basil Henriques was 'clearly a saint'.

At her second at-home 'masses of people came, mostly nice-ish but a bit dull'. Colin also took Mary to visit Miss Fosset:

> She lies all day in a marvellous Edwardian bedroom, beautifully got up with a lilac bed jacket trimmed with lace and ribbons, with her white hair arranged in a marvellous coiffure like Queen Alexandra. I took her some roses out of the garden and she gave me 10/- worth of farthings which she had collected for the church. Coin is so sweet with these old people and they do love him so, and I am sure feel his visits give the greatest comfort and help.

Mary confessed that she had at first felt some resentment that Colin's powers were wasted on a ministry of 'being nice to old ladies'. But when she left Miss Fosset she 'felt suddenly that it was really worth while and that it was not work that *anyone* could do'.

> Most of his congregation (are) old, many of them ill, and their lives have been barren of most things and most of all of family affection and the affection and devotion of children. Lots of them have no relations, no jobs, not even any friends to speak of. [This description strongly recalls the social world of Mrs Gaskell's novel *Cranford*] It is only right that at some moment of their lives they should be served with a kindness which is born of love by those who have all the advantages on their side.

A day or two later they went up to London to see the Russian Ballet, and particularly liked *The Firebird*. Mary still hadn't heard from the school, but was writing a popular lecture on Socrates 'mainly for practice'.

In September they had their much needed holiday. They stayed first in the Western Pyrenees at Luz S. Sauveur, which turned out to be a '*Station Thermale Gynaecologique*', where Mary much excited the proprietress by explaining they were really on their '*voyage de noces*', and also obtained from her (the account reinforced with vigorous gestures) the house recipe for mayonnaise. Her letters to Ida are mostly full of descriptions of the wonderful scenery around them. By 12 September, she reported, Colin had 'quite lost his peaked look and says he feels quite a new man'. They then went via Pau, where they stayed the night, and the vast frontier station at Canfranc, to Zaragoza in Aragon. Colin found much of liturgical interest here in the old Cathedral, Lo Seo, and wrote it all into another *Guardian* article, 'Some Spanish Ways'.

In contrast to El Pilar, the new cathedral, which contains 'the jasper pillar on which our Lady is said to have appeared to St James' and is really a pilgrimage church catering largely for 'the satisfaction of individual devotion', Lo Seo still embodies the ancient view of cathedrals, that they were primarily for 'the continuous offering of liturgical worship' by the Canons, whose raison d'être is precisely to do that. He observes that, 'Out of service time, the (High) altar is completely uncovered and is destitute of any ornament whatsoever', and during a Mass 'only what is necessary for the offering of the Eucharist' is placed on it. He was also struck by the fact that clergy and people alike varied greatly in their outward signs of reverence for it: 'The principle seemed to be that of the First Prayer-book [1549]: "As touching kneeling, crossing ... and other gestures: they may be used or left as every man's devotion serveth without blame."' But the great survival from Catholic antiquity, not only to be found in Zaragoza, but elsewhere in Spain (and some other places),

> is the fact that all the Chapter Masses and the Offices are sung by the clergy and not by paid deputies. ... Their voices may be like those of corn-crakes, but they

upraise them lustily and with a good courage in psalm and office hymn, in
introit and gradual'.

He ends with a plea:

> that our own Church, with its fine appeal to an earlier and healthier Catholicism,
> should do something to make chapter-worship more of a reality than it too
> commonly appears to be.

The holiday ended with an overnight stop at Tudela (which the architect
G.E. Street called the most satisfactory Gothic church in Europe), and a few
days in San Sebastian – 'the exact equivalent of Brighton' – as Mary called it
in her letter. Neither Colin nor Mary were now fit for a lot more sightseeing, so
the pleasures of a beach resort was what they needed, together with time for
Colin to go on preparing a course of lectures on the Book of Common Prayer,
and Mary to read Father D'Arcy's book on St Thomas Aquinas. They were
home by the end of September, and Colin was plunged once more into the
strenuous round of visiting and services with occasional help, which resumed
with daily celebrations of the Eucharist during the octave of St Michael and All
Angels.

This week was followed by the Dedication Festival Celebrations on 6
October, when Colin's friend Will Porter stayed for two nights and preached at
the morning service. In the *Chichester Diocesan Gazette* Colin had announced
that 'in order to impart an added spirit of joy and gladness to our worship on
this Sunday the choir will be augmented by the large choir ['The Heavenly
Host'] which the late Mr Gustav Holst had gathered round him', adding that
they and a small string orchestra would be conducted by Miss Lasker (they
were to come again at Passiontide the next year, when Colin devised a service
with scriptural readings alternating with choral items illustrative of the theme).
The *Sussex Daily News* carried a report of the Festival services, pointing out
that the visiting musicians came without any reward except free 'hospitality for
the weekend' in houses of the parishioners. At the festival Eucharist:

> Vaughan Williams' Mass in G minor was rendered, and the same great
> composer's Magnificat and Nunc Dimittis were sung in the evening. In the
> Procession at the latter service, St Thomas's choir sang a short motet at the three
> stations that were made [Chapel of the Blessed Sacrament, Lady Chapel and
> Font], a memorable Festival Day concluding with the singing of Holst's Te
> Deum as a great act of thanksgiving.

The report finished by mentioning:

> the beautiful incident at the Eucharist (of) Mr Dunlop's invocation to remember
> his three predecessors at St Thomas's ... who had played so important a part in
> the building up of the church and its traditions.

Next Sunday (13 October) came the Harvest Festival, when another old friend, Philip Usher, also stayed for two nights to help, taking 8 o'clock Communion, 'School Service' (possibly next morning) and the Sunday 11.00 service of Procession, Solemn Eucharist and Sermon. Later in the week Gabriel Hebert, SSM (author of *Liturgy and Society*), also stayed a night and celebrated the next morning. On 24 October Mary and Colin had a visit from Deaconess Batho, who 'was very interesting indeed about the Priesthood of Women'. The Archbishop had set up a commission

> to determine the theological objections, if any. The majority report purports to have found and defined the objections. There is also a minority report of *one* – the Dean of St Paul's. He finds that the objections do not in fact exist! Bad – but interesting, isn't it?

She also told them of the 'almost unbelievable' prejudice there was then against deaconesses.

> As Colin says, the only consolation is that there have been, and are, so many subjects on which the majority of church people have held totally unchristian views and either have been, or are, in slow process of being converted; so we can hope on.

There is no indication that Colin raised the question to his own parishioners.

Most of his attempts to bring changes to St Thomas's were focussed on the encouragement of more congregational participation in services and the attempt to get them to see themselves more as a Church Family than as a collection of individual worshippers. During Lent 1936 he preached a series of sermons on the general theme 'Family Life in the Church'. In the summer of 1935 he had introduced the corporate singing of the psalms at Evensong in the hope that more people might be attracted to the service, though, after a few months' trial, had to revert to singing them to Plainsong, which not everyone could do, as the numbers had not risen significantly. He also introduced the censing of the congregation during the Magnificat, writing that they should return the thurifer's bow, as a 'symbol of their ingathering into the prayer and thanksgiving of the whole Church, which ascend in and with Christ's prayer, to the father'. These changes were accompanied by simplifications of the Introit at the Solemn Eucharist.

Then, at the Bishop's suggestion, he invited Henry de Candole, who was chaplain of the Theological College at Chichester and author of *The Sacraments and the Church*, to come and lead a Liturgical Mission in the parish in January 1936. Colin already knew him well, and was on friendly terms with him. When he was at St Mary's, Primrose Hill, de Candole gave four sermons during Holy Week while D-J was in the USA and Colin was in charge of the parish. Now, in Hove, he and de Candole carefully planned the details of the mission together, and Colin explained in the Parish Magazine that: they were to have a 'Liturgical Week' when the speaker would give:

instruction on the Eucharist and the ways in which the worshippers can take full part in the service, showing at the same time the meaning of many of the ceremonies at the Sung Eucharist. ... It is really a sort of Mission of a new kind, and is being very successful and popular among Catholics in Holland, Belgium, Germany, Austria and France. By means of it many people, formerly alienated from the Church, are finding in public liturgical worship just that religious experience which they have sought for in vain in other directions or which they had given up seeking anywhere.

This led him to encourage parishioners to take the opportunity of bringing a friend or acquaintance to the evening instruction. There were three evening sessions at which de Candole expounded the idea, first, of worship as corporate activity, second, an outline of the service itself, third, personal preparation along 'corporate' lines. The expositions were illustrated by 'enactions' of parts of the service, and by rehearsals of the music, processions, etc. Colin followed this up at the Annual Church Meeting on 6 February (when Mr Parfrey, Vicar's Warden, 'made a most touching little speech about Colin') by announcing that he would write to all on the Electoral Roll asking them what they thought of the proposal to have a weekly Parish Eucharist at 9.15 followed by a Parish Breakfast, when all the Sunday communicants would be present. 113 people replied, 29 being against any change, 30 wanting the 9.15 every week, and 54 wanting it once a month. Colin therefore felt he could not introduce the *weekly* Parish Eucharist, and had to compromise by holding it once a month, on which occasions there would be no 11.00 High Mass, as there was on other Sundays. After the mission he wrote to de Candole telling him that he had a real genius for teaching and exposition, adding: 'You will be glad to hear that one person thought you were the Bishop!'

Apart from his efforts to encourage a parish Eucharist, Colin also organised a successful Parish Outing, and a Parish Pilgrimage to Chichester, when those participating would be able to see inside the Bishop's Palace. He was cheered by the fact that the Easter Offering for 1936 of £46/9/2 was also £10 up on that for 1935. He and Mary also had 'all the parish round to parties gradually'. Christmas 1935 had also brought him and Mary a good many presents from parishioners and 210 cards, 'which (Mary wrote) even Colin is satisfied with'. She was able to tell Ida that 'despite troubles and vexations ... they were very happy', though, besides Midnight Mass, the Christmas Day service list was still as extensive as ever. Colin took the 7.0 Mass, but the Bishop drove over from Chichester to take the 8.0. Then Colin had to take Mattins, and then High Mass followed immediately by Evensong before they were free to relax at home.

But despite all the growing good-will and co-operation of most parishioners, Colin still continued to get painfully over-tired, and sometimes to be ill enough to have to stay in bed for a day or two. There was periodic trouble with the organist. This seems to have been partly a matter of salary, partly the result of Colin's requests for new kinds of music (such as the Folk Mass), and partly due to the poor relationship between organist and the choir trainer (Colin may even have introduced the latter post for the first time). Then the verger and his assistant were both ill in bed at the same time, which resulted, wrote Mary, in their 'needing constant visits, with Lent coming on', which made life very hectic. Beyond the parish there were, of course, lectures elsewhere in the diocese, and, for a time, a regular class at Roedean, and he was asked to take a part at the BBC in a discussion on religious broadcasting, and there were meetings of the Foreign Relations Council and the Alcuin Club Committee.

But of course Colin now had in Mary a very willing partner in pastoral matters. Quite soon after they returned from their short wedding tour of English churches Fr Clarke, Colin's predecessor at St Thomas's, died, leaving an utterly distraught widow who had had hardly any life of her own outside the compass of her husband's duties and interests, and a teenage boy. There were a requiem and a solemn requiem, the flowers had to be looked after and the accompanying cards recorded, numerous old lady parishioners who had doted on him had to be given what comfort was possible in such a case. All this was almost immediately followed by a long-drawn out engagement with Mrs Taylor, whose husband had deserted her for another woman and left her with hardly any money to live on but two children, one at boarding school and on the point of sitting her School Certificate (they could not therefore tell her straight away), and one at home – and to top it all, she was in great pain from either gallstones or an ulcer.

After three weeks on nothing but milk, Mary wrote, 'she could do nothing but cry and cry', while her daughter at home was 'bearing the brunt of everything', getting up frequently during the night to go to her mother and attending school by day. 'All this coming on top of the funeral was rather exhausting' – and, of course, there were no social services which could be called in for such cases. Very soon after her came Mrs Fraser, who was clearly heading for a nervous breakdown. After a while she was taken to a mental hospital, and then escaped and turned up at the Vicarage saying that Colin and Mary 'were her only sanctuary', and that all the male medical staff in the hospital had 'designs on her'. Some time later they put her up for a week in the vicarage while she was waiting to go to some relations or friends in Weymouth.

Mary's activities had meanwhile widened greatly in scope. She gave frequent lectures (subjects included Socrates, Andorra, 'Education and Family Life'), many of them to schools, but also to the University Extension Club. Then she was frequently asked to give talks to branches of the Mothers' Union, including one on Peace, despite the rather discouraging attitude of the Diocesan MU officials. She also wrote an article on a book by Alfred Zimmern. There was also her coaching; after a year or so she was taking on several students for University Entrance, etc. Her time at Oxford, where she had acted in and produced college plays, had given her a taste for dramatic production, which was put to very good effect at Hove. Her Nativity play for the children was perfomed at Epiphany, 1936, and very favourably noticed by the *Chichester Diocesan Gazette*, where the reviewer wrote 'it was beautifully acted by the children, who were very natural without any striving after theatrical effect'. This was followed by *Outward Bound*, for the St Thomas's Players, in which she also had to act herself. As a result of this she was coopted onto the Diocesan Drama Committee.

She also became a member of the Hospital Council, and wrote reports for it. When Colin was ill she would take the Children's Service for him. Much, but not all of this, must have gratified Ida very much, since she wanted her to succeed academically or as a non-institutional intellectual, but Mary told her in a letter when she had been reading in the Bodleian, while staying with the Collingwoods in Oxford, that she found 'working with her mind' very difficult without some kind of extrinsic stimulus. It is worth referring back at this point to a very interesting and significant passage in her letter of 2 December 1935. Ida has clearly been trying to persuade her to call herself 'O'Malley-Dunlop', to which she replies:

> I am sorry but I really can't agree with you about the names question. I can't see that it's important except as regards convenience. I can't see that my taking an immensely cumbersome and really absurd sounding name would do any good at all in asserting a principle about marriage.

Mary argues her point for almost half the letter, a sign of how painful it must have been for her to go against her adopted mother, someone she dearly loved and revered, who would obviously be very disappointed at her attitude – and perhaps everything was made worse by Ida's breast cancer for which she was then, and would be for some time to come, under treatment.

During all this time the political situation in Europe was continually deteriorating, and war with Germany seemed ever more possible. Hence the frequent mention of Peace in Mary's letters to Ida (and, presumably, in hers to Mary). In her letter of 6 November 1935, Mary first mentions that they have had a Mr Foxe to stay, of the World Alliance for International Friendship through the Churches. Then, a few days later, that she 'had to go to an awful meeting and sit on the platform to support a Pacifist member of the LCC speaking against aerial warfare'. She 'dearly liked' the man, but came away still feeling very uncertain about the pacifist cause.

'I wish I could be as certain as you are now', but, she continues, 'we are apt to get obsessed with the physical horrors of war, and not realize that there are things just as horrible and wrong that we are doing and that are being done; that merely keeping our hands clean over the question ... of gas attacks is not going to make us in the right'. Mary seems here to be implying that the pacifist reaction to violence cannot be the right one, that sometimes one has to fight, but cannot quite bring herself to say this clearly to Ida. However, Colin encourages his parishioners to join him in walking in the peace procession in Brighton on 27 June ('I *hate* walking in procession through the streets, but these things really do good. Governments notice them'), but at the back of this is the need to stop Italy's rape of Abyssinia. His notes at the beginning of the Parish Magazine for July start like this:

> Prayer for the world. It now appears that the powerful nations of the world have frankly abandoned the attempt to live together on a basis of collective security. The lesson of the Great War, which so many men and women died to teach, has been forgotten or disregarded. We are back where we were in 1914. ... Yet tragedy may be Christ's opportunity, the Christian Church itself was born out of the tragedy of the Cross ...

He goes on to thank the parishioners for standing after the Absolution and before the Comfortable Words of the Eucharist (as they passed from penitence to praise), in accordance with his request in the Parish Magazine.

Mary's sister Honor spent Christmas 1935 with them. She longed to find some permanent work with children or looking after the sick, but had no qualifications, and whenever she was taken on by someone as a helper, never managed to keep her position for very long. But she was a very devout Anglo-Catholic, and attended every single service at St Thomas's over the Christmas she spent at Hove. She was invited to tea with the Miles, and got to know other parish members, among them the Captain of the St Thomas's Rangers, who was very keen that Honor (a Ranger herself) should accompany the local troop to an 'international chalet' at Adelboden in Switzerland, but nothing seems to have come of this. However, the Jumble Sale the Rangers put on to raise money for the trip certainly did take place when Honor stayed with them again next May, and caused a lot of anxiety for Mary on her account when she heard about the 'precautions' the organisers had taken – and always did take – for such sales. It 'was an indescribable scene of chaos', Mary wrote to Ida:

> like being stampeded by a herd of wild elephants. However we had ... engaged a policeman and several sturdy young men to be chuckers out, and barricaded the saleswomen behind irremovable barriers ...

Honor 'survived, but got a headache and came home and went straight to bed when it was all over', sleeping for three hours before coming down to eat a good supper... 'so I hope it did her no harm'. It clearly affected Mary herself a lot, as she describes 'A mass of wild women from the poor parts of the town ... (who) besiege(d) the stalls with cries and grabs and pushings and yells. It's quite frightening. Apparently it always happens.' It was a far cry from the 'drawing room of a parish' they inhabited.

After the hard work of Lent and Easter 1936 they spent several days at the cottage in Old Felixstowe where Sibyl and Nana lived most of the time now. It was very close to Felixstowe Ferry, where Colin had spent his summer holidays as a child. Mary's letter to Ida (22 April) contains much enraptured description of East Suffolk, which she was 'discovering' for the first time, and they both felt greatly relaxed and invigorated when they had to return to Hove – Mary excited at the 'prospect of a very nice intelligent pupil in 4 languages next autumn' (Latin, Greek, English and French). In the August Parish Magazine Colin announced that he would be lecturing at the Sunday School Teachers' Summer School at Weymouth. He would then be on holiday until 31 August. Then, he continues, 'I go to represent the Church of England with others at a conference in Norway' and will be back about 12 September. While he was away the Revd Percy Rushmere would deputise for him without remuneration from the Parish, but live in the vicarage.

During the summer they had opportunities to go out riding together, an activity adopted by Mary in order to hasten conception, but very worth while in itself, especially on the downs behind Brighton. The summer holiday took them to Copenhagen, then to Gotland in the Baltic, and then to Stockholm, and Mary shows herself very much in tune with Scandinavian ways, much appreciating the beauties of the two capital cities and the marvellous medieval churches of Gotland, and the general orderliness everywhere.

One of her letters to Ida during this holiday contains the information that Colin 'has accepted the Bishop's offer of Henfield', which the letter itself suggests that Ida already knew about. I shall return to this matter of a new incumbency, of which this is the earliest mention I have seen, below, but first say something about the conference. From Stockholm they took a Norwegian sleeping car on the Oslo train, and were actually brought breakfast in bed at about 7.00 am, 'coffee in a thermos, cream in a little bottle, two eggs, rolls and butter, all complete in a little basket'. At Oslo, Mary goes on in her letter to Ida:

> we fetched up with the Norwegian pastors of this conference, and the Bishops of Strängnäs and Southwark. All of them disguised as men on a holiday – light suits, and no dog collars to be seen. One of them – Finnish actually – soon got very friendly with Colin and they began tremendous theological discussions which lasted all the way to Larvik [where the conference was held], with occasional interruptions to say 'Look look, how fine' about the scenery, or to offer us refreshment. 'I have here some ploms which I beg you to eat'. It is all very funny – Colin nearly laughed himself into hysterics last night because the Conference is supposed to close every day with 'Norwegian Evening prayer'... Larvik is rather fascinating – a funny little town at the end of a marvellous fjord, and this is a funny old-fashioned hotel. But we have a very nice room and the food seems good. The view is quite lovely.

Colin's participation in this one-week conference seems to have been on the recommendation of Fr. Hebert, SSM, who had now twice stayed the night at St Thomas's Vicarage and probably knew him through the Alcuin Club in addition. It was the fourth of an annual series which seems to have been set up, at least partly, by Mr and Mrs Treschow, who treated the delegates as their guests at their residence, Fritzøhus, Larvik. All participants were asked to bring '*either* evening dress *or* cassock for evening wear'. Hopes for closer communion with one or more of the Scandinavian national churches, which were Lutheran, were high at the time, and therefore it was hoped that this small gathering of members of the five (or six, counting Iceland separately) national churches would come to understand each other better and pave the way for something more important. Members of the small group included several whom Colin already knew, including Philip Usher, and possibly one or two of the Swedes. One of the Norwegian participants was Eivind Berggrav, Bishop of Halogaland, whom Colin liked and met up with again at the Michael Agricola celebrations in Finland in 1948. During the war, after the Germans had invaded Norway in 1940, Bp Berggrav was at the centre of resistance to the German occupation.

The subject for the congress was 'The Church', and Colin's task was to produce one of the two papers in the session on 'The Church's preaching of the Gospel', the other to be provided by a Scandinavian. Colin reminds his audience that the early church's proclamation of the Good News was, firstly, its immediate (corporate) response to the gift of the Holy Spirit, so not a kind of personal self-expression, and secondly that it consisted in its *living* of the good news with sins forgiven and new life bestowed, as reflected in its worship. He then goes on to specify symptoms of the contemporary neglect of these things: a stress on the personal and individual in worship, an unreal contrast between doctrine and life, the over-defensiveness of much Christian preaching, and the neglect of *un*felt or *un*conscious needs which is all too often associated with the stress on relevance to the satisfaction of more 'worldly' human needs. In this situation, we need to recover an understanding of the Gospel as a way of life dependent on historical events in Christ's life, continued and fruitful in the life of the Church, and on the Eucharist as 'the normal and regular climax of public worship as the Church's self-offering in Christ and a showing of the unity of all Christian people'.

Colin's published writings show a marked decline in number during his time at Hove, but it is worth saying something about the fruit of his temporary halt at Lyon on his way back to England from Iraq in October 1934. The 1934 Annual Report of the Alcuin Club announces that the Committee 'had in view for future publication (Colin's) translation of a French account of the Lyons Rite', but I have seen no further reference to it. However, he was asked to read a paper on the subject at the AGM in December 1935. It seems likely that the very short paper he published in *Theology* in the April 1936 issue contains the gist of it.

In this paper he returns to the issues he had tackled in his Alcuin Club pamphlet *What is the English Use?*, although, instead of talking of the 'spirit' of a liturgy as he does there, he uses the term 'genius'. He begins by referring to Fr Hebert's article in the previous number of *Theology*, which discussed the origin of the Use of the Church of Lyons. Fr Hebert had referred to a French book by Dom Buenner, *L'ancienne liturgie romaine: le rite Lyonnais* (quite likely the book Colin had offered to translate), where the writer established that the Lyons Use 'reproduces very adequately many of the ceremonial features of the Church of Rome in, and before, the days of Charlemagne'. Colin now goes further, and claims that the book also shows that 'prominent features of the

Lyons Use are at once recognisable as prominent features also of the Sarum and other ancient English Uses'. By 'prominent' he means not those immediately apparent, but

> those that compose the ground-plan, the underlying structure, the genius of the whole. That common ground-plan represents the genius of the Roman Use before it became overlaid with odds and ends of ceremonies, culled from all manner of sources with a reckless disregard for the balance and coherence of the whole.

After remarking that 'many Anglican churchmen today feel an instinctive affinity with a ceremonial based upon the ground-plan of old English Uses, he argues that both the English genius and the old Roman can be characterised by 'the love of what is practical rather than what is purely symbolical in ceremonies, the desire for splendour modified by austerity and the checking of piety with a strong dash of reserve', and that they can also be found reflected in the prefaces to and the rubrics of the Book of Common Prayer. He goes on to remind the reader that, if the Anglican Church's claim to catholicity is based partly on doctrinal continuity with the pre-medieval Church, then we can hardly be surprised at the corresponding continuity in liturgy. And when we become aware that the Liturgical Movement in the Roman Church itself looks back to this early period 'with longing eyes' (a longing hampered by 'the newer laws of the Sacred Congregations'), how foolish it seems to look for what is 'Western' and up-to-date in the post-reformation Roman liturgy.

When Colin and Mary returned to Hove from Norway, slightly less than two years after Colin began his ministry there, the parish already knew that they would be leaving them for Henfield, and it cannot have been easy for them to face the congregation, who were both surprised and also very sad to be losing them. The PCC minutes record that his resignation had been 'accepted with surprise and regret', and the Parish Magazine for September contains an announcement, probably by one or both Churchwardens, that the PCC 'hears with great regret the resignation of Fr Dunlop, particularly after so short an incumbency'. Colin's own self-accounting in the same number of the magazine reads as follows:

> It has not been easy to accept the Bishop's offer of Henfield. I have not been long at St Thomas's and the time has been a happy one for me. You have all been most kind to Mrs Dunlop and myself. ... Even before I came I was most attached to the traditions of worship at St Thomas's and to the general scheme of things at the church. I have made many friendships which I value most highly and which I hope will not now come to an end.

Among these friendships was that with Ronald Humphries, a naval officer, who was asked to be one of my godfathers, but who was killed in the war, so I have no memories of him. 'On the other hand', Colin goes on:

I am only too conscious of defects and shortcomings which have made me unsuitable for a Parish such as St Thomas's, defects with which you have always been extremely patient and tolerant. In addition, I have always wanted to be the parish priest of a country town, and especially of a parish where there are Church Day Schools....

Colin was instituted at Henfield on 26 September, but immediately returned to Hove and stayed until the middle of October, in order to be a guiding and ministering presence at the Dedication and Harvest Festivals. This peculiar arrangement was resorted to, with the agreement of the Bishop, because the vicar's stipend at Henfield was, Colin wrote, 'derived largely from tithes', but 'under the recently passed Tithe Bill the value of all Tithe Livings will be largely diminished after October 2nd'. His contribution to the October Parish Magazine contains a defence of the use of 'secular' heraldry on the new pulpit in memory of Fr Dom Markham (who had preached at St Thomas's more than once), largely because 'it conveys a sense of history, of our being heirs of a long and ancient tradition stretching back to Galilee and Jerusalem', and commemorates 'the great men and great deeds of the past'. He follows this by reminding readers that we are bidden to worship God 'with all our mind', and commends to them the Brighton School of Religious Study, since the parish itself contains no Study Circles. He also tells them that the Sussex Church Builders Pageant raised £50, of which the parish's own share was £3 (The Sussex Church Builders was a charity started by Bishop Bell in order to raise money to meet the need for new churches in places where there was a great deal of new housing). Colin's Cuttings Book contains a Press photograph of a long procession of people in vaguely 'religious' or 'medieval' costumes, among whom he and Mary are clearly portrayed.

In the November magazine he wrote: 'To my great regret I was unable to come and say Goodbye to many of you before I left. During my last two weeks I was laid up nearly all the time with a bronchial cold which kept me in bed and unable to get out of doors. ... The unpleasantness of leaving is to some extent lightened by the knowledge that in the Revd Jerom Victor you have a priest who fully appreciates the best things St Thomas's stands for, and who will serve you faithfully.' As a parting gift, Colin and Mary gave the church a new Altar Rail Kneeler and a new matching cover for the Altar Cushion. The February PCC minutes record that 'Mr Parfrey's proposition that the (new) Vicar 'institute a brighter type of service' was carried *nem. con.* But it was also agreed to hang a 'portrait' of Colin in the vestry alongside former vicars.

It is not easy to be sure why Colin did not wish to remain longer in Hove when he was clearly much appreciated by large numbers of parishioners, and, as he wrote himself, counted his time there as a happy one and made some good friends. But Colin's 'self-accounting' letter in the September Parish Magazine may give an important clue in the last sentence I quote – his long-cherished desire to be the priest of a country town. This was also Mary's wish. Although Colin had spent much of his childhood in Beckenham, when it still had a village-like appearance in parts, it was full of London commuters, living in their own newly built houses, and rapidly losing its rural character and sense of being a settled community. Henfield still had this. Although it also contained artists and intellectuals, and probably also a few Brighton commuters, it still also had farms and other country businesses, and more than one church school. Even today it has a surprisingly rural feel about it.

Whatever the reason, the Bishop must have thought it good enough for him to move under the circumstances, or he would not have offered him the living of Henfield (and soon afterwards a non-residentiary canonry in the cathedral). It is also worth quoting here from a letter Mary sent to Ida on 10 October. She tells Ida that, during the past fortnight, they have made several trips to Henfield. One was with Colin's cousin Ruth Anderson, whom they took there to see the vicarage. She then introduced them to 'a family called Milne, with a lovely garden ... Mr Milne paints; she also took us to Mr Squire, an art critic. ... *we are very encouraged to find such people in Henfield.* ... We *shall* miss the music in Hove', but the organist at Henfield, she adds, has excellent taste for Bach and Plainsong and is a good choir trainer, 'so we shall have a marvellous ally in him'; ... there's also the schoolmaster of the boys' school: 'Colin is *so* delighted'. These, of course, are largely 'worldly' or 'fleshly' considerations, not purely spiritual. But in her letter to Ida of 24 November, which I will discuss below, she writes: 'When we came to Henfield it was not only a call to Colin but a call to me.' They moved in mid-October, and seem to have felt from the first that they had done the right thing.

Postscript: St Thomas's was declared redundant in 1993. The church building had been begun in 1909 under the architectural firm Clayton & Black of Brighton. After 1993 It was bought by the Coptic Orthodox Church for the community of Sudanese who found refuge in the area after the 2nd Sudanese Civil War. The congregation now includes Egyptians as well. The Stations of the Cross were moved to St Mary's Kemptown (St Mary the Virgin, Brighton).

12

HENFIELD

C OLIN'S FIRST ALTAR SERVER at St Peter's, Henfield, was the sixteen-
year-old Douglas Tucker, whose parents lived in the large village but
did not themselves regularly come to church. Douglas Tucker worked
for the local branch of Barclay's Bank, and later became Chairman of the
Shoreham-by-Sea Citizen's Advice Bureau. His son was ordained, and later
worked for a time as Chaplain of Colin's old college at Oxford. He told me that
Colin 'really brought the parish to life', and 'revolutionised the services'. The
previous vicar had been in Henfield for over 23 years, and most of his
congregation were probably ready for a change, so it is not surprising that they
'took to it gladly'. Canon Lea himself, employing the Pauline athletics imagery
so beloved by Church of England clergy at that time, wrote in the Parish
Magazine:

Now my relay is over, and the flag passes to the next runner. Young, well
trained, keen and vigorous, the race is in good hands and I am confident for the
future. Will you help the new runner, as you have the one just finished, with
your prayers, your cheers, and encouragement? A good start means so much,
and loyalty, friendliness and sympathy are needed now, and always.

Colin, back in Hove after his institution, wrote in the same number of the
Parish Magazine, in what must now to the reader be familiar fashion: 'I am
afraid I shall be but a poor successor to Canon Lea, so I must ask you to be
indulgent and to overlook many shortcomings and, above all, expect me to do
my best.' Colin's nearly three and a half years at Henfield were clearly very
successful ones, despite the sickness and pain which, as I shall set out below,
overshadowed the 'private' lives of himself and those dearest to him. And the
fact that Mary and he spent the years of his retirement there seems to bear out
what Denis Lant wrote to my mother on Colin's death (my italics):

He was so kind to me and when I was a theological student, his preaching was
rather a model to me. I always said that I never heard such a consistently good
preacher. But it is as a man that I remember him with affection. My father [one
of the lay-readers] thought so much of him. ... *I suspect that he was never
happier than when he was vicar of Henfield, and certainly the village was never
happier than when he was vicar.* ... I salute a good man and a real friend.

205

They moved in to the spacious vicarage, with its large and beautiful garden, on 14 October 1936. Mary soon wrote to Ida 'If only we could get some devoted servants, we would be ideally happy here', and three days later told her that Colin, arriving home one afternoon, said to her straight out 'This is going to be a *wonderful* job'. The place itself, half way between large village and country town, with a population then of a little over 2000, was a much more welcoming environment than that of St Thomas's, Hove. Instead of the long straight streets, terraces and 'semis' of a Victorian suburb, there were houses and cottages of all periods, with winding lanes, shops and businesses mostly concentrated on the main street, trees and gardens everywhere, a very picturesque churchyard, and a lovely and varied countryside all around. In addition there were rail and bus connections with Brighton, Horsham and other places.

Henfield also possessed its own Assembly Rooms, and a pleasantly rural area of Common land, which made it all so much easier to 'reach out' to the non-church-going population of the parish. There was also a curate, Mr Blaikie, already a priest, to show Colin round and take some of the services, who would be staying on into 1937 and then replaced, and, as Douglas Tucker, said, the congregation were ready for changes. In his November Vicar's Notes for the Parish Magazine, after saying how much he was enjoying Henfield, Colin told his parishioners that, for financial reasons, Mary and he might not be able to continue living in the 'very homely house with its delightful garden', though they would try, that he hoped to start visiting as soon as they were 'straight', and that he would not make any changes until he had got to know them well.

He also added that, having lived abroad, he was keen to get them to know what was happening on the 'front line'. Accordingly, on 18 November, the Revd A. Bulstrode would tell them about the work of the Church in Palestine, 'a country for which we are responsible to the League of Nations Union. Nearly all its problems are, at bottom, religious ones, as is nearly always the case. Do try and be present.' It is worth adding here that Colin's worries about not being able to afford to live in the Vicarage were well-founded, and that on one occasion in 1938, Mrs Hicks, a member of the Ladies Care Committee (mentioned below), who was a wealthy widow and lived with her daughter in Chestham Park, was good enough to help them financially in some way. Both Colin and Mary were very surprised to find how expensive living in the country actually was.

About a month after their arrival Mary wrote to Ida:

We have been discussing what we ought to do in the way of a 'Mission' service on Good Friday. We thought at first of a procession all through the village onto the Common, and a short service there. However, Good Friday comes in the middle of March this year, so the weather will probably be terribly cold and trying; so we have now a new idea. This is to book the Assembly Rooms, and get the Oberammergau slides, and show them, only instead of having an explanatory lecture, to have quite simply the Gospels, of which the pictures are illustrations, read *dramatically*, i.e. with different voices for the narrator and the speakers, and interspersed at certain points with solemn chorales and motets – meditations on the words and scenes. I believe this would be very *popular*, and yet would be a really solemn and impressive missionary service for Good Friday. Colin is at any rate going to book the slides now.

In his 'Vicar's Letter' for the month following Easter Colin reports that the Assembly House had been full. The first and rejected alternative for the mission service became a monthly open air ecumenical service on the Common during the summer months, with the co-operation of the two non-conformist congregations in the parish, the Congregationalists and the 'Nep Town Mission'. He did this every summer of his work in Henfield, and the venture seems to have worked well, and even to have drawn in passing motorists.

The letters that Mary wrote to Ida give a very good impression of the busy life she lived while at Henfield, with frequent references to Colin also. In her letter of 1 November, she first tells about a visit from Evelyn, during which, despite her streaming cold 'she was in high spirits and finally I had to play the gramophone to keep her and Colin from talking and laughing too much, and bringing on his cough'. At church (it was All Saints Day), 'we had the Vaughan-Williams tune for the first time, everyone sang lustily'. They dined with the Mayes, who ran an educational coaching establishment (and went on to become good friends with them). Mary probably did some work for him later.

Next day she chaired the Ladies Care Committee in the Vicarage. She found 'an eager anticipation of new doings instead of the dread of changes she had expected', and found them 'mostly very nice and sensible; they are under the PCC and take care of things in the church'. After naming them, she goes on: 'none of them are young, but none of them are "dead" still less buried as many were at St Thomas's'. Ida was clearly hoping for a visit soon, as Mary goes on to say that she couldn't come next week as the Andersons (a married couple who were coming to do the work of the house in exchange for the use of the empty wing of the vicarage, heating, lighting and £1 a week each) were arriving on the Monday; then she had two rehearsals and two committees she felt she ought not to miss; it wouldn't be worth coming for a single day but she hoped they could both come the week after for two days. Colin wanted to go to the British Museum and she to look for books about Visby (in Gotland) in connection with some articles she was writing; alternatively she could help Ida instead.

The day before they had both been at the Diocesan Conference; 'Lord Robert Cecil spoke for an hour on the Church-State report; Joynson-Hicks spoke for an hour against it, implying that the House of Commons was more representative of the Church of England than the Church Assembly or Convocations.' There had been a splendid speech by D-J after lunch; then there were other speakers, some of them 'lunatics'; Lord Robert summed up extremely well; '*such* an example of Christian righteousness and a witness to the need and effectiveness of spiritual liberty'. A resolution commending certain vital points to the immediate notice of Convocation was carried with acclamation by a large majority. She ends: 'I must now go to Brighton to help receive Princess Louise', who was going to open the Winter Show and Bazaar in aid of the New Sussex Hospital.

A week later she writes that the Princess had been ill and never came, but that Lady Leconfield, her stand-in, made an excellent speech:

> The bazaar was of the usual description – masses of unwanted objects extravagantly priced, being sold by elderly ladies dressed as Hungarians while a band played Gypsy dances by Brahms, very hot and crowded.

However, a lot of money was raised. Mary had left before the end, to get back to Henfield in time for tea with the Maidments, who lived in a lovely Tudor house with Queen Anne additions. On the next day she went to the meeting of the GFS (Girls' Friendly Society), with which she had a lot to do while at Henfield. 'I played guessing games with a lot of little girls whom I am afterwards going to teach some scenes out of the *Water Babies* for a competition. They are a very nice lot of children here.' On Sunday, she reports,

> we paid a visit to Chailey [a boarding school for severely physically handicapped children]. Colin preached a splendid sermon to the crippled boys and we both so much enjoyed the service. They sang so delightfully, and the lessons were read by two very rough, *very* lame, boys – one Yorkshire and one a Cockney, I think – but *so* well in spite of the accents; it was really very touching.

Afterwards they were presented with 'two specimens of their carving – bookends and a cigarette box'. There follows a long and dramatic account of a great storm during the night when some damage was done to the Vicarage because the leaves had not been cleared from the gutters, and quite a lot of water came in. Then, next day:

> The Andersons arrived with all their household goods. I spent an almost sleepless night with the prospect of what would happen if they (did) *not* turn out well – but still, in the light of day, I think it is going to be all right. They seem very promising.

After a few days they paid a very brief visit to London, when Mary stayed with Colin's brother Walter and his wife Irene, 'who had been asking her to for ages', while Colin stayed at Steele's Road, where they all met for lunch, though Mary had arranged to arrive as soon as she could in the morning. She also told Ida that they had the two schoolmistresses to supper the night before, who expressed much excitement about the new Education Act, which would probably mean 'a new central senior school (a church school) here', and have repercussions on the exisiting junior schools in the village (it also meant that Mary did in fact have to make time for School Managers' meetings, as well as many others). In her letter of a week later she wrote first about a lunch with the Rothereys. He was an engineer and had been in Peru when her grandfather Carroll was there and knew him quite well. Colin liked him a lot, and they both went on to think of the Rothereys as among the nicest of their parishioners. Then she mentioned a visit to tea from Helen Royden, Maude's daughter, 'an ordinary child of extraordinary parents', who was teaching at St Mary's Hall, and 'in a slight state of conflict against her upbringing'. Mary goes on to report a visit from the GFS Branch Secretary, Miss Knowles, who

> came in, in a state of great consternation, to say that the young lady who is producing the GFS Christmas play, has been ordered by her doctor to have a complete rest! ... I have taken over the whole thing, lock, stock and barrel. ... In producing, (she adds) especially in a semi-original composition as last year, I find all the satisfaction of my aesthetic creative instincts... It is to me what painting a picture, or writing a sonnet or composing a song are to those who can.

She had also been roped in to perform with a local drama group:

> The day before was the performance of that despicable little play *Me and Me Roses* at Keymer. I felt ashamed to be in it – I really did. However, it went off very well, and I was much congratulated – but O, what *stuff* this rotten little modern thing is.'

This letter was continued the next day, as Ida's previous letter contained a great deal that required very serious consideration. Ida, who was, in fact, still under treatment for her breast cancer, had asked Mary whether, instead of coming to London for the odd day or two, she could come to Steele's Road for much longer visits. It sounds from Mary's reply that Ida had spent some time giving her reasons why she should do this (Ida's letter does not survive). Behind this issue, Mary agrees, is the need for both herself and Ida to adjust to their new relationship – harder for Ida, Mary suggests, since she has never had a husband, and the serious conflicts in her life have only been between children and work, not between children and a man.

There is also, running through what Mary writes, an implication that the kind of things that constituted much of her life as Vicar's wife in Henfield were regarded by Ida as rather trivial or unimportant in comparison with direct contributions to the 'big movements' (such as women's emancipation, peace and international organs for keeping it, or literary and scholarly achievements which could change for good the consciousness of a generation) where Mary's work, she hoped, would be concentrated. Mary replies to this that her 'genius in so far as I have any is not primarily for a student's life, or a life given over to literature'. But she *was* trying 'to dedicate my talents to God, and my fellow men'. This means that she *cannot* 'leave my life here and stay in London for long periods' at her own convenience. What, in Ida's terms, she is trying to do, is help to build up the kind of spirit 'which will be useful to the big movements'.

What is more, Henfield is the kind of place where this is most possible, since 'big towns are (being) usurped by forces of the devil'. This is why she has been longing to live in the country. She also stresses that in all this she is not merely adopting Colin's own ideas – though she did share his sense of a vocation to a community like Henfield. Indeed, *she* is changing *Colin* in various respects! Ida replied that Mary's idea of Christianity in village communities was rather fanciful; and that she herself could not turn her back on 'my darling people of London'. There would always be men of goodwill, she went on, in whom is 'the spirit of Christianity':

> if they are killed it will spring up again from the blood of the martyrs; whereas you identify the Church with the Church of England or organised religion, I identify it more and more with men of good will, whether they profess Christ or not.

The question of how Mary should be using her gifts is not raised again in the letters that have survived.

Mindful, perhaps, of his Hove ministry, Colin had promised in the Parish Magazine for November 1936 not to change anything in the service pattern at St Peter's before he had got to know his regular congregation – though he did make a determined effort to get people to join him for Morning and Evening Prayer in church. How successful he was in this is not clear, since the appeal recurs in more than one of his monthly contributions to the Magazine. But he seems to have had no difficulty (nor does this seem to have been difficult at Hove) in persuading the PCC to support his introduction of a 'Liturgical Three Hours' on Good Friday instead of a service made up primarily of seven sermons, or meditations, on the 'seven words' the four Gospel-writers severally record as uttered by Christ on the Cross.

Colin also seems to have introduced an Easter Carol Service, and also a regular afternoon service in church for children, and to have divided the existing Sunday School into several classes according to its different age-groups. Apart from changes to services he also introduced a Study Circle, which would probably not have been possible in Hove. Subjects included 'Liturgy' and 'The Thirty-Nine Articles', which formalise the attempt by the Church of England of the days of Elizabeth I to distinguish its own teaching from that of Roman Catholics on the one hand, Calvinists and Anabaptists on the other, in such a way as to avoid unduly narrow definition. Colin also re-introduced the ancient practice of holding baptisms during Mattins and Evensong, the rationale of which he set out in his Vicar's Notes for May 1937:

Many have expressed to me their satisfaction at the administration of baptism during Mattins on Easter day. It was one of the great aims of the reformers in this country to rescue Baptism from being a private, hole-in-corner rite, to its primitive dignity as a public act, only to be held when 'the most number of people come together' (as the Prayer Book directs). It is the reception of a new member into the family of God, and the family as a whole ought to be there when it is received.

He adds at the end that, provided due notice is given, the bell-ringers will always be glad to 'ring in' with a joyful peal a 'new child of God in this way'.

As he did at Hove, Colin also introduced his new parishioners to the Parish Eucharist, after initially inviting reactions at the Parish Annual General Meeting in March 1937. This encouraged him to put on the service 'as an experiment' in October. In next month's Vicar's Notes he began a section on the Parish Eucharist as follows:

> The Parish Eucharist has started well. I am perfectly certain that in this return to the ideals of worship held by the church in its great days we shall find new meaning in Holy Communion. It is the ideal which our own Reformers tried to recapture when the Prayer Book was drawn up, but they were prevented because the slack habits of the Middle Ages as regards communion were so deeply engrained. The idea of making 'my communion' (as we put it) at a service in which our private prayers are continually interrupted by the necessity of joining in responsorial or community prayer is strange and difficult to many of us.

He goes on to acknowledge the power of habit in human life. 'But the way of adventure is the Christian way, and if we face the strangeness and difficulty of innovation with hope and courage we shall not regret it.' He concludes by asking his readers

> to give it a try, if only for the sake of the younger people, who seem unanimous in approval of it. I am not going to stop the 8 a.m. celebration; do meet me half-way by trying the 9.30 service at frequent intervals. I am only doing it because it is the ideal of the Church which commissioned me as a 'messenger, watchman and steward of the Lord'.

Colin's attempt at Hove to hold a Parish Eucharist every Sunday had not succeeded, despite the help of his friend, Henry de Candole and his teaching on the subject. But de Candole, the Liturgical Missioner for Chichester Diocese (who became one of the leading proponents of the Parish Eucharist in the Church of England and was eventually made Bishop of Knaresborough) had had great hopes of Henfield. He did, in fact, succeed Colin as Vicar there. Peter Jagger, in his book *Bishop Henry de Candole: His Life and Times 1895–1971* (Leighton Buzzard: The Faith Press, 1975), was able to shed much light on this particular issue, thanks to the extensive diary material de Candole left when he died. As a result he was able to write that de Candole was 'deeply impressed' by two parishes in Chichester Diocese especially. One was Henfield, 'where Henry's old friend Colin Dunlop had introduced a 9.30 a.m. Parish

Communion soon after becoming Vicar' – though, as at Hove, he was never able to make it the most important Sunday service, which would more nearly enable the committed Anglicans to meet together every Sunday at the Lord's Table as 'one body'. On the other hand Colin had laid sure foundations for de Candole, enabling him 'to work out ... the principles of the Liturgical Movement' and make it the main Sunday service:

Colin's framework was, he believed, excellent and carefully thought out, in that there was a regular Parish Communion at 9.30 sung to Merbecke; there were two servers to assist, an Offertory Procession by three girls, mostly members of the GFS, and a short sermon, the Epistle being read by a rota of laymen. All ages were present, but mostly the newly confirmed and a few children. There were about 40 communicants.

However, 'Henry felt', wrote Jagger, 'that Dunlop, who was very much in touch with the Alcuin Club, was perhaps more interested in the academic and the ceremonial aspects of liturgy than in the pastoral, which was, of course, Henry's chief concern'. He also felt that the Henfield Parish Eucharist 'was good but rather "starchy", "liturgical" rather than "homely"', and created a freer and more 'corporate' atmosphere. Jagger goes on to add to de Candole's further impressions of Colin:

> He was a very gifted man, artistic, musical and a good preacher; he improved the church, its ceremonial and music ... On the whole he brought a more modern spirit to the parish and livened things up in general. In spite of Colin's many gifts, Henry wrote of his friend and predecessor; 'But I don't really think (and I think he would agree) [he was cut out to be] a parish priest, though he visited faithfully and left me an invaluable parish register.'

However, de Candole's efforts to 'downgrade Mattins' and 'emphasise the centrality of the Parish Eucharist led to a number of conflicts'. His first curate, Martin Pierce, originally appointed by Colin, told Peter Jagger that he:

> felt that Henry's single-mindedness about the Parish Communion left him 'little real sympathy with those who did not share his feelings'. But he concentrated on confirmation candidates, teaching them 'that attendance at Parish Communion was a 'must'.' Eventually attendance at it outstripped the other [services], and the statistics of attendance show a marked rise in his 9 years at Henfield; this had results in revitalising 'the whole life and work of the church', despite some 'conflicts and misunderstandings'.

Henry de Candole certainly did have a reputation for insisting that his own liturgical judgments were right, or, as the Bishop wrote to Colin (letter of 9/2/39), that he could be 'very hustling'. Colin, by contrast, temperamentally not very sure of himself, was probably far more ready to see the other person's point of view than impose on them his own opinion. However, he fully recognised his friend's gifts as a preacher, and asked Henry to deliver three addresses at the Henfield 'Liturgical Three Hours' on Good Friday, 1938.

Colin had never had a curate at Hove, though when he became Vicar of Henfield, he 'inherited' the Revd S.G. Blaikie, who stayed with him until May 1937, when he accepted the living of Crawley Down, also in Sussex. In the valedictory paragraph of his Vicar's Letter, Colin lays special stress on 'his help during my first six months here, and for the entirely selfless way in which he has co-operated with me from first to last', and talks of him as 'a trusted and valued friend and pastor', mentioning also his 'quiet sincerity and his faithfulness to his calling'. When he left, some of the curate's work was carried out by a Church Army Sister, Sister Evans, who left in her turn in June 1938. 'She will be greatly missed', wrote Colin, for

she has thrown herself with whole-hearted enthusiasm into our life at Henfield, and many lonely people will sadly miss her frequent visits and spiritual help. We shall all remember with gratitude the sight of her small but stalwart figure striding through our streets and lanes in all weathers on her visits to our houses.

Colin had clearly hoped that he had found a successor to Mr Blaikie who would come almost as soon as the latter left. But in his August 1937 Vicar's letter he announces that, although he has secured a successor, Martin Pierce, he would not be able to come until the following summer, since he had been chosen to spend a year with the Orthodox church in Romania as part of a regular interchange. However, he had known him for about seven years and was confident that, when he did come, he would be 'a faithful and devoted partner', as indeed it proved. On return from Romania, he was made deacon in June 1938, and priested in June 1939 (when he was awarded the Bishop's Ordination Prize for the best work during training). But despite the work of these curates and help on the pastoral side by Sister Evans while he had no curate, Colin still needed outside help (especially to celebrate Holy Communion). Much of this was given on a regular basis from October 1937 to August 1938 by a retired priest, Mr C.E. Tuppen, who, as Colin's Vicar's Notes recorded in August 1938,

not only helped with the services on Sundays, but has willingly driven over from his distant home, often several times a week ... What the Vicar could have done without him, he hardly knows. His dignified stance at the altar, his thoughtful words from the pulpit and his genial presence at all times will be greatly missed. He never let his occasional illness interfere with his duties or with those extra services which he so kindly offered to perform. We are very grateful to him.

There was also occasional help from Lay Readers and from other clergy. Despite all this, he often found Sundays exhausting, as he had at Hove.

Colin's health was in fact still giving Mary cause for concern. Whenever there was a change in the weather he seemed to develop a head cold, which frequently settled on his chest. Here is an extract from Mary's letter to Ida of Sunday, 9 September 1937:

The sudden cold weather made him start a cold, and though he went to bed early on Friday and stayed there yesterday morning he did not seem to shake it off, though it was still in his head. Then yesterday afternoon he got up, in preparation for today, and by the evening he was really bad. When I got him to bed I didn't see how he could be fit for any services today. I was at my wits' end. There was no chance of getting [a substitute] you see. However by some miracle he was able to get up today, and doesn't seem any the worse. I filled him up with quinine and aspirin and ephedrine last night, rubbed his chest with camphorated oil, ending up with a stiff dose of whiskey. Then this morning he was plied with hot Ovaltine before going to church, and as I say, he really does seem all right – only a little drugged.

Miss Knowles, one of the kindest and most generous of their Henfield friends, had 'sent round a half bottle of champagne to get him through today, and a bottle of port "to be administered as a daily tonic"!', and he was able to manage '2 Celebrations, Mattins and Sermon, and a children's service, and has appeared almost normal, eaten hearty meals, and even ventured on a pipe this evening'. A letter from Mary to Ida after their brief visit to Steele's Road at the end of November 1937, tells of another bad cold, caught when visiting Evelyn. But Mary goes on to say that, despite physical improvement, 'Colin is rather pulled down and his spirits are low. ... It's really due to overwork – he has *so* much on his mind', and 'no amount of sympathy and support from one's friends or even one's wife can quite make up for not having a *professional* colleague to share the responsibility with'.

An earlier letter from Mary to Ida (28/4/37) alludes, à propos of Honor's psychological problems, to the fact that Colin had at some time consulted Leonard Browne, who 'has helped Colin so very much over various little nervous difficulties, and being a Christian and a Churchman, would know the way to help Honor through her religion'. Leonard Browne 'help(ed) people to understand their own reactions, and also, by disentangling things, he gives free play to the work of Grace (in them)'. However, Colin's problem certainly did have a strong physical basis; over Easter in 1938 he had an attack of tonsillitis, such that he could take no services at all, and Mr Tuppen had to do all the services himself.

At the beginning of December 1939, when Colin's appointment to Edinburgh was announced in the *Sussex Daily News*, the writer added: 'Colin Dunlop has been convalescing from a serious illness, and has not yet regained his normal vigour.' Then, in the January 1940, Parish Magazine, Colin writes that his tonsils will be removed on 4 January, and he will be away for about three weeks. In February's magazine he says that the surgeon reports him in a 'low state of health', and he must not return to work till 10 March. It was just as well that Martin Pierce was such a competent colleague.

It should be added here that Colin's tendency to 'days off sick' had not prevented George Bell from making him a non-residentiary Canon of Chichester. He was installed as 'Prebendary of Windham' in January 1937, and had to preach in the Cathedral every so often and attend Great Chapter

Meetings. In October 1938, the Bishop asked him to conduct a 'weekend campaign' in the parish of Bury, just as he himself had conducted one in Henfield the year before. Their purpose was to stimulate church congregations to think how to live as a Christian under the rapidly changing conditions of modern life. Colin was also asked by him to join a Diocesan Liturgical Committee. In the original letter of 10/7/37 he told Colin that his idea was to get Canon How as chairman, with Canon Frith, Colin and The Revd E.C. Ratcliffe, an important liturgical scholar, as members.

Soon afterwards Henry de Candole and the Revd W. Westall were added to their number. Their brief was to look into the whole question of 'additional weekday Masses, Holy Week services and other special services'. It seems from the records I have seen that many of the special services, with special collects, epistles and gospels, were to cater for figures like St Richard of Chichester, for whom there were no special services, as there were in the case of the best-known saints. Colin made many suggestions for proper readings and composed special collects, or adapted existing ones, for such local figures. But after he became chairman of the committee in January 1939 (Canon How had become Bishop of Glasgow), he strongly opposed any work on special prayers and readings for St Joseph's Day and the Assumption of the Virgin, when these were proposed.

The main reason was that this was outside the committee's brief, since this was of national, not merely local, significance; it was, of course, also a matter which greatly interested the 'Romanisers' on the committee, whom the Bishop scrupulously included. These extreme Anglo-Catholics had also earlier wanted him to authorise the Good Friday Mass of the Presanctified, which consists of the early part of the Communion service but omits the Consecration, and proceeds directly to the consumption of wafer-bread and wine consecrated on the previous day, which had in the interval been left to lie on the 'Altar of Repose'.

The records of the committee show that Colin set out his reasons against this very clearly, his chief one being that the events of the evening and night of Maunday Thursday (that is, the Thursday before the first Good Friday, when Jesus Christ was crucified) were far from reposeful. After much discussion the Bishop ruled the service out as 'inconsistent with what I believe the Bishops can allow', though at the beginning of their discussions he had expressed himself as 'unwilling to rule out altogether the possibility of such a service'. This may have been what lay behind this otherwise surprising passage from Mary's letter to Ida on 16/8/38. It runs as follows:

When I got home I found Colin very tired and rather upset about a meeting of the Bishop's Liturgical Committee. The Bishop, after writing his charge and telling them all they must obey the Prayerbook and not have any services that were not allowed by authority, is now apparently going to allow them to have any services they like, including Benediction and the Mass of the Presanctified, etc, etc. In other words they may do as they like provided they ask him first. I must say if the authority is only going to be the whim of an individual Bishop instead of the whim of an individual Parish Priest, I don't think it is any gain. It is all very odd. 'They' are the Anglo-Catholics, for as yet he has not seen fit to grant any indulgences to the Evangelicals, whose party is not so strong in Sussex.

Colin is fearfully upset about it, not so much because he dislikes these services and thinks they are unnecessary and do harm, but because he can't understand what the Bishop is up to. When he delivered the charge he said distinctly that the standard of what was to be 'lawful' was to be the 1928 Prayerbook supplementing the old one. Then he set up the Liturgical Committee, with 3 Anglo Catholics, two 'Prayerbook' Catholics [including Colin] and one Evangelical on it, to draw up supplementary services which are not provided in 1928. But the Committee has turned into a sort of bargain counter when the A.C. clergy say: 'now if we obey you about this, will you let us do so and so?' – pressing him for more and more 'concessions', and the Bishop is giving in to it, and apparently playing the game with zest. Colin wonders whether to resign or not. It seems so shocking to him because no principles are being invoked, and the whole of the spirit of the charge seems gone to the wind. It is rather awful because I fear he has ceased to respect the Bishop now, which makes it so much more difficult to work under and for him. It is all very odd. He really does seem to say one thing and do another.

That this committee meeting really led to withdrawal of respect on Colin's part is not easy to believe. I have not found any reason for thinking that relations between Colin and the Bishop permanently changed about this time, so it seems easier to think that Colin was certainly very tired and temporarily upset, but that later, when he had regained his equilibrium, his indignation lost much of its force.

The paucity of information about the later part of Colin's time in Henfield arises partly also from the complications of two births, more serious illness and Ida's death. The first of these events was the birth of Francis Ninian (the author of this biography) on 5 October 1937. In the early months of her pregnancy Mary had suffered from often very severe bouts of sickness, and, when her time was approaching, she and Colin were advised that, rather than having the baby at home, as they had hoped, Mary should go to 67 Brunswick Place, a Nursing Home in Hove, in case there were complications. But all went off well, apart from a small tear, which was 'beautifully healed' when she and the baby returned home on 23 October. But on 3 March 1938, Mary 'was taken into Tregarthyn House Nursing Home, so very very ill' (she came near to death), and, on the 10th she wrote a short note to Ida from the New Sussex Hospital, where the 'horrid old tube' was removed from her and she was hoping she would be allowed home soon. Later, she wrote to Ida that she had 'never felt the presence of God so vividly as during the worst part of my illness'. Ida mentioned the terrible shock it gave her, but told Mary that what made it *bearable* was the way you behaved yourself. If you had been frightened and miserable, I don't know how I should have held up. But you were so much yourself, that I felt that even if you did die, I should not think of you as dead ... If you could be so near death and yet behave like that, then I thought I should be able to go on realising that death does not matter so very much. Of course what would have happened if you had died, I can't tell!

There is no mention in the correspondence of what exactly had been wrong with Mary, but Colin got a night nurse to help her when she did get home, and there is a reference in a letter of the second week of May where she says that she has just been to church for the first time in two and a half months. Many parishioners, both in Henfield and also in Hove, rallied round to help, especially with the problems raised by Francis's helpless presence (indeed he could not stay with her in the hospital, but was taken to be looked after for some time by Mrs Freeman in Henfield, with daily 'visits' to the hospital), though it seems that Peggy, his fifteen-year-old nanny, recruited from a large family in the village, turned out to be an excellent nurse and devoted to the baby. Later in the year Mary's bodily fitness suffered another quite serious setback with in-growing toenails, which entailed the removal of the nail and inability to walk for some time afterwards.

As for Ida's death, she had struggled with undaunted courage against her breast cancer, often feeling extremely wretched as a result of the radium treatment she was given (especially after a nasty burn appeared on her arm as an accidental by-product), and then briefly rising above it to continue the literary work she needed to do to keep the Steele's Road household going. After many visits from close friends and relations, she died at home tended by her cousin Ethel Sprigge, with a resident night nurse, on 10 April 1939. Mary had been quite ill herself from a 'bug' that was prevalent in the village, and was thus unable to go to see her during this time when Ida's end seemed near. Thus, Ida never saw Mary's second child, Philip James, who was born on 7 May of that year.

Apart from Peggy, who stayed with the Dunlop family as the babies' nurse until she was called up during the war, when they were in Edinburgh, the other reliable standby in the vicarage was Elsie Aukett, who cooked and cleaned the house. For a year or so Colin and Mary had let the empty wing of the vicarage to the Andersons. He was at the time unemployed, but had been 'an engineer, mechanic, chauffeur, etc.' and would do all the heavy and 'odd' jobs that needed attention in house and garden, while his wife, a dressmaker, would cook and clean the house. All went well for some months after their arrival in November 1936, but during 1937 they became difficult, rude and uncooperative, letting the kitchen get more and more squalid. Ida felt that the house was in fact too large for Mrs Anderson to keep clean, as well as cooking, and so on. But in December Colin felt he had no alternative but to tell them to look out for some other position. In the event they were not able to move until the summer of 1938, as they had nowhere to go. Early in that year Mrs Aukett, a widow, who had 'looked after' the Assembly Rooms, and her daughter, had also taken up residence in the vicarage. When Colin and Mary moved back to Henfield after Colin's retirement in 1964, Mary wrote about her in glowing terms in the Parish Magazine:

> I don't know whose inspiration it was that her difficulties and ours might be solved in one, but it was decided that she and Enid should come into the empty kitchen wing of the vicarage and Mrs Aukett would 'do' for us. I remember my husband coming in one day and saying 'I've just seen Mrs Aukett. She came out of the Assembly Rooms to shake out a duster, and something about the way she did it gave me complete confidence.' How right he was! Her coming brought a stability and comfort to the vicarage that we had not yet known. ... She was still here when we moved back in 1964. During her last illness she suffered much. When I last visited her, she admitted this very briefly, but it was my husband's health, not hers, that we talked about. We owe a lot to her.

As her daughter, who worked in Horsham, paid for her board and lodging, they were able to hire a man to stoke the boiler, a gardener for one day a week and a fortnightly charwoman.

So far, I may have given the impression that everything ran smoothly in the houses where Colin and Mary visited. Several of his 'Vicar's Notes' mention the gift of fine new ornaments for the Church, and strengthen the impression of a parish whose members were all comfortably off. But in her letters to Ida Mary naturally concentrated on their own doings and on the parishioners she knew best. But she did record three rather different pastoral contacts. Here is the first:

> We went to visit such a charming household on Sunday: a little old cottage on the edge of Broadmere Common – the other common, much wilder and with pools in it – where live an old man and an old woman and their two daughters, two elderly girls. They were all ill. The old man was in bed in one room, with a huge beard, and the two old girls in the other, and the mother was hobbling about crippled with rheumatism, and their son had come over for the day to help. There they all were as merry as gigs – shouting to each other from their beds (2 of them are quite deaf). *So* pleased to have visitors and the old woman said: 'Oh we don't make much of trouble, we don't believe in making much of it'. I wish I could always feel like that! (Letter of 21/1/37)

The second began in late August of the same year:

> On Saturday morning ... the wife of a small shopkeeper called at the vicarage in a terrible state, to tell Colin that her husband had committed suicide. Apparently on Friday night she had found him in a van in their garage, suffocated with deadly fumes from cyanide, which are used, it seems, for destroying pests in greenhouses. There was no question of anything but suicide. They had only been married just a year, and it seems to have been a dreadful year for her – not only money difficulties, and trouble caused by the inability of the man to do any work, or keep anything going, but also by his unkindness to her, dreadful fits of

anger and so on – all pointing to the fact that his mind was deranged. The day of his suicide was actually the eve of their wedding anniversary.

She was in such a dreadful state both mental and physical when she came round that we felt we could not allow her to return home alone, and none of her relations seemed suitable for looking after her. Her own sister had to return to Portslade to look after husband and children and invalid parent, and her husband's relatives were not being at all kind to her – at least they were trying to be, I think, but she feels that they blame her somehow for what happened. Anyway we felt we must do something so on Saturday evening we fetched her here. I rang up the doctor and got him to bring round some bromide, and after a good deal of patient listening we got her into bed and drowsy. She was fairly quiet most of the night and did not keep me awake, but next morning she was pretty bad again and continued so all Sunday. She was seized with dreadful pains, poor thing, as the result of the shock, so I had to keep her in bed and dope her with aspirin. Then on Monday fortunately I managed to get the doctor to her and he dosed her with bromide, and with that and hot cups of tea and bovril we got her sufficiently braced up and quieted down for the inquest. Colin and I both went with her to that. ... (Afterwards) We brought her back for a little restorative and then sent her into Brighton with her sister to buy mourning and a wreath and so on. When she returned she was very much better and after a few more doses of bromide I was able to leave her alone. ... They had the funeral this afternoon. Mrs Skipper broke down at the grave, I hear, and was brought back a little hysterical, but we made her drink very hot sweet coffee, and she is now quite calm and lying down. I have arranged for her to stay here for one more night. Tomorrow she will have to return either to some of her relations or go home.

In March 1939, they became much concerned about the situation of a child of about eleven or twelve, who (Mary wrote to Ida):

lives, not at home , though she has parents and four or five brothers and sisters, but with an old grandmother, who is nearly blind and rather infirm, and one brother who works and lives there too. The child, apparently, has been for some time past cooking breakfast for herself and brother and granny, making the beds and doing all the work of the house, *and* the household shopping before coming to school every day! She arrives of course very late, and much too tired to do anything else.

Colin and Mary weren't quite sure at first what could be done, but Mary went to see the School Medical Inspector next day:

armed with the headmistress's report, and also the evidence of neighbours that the granny is not even very kind to the child, but always nagging at her and scolding her. ... [In her next letter she continues:] In the case of that child I wrote about last week, the School Nurse has discovered a means of getting at the grandmother and we are hoping to stop the exploitation of the child. But it *is* a very difficult situation because the family are so poor, and the old woman is so helpless.

Because of the still rapidly deteriorating international situation Colin and Mary had fewer continental holidays while they were at Henfield. The only fairly long one was in May–June 1937, spent largely at Champéry in Switzerland, in the Châlet Anglais, a small hotel in a little village in the Canton of Vallais, where they spent much time revelling in the lovely countryside around – though by this time in her pregnancy Mary found she got very short of breath walking uphill, so could not accompany Colin on the longer and steeper walks. On their first Sunday Colin volunteered to celebrate in the English church at 8.00, in the absence of the Chaplain, and then take Morning Prayer for the benefit of the English Girls' School nearby. Mary wrote:

> The chaplaincy is under the Colonial and Continental Church Society – very Evangelical – and the church is unspeakably ugly and very ill-furnished. We could hardly find a decent linen cloth to cover the Altar for the Holy Communion, the Hymn Book was *The Hymnal Companion* and altogether the surroundings were depressing in the extreme. I felt sorry for the poor girls having such a church to go to ... The Sunday before we came ... they were marched down to the Châlet Anglais and all sat round in the tiny stuffy little salon, listening to a Methodist service on the wireless!

During the week the Chaplain returned with a large party of friends and relations which made it almost impossible to sit and relax anywhere in the hotel except their own room. Next Sunday, Mary wrote, they had

> rather a trying day, as the rabid, almost fanatical Evangelicalism of the Chaplain and his party of friends broke out in force. The eight o'clock Celebration produced nothing worse than 'taking the North end' [of the altar], and addressing all the prayers to the Congregation as though they were exhortations ... and a curious lack of reverence in Celebrating. But mattins, I gather, [M didn't go] was dreadful. Emotionalism ran riot throughout the service and the sermon made Colin's hair stand on end. It was delivered ... in an awful clerical whine, with a fixed and deadly smile!
> [After tea I] got into terrible disgrace by sitting sewing in the garden, ... (and) finally we both put ourselves beyond the pale by not going to the evening prayer meeting, which was advertised as 'a *very* short service not lasting more than an hour'. Since then they will hardly speak to us. [However] we both feel ashamed of ourselves for feeling so irritated – but it is not *merely* the difference in ideas and opinions that worries, but the feeling of strong disapproval and terrible smugness. However, perhaps we are being smug too.

Then, in June 1938, they paid a brief but very happy visit to Rouen; and 'It was so lovely coming home to find a Francis and no Andersons!' One day they visited Evreux:

> The sad thing about the ['glorious'] cathedral was the utter poverty of all the furnishings and the terribly neglected and uncared-for look. The *dirt* was appalling. I believe they are very poor indeed – but one felt they might have had

the place *cleaned* by voluntary effort. There were plenty of pious widows praying there and putting candles about, who would surely have loved to have a go at washing and dusting!

In her letter (11/6/38) Mary goes on as follows:

Talking of candles – you would have been amused. In the cathedrals of France as you perhaps know there is a perpetual tendency to replace the old Saints by newer ones – e.g. St John will go out before Blessed John Bosco, etc – but *chiefly* the popular objects which you find everywhere are N(ôtre) D(ame) of the Immaculate Conception, and the Little Flower (Thérèse of Lisieux). Well – in the Cathedral of Rouen the Chapel of Joan of Arc is now almost filled up with a disgusting statue of said Little Flower surrounded with hosts of candles, while Joan of Arc had none. Colin was so furious that he bought 5 francs worth of candles and stuck them up in front of Joan of Arc!

Otherwise they took their holidays in England, spending two short periods at Sibyl's country retreat at Old Felixstowe, in January 1938 and then again in late July after their Rouen trip, once Martin Pierce had arrived and settled in. Hill Cottages stands on its own at the end of a lane out of sight of any other house, with a view from the garden out over the marshy fields bordering the Orwell River, and of the northern bank beyond. Colin and Mary spent most of their days driving about the then unspoilt countryside of East Suffolk, with excursions to Bury St Edmunds and Norwich, and twice to Bungay, where Mary's father Charles was now working as a proof-reader at a well-known printer's. Most of the letters she wrote to Ida are full of Mary's enthusiastic descriptions of the many lovely churches they visited. The same is true of her letters from Penzance, where they spent nearly three weeks in February 1939 (a very early holiday as Mary was 'expecting' in May), reading a good deal, each reviewing several books and being greatly revived by the mild winter climate of Cornwall.

As the months of Colin's incumbency passed by, virtually all his 'Vicar's notes' and a great many of Mary's letters to Ida and hers to Mary contained references to and reflections on events in the wider world. During Colin's incumbency at Hove King George V died and was succeeded by his son Edward VIII. But Edward was deeply in love with an American woman, Mrs Wallace Simpson, who had already divorced one husband and now wanted to divorce the second, so that she would be free to marry the King. Eventually she did divorce him, and, after much pressure from various sources, including the Archbishop of Canterbury, Edward chose marriage rather than kingship in December 1936, and was succeeded by his brother George VI. I have seen no reference by Colin to these both unedifying and also embarrassing events, which the Press had for long refrained from mentioning, but he did include in his Vicar's notes for June 1937 a very cheering account of King George VI's Coronation, which was broadcast and found deeply moving by many of his subjects:

Here was our King, set in authority over a vast Empire. Yet in spite of its strength and vastness, he was conscious that he himself is but the servant of the King of Kings. So he went to the Abbey to acknowledge Him as his King, and to promise obedience to God's laws. ... The way King George made his oaths and the way he moved around the Abbey from place to place showed as clearly as possible his inner concentration upon the meaning of the service, namely dedication to God and reception of power from on high to perform his task. I heard from one who was in the Abbey during the service that there was an atmosphere of worship rare in its intensity. It was certainly an imperial function and a demonstration of historic pageantry, but it was much more than this.

In Henfield itself, the ecumenical, or 'United', service it had been planned to hold on the Common had to be held in the Parish Church because of rain. Colin asked three others to help conduct it, and about 500 people were present.

Two months before, he had drawn special attention to the continuing plight of the unemployed:

The distressed areas of our country give many Christians a severe twinge of conscience. It is dreadful to think of so many men, women and children, who, because of the selfishness of our economic life are given no chance of earning their daily bread, and live in a state of want and despondency which is often sheer despair. Henfield people have often felt the shame of that, and have frequently, in the past, sent money and the necessities of life to the relief of these people.

Colin then goes on to outline a new way of doing something about this, which had been tried successfully in one or two parishes:

An out-of-work man in a distressed area is chosen by his local branch of Toc H and his character vouched for. The Ministry of Labour pays his fare to Henfield. In Henfield, 53 people undertake to give this man four hours work a month. They pay to the local secretary of the effort 1/- per week for this four hours a month casual labour. The man works 50 hours a week, doing periods of four hours' work in the houses or farms of subscribers to the scheme. ... If he gives satisfaction the Ministry of labour will pay for the removal of his furniture and, if he has them, wife and children.

Colin admits that the scheme might not work, but reminds his readers 'that nothing worth while can be done without taking risks'. He ends by asking:

what people think of this plan. It is only a drop in the ocean, but even a drop is some use. The great thing is that we should be trying to do something to diminish the misery of the distressed areas.

The parish also regularly sent Christmas gifts for the unemployed and their families at Tonypandy in the Rhondda valley. In February 1939 Colin announces the great increase on the previous year's gifts, and reports that 'the Vicar there wishes to say that Henfield has been a real friend to the parish'.

But it was, of course, the rise to supreme power of Hitler and Britain's response to it which affected people most. When the anti-Jewish legislation in Germany was passed, many Jews took refuge in England, and many welcomed them. In the summer of 1937 Colin and Mary offered summer holiday hospitality to two young German Christians of Jewish descent who were being given free schooling in England. Heinz and Inge Mendelssohn, brother and sister, were for some reason in different institutions, and it was therefore difficult to obtain permission for them to come at the same time. But they were eventually able to come for a shorter time than they would have liked so as to be together. Mary tells Ida of their 'rapture at meeting ... (it was) most moving to behold'.

They came also at Christmas 1938. The Soviet Union was also creating great difficulties for Christians as such. After recording the PCC's unanimous vote of thanks and appreciation for the Holiday Singers, who had come to sing during their Patronal Festival (as they had done more than once at Hove while Colin was there), Colin used the opportunity in the August 1938 Magazine to draw attention to the plight of:

> the Russian Choir which has sung in many churches and cathedrals in England from time to time. It is made up of students from the Russian Theological Academy in Paris, where clergy are trained for the Russian Orthodox Church. With the present regime in power it is the only institution in the world existing for this purpose. Most of the exiles live in a state of great poverty themselves, and now the academy, which has always existed on a bare minimum of income, is in such financial straits that it is in grave danger of being forced to close.

If that happened there would be no way the Russian Orthodox Church could train a new generation of clergy. Colin asks anyone who could help to get in touch with Mr Pierce (the curate) and also to offer:

> hospitality for a week or more to young Russians (mostly students) who are brought over to England for a holiday from their crowded home conditions in Paris during the summer months. Such actions as these are practical expressions of our desire for unity between separated Christians, and of belief in our essential oneness in Christ as a fact which transcends all outward divisions.

In March 1939 Colin got his Russian friend Nicholas Zernov, whom he had got to know at Oxford while he was at New College, to come and preach, and also talk informally about his church. Zernov was a historian of Russian Orthodoxy, and strongly hoped for the reunion of Eastern and Western Christendom.

This is perhaps the place to insert some more on the theme of 'overseas missions', to which Colin attached much importance:

> On Saturday 19th June (1937), at 4 p.m., there will be an opportunity to meet and listen to two remarkable men in the Vicarage Garden. The first is Dr Horace

Crotty, who was till recently the Bishop of Bathurst, in New South Wales; the other is the Rev. T.B. Benjamin, a native Indian priest from Travancore. They will tell us what the Church is doing to bring the knowledge of Christ to those in overseas countries who do not possess that knowledge; Mr Benjamin will especially dwell upon what Christ can do for the people of India and what contribution a Christian India could make to the whole Church. An American-born priest, the Rev Horace Fort, Rector of St Mary's, Bedford, will also show us in a most vivid and interesting way what Christianity can mean to a primitive people. He was brought up by a negro nurse and saw much of the negro life in America as a boy. He has a fine voice and will sing some Negro Spirituals. To listen to these is to understand some of the ways in which the Christian religion brings salvation to a primitive people.

Despite various 'counter-attractions' over 100 people attended the meeting. Mary briefly describes to Ida another Missionary Afternoon in December 1938. She first confesses that she had been 'horribly dreading' it, but, she goes on:

it was really very enjoyable ... because the woman who came to speak was so very nice. Except that she was not Scotch she reminded me of Mary Slessor [one of the 'Great Englishwomen' Ida writes about in her little book of that title] – she seemed to have the same kind of overflowing generous affection, mingled with shrewd commonsense, for the people (Africans of Uganda) she worked for, and she described it all very vividly and amusingly in a homely simple sort of way, without any of the pietism one gets to associate with her particular brand of Evangelical missionary zeal (she is a CMS worker).

Mary immediately goes on to say:

I had the Mothers' Union and gave them a talk on Bringing up children and all the problems involved. I spoke some fairly winged words on some points. I hope none of them will leave.

But we must return now to the international situation in 1938. It was in the autumn and early winter months that the 'Munich crisis' and its aftermath took place. Hitler, head of state in Germany since 1934, and intent on the creation of a new pan-German empire under his sole control, had already annexed Austria in 1937. Now, on the pretext that the German minority in Czechoslovakia (that of the 'Sudeten Germans') was being persecuted and denied its rights, he threatened to support them by force unless the Sudeten Lands, nearly all of whose inhabitants lived alongside the German and Austrian borders, were handed over to Germany peacefully, adding the 'reassurance' that this would be his 'last territorial demand in Europe'. Neither the English nor the French Government were taking a really firm line about this, but still seemed under the illusion that Hitler was amenable to sweet reason.

Ida's letter to Mary of 24 September is a response to her 'most cheering' telegram, in which she and Colin had offered her and her household asylum in Henfield, should it come to war and the danger of bombing or civil unrest in

London. 'Already there seems to be a rush out of London', she writes, and repeats what her friend Miss Savage has told her about the apparent demoralisation in government offices. She also refers to the French General Faucher who has openly said that he 'feels ashamed of being a Frenchman', and that her own doctor has said the same about being an Englishman.

It is horrible that we are all so divided, and that one side feels that its opponents are trying to have war and the other that its opponents are sacrificing the honour of the Country and betraying all that England should stand for. The Peace Pledge Union seems able to combine both points of view, abusing the Government *both* for proposing to have a war and also for betraying Czechoslovakia! ... I feel that almost the only thing we not very able bodied citizens can do at the moment, is to refrain from adding to the atmosphere of anger and fear and hatred that war breeds, to pray without ceasing that God will give us all love and the courage that comes of it.

Ida goes on to say that she is sure her own servants, Gladys and Jack, will get on well with Mrs Aukett, if they come to Henfield, and prove really useful. They have now all been measured for and provided with gas masks, and can take them, with the other things they will need, out of London with them.

Colin's October contribution to the Magazine, which talks of the proximity of 'Judgement Hour' for Europe and the ever increasing need to pray for the powers that be, was clearly written a few days before the Prime Minister, Neville Chamberlain, flew to Munich, and then, a day later, stepped off the aircraft in England waving a piece of paper on which was the text of the 'Munich Settlement', which he described as delivering 'Peace with Honour' and 'Peace by Agreement'. In recalling the Harvest Festival, held at 'one of the most critical moments of this crisis', Colin points out how it made our 'sense of dependence upon God and gratitude for his past care for our physical wellbeing' even more telling than usual. ...

Once again we saw how marvellously the liturgy of our Church, its Psalms and Bible readings and Collect, is able to voice the profoundest sentiments and thoughts of the human heart and to lead them up to God. I am quite sure that it was the dependence upon God, aroused and deepened in worship, which made the Harvest Home party which immediately followed such a genuinely friendly and happy occasion.

It was good to see so many in church during the crisis, he added. 'But it would be an even more encouraging sight if, now that immediate danger to ourselves is past, the church were just as frequented. Do come at 10 or 4 for joint prayer for the world.'

His November 1938 Vicar's Notes begin as follows:

None of us can help being grateful that we are not now engaged in a dreadful and diabolical war. But we should be foolish if we thought that the events of the past weeks have made war for ever impossible. Peace cannot be secured by the mere strokes of a pen, however well-intentioned the men who hold the pen. Peace is a spiritual condition, and can be only brought about by spiritual means. The decision between peace or war rests not with Mr Hitler or Mr Chamberlain but with the ordinary people in Europe like you or me. Nor is peace a question of whether you or I earnestly long for peace. Of course we do. But with our desire for peace we only too often desire other things which make peace impossible. Are you a selfish person, bent on getting your own way in everything? Then you are helping to make war. And so on. A change in the European situation must mean first and foremost a change in your own heart.

Ida wrote again to Mary on 10 November, adding a postscript which began:

Did you listen to Chamberlain last night? I should be sorry for him if he were not so dreadfully complacent. I listened to every word he said with attention and tried to see his point of view. I am sure he is sincere and in earnest, but dreadfully stupid and ignorant. It is appalling to be in the hands of a man of such limited vision and insensitive mind.

Colin and Martin Pierce had organised a Quiet Afternoon on 4 December to enable their parishioners to meet the challenges of the time closer to God. Here is Mary's account of it in her letter to Ida two days later:

(The Quiet Afternoon) was taken by a Mirfield father, called Biggart, who is a great Walsingham Preacher, I believe, so perhaps Honor will know of him. Colin and I viewed his coming with the deepest distrust in case he should turn out a fearful 'spike' and drive half the congregation away. But he turned out to be not only a most delightful man, quite willing to play up, or rather *down*, to our moderate Catholicism, but also a really inspiring and fascinating preacher. We both felt enormously exhilarated and refreshed by his words and his personality. ... Then yesterday Toc H had their Annual Rededication service and social meeting after, and at that there was a wonderful speech on the world situation and what we had to think and do about it. It really was splendid. The speaker was one of the Toc H padres, a Northcountryman I should think, and all that he said was so true and sensible , as well as being most moving. I feel sure that it made a great impression on many people who were there who are not churchgoers, as well as on those who are.

Then, for the Vicar's Notes of January 1939, Colin began:

A Happy New Year to all readers. It seems almost ironical in these uncertain days to breathe such a wish – unless you believe in God. If you believe in God and commit your whole life to Him, knowing how helpless you are, out of despair at man's folly and blindness will be born a faith in the mighty power of God to overrule human sin and wickedness. And that faith brings a joy which is able to flourish and abound even in the midst of troubles and sufferings of all kinds. This is the joy which our Lord bequeathed to his Church, and said of it: 'Your joy no man taketh from you'. May this joy be in us at the beginning of this new year.

In March 1939 Hitler invaded and quickly overran a Czechoslovakia now deprived of territory, factories and raw materials which would have enabled a vastly more effective resistance, and then, after another five months, invaded Poland, having just concluded with the Soviet Union a non-aggression treaty. The Second World War was the inevitable response of Great Britain and France; Colin and his family – now numbering two children – went north to Edinburgh in April 1940, leaving almost nothing I could discover in the way of letters or other writings as responses to these events, except what I have already recounted earlier in this chapter about Colin's illness.

Colin appears to have written very little for publication during his time at Henfield. But two cuttings in his scrap book give us some idea of his thoughts on women's ordination at this time. The first is a *Times* report on a meeting at Mary Sumner House, London S.W., organised by the Anglican Group for the ordination of women to the historic Ministry of the Church. Four speeches are summarised, Colin's at considerably greater length than the others. He does not directly argue in favour of women's ordination to the clergy, but seeks to establish essential conditions for it, such that, if they were realised, women's ordination would be seen to follow automatically.

The main problem we had to face, he argues, drawing on his own parochial experience of confirmation candidates, was the conception of the church as a collection of individuals who might or might not join it, rather than as 'a family, of which (individuals) were vitally important members'. It was regarded as 'a body which arranged improving entertainment for the Public on Sundays, to engender a serious moral outlook and help them to live straight lives on weekdays'. But 'Christian fellowship ... must arise within the building, at worship, when the church was most truly herself'. Worship is 'the offering of the whole family to God'; the core of fellowship 'must be the Holy Communion'. 'Only in that atmosphere could a desire for service grow in young and old.'

The second contains an article in the *G.F.S. Review* which appeared two years later. The Bishop of Dorchester had written condemning 'the decision of Convocation to permit women to undertake liturgical functions in church'. In his reply, Colin once more did not directly address the priesthood of women, only subordinate liturgical functions. The Bishop's first point, Colin writes, is that woman's 'supreme task' is motherhood. But even if all could be mothers, why does that fact by itself debar them from liturgical function? But it becomes clear that it is sex that is for him the real barrier. But, Colin argues, don't some women occasionally feel aroused by the service of men at the altar? In a world of sin it could not be otherwise. But, he goes on, I can assure the Bishop that at Henfield GFS members regularly bring up the oblations of bread and wine, while the young men follow with the alms. Even in our 'conservative country parish' no-one has complained that this has 'spiritually or emotionally degraded the atmosphere of worship'.

But the Bishop makes his greatest error when he assumes that the Eastern Church supports him. In Paris at the Russian churches women regularly lead the choir (more of a liturgical function than in the Church of England), read the Epistle at Holy Communion and psalms and prayers at Mattins and Vespers. He goes on to adduce other examples from Tsarist Russia and Armenia which contradict the Bishop's assumption. These two cuttings do not seem to me to show that Colin was wholeheartedly in favour of women priests, or even deacons, but that he was completely in agreement that women should be allowed to perform 'subordinate liturgical functions', as they were already doing at Henfield, probably at his instigation, and at least still open to the idea of their being deacons and priests as well. This certainly seems to follow from his general social and political attitudes at the time.

In Colin's valedictory Vicar's Notes in the Parish Magazine, he tells the reader that he has much enjoyed his time at Henfield, though now feels he could have done much better, and is full of complements for Henry de Candole, who would be succeeding him, and for Martin Pierce, who would be carrying on for a time as Assistant Curate. Martin himself wrote: 'Henfield has been incalculably enriched by having had him here and his going will be to many people the loss of a real friend.' After Colin's death he wrote to Mary:

> few though contacts were after Henfield days I think it is true that his has been one of the strongest influences in my life. He laid foundations for me in those early days and I have so often related my thinking to what he stood for and how he might see things.

Photos 12 (*above*) **and 13** (*right*): Babylon signage, 1932.

Photo 14: Colin with pipe and dog collar, 1930s.

Photo 15: Colin in shirt and tie, 1930s.

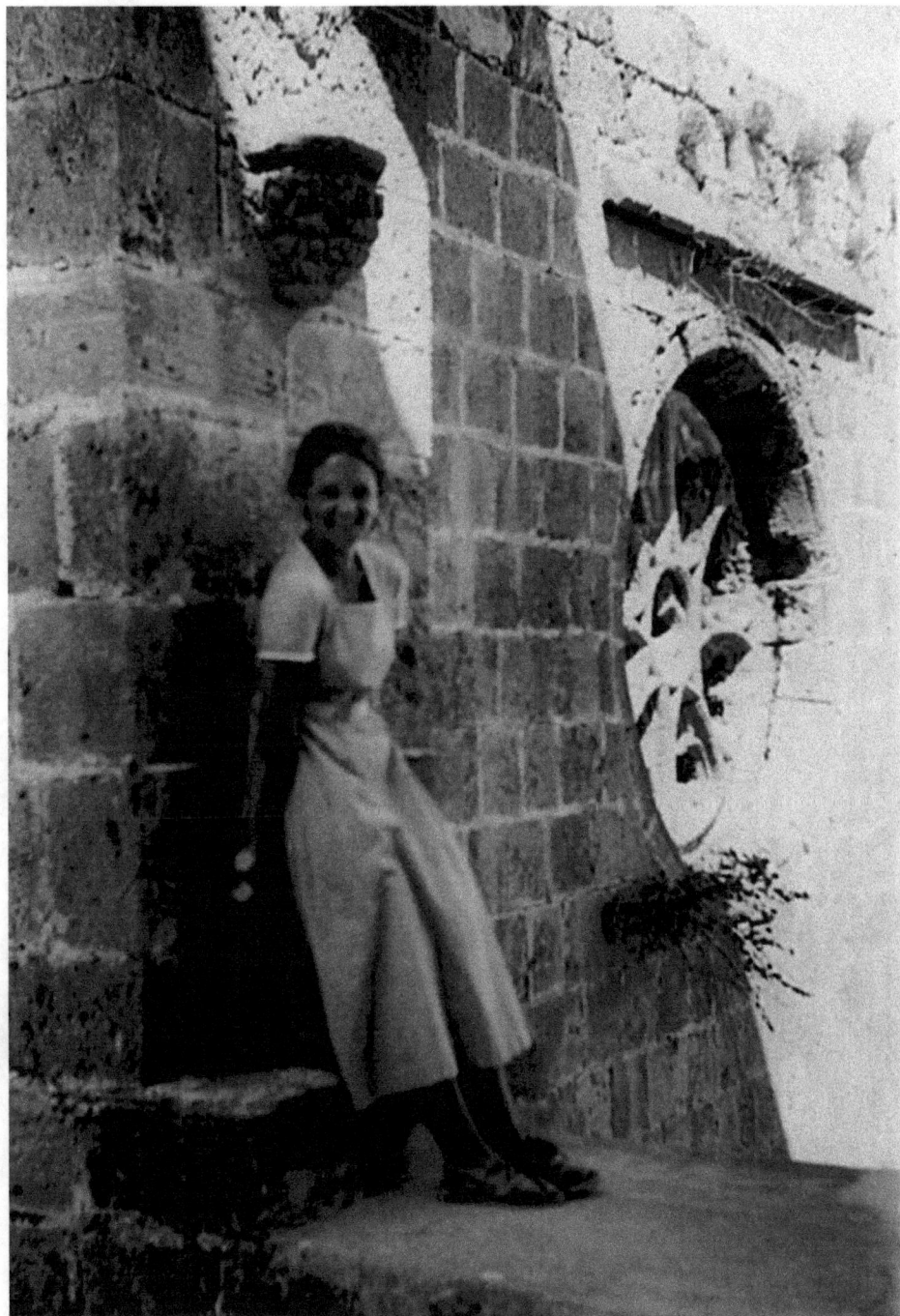

Photo 16: Colin's fiancée Mary O'Malley at church in Kyrenia (Cyprus).

Photo 17: Colin with Francis on his knee, 1938.

13

EDINBURGH

C OLIN'S NEW POST in Edinburgh was that of Provost in the Cathedral of the Scottish Episcopal Church, which is part of the Anglican Communion – quite distinct from the Church of Scotland, which is Presbyterian, the Church to which his father had belonged. St Mary's Episcopalian Cathedral, by Sir George Gilbert Scott, with its three lofty spires, is a prominent landmark at the west end of Edinburgh's largely Georgian 'New Town'. As D-J told Jack Arnold after a visit there to preach, 'It is a glorious church , and Colin's house (8 Lansdowne Crescent) is stately and fine in a kind of sober, stern Scottish Belgravia.'

The vacancy had come about with the elevation of the previous Provost, Logie Danson, to be Bishop of Edinburgh, who had thus become, *ex officio*, patron of his old post. Bishop Danson had written to Cosmo Gordon Lang, Archbishop of Canterbury (himself of Scottish descent) to ask if there were anyone from England he could recommend for the Provostship, 'one of the really key jobs in the Scottish Episcopal Church'. Danson's letter had stressed that the successful candidate ought to be a really good preacher, able in some measure to hold his own with the many Presbyterians in the city and to be a moderate Catholic.

In his reply, Lang mentioned the names of two people who had already been suggested to him, but added that he himself had another suggestion which he was 'inclined to think the most likely of those he had mentioned'. This was Colin, Scottish by birth and 'as a great friend of his puts it, very characteristically Scottish in temperament and mentality. He is a very successful parish priest, an excellent preacher and has something of the capacity of a Dwelly for running a great church without the latter's deficiencies. He is also a convinced but a sensible and restrained Catholic.' Lang adds that he believes Dunlop 'verted' at about twelve years old from the Presbyterian to the Anglican Church. Returning to his CV, he mentions Baghdad:

where he did excellent work and showed a commendable spirit of independence in his relations with the then British Ambassador in Iraq. He is a man of very attractive personality and appearance and has lots of go about him. I really think you would be well advised to give him serious consideration if you are on the look-out for a Scotsman over the Border. ... The Bishop of Chichester could tell you all about him. He is a member of the Church of England Council for Foreign Relations and takes a great interest in our relations with other churches. In fact a good all round fellow.

Danson wrote again two days later, saying that he is giving serious consideration to all three of the suggested names, but that he thought Colin was 'quite the best – strongly recommended by his Bishop [Bell] and yourself. If the Bp of Glasgow agrees [Bishop How, ex-vicar of Brighton, whom Colin knew from Sussex], I shall write inviting him to come here and talk it over.' The other two 'names', he goes on, were strongly recommended by their bishops but had no Scottish connection. Then, in a postscript, he says the Bishop of Glasgow has just expressed his agreement with Lang and Bishop Bell. So he's going to write to Dunlop.

To avoid confusion in this chapter, I should add here that the term 'dean' is also used in the Scottish Episcopal Church, but to designate a Diocesan official with many of the functions of an Archdeacon in the Church of England. The provost of a Scottish Episcopal Cathedral is the senior clergyman on its staff, as is also the case in many recent Anglican cathedrals. What made the Provost of Edinburgh more than locally important was that Edinburgh had the biggest Scottish cathedral, with 1100 on the roll of communicants – quite apart from the city's secular importance in Scottish history and culture. The diocese had been carved out of the Diocese of St Andrews by the Stuart King Charles I, whereas the other Scottish dioceses had remained territorially much the same as those in the pre-Reformation Church in Scotland.

Colin went to Edinburgh to see the Bishop at the end of November or beginning of December 1939, and, as a result, felt able to accept the Bishop's offer. Press announcements followed near the beginning of December, but, because of the operation on his tonsils scheduled for the beginning of January and the surgeon's warning that he would not really be fit enough to take up a new appointment until the beginning of April, Colin was not installed until 4 April. The Chapter Minutes for 11 January 1940, record that the Bishop had formally announced the appointment, and had added that Colin would also be asking the Chapter if he might temporarily hold the office of Precentor himself, and thus have some control over the music. As the Cathedral finances were not then in a good state, it might seem that the post had been kept vacant as an economy measure, but in fact none of the Canonries at Edinburgh were specifically devoted to the precentorship, as is usually the case in English cathedrals, and any of the Canons could take it.

Colin, having all the musical knowledge, taste and abilities it required, was no doubt eager to take on the work in addition to that of his provostship; it would also provide him with much satisfaction. This was agreed at Colin's first Chapter meeting on 11 April, chaired, as always in the Scottish Episcopal Church, by the Bishop. Some of the functions of an Anglican Cathedral Chapter in England, mainly the financial ones, were performed by the Board of

Management (also known as 'The Cathedral Board'), which was chaired by the Provost. We learn from the minutes of the Board that, as there was no precedent for paying the removal expenses of a provost, no exception would be made in Colin's case, especially under the Cathedral's straightened circumstances at the time. The Cathedral would directly benefit from the sale of those items of furniture left by the Dansons which Colin did not need; money from the sale of these probably offset the fitting and insertion of a Nursery gate at the top of the (steep) stairs, as requested by Colin and charged to the Cathedral Furniture Fund.

Before the move to Edinburgh Colin was asked to write and introduce himself in the *Cathedral Monthly Paper*. This is what he said:

> Dear People, the Vice-Provost asks me to write a letter for the April Monthly paper. But as it is the middle of Holy Week, and as I do not find it easy to write to people I do not know, I am sure you will excuse a very brief note. I should like to say how proud I am at the prospect of becoming a Scottish churchman, and being allowed to serve a branch of the church which has such a noble history. It is also a peculiar satisfaction to be called to serve a diocese founded by one who has increasingly been one of my heroes, His Majesty King Charles the Martyr. It is an added joy that I shall serve under a bishop who made a deep impression on me the first Sunday after my ordination, and whose words in the pulpit about the duty of priests to consider work overseas remained with me many years till the opportunity came and was accepted. These are three reasons why I look forward to April 4th with pleasure.

The brief report in *The Scotsman* of 5 April tells us a little more about the parochial aspects of the Provost's position:

> The Rev David Colin Dunlop ... was installed last night as Provost of St Mary's Cathedral, Edinburgh, and Rector of the congregation. The Right Rev. Bishop Logie Danson, whom he succeeds, officiated, and the new Provost was presented to the Bishop by the Very Rev. Dean Mackay, to become a member of the Chapter. A social function was then held in the Walpole Hall after the installation, when Mr Dunlop, who comes of an Edinburgh family, was welcomed.

Colin's 'Provost's Notes' for May express gratitude for his warm welcome; he then confesses that he had been very nervous but soon felt at home with the well-ordered service and the 'stately movements of clergy and choir'. Even his speech in the Walpole Hall, he goes on, was 'emptied of most of its terrors'. In the same 'notes' he refers to the war as 'really a religious war', with Hitler as Antichrist, and then In June refers to it as a 'struggle for the human soul', and the practice of religion as a kind of war-service.

On 12 June he wrote a revealing letter to his great Henfield friend, Eric Whittome, one of the few which has survived from this period:

We are trying our best to like Edinburgh and are succeeding on the whole, but frankly it is a conscious effort. We still miss Henfield rather sorely, and by Henfield I mean not merely a geographical expression but all that the place stands for, especially friends. This is not a time for striking new roots and we have not made any absolute friends here, though we have met many friendly people whom we quite like. On the other hand politically this place and society is definitely sounder than the South. Of course it may really be the unifying power of disaster which gives us this sense of political solidarity, but I believe not only. Actually of course politics have almost ceased to be an interest; it's entirely a matter of power and nerve now and as to that one can only have hopes, not informed opinions. Dunkirk and our air successes have been most encouraging as evidence of superior nerve and I suppose there comes a point when superior power gives way to superior nerve. This is no doubt partly what is meant when the Bible says 'The Lord can save by many or by few'.

But what a legacy of past misgovernment our physical deficiencies in arms is. Are Christine, or Dykes, still impenitently Chamberlainites? Doubtless also Maurice Bell is regretting his championship of Mussolini as a Christian hero. Even in the midst of disaster it is a glowing satisfaction to know that on the main issue you and I represented sanity and realism in Henfield opinion! On the whole the worse things get the more easy I feel in my mind. Is this callousness or numbness or the Grace of God? I really believe it is the last-mentioned , though of course I am prejudiced.

I hope you like Henry de Candole. I have never talked to him on subjects other than ecclesiastical, but I have always felt he had the authentic divine spark in him.

Colin ends by telling Eric that he 'spent most of last week at a murder trial' and found it highly absorbing, but doesn't say why he was there or how he found the time!

Colin was to remain Provost of St Mary's for four years, but he spent most of 1943 away from Edinburgh with the RAF, a year punctuated by one month's 'leave', and a good many brief visits to 8 Lansdowne Crescent to be with the family (Mary was now expecting her third child) and trying not to get too much involved in Cathedral affairs. The Bishops of the Church of England, headed by the two Archbishops, Temple (Canterbury) and Garbett (York), had become much concerned about what the war would do for the Christian faith in this country. Many of the chaplains to the armed forces were new to their work, and many, again, would be seeking 'civilian' clerical employment when it was all over. At the same time, these concerns had been current in the Chaplain's department of the RAF.

As a result the Air Council had themselves raised the matter with the Archbishops, who decided to appoint a small number of senior clergy as 'Archbishops' Visitors', relieve them for a year from all the responsibilities arising directly from their jobs, and put them at the disposal of the Air Force. Colin was one of five who presented themselves at the Air Ministry at 3.00 p.m. on 30 November 1942. He had not completely understood what his 'Call' would involve, but he now learned that he and his four co-workers would, as he put it in his diary, 'travel about visiting aerodromes (in Scotland for me) staying at each about ten days and doing what we can to ginger up religion. It is an awesome task for which I feel my qualifications are few.' Colin's area of operations would also include Northern Ireland and, as he discovered later, Iceland. Needless to say, his acceptance of the call had already been sanctioned by the Bishop of Edinburgh, who had been approached first by the Archbishops. As Colin put it to Temple in his letter of acceptance:

> With his permission and sanction I write to say that I am at your Graces's disposal for this work in the RAF. I accept, not because I fully understand what the work is or from any conviction that I am capable of doing it, but simply in response to the urgency, rather than invitation, of the call that you make.

Colin's work in the many airfields around Scotland, Northern Ireland and Iceland is of great interest, and I shall, of course, be saying a lot more about it below. His visits to report to the Air Ministry or Lambeth on this RAF business, of which there were at least three altogether, also gave him the chance to catch up with friends, visit Mowbrays and the Warham Guild, and so on, things that would otherwise have been very difficult under wartime conditions.

Meanwhile I shall return to his profession of veneration for King Charles the Martyr, which he announced in his self-introductory article in the *Cathedral Monthly Magazine*. It was soon to be gratified. In the Chapter meeting for October 1940, he is recorded as having mentioned 'Miss Donaldson's desire to provide a Memorial for Episcopalians martyred in the Covenanting times'. The Scottish Covenanters, of whom there were several different groups during the sixteenth and seventeenth centuries, bound themselves by an oath to uphold the cause of Presbyterianism, which meant above all opposing episcopacy. In view of the fact that putting memorial tablets on the walls of churches was no longer permissible, it was agreed by the Chapter that the memorial could consist in adornments and other improvements to All Saints Chapel, if the would-be donor was satisfied.

After talking to her, Colin was able to report at the next chapter meeting, in January 1941, that Miss Donaldson had now agreed that the Memorial would be to King Charles the Martyr and 'other martyrs for Episcopacy', and was happy about the terms and conditions he and the Chapter Clerk had worked out together. There would be printed descriptions of the victims, and all the alterations to the chapel itself would be done in accordance with the 'ancient ecclesiological usages of Britain' and not in obedience to modern or continental 'fashions or requirements'. He hoped that Randoll Blacking, or someone of comparable reputation, would be able to take charge of the decoration. The Chapter approved of all this, and Colin was authorised to attend to the details.

He followed this up with a Cathedral sermon on King Charles the Martyr three days after the anniversary of his execution on 30 January 1649. It was printed in *The Scottish Guardian* on 14 February. He first points to the strangeness of the fact that the anniversary was ignored by both the city, which would still be a 'mere borough' if it were not for Charles I, and by the Church, especially the Church in Edinburgh, whose diocese was founded by the King, who also gave the Episcopalians their own Scottish Prayer Book, with a liturgy which 'has resulted in a form of service universally regarded as one of the most precious jewels of the liturgical treasury of the whole Church', and 'has powerfully influenced the liturgy of the Church of America, of the South African Church, of the Indian and Ceylon Churches, and the revised Prayer Book of England [the '1928'] itself'.

Colin goes on to point out that 'to honour King Charles does not mean that we are obliged to approve and applaud everything he thought or did. ... Saints are not endowed with all God's gifts.' But, for all his many faults, Charles also had many great virtues. Yet 'it is not merely for these that the royal name finds a place in our Church Calendar among the Saints of the Church. ... He is placed there because he preferred death rather than betray his church', though the Covenanters, into whose hands he had fallen, 'would have spared his life had he agreed to abolish Episcopacy in England and to force the English Church to become Presbyterian'. As it was, he was handed over to certain death, and executed in London. Colin goes on to remind us that it is the existence of bishops that links us:

> by the Apostolic Succession to the ministry of the Apostles, and so to the ministry of Christ Himself. ... It was to preserve this sacred thing that King Charles died. It is because we share his faith that we are here today... and are called upon to continue Charles's witness to the Apostolic nature of the Church. But do not let us get swept away by the angry passions which wrought such havoc to the Church in the seventeenth century. If we are to commend Episcopacy to our fellow-countrymen it must not be by hatred or contempt or by jealous feelings. Our attitude towards our brethren of the Presbytery must not be like that of the Roman Catholic Church in England towards the Church of England. Do not brood over the past. Anyone can work themselves into a pitch of fury and indignation by reading history – especially if they don't read very much. ... True tolerance combines a passionate love of truth with a deep respect for human personality, even if you believe it to be in error. In the words of St Peter our attitude must be 'not as being lords over God's heritage, but being ensamples to the flock.' So let us try to give our witness with the same faithfulness as King Charles gave his.

In the first quarter of 1942, Colin was able to report in the Cathedral's official 'Quarterly Record' that the anniversary of King Charles's execution had (with the sanction of the Bishop) been celebrated in the Cathedral as a Red Letter Day.

The last part of Colin's sermon alludes to an issue which greatly concerned him – that of relations between Episcopalians and the far more numerous clergy of the Church of Scotland. Naturally, most churchmen on either side believed themselves to have made the right choice. But how were they to live with the difference? A paragraph in another letter Colin wrote to Eric Whittome tells us something about Colin's attitude. It is dated 28/11/42:

> I have found myself a leader and protagonist here in the question of reunion with the Presbyterians and have already acquired a considerable degree of suspicion from my fellow clergy. So far I have carried my Bishop ('dragged' would be better) with me. I had to address a public meeting with the ex-Moderator last Thursday. It's the first time I have ever found myself forced to the front (merely on the strength of a moderate letter in *The Scotsman*), and at present I am dizzy to think that what seemed common sense is regarded as dangerous innovation. So I must go ahead, though I did not choose the path.

His Provost's Notes in the *Cathedral Monthly Paper* for December 1942 show us one way in which he felt the aspiration might be realised:

> Ultimately both Church unity and World Evangelism depend upon the intensity of desire for these objects in every member of the Church. If *you* do not care much, one way or the other, for these things their coming will be greatly hindered and delayed. But if every member of the Church really cares, the formidable difficulty in the path will be steadily overcome. '*Desire* of me, and I shall give thee the heathen for thine inheritance.' So speaks God through the inspired voice of the writer of the second psalm. And one way to deepen our desire is to act as though we desired deeply. With that end in view I ask you to attend the Usher Hall meeting on Tuesday, December 1st, at 7.30 p.m.

When Colin visited Iceland in 1943 (see below) and preached at the 'Lakeside Church' in Reykjavik (temporarily loaned to the British forces stationed there), the event was announced beforehand in a forces' newspaper. Colin was said to be 'well-known in Edinburgh and elsewhere for his eloquence and vigour in preaching, and for his energy in promoting the cause of Church Unity, especially between the Episcopal and Presbyterian churches in Scotland'.

The Second World War saw many Polish and Russian troops temporarily living in Scotland. The Chapter of St Mary's Cathedral was perfectly happy to allow the building to be used for Orthodox services. In the Quarterly Records it was now the Provost's task to complete, Colin reported that In the first quarter of 1941 there were two services taken by the Orthodox chaplain for Polish troops; in the second quarter of 1942 there was a Russian Orthodox celebration of the Eucharist, and in the fourth a celebration for Poles, Russians and others, following a lecture on the Eastern Churches. Here are two passages from his diary describing personal contacts with a Polish Bishop:

> 4.1.44 Bishop Savva of Grodno (Poland) came to tea with me bringing two Polish officers. We arranged about tomorrow's celebration of the Orthodox Liturgy in the Cathedral. I succeeded in overturning the tea tray and breaking a plate and saucer besides scattering biscuits and scones all over the floor. He

came to Evensong after, sitting in the Dean's stall and joining with melodious grunts in the singing. He blessed us from his stall at the end.

7.2.44 This afternoon the Polish Orthodox Bishop Savva of Grodno came to see me again, bringing with him the Rev. Jan Panir who is chaplain to the Polish Lutherans. They seem very friendly, admittedly largely for political reasons, neither desiring to see Poland dominated by Roman Catholic Fascism. Panir even hinted that his leaving Canada to take up work with Polish troops in Britain was as much due to hopes of opportunities for political propaganda as for openings for religious ministration. Apparently the Polish Lutheran Church dates from the time of the Reformation and its principle seat is in Silesia, which he said was called 'Old Poland'. Bishop Savva spoke well of the Polish Lutherans from the ecclesiastical as well as the political standpoint. He, the Bishop, is anxious to celebrate the Polish Orthodox Paschal night office in my cathedral, a week later than our Easter.

Colin also records another contact with the Lutheran Church, this time of Sweden, when he mentions the presence in the Cathedral, at a choral recital of Tudor Church music, of Bishop Ingve Brilioth, who had stayed at 8 Lansdowne Crescent in November 1942. Brilioth knew Bishop Bell, and Colin had very likely met him while he was Bell's Chaplain. There would not have been any difficulty about Orthodox or Swedish Lutheran Bishops performing liturgical functions, or occasionally holding their own services in the Cathedral.

But close religious contact between Presbyterians and Episcopalians (or 'Presbies and Piskies') usually had to contend with strong hostile prejudices on either side originating in the religious wars of the sixteenth and seventeenth centuries, and closely entangled with nationalist loyalties. Even Colin had had to overcome the effects of the religion and culture of his father, in which (see above in Chapter 3) he had found very little joy or penitence. There are perhaps echoes of it in two short extracts from his diary. In one of them he records having to take the funeral of the Piskie Colonel Kirkpatrick: 'We were held up by a(nother) funeral conducted in that ultraformal informality which characterises the outward observances of the Kirk. The congregation was wallowing in gloom.' He also recalls 'a Missionary brains trust at Lusk's church which was good but, like so many Presbyterian activities, far too Teutonically long'. On the other hand, he mentions:

A pleasant talk before dinner [at RAF Errol] with the Presbyterian officiating chaplain, the parish minister, a Mr Morgan. He is a well-read cultivated man and we found in common an admiration for Archdeacon Grantly [the unforgettable, wealthy, ultra-conservative Church dignitary in Trollope's Barsetshire novels]! Theologically too I felt much common ground with him. He has a high opinion of Metcalfe's work as a (C of E) padre. He says that he is really growing into his work, that he is a real friend to all on the station and that if a vote were to be taken there would be few on the station who would vote for his dismissal.

Quite apart from individual exceptions to the stereotype, Colin emphasises strongly in his Provost's Letter in the November 1943 number of the *Cathedral Monthly Paper* 'the cordial welcome I always receive from the Church of Scotland padré'. This is a completely general tribute, by no means confined to 'High Church' Presbyterian ministers, such as John Begg, the young Parish Minister of Tain, with whom he lunched one day during his RAF duty in the town, and whom he describes in his diary as 'setting the place by the ears'.

But the following passage from the same source seems to encapsulate both Colin's hopes and his worries in the matter of the unification of the two churches, which he stood for. The starting point is his visit to St James's Episcopalian Church in Stranraer, which he called 'an untidy ugly little place':

What a tragedy it is that in this country, where our 'ecclesiology' should be at its best in order to impress Presbyterians, our churches are on the whole far below the English average and the parsons unconscious of the great appeal which Anglicanism can make to Scottish people. Our Scottish clergy regard their missionary role as consisting almost exclusively in the adoption of a sneering attitude to the presbies while either through ignorance or laziness they appear to take little trouble to make our services and church buildings express that austere beauty which is our especial contribution.

Here again is his impression of Sunday Evensong at the Episcopalian Cathedral of Oban:

It is difficult to think that the Anglican liturgy could be celebrated in a more slovenly or unimaginative way. A choir of 4 boys and one man and a congregation of about 30-40 huddled at the back of the nave was a bad start. The Provost and the Synod Clerk ... appeared in cottas. The organist couldn't get through a hymn tune without several mistakes in a verse. The actual building is pretentious and cheap-looking, utterly lacking in dignity or grandeur. The Provost's sermon stressed the high standard of service and surrender expected by our Lord in his service, but the only example provided by the preacher was that it meant that Episcopalians must keep Presbyterians at a distance.

Elsewhere (*Cathedral Monthly* paper, December 1941) he cites a characteristic Episcopalian excuse for this active aloofness: a fear that, if they did not, they would 'compromise their position'. The reference to the wearing of cottas at Oban is a reminder of the 'unintelligent catholicism' that, in Colin's view, typified most of the Episcopalian clergy, since cottas, a shortened form of the surplice, were a post-Tridentine fashion in the Roman church which, even when Colin wrote, was gradually being replaced by the full length surplice of the Middle Ages. Despite his irritation at so much in the Cathedral and the service, Colin recorded in his diary a pleasant evening he spent two days later at the Rectory, where the Provost, D.A.G. Muir, and his wife lived. He found they had 'a host of friends in common'. He was in fact a convert from Presbyterianism, but left Colin with a strong impression that he chose the Church of England ... as the most suitable sphere available for the preaching of certain doctrines and the inculcating of certain piety rather than from an appreciation of the nature and history of the Community itself he joined.

It is this sort of thing, he goes on, that 'characterises so much Anglo Catholicism and gives it that *déraciné* existence which will in the end be its own destruction'.

But the following letter from Colin to The Revd Donald MacLean of Galashiels also adds another reason for deprecating 'Anglo-Romanism':

Dear Donald, I congratulate the Vestry of Fort William or whoever is responsible, on the appointment of their new rector. I have just seen the announcement in the Glasgow Herald & it has filled me with satisfaction. You are just the man to rebuild the devastation caused by the last rector & in your work of re-establishing Anglican religion there you will have the support, not only of the magnates such as Lochiel & Lord Abinger, but probably of a suffering majority of the congregation who dislike or are mystified by Anglo-Romanism. It is always a good thing when a defection to Rome on the part of an incumbent is followed by the arrival of an Anglican who knows why he is an Anglican & is proud of it. I hope & believe that you have a valuable ministry before you at Fort William....
Yours ever, Colin Dunlop.

His son Alan, who sent me the text of this letter, adds that 'it did not work out, as my father was very unhappy at Fort William, with an impossible Bishop'. He added an amusing anecdote that, he said, his father often used to repeat about his and Colin's first meeting; Donald MacLean speaks first:

'Provost, I wonder if you have met Hector MacLean, the Vicar of Woodmancote, near Henfield?'
'Yes, I have; the only clergyman in the Church of England who plays the concertina in church.'
'He's my uncle.'
'Oh, he plays the concertina *very* well!'

The faults of both Presbies and Piskies recur in different form in Colin's account of a talk with Mr Sutherland-Graeme, whose house, Graemeshall, had been lived in by his family since 1615, when it was built by his ancestor the Bishop of Orkney, who refused to accept the Presbyterian re-ordering of the Scottish Church, resigning his see in 1638. Colin was taken there on an afternoon in August by the padré at Kirkwall, Mr Bowen. He describes 'S-G' as 'a nice country gentleman and a stray Episcopalian':

We spoke of the recent Episcopal election at Aberdeen in which S-G had proposed the Rev: Pat Lennard, Vicar of Hatfield, and got much vilified for proposing an Englishman. We spoke at full agreement of the dangerous Romanising and anti-Presbyterian drift in the Episcopal Church.

Colin's host bewailed the new Bishop's announcement that he would not visit Orkney till next Easter. So Colin undertook to tell the new bishop 'how vast an assembly of Anglicans the forces constitute in the diocese and how essential it is for him to visit them as soon as he can after his enthronement.' The visits of his predecessor, Bishop Deane, had raised the standing of Episcopalianism to a very high level. It would be a tragedy to let this fall again. S-G was delighted at this proposal. But it was not until he was sent to Northern Ireland in October that Colin met an 'English Use' padré in the RAF – Cooke, of Aldergrove, who sounds an ideal chaplain. But, for all Colin's personal allegiances in the matter of churchmanship, which he saw as historically justified, one thing he says he learnt from his year with the RAF was that 'Evangelicals make the best chaplains.'

I must end this section on relations between Episcopalians and Presbyterians in Scotland by first mentioning the Leighton Club in Edinburgh, named after a Scottish Archbishop of the seventeenth century who laboured hard to reconcile Presbies and Piskies, even preparing to resign his Bishoprick of Dunblane because the Government persecuted the Covenanters. Charles II managed to give him reassurances such that he withdrew his resignation, but in the end, after further fruitless efforts towards union, he resigned his archbishopric. We have already quoted Colin's letter to Eric Whittome in which he tells his friend about the leading position he has found himself holding on the issue. He implies that, although he has persuaded Bishop Danson to take the issue seriously, the latter (despite attending at least one meeting of the Leighton Club) is reluctant to become too involved. This explains an entry Colin made in his diary about the bishop during his last months in Edinburgh, in early 1944. The Primus, he writes (that is, the 'Presiding Bishop', a position to which he had now been raised by the election of his fellow bishops), had consulted him about his successor as Provost. Donald Sinclair, the Chapter Clerk, had recommended Lancelot Fleming:

> The primus spoke coolly of the plan and said that Fleming 'is too much a C.of E. man, more at home at St John's than the Cathedral'. I fear he intends to take the bit between his teeth and appoint what he likes to call a 'sane Catholic' who will almost certainly be a mildly Romanising spike. He seems to have no conception of the vocation of the Episcopal Church other than that of a not too extreme but uniform sect of holders of 'definite Catholic principles'. What they are to witness to or to become perhaps doesn't bother him. They are certainly to have a 'short way with Presbyterians'.

Despite their disagreement on these matters, Colin was able to write a fortnight later that 'The Primus made a very generous speech about me at the Clergy Society Meeting yesterday which surprised me by its warmth'. But he was not at all happy when the Primus told him to whom he had offered the provostship. As regards the mutual disdain of Piskies and Presbies, this lasted at least into the 1970s, though at that time it was 'fast vanishing on both sides' (letter of December 2007 from the Revd Canon Philip Crosfield, OBE).

Colin's post as Provost, together with his accompanying Precentorship, meant that, in matters of cathedral liturgy and music, he was probably the author or instigator of many, perhaps most, of the changes and innovations mentioned in the Chapter Minutes, Records of Board of Management Meetings, Quarterly Cathedral Records and the *Cathedral Monthly Paper*, quite apart from his diary and one or two letters. It is easy to see in some of the official 'it-was-agreed-thats' the influence of Colin's concern to make communal worship strengthen the sense of community in the participants, or, in one word, to edify, and at the same time to show forth the beauty of holiness and of good order.

At their October meeting in 1940, the Chapter agreed to hold its meetings after a celebration of Communion and a communal breakfast. Shortly afterwards we read of the inauguration on Advent Sunday of a weekly Sung Eucharist and short address at 9.15 for all, followed by breakfast. This change was supported by many worshippers, especially after Colin had pointed out in the Monthly Paper that the sharing of a communal meal is a time-honoured way to encourage the growth of community. The Chapter also agreed in October to observe a resolution passed in 1899, and still in force, that scripture readings for Sundays and Holy Days should, except on certain occasions, be taken from the Authorised version (King James's Bible), not from the Revised version, as was presumably being done.

They also agreed in January 1941 that all its members should wear cassock, surplice, hood and scarf for the Communion and cassocks for the meeting itself. In October 1941, Colin is mentioned as the one who proposed moving the font from under the south-west tower, where it was rarely seen, into a position at the west end of the nave near the main entrance, where it could 'greet' people as they came in or form the basis of a processional 'station'. After consulting Francis Eeles, an acknowledged expert on ecclesiological matters, who suggested a position under the south-west arch of the aisle arcade, it was moved in 1942.

In January of that year, under an agendum headed 'Naming of Stalls', Colin is recorded as having submitted 'a list of Saints and other worthy persons prepared by himself and the Dean', which was accepted with a few amendments, and shortly afterwards applied to identify the seats in the back row of the Choir Stalls. As pointed out above, the Board of Management dealt chiefly with financial matters.

In March 1943 Colin suggested that something should be done about pensions for vergers, which was soon acted on in at least one case. Soon after his arrival, despite the poor financial state of the cathedral, he had deplored the Bishop's decision not to appoint a new Vice-Provost after the departure of Vice-Provost Broun in September 1940, since this would bear hard on the parochial work of the cathedral, especially visiting. He proposed that a temporary woman worker should be appointed until the Vice-Provost's post was once more filled.

The Chapter agreed and the position was advertised, but there were no applicants. Not long after, a new Vice-Provost *was* appointed, and Colin was also thanked in December 1941 for 'the very satisfactory results as to finance', in which he had reduced the annual deficit from £412 to about £5. The financial improvement seems to have continued until at least the end of 1943. It is very probable that the visits of Martin Browne and The Pilgrim Players in 1941 and 1942, during which they put on more than one performance of T.S. Eliot's *Murder in the Cathedral*, at least one to a 'packed house', together with performances of André Obey's *Noah*, and Henri Ohéon's *Way of the Cross*, contributed to the financial turn-round, and that Colin was instrumental in getting his old friend, with his wife and fellow players, to come.

Financial concerns may also have suggested some of the non-liturgical events in the Cathedral during his time in Edinburgh. Colin was blessed with a very good organist and first-rate choir trainer in Dr Head, though, according to Alan MacLean, he was reputed to have hated clergymen, even to the extent of egging on choirboys to give silly answers to the clergy when questioned by them (D-J reported to Jack Arnold that he was 'impossibly silly'). I have no idea how Colin got on with Dr Head, though it is likely that the musical scholar in Head responded to Colin's extensive knowledge and love of good church music, and to his melodious voice, quite apart from his personality. It is possible, however, that two of Colin's decisions as Precentor may have irritated him.

The first was his decision, announced in the Monthly Paper for September 1940, that the Nicene Creed in the Eucharist (as opposed to the Kyrie, Gloria, Sanctus and Benedictus) would always be singable by the congregation. The announcement suggests that this might well be to the great Tudor setting of Merbecke (which I enjoyed singing again on my visit to the cathedral in 2007). Then, in March 1942, Colin announced his policy over introducing hymns – that in each service three were to be known already and only one new. He also seems to have got Head to start Congregational Practices on Thursday evenings which would make the introduction of new hymns and possibly some plainsong easier. But one of the potential money-making performances directly involved Colin, and may well have been suggested by him. It was in the second quarter of 1942, when the choir gave a recital of Anglican Church Music to show how it developed from Plainsong to the Edwardian style of Parry and Wood, while Colin gave a verbal introduction to each work or composer.

On another occasion they gave a recital of Tudor Church Music to accompany a lecture by the Reid Professor of Music. As an organist, Head was highly skilled, but Colin does complain in his diary after a Carol Service of his 'excessive rallentandos', over-accompaniment and occasional 'vulgarity of treatment'. However, he did full justice to Head as a choir-trainer. Here is what he wrote in his diary after the Dedication Festival on 31 October 1943. 'The choir has sung magnificently all day. Weelkes's *O Lord Arise* was beyond all praise. The new responses lacked resilience and rhythm, but I have realised that our choir advances by slow but sure stages to perfection, and in a month or two it will take them in its stride.' He persuaded Head to enlarge the repertoire with some works chosen by himself every year. When Colin was at Durham, and Sir Sydney Nicholson brought a choir to take the place of the Cathedral choir on holiday, he tried to interest Sir Sydney in getting Dr Head an Organist's post in an English cathedral.

At the beginning of July 1941, N.J. Cockburn began his work at the Cathedral as Vice-provost. Colin gives him a glowing welcome in the *Cathedral Monthly Paper*, and in the Quarterly Record stresses the great value of his experience and enthusiasm. Among his other duties he is asked to take charge of the Cathedral's youth work. He seems to have had some experience of, or at any rate interest in, the Russian Orthodox Church, since he writes about the Fellowship of St Alban and St Sergius in the November number of the Monthly Paper, while announcing the approaching visit of Nicholas Zernov. Before he began his work for the RAF, Colin records in his diary for 8 December 1942, that he 'had a talk with Norman Cockburn about work in my absence', without any further comment. Then, on the 20th he analyses his preaching as follows:

> Cockburn's Mattins sermon was doubtless sound theology but I doubt if it gripped anyone. He doesn't seem to know, sympathetic and human soul as he is, the way ordinary people think; nor yet the difference between a sermon and an essay. A sermon must not only be reasonable or reasoning but it must be able, all along the line, to awaken and startle and challenge. To use well-worn conventional phrases, even in conjunction with sound thoughts, is to invite apathy in your hearers, especially in a large building where personality gets little chance of communicating itself.

But the Monthly Magazine for January has a paragraph expressing Colin's confidence that he will be a good leader of the cathedral staff. However, three or four months later, while temporarily at home in Lansdowne Crescent, he wrote:

> 23.3.43: Norman Cockburn bearded me in the Cathedral this morning and asked for a talk. He told me frankly that he felt things were not right between us, and explained what he found to be obstacles to friendship and cooperation in my conduct. I replied by detailing my grievances and as a result I feel we understand one another better. On the whole he was just in what he said: I had no idea though that my excitable manner can actually terrify people, but this seems to be the case. I hope we shall get on better now and that we shall be more mutually understanding.

While Colin was at home again in June, it seems that Cockburn had asked him whether he could make the Sunday evening service much more accessible to younger worshippers and servicemen when Colin was away. Colin had told him that he could not give him a completely free rein in this, and went over the ground again in a letter written from Peterhead and copied into his diary:

> I write to confirm what I said to you the other evening, i.e. that I view with sympathy and gratitude your desire to make the 6.30 pm service on Sundays such that especially young men of the services may find in it something that more readily meets their aspirations and does not present them with something that is unfamiliar. It is understood that the 'framework' of Evensong is to remain untouched, but that Psalms are to be rendered to Anglican Chants, the Hymn before the Magnificat eliminated, and the Prayers after the 3rd Collect to be conducted less formally than hitherto. The only exception or caveat I would put in is that on those occasions when the office of Evensong is not sung at 3.30 the full Psalms appointed shall be read. I believe that a Cathedral is uniquely and especially bound to use the Office the Church prescribes every day and especially Sunday. But when Evensong has been sung at 3.30, the choice of Psalms and Lessons at 6.30 shall be at the discretion of the priest responsible for the service.

On 5 July he was at home again, and records that he 'wrote to Primus suggesting Norman Cockburn for Portobello and Sandford Canonry, should Hall (the existing incumbent) go to Aberdeen'. Then, on 14 September he wrote:

> This morning Andrew came round and in conversation enlightened me more about the misrule of the Cathedral by the Vice Provost in my absence. The more I hear of it the more the conviction grows that Cockburn is actuated by a malicious jealousy of massive proportions in his attitude to Andrew and through Andrew is endeavouring to strike at me. It is a deplorable and tragic situation.

On 3 November he wrote from where he was staying in Glasgow:

> Had Cockburn round for a talk about the recent crisis in his relationship with Andrew over the service at Dalry. He seems to me scarcely sane. He claims of course to be quite in the right, for is not his every step 'guided by God?' Therefore everyone else is wrong. I have of course been led into error by my 'natural' affection for Andrew as an old friend (an excellent thing in itself, he hastened to reassure me), but he (Cockburn) has thought only of Andrew's highest good and is convinced that the Spirit of God is struggling for mastery within his soul and that God will prevail there. I asked him whether he thought it was consistent with his position of responsibility to me as Provost to inaugurate changes in the institutions and life of the Cathedral without consulting me first. He affirmed that his view of his position was not mere carrying on, but a 'creative task' which must continually find new means of expression. When I asked him why in that case he had in fact consulted me about two named matters of change, which seemed to imply an obligation to consult, he referred the matter to a question of 'intuitive guidance'. It was just like talking to Hitler. He even referred to his decision to make no further effort at present to secure a residence nearer the Cathedral than Liberton as a waiting

for the guidance of God. I recall Oliver Quick's dictum about Oxford Groupers: 'These people would be pathological cases if they were genuine.'

On 30 December Colin wrote:

Cockburn being in urgent need of rest the Primus has asked Wright to excuse me from returning to R.A.F. for the first 14 days of January in which I should have completed my agreed year's service. Wright has of course done so and suddenly I find myself Provost of St Mary's again.

The *Cathedral Monthly* paper for February reported Cockburn's sick-leave.

The 'Andrew' mentioned in the sequence of diary entries just quoted was Andrew Duncan-Jones, one of the two Cathedral Chaplains. He was one of the sons of D-J, whom Colin had known ever since his days at St Mary's Primrose Hill. The Edinburgh appointment was his first close encounter with the Scottish Episcopal Church as it was also in Colin's case. It was therefore natural that both should feel drawn closer in this unfamiliar environment, which Colin describes as 'being among a set of clergy & bishops whose language, with few exceptions, I do not (psychologically speaking) share'. This must have led to mutual confidences about the people among whom they now both worked. Hence the 'jealousy' of Andrew that Colin ascribes to the Vice-Provost.

It was not only Colin who found the Edinburgh environment a difficult one to come to terms with. Mary used to recall with horror the cold and damp of the Edinburgh climate. This, of course, did not stop her making considerable contributions to the life of the cathedral. She wrote articles and book reviews for the Monthly Paper, composed and produced a Nativity Play for Young People who were under the Vice-provosts's leadership, organised an 'entertainment' for the Forces Rest Centre run by Lilias Johnston in the Water of Leith Church Hall and sang solos in various money-raising concerts in the Cathedral's own Walpole Hall and in St John's Church at the west end of Princes Street Gardens.

But at the end of 1942, much of this came to an end. She began to suffer from morning sickness, which led on to the birth, after a very difficult labour, of her third son, Charles Leo, on 4 July 1943. Until she was called up for 'war work', Peggy, who had first been employed as nanny in Henfield, had come with the family to Edinburgh, which made it possible for Colin and Mary to go out together for excursions into the country or to films and concerts in the town. After Peggy was called up her place was taken by one or more people who did not stay long. There was also a 'daily', Christina, for some time. But at the end of August 1943, Colin wrote: 'The end of the holiday was clouded over by the "falling through" of a nanny who was expected to arrive next month. After the first shock of disappointment Mary is inclined to feel she is well quit of that particular nanny.' When Colin left for the north of Scotland in September, it was 'with a rather heavy heart' that he noted:

the enormous pressure of work which increasingly devolves on Mary. She is scarcely ever free, and with the continual strain of Francis, Philip and Charles it will wear her down. God grant that we get a nanny for I do not see how she can bear it under the conditions we are forced to live in in Edinburgh, a vast house and the need for me to have the seclusion of a study and to entertain mildly.

But of course she did bear it, together with the common shortages of war, like the vast majority of the British people. And, on the other hand, there were almost no air raids on the city of Edinburgh, unlike the Port of Leith a mile or two to the north; the nearby Forth Bridge, a vital communications link, was extremely well defended, and what raids there were did remarkably little damage, Edinburgh houses being for the most part very solidly built of stone.

On 12 January 1943, Colin spent a few days at the Diocesan Retreat House at Walkerburn in preparation for his RAF work. On the second day he wrote:

I have had much 'sensible' devotion since I have been here, more than ever I have had for a long time. It probably is preparing me for the difficult days ahead, something to go in the strength of, 40 days and 40 nights. I am amazed at the way the prospect of my new work has changed from icy dread to quite eager desire. It seems such a clear case of a call from God. ... I believe that the conscious attraction the work has now been made to have for me, is an earnest that God has also given me what I need to do it. The great thing seems to be to aim at faithfulness, not at success, in it. ... I need a great stirring of love for those to whom I have to minister, for it is only love that can make my powers of sympathy, insight and concentration work at adequate pressure.

Colin's itinerary has a certain randomness about it, which is no doubt easily attributable to 'the war'. His first station was Prestwick, near Glasgow, which was primarily used for Transatlantic traffic; he then went to Lossiemouth, on the Moray Firth, and, after a few days at home, to St Andrews and Leuchars in Fife, then further up the coast to Arbroath, before travelling down to London, to report to both the Air Ministry and the Archbishop (Temple) at Lambeth Palace. This gave him the chance to see family and friends at Windsor and near High Wycombe and then in London, before his next assignments on the Firth of Tay (Errol) and the Dornoch Firth (Tain), before spending four days with Mary at Pitlochry and Holy Week in Edinburgh, after which it was south-west to Wig Bay, near Stranraer. Then he was hard at work at Wick, in Caithness, and expecting to go on to the Orkneys, but instead he was flown to Iceland, where the main base was near Reykjavik.

From Iceland he returned on a troop ship to Greenock and found himself briefly at home again after a long train journey. Then he was off again, to Peterhead in the north-west, before spending a month at home to catch the birth of the new baby. After that it was Sumburgh, on the extreme southerly tip of the Shetlands, then down to Lyness on Hoy and Kirkwall on Mainland, both in the Orkneys. After a week at home it was north-east to Stornoway on the Isle of Lewis in the Hebrides, then Islay, further south, before another brief day or so at Elie in Fife, where the family were holidaying, and Edinburgh, and then another trip up to the far north of mainland Scotland for a stay at Castletown, near Thurso, before plunging south-west to Oban. From there he went to Northern Ireland, managing to get a few days in Dublin and Belfast before work at Limavady, on Loch Foyle not far from Derry, Aldergrove, near Belfast, and Castle Archdale, a few miles down Lower Loch Erne from Enniskillen.

Then he had a few days at home again before Bishopbriggs (part of Glasgow) and then London, for a 'Quiet Day' with RAF Chaplains and another meeting with the Archbishop. Then came another assignment on the Moray Firth, at Kinloss (about fifteen miles from the second station he had visited back in January), and then to Montrose (about 13 miles north of the fifth station). Then came another brief home visit, and work at Scone, near Perth, and at Charterhall, near Duns, in the Lowlands. He was home on 19 December for the crisis of the Vice-Provost's breakdown which triggered the Bishop's successful request that he should be excused the last two weeks of his contract in January. It was as well that Colin greatly enjoyed travelling, and, for us, that he kept a lengthy diary of it all. He had clocked up 51 hours and 40 minutes flying time in a surprisingly large number of types of aircraft, travelled on many trains, in RAF cars and launches, and given 328 talks (many of them often repeated), including sermons, in an enormous variety of stations and airfields in virtually all the 'commands' of the Air Force, including tiny signal stations several miles from the main bases to which they were attached.

On 8 April 1943, Colin wrote again to Eric Whittome who had asked him for 'hints on talking to the Forces about religion'. He writes:

> I am more than ever conscious, after 3 months of this work, of the apparent lack of almost any convictions among the men, not only about religion but about anything. There is no hostility towards religion or the church that I can see, but I think the interest which the men appear to have when one speaks to them of these things is proof that they are beginning to realise there is a gap within their lives, that they miss having a faith and want to have one. If they don't learn to believe in the truth *soon* they will be a prey for any plausible agitator who comes along, be he Left of Right, Spiritualist or Jehovah's Witness. If only one could teach them to *think*, even if their thought *at first* led them away from Christianity, it would be a gain – a foundation would be laid. The line I usually take with the men I speak to is this: I try to awake in their minds the knowledge that they have a 'religious instinct', an urge (e.g.) to pray; but is this instinct trustworthy or is it 'escape mechanism' or wishful thinking? I give reasons for denying it is wishful thinking; then I bring them back to the fact that they have the instinct, that all other instincts are implanted in order to stir man up to harmonise with or meet the demands of his real environment ... and it is unreasonable to deny to the religious instinct the same validity as the other instincts, and that the religious instinct may be accepted as a rational basis for belief in God. Then I speak of the necessity of faith to supplement reason and so on. Whether they understand it I don't know but they always listen and they are always stirred to bombard me with questions. The questions thay ask *always*

seem prompted by a desire to know and not by a wish to try and trip me up or catch me out.

At Kirkwall on 18 August he reflects again about what he has been doing:
]

More and more, the questions and comments I get deal only with the defects of the visible church given usually as excuse for not being identified with that church. Hardly ever is a question raised dealing with first things or showing any desire to understand the truth. That hasn't always been my experience but it is increasingly becoming so. But I don't think that anywhere has anyone ever shown the faintest interest in the life and death and resurrection of our Lord, or even referred to him. It is just assumed that Christianity means the promotion of decent conduct or a square deal for the masses and that the Church is uninterested in that. The entire theological background, the life of prayer, the striving for perfection, the walk with God, none of these appears as being considered as even relevant to one 'interested in religion'. Only once, I think, in my visits has Hell been referred to; the miracles of Christ never, the Cross never, Forgiveness never. And so on. ... People have almost completely forgotten what Christianity is. It is as unknown as Buddhism. Above all it is the inability to reason which is so marked. Sometimes complacent young airmen say that people have given up Christianity and the Church because they have learned to 'think for themselves'. But it is just the absence of evidence for the capacity or practice of thought which is the most alarming characteristic of the rising generation. ... And yet they have brains which can be applied with astonishing success to the details of their technical task.

The following entry was written on 2 September at Stornoway:

My programme has been unusually full here and the difficulties of keeping up this journal immense. I have made more personal contacts than usual – largely owing to the zeal of the padré, Dodson, and have had a succession of long private interviews, e.g. with an air-crew sergeant about training for ordination ..., with a WAAF officer about sex problems in view of her marriage in a few weeks, with a corporal who thinks he is a Rationalist and so on. The general talks have been better than usual. I have been in better form and the discussions have been about less superficial matters. Lately they had degenerated into mere testimony to unfortunate personal experience of the clergy and congregations, and rather superficial criticisms beginning 'Don't you think that the Church ought to ... ?' usually recommending something which the Church has been doing for years rather well. Such discussions do at any rate mean this. First that the Church has certainly failed to capture the imagination of the younger generation and second that the Church gets a very poor Press and people know very little about it.

Here we have had better discussions. An air-crew officer stated the case for pacifism and conscientious objection (the second occasion in my experience) which led to a close debate on a fairly high level. Indeed I enjoyed this discussion with 518 Squadron officers very much – more than the usual air-crew talks. At the general meeting of officers yesterday another young air-crew officer asked what was the difference between British administration of India and Nazi rule in Czechoslovakia, hinting that both were based upon the same force-philosophy. I am impressed with the fact how widespread is our intellectual defeatism. So few seem coherently and consciously to realise what is at stake in this war in terms of ultimate spiritual ends and seem content to regard it as a dogfight without spiritual significance in which they have no insuperable objection to joining in. Last night at Broad Bay the question of the credibility of Holy Scripture and the Divinity of Our Lord came up, and the men listened with deep attention to my lengthy replies. At Rodel the other night a very young airman said epigrammatically 'It is hard to think of God when you are standing by an aeroplane.' How parabolically true that is of our generation.

This entry finished in a rather different key:

> The drive down to Rodel was full of beauties and wonders and I shall not quickly forget the savage splendour of much of the scenery and the sublime beauty of the view down Loch Seaforth across to the blue mountains of Skye. St Clement's Church at Rodel is 'a vision to keep'; its sturdy yet graceful rectangular bulk standing on its rock by the raging sea.

After lunch Colin fulfilled a promise he had made to a Group Captain at Leuchars; to send him a box of Stornaway kippers. Being extremely fond of kippers himself, he noted in the margin: 'For Stornoway Kippers write to Duncan MacIver Ltd., Stornoway. 10/- a box containing 18-22 pairs.'

For his visit to Iceland Colin was accompanied by Gerard Wright, the RAF Chaplain-in-Chief. Their flight from Wick in a Hudson took 4½ hours, in very mixed weather. 'I beguiled the time', wrote Colin,

> stretched upon a heap of parachutes reading Saki's stories. They seemed to give me more amusement than ever. We had spam and cheese sandwiches, and masses of chocolate which Miss Rattray of the Wick YMCA provided us with. ... No one wore parachutes or Mae Wests – we were quite informal.

After crossing the coast, there seemed no sign of life for some time in the utterly bare 'geological' landscape, until:

> Suddenly a ribbon appeared below meandering across the lava and along the ribbon a moving object followed by dust – a motor lorry going along a road. ... After a bit, clusters of houses, then across a firth a largish village, and finally in the distance the runways of an aerodrome standing out sharp, after which Reykjavik itself took shape. The sun was fully out now, and as we circled round over the town and harbour every building shone with colour and brightness. After circling three times we landed beautifully. We were met by the C.O. of the station and the padré, Betts, a young man in spectacles who reminded me of Harold Collingham. 'My name's Gabriel', said the Group Captain smilingly. It was his surname. 'It's only 2.30 by our time (our watches said 4.30), do you want lunch or tea?' We plumped for lunch and were soon eating what I should have called breakfast, for we had bacon (thick mild stuff) and beans and a fried egg *and* white, utterly white, bread, with tea.

Later, in the Operations Room, they were shown

> the progress of today's instalment in the unending Battle of the Atlantic. 'Down there you can see a convoy going from Britain to America and those white things are U-boats following it which our planes have spotted. We are on the way to attack them now.' It was fascinating.

Next day they went into Reykjavik from 'Atlantic Camp', a colony of Air Force and Naval personnel where they were based. Colin found the capital 'very like any other Scandinavian town except that they seem devoted to covering their houses with corrugated iron', which, especially when painted beige, gives 'an impression of squalor'. Though prices were high (Colin was horrified to have to pay 4/-, including tip, for a hair cut), the shops manifested 'a material plenty unknown in our own land at present', and he found 'the dress of the elder women' to be 'refreshingly dignified – a long skirt, over it a brightly coloured silk apron and then over the shoulder a shawl, their hair hanging down behind in two looped plaits'. The material plenty Colin refers to was an indirect result of the British occupation of Iceland in 1940, designed to prevent the Germans from seizing it after they had made themselves secure in Denmark and Norway. The AOC of Iceland, Air Commodore Lloyd, explained that:

> at first the country resented our occupation, but finding us ready to pay almost anything they asked for occupation costs and services rendered, is now quite friendly in a condescending, pitying way. They cannot understand how we can be so foolish as to pay any figure they quote, but finding we in fact do, they ask any fantastic sum that occurs to them.

Colin also learnt that Iceland had now broken with Denmark, and was likely to declare itself a republic after the war – which did in fact happen. Meanwhile those functions once carried out by the Danish Crown had been entrusted to a Regent. At a fine dinner with the AOC – 'fried plaice and delicious sauce tartare, tournedos with fried potatoes, peas and thin slices of parsnip, a sweet which I cannot recall but which I remember to have been excellent, together with sherry, beer, drambuie and a final whisky and soda' – the Intelligence Officer, Gwynne Vevers, was present, 'who used to be in my Catechism at Primrose Hill'.

Next morning Colin wrote an address he was to give on Icelandic radio the next day, and after lunch he and Wright called on the Bishop of Iceland, who 'received (them) most warmly'. Colin:

> explained that though he was here with the Archbishops' commission to minister to the R.A.F. in general, his visit was planned rather suddenly and he had had no time to communicate with Lambeth to get the message which he was sure his Grace would have wished to send by him. He was pleased at my little

speech and pointed to a framed coloured picture of the Archbishop of Canterbury in cope and mitre which hung on his study wall.

They were given a delicious tea, and the bishop told them much of interest about his church (Lutheran) in Iceland. He pressed Colin to call again and hoped he could introduce him to the Regent and show him some of the surrounding country on the way. Next day, Sunday, after preaching at the Parade Service in the camp Cinema and resting in the afternoon he and Wright visited the RC Cathedral ('as was to be expected, it was furnished in poor taste'). They then arrived at 'the local broadcasting house', where 'the airmen's choir and padré Betts were already assembled'. There was a short practice and then the broadcast started. Colin preached on the theme 'endure hardness' for eight minutes. At 7.30 came the service at the Lakeside Church, a building loaned to the British forces by the Icelandic Free Church, who, on principle, would not accept money from the State. At this service Colin was 'deeply touched' to see the Bishop of Iceland and his wife 'in mufti' sitting in a front pew, a fact he acknowledged at the beginning of his sermon ('Be not anxious'). He records:

> a large congregation of air force and navy, officers and men, and a few American officers. Singing was good and hearty. I was in fairly good form. We went down to the door to say good night to the worshippers. The Bishop pressed my hand and thanked me with gravity and emotion for my sermon.

A couple of days later they went again to the Bishop's, who drove them out to the Regent's house in his car, 'a magnificent American affair', and on the way they 'listened to the 6 o'clock news from London. A strange situation'. The house, built in 1760, 'is one of the very few old ones in the country', and was situated 'at an isolated point' some way from Reykjavik, but with a wonderful view of it and a 'wide circle of snow-covered mountains' beyond. It was furnished with Chippendale and other old English furniture and some modern Icelandic pictures. The Regent was an 'old lawyer called Björnson who for many years represented Iceland in Copenhagen. He has a crinkled parchment skin but lovely clear blue eyes. Our conversation was not interesting. They gave us whisky and nice nutty biscuits.' Back at the Mess after dinner Colin met Air Chief Marshall Courtney, who was en route for Montreal. 'I had not seen him since Baghdad days. He was friendly and forthcoming.'

On 3 June, which was Ascension Day, they flew to Höfn in another Hudson:

> over the snow-covered hills to the east of Reykjavik and down to the south coast above Kaldadarness. The first sight of Hekla, alone and majestic, snow-covered and infinitely beautiful. It was incredible to reflect that at the last eruption stones from this volcano killed cattle in N Scotland and sent dust as far as Siberia. To the south were the Westmann Islands. From here we flew along the

coast. At times the weather was appalling, heavy rain and thick mist. The pilot was within an ace of turning back ... From Höfdhabreka to Ingolf's Head the coast is desolate beyond description – wide forlorn flats of powdered lava across which mighty rivers meander delta-wise. It was often uncomfortably bumpy but Saki's stories kept up my spirits. Then came the great series of gigantic glaciers from Vatna Jökull and finally the semi-circular flat, surrounded by great hills and no fewer than four glaciers in which Höfn lies. We landed on a narrow spit of land on which is an abandoned landing ground. The prospect was wonderful and I cannot attempt to describe the beauty and majesty of the great semi-circle of gigantic hills which at a pleasant distance hedged us in. We lunched crudely but plentifully in the Sergeants' Mess off 'braised' bully beef and tinned peas, followed by tinned peaches and tinned milk (all on tin plates). Then came a talk to the men who are a rather 'browned off' despondent crowd, referring to themselves as the 'legion of forgotten men'. Wright said he thought I would not bring off a talk to them but was full of delight at the way their bored and rather hostile expressions gave place to absorbed interest. I talked on prayer and one of the men said life was too monotonous at Höfn to bother about God or prayer. At the end I had talks with several of the men and two rushed up gleefully and asked me if I remembered them at Arbroath.

After this a launch took them over the now very rough water to the jetty of the tiny village on the mainland, where they had a walk to the Signals Station:

> 1½ miles along one of the world's stoniest roads. By this time it was about 5 and we were treated to tea and fried eggs in the officer's office-cum mess-cum bedroon in half a Nissen hut. Then at 6 a talk to the men on faith and a nice discussion. I felt in better form than before.

They were back at the landing ground and the huts of the 'Works Squadron' at about 8.15 and left at 8.45pm. 'Circumstances made our take-off a hazardous affair but the pilot managed it in a way that Wright (who has been a pilot) said was superb. We sailed up into the sky of cloudless blue.' There were more wonderful views of the icy wilderness of Vatna Jökull, and then more rain and cloud and mist – 'the bumpiness worse than on the outward journey' – before they landed 'gracefully' at 10.30 pm and were regaled by 'a glorious supper of bacon and eggs and tea', before they reached their hut at midnight. 'A wonderful day in which the happiness and interest were spiced with moments of uneasiness and foreboding.' Dietary enthusiasts would, one hopes, have had their fears about camp food somewhat mollified by Colin's earlier observation that 'they give you 2 little pills at meals here – it gives you medicinally what green vegetables give you gastronomically'.

Next day the CO took him on an excursion to Geysir and Gullfoss, for which he had been advised to wear 'full winter clothes and my ulster'. It was a good road at first, running through 'many American camps'; they stopped for:

> coffee and cakes at a charming little ski-ing restaurant. Kolvidarhall is an ugly assemblage of little wooden houses faced with corrugated iron and looking like

an Icelandic Peacehaven – all very rectangular and yet haphazard. Steam from hot springs blew about.

Soon they had left the lava country:

small bushes, rather like heath, and quite green grew thickly part of the way. At about 1.30pm we reached Geysir and saw the renowned boiling gushers. The large one was quiescent, not having erupted since the day before yesterday. It was quite thrilling to look into its bottomless pool of practically boiling water. The two little ones were bubbling a little but not spouting. Some airmen there had thrown in the necessary soap the day before and one had erupted – 'we only had to show a piece of soap to the other and up it came', they said. Then we drove up to Gullfoss – about 15 miles off by road. When I say 'road' I mean a very bad cart-track – it took us an hour. But what a reward. At a distance we saw the spray which was one vast rainbow and you walk about in a halo of colour. The waterfall was superb and terrifying. It comes down in three stages, each deeper than the last. The final cascade is almost the most awful thing I have ever seen. I wanted to pray. The water hurled itself down into what seemed an infinite depth and the spray rose up like smoke from Hell.

On the way back the car had to make a detour to drop off an officer:

I decided to get out and walk, to be picked up again by the car after it had done its journey. It was a strange feeling, when the car was out of sight, to find myself alone in the vast, barren, contorted wilderness, with the great mountains and trackless glaciers all around. Not a sound to be heard except the blowing of the wind. The car overtook me after I had trudged along the stony track for 40 minutes.

Next day Colin wrote in his diary:

The kindness and friendliness of the officers here is unparalleled so far in my RAF experience. They come up and talk to me and ask how I am liking the place. They ask what one has been doing and generally act the host. Always before it was I who had to take the initiative. ... Drinks and cigars are showered on me. What can one do to repay all this?

Ever since his conversations with the Bishop, Colin had been considering what was likely to happen to the Icelandic Church after the war, when normal inter-state and inter-church relations would generally resume. But since Iceland had already severed political relations with German-occupied Denmark, and intended to become a republic, might it not be extremely difficult for it to resume close inter-church links with Denmark, especially as, unlike Sweden and Norway, Denmark had no Apostolic Succession in its episcopacy, whereas Iceland had, not all that long ago, actively sought it? So, meeting Captain Stevenson, a young man from Edinburgh who attended St Mary's and acted as the liaison officer at America House, and was also a friend of the Bishop of

Iceland, he asked him whether he thought the Icelandic Church would welcome the growth of closer links with the Church of England.

Suppose, as a first move, he could get Bishop Bell, say, or D-J, to spend a month in Reykjavik as guest of the Bishop, followed by a return visit of the Bishop to Lambeth? The Bishop had after all 'made no secret of his satisfaction at his (Colin's) visit and was definitely sympathetic with Anglicanism.' Stevenson was very enthusiastic and wanted to ask the Bishop at once, but Colin made him see that the first move must come from Lambeth, and asked Stevenson to find out more exactly about 'the 19th century movement to get Apostolic Succession for Iceland from Sweden or England about which Sira Arnie (pastor of the Lakeside Church) had told him the other day'. Colin himself contacted Archbishop Temple and Bishop Headlam, Chairman of the C of E Foreign Relations Committee, about all this, and soon heard from Bishop Headlam that the Archbishop had written to the Bishop of Iceland according to Colin's suggestion. But the scheme seems to have fallen foul of wartime regulations about travel between Britain and Iceland, and perhaps from opposition within the Church of Iceland itself, about which Colin might not have been told.

His last talks were held at Kaldadarness, 'an aerodrome disused now for operations and indeed all flying owing to a flood of the River Hvita last March which is held to have spoiled the runways'. But there were still a large number of officers and men awaiting the final closure of the station.

As we drove along the bumpy road through the lava-covered ground or through the melancholy tufted and stone-sprinkled grassland, with the glorious yet menacing mountains all around, I speculated upon the effect that Nature, as known to Icelanders, must have upon their minds and imaginations. To us in Britain nature means something calm and serene and domestic. ... To believe in nature red in tooth and claw is an effort of abstraction. Nature seems on the whole on man's side. But here all is different, and there is perpetual evidence of an apparent hostility to man and all his works on the part of nature. ... People say that the Icelander is suspicious and unreliable. If he is, it is scarcely to be wondered at. The marvel is that man has ever succeeded in bare survival in the teeth of such opposition. How easy it is to see why Lutheranism so easily dispossessed the accommodating Catholicism of the Mediterranean, but what a miracle that Christ has ever taken the place of the savage old Norse gods.

Colin's first talk was to about 150 airmen, where his theme was loving your neighbour, loving your enemies and the love of God. He felt on good form, and they had a 'merry discussion, and I got a resounding clap'. Then after lunch in the mess he talked to the officers in the ante-room:

ending up with my usual appeal to them to be real officers, i.e. shepherds of their men and not mere executives or technical experts. [The CO] asked me why I did this and I replied that in my experience R.A.F. officers were deficient in those qualities of fatherly leadership which seem to me so necessary. He said that for long he had been meditating talking to them on that very theme but that

I had taken the words out of his mouth. Then off we went to a further talk to another 150 men. And then off in the car for home, but the steering wheel went wrong and we landed in the ditch. By the mercy of God it did *not* go wrong as we passed over the very dangerous road across the great pass between Reykjavik and Kaldadarness where we would have been hurled down a precipice! With the help of another car's chauffeur the mechanism was righted and we drove quietly home.

On his last scheduled day in Iceland, Colin was approached by '16 air-crew sergeants who were at the general talk but wanted to take things further with me'. Nearly everyone contributed to the discussion, and many different themes were touched on. 'I felt we really "got down to things" and when (after *two* hours) I asked them to join me in prayer I discerned an eagerness in their response which was most marked. Betts, the chaplain, said that if I had done nothing else in Iceland the visit was worth while for this session alone, for, he said, the Air Crew sergeants are the section of RAF society most difficult to get at.' Afterwards Colin and Gerard Wright made a shopping expedition to town, but felt frustrated because of the very limited room there would be on the plane next morning. But, as it happened, it was cancelled at the last minute because of bad weather, and they were strongly advised to go after all on the troop ship which had just docked, since the weather forecast for the next few days in the direction of Scotland was very poor. So they went on board and cabins were assigned to them.

We had a miserable evening meal of a single slab of bully beef, two pieces of dry bread and a little butter, plus tea. We are waited upon by Chinamen. The ship is full of RAF officers and men going on leave or returning from service elsewhere, while there are also naval people, Americans, merchant seamen, and a few soldiers among whom is Captain Stevenson. ... I managed to get to sleep in spite of much deck-trampling above my head and all the other sounds which appear to be necessary at sea. After my hard little couch at Reykjavik, the bunk here was paradise.

The two escorting destroyers had nothing to do but escort, though they woke on Whitsunday to the sight of a 'sullen grey sea with white crests, and a leaden sky thick with menacing cloud. And yet', he calls to mind, "The Spirit of the Lord filleth the whole world and that which containeth all things hath knowledge of the voice." Next day, Whitsunday, Wright celebrated Holy Communion at 7.30am in the Warrant Officers' Lounge to a devout congregation of about 14, mostly airmen, and, despite the rolling of the ship, which made kneeling and standing hazardous, Colin was not seasick. Meanwhile he finished LeFanu's *The House By the Churchyard*, a book which gave him 'intense and prolonged delight', and started *Pride and Prejudice*. At other times he talked to Captain Stevenson and others, and the time passed quickly enough. This Icelandic interlude had been for him a time of 'great happiness', in which he had felt the enabling power of God in an extraordinarily stimulating environment. He was at home for a few days before his visit of ten days to Peterhead in the north-east, and then home again on 2 July for a whole month, just in time to catch the birth of the new baby, Charles.

While he was with the RAF in the Orkneys, he paid 'a visit of courtesy upon the charming Admiral commanding Orkneys and Shetlands (Vice Admiral Wells)' and discovered that his old Oxford friend Val Elwes was RC chaplain on HMS *Tyne*, 'the depôt ship for destroyers in Scapa Flow'. Colin got into touch and was invited for lunch:

To his ship I sailed in the C.O.'s impressive if antiquated pinnace and on the deck found not Elwes but Nankivell awaiting me, looking immense and jolly in his cassock. Soon we were in the Ward Room drinking brown sherry and then Val came in. Simultaneously we exclaimed 'How little you've changed'. But I felt that Val had changed in the sense that he was now more his true self than he had been. It is refreshing when one sees that: change without decay, growth without alteration. The same spirit looked out of his fine brown eyes, though a spirit chastened and deepened. He is somewhat at a loss still without his old chief Cardinal Hinsley. When I asked him what kind of a Monsignore he is he replied 'The lowest that you can be'. When I enquired after his uncle Bp Elwes (now, it appears, deceased) he told me that as a boy he visited Pius XII in his uncle's company. Val was deeply impressed and full of ecstatic reverence in the presence of the Pontiff, but somewhat shocked when his uncle, rejoining him after receiving the customary kiss on both cheeks bestowed upon diocesan bishops, remarked in a husky whisper 'The Holy father hasn't shaved this morning'. ... The pinnace called for me after lunch and I returned to the pier where I was picked up by Bruce the padré.

... Visibility was amazingly good and we saw with startling clarity the line of the Caithness coast, even the hotel on John o'Groats being clearly discerned. Stroma, Swara, South Ronaldsay lay before us clear cut in the utterly ripple-less sea. In Long Hope, which separates South Walls from Hoy, lies the old Iron Duke, now used as a depôt ship and recalling the pictures in *Chums* which I conned at school over legends such as 'Britain's latest Dreadnought'. She looked as pathetic as a faded actor touring the Provinces and with the same sort of dignity beneath. Out in the Flow are exquisite moderns such as the Anson and the Duke of York, but the Iron Duke wistfully recalls the happy Edwardian past.

In September he found himself in the Hebridean island of Islay:

Arrived at this unprepossessing spot at 5.15 today after flying from Stornoway in a Dominie. I cannot pretend to have enjoyed the trip. The wind began to blow a gale, it was raining, visibility at most times was almost nil. We 'bumped' atrociously as we flew at 300 feet over a raging sea. At times I thought the wind would blow us over or that a deep bump would land us in the waves below. Dimly and menacingly the mountains of Skye loomed through the mist as we passed the coast. Except for that and the island of Tyree, over which we passed, we saw no land till we reached these shores. Only the frenzied sea beneath and the mist all around. I was not sorry to land here: my stomach was beginning to feel a little uncomfortable. ... Besides myself there were two passengers and the crew was a Warrant Officer pilot and a sergeant W/T operator – both nice fellows. I was almost blown off my feet as I stepped from the plane on to the runway, which seemed ½' deep in water. My luggage and I were bundled onto a dripping wet lorry and conveyed to the Mess where I had tea with the Education Officer. There is no padré here, the last incumbent having been suddenly posted overseas. It will be a new experience to manage a 'visit' on my own. ... After dinner I staggered up to my quarters carrying my luggage, almost blown backwards by the demoniac wind and cut by the furious rain. I am to live in a 'bunk' which looks like a rather superior prison cell. However, the nice batman from Leeds has put a fire in my stove and the room is getting cosy. The wind is a raging tornado outside. I suppose I shall sleep. I didn't get to bed till about 2am this morning when we returned from the Butt of Lewis (Eorodale) where I gave a talk to 8 men after a drive of 35 miles!

Three days later he and 'Goff' (unidentified):

fixed up with the Minister at Bowmore about Church Parade next Sunday in his quaint circular church at the top of the hill which is the main village street. Then a talk to a voluntary meeting in the airmen's dining room into which the kitchen officials gradually edged so that in the end they became part of the meeting and the leaders of the discussions. It was comic but gratifying. Lunch in the rather primitive Mess off roast beef and treacle tart. I sat next to W/Cmdr Sney the C.O. of 422 Squadron (Sunderlands). He is a tall Canadian, very gentle and quiet in manner, simple and human, and underneath a spirit of steel. Talked to the WAAFs after on Marriage, and got a little discussion going. Two stayed behind for short private talks.

Two days later he wrote: 'After dinner the C.O. came into the Mess and asked me and one or two others to come over to his quarters to "celebrate" the Italian surrender. He has evidently repented his former standoffishness.'

In October he was in Northern Ireland, and got a chance to spend a few days with Gerard Wright in Dublin. The first part of his account reads rather breathlessly:

Arrived here yesterday at 4pm. These two days have been packed with delights: Boarding the train at Belfast in the bright sunshine; the charming, airy, 3rd class saloon carriage; no fuss, no crowds; lunch at the other end of the coach; the customs examinations on the Ulster and Free State sides of the frontier; the wonder that my simple identification card was sufficient to carry me into Eire; the Mountains of Mourne; the first glimpse of Dublin harbour; the ride from Amiens Street station to the Wicklow Hotel in a jaunting car; afternoon tea with iced cakes at Mitchell's in Grafton Street; the Hall of Trinity College with portraits of Bishop Berkeley, Dean Swift and Abp Ussher; the classical Chapel; the elegant façades; the autumn tints on the trees round the playing fields; the walk up Grafton Street, through St Stephen's Green to Merrion Square where we halted in front of no: 18 where J.S. LeFanu died; dinner at Jammet's in Nassau Street (dressed crab, petite Marmite, entrecôte poêllé, Beaujolais); the comfortable bed at the Wicklow with hot water bottle; the lit streets; undressing with the lights on and the blind up; the public notices in Irish as well as English. Today has been grey and drizzling at times but very happy. The maid at breakfast reproved my eagerness for bacon with a gentle but firm: 'Seeing that today is Friday ...' To Kingstown in the morning with Gerard Wright, passing the German Legation in Northumberland Street where the Nazi flag is no longer flown ...

After lunch he found and bought a second-hand copy of another Lefanu novel (*The Wyvern Mystery*), attended evensong (or part of it) at both Christ Church and St Patrick's cathedrals, writing detailed comments on liturgy and music, before going with Wright to meet the Archbishop, Dr Barton, at the University Club at 17 St Stephen's Green. They were both 'delighted by his friendly welcome and talk, and his lovely Irish brogue'. Next day Wright went off 'on a sentimental pilgrimage to Wicklow and the scenes of his youth'.

I strolled about the city in the morning. I was pressed to buy a flag by a girl. 'What is the flag-day for?', I asked, 'Och, and I've forgotten! (then, looking at her money-box) Sure it's for the *Regina Coeli* home for the gells'. I bought one and said: 'You've sold one to a black Protestant!' She looked scared and hurried off. I found myself at Dublin Castle, and said to a brawny policeman at the gate: 'Am I allowed to come in?' He replied 'Oh, you are'. I ambled about the spacious courtyards of the severe Georgian buildings, lit by the mellow autumn sun. The Military Chapel, which adjoins the ancient keep, could be described as being in the Flamboyant Strawberry Hill style. Inside it is very ornate in a manner characteristic of ancient established Anglicanism. The pews are many and heavily carved: upon the richly sculptured galleries are displayed in uncoloured wood the arms of the Lords Lieutenant of Ireland with their names beneath. I noted the luckless Strafford's. Until the last 6 months this chapel was preserved as a show-place only; it is now a place of Roman Catholic worship, and the Roman altar with its tabernacle and six candles looks queer in the ineradicably Protestant setting. Even the British Royal Arms remains *in situ* beneath the organ at the west end.
I feel everywhere here a strong defensive attitude towards the Britisher, an attitude which at times seems on the verge of hostility. The rector of Chapelizod, whom I visited in the afternoon (Canon Strong) told me that there is still strong and bitter hatred of England everywhere, and even a strong pro-German sentiment in places, which meets every condemnation of Nazi ideals and methods with the cry 'Just English propaganda'. On the other hand people who sat at the same table at lunch here in the hotel say that Germany has lost caste and that the Legation folk are modest and retiring in public appearance.
In the streets I am continually subjected to a wide range of emotional reaction on the part of others. Either I am scowled at by Roman priests for a Black Protestant and an Englishman, or I am saluted by soldiers (Free State) under the impression that I am a Papal dignitary. Police occasionally do the same.

Here is Colin's summary of his impressions of the (Anglican) Church of Ireland in his November Provost's Letter to the *Cathedral Monthly* paper at St Mary's:

During October my R.A.F. work has taken me to Northern Ireland, and for a few days I was able to slip down to the Free State for a visit to Dublin. I have taken every opportunity of making contacts with the Church of Ireland, and this has been of intense interest to me, for in some ways their position is similar to that of the Episcopal Church in Scotland. Like us they are a disestablished Church, though their becoming so is comparatively recent history. Like us they are a minority Church, representing about the same proportion of the inhabitants of Ireland as our Church does in Scotland. Like us they have their own Prayer Book, which, however, differs much less from the English book than does ours. They also have their own Canons and Constitution, and, of course, elect their own Bishops through the Synods. They have 13 dioceses, and are organised in two provinces under the Archbishops of Armagh and Dublin.

The points of difference are equally interesting. Owing to the fact that they live in a predominantly Roman Catholic country Irish Anglicans are, in reaction, mostly what we would call Low Church, whereas in Scotland, in a predominantly Presbyterian environment, the Episcopal Church is for the most part High Church. But there is a very important point to notice here. Though Irish churchmen are Low Church in that they tend to be shy of external ceremonies and church ornaments, which remind them of Roman Catholic worship, they are intensely loyal to their Prayer Book. They have a very strong Church sense, and are not merely vaguely 'Evangelical'. To them, being a churchman means doing what they are told and living and worshipping in accordance with the mind and the discipline of their Church. This is a very precious element of true Catholicism, far more precious than an abundance of Catholic piety and traditional ceremony introduced on merely individual preference and in despite of the liturgy and rubrics of the Prayer Book. Much that passes, both in Scotland and in England, for a revival of the Catholic element in religion is mere self-assertion and ecclesiastical Bolshevism: besides this, the worship of the Church of Ireland, though superficially it may look bleak and jejune, has a true Catholic dignity and order which we may well envy. The other great difference is that the Church of Ireland has in its midst a theological faculty in a University founded by Anglican churchmen, in which an Anglican atmosphere prevails. Trinity College, Dublin, is a centre of theological thought and study from which the whole Church of Ireland directly benefits. In Scotland we have no such foundation, though our Presbyterian brethren are rich in their Scottish centres of sacred study.

I mention these reflections upon the condition of our fellow-churchmen in Ireland partly because of their intrinsic interest, and partly to enable worshippers at the Eucharist in St Mary's to have some knowledge of those dioceses in Ireland for which their prayers are asked in rotation with other Anglican dioceses throughout the world.

Here, to conclude this series of long extracts from Colin's diaries of his RAF work, is part of his last 'Provost's letter' to the congregation of St Mary's:

Dear Friends,

I shall (shortly) be giving up my work with the R.A.F. with one or two very definite convictions which I find stimulating and encouraging in facing the future. One of them is this. Though there is among the young men and women, with whom it has been my good fortune to be in contact, a great deal of criticism of Church members, both clerical and lay, yet I have discerned beneath all this a deep and mysterious respect for the Church itself. I have heard many complaints about the shortcoming of both parsons and laymen, some fair but some unfair. These complaints, if lodged against some purely human institution, would probably have caused those who made them to bother no more and to regard the said institution as not worth thinking about again. But this is just what they don't do. In spite of often searching condemnation of us Church folk, our young people continue to look to the Church and to expect great things. Very dimly they grasp the doctrine that though the Church is composed of many weak and sinful members, yet that it is, notwithstanding, the Body of Christ; more than a mere institution: rather, a supernatural mystery. That is why they cannot ignore the Church, but regard it with both bewilderment and awe. That is our opportunity. If we are going to serve the modern world and help it in the mighty tasks which confront it, we must learn to be both humble about ourselves, and our own attainments, and yet proud and confident in the fact that as Baptised Christians we are members of a victorious supernatural Body, the Body of Him who goes forth conquering and to conquer.

Colin's contributions to the *Cathedral Monthly Paper* are often very imaginative, and frequently have a direct bearing on the war. The May 1942 'Provost's Notes' are an excellent example, entitled 'Thomas à Becket is not Dead':

The story, both in its outward and inward aspects, of the murder of Archbishop Becket was nobly presented in the Cathedral by the Pilgrim Players on Palm Sunday. Mr T.S. Eliot, interpreted by Mr Martin Browne and his company, has shown us that what the world may call the deliverance of the State from the machinations of a turbulent priest was in reality the promotion of the Archbishop to the noble army of martyrs, and that we do right to call him St. Thomas of Canterbury. At the very moment when this play was being presented in our Cathedral, a similar drama was being played out in real life. I refer, of course, to the conflict between Nazi-ism and the Church of Norway in which King Henry II is being played by Quisling and St. Thomas by Bishop Berggrav, the Primate of the Norwegian Church and Bishop of Oslo. The story of the interview of the four knights with Becket is closely repeated in an interview between Quisling and Berggrav. 'You triple traitor, you deserve to be beheaded,' shouted Quisling (so it is credibly reported). To which the Bishop quietly replied: 'Well, I am here.' Now, as well as all the Bishops, all the clergy, except a tiny minority, have followed the Primate's lead and resigned their State appointments, thus resigning their stipends and means of livelihood. Our thoughts and prayers will be with the suffering Church of Norway at this time, and our thanksgivings for their noble and heroic defence of Christendom against the servants of 'the Beast' will be fervent and genuine. May they be strengthened in the deadly conflict which has been forced upon them.

It must come as a great surprise to people who assume that 'the Church is dead' or that 'the Church does nothing' to see that wherever the might of Nazi-ism tries to assert itself it always finds that the Church is a formidable obstacle in its path. Doubtless it would prefer to ignore the Church and quietly to silence the more active opposition to its New Order. But it is never able to do this. The strength of the Church is such that everywhere the struggle is forced out into the open. How little even keen churchpeople realise the inherent strength of the Church and the deep reality of its faith. What an inspiration all these happenings must be to him who 'discerns the signs of the times'.

The Notes for November 1942 begin:

'IT COULD NOT HAPPEN HERE'. 'The Germans, immediately after the occupation of Scotland, imprisoned the Head of our Scottish Episcopal Church, the Most Rev. A.J. Maclean. They even maltreated him physically. He is now imprisoned in the College at Cumbrae and thus deprived of the possibility of exercising his functions as Primus. The Bishop of Aberdeen was flogged by S.S. officials and expelled to Edinburgh, where he is now lying in hospital recovering from his wounds. The Bishop of Edinburgh was wickedly tortured by the Gestapo who beat him, cut off his hands and feet, tied a stone round his neck and threw him into the Forth, from which the people of South Queensferry, a few days later, recovered his body and buried it.' It sounds fantastic and utterly impossible. Yet this is a section of a letter from the chaplain of the Yugoslav Embassy in Turkey to the Archbishop of Canterbury, with only the names of people and places altered. These things have happened and are still happening all over Europe. When we are tempted to pity ourselves for the hardships and inconveniences and anxieties this war is causing to us, let us try and remember what is happening to others. The remembrance should move us to deep thanksgiving, but even more to a deep sense of responsibility. 'To whom much is given, of him shall much be required'. We who have been given so much shelter and protection from the awful scourge now afflicting Europe, should show our gratitude by a strenuous loyalty to God and his laws, as well as to our country and its cause.

Colin's Cuttings Book contains a few other items of interest. Here is Colin on Praying for Victory, as reported by *The Scotsman* on 9 January 1941:

'I cannot agree with those who say that it is wrong for Christians to pray for victory,' declared the Very Rev. Provost Dunlop, St. Mary's Cathedral, when he spoke at the third meeting of the World's Evangelical Alliance Universal Week of Prayer in the Church of Scotland Hall, George Street, Edinburgh.
It was not for anyone to say what were the inscrutable purposes of God for the nations of the world. We could never know absolutely what was the will of God. But it had to be remembered that He had given us reason and moral sense. It was wrong, therefore, not to pray for victory, because, without that, all the things we held dear and cherished would be trampled upon. In so far as our conscience and reason was concerned, it was right that we should pray for victory, because we believed that God's kingdom would best be served by victory for ourselves.
That, however, was not the most fundamental thing. There always came a time in the history of nations when they became drunk with pride of our human achievements, when they began to think that man was sufficient unto himself,

and that by his own efforts and with purely human resources, he could build up a perfect civilization, and that God could be dispensed with. 'That is the sin of Germany, Russia and Italy', said the speaker, 'but it is only true of these countries. It is a sin to which we, to some extent, share – that secure civilization with windows not open to Jerusalem. That sin is self-sufficiency, or trying to organise life apart from God. That is the sin of which we must repent. We must pray that men may come to see that it is the Most High who always rules, and that our rulers must not think it is their function to control the whole of human destiny.'

Rulers had to realise that their task was not to control the whole of life. Their function was to safeguard the freedom of the individual and the Church, in order that the individual might become the son of God, and that the Church could preach His word without interference.

Presiding at the meeting was the Rev. Dr J.R. Aitken, Church of Scotland.

There is also a letter from Colin to the Editor of *The Guardian* on 'The Diaconate'. In a Leading Article, deploring the 'virtual eclipse' of the Diaconate in the Anglican Church, it had been suggested that the order might be revived by 'laying hands upon lay readers'. But the function of lay readers is to assist the parish priest in the Ministry of the Word, while the Order of deacons arose 'to serve tables' so as to free others for the Ministry of the Word'. But table-serving, that is, organising finance, running church organisations, etc., calls for gifts which the clergy need not have in order to be good priests. Many laymen do certainly have them, but many church people won't accept the leadership of laymen in Church business.

Perhaps this instinct is right, a dim realisation that table-serving in the Church is a spiritual office demanding an ordained ministry. (So) why not lay hands on one or more laymen ... for the work which they are anxious to do, but cannot do adequately without the Grace and standing which Holy Order gives? ...The Church's ministry would thus be really three-fold once more, and the parish priest have more time and energy to be a real priest.

A flyer pasted into the Cuttings Book also announces that Colin will be conducting a Convention for the Deepening of the Spiritual Life in St. Cuthbert's Church, Carlisle, on 21, 22, 23 and 24 September, to the theme of The Gospel and our Human Needs. The year is not given, but it is probable that Logie Danson, Colin's bishop, who was at Carlisle before being Provost of Edinburgh, recommended him. It probably took place in 1942. Another cutting, from *The Orkney Blast* of 20 August 1943, adds a footnote to Colin's progress through the Scottish Islands:

When asked about his impressions of Orkney the Provost said that he had been very pleasantly surprised at the 'domestication' of the place, having expected to find it much more barren and much less inhabited.... He had been particularly pleased with St Magnus Cathedral – where he preached during the R.A.F. church service – which he says is one of the finest buildings he has ever seen;

and that from someone who has seen many, many cathedrals and fine buildings is praise indeed.

In the Episcopal Church of Scotland Bishops are elected by clergy and lay representatives of the diocese concerned at an electoral synod. When Colin was at Arbroath in March 1943, he wrote in his diary that he had had a letter from Lord Glentanar (who had experience of his ministry at St Mary's Cathedral):

> asking for my consent to put my name forward for the Bishoprick of Aberdeen. I have known for some time that my name has been mooted but have decided to decline. I do not really feel mature enough for the office for one thing. Indeed I feel I am barely mature enough for the office I at present hold, though I am filling it more adequately than I had expected. ... Mary and I have talked it over and though we both feel the attraction of Aberdeen both agree that the time is not yet ripe for a move, failing any strong positive indication to the contrary.

On the very next day he wrote that 'an invitation has come from Canon Wolf of Aberlour that I allow my name to be put forward as Bishop of Moray!' Both these invitations were refused. But about ten months later, on 6 January 1944, he had a letter 'from the Bishop of Durham asking whether I would consider becoming Bishop of Jarrow':

> This requires consideration, for some of the reasons which led me to decline being thought of for the sees of Aberdeen and Moray do not apply here. For instance my consciousness of personal and spiritual immaturity is less important when the bishopric is not a diocesan cure but only a suffragan. The same applies to the possession of a young family which would penalise a diocesan bishop but far less a 'curate' bishop. The question whether I am justified, even if I really want to, in leaving St Mary's after four years, of which one has been spent in absence with the R.A.F., still remains. On this I shall consult the Bishop of Glasgow tomorrow. Durham exercises an almost magical spell upon my imagination. The Chapter there seemed a happy one and I believe I would like serving under Alington as Dean (for the Bishop of Jarrow is a Residentiary Canon, as also Archdeacon of Auckland). The prospect of more money is undeniably attractive – I would be receiving £1300, an uncrease of £500 p.a.. But what about the domestic element? Servants? Furniture? – really acute problems in these days.
>
> It is strange how events seem to be pushing me towards the Episcopate. Until March 1943 the possibility of my being a bishop had not seriously occurred to me as my vocation. The height of my ambition was to be a Dean. I do not like most of what experience has shown me to be a bishop's work. I feel destitute of most of the gifts the office demands. I genuinely feel unworthiness and unsuitability. Yet not only do events begin edging me towards the office with a gathering momentum, but friends such as Tom (Stavely, from Oxford days) do not consider the prospect ridiculous, while my confessor thinks I have the right gifts, at least in embryo. Mary thinks so too. What a revolution it all is!

On 12 January Colin wrote in his diary:

I have been down to Durham where I lunched with the Alingtons, saw Leslie Owen the retiring Bishop of Jarrow and stayed the night at Bishop Auckland with Dr Williams. Alington has no shadow of doubt I ought to come – indeed he almost admitted it was his suggestion. He thinks it is the very thing for me and waived away all my scruples about Edinburgh's claim. In a far more reserved way the Bishop of Durham did the same and he has since written to me to say he hopes I will come. I was much impressed by and attracted to him. I arrived at Auckland castle at tea-time having gone over by the bus from Durham. In my ignorance I arrived at the Castle by the back door (it all looked so magnificent) and was conducted by the perfect butler, who had magically appeared at the door just as I came up, to the Library where the Bishop and Mrs Williams were. The Bishop is tall and young-looking with a face of much kindliness, shrewdness, moral power and serenity. I have scarcely analysed my impressions of him, which were wholly favourable. I find it easy to talk to him and enjoy doing so. I can imagine it would be a delight and a blessing to work with him. He felt that my difficulties about leaving Edinburgh so soon would only be serious if I had there started an important piece of work which couldn't get on without me. This of course is not the case. He thinks that this is a strategic moment for either taking up new work or remaining where one is for 4 or 5 years. I don't believe I could keep Mary here as long as that [long after Colin's death she reflected that the four years in Edinburgh, with no visits to England, had rather cut her off from her own relations] and as Alington says 'You've got to be a bishop and this is the best possible way of starting it'. Leslie Owen told him about the opportunities of speaking to the men in the shipyards; the Bishop about the ministry a Suffragan should have with the clergy of the diocese. Both these tasks seem to have been prepared for by my R.A.F. experiences.

The House question does not exist as an obstacle, for the house in The College is far more convenient than this. I have spoken to the Primus about the growing attraction of the post and office. He has been sympathetic and judicial and though he doesn't want me to go refuses to say so in terms which would unduly influence me. He said with his characteristic meekness and humility 'If you do accept, I do hope you will ask me to take part in your consecration'. How good people are and how little one deserves it. Am I ever as good to anyone as people daily are to me?

On 16 January he was surer that being Bishop of Jarrow 'will claim more of me than the post here', where he felt continually inhibited by the prevailing assumptions of most of his fellow clergy. 'I am not an Athanasius who can stand alone for an "unclerical" Church and re-union with the Presbytery. As a bishop here I would cut no ice, and a bishop it seems I must be. Baptised Mrs Daunt's baby girl at 3.30 Evensong. The choir's singing of the Purcell "Nunc Dimittis" in procession back from the font was perfect. Talked to the Youth fellowship about Ireland after supper.' Next day (17th) he telegraphed to the Bishop and to Alington accepting the former's offer. 'Mary and I knelt down and offered our decision to God. I believe we are right. But how agonising are the conflicts involved.'

Official confirmation from the Prime Minister took about three weeks, which often made it hard for Colin to concentrate on his pastoral and other duties without accidentally blurting it out (Churchill, who kept the conduct of the war so closely within his grasp, was notoriously uninterested in religious affairs). But, of course, life at St Mary's continued much as usual. At the Commemoration of King Charles the Martyr on 30 January Colin recorded '11th hour qualms that I was overdoing it. But I think the emphasis has commended itself to most people.' Bishop Deane, ex-Bishop of Aberdeen, was the preacher. After lunch at 8 Lansdowne Crescent:

> he tried to convince me that Russia is behaving well and Poland badly over the frontier question. I think the vehemence and reasonableness of my rejoinder surprised him and he did not relish my suggestion that his championship of Russia at this juncture was morally indistinguishable from the appeasement of Germany at the time of Munich – an event of which he is a very vocal critic.

On 2 February Colin conducted a Quiet Day for about 20 Army Chaplains. 'Though I announced two periods when I would be available for interviews or confessions, none took advantage of the offer. They listened to my address with attention and apparent interest. I suppose I speak to the head and to the will rather than to the affections.' His plea to observe 'the discipline of silence ... was almost unanimously disregarded. Still no word from the Crown'. On 8 February it came, and he attended the Leighton Club in the morning, and the Theological Club in the afternoon. Two days later he 'Took the Sacrament to the Rev. C. Kirk and to Mrs Stevenson (mother of Captain Stevenson) and then wrote a sermon for Sunday on the fall of Man.'

After evensong Gerard Wright called. He had felt so sure of Colin's 'elevation to the episcopate' that 'he had in the autumn bought a shepherd's crook in a Highland village' which he intended to give to Colin as a Pastoral Staff. 'What a good friend he is.' (Colin virtually always used this in preference to the very heavy and ornate staff given later for the use of the Bishop of Jarrow. The lovely light brown crook was eventually presented to Henfield Church by Mary.) Meanwhile Colin was receiving many letters about his new appointment, some of which 'deeply touched' him, especially those from Presbyterian ministers. Then, on 22 February he records a visit to:

> a Mrs Bennett, a protégé of Miss McNair's. Her husband, a D.F.C., was killed test-flying 6 or 7 months ago. Now she wants her 2 months old baby baptised. She told me that before her husband's death religion had meant little to her but that now God seemed to her real and alive. There was a subdued radiance about her; evidence of a real inner calm and serenity. This, as a result of a staggering blow, should make people think who speak too easily of war and suffering as necessarily destructive of faith in God. I feel better for having talked to her.

Two days later, he:

visited Miss Kirkwood who has practically gone blind. She was quite radiantly happy and cheerful. The second instance in the week of the supernatural growth possible in suffering. There seems to be less a problem of evil than a problem of why people who do not suffer should lead such humdrum and unadventurous lives without much trace of real deep joy. The capacity for joy seems to grow with the suffering endured.

On 15 March Colin's diary records some familial matters:

> Yesterday at tea time poor little Charles got rather badly scalded by pulling a table-cloth off a table on which was a newly filled teapot, which thereupon disgorged its contents into the baby's basket [where he was lying]. We rushed him up to the Children's Hospital where he has been properly taken care of and is now doing well. He behaved so well, poor little dear. We also got news yesterday that Honor has offered herself and has been accepted as a Postulant at the Rottingdean Convent. Presumably each party concerned has more or less counted the cost. I hope she has done right. If it is right, it solves many difficulties for everyone concerned. Audrey [Colin's niece] arrived last night and is staying at any rate until my Consecration. My episcopal robes are beginning to arrive and the Board of trade have allowed one 84 additional clothes coupons. Adeney has made me a black cloth chimere in accordance with special directions which he has carried out well.

Then, on the 21st, came Colin's installation and collation (first as Archdeacon of Auckland, then as Canon of Durham) in Durham Cathedral, after leaving Edinburgh at 6.50 am. 'The ceremony and ritual seemed both solemn and homely. I felt curiously at home; presumptuously so, in view of the majesty of the cathedral and the distinction of my predecessors in office and of the Durham "familia" in general.' He chose Stanford's beautiful 'Beati Quorum' as anthem, 'in honour of St Cuthbert's day and as my personal aspiration. ... In the Chapter House afterwards I stumbled shockingly through the Latin oath, like a boy construing an unprepared passage, giving scant proof of that learning demanded of a Canon of Durham. What the Bishop and the Dean, both ex-headmasters [of Public Schools], thought of it, I do not care to ask.'

Then he stayed the night at Auckland Castle, after which he travelled 'by slow and crowded stages, ... via Darlington, York and Malton', to Birdsall Grange, where 'Bill and Rose are looking after me wonderfully'. On the 26th came the Consecration in York Minster, by Dr Cyril Garbett, the Archbishop. *The Scotsman* report informs us that five other Bishops were present, 'Durham, Newcastle, Ripon, Whitby and Selby, all of whom laid hands on the new Bishop. The Civic life of Jarrow was represented by the Mayor and Mayoress and the Town Clerk.' Colin records that:

> Among those present were (from Edinburgh), 4 of the Chapter (Dean Mackay, Chancellor Hall, Canons Perry and Ballard) and Andrew. D-J preached, a remarkable discourse, most powerful but rather spoiled because it was so plain

(to me) that most of it was meant to be reproof to the Archbishop for his Russian 'flirtation' and because of the South India scheme. All the same it was a fine sermon and his few personal words to me at the end were austere, reserved, but full of power. ... Phillips [from St Mary's] attended me as verger with his characteristic blend of decorum and efficiency. ... I was deeply touched by D-J giving me his sapphire ring. ... If it can bring me some of his courage and clearness of thought, as well as his underlying simplicity of heart, I shall be grateful.

They returned to Durham by train – the Bishop and Mrs Williams with us in the carriage. Audrey remained in the train bound for Edinburgh. Mary (who had not been able to attend the installation and collation) and he 'walked up to the Alingtons through the sunny crowded streets and then up the peaceful river bank to The College'.

By the time of his next entry in the diary on 29 March, Colin was back at Edinburgh, having already taken two confirmations,

the first at Cornforth, an ugly mining village with a little rustic heart to it, in a raw, red-brick church, the air sibillant with gas-lamps burning. About 80 candidates, whom I confirmed in pairs. Church crammed. I felt very new to the job at first, but as the laying on of hands proceeded I got the feeling of being quite used to it. ... I met the Vicar of Ferryhill, an ex-miner named MacManners who was at Chichester in Pass's time. The confirmation next day was at Kelloe, in the ancient church there. ... I felt quite at home at the service which I enjoyed very much.

Next day Mary and I visited Charles, still in hospital, and for the first time we were allowed to see him face to face. But (he) stared at us with uncomprehending and unrecognising eyes! In 16 days he has learned to forget us. He looked well and serene, somewhat older and more of a 'little boy'. He was still on his tummy, and it was uncertain when he would be healed up and able to come back.

On 3 April Colin celebrated at 11, then coached Bill Harvey, one of the chaplains, in singing the part of Narrator in the Byrd Passion. 'Dean Carpenter of Exeter', the evening's preacher, 'and his wife came to lunch; after which I motored him out to call on old Professor A.E. Taylor. Mary and I visited Charles in hospital, and he greeted us with coos of delight. But it is going to be some time before he gets out, alas.' They had, in fact, to wait until after Easter. Colin's niece Audrey was still with them to help with the move, and 'being more useful and nicer every day'.

The last thing Colin records concerning his cathedral work was the handing over to Donald Sinclair, the Chapter Clerk, of 'the correspondence relating to the Durham Screen'. This had begun with a letter from Dean Alington to Colin on 8 November 1942:

My dear Provost, here's a letter on what may be the wildest of wild goose-chases! Some 60 years ago Gilbert Scott put up in this cathedral a choir screen of marble and alabaster – very good of its kind but very ill-placed at Durham.

We have been long considering its removal, but one of the difficulties has always been where it could go. It has been suggested to me – it ought to have struck me independently – that it might find a home with you. As I say, it really is good Gilbert Scott, and I have come to like it the better the longer I've known it, but Gothic and Norman work don't suit very well. My reason for writing now is that if you think there is or might be anything in the idea you could before your visit here (to which we're much looking forward) take a few rough measurements, and have your chancel rather clearly in your eye. ...

As St Mary's does not have a screen, but a very low 'wall', this seemed to Colin a very good idea, so he had written to Francis Eeles, who recommended its acceptance. The Cathedral Board were naturally worried about possible costs, but gave the general idea a fairly cautious welcome. Colin took soundings and found a rather mixed reception, but, in any case, as Colin's RAF work was just starting the scheme had to be shelved to wait until his release. Now, in 1944, especially after his entertainment by Alington and greater familiarity with the screen itself, Colin seems to have reintroduced the idea by reading a letter from Sir Gilbert Scott published in *The Builder* in 1873, in which he said that he would certainly have liked to add a high screen to his plan for St Mary's Cathedral, but, understanding that there might be local objection, he had substituted a low wall as at Florence, Monreale, etc.

Colin had also got Audrey to produce an 'Artist's impression' of what the screen might look like in St Mary's, which she did very well. At the Chapter meeting on 14 April 1944, the offer was accepted unanimously in principle, but without any commitment to financial liability. Entries in Colin's diary suggest that the idea was for some time not properly discussed by the Durham Chapter. Then, in the February 1946 edition of the Durham Diocesan Magazine, *The Bishoprick*, readers were told:

No new plans have yet been developed for the removal of the Scott screen: the authorities of the Cathedral in Edinburgh, who at one time seemed disposed to welcome it, have somewhat changed their mind, and the Chapter, though unanimous in hoping to see it go, are not agreed as to the next step.

In the event, the idea seems to have been quietly abandoned.

Colin's published farewell to St Mary's reads as follows:

Saying Good-bye is always unpleasant and, for a Rector with a large congregation, difficult. In war time, with its petrol restrictions and with a very much scattered congregation (as the Cathedral's is), it becomes impossible to visit everybody for a farewell. So I hope that the large number of friends to whom I have not been able personally to say 'Good-bye' will excuse me and accept the will for the deed. I am deeply grateful for the confidence, loyalty and support I have unfailingly received during my four years ministry among you, and for friendships which will not easily be forgotten or broken. During my time here our nation has gone through some difficult days, and in those days I have felt something of the united strength and faith of our community at St

Mary's which has buoyed up and increased my own. When, in happier times, we are all able to look back with some detachment on those critical months of the summer of 1940, I shall always remember with gratefulness the little band of worshippers at the 12 o'clock intercession service and the sea of faces in the nave at Sunday Mattins, and recall the sense of confidence in God's faithfulness which those experiences brought to me.

14

DURHAM

COLIN'S DUTIES as Provost of Edinburgh had been reasonably clear-cut. The provost of an Episcopalian Cathedral is also the rector of its congregation, so his sphere of essential duties was centred on the Cathedral, and to those who worked and worshipped there. But now, at Durham, he had three quite different spheres of responsibility. The first was that of Bishop of Jarrow, whose prime function was to assist the Bishop of Durham, the supreme spiritual head and pastor of the Diocese of Durham. As such, he was entitled 'The Right Reverend David Colin Dunlop', and signed himself 'Colinus Jarven' (the latter word being Latin for Jarrow), and the most obvious aspect of his duties was the taking of Confirmations in the diocese, which only bishops can do.

As recorded at the end of the previous chapter, Colin had already been asked to do two confirmations immediately after his consecration as bishop – such was the backlog arising from the departure of his predecessor, Leslie Owen. The Bishop of Durham might also ask him, as fellow bishop, to join him in ordinations, which were held in the cathedral. His second *persona* was that of Archdeacon of Auckland, and as such, he was entitled 'The Venerable'. Dioceses are divided into archdeaconries, and, when Colin was an archdeacon there were two in the diocese, Durham and Auckland, to which a third, that of Sunderland, was added after his time. Archdeacons, like suffragans, are directly responsible to the diocesan bishop, as spiritual head of the diocese, with a special responsibility for the parochial clergy and church buildings, including vicarages, within the geographical bounds of their archdeaconries, and also for carrying out diocesan policy.

Every few years they hold Visitations, at which churchwardens and clergy are 'officially' surveyed and a service is held in one of the churches of the Deaneries into which the Archdeaconry is divided. Colin's third sphere of activity was that of a residentiary Canon of Durham, and therefore a member of the Durham Cathedral Chapter – the Cathedral Foundation – under the Dean and on a par with four others, who were together responsible for the cathedral building and what went on in it, and also for property, leases, employment and anything else which was the legal concern of the Corporate body 'The Dean and Chapter of Durham'. A member of a cathedral chapter need have no other title than that of 'The Reverend', or 'Canon', though in practice the ministers of a cathedral are rarely just 'The Reverend Canon'.

In Colin's time at Durham, the Chapter included the Archdeacon of Durham, Egbert Lucas, and there were also three who were closely involved in the teaching of theology – Michael Ramsey, who was already Regius Professor at Durham and later to be Archbishop of Canterbury, Alan Richardson, who had for some time worked with the SCM, and Stanley Greenslade, shortly to be made a Professor. The Very Reverend Cyril Argentine Alington, the Dean, had been Headmaster of Eton, and before that a prize Fellow at All Souls, Oxford. All this accounts for Colin's dismay at having made a hash of the Latin oath he was required to swear on his collation to the Canonry, as recorded in the last chapter.

Members of cathedral chapters often live in a cathedral close. This was called 'The College' in Durham – a completely enclosed space, mostly covered with grass, with several fine trees and a large ancient pump in a wooden case, on the south side of the Cathedral. The houses which surround it, including the mostly medieval Deanery and the Canon's houses, included houses for the organist, one or two of the 'Minor Canons', who assist the Chapter in the round of Cathedral worship, a small number of other Cathedral officials, and also, housed in a grand old house in one corner with its own entrance gate, living quarters for students at Hatfield College, which was part of the University.

Another large house, a plain Georgian building, housed the Choir School. There was a gate and medieval gatehouse at the east entrance of the College, with a resident porter, and another entrance on the west side, consisting of a long sloping pedestrian tunnel, called 'The Dark Entry', locked at night, which led down to 'The Banks'. This is the name of the wooded gorge, with its numerous paths at different levels on both sides of the River Wear, which forms a narrow loop around the small plateau on which the old fortress-like Cathedral, Monastery and Castle of Durham were built. The main gateway of The College opens onto the North and South Baileys, no longer of obvious defensive significance, but now the names of two streets full of old houses, two little churches, and, when we lived in Durham, two theological colleges.

Beyond the gateway that ends South Bailey is a steep hill leading down to Prebends' Bridge, and North Bailey eventually descends into the mediieval and new towns. On the north side of the Cathedral is a rectangular open space known as 'The Palace Green', bounded to its north by the Castle, which once housed the Bishop's palace, but which later became University College of the University of Durham, founded by Bishop Van Mildert in 1832. Another little street leads downhill from here to join North Bailey and the city itself, still very small in the 1940s. When Colin was appointed, some of the narrow streets of the older parts were still crammed with the through traffic of the Great North Road (the A1), which cut through the neck of the Cathedral-Castle peninsula in Durham market place and crossed the Wear by Elvet and Framwellgate Bridges.

One place I especially remember from childhood is a rough path which led below the old castle walls on their north side, and adjoined the gardens of small houses where one might see a Durham miner or two, still dressed as such, with the whippet dogs they fancied. If the overwhelming impression of Durham City is of the Cathedral and Castle, dominating and enclosed by the thickly wooded loop and gorge of the river, the County of Durham – with the exception of the extensive and isolated moorland to the west and the heavily populated urban and industrial areas – stood for coal mining. Much of this once lovely county of rolling hills was covered with mining villages, each with one or more 'pits' and continuously growing conical slag heaps, and with a great number of railway lines. There were even two pits on the outskirts of the City itself. Neverless, Colin could write in his diary, 'Motoring in Durham' – of which he had to do a great deal – 'is pleasant, for the undulating country nearly always provides good and distant views, a great help when the foreground of mining villages and their neighbourhood is so constant and so mournful a feature'.

I do not know how Colin and Dean Alington first met, but Colin had been asked to preach in Durham cathedral while still at Edinburgh, and the Dean had clearly learnt quite a lot about him before approving, or, as Colin surmised, even suggesting, his appointment as Bishop of Jarrow, and hence his two other spheres of duty as well. It is possible they met through the agency of Colin's brother Walter, who taught Classics at Eton for a time during the war. But in any case Colin was by now quite well-known among Anglican clergy for his not primarily scholarly, let alone academic, but practical interest in and knowledge of liturgy, church ornaments, decoration and music, as, among other things, an active and office-holding member of both the Alcuin Club and Warham Guild and also the Board of the English Hymnal, of which he later became chairman.

The Durham Cathedral Chapter minutes show that, right from the start of his new ministry, his expertise in these fields was recognised and put to work. At his first Chapter meeting, for instance, Colin undertook to buy new material to decorate the Bishop's throne and, after a year or two, was asked to buy a new chasuble for the cathedral and to see to the design of an appropriate flag to fly on the tower. He also agreed to call in appropriate experts to give advice about the feretory, the shrine of St Cuthbert, the saintly Abbot of Lindisfarne who is so important in the history of Durham Cathedral. Colin also introduced on his own initiative the matter of who should sing the service and read the lessons at the daily offices of Mattins and Evensong.

The established custom was that the Minor Canon on duty should sing the service and read the first lesson. Colin was sure that this 'was a relic of the days when the Canons of the Cathedral Chapter were non-resident or at least non-churchgoers' and suggested that they should start to divide these tasks among those canons actually present on each occasion, and thereby observe a principle of variety. The matter was left on the table but was passed at the next meeting. Colin was also asked to work with the Precentor (a Minor Canon) in suggesting ways in which the days commemorating the three great saints associated with Durham Diocese – St Cuthbert, St Oswald and the Venerable Bede – could be more fittingly celebrated.

The consulting of the Precentor in this matter shows that an important part would be the provision of suitable music, much of it sung by the choir. The Dean also got Colin to write a special service to give thanks for the Armistice, which all knew could not be long delayed after the summer of 1944. This was duly used in the Cathedral on the appropriate Sunday. He also wrote for the Cathedral a Youth service for the Whit Monday of 1947. Judging by his note about the Diocesan Youth Conference in January 1948, during which '180 young people of both sexes were present and communicated' at a Sung Eucharist he celebrated for them in the Chapel of Bede College, this side of church life was thriving. During this year he also 'compos(ed) a service in which the Recital of the County Music Festival could be effectively set', and no doubt there were other special services too.

His liturgical expertise was also called on by the Bishop of Durham, who announced in *The Bishoprick* for November 1947 that there would soon be a new authorised form of Institution in the Diocese, to which 'the Bishop of Jarrow has given much time and attention' (he may well have suggested it in the first place). The Bishop of Durham thought it would be 'generally welcomed'. In February 1949 he announced that it had won general approval in use. He and the Bishop of Jarrow had noticed one or two places where improvement was possible, and they would take account of them. Later in 1949 the Chapter minutes record their 'warm approval' of Colin's proposals for the revision of the list of daily intercessions in cathedral services, and the empowering of the archdeacons (Colin of course was one) to revise the list and give instructions to the precentor to alter the service books accordingly.

We should note here too that Colin was asked to write a short pamphlet, entitled 'Evensong in Durham Cathedral', presumably to be made available to cathedral visitors unaccustomed to services held there. It is clear from this that Colin was already thinking in terms of the book he published when at Lincoln, *Anglican Public Worship*. The pamphlet introduces visitors to the meaning and purpose of worship, and the place of cathedrals in it, and then explains the significance of the different stages of Evensong itself. Whether or not he was thought to be an expert on change-ringing, he was also asked, along with the Sub-Dean, to negotiate with the Cathedral bell-ringers after they had asked for a rise in pay.

He contacted the Ringers' association, and, after talking to the ringers, wrote in his diary: 'We want real ringing; they think chiming sufficient, except on great occasions. I didn't much admire their spirit. They seem to care much more for the money than the bells.' (As far as I know, Colin's undoubted interest in ringing was never taken very far; indeed, on one occasion, when invited to 'have a go' when watching the ringers in action in some church tower, he let the bell go off balance, and found himself being carried off the ground by the weight of the bell, and had to let go of the rope!) The Minutes also record a financial shortfall around this time.

One of Colin's suggestions was to raise the fee for going up the tower, which, of course, meant approaching other cathedrals to find out what they charged. Another matter raised by Colin at these meetings was the privacy of the College. As there was a direct entry from it into the Cathedral, visitors to the building who had left by that route sometimes 'camped out' on one of the grassy plots for a picnic lunch and a rest. Colin records an occasion when he saw an 'amorous couple' indulging in some 'rough horse play' in full public view. Whatever form it took, he did not want his children to see it. So, in a very practical spirit, he suggested the wording of a notice to be posted where visitors could read it: 'This open space is a private garden. Visitors to the cathedral may pass through it, but they must keep to the paths.' People who don't look after their own property, he observes in his diary, perhaps don't deserve to possess it.

One very important change he brought about during his time at Durham may have been suggested partly by the disquiet of some Chapter members at the Dean's keenness to give the Gilbert Scott screen to Edinburgh Cathedral, as recorded at the end of the last chapter, though probably even more by what he saw as a disastrous neglect in the whole diocese of the statutory procedures for any alterations in churches which would greatly change their appearance. When, as Archdeacon of Auckland, Colin made his first Visitation in 1944 (in 1946 he had to make five in all) to the Stockton and Darlington deaneries of his archdeaconry, although he was able to praise the sense of responsibility of the churchwardens towards the incumbents, and to deplore the serious situation brought about by the shortage of clergy, he was appalled by

the prevailing indifference to law and order exhibited in disregard of Faculty Jurisdiction and the lack of proper concern for the well-being of ancient buildings. That element in the administration of the diocese seems to be extraordinarily weak and ineffective.

He adduced the example of the vicar of Stockton, with an important (Georgian) church, who 'spoke gaily of his intentions about his church without a thought that he is not legally a free agent in its alteration and "improvement"' (31/5/44). Later in the year, after a Faculties Committee meeting about changes to the internationally celebrated Saxon church at Escomb, he bewailed the fact that the faculties committee met very seldom, and, when it did, it relied on notes made by each member in isolation without common discussion. Yet, 'In no subject is lack of common discussion more disastrous than in the assessment of Church ornaments and decoration.' (5/11/44). Even in January 1948 he could still write:

These meetings fill me with dismay. Hardly anyone on our committee seems to have any knowledge or experience of good church furniture and ornaments and nearly all are prepared to pass anything. Romans, the master of Sherburn Hospital, is especially dangerous. His undoubted archaeological knowledge is thought by other members to give him a preeminence of artistic taste of which he is curiously destitute. Still it is an undoubtedly difficult task we have to exercise. Hardly any proposal which has come before us in my time has been really good. The standard of what is commonly desired hardly ever rises above what is barely tolerable. Are we just to refuse everything or to refuse only what is not frankly barbarous? To establish even a very banal standard would mean that we must turn down about 50 per cent of what comes before us.

It is against this background that we should note the September 1946, resolution of the Cathedral Chapter 'that in future the Chapter should submit any considerable proposals for adorning or furnishing the Cathedral to the Central Advisory Council for the Care of Churches for their comments'. Thus, when the Chapter discussed the substitution of a stained glass RAF war memorial window for the existing clear glass, Colin was deputed to consult the Central Council about artists to decorate the wall arcading below it. As for the window itself, the Dean strongly supported the design of Hugh Easton, whereas Colin, having consulted Francis Eeles, suggested asking Harry Stammers for a design.

In his diary he wrote, after a Chapter meeting: 'I strongly criticised the design for the RAF window, feeling that the very crude comparing of an airman's death in action to the death of Christ on the Cross is presumptuous and sentimental.' He hated having to express disagreement with Alington on this matter, as he knew the Dean's son had been recently killed in action. No one gave him verbal support, but Colin 'felt that other members of the chapter were with (him)'. But Alington did in fact accept Colin's suggestion of Stammers and wrote to ask him. In the end the Hugh Easton design was chosen after all, since Stammers was too busy with existing commissions to produce a design for some time, and the Air Ministry had approved Easton's.

While he was Bishop of Jarrow, Colin officiated at 170 different confirmation services in Durham diocese. At least one was in Durham Prison, where he confirmed two candidates on the same visit, several were in hospitals, and also in the chapel of Brancepeth Castle which was largely occupied by soldiers. On various occasions, Colin mentions that some of the candidates were suffering from tuberculosis. In May 1944, he writes:

> Drove over to South Shields through Houghton-le-Spring and Sunderland for lunch with Squance of South Westoe, at whose church I afterwards confirmed 182 souls (one a woman dying of consumption in her slummy home). The candidates seemed well-prepared and were quiet and collected.

A month later: 'after tea I motored to South Hylton where I confirmed six TB girl patients in a ward'. Then, on 1 August of the same year he wrote in his diary:

> After tea at Jack Richardson's a confirmation at the Municipal Hospital which the Mayor and Mayoress (Wesleyan) attended. A very large number of the female staff were confirmed (the chaplain has only been in office since Easter) and a few patients, some almost certainly incurable TB cases.

This special interest in TB patients (the disease was clearly not uncommon in the north-east of Durham County) can be explained when we recall that, when Colin had a medical examination in 1932 to check whether he was fit to work for some time in India, an X-ray of his lungs had revealed that he had once suffered from the disease himself, which he probably caught in the trenches of the First World War battlefields. In November he records a different type of illness:

I went over in the rain to W Hartlepool to confirm George Major, a young man of 35 who for some years has been confined to his bed with spinal arthritis. He cannot move a muscle, though he can speak and eat – lies stretched out helpless and motionless. In the small kitchen where he lay were his mother and other relations and some representatives of S.Luke's Church Council. It was a moving occasion and obviously meant much to the young man. I felt as never before the wonder of the drama of Catholic worship of which the significance is almost heightened when its theatre is not a noble church but a cottage sick room.

Colin's cuttings book also contains a newspaper photo taken in Dryburn Emergency Hospital, Durham. It shows Colin in cope and mitre, carrying his shepherd's crook in his left hand and, with his right, shaking hands with Private H. Woodland, who is lying prone on a bed, his head supported by four pillows, while two nurses and another priest, probably the hospital chaplain, stand round it. The caption reads: 'The Bishop of Jarrow, the Right Rev. D.C. Dunlop, wishing Private H.W. Woodland, of the Durham Light Infantry, a speedy recovery after the soldier had been confirmed by the Bishop at a service held in the hospital. Infantryman Woodland was seriously wounded in Belgium in September, 1944.' In August of that year he had visited, 'with the ubiquitous mayor and a following of councillors', in Sunderland Municipal Hospital ... 'some of the men wounded on D-day in Normandy; mostly shellshock cases, or "exhaustion" as modern euphony insists upon', and then taken a short service in the chapel, where he dedicated a combined chalice and paten.

The visits to hospitals and sick-rooms away from Durham City were, like most of his travelling, usually combined with other things. After the South Hylton confirmation Colin went to Bishopwearmouth Parish Church and

(25/6/44) preached at the Industrial Service. It is a fine graceful church well restored by Caroë. The Mayor was there and thanked me effusively for my discourse as did the Mayoress and Town Clerk's wife.

In the morning before the service at Sunderland Municipal Hospital, he went with Jack Richardson

to visit the canteen at Laing's shipyard in dinner-hour and sat talking to 4 or 5 men, grimy with toil, but friendly and conversational. Then lunch with the bosses and after that a walk round the yard and a visit to an almost finished oil tanker on which I was allowed to manipulate a compressed-air rivetter.

One of the problems a bishop sometimes faces at confirmations is that of grasping the exact names of the candidates. Colin, whose love of 'godliness and good order' was also strongly allied to a love of practical common-sense, records a confirmation at Longbenton, a suburb of Newcastle. After staying the night at the vicarage, he wrote:

(13/5/45) ...At 9am this morning confirmed 60 candidates and then celebrated the Parish Communion, giving the Sacrament to the newly confirmed. Each candidate had a confirmation sponsor who, standing by his side, displayed a card with the candidate's Christian name written upon it, so that I could call him by name. A pleasing custom of real spiritual value, I should judge.

After another confirmation he took at South Hylton in 1947 he writes: 'I named each candidate as I laid hands on them – what a hush comes over people at the naming of a name on such occasions!' In 1949 he wrote a short article in *The Bishoprick* (the Durham Diocesan Magazine) entitled 'Confirmation Service Arrangements', in which he commended much in the churches where he had confirmed ('Durham sets a high standard'), and gave good advice to those where things hadn't gone so well. One is struck once more with the good sense and human understanding Colin brought to practical matters in the work of the Church.

Colin's diary entries about his clergy contacts in Durham diocese, of which there are far more in the first year of his time at Durham than they became later, when he felt too busy to write regularly, illustrate the great variety of clergy in the diocese, and of occasions for the meeting. Here are some extracts:

6/6/44: I had a talk with Hudson the prison chaplain about his work, and at 7pm attended a Missionary Meeting addressed by Dr Heywood the late Bishop of Mombasa. Gordon Hopkins the vicar of St Luke's Sunderland came to talk to me about the shipyards in the afternoon.

15/8/44: Lunched with Lomax, rector of Washington since 1899 (he had been his father's curate there since 1897!). A charming old man who had intended to become an Army Chaplain. He has hunted a lot, as pictures and trophies on the walls witness. A real parson. In the streets no passer-by failed to greet him. I preached to a MU gathering in his barn-like church.

30/8/44: In the afternoon Mary and I motored over to Murton near Seaham for a parish tea to which she had been bidden. On the way we called on the Andersons at South Hetton vicarage. He has the quiet strength and happy gentleness of a true saint. He is very poor, though says nothing of it. At the most he gets £400 p.a. but both his son and daughter have been trained as doctors at Newcastle. His parish is raw and unattractive to behold while the mean little church must be a constant grief to him. Yet he has not a word of complaint.

1/10/44: I had tea with Casey in his remote vicarage at Quarrington and met his twin girls and his baby son. Harvest Evensong at this church defied every law of ecclesiological science, though the vicar loyally stuck to the liturgy. But the service was devout and hearty and I enjoyed it. Motored back over wet roads gleaming in the pale yellow of late sunset. 27/4/45: In the afternoon Mary motored with me by devious and pleasant roads to Coniscliffe-on-Tees where I called upon the bed-ridden and plainly dying vicar.

13/9/45: Set off with Mary and the children in the car via Willington and Stanhope to Westgate where the Vicar, old Perry (78), is ill. He has had pneumonia but is now better. He wants to retire but finds it hard to face the financial consequences. If only Westgate could be united to S. John's Chapel and Perry allowed to end his days in the Vicarage. But that would mean getting Darling out of St John's Chapel. But he is a bounder, idle and graceless. Meanwhile the sun had come out. We went on to Rookhope, via Eastgate, where the vicarage garden has grown up round the vicarage like the Sleeping Beauty. Unutterable decay and neglect. The vicar was out. Rookhope is a little slum in the midst of wild and remote country – I've never seen its like. [There had once been much lead-mining in this moorland area.]

22/1/46 Went on to see old Perry of Westgate who is in hospital in Newcastle. He welcomed me with affection. They say he is unlikely to get up again, but I'm not so sure.

14/1/48: Called on the Vicar and Mrs Fryar at Langdon Beck [in Upper Teesdale]. He is a pathetic object. It seems wrong that he should have been left in so bleak and remote a spot for 20 years. His clothes were quite literally in rags and I doubt if he had shaved for two days. I could not think of any way to help him: I feel ashamed that I did nothing ministerially for him.

3/1/50: 2 drives with Francis and Philip to say farewell to Norton (Mrs Edwards) and Seaton Carew (Canon and Mrs Booth), then next day to Stanhope (Knightall) and Frosterley (Jackson).

It is worth adding one more visit here. In his reply to my appeal in the *Durham Newslink* asking if anyone had any reminiscences of Colin, Professor P.G. Britton told me that he had been brought up in the vicarage of Tudhoe, not far from Durham City. Though too young to recall anything directly himself, he remembers his father telling him that very early on Christmas Eve, 1944,

a stray doodlebug [a V2] exploded in the playing field adjoining the Vicarage. ...This caused great damage to the Vicarage and surroundings although, thankfully, our family was not seriously injured. My father used to recall the Bishop of Jarrow ... turning up on the Sunday and picking his way through the debris to offer support and help. I am sure that he did help with the services on that day and Christmas Day. There is also a story about him turning up later with some presents for me (then 4) as Christmas had been blown away! My father also had a very positive regard for the help of Bp Dunlop in the period of resettlement into a colliery terrace which followed and the eventual move in December 1945 to a new living at Eighton Banks.

The damage done to Church property by bombs and rockets was a common problem in many English dioceses. But, as was no doubt the case in some others, church property also suffered the effects of industry. In a report in *The Bishoprick* Colin drew attention to the objectionable fumes from the ICI works at Haverton Hill, on the Tees. But coal-mining was probably a worse culprit in County Durham. After a Dilapidations Committee meeting Colin wrote: '17/12/46: The vicarage at Felling is collapsing owing to coal subsidence.' What is more, 'the Colliery Company who are liable refuse to do anything as the mines pass to the state on 1 Jan. Where can we appeal?' The virtual ubiquity of coal also had its entertaining side: after a visitation Colin held in Auckland Castle on 25/4/44 he wrote: 'The Visitation was held in Cosin's lovely chapel. One of the church wardens turned up black from his coal-pit – a fine example of real enthusiasm.'

I think, though I am not sure, that Colin made it his business while at Durham to arrange a visit down a mine and to see work at the coal face. But no record of this has survived. But here are some other 'industrial' visits which he did record:

22/6/44: Drove over to Hebburn with Mary D-J. On arrival she set out for a visit to Jarrow while I went with Cameron on a visit to Reyrolle's Electrical Works, the largest industrial plant I have ever been over, employing about 8,000 people. Col: Leeson the Managing Director devoted 5 hours to showing me over and explaining things. First we attended a choral concert in a canteen where the singing was excellent. After lunch we went round the works where I was amazed at the variety of output. Leeson seemed most anxious to show me what the firm is doing both technically and socially in service of the community, and of the employees. They have a fine education and apprentice scheme working in with university and school curricula. How absorbing a technical career must be of a man's mind and heart! Small wonder that many have no time left for religion, in view of their earlier training. Such a works with its social life provides material for what must seem a full enough culture to those whose hearts have never been awakened to the call of God.

2/10/44: Yesterday, Mary, Francis, Philip and I went to Hebburn for the launching of the aircraft carrier 'Triumph' built by Hawthorn, Leslie & Co. The day was dull and cold and we had to wait longer than anticipated for the strategic moment when river traffic and tide were just right. Lady Louis Mountbatten did the 'christening' and I recited the prayers – prayers for the men who would serve the ship. On the launching platform I met several old acquaintances – Col. Leeson of Reyrolles, Charles Brackenbury whom I had not seen since Oxford days and whom a moustache failed to disguise, Air Marshall Gossage whom I had not seen since 1934 in Baghdad and Col. Wannop, a solicitor in Chichester, now GSOI of Northern Command. The actual launching of so vast a ship (15,000 tons) and of so elegant a build was a sight of unique fascination, and its plunge into the river almost awesome in character. A plentiful tea was provided for the guests of the Company, and I had some words with Ravell, the Managing Director. Mr Smith, a sort of very senior employee, looked after me with courteous efficiency. The boys' kilts were much admired and we all enjoyed the whole proceedings, though I believe the sight of a travelling fair at Chester-le-Street on the way there and back was the high watermark of the children's enjoyment.

12/2/45: Motored into Sunderland and picking up Gordon Hopkins at St Luke's, Pallion, went to the Sunderland Forge, a large electrical works. I then addressed a meeting of men and women in the canteen and told them about my work with the RAF. It was a good audience and I was in good form. I had a word after with two Shop Stewards who deplored the lack of responsibility in the men in Trade Union matters. At lunch I sat next to Cooke, the Chief Constable for Sunderland, a pleasant man who can, I should say, be extremely truculent. Griffin, the Chief Accountant, showed me round his office with its amazing assemblage of labour-saving devices. All calculations are mechanical. Then I went on to Shortt's and saw a 10,000 ton cargo ship launched in the pouring rain. Had tea with the Directors and then on to see Troop at Sunderland Rectory. Returned in time to hear the boys their prayers and to read to them.

Towards the end of his time at Durham, I well remember Colin's eagerness to satisfy my desire, as a keen juvenile 'train spotter', to visit the old LNER Steam-Engine Railway Shed at Gateshead, telling me that he would be happy to arrange a visit. He often recalled the shedmaster's welcome on our arrival and particularly his immediate grasp of the situation, suggesting at once a division between Philip and myself on the one hand, who were probably, as he put it, 'number snatchers', and Colin on the other, who had, perhaps (here he smiled engagingly) 'a mild interest in the workings of the railway', whom he himself would take round. Colin often recalled this visit with respect and amusement.

In view of all this, it may not be surprising to hear of his interest in and promotion of the work of industrial chaplains in the diocese. *The Bishoprick* for November 1945 records him as having 'spoken at the Diocesan Conference' on the 'ministrations of industrial chaplains in factories, trading estates and shipyards', and appealed for some sort of cooperation and sharing of experiences. Elsewhere in the same number of the magazine Colin himself announces a meeting of industrial chaplains. Another report in this number concerns the Church Lads' Brigade, who had held their usual summer camp for the NE region. The writer of the report speaks of Colin's interest in and appreciation of what he saw and heard, and of how he 'inspired officers and lads to further efforts by encouraging words'.

Among his papers is an Officer's Commission, which 'grants to the Rt Reverend D.C. Dunlop ... the rank of Assistant Regimental Chaplain' in the Brigade, dated 21/3/47. Though I have found no diary entry about his work in this sphere, when Colin was appointed to Lincoln in late 1949, the reporter from *The Yorkshire Post* included it in a summary of the special things he was known for at Durham. He also seems to have had a good many requests to speak to Rotary Clubs. A favourite topic was, as we might expect, his work for the RAF and other forces. Rotary Clubs are primarily social and philanthropic organisations, giving generously to various charitable causes. But Colin's diary entry for 17/12/46 contains the passage: 'Did notes for Rotary Club lunch on Thursday – a "Christmas message". They are supposed to bar religion and politics but I fear they'll get a sermon from me.' Unfortunately there is no further entry until 3/9/47, so it's not clear what the result of this was, though Colin's 'message' is very unlikely to have offended most of them.

At Durham Colin continued his work for women's ministry in the Church, and, in his farewell article about Colin in *The Bishoprick* the Bishop of Durham paid special attention to, among other things, 'his wardenship of the Society of Christ and Blessed Mary the Virgin and his care for Women's work in general'. In September 1944 Colin took a retreat for women workers and deaconesses. Conducting retreats was something he had not done for a long time – possibly not since he took an ordination retreat in Jerusalem during his time in Baghdad and – and he records now that he found the writing of retreat addresses very difficult, largely because, although he had for some time been invited to preach in many places away from his home ground, he knew that retreat addresses require a quite different technique from sermons. When the retreat was over he was fairly satisfied with how it had gone, but felt completely exhausted by it. In January 1945 he wrote in his diary:

> At 5pm presided at an informal meeting of the Training Committee of the Women's Work Board arranging details for a special meeting of teachers and youth workers who are to hear the Bp of Sheffield speak on openings for women in the work of the Church.

In the same month he preached at Richmond, 'for some Ripon diocesan function' on women's ministry. In *The Bishoprick* for September of that year, we read that Colin 'announced a "School of Prayer"' for women on 1–3 October; the August 1947 number tells us that at the Diocesan Conference for that year 'attentive hearing was given to the Bishop of Jarrow when he appealed for women to be trained to work in the diocese'. I shall end this paragraph on Colin's engagements with identifiable groups and causes with a report in *The Bishoprick* on religious education. In the 'Diocesan Synod', the recorder writes: 'there followed a short but telling speech by the Bishop of Jarrow. He reminded the Conference that religious teaching in schools often made indelible impressions on the minds of receptive children. It also created a subtle atmosphere that touched the inward spirit.' He may well here have been thinking of the teaching he received at Radley, the intellectual basis for his turn away from Presbyterianism towards some variant of Anglo-Catholicism.

Colin's diary entries about the services at Durham Cathedral contain, as we might expect by now, a good many references to the choir and its trainer, Conrad Eden, the Cathedral organist. They make the Dean's announcement in *The Bishoprick* of February 1947: 'the choir has repeatedly been asked to broadcast', rather surprising. Some of Colin's adverse comments are very unspecific, as when he writes of the 'unbelievable dreariness of our services', and, elsewhere, the 'dullness' of the choir, and says 'The men's choir [which took the place of the full choir during their holidays] is a great affliction, especially when used so unintelligently. Eden has no flexibility of mind or imagination.'

But when he talks of Durham Cathedral as 'this centre of Victorian taste in music', and contrasts its choir with Sir Sydney Nicholson's amateur stand-in choir (which was in Durham during the summer holidays of 1944), and which, despite their 'poor voices', performed with 'dash and courage and movement, without which most choral music is a poor thing', adding that he 'prefers the service as sung by them to those sung by our trained but dull choir', we get a better idea of why he was so negative about it. On 25/10/44 he is even more specific:

> at evensong we had Byrd's 2nd Service which was taken far too slow and with that absence of vivacity which can make even Tudor music seem dull. Of deliberate policy 'generations' is sung as four syllables – while Byrd's intention was for five: 'Gen-er-a-ti-ons', and so with similar words – thus cloying the texture of the music.'

On 29/11/46 he writes again:

> attended evensong. Byrd's short service and Victoria's 'Glorious in Heaven'. I would sooner have polyphonic music than any other, yet how how hard it is to endure our choir's arid and wooden performance of it.

Colin here reveals himself as a champion of what was then a relatively new movement in Church and secular music, the revival of English Tudor polyphony, and similar styles abroad (especially Flanders, Italy and Spain), of which Michael Howard, founder of the Renaissance Society in 1944, with its performing branch, 'The Renaissance Singers' was an important pioneer. In his aptly entitled autobiography, *Thine Adversaries Roar,* Howard tells us that, among the vice-presidents of his choir were D-J and Colin, and that he had first met Colin while he was organist of Christ Church, Woburn Square, probably when Colin preached there on Remembrance Day, 1946.

After a few years, the Renaissance Singers began to receive much support from Benjamin Britten and Peter Pears, and their 'eventual president' was Vaughan Williams, whom Colin had got to know because of their common involvement with the English Hymnal. Michael Howard came for short stays with us in Durham three times, in 1947, 1948 and 1949. He married six times, and his autobiography makes no attempt to conceal the serious psychological problems that wrought havoc in his life, but, as Colin never mentions him in his diaries, and I have seen no letters he wrote referring to him, I have no idea what became of Colin's support and friendship with him after Howard's appointment to Ely Cathedral. However, while Colin was Dean of Lincoln, Mary records that they 'had quite a little chat' with him on 23 June 1954, at the Aldeburgh Festival, when the Renaissance Singers sang and Colin read a sermon by John Donne at the Festival Evensong, but she does not comment on this reunion.

Howard writes in the autobiography that he had asked Colin if the fact that he had divorced his first wife (it had been a 'shotgun marriage') would prevent him from getting a Cathedral organist's post. He records that Colin told him: 'there need be no adverse effects provided that I do not marry again'. He did apply for Ely in 1949, and was shortlisted but not appointed. But when Howard visited us in 1948, he was accompanied by someone called 'Nicolette Howard'. Whether she was his second or later wife, or his sister or mother, I don't know, but Colin, together with Professor Hutchings (Professor of Music at Durham and a good friend of Colin's) did support his second application for Ely in 1953, and this time he was successful. He only stayed at Ely a short time, resigning in 1958, but in that time he seems to have inaugurated the practice of leaving much of the organ-playing during services to his assistant, and to have conducted the choral singing himself, to ensure that the choir knew exactly what he wanted from them. Ely Cathedral became well known for the quality of tone and performance he elicited, and Howard's approach, which had the Dean's full backing, became widely adopted.

The high standards Colin looked for in cathedral music he also looked for in the spoken word. An undated typescript lecture entitled 'The Conduct of Public Worship with Special Reference to Music', which he probably composed for a talk to ordinands or clergy in post-ordination training, has a useful section on voice production, in which he points out that

> many of us can only achieve the art of speaking and reading in church by real effort. When that is so we should make the effort. A clear and intelligent reading of the bible and recital of the prayers can be almost a means of grace to the people. Lack of attention to this art can be the cause of widespread dissatisfaction, a real deprivation from the people of what they are entitled to.

If necessary, clergy 'should take a course of lessons from a teacher of singing or an actor', and he goes on to talk about the appropriate tone to adopt. A diary entry on the provision of microphones in the pulpit makes it sound as though this was a comparatively new practice, and certainly one that he felt uncomfortable with, as it seemed to put a barrier between him and the congregation – however much it might help others. His diaries also show that he gave much thought to the art of preaching (as part of a church service), contrasting sermons with the more intimate Retreat Addresses, and the more informative and factual Lectures, as we have already noted. 'The style and manner of preaching' was the title of a paper he read to a gathering of clergy in Chichester Diocese when he was visiting D-J at Chichester after Church Assembly Week in November 1944. On 8/1/48 we find an entry on 'exhortatory' sermons:

> In the morning I began a sermon for the Cathedral on Sunday upon the Missionary task of the Church. I find such exhortations difficult and the effort to produce them tends to lead me into unreality and overexpression. This is often the case with sermons trying to create enthusiasm for a cause. Somehow I begin at the wrong end.

Nevertheless, Colin several times emphasises in sermons that a church which ignores Mission will completely fail in its task at home, and he was clearly much involved with Mission in one form or other at Durham. For example, *The Bishoprick* reports in 1949: 'The Bishop of Jarrow chaired a 1-day conference of younger clergy in the diocese, arranged by the Younger Clergy Missionary Fellowship – "presenting the work of the Church overseas to the congregations at home in a living and challenging way"', and he was at least once involved in the week-long Summer Holidays 'Sands' Mission on the beach at Roker, near Sunderland, though there is no personal reference to this.

During Colin's time at Durham, when the difficulties of travel began to ease after the war, he received an increasing number of requests to preach beyond his home ground. He nearly always wrote out his sermons in full, and added the name of the church, or churches, where the sermon was preached – though, as he learnt his sermons almost by heart, and did not invariably stick to the written text, he hardly ever sounded like someone who was simply reading one. Among his 'aways' when at Durham, were Glenalmond (a public school in Perthshire, where he gave a course of Holy Week addresses), St Matthew's Northampton, where the incumbent was Walter Hussey, the well-known connoisseur of modern church art, later to become Dean of Chichester – 'The parish life and worship is vigorous and wholesome but I doubt if it is much influenced by the aesthetic interests of the vicar' – Great St Mary's, Cambridge (for a university sermon), Birmingham University (another university sermon, in a large hall got up to look like a chapel – the arch-liberal Bishop Barnes was present, 'wary and ill at ease', but also Austin Duncan-Jones, D-J's oldest son, later to be Professor of Philosophy, and his wife Elsie).

There was also York Minster, where he preached about Moral Welfare work on 30/6/45 'before a large congregation of women and clergymen including the Archbishop and his three suffragans'. Several sermons he gave in Ireland were woven into a holiday he and Mary made in 1945 (no doubt the foundation for this was laid during his visit to Dublin in 1943). In Dublin he preached at both St Patrick's (twice) and at Christ Church cathedrals, and also at St Bartholomew's Church. They stayed twice at the boy's public school, St Columba's, Rathfarnham, a Dublin suburb (the school is now a very exclusive co-educational boarding school for the children of the wealthy).

Both here and in Oughterard, County Galway (incumbent the Revd D.L.C. Dunlop – no relation!), Colin's sermon was a return for hospitality, as were his sermons at Woodenbridge, County Wicklow, and his celebration of Holy Communion (and, no doubt, short address) at Christ Church Cathedral, Dublin, since they stayed a day or two with the Dean, The Ven. Lewis-Crosby, at the

Grange, Stillorgan, before leaving for the ferry from Kingstown (Dun Laoghaire). During Colin's time at Durham, and then later at Lincoln, he 'did duty' two or three times for the vicar of Hintlesham, near Ipswich (he was father of a Durham chorister), where we could have a family holiday not far from both Sibyl's cottage, and the retirement home of the Martin Shaws, and was responsible for taking all the services and preaching during the month we were all there.

Colin's series of preaching visits to Liverpool Cathedral, where his friend Dwelly was still Dean, was extended by three during the Durham years. The first of the three sermons was due to be preached on 6 May 1945, the day before the Germans 'unconditionally' surrendered to the Allies. Colin wrote: 'We are all expecting hourly the declaration of victory in the West', and he had been 'dreading lest (his) prepared discourses would have to be scrapped'. But he much enjoyed his visit, as usual, sleeping at the Adelphi Hotel and spending the day with Dwelly, who was finding it difficult to 'get the measure of' his new Bishop (Clifford Martin). 'At my request the choir did Weelkes' "Two trebles" service on Sunday afternoon.' Next year Colin was asked to preach again, and his sermon was printed, and entitled 'The Ascensiontide Sermon of the Year after the Days of Victory, 1946'.

It is, to my mind, an extremely fine sermon, its main point being that we should take much more seriously the nature of Christianity as preparation for Heaven, since Heaven is what man was made for. An exclusive attention to improving the things of this world should be the direct result of a preparation for the next, not replace it, as is, Colin insists, far too common today. The half-column devoted to the sermon by 'Layman' in *The Liverpool Echo's*, 'Weekly Causerie on Pulpit and Pew', is most warm in its praise.

Colin's third visit from Durham came at the end of 1949, when he preached on Remembrance Sunday. By this time, in the shadow of the atomic bomb, public concern with things military had lost much of the thankful and approving tone it had had during the war. The 'Weekly Causerie' was now clearly written by a different layman, who was hearing Colin for the first time, and wrote:

> Would that the Church of England were richer in preachers of his calibre. Earnestness, eloquence, frankness, the conviction he has something to say, and wanted all his listeners to hear him, and not merely those close to the pulpit – these were the impressions he left with one, and for once the sermon was worthy of the occasion.

It has been fashionable to debunk the soldier (I here draw on 'Layman's' brief summary); there has been much submission to pacifist claims; yet it is historically the case that the Christian elements in our society were fought for; the people we honour today protected Christendom from 'the wolf without and the enemy within'. We must never relax our state of readiness to defend our heritage of Christian civilisation. 'Words, clever diplomacy, ingenious subterfuge' may all fail. 'Layman' summed up the sermon as 'A defence of the soldier', and was 'convinced it made a deep impression on the vast congregation'.

We must end this section on Colin's growing reputation as a preacher with a characteristic reference to his self-examination after spending:

> most of a day writing a sermon for the initiation of the Lambeth Campaign in Newcastle Cathedral on Saturday. I sometimes wonder whether I am right to put such furious energy into sermon composition. Much of the stimulus to such compositions is definitely self-regarding – a desire to justify myself and 'hear myself saying true things' in a vast assembly. On the other hand it is the thing I seem to be able to do best, so why not try to do it well and gradually to purify the motive?

In 1946 the Bishop of Gibraltar wrote to the Archbishop of Canterbury asking him for his permission to retire from the see, in which, he said, he had been no more than a stop-gap. The Archbishop suggested possible successors for his consideration, and on 23 July 1946 he added: 'Another suggestion – possibly the best of all – comes to my mind – the Bishop of Jarrow.' Before contacting Colin he wrote to Dr Williams, the Bishop of Durham (1/8/46), whom he knew would not wish to lose him so soon, with his own view of the 'pros and cons' of such a move. Against it were the 'bad luck' to Durham Diocese, and the fact that Colin had for the last twenty years 'jumped about from one job to another'.

On the other side, Colin had all the many different qualities needed: he was a staunch Church of England man, who would therefore be at home in all the varied Anglican chaplaincies in the diocese (those in the southern half of Europe), he was used to working with members of the armed forces as he would have to do in Gibraltar itself, familiar with orthodox churches and interested in ecumenism, and so on – all in all, he thought him 'much more convincing than any other candidate'.

The Bishop of Durham replied that he didn't doubt that Dunlop 'would fill the position extremely well'. But it 'would on all grounds be a very serious loss [to the diocese], especially *now*. He's just settled in and begun to know the people and problems.' He would not be at all happy to lose him, and it would be better for him to be 'longer at one big piece of work'. However, he accepted that the Diocese of Gibraltar's interests must have priority over those of Durham. The Archbishop, after consulting his fellow of York, wrote to the incumbent holder of the see that, as Colin's name 'stood out' so clearly, he proposed to invite him (the Crown, in the person of the Prime Minister, would of course have to agree too).

The Archbishop then wrote to Colin, stressing that the arguments against his accepting were 'completely overweighed by your own special qualities for this work.' Colin replied that he was very grateful to be so honoured and would give the offer his 'fullest and deepest consideration'. After three or four days he wrote again saying that he did not think it would be right to accept. Since 1927 he had been nowhere longer than four years, and he only accepted Jarrow after much hesitation because of the very pressing invitation of both the Bishop and the Dean of Durham. He felt that his quick moves had not been good for him, as he had never had to keep on sticking to his work despite boredom or accumulating difficulties. To accept would therefore not be good for his soul. Apart from that, he could not, under post-war circumstances, adequately perform the duties of a father as a largely itinerant bishop. This firm refusal was accepted by the Archbishop.

It seems clear that Colin was during these years considered likely by some other church dignitaries to be offered a diocese sooner or later. Dean Alington – who had written to Colin 'you have got to be a bishop some time and Jarrow would be a good place to start' – was certainly one of them. Apart from the definite offer of Gibraltar, Mary used to tell my brothers and myself that he was once offered the see of Hereford, but I have searched in the library at Lambeth (whose detailed records sometimes have obvious gaps in them) and found no reference to his having been officially considered for this. The most important point against his being offered a diocese in England (Gibraltar was in fact a rather special case) seems to have been what Archbishop Garbett (of York) called his 'uncertain temper'.

When, almost ten years later, Fisher was looking for someone to chair the new Church of England Liturgical Commission, for which Colin seemed to him an extremely suitable candidate, he wrote to Garbett to ask whether he thought he would fill the position well. Garbett thought that he would be very suitable, and agreed with Bishop Williams and also with Bishop Harland of Lincoln, where Colin had become Dean, who had already supported Archbishop Fisher's suggestion. Garbett also mentioned that he himself had been approached by someone (unnamed) who wondered whether Colin would be suitable for the see of Chester, and had given an 'emphatic negative', citing the psychological defect mentioned above.

'Proneness to irritation' can, of course, be controlled, though it may well produce a psychological *persona* rather unsuited for the pastoral work of a bishop. When I discussed this matter with Bishop Michael Manktelow, who had been Suffragan Bishop of Basingstoke and knew Colin well as Dean of Lincoln and had a high opinion of him, he went, I think, more to the heart of the matter. As he put it, Colin was 'too sensitive', and would not have coped at all well with the ever-increasing load of administration today's diocesan bishops have to undertake. I believe he was right on both counts.

Colin's over-sensitiveness, which brought with it a proneness to irritation, comes out clearly in his increasingly critical attitude towards Alington in the Durham days, especially his conduct of Chapter meetings. The diary account of his first such meeting, dated 13/5/44, has no trace of this: 'Alington hobbled about the room excitedly, talking enthusiastically and generously about being willing and eager for full cooperation of and suggestions from Chapter and not leaving it all to the Dean.'

When, after next month's meeting, Canons Greenslade and Richardson both independently approached Colin because of their 'alarm' at Alington's concern to hurry a decision about transferring the cathedral chancel screen to Edinburgh, he wrote: 'I am back in my old role of peacemaker. Being fond of A is going to be as difficult as being fond of D-J.' Two months after that his diary entry reads: 'A pitiable Chapter meeting this morning; A's vagueness and refusal to consider *ex animo* with any seriousness questions not originated by himself are exasperating beyond words.' By 30 June of the following year he writes:

Today was a chapter meeting, up to the usual standard of tiresomeness and nerve racking – the Dean restlessly walking to & fro and uttering incomplete vague sentences, indirectly claiming for himself all possible virtues such as magnanimity, impartiality, thirst for justice and above all a deep reverence for the opinions of the canons; and yet always ready to make anyone voicing an opinion feel both a knave and a fool should his view run counter to the Dean's. His perpetual decrying of 'legalism' and 'legality' in Chapter concerns enforces, in his own belief, the notion that 'we all want to be just a body of friends talking things over' – really it is a plea for the supremacy of his own unfettered whims and a dislike of all that stands in its way. I find these capitular gatherings all but unbearable.

As the reader might by now expect, Colin does not spare himself from criticism; on 8 January 1948, he writes:

Increasingly I find that in talking to my brother canons the subject that presses to the front is the maladministration of the Cathedral or I feel constrained to point out deficiencies somewhere. I find the desire to pull the mote out of my brother's eye is getting too strong to be healthy.

The fact is that Colin was finding the work at Durham, into which he put a great deal, a severe strain. His diary entries frequently reveal how tired and exhausted he is, and, indeed, as they get more and more occasional they read more and more like the outflow of safety valves, hinting at great tensions beneath the surface. Colin was on good terms with his fellow canons but never felt really at ease with any of them, though he quite liked the strangely 'abstract' Richardson. Both Greenslade and Lucas are once or twice the subjects of his criticism, but not Ramsey, who is in fact barely mentioned (although, after Colin's move to Lincoln, he wrote to Ramsey on 19 June 1952, saying how 'deeply moved' he had been when Ramsey had told him about his appointment to the see of Durham before it was made public; adding that this departure from the 'beaten track' of episcopal appointments was 'a great event, a landmark and dare one think also a beginning of better things?'). But, on the topic of relations with colleagues in general, the following extract (dating from 1945) is of importance:

Since Saturday I have been overcome by a more paralysing lassitude than I have ever known. I spent Saturday and most of today (Monday) in bed. Still I do not feel rested. It extends from the body to the mind and spirit and makes me very unpleasant to Mary. Yesterday I had to deputise for the Bishop at the Cathedral Carol Service and confess that I enjoyed with zest this temporary preeminence among my colleagues. How tiny we all are (or at least some of us)! It was nice doing well what is too often done ill.

The last sentence of this extract is a reference to the conduct of worship in a wide sense. Colin's faithfulness to the St Mary's Primrose Hill (or the Percy Dearmer) way of doing things, and the fact that it was consonant with his own strongly felt aesthetic tastes, meant that the failure of his colleagues to come up to these standards (which was almost inevitable at times), felt to him, especially when he was tired and depressed, almost like a personal affront. Hence the zest with which he responded to the chance to 'show them how things *should* be done'.

The reference to Mary is also significant here. Although Colin's work was sometimes very tiring (recall that he had to 'wear three hats'), much of it was extremely stimulating, especially when we consider the short trips he made to British forces in Belgium and Holland in late 1944, and then the month-long trip to the Middle East in late 1945, largely to take confirmations. (I shall give an account of the trips abroad in the separate chapter which follows this.) Meanwhile Mary had given birth to a fourth son, Michael Bede, and became herself extremely tired from looking after the younger children and battling to keep the house presentable when it was extremely difficult to find any kind of servants or a good nanny, at a time when labour-saving equipment was still rare.

Mary did manage to give a few talks (a cutting from *The Gateshead Post*, dated 14/5/48, records a speech she made at a meeting of the Gateshead Moral Welfare Association), and also to present prizes at the Church Lads Brigade sports, to continue her work with the Mothers' Union, and other church work, especially in the early days, but she may well have had to give it all up for quite long periods. Colin's diaries do mention various people (including relations and friends) who helped in the house or with us children for longer or (usually) shorter periods in one capacity or another (a daily woman called Lily stole some of Mary's best Sibyl Dunlop jewellery), but the search for a good nanny was not solved until 1948, and that for someone to cook and clean never achieved a lasting solution at Durham.This situation must itself have contributed to Colin's feelings of tiredness. Here is what he wrote in August, 1945:

I had been looking forward to August as a month of comparative leisure in which I could do some writing for the Alcuin Club and prepare some mission addresses. But it has been a month of unremitting toil and distraction. The preparations for VJ [Victory over Japan] day and then a series of illnesses (minor) overcoming each member of the family have made any leisure or repose impossible. Now at last we have a resident maid which may perhaps bring relief from domestic cares [she can't have lasted long!]. Up to now I have been wholly unable to get away from them in order to give my mind to my work. If this proves impossible I shall seriously have to consider resigning my post. ... As I write my letters or try to master reports I keep wondering whether Philip will have any clean trousers tomorrow, whether Francis is not getting out of the habit of brushing his teeth, can Mary stand the strain etc etc and then when my mind is stilled the boys rush with a whoop past my two doors and perhaps burst into the study – and away again goes my mind from my work.

There was, of course, much less of this during school hours in term-time, and still less when I started at a prep school in Buxton in October 1945 and Philip at Christchurch Choir School, Oxford, two years later. But Colin must often have compared his own interesting and stimulating work, with its frequent changes of scene, with Mary's difficulties at home, and felt a little guilty about the contrast.

Colin did have some secretarial help, even in those early days near the end of the war. He began with a shorthand typist, Miss Harrison, who turned out to be 'poor at the work, inaccurate and muddling, and above all will try to be helpful when I pause in dictation to think for a word – a disastrous habit which causes nervousness, uncertainty and confusion in my mind'. But on 25/1/46 he asked Miss Greenfield, daughter of the Vicar of Brandon, who had been in the Women's Royal Navy Service (hence a 'wren'), to come for an interview. He told her that she would have to 'go on errands, see to the car, etc', as well as typing and shorthand. She replied, to his amusement, that she would quite enjoy being his 'stooge'. Colin employed her at £1 a week for five half-days, and she started on or soon after 22/2/46. As there is no further reference to this topic it is likely that they got on well together.

The following letter from Mary to her friend Barbara Halpern outlines some of the domestic problems and a few hitherto unmentioned advantages from her point of view. It was written about a year before Michael Bede's arrival, on 15/9/44:

The Durham house is a very nice old house ... We simply love the surroundings, and our neighbours, and Colin enjoys being a bishop very much, I think. I have no time to be a bishop's wife, as I am cook, nursemaid and charwoman. I have had no nurse since ... Charles arrived, so I am very tied. I have got a good sort of working housekeeper who can cook nicely and doesn't much mind what else she does. The only snag about her is that she also breeds King Charles spaniels – we have *nine* of them in the house, which makes an additional difficulty over cleaning and catering – however it's better to have a maid and dogs than no one – and there was no choice. My sole other domestic staff is a woman who comes from 10-5 to do the washing and 'mind' Charles and keep the nurseries clean. She is quite nice and quite efficient, but her hours of work leave both the rush periods of the day on my hands – ie the getting up and putting to bed. It takes me about an hour to get the three up and washed and Charles given his breakfast, and an hour and a half to two hours to get the three put to bed, and I must say that doing it every single day without exception gets very wearing. I pine for one day off in the week but can't get it of course. [At a later date Colin wrote in his diary that he had taken over the job of getting F and P up and putting them to bed, and that he much enjoyed it.]

The children are quite blooming. The end of the school holidays is approaching thank goodness, and when they are at school Francis stays all day on four days a week, which is a help. They have much more fun here than in Edinburgh, as they have all the College to run about in, and a playground with a swing and a sandpit and a seesaw outside, and inside an empty room for wet days in which they can make a huge model with railway things and buildings, and leave it on the floor. This is in addition to the proper nursery. They have lots of children to play with too as several of the college houses have young children in, and there are also others who come in from close by to play.

It is perhaps of interest that the swing, sandpit and seesaw were specially made by the Cathedral staff for the enclosed green space [the 'Monk's Bowling Green'] south of the Galilee Chapel, and virtually adjoining our garage and back yard, to entertain refugees from London after the flying bombs began to displace many more people. Colin records that three refugees from London (two children and their grandmother) did arrive at our house, but the grandmother did not think the accommodation we had to offer was good enough, and they went away again.

In January 1945, Mary was able to get away for three days to go to Sussex and sort out her sister, Honor's, troubles at the Convent, and Honor paid a short visit to Durham. It may well have been while Mary was away that Colin recorded how much he enjoyed helping Francis and Philip to dress and get presentable for the day. 'After evensong', he wrote:

I took the boys out tobogganing on the hill which lies to the South of Durham School grounds. We all enjoyed our half-hour there in the crisp cold air and brilliant clear evening sunlight. As we came back across Prebends' Bridge the Cathedral stood out a mass of gold and orange – indescribably glorious.

But Honor died in early February 1946, and the manner of her death was a very shocking occurrence, so that a coroner's inquest was held. Colin wrote thus in his diary:

Mary and I returned yesterday from Sussex where we went on Feb 13th on receipt of the news of Honor's death. Mary has born very well the shock of the news, the exhaustion of travel and the painful situation at the inquest in Brighton, all the more praiseworthy in view of her being in the early months of pregnancy. To any who knew her the interpretation of suicide can be ruled out in any attempt to account for Honor's fall from the window, and even the coroner had, on the lack of evidence, to return an open verdict. We were on the whole delighted with the evidence of the loving care shown by the community at Rottingdean Convent for Honor. Only religious are capable, it would seem, of the unwearying patience and forbearance necessary for the care of the defective: we are deeply grateful for what they have done, these four years past. The funeral rites, for which Leo joined us, were wholly illegal and indefensible in the C of E but they were consoling and gratifying in a way in which parallel illegalities, fashionable everywhere, are not.

In his letter to Jack Arnold, dated 27 February, Colin writes: the words 'delivered from the burden of the flesh and out of the miseries of this sinful world' have seldom seemed less of an overstatement than at her funeral.'

Before I record some of Colin's reactions to the 1948 Lambeth Conference, I shall mention one or two other matters that occupied him at Durham. One thing that he was asked to do was to dedicate the first new house in Newton Aycliffe, which was itself the first new town in the north-east. *The Northern Echo*, in its 'Archive' for the north-east, published on 20 August 2005, began as follows:

It began life as a humble farm, and 50 wonderful years later at St Clare's, at Newton Aycliffe, it's time for some golden celebrations. 'May a town arise here fair and lovely for the eye to see, noble in its proportions, majestic in its beauty, homely in its charm. May its houses be worthy homes for children of God, its schools true nurseries of wisdom, its industries such as will ennoble men's lives' – The Rt Rev D C Dunlop, Bishop of Jarrow. The Bishop was talking of Newton Aycliffe of course, though to what extent that vision has been fulfilled is for others to determine. It was on Nov 9, 1948, Bishop Dunlop present to dedicate the new town's first house – 9 Clarence Green – after its keys were officially handed over. The population was still fewer than 100.

The article then describes how the village acquired its clergy house in 'the then unused Clarence Farm', how the money was raised in the village to build in July 1955 'St Claire's parish church in the burgeoning town centre. ... It cost £15,000 and was dedicated by the Rt Rev Michael Ramsey, a future Archbishop of Canterbury' [but then Bishop of Durham]. The writer goes on to describe other landmarks in the life of the town and the church, ending with the great Jubilee celebrations in 2005, including a special service in the church. 'It was a most enjoyable service and the most perfect summer Sunday.' One could easily 'believe, on strolling back through the rather unmajestic town centre that God was in his heaven and that Bishop Dunlop's prayers had been answered after all'.

In August 1944, Colin visited his old Oxford theology teacher, Bishop Arthur Cayley Headlam, whom he had met quite often in recent years when serving on the Church of England Council for Foreign Relations, of which Headlam was then Chairman. The bishop was staying in his sister's cottage at Whorlton, a village on the Tees near Barnard Castle where his father had once been Vicar. Colin describes his visit as follows:

Headlam appeared dressed in a grey flannel knickerbocker suit and a white tie and green pork pie hat looking most leisurely, comfortable and countrified. He took us over the garden of his house (at present occupied by a school) and showed us his rhododendrons and rock garden. 'In its present state of neglect the garden is well suited for botanical research', he remarked. We talked about Russia, a propos his *Times* letter on the Baltic States, then about Iceland. He says he wants to resign next Easter but wonders whether he ought to refrain in order to be 'a bridge' with the German Church after the war. I can scarcely believe this alternative plan to be a useful one in view of his past record. We had a pleasant tea ...

By 'past record' Colin alludes to the fact that, when the Nazis set up the Reich or German church before the war, which enabled them to exercise considerable control over it, Headlam supported it as against the 'Confessing Church', many of whose members, perhaps the most famous of whom was Dietrich Bonhoeffer, were persecuted and some killed in Nazi death camps. Despite this error of judgment, Bishop Headlam was widely respected in the church, and had an impressive intellectual record. He died during Colin's time at Durham, and Colin was able to take a part in the funeral service. The obituary in the *Richmond Chronicle* reports: 'The Vicar, the Rev C.F. Porteous officiated, and the funeral prayers were said by the Bp of Jarrow, the Rt Rev. Colin Dunlop, an outstanding young prelate with a beautifully modulated voice.' The Bishop of Durham pronounced the Committal Sentences and the Dean read the lesson.

Another even more controversial Bishop of the Church of England with whom Colin records some Durham-based contact was Herbert Hensley Henson. Henson had retired to Hintlesham, near Ipswich, where, as recorded above, our family had two or three summer holidays in the Vicarage. Henson had been both Dean and then Bishop of Durham, so Colin was sure that he would welcome his stand-in vicar, with the latest tidings of Durham. His first visit was on 21 June 1945: 'I visited Dr and Mrs Hensley Henson at their little country home near

Ipswich and was charmed with my visit. The Bishop was at the station to meet me, a little bowed and shuffling in his gait but with the quick alert and lively eyes which I had expected and a spirit too vivacious for his aging frame. In the spacious study which he has added to the little house we had a delightful talk. He plunged almost without preliminary into disestablishment, ecclesiastical discipline, artificial insemination and other topics. He wriggled with delight when after his frequent biting comments upon persons and things I laughed aloud at them. This revealed the measure of his present isolation. His expression is at once kind and puckish: his eagerness to discover the views of whoever talks to him is dictated not only by a desire to counter them. He spoke of Bishop Barnes as 'continuing in his relentless crudity'; ... he thought Alington goes too fast in his improvements and changes in the cathedral: he lectured me with his hand on my shoulder, upon the unessentiality and the bad record of episcopacy as a principle of church government; and – if I understand him right – of the needlessness of monarchs for 'there are no real nations'. I couldn't quite follow him here.

A published collection of Henson's letters contains an account of Colin's visit as told to Dean Alington. It is dated 1 July:

> We were charmed with the Bishop of Jarrow, and would have been pleased if we could have seen more of him. What an unusually interesting career he has had! That he should have emerged from it with such admirable balance and good sense, discloses qualities of a high order, and he has a taking aspect and manner to provide a suitable 'shop-window' for the goods beneath the counter!

In another letter to Alington of 30 January 1946, he returns to Colin:

> If, as you assure me, the Bishop of Jarrow's arrangement of the Commemoration Service justified itself in experience, I have no reasonable ground for objecting to it, and the less since in itself it appears to be admirably conceived. The liturgical trick of breaking up forms into fragments, duly introduced with more or less appropriate tags from the Scripture, is now so well established that (after having successfully played its part in discrediting the Revised Prayerbook), it may very well determine the procedure in other compositions!!!!!

From 5 July 1948 Colin and the family had the use of the Vicarage of St Mary's, Primrose Hill, to enable Colin to attend the Lambeth Conference without leaving Mary and the children behind in Durham for a month or more. The first Lambeth conference had been called in 1867, and the intention was that they should be repeated every ten years to enable all the bishops of the Anglican Communion to discuss questions and problems of importance, and, if possible to come to a common mind on them, though, since each Anglican church is autonomous, its decisions are not binding on all constituent churches. Colin's diary has relatively few entries in 1946–8, so he started on a new one to mark the occasion. What follows is an abbreviated version, with occasional summaries and omissions, of what he wrote.

1/7/48 Opening day of Lambeth Conference. Left Stanmore [where the Arnolds lived] at 8am and boarded the special train for Canterbury at Victoria ... Hoards of Bishops and their wives and other camp followers – Bishops in all sorts of dress from orthodox gaiters to bright purple cassock under overcoat. American Bishops in wide-brimmed light grey hats, shouting American slang-greetings at one another. We lunched at S. Augustine's College in a fine Gothic crypt. I sat between the Bishop of Moray and the Bishop of Wangaratta with the Bishop of Argyll and Bishop Mounsey opposite. At the cathedral we robed at congested ranks of chairs in the Chapter House ... (not well managed), and processed by Provinces (York and Canterbury last). Greeted by Dean and Chapter at West door, then processed up the nave and the 'wonderful' steps into the Presbytery. Fanfare at entry of Archbishop of Canterbury. The Archbishop's address hardly rose to the occasion, and indeed seemed to me a little ominous. Overmuch time was devoted to Reunion – presumably with Free Churchmen and non-episcopal bodies; nothing was said at all openly of the challenge of Communism and of the Church's danger there and of the Church's opportunity.

4/7/48 The St Paul's service. I went off there from John Jagoe's flat without breakfast. We all had to robe in the crypt and wait about for a very long time before we were marshalled for the Procession. Our waiting place was a large chapel in which all seats were ranged with their backs to the altar. Whether this fact was responsible for the lack of any mental or spiritual preparation displayed on all sides I do not know. It was somewhat unedifying that talking and laughing was all but universally indulged in and no inclination for silence and collection made itself apparent. (They were waiting for a Communion service at which they had all been urged to be present, even if they found it inconvenient.)

Colin was pleased that the Dean had apparently acceded to his suggestion that the Creed be sung to Merbecke and not some elaborate setting. However the American Bishops didn't seem to know it. The presiding Bishop of the American Church preached a sermon which was long and dull. However, on the whole the service was a great occasion.

8/7/48 Yesterday's Session on the Apostolic Ministry. Following the excellent speech of George of Chichester (excellent though based throughout on pragmatic assumptions), the Archbishop of Armagh, Dr Gregg's, speech nevertheless stood out in every way as the utterance of a great theologian and a great ecclesiastic: his words brought consolation and reassurance to many who had begun to feel that the issue of reunion was to be decided on grounds of sentiment and face-saving only. George said that, before the Tractarians, non-Episcopal churches were always recognised as spiritual equals; Dr Gregg brought striking evidence of another view long before the Tractarians. Afterwards visited Ruth and then joined Mary at dinner with the Jagoes.

This morning I sang High Mass in St Margaret's Westminster for the Anglican Society [founded in the USA in 1932].

The afternoon session very dull. It becomes apparent that the English Bishops have little intellectual preeminence over Bishops from other countries, nor is their understanding of matters at issue more profound. The Archbishop of Armagh enjoys a solitary eminence.

11/7/48 I sang the 10 and 11.15 celebrations at St Mary's, Noel Davey having been responsible for 8. He also chanted the litany in Procession. ... I preached on public worship as exercise, an old sermon.

15/7/48 The very crowded programme and tiringness of most days leaves little leisure for diary writing. I leave after breakfast and sometimes don't get back till 10pm. I'm pleasantly surprised at some of the American Bishops' attitudes, eg they want unconditional equality between black and white and joint worship in churches (our Bishop of Johannesburg is more guarded and prudent). On the 'lack of fellowship' shown among worshippers in the Church of England, the Americans warned of the danger of pressing this so far that the fellowship of worship becomes overlooked – a real danger, it seems, in the USA.

[Receptions at the House of Lords, Mansion House, and Buckingham Palace, as well as Dunlop family outings, omitted here.]

27/7/48 In the afternoon I spoke in full session on that section of Committee 2's report dealing with Communism: saying that if the very dispassionate and academic analysis of Communism were to be our only word, we should be failing to realise how different it appeared to the Christians who found themselves under Communist rule. I gave notice of a resolution conveying the sympathy of the Conference with them. Mild applause greeted my speech. The Bishop of Grantham followed with a very strong denunciation of the report and this brought the Archbishop of York to his feet in an emotional defence of 'Christian Communists'. Who or where these are I still fail to understand. The Bishop of Gibraltar said that my resolution might bring even more trouble on the Christians of Yugoslavia. But even if true, might not the knowledge that other Christians cared for them ... outweigh the bitterness of increased persecution?

1/8/48 (A full session.) Colin is very worried that so much of what the bishops say in debate seems calculated to earn them a 'progressive' reputation among the young. This is far removed from the historic Anglican soberness and learning, and is based to an alarming degree on sentiment. This attitude dominates more and more. (On 3/8 he criticises many of the opinions expressed in the Marriage Debate on the same grounds.)

I duly propounded my resolution of sympathy with the victims of Communism but the Archbishop of York sprang to his feet and hurled himself with all the fervour of which he was capable against my view. I believe I was only supported by Nyasaland and Roscoe Shedden. I still believe I was right.

6/8/48 (The penultimate day of the Conference) I feel more tired mentally and physically than I ever remember being before. ... I wish I could feel some of the exhilaration which the writer of the Encyclical appears to experience. I think everything about the Conference has been excellent and well worth while *except* the written reports, resolutions and encyclical which we are to send out to the world. The meeting together, the debating, the personal contacts have all been of immense value, but if only we might stop there and not broadcast any message.

Colin's concern about the Soviet Union, and in particular, its attitude to Christians, and his feeling that the Conference did not take it seriously enough had been greatly increased by various conversations he had had with High ranking officers in the armed forces. Here are two diary entries from his Middle Eastern tour in late 1945, about which I shall say more in the next chapter:

The CO at Abu Sueir, Gp Capt Ellison, has served for 18 months in Moscow on the British Military Mission. His impression of the Soviet Regime and its intentions towards the rest of the world are not re-assuring. The Mission were systematically ignored and despised by the Soviet authorities and every hindrance placed in the path of their work. They were spied upon incessantly, as a matter of routine. He has seen from his windows the long queues at the bread shops during which men or women fainted from exhaustion and perished upon the street kerb. Yet officials, soldiers and others lived on the fat of the land. When British ships brought war supplies to Murmansk the unloading was done, not by eager, satisfied, Russian workers, but by groups of half-starved foreign slaves driven upon the ship at the point of a bayonet. So much for the country where 'the plain man gets a square deal'.

And here is a very different kind of witness, but in substantial agreement with the Group captain: the Orthodox Patriarch of Alexandria, Christophoros II.

> He told me something of his impressions of Russia whither he has recently journeyed for the enthronement of the Russian Patriarch. He seems to have few illusions as to the moral and physical security of the church in Russia. While in Moscow no Greeks [i.e. Greek orthodox] were allowed to visit him, though one succeeded in eluding the guard. These impressions of the Patriarch and of Gp Capt Ellison make the Abp of York's eulogies all the more disingenuous...

A few months before he had spoken in Durham with:

> The A.V.M. of the Western Approaches Group, Sir Leonard Slatter, (who) came to supper in the crypt on Sunday night – a tough, jolly and highly intelligent South African who won the Schneider Trophy. He spoke with anxiety about the Russians, mentioning among other things that in Iceland, where there are no Russian residents, they have recently established a consulate with a staff of 25.

On 2/9/44 Colin had noted in his diary, among other news items, that:

> the Russians are flooding Roumania. The Russians incidentally are refusing point blank to allow British and American planes to take armaments to the unfortunate Poles in Warsaw who in obedience to Russian radio incitements rose against the Germans in their capital at the approach of the Russian armies, which have since been held up outside.

Lying behind this delay was, of course, the fact that by no means all Poles wished for a Communist government when peace came again. So it was important for Russian political policy that as many as possible of the Polish army be destroyed by the Germans, before their own armies entered Warsaw to mop up residuary German resistance.

The diary pages in which Colin gives his reactions to Lambeth 48 are followed by an account of a family holiday at Hintlesham in the summer of 1949, which is preceded by a single entry, entitled '30th July 1949 Durham':

> The Dean told me this morning that he had discussed with the Prime Minister (Attlee) the possibility of my being offered the Deanery of Lincoln and that the Bp of Durham had written to Anthony Beevir [the Prime Minister's Appointments Secretary] making the same suggestion. This is interesting. Early

in July I met Eeles in London who said he hoped I might become Dean of Wells or Lincoln. I said I preferred Lincoln. On my return from London Alington told me that the Prime Minister was to be present in Durham Cathedral on Sunday, 24th July, when I would be due to preach.

In forecasting my sermon I found a tendency to aim at a sermon which should please the PM (for I could not forget the impending vacancies at Lincoln and Wells). So I decided to preach a compromising sermon upon an unpopular subject in order not to insinuate myself into the PM's good opinion. I selected the subject of Confession, auricular and otherwise, which would arise out of the psalm appointed, Psalm 32. Then I heard that the Dean of Lincoln was dead! On Sunday 24th July I accordingly preached on Confession before the Prime Minister. And now I hear the news from Alington. I set this down in order to show that though I would like almost above all things to be Dean of Lincoln I have not tried to ingratiate myself with the PM in order to facilitate an appointment of my unworthy self. I wonder what will happen.

Two days later, on the lengthy but leisurely drive to Hintlesham, they stopped for lunch at the White Hart in the shadow of Lincoln Cathedral, and inspected the outside of the Deanery – a 'vast and unattractive edifice'. After a month of mostly glorious weather, filled with family outings to nearby beaches, cycle rides with Philip and myself, French cricket after supper in the garden, reunions with friends and relations (especially the Martin Shaws, Sibyl and Audrey) and numerous church crawls with Mary (in the diary Colin rails characteristically at ugly modern furniture placed next to some of the finest fifteenth- and sixteenth-century church screens and pews, etc – 'one wonders whether the man who designed such poor work really had the use of his eyes'). But he had still not heard anything about the Deanery of Lincoln. Then, on 3 September came the letter from 10 Downing Street, asking if he would allow his name to be put forward, and the agony of waiting was over. He asked for a few days grace in order to consult the Bishop of Lincoln and members of the Cathedral Chapter. After a night at Bishops' House in Lincoln and meetings with Chapter members, from whom he received the encouragement he was hoping for, he was able to accept the appointment on the 8th, though had to wait another eight days to hear that the King had approved it.

Reactions in Durham Diocese were mixed. The 1950 Diocesan Annual report contains the following statement:

The Diocese received the news of Bishop Dunlop's appointment as Dean of Lincoln with very mixed feelings. There was much satisfaction that his outstanding qualifications to preside over the destinies of a great Cathedral Church had been recognised in this way, but there was very real regret at his departure from the Suffragan see of Jarrow and the Archdeaconry of Auckland, in both of which offices he has rendered such signal service to the Diocese during the last six years. During that period he had earned for himself a most affectionate regard, and he and Mrs Dunlop will carry with them to Lincoln the heartfelt gratitude and good wishes of the whole Diocese for their happiness and success in their new sphere of activity.

The Bishop of Durham wrote as follows in *The Bishoprick*:

> The Diocese will say goodbye to the Bishop of Jarrow with great regret when he goes to the Deanery of Lincoln. He has made many lasting contributions to our life in the years since 1944, combining his work all over the county with his special concern for the Archdeaconry of Auckland. Perhaps we shall remember in particular his preaching, his interest in young people, his wardenship of the Society of Christ and Blessed Mary the Virgin and his care for Women's Work in general, together with his work and practical skill in all matters of liturgiology and 'the care of churches'.
>
> We all wish him and Mrs Dunlop, who has so ably helped him and us, happiness in the work to which they go, and we know that no-one could be better fitted than he to guide the worship of one of the greatest and most lovely of our cathedrals.

The *Durham County Advertiser* adds the intriguing detail that 'Bishop Dunlop ... 'has done much to raise the standard of churchmanship' (23/9/49). The Cathedral Chapter added the following in *The Bishoprick*: 'The Chapter wishes to record its gratitude to the late Bishop of Jarrow for his work in Durham, and in particular for the help he has given in ordering the Cathedral services and by his intimate knowledge of the clergy in his Archdeaconry' (this last was an important consideration when it came to filling Chapter livings).

Colin's installation at Lincoln took place on 15/12/49. The elaborate ceremony was described in detail by *The Lincolnshire Echo* next day. He was installed both as Dean and also as Prebendary of Aylesbury in Buckinghamshire, a stall whose painted identification on its canopy reminds one of the fact that the Diocese of Lincoln once extended as far as the Thames. The *Echo* report told its readers that the 'prebend ... dates back to the earliest days of diocesan history. Until the middle of the 13th century, this stall was always held by the Deans of Lincoln Cathedral, and with the installation of Dean Dunlop, the former custom has been restored. Unlike his predessors, the late Dean Mitchell did not hold a prebendal stall'.

It seems very probable that Colin himself encouraged the resumption of the ancient custom, recalling, perhaps, his former position as Prebendary of Wyndham in Chichester Diocese. Prebends have long been disendowed, and the title of prebendary is now little more than the name of a particular stall in the Cathedral Choir, with which a canon of a certain seniority can be associated, and regularly preach in the cathedral. The ancient practice was also in keeping with Colin's view that the ownership of Auckland Castle should remain in the hands of the Bishop of Durham and not be transferred to the Church Commissioners. The accompanying press photograph shows him 'seated in the chief seat in the Chapter House', while the Vicar of Boston, one of the canons of the Great Chapter, walks away after promising obedience to the new dean. The ceremony was, of course, attended by the Lord Lieutenant of the County, the MP of Lincoln, the Chief Constable and other leading representatives of the armed services, and of law, education, and other branches of civic life.

After the service Colin gave a 'brief, informal, premeditated address' to the chapter:

> Brothers and fellow canons; it is a proud moment for a man to find himself Dean of Lincoln. At the moment I feel almost dazed with the majesty and glory of this church I have been called to serve. I find it therefore hard even to attempt to put into words my feelings on this occasion. I can only hope and pray that this sense of the greatness of my inheritance may translate itself into a life of faithful and loyal service in the post I now hold. That will be my endeavour. In the meanwhile I will content myself with thanking you all for attending this ceremony. For many it must have involved a long and inconvenient journey at a time when it is particularly irksome. I would only ask you to follow up this kindness by remembering me in your prayers. For with the sense of the greatness of my inheritance comes the sense of my personal inadequacy and the need to be upheld at every step by the grace of Almighty God.

They did not move to Lincoln until 25/1/50, after Colin had officiated in Durham for a month, 'with a commission to act as Assistant Bishop' (as *The Times* put it). Once in Lincoln, they stayed three nights with the Srawleys (Colin knew the former Chancellor from his scholarly liturgical work). Finally, on 28/1/50, they were able to move in to their new home.

15

OFFICIAL TRIPS ABROAD FROM DURHAM

THESE FOUR work-related trips to foreign countries are all recorded In Colin's diaries. I have edited them and, in most cases abbreviated them. Passages written by Colin are either in quotes or indented in the main text.

1 *Confirmation trip from Durham to Brussels and Eindhoven with the RAF, 18–23 December 1944*

Colin's diary entry for 6 December 1944, begins: 'Was rung up just after breakfast by the Archbishop of York asking me if I would go to France and hold some confirmations for the RAF [in the event they took place in Belgium and Holland!]'. After consultation with the Bp of Durham I joyfully agreed and have said I can go in the week previous to Christmas.' On the 17th he dated his entry from de Vere Gardens, Kensington, where John Jagoe, now RAF Chaplain-in-Chief, lived, and begins: 'arrived here by plane from Thornaby in time for tea after a strenuous morning', in which he took a confirmation of '40-odd' in Sunderland, followed by a Parish Eucharist and breakfast 'with the four clergy in their artisans' dwelling on the [Ford] estate', and then another confirmation of

> two women patients in the hospital – in the open ward. The rite was followed with intense interest by all in the beds. Then I drove like Jehu back to Durham whence, after hurried packing and a hurried lunch, I sped down to Thornaby [SE of Stockton] from which a Hudson conveyed me to Hendon.

Though very bumpy in the stormy head wind, the flight took much less time than he had been warned. He was met by RAF chaplain Cocks, whom he knew, and taken 'in a fine car ... to Jagoe's flat. Before dinner he managed to squeeze in a visit to his cousin Ruth, 'tired and dispirited, yet ... as charming as ever'. Next morning he was taken to the BOAC office with unexpected time to kill, and 'found [him]self at the Capitular High Mass in Westminster Cathedral. I was intensely moved by the service: the severe plainsong of Advent, and the well known yet foreign ceremonial.' After buying gloves at the Army and

311

Navy Stores, he returned to the BOAC office, whence the airline bus took him to Croydon. 'After many formalities' they took off in a two-engined Dakota and touched down in Brussels at 4. He was met by Stanley Betts (again well-known to him) and 'the senior chaplain Wilkie', who

> rushed me off in a car to 2nd T.A.F. Hqrs. Parts of Brussels have been battered by flying bombs but it was lovely to be on the Continent once more and to see some of the long-lost sights as we sped along the *pavé* road. ... Then after a talk about what I'm to do, I was taken round to my quarters in the Hotel Astoria, Rue Royale, maintained by the Army and RAF for 'distinguished visitors' but served by the Belgian staff.

Later, sitting in his luxurious suite unable to sleep, he recorded with a smile:

> Mary's indignation yesterday that I was referred to as 'Canon Dunlop'. But the temperature sank still lower when at Croydon this morning I was cited as 'the Reverend Dunlop'. But all is now well for I observed that the reception Clerk of this hotel entered me in the Register as 'Monseigneur Dunlop!'

> *Brussels 19.xii.44*: As one goes about in the streets one is struck with the normality of life in this city. You would never think it had been under a foreign oppressor for four and a half years, liberated only a month or two ago and since then suffered an internal social and political crisis. ... The shops seem full of good things: indeed I have been able to buy toys for the children such as one cannot get at home, and eau de Cologne for Mary and a lace handkerchief for Ruth. Paris I am told is very different.

In the morning he was taken to the 'Luther Kirk', which the padres had taken over for Moral Leadership Courses, designed to enliven the faith of picked men 'so that they may realise their vocations as Christians in the modern world'. After an afternoon of calling on various high-ranking officers, he felt so exhausted that he returned to the Astoria for more reading and writing. In the evening he:

> dined with Air Marshall Sir Arthur Conyngham ..., conveyed to his house in a dense fog in a car. A Belgian peer, Baron Braun, and a captain of Belgian industry called Germanis were present and a few senior RAF officers. We had a superb dinner of which roast turkey and, almost paradoxically, brussels sprouts, was the *pièce de resistance* as to food. We drank hock with the fish, a cosy claret with the turkey, followed by satisfying champagne. With coffee we had mellow brandy in immense globular glasses. ... I had some talk with M Germanis, a pleasant forthcoming elderly man. I asked him how the Belgian church had fared under the Germans and whether the hierarchy had been persecuted. He replied that as the Cardinal Primate had quite firmly defied the Nazis at the start, they had made no move, remembering their experience of Cardinal Mercier in the last war. He quoted a Belgian proverb *'Qui mange le curé en meurt'* which he said the Germans in Belgium at least had taken to heart. ... I had some talk with Sir Arthur, a pleasant man with an almost boyish

manner. He told me that Churchill disliked William Temple exceedingly, not because of his political opinions but because he was jealous of his powers as a speaker and of his popularity. He did not think Stalin had had any hand in the recent Belgian troubles, ascribing them wholly to the difficulties of life created by the withdrawal of the Germans and the necessary gap before we could get supplies and transport working normally.

Next day he wrote:

I am just back from the Confirmation in the Church of the Resurrection where I laid hands on 37 candidates, one of whom was a Squadron Leader with DFC who lives at Burgess Hill. In spite of two flying bombs passing over us during the service, the rite was accomplished with a solemnity and dignity I have seldom known excelled. I had lumps in my throat several times as these fine young men one by one knelt before me for the laying on of hands and I realised the effort and moral courage needed to bring them to the service. All the chaplains stood round and behind me in a semi-circle as I recited the prayer for the 7-fold gifts and laid on hands, all of them firmly repeating the Amen at the end of each 'Defend O lord...'. This added greatly to the solemnity of the service.

After an early lunch at the TAF Main Hqrs Mess Wilkie and I set off in a Staff car of immense size for Eindhoven in Holland. First we went to Malines where I called upon the Primate, Cardinal van Roey. The *Archevêché* is a large white building in a quiet square to the north of the lovely cathedral. ... A chaplain ushered us along passages and up some stairs to a very simply furnished room, into which the aged cardinal soon came. He has thick white hair, and a ruddy and rugged peasant's face of a somewhat severe expression. He does not smile much but his manner was distinctly friendly. I told him how much we in England had admired the courage and dignity he had displayed vis a vis the Nazis, which did not displease him. He talked of the abomination of the Nazi regime and of the noticeable moral and spiritual deterioration of the German soldier since the last war (he, poor man, has lived in the same Palace under two German occupations, last time as Vicar General of Cardinal Mercier). I said something about the same anti-religious character of the Russians but he maintained an eloquent silence. We talked of the churches in Belgium which had been destroyed, and of the Anglican members of the Malines Conversations. He asked about Frere and Kidd and Armytage Robinson. I stayed about 15 minutes and then we continued our journey. At the Albert Canal we were held up for some time by an armoured Division of ours on its way from Holland to help the Americans in S Belgium stem the Nazi break-through. We reached Eindhoven, through country which became ever more bleak and featureless, at nightfall. The Dutch Reformed Church – a nice modern building – where the confirmation was to be held was, however, along with the rest of the town, destitute of electric power this evening. However, Padre Goodrich in less than 10 minutes laid his hands upon about 80 candles by the light of which we held the confirmation. Among the padres present were Blacktop, Goodchild (of Islay), and Fayne (of Castle Kennedy, son of an Irish bishop) – 6 in all. About 40–50 candidates. At intervals you could hear the guns or bombs in the distance. We had some tea and buns in a room over the vestry and I shook hands with a good many of the men and signed my name in their bibles or prayer books. I was amazed at there being so many candidates in active service under front conditions. I don't remember ever hearing of a confirmation or classes in the last war. Wilkie and I had some supper in a Dutch house of some comfort and then set off on our three hours drive through the foggy night back to Brussels, which we reached at 12.30.

Next morning we drove off in the same car to Ostende. I was transported across to Dover in a high-speed rescue launch along with about 10 officers. Fortunately the weather was comparatively calm and not very cold and I enjoyed the trip. We passed Merchant Ships in convoys and a number of smaller warships. We made for North Foreland, it seems, and then ran down the coast to Dover. The crossing was just under four hours. After dinner at Dover we crawled in two trains to London and thence I went on by sleeper to Newcastle. A memorable trip.

2. Visit to Air Force, Army and Naval bases in the Middle East, 2 October to 4 November 1945

2/10/45 Sandacres Hotel, Sandbanks (Bournemouth) Came down from Durham in a 3rd Sleeper last night. At Kings X I came across a sergeant in paroxysms of tears who told me he is suffering from accumulated war strain and unhappiness. I took him in the Staff Car awaiting me to a military hospital for which he seemed grateful. Bathed, shaved and breakfasted in John Jagoe's flat, after which we went along to his department of the Air Ministry near Olympia. I called in at 7 Argyll Mansions and saw Leo for a few minutes. Lunch at the RAF Club in Piccadilly ... Met several old friends, Ronnie Graham, now an AVM and Head of the Staff College, also AVM Champian de Crespigny who stood unsuccessfully as Labour Candidate for Newark and who seems to have leanings towards the Oxford Groups. He thinks Socialism and Christianity go hand in hand. We had some words about the Assyrians. After lunch John and I visited CACTM and I listened to their plans for the training and financing of service ordinands.

At about 7 I left the British Airways private railway station in a special train, on which we had a well cooked but exiguous dinner. Three Army Officers at my table (in a sort of coupée) were agreeable en route. Everything is planned in my journey down to the smallest detail. There is no need to think till I get to Cairo.

3/10/45 Malta: We set off from our hotel at ... 9.45 for Hurn Aerodrome. Here were done the embarkation and customs formalities – all with quiet and respectful efficiency and brevity, and after being regaled with coffee we were put on board the Dakota. I was allotted a good seat near the front from which I saw quite a lot en route ... We took off at once and crossed the Channel above the clouds ... As we reached Cherbourg the cloud dispersed and we had a sunny and delightful trip over the Beauce Region and Le Mans, and down over the Gorge du Tarne (which I recognised) to the Rhone Valley and so to Istres where we touched down... We were given lunch at a transit Mess (hors d'oeuvres, filet de veau, tea, bread and marmalade) and waited on by French girls. One of my fellow travellers is called de Ferranti, and his brothers were at school with me at Heddon Court. We set off again across the Mediterranean at 4.30 and passing over Sardinia reached Malta at 8.30, two hours after dark. My first experience of night flying and night landing... It is warmer here but not hot, and I feel quite comfortable in my gaiters. We had a good dinner in the Mess with lots of grapes, and I sleep in an austere but comfortable room in the VIPs' quarters. We rise tomorrow at 4 a.m.

5/10/45 Cairo: Our plane reached here from Malta yesterday at about 2.20 p.m. We took off about 5.30 a.m and could look down on the island in the light of dawn. My principle impression was the multitude of walls everywhere, like a maze, due I am told to the need for husbanding such soil as exists. We passed a town with a large church and two baroque towers. Soon we were well out over the Mediterranean... We reached the African coast a little North of Benghazi... We touched down at El Aden – about 10 miles south of Tobruk and sat down before our unappetising mixture of lunch and breakfast. Then on again past Bardia, Siddi Barrani, Mersa Matruk etc none of which I could really see. Except for occasional views of conglomerations of wheel tracks there was no visible evidence of the recent battles from where we flew. Then suddenly the Nile appeared and the abrupt beginning of cultivation after miles of barren ground. Almost at once we were over Cairo and I got a glimpse of the Pyramids. Shapley, the Assistant Chaplain in Chief, met me, and after going through Immigration and Customs we had a meal in some mess or other and then motored to the Archdeacon [of Cairo]'s house, where I am staying. I had no idea of the great extent of Cairo and its suburbs Heliopolis, Abassia, etc. It was about ½ hour's drive from the airport to this house, next to the new and very fine cathedral on the Nile bank. It's a far more 'civilised' place than Jerusalem or Baghdad – I knew that before – but I hadn't pictured it quite as large and handsome a place as it is. It is beautifully warm and seems hot coming from NE England, but how delightful it is to be really warm again. I slept beautifully all night and woke refreshed and ready to get up at 6.45. Last night there was a meeting of the Cathedral Fellowship – mostly troops – who were considering the Report on the Evangelisation of England. I spoke to them for some minutes on the great movement of our day – the rediscovery of itself by the Church. Amongst the troops were one or two officers including an AVM.

The news has just come that no troops are to be allowed in the city for three days! It looks like political trouble. I now expect to be shipped home on the next plane!

6/10/45 Cairo: Yesterday afternoon I renewed the siesta habit, broken the last 11 years, and felt all the better for it. I also feel the better for the excellent food here. Having three poached eggs for breakfast is a new sensation. There is no shortage of anything. The archdeacon's house is like a pre-war house, clean and fresh with efficient quiet service by white-clad be-fezzed Egyptians. After tea yesterday, Shapley and I set out for Tura, about 15 miles south of Cairo. In the very quarries whence the stone for the far-famed Pyramids was hewn there is an RAF Maintenance Unit. In the stone church, built and equipped by officers and men, I confirmed 5 airmen and 1 WAAF. The Group Captain, about 12 more officers and about 40 other ranks were present in the church for the service. The church is modelled upon an English village church with squat square tower, nave and aisles, and though of course one sees what they mean it doesn't quite look like it! But it is a noble effort, and a tribute to the imagination and faith of the padre who initiated the work. One of the candidates was a lad from

Squance's parish in South Shields. He seemed genuinely pleased and struck with being confirmed by 'his own bishop' so far from home. We dined in the mess after, where I met the very pleasant company of officers. The padre, J.H. Piper, comes from Exeter diocese. I like Shapley, the Assistant Chaplain in Chief. His rather extreme Anglo-Catholicism has not warped his ordinary powers of judgment. He is shrewd and steady; not brilliant.

This morning I have been touching up sermon notes for tomorrow.

It is a little tantalising being the guest here of busy people. I long to sight-see, but they have no time to take me and I don't know where to go. Also it is inadvisable to be in the streets this weekend as some political demonstration with probable violence is expected. However, I *have* seen the Pyramids in the distance.

8/10/45 Cairo: Yesterday, Sunday, I celebrated in the Cathedral. Congregation 60% military. For the first time, and partly at my instigation, the Archdeacon put on a Parish Breakfast. I sat between 2 women missionaries. At 9.15 I was fetched and taken to Abassia to preach at the voluntary church parade in the Transit Camp barracks – soldiers and airmen. The Brigadier commanding the area turned out to be Hayman-Joyce whom I had not seen since 1914 at Radley. He is very much the same, holds himself still with a slightly exaggerated erectness, has the same tendency to stutter, but he looks a fine fellow. I am struck here with the smart and clean appearance of everybody in the forces, from the Generals down to the ranks. Everyone looks so young, and alert, and glowing with health and intelligence. Shirt and shorts help to give this impression, no doubt, but are not entirely responsible. After the service I interviewed informally a number of ordinands. Two, who held the rank of Captain, seemed very fine quality, especially the one (whose name I forget) who was not quite sure of his future. In my talk to him about the Ministry, I laid stress on the need to remain single during the early years, afterwards discovering that it is a girl who is partly responsible for his hesitation.

Evensong in the Cathedral was a remarkable experience. About 2000 people present, 85% military. I suppose the average age could not have been much above 25. I have never heard such congregational singing. 'Come ye thankful people come' almost took my breath away as sung by this concourse of youth. The service was straight Prayer Book (though only one psalm). The cathedral is by Adrian Scott and quite fine and impressive, all white and Byzantine within. It is well lit with large and prominent gilt lamps which yet do not dazzle the eye as you look up or down the church. I enjoyed preaching to so attentive a congregation. John and Mrs Badeau were there. They came into supper after I had lunched with them in their flat the day previous. I feel they are real friends, and I enjoy talking to them and being with them so much... John is Head of some Missionary University. He had very interesting things to say.

The churchwarden of the cathedral told me how disastrous it is that Bishop Gwynne, at present on leave in England, is coming back. He is over 80 and quite failing in grip. The churchwarden told me that this, combined with the bishop's cheerful obstinacy, will bring the diocese to a very low level; indeed it is there already. He relies entirely on military chaplains' ministrations and hardly has a priest of his own in all Egypt (3 to be correct).

At 10.30 Parry came and took me round in his car to call upon the locum tenens of the Coptic Patriarchate. We drove through the busy, French-looking streets in our cassocks. Driving into the courtyard we saw a number of dusty, black-robed clergy sitting about, and the usual quantity of lay hangers-on in their suits and red tarbouches. We were ushered into a reception room, with armchairs ranged along the walls, and a special chair for the Patriarch. The wall was hung with portraits. Turkish coffee was served. Several bishops appeared in bottle-green silk cassocks covered by their black mantles. Their head-dress resembles that of the Syrian Orthodox or Jacobite clergy. We visited the patriarchal church, a roomy structure of the nineteenth century with the curious appearance of a blend between drill-hall and drawing room that such buildings have. It was far more like a Greek or Russian church than an Abyssinian or Chaldaean. Their baptistery was a sorry affair, having the aspect of an abandoned laundry in some country house.

10/10/45 Abu Sueir (near Ismailia): We left Cairo by car yesterday for visits to units in the Suez Canal area. I was struck by the wonderful fertility of the country between Cairo and the canal and the real beauty of the scenery. With all its irrigation there is nothing like either in Iraq, which never loses its dusty barren look.

I celebrated this morning in the very dignified little stone camp church of 107 M.U. not far from Suez. A congregation of nine airmen made the responses with real liturgical vigour and there was an air of corporate worship I have not often met. The padre, Birmingham, comes from the Chichester diocese. I addressed an immense concourse of men being drafted off to England from the Middle East, at about 9 a.m. They were all very sorry for themselves and were loud in complaints about 'official' bungling of trooping and demobilisation, full of accusations of unfairness and discrimination. In my innocence I had expected to be talking to a crowd of men all happy to be going home. The men were at bottom good humoured. Probably their critical temper is the result of the climate coupled with natural impatience to be home again. I got inoculated after and don't feel very grand now, though not nearly so bad as after the first, done at home. I have a meeting tonight to address and see no reason for crying off. The Suez Canal was interesting to see. We drove down the bank for miles. I ought to add that Scott, the padre of the camp where the draft was, seemed to me an excellent priest and one who had in a marked degree the confidence and affection of the men. When he joined up he was curate at St Mark's, Gloucester.

13/10/45 Alexandria: The CO at Abu Sueir, Grp Capt Ellison, has served for 18 months in Moscow on the British Mission. His impression of the Soviet regime and its intentions towards the rest of the world were not reassuring. The Mission were systematically ignored and despised by the Soviet authorities and every hindrance placed in the path of their work. They were spied upon incessantly, as a matter of routine. He has seen from his windows the long queues at the bread shops, during which men or women fainted from exhaustion and perished upon the street kerb. Yet 'officials', soldiers and others, lived on the fat of the land. When British ships brought war supplies to Murmansk the unloading was done not by eager, satisfied Russian workers, but by a group of half-starved Russian slaves driven upon the ship at the point of the bayonet. So much for the country where 'the plain man gets a square deal'.

In order not to confine my attention to large and comfortable stations I visited a little camp out in the country near Ismailia and joined in their 'Fellowship' evening. We had evensong, said, in the tent church, then the Bible

Study, and finally Compline. One of the airmen was the son of the Rector of Wick, Webber, who used to be at Edinburgh Theological College while I was Provost at the Cathedral. Another airman told me that when I came into the hut he experienced a feeling of happiness which made him want to laugh. Later he had seen the Devil perched upon my shoulder endeavouring to no purpose to attract my attention which was all being given to the good spirits on the other shoulder. He exhibited no other sign of oddity, but I think the climate cannot suit him.

We stayed last night at the Hotel Beau Rivage on the Corniche. Alexandria extends like a ribbon development for 10 miles along the coast. I hope I shall have more chance of exploring it than I have so far had in Cairo. It is definitely getting cooler. I am not only wearing my grey suit with no white coat, but a waistcoat, and feel very comfortable. I have not worn gaiters since my arrival.

14/10/45 Alexandria: Celebrated at 7.15 in a NAAFI canteen in very picknicky circumstances. Shapley, Langmead (the chaplain here) and 1 WAAF formed the congregation. After breakfast of bananas, grapes, eggs and bacon and coffee a naval Staff Car took me to the Naval Headquarters not far from this hotel where we had Mattins for the HQ staff at which I preached. Then we went on in the car to the dockyard where a little launch sped us to a depot ship, Blenheim. There we had a service for quite a large congregation of officers, petty officers and ratings on the deck under an awning. I had some talk with the Captain in his comfortable cabin after, and then we went in and met other officers in the ward room. A very nice friendly and serious lot. Lunch followed. I had some talk with the chaplain, the Rev J.S. Clarke, of Caius, Cambridge, whom I liked very much. He is married and has one son aged 5. We went over the ship and at 2 p.m., with usual naval pomp and good manners, were shown off.

16/10/45 Alexandria: I am fuller than ever of admiration for the Navy after spending most of Sunday and all of Monday with it. It is almost the only circle in which good manners are regarded as important, and a necessity of life. This, no doubt, is not unconnected also with the extreme efficiency of that service. Even if they don't like you, naval officers treat you with respect and feel a duty to make the best of you.

On Sunday I preached to a small congregation of Headquarters naval staff in some large-ish room rigged up as a chapel. The Admiral's wife was there. She thanked me for my sermon. I delivered the same address on the deck of a depot ship, HMS Blenheim, to a large Church Parade. Here we had lunch and I had some talk with the Captain in his cabin, and also with the padre, the Rev. J.S. Clarke, to whom I greatly took. In the evening I preached at St Mark's, the civilian church, erected in a semi-oriental style in Mohammed Ali Square on ground given by that 19th century potentate, an Albanian, who had made himself master of Egypt and of whom the present King is decended. The service was attended by many service men and women, but not on the same scale as at Cairo.

On Monday, the Senior Naval Chaplain, Gover, took us round a number of naval units, mostly on shore, eg Sphinx, Nile, Grebe; we visited a cruiser, HMS Sirius; we lunched sumptuously with Admiral Tennant, and we visited the Fleet Club, an amazing institution. It extends over 6 acres of ground and includes a beer garden with a stage upon which the sailors themselves are encouraged to come up and sing their own songs and otherwise go through their hoops. This provides a never-ending programme to which all listen with enjoyment or at least respect. It seemed to be an unusual and peculiarly valuable feature of the place. The club leader, Dick Vines, seemed a good man in almost every sense of the word. We dined with Gover at a café run by a Greek called the Union, and had pâté de fois gras, dover sole, chocolate mousse, local cheese and a local white wine of the dry, Chablis, type.

This morning I waited upon the Orthodox Patriarch of Alexandria, Christophoros II. I was accompanied by James Anderson, the English Civil Chaplain. We found his Holiness sitting in his throne room dealing with matters of business. He dismissed his company and drew me to a chair on his right. We exchanged formalities and then he told me something of his impressions of Russia whither he has recently journeyed for the enthronement of the Russian Patriarch. He seems to have few illusions as to the moral or physical security of the Church in Russia. While in Moscow no Greeks were allowed to visit him, though one succeeded in eluding the guard. These impressions of the Patriarch and of Grp Capt Ellison make the Archbishop of York's eulogies all the more disingenuous. On leaving the Patriarch, Shapley and I motored to Aboukir for lunch at the RAF station. It is very well equipped and I never ate a better curry. The padré, Baker, is an elderly man to whom I was strongly attracted. We drove past King Farouk's summer palace, an ostentatious but not unpleasant edifice to the east of Alexandria.

18/10/45 Alexandria: Celebrated at 8 at St Mark's and breakfasted with chaplains of all services after. Gave them a talk and answered questions about their getting work in the civilian church after demobilisation. Returned to Beau Rivage where I did a sermon for Sunday. Back to St Mark's at 5 for a confirmation of two marines, two sailors, an army captain, a WAAF and a civilian girl. It takes over 20 minutes in a fast car to get to St Mark's.

Yesterday I was with the Army and did a lot of visiting. This I find tiring and exacting. To walk round a hospital ward accompanied by the CO and four or five other officers and say the right thing to man after man in bed in the hearing of all is not easy. I begin to sympathise with Royalty.

20/10/45 Jerusalem: I suddenly found myself with an absolutely free morning in Cairo, so I asked John Badeau to take me to see some of the old mosques. He drove me off first to see the Ibn Tulun mosque. It was built in AD 879 and is of the large congregational type, rather like that of Samarra in Iraq. The piers and arches are astonishingly like those of an ancient Transitional Gothic cathedral. Some of the stucco decoration, done in the wet plaster by hand and not moulded, was very pleasant. The minaret is ascended by an outside circular staircase, again as at Samarra and nowhere else (except *one* other Mesopotamian mosque). We climbed up to its top and had a fine view of the ancient part of Cairo with its attractive and very varied minarets and domes. The modern Citadel mosque looked very fine and majestic in its Byzantine mass upon the hillside. Then we drove along the narrow streets to see the mosque enshrining the tomb of Kalaun, a fine lofty structure of the 14th century with much attractive stained glass. The whole beauty of these mosques lies in the attached decoration and only very secondarily in the structure. They are more pretty than beautiful though their prettiness is often very considerable. As ususal I enjoyed the talk I had with John.

At 2 we left Heliopolis in an Anson and flew over the delta, the Suez Canal, the Sinai peninsula and the sea to Lydda. Coming down in the Palestine scene was almost like coming down in Europe. George and Dorothy Reed were at the airport and drove me up to Jerusalem. It was lovely to see them again. Shapley and I are staying with the Bishop and Mrs Stewart at St George's. My programme for tomorrow is different from what I had expected. I am not equipped for these swift changes of plan and the need for extemporisation they require. I feel rather cross that I am worked so hard, with so little regard for my own convenience, and am manoeuvred away from any plans I project for my own delight, eg staying with the Reeds, or getting a free morning now and then for thought, reading and preparation.

Sunday 21/10/45 Jerusalem: Celebrated at 8, assisted by Whitton Davies, the Hebraist specialist on the cathedral staff. Douglas Tucker [a server at Henfield] in the congregation. At 9 after a rapid breakfast I preached at a combined Army and Air Force Church Parade which quite filled the Cathedral – George Reed at the organ. When the cathedral congregation come out of the 10 am service they have tea at the Bishop's garden and I met there one Bertram Thomas who runs a political school for service officers and others. He used to be in Iraq. Then I went back with George and Dorothy to lunch in their old flat in the German colony. We talked reminiscences mostly, with some reference to events since we last met in London just before Francis was born. At 4 Shapley and I visited the Prevocational Training School for ordinands of all denominations. It is housed in a Greek monastery. I talked to nearly all the students individually, including three West Africans.

At 6.30 I read a sermon to a congregation consisting mostly of troops in the cathedral. The Bishop was there. I preached on the text 'The Lord thy God is a jealous God' and of the importance of recognising the inexorability of the laws of moral and spiritual nature. An impressive officer in the Coldstream Guards thanked me for the sermon which he thought timely. At supper, one Morrison of the British Council but newly appointed Professor of Greek at Durham appeared.

23/10/45 Ein Shemer: We stayed last night at the RAF station (Fighters) at Petah Tigrah where I had the good fortune to meet W/Cdr Goldthorpe, the CO. He is very young and very good looking, his face radiating goodness and courage and godliness. He is respected but not altogether understood by his officers, which is perhaps not surprising, for they cannot often have met his like. He lives near Halifax in Yorkshire, and his father, Col Goldthorpe, is a member of the house of Laity for the Wakefield diocese. I dedicated the camp church there. Our quarters were rude and primitive. At 9 this morning we flew to Haifa. We went in a small single-engined plane called a Fairchild Argus, a neat little machine with an inside like my Morris 8. One could see beautifully, as the cabin is slung beneath the wings. We saw Caesarea on our left, and later on I could see Nazareth away on the Right front. We flew over Mt Carmel and I thought I could distinguish the place by the trees where Mary and I made up our first quarrel just over 12 years ago! The padré, Langford-Sainsbury, met us. He strongly resembled my mental picture of his brother whom I have not seen since

1914 [Radley]. We spent a rushed time in his company which included a blow
out to sea in a high-speed launch. We lunched with a RAF Regiment Wing near
Acre. Their task is to guard the one British Ammunition Dump in Palestine,
upon which the militant Jews cast eager eyes. Trouble is expected here very
soon. I hope for Mary's sake I shall be out of the country before it begins. I
should be quite safe, but naturally she would be uneasy. We looked over the
said dump later and came back to Haifa making a detour through the narrow
streets of ancient Acre, a 100% Arab city. We then boarded our Fairchild and
came to this station flying over land looking sleepy and peaceful in the
afternoon sunlight. I am dreadfully tired.

25/10/45 Lydda: We returned from Ein Shemer to Jerusalem flying in our
Fairchild 'taxi' to Kolundia, a semi-emergency landing ground in the hills near
the holy city. It was hard to imagine that in the tranquil-looking villages beneath
us quantities of arms are stored and quantities of men are living ready and eager
to use them in fruitless violence. How lovely is the red earth of Palestine and the
green of the olive groves. We stayed with the bishop again. In his company I
called upon the Armenian Patriarch, Cyril; upon the Greek Patriarch, Timothy;
upon the Latin Patriarch, an Italian; and upon the locum tenens of the Jacobite
archbishopric. The Armenian received us with much splendour. I have never
seen so sumptuous an audience chamber as was his. The whole patriarchal
establishment wore an air of wealth unusual in oriental ecclesiastical residences.
The Patriarch is a plump, jolly prelate, talks English well and is a man of
extensive and rambling information. He seemed pleased when I admired his fine
pectoral cross with its massive topazes. Cherry brandy, cigarettes and Turkish
coffee were produced at the statutory intervals. The Greek and Latin Patriarchs
were not to be seen, the first being engaged with a synod, the second ill in bed.
The Jacobites received us with much pleasure and respect. The locum tenens of
the see had a strikingly youthful face, illuminated with both sanctity and
intelligence. It seems the incumbent of the Jerusalem see is not elected by the
clergy and people, but nominated by the Catholikos of Echmiadzin in view of
the peculiar influence of the Archbishopric. To all the residences of these
ecclesiastics we walked on foot in our cassocks, preceded by a kavass wearing a
tarboosh and wielding a verge with which he made way for us through the
crowds. Our progress was greeted with universal interest and a good deal of
reverent respect.

I lunched with Col Bertram Thomas, the oriental explorer and authority on
Middle Eastern politics, whom I had previously met. He is the Director of a
training school for political officers in Moslem countries. The school is attended
by officers of the forces and the course lasts one year; it is housed in the
spacious Austrian hospice, situated in the old city at a corner of the Via
Dolorosa. At lunch were also the AOC Air Commodore McGregor, a young and
able officer, together with one Shaw, with wife, who is Second in command at
Government House. Conversation was general, easy and interesting.

Shapley and I made a pilgrimage to the Church of the Holy Sepulchre,
praying at Golgotha and at the Anastasis. The church is full of scaffolding and
props and hard to see at all. I was much struck with the chapel of St Helena,
allocated to the Armenians.

This morning I talked to the service ordinands from the RAF at their
Selection course at Carlile House. There were about 20 and the number included

3 or 4 officers. In the afternoon we drove to Ramleh where we visited Philip Usher's grave. Shapley had actually buried him. His grave has only a rough wood cross, painted white, with his name upon it. The cemetery is well kept and I picked a sprig of the rosemary which grows thickly all around to send to Irene Usher. Hibiscus and Oleander give colour to the place.

In the evening I talked to united fellowships from 4 RAF stations. The chaplain of Ramleh, one Crosse, seemed pleased with what I said to them. We then drove to this aerodrome through the dark orange-lined woods, with a vast red moon rising over the Judaean hills. It is hard to realise how near at hand may be bloodshed and terrorism.

26/10/45 Habaniyah: We left Lydda at 10 in a Transport Command Dakota, flying high over the Judaean plateau, and over the wilderness sloping down to Jordan; then over the Mountains of Moab, across the lava country and out across the Syrian desert. Our altitude being considerable it soon became very cold until the heating was turned on. The journey was smooth and un-bumpy. When you first see the Euphrates from a height it looks like a mere stream set abruptly in the desert; not till one comes down lower does the thin belt of vegetation on either side take substance. Soon we saw Lake Habbaniyah and not long after we touched down at the magnificent airport [which when Colin was chaplain in Baghdad only existed on paper]. It looks now ... as tho it had been here for 30 years at least. We are living in the AOC's Staff Mess in fine quarters. I have a private bathroom, and all the appointments are far above those of the average station. And well it should be so, for life in this station must be prison-like. Outside is mere desert, and life is bounded by the barbed-wire fence surrounding. People here seem touchy on the point and do not like favourable comment on the station's amenities. In the mess I met Patrick King whom I knew in Hinaidi days. He is now a Group Captain and fatter than ever. I have little 'laid on' for me to do here; only a confirmation on Sunday night. Tomorrow I go in to Baghdad. My tour, as regards work, is all but over.

28/10/45 Baghdad: I was brought over here yesterday in a Proctor, a small single-engined 3-seater. We flew over Felujah and the Aka Kuf (where they have been digging, and discovering great things about the Kassite Empire) and then we 'shot up' Khadimain and flew round the twin golden domes which I had never seen to such advantage before. They look tarnished, however, and the whole city from the air looks dusty and dilapidated. From here we came down the Tigris low over the city and landed at the civil airport. Baghdad has grown in size, but not in quality. Walking down Al Raschid Street one passes the same endless succession of miserable open-fronted shops displaying cheap and unappetising goods. The gramophones still blare forth in the comfortless cafes and chikhanas; the pavement is still rough and broken, with muddy gaps. Arebanas with pairs of worn-out horses ply for hire, though in slightly smaller numbers. Jack Finch thinks that the mere fact that Baghdad has not dropped back into old Turkish ways is proof that the British mandate did permanent good, despite the low level actually reached. The greatest physical difference is the presence of the two great bridges across the Tigris which have now replaced the bridges of boats. They arch over the river at a considerable height and give the passers by a fine view of the city and river fronts never before accessible. Jack Finch and I strolled about in the streets in the afternoon, and I bought some stamps for Francis in the old post office near Bill Bailey's house under the wireless masts.

The new English church is undoubtedly good, and I was pleasantly surprised at it. The glass windows are, however, poor and though the vault has been whitened, the walls and piers call for similar treatment. I met a number of the English community at a tea party at Roach's house (Roach is the Civil Chaplain) including Scaife, Col Ashton, the Caparns, 'Mossie' Murdoch, Lucie-Smith, Daniel Isa and Mme Krummins. The last mentioned embraced me with vigour to Jack's delight who only wished the event had taken place at a stage in the party when more were present to witness it! The Ambassador was present and Neil Hogg the 2nd Secretary. The former seemed rather colourless, I thought. I dined with General Savory, whose mess is in Cornwallis's old house by the river. I liked him very much, and he spoke long and earnestly to me in the garden, saying at the end 'I don't talk like this because you are a bishop; we talk like this among ourselves'. He is typical, I hope, of the new spirit in the forces. He gave us a fine dinner, with partridges and Persian white wine. This morning I celebrated at 7 and preached at 9.30 Mattins to a congregation mostly military, but including Scaife and Jack and poor Mme Halyoutin.

29/10/45 Cairo: We left Habbaniyah after breakfast and took off from the great lake there in a Sunderland which had come from Karadir. I was treated with much formality by the captain and shown to a good seat in the luxurious saloon of the craft. We passed by Rutbah, of which I got a glimpse, but on the whole of course the passage over the desert was without interest. I read E.B. Soane's 'To Kurdistan in Disguise' most of the way and slept for part. I was interested in our flight over Transjordan where we got a fine view over Amman. This capital city sprawls over several high hills with the aerodrome well to the East. Soon after this we crossed over the watershed of the Mountains of Moab at only a few hundred feet and were soon dropping down to the Dead Sea. We disembarked at Kallia, the name given to that assemblage of modern dwellings where I bathed with the Reeds in 1934. We were given a beautifully served and cooked luncheon in a new hotel by the sea, though I could have eaten twice the quantity provided. After lunch we took off again and sped down almost the whole length of the Dead Sea, finally, when high enough, turning S.W. over the wilderness of Jeshimmon. I tried to imagine Amos the prophet cultivating his 'trees' there in that bleak and haggard land. We had a good view of Hebron and then of Gaza; but the afternoon journey was all very bumpy, though a Sunderland bumps in a very genteel manner. We touched down on the Nile in Cairo at about 4.30.

My actual work is now over. I hope its quality has been better than it seems to me and that it was worthwhile doing. I am still too near it to make any profitable reflections. All I know is that I am exceedingly tired. One strong impression however survives fatigue – the amazing kindness and generosity of almost all with whom I have come into contact, from Archdeacon and Mrs Johnston down to the airman at Kolundia who rushed about on a grilling hot day to find some petrol for my lighter.

30/10/45 Cairo: Bishop Gwynne, with whom I am staying, told me last night that when the C of E padres in Italy instigated men who were marrying Italian girls to insist that *they* should join the C of E rather than the men becoming Papists, they were enormously successful. At one time the C of E padres had 70

Italian RC girls under instruction. He also told me that when Alexis, the new Patriarch of Moscow, was here recently he was ceremonially visited by the heads of the Maronite and Melchite uniat churches, who paid him much respect. These Eastern Christians originally went over to Rome in order to secure the protection in the Levant of that French pro-Roman policy which is now beginning to wane owing to the eclipse of the French influence here since the war. The rising political star, from whom Eastern Christianity seems to expect help, is then Russia! In the evening Baron de Bildt, once Swedish Consul General, came to dinner. He is a cousin of Axel Bildt, who, he tells me, is now dead. The Baron is a fine figure of a man, a Quaker originally, but a regular attender of the Anglican Cathedral services. I had much to say to him and he to me, but Bishop Gwynne held the initiative in conversation for the entire evening.

31/10/45 Cairo: John and Margaret Badeau took me to visit the Coptic churches and the Coptic museum of Old Cairo this morning. We then shopped in the souk, after which we lunched at the Gezirah Sporting Club, of which one has always heard so much. I am too hot to describe our excursion in detail. At a 'Prayer Meeting' tonight in the Cathedral Hall an American spoke upon 'Some atheisms to which Missionaries are susceptible', eg Worry, Impatience, Doubt of God's magnanimity, etc. He said that Christian Ministers and workers ought to go about with a placard round their necks: 'This is *not* the best the Grace of God can do'. He spoke of a man who went to meet a parson whom he had not seen at a station. One man stood apart from the crowd disembarking from a train. 'Are you a minister?' said the meeter; 'No, I'm not. It's indigestion which makes me look that way'. But it was a good talk, if superficial. Is my discomfort at 'Prayer Meetings' good or bad? I only went for Frank Johnston's sake.

3/11/45 London: I got away from Cairo yesterday morning just before the anti-Jewish riots started which have resulted in 600 people being injured – the Arab way of protesting at the anniversary of the Balfour declaration. Shapley and Keeling came and saw me off at Asmara in the glittering silver Dakota which left at 7 a.m. We touched down at El Aden in Cyrenaica and again at the Luda airfield outside Valetta. At each place we had a meal, while in transit we had a good lunch box apiece. One Colonel Teague, an Intelligence Officer from Cairo, sat next to me and with him I conversed and also shared a room for the night at Sardinia. He knows George Reed who, in a sense, 'works for' him. Malta is very small. Most islands when you get to them always appear far larger than you expected. But as you approach Malta by air you take in the whole, with Gozo, in a single *coup d'oeil*. It is quite obviously too the most crowded place in the world. It is a mass of towns and villages which jostle one another in their effort to retain a place upon the island. I retain an impression of brown-red earth, of great quarries cut out of the surface, of multitudinous field-walls, of two-towered churches all looking baroque and magnificent.

Before reaching Malta, the cone of Etna, distant about 120 miles, showed itself out of the sea, a rare event, owing to perfect visibility. As we left Malta the whole of the S.W. Sicilian coast clearly appeared, blue and sharp-cut against the horizon. We reached Sardinia about 5.30 and swooped down upon Elmas, the airport outside the capital, situated by a large lake bordered by a high serrated line of hills above which the crimson of the sunset flashed and glowed.

Here we stayed for the night in crude and sparse quarters. Col Teague and I shared a bleak barrack room with two canvas beds, no chairs, no electric light or hot water. We went for a walk in the darkness by the lake, drank whisky with the CO (a nice South African) and retired to bed at 8.30 pm.

Our flight from Sardinia to Hurn was without break and the journey over France was above cloud all the way except for glimpses of Marseille and Caen. The latter looked very devastated. We passed over the Isle of Wight and, to our surprise, found England bathed in warm and genial sunshine. A special train, on which we lunched, brought us comfortably to London. How lovely was the English countryside in the mellow warmth of this autumn sun – Brockenhurst, Winchester, Fleet and many other familiar places.

Here I am in John Jagoe's flat, wondering how soon I can decently fly off to Mary and the boys.

3. Visit to Finland as representative of the Church of England at the celebration of the fourth Centenary of Michael Agricola's translation of the New Testament into Finnish, 20 September to 8 October 1948

Not long after after the 1948 Lambeth Conference Colin received a letter from Bishop George Bell, who was now the Chairman of the Archbishop's Foreign Relations Council, asking him to go to Finland to represent the Church of England in the events organised to celebrate the Fourth Centenary of the Translation of the New Testament into Finnish by the Finn, Michael Agricola [who is also remembered yearly today on 'Finnish Language Day']. The invitation had originated with Archbishop Fisher, who had first approached a Diocesan Bishop, Leslie Hunter of Sheffield, who had already visited Finland, but was unable to go at this time.

In his reply Colin says he is glad to accept, though his knowledge of the Lutheran Churches of Scandinavia is no more than 'superficial', which makes him wonder whether, as a Suffragan, he won't be considered 'rather small beer' as sole representative of the C of E. He also raises the question of what he should do if asked to take part in any celebrations of Holy Communion, since the C of E is not in communion with the Finnish Church. He would not like to 'hurt the feelings of a church which has borne and is bearing so much of the "burden and heat of the day" in its remote Christian bastion'. But he will do what the Archbishop tells him. After an exchange of letters with the Archbishop's chaplain the latter relays to Colin Geoffrey Fisher's own judgement: 'if asked, I would say he should *either* robe and sit in the sanctuary and *not* communicate, *or* sit in the congregation and feel free to do so if he wishes. But if they *permit* him to do so, "the Bp of Jarrow could certainly avail himself of this permission".'

Colin took the opportunity offered by his rail and steamer journey to Finland to spend two or three days in Sweden en route. He left Durham early in the morning of 20 September, leaving himself a few hours in London, where he first went to the Head Office of Barclays Bank to have an error in his Foreign

Currency allowance rectified, and then watched a 'magnificent' French film on the life of St Vincent de Paul before catching the old boat-train from Liverpool Street to Harwich, Parkeston Quay. After recording the crossing to the Hook of Holland, made tolerable by 'Kwells', he describes salient facts and incidents of his luxurious journey by first class sleeper through Holland, Germany and Denmark: the well-cooked meals taken in the dining-car ('Lunch was excellent: Hors d'oeuvres and a glass of Hollands, *poulet en casserôle* – the vegetables had undoubtedly been packed in layers – jam tartlets and cream and a fine pear'); the 'neat and clean' towns, villages and stations in Holland; the striking difference between frontier formalities when leaving Holland ('all was quiet, efficient and convenient') and those when entering the British zone of Germany ('an atmosphere of confusion and over-crowding', not to mention queuing in a shower of hail); 'the old abbey church at Bassum was a pleasant sight', though 'Osnabrück looked a bit down at heel' and 'the outskirts of Bremen more seriously battered'; nevertheless, Bremen cathedral spires reminded him of Lübeck; the last detail he notes is his view of 'a dachshund gallop(ing) over the furrows (of a ploughed field)'!

On 23 September he wrote in the train from Växjö in Sweden to Stockholm, after staying the night of the 22nd with Bishop Brilioth in 'the episcopal house, an attractive eighteen-century wooden building' overlooking the town. He then goes on to summarise the main architectural features of the Cathedral (and its need of internal redecoration) and records his pleasure at hearing Bach and Buxtehude played on the fine organ after dinner. Colin was also extremely interested to hear Bishop Brilioth talk about the details of his work. For example:

> When he does 'visit' a parish officially it is a formidable affair with much preaching (he hears the local clergy preach), much catechising of the youth and much economic inquisition such as archdeacons do, or are supposed to do, in England. The local schools occupy much of his attention on such occasions... He tells me that a good parish pastor will give 100 hours instruction to Confirmation candidates.

Next day his diary entry was written in the British Embassy in Stockholm:

> It is so novel an experience to be in a country which was not in the war and to see all those evidences of continuity with the past unbroken by catastrophe and cataclysms both moral and physical. Alone of places I have visited since the war Stockholm seems unchanged, in spite of the few obvious developments... It was touching to be remembered with such effusive affection by both men and women whom I have not seen for almost 20 years and whom the Ambassador's reception enabled me to meet again.

After a night in his 'impressive and comfortable suite' in the Embassy he left Stockholm at 4.30 p.m. by ferry across the Gulf of Bothnia in the Baltic Sea. 'The city looked wonderfully beautiful. A feeling of melancholy came over me at leaving this familiar and lovely scene as we steamed ... toward the heathen East'. But it was not long before Colin was cheered up by finding in his cabin companion 'a friendly and charming Finn' – a professor of constitutional law at Helsinki University – who was just returning from a Moral Rearmament conference in Switzerland. 'Though much stirred, he was nevertheless critical and we had some interesting talk.' Colin was disappointed to find that 'though new belief in the reality and sovereignty of God had plainly been born', it didn't seem to have given rise to any 'desire for closer Church membership'. They then got on to Finnish politics and the attitude of Russia. 'I was a bit diffident', he writes, 'since Moss [one of the Archbishop's chaplains] had warned [him] "not so much as to mention Russia".'

Both Professor Kastari and all Finns I have met since seem unaware of such a necessity. They discuss it loudly and publicly. The great tonic one gets here is the supreme contempt the people have for Russia – a contempt which broadens into amusement. Nevertheless I had become somewhat nervous of the prospective train journey from Åbo [where his sea journey ended] to Helsingfors [Swedish for Helsinki]. The trains go through the Russian zone and are driven and officered by Russians during that period, the carriage windows being shuttered so that no one shall get a glimpse of what goes on. My fears were needless for on arrival at Åbo I was met by the British Consul in Helsingfors, who conveyed me and Professor Kastari in the legation car by road.

Colin sometimes uses the Swedish name for places, sometimes the Finnish (thus Åbo is the Swedish name for Turku). Finland was part of Sweden for many years (many Finns are still bilingual in Finnish and Swedish), and then, during most of the nineteenth century, it was part of Russia – though in both cases with a good deal of self-government. Russian policy towards Finland has long been influenced by the fact that, until well on in the twentieth century, the Finnish-Russian frontier was extremely close to Russia's second city, St Petersburg, and Finland could therefore become a convenient jumping-off point for, say, Germany to invade them.

There were, in fact, two periods of warfare between Finland itself and Russia during the Second World War – the Winter War (1939–40), when the Soviet Union attacked Finland but never managed to occupy it, since the Finns were greatly superior to Russians in fighting in ice and snow, and the so-called 'Continuation War', when Finland attacked Russia as an ally of Hitler's Germany, in the hope that they would get back what they had lost in the Winter War. The outcome of all this was the loss to Russia of Finland's eastern province, Karelia, which is still Russian (the entire population either moved to other parts of Finland or to other countries), and, until 1955, the loss of a small coastal zone to the West of Helsinki, besides extensive reparations in kind. It is the small coastal zone to which Colin refers in the diary passage preceding this note.

On arrival in Helsinki Colin had lunch with Sydney Linton and his Swedish wife. He had just been appointed English chaplain in the capital city, and,

Colin writes in his diary, 'I (found them) delightful and altogether admirable', despite their being 'moral Rearmament'. On the following day, Sunday, at the 11.15 service, Colin 'gave an informal inauguration of Linton's ministry and said some prayers 'over' him' in the British church, which in those days was no more than 'a large room in a corner block of flats. The altar stands in a corner and the 'nave' broadens out westwards like a fan.' In his report on his visit Colin says that Linton is likely to become 'a very valuable agent of the Church of England both as pastor of the English congregation and community, and as liaison with the Finnish Church'. Earlier he had celebrated and then breakfasted with

> a Miss Henley who lived in St Petersburg in the old days and who has seldom been far away from that city. She lives in one room which she shares with her faithful servant Miss Alexandrov. In spite of her exile life and her horribly cramped circumstances she is a typical English lady, her room is elegant and her clothes and general appearance are really chic. She is a wonderful embodiment of the wholesome strength and tenacity of our English middle class and of the quiet uncomplaining courage of a tradition now passing away, of its adaptability to changing and worsening circumstances without any loss of essential characteristics.

'We lunched with the American Minister, a Mr Warren, a man totally unlike any American I had ever previously met.' Fellow guests included a variety of diplomats, and also the famous violinist, Yehudi Menuhin. 'We were waited on by a butler and three maids in lovely Edwardian frilly aprons. Everything was sumptuous, both to look at and to taste. It is wonderful to be able to eat too much again.' While in Helsinki he was given bed and breakfast by Mr and Mrs Snelman. He was a leading portrait painter, whilst his wife painted china. 'The view from my window over the whole of Helsinki and its sea approaches will be hard to forget.'

On Monday the 27th he 'waited upon' Archbishop Hermann of the Finnish Orthodox Church, an Estonian:

> the first Orthodox prelate in my experience to be beardless. It was striking to realise how much this increased his approachability. He has no English and we shot observations and questions at one another through the medium of his daughter-in-law. He spoke of the blow to his church through the Russian annexation of Karelia where most of his people and church property were. Now they are scattered all over Finland and it is hard to minister to the countless tiny groups. He is grateful to the C of E for their help and showed me his cassock made of English cloth.... We went into another room for tea, where the great feature was a wonderful confection of strawberries in a thick syrup. Jam would be a derogatory name: I noticed that the Abp put two spoonfuls of it into his tea, while he put 3 lumps of sugar on to his plate!
>
> On Tuesday morning I spoke to the Oecumenical Committee of the Church about the origin and growth of the Anglican Communion. Gulin [whom Colin had met at the Anglo-Scandinavian churches conference in 1936] was in the

chair and gave me a magnificent welcome. ... I was greatly impressed with Gulin. I was hardly prepared for his obvious growth in spiritual stature. He was always attractive and striking, but now he is almost a Luther. ... We drank coffee and ate biscuits during the meeting. At lunch with Dr Grundy, the head of the British Council, I met the RC Apostolic Delegate, a sprightly Dutchman who rules over the very small R.C. community, and the Chaplain General of the Finnish forces. The latter calls himself a bishop, and over his grey-green military uniform wears a gold pectoral cross which Mannerheim gave him. But he isn't a bishop. He only spoke German but his charming wife interpreted. ...

At 4 a reception at which I met the English congregation. At 8 a dinner with Magill (Shamus Magill) the Military Attaché at which Enckell, the Finnish Foreign Minister, was present. I had a very long talk with him but missed a good deal of what he said. He started life as a cadet in the Russian Imperial Guard, he was a Finnish representative in St Petersburg at the Revolution and had to negotiate with Lenin. This last February he had to negotiate with Stalin in Moscow. I wish he had spoken more clearly, that I were not so deaf and that the others had not talked so loud, for I would have liked to have heard all he said.

On Wednesday, 29 September Colin was driven back to Åbo/Turku in the Legation car, three days before the Michael Agricola ceremonies were due to start:

On arrival here we went straight to Archbishop Lehtonen's house and paid our respects. He reminds me of a Nordic Adam Fox. He has great charm and a delightful atmosphere pervades his house. I am most comfortably lodged in this hotel (the Societetshuset), with a private bathroom (no hot water) and a good writing table and two (!) WCs. I supped with Samuel Lehtonen, the Abp's son and chaplain and a Herr Winter, the Secretary of the Bible Society, whom I did not specially like.

Next day he visited the Cathedral and St Catherine's Church:

in the afternoon we visited three country churches. We lunched in the hotel off porridge and milk followed by a nice sort of meat and potatoe pie with a fried egg. Our drive into the country was in a vast Buick which for some reason or other was driven by a vast bull-necked policeman. I was told the reason but did not follow it. It was a glorious afternoon of autumn sunshine and the country looked superb. In one vicarage we entered, a prie-dieu in the study carried an open English bible with a rosary!

There follow many details of the churches' fabric (largely granite), and of particular objects in them, some dating from mediieval times.

In the parsonage at Reisio I was shown one of the few existing copies of Missale Aboensis (late XV or early XVI century) printed at Lübeck and a fine example of printing in Black Letter. It is in beautiful condition and seemed complete. The calendar was interesting – not too many saints – and included St Henry on 20th January, St Eric, St Olav. ... At the most distant of the churches was an ancient shrine of St Henry which used to contain some relics of the saint.

It is in shape like an altar tomb with a fine brass of the saint in full pontificals on the top. Round the sides the story of his life and of miracles after his death is done in small brasses in a most spirited manner.

Marti Paavio, an infantry officer in the first of the two Finnish-Russian wars, i.e. in 1939-1940, dined with me and took me to have a Finnish bath at 8.30. The heat was terrific but the whole process leaves one with the impression that one has never been clean before. Paavio duly beat me with birch branches and it seemed just the right climax to 15 minutes sweating on top of the high bench. I was washed with loofah and soap by an old woman with incredible efficiency and then had a cold shower. A quiet lie down came next and then the old woman came and dried me with much smacking and slapping. I feel a new man, as light as air.

Next day Samuel Lehtonen took him to two museums before lunch. In one there was 'A little series of engravings illustrating the Lord's Prayer. 'Forgive us our trespasses as we forgive ...' was illustrated by an outraged husband laying his hand gently on the shoulder of the adulterer caught almost in the act':

I had tea with the Abp and his family: for my special benefit there was strong tea, bread, butter, marmalade. Both the Abp and his wife are irresistibly attractive. He is the incarnation of kindness, natural dignity and an impish humour. I read my paper to the Bible Societies in the Chapter House, a fine 18th century house which contains a great hall (where the Finnish Church Assembly has today begun its quinquennial month-long meeting – Gulin waved enthusiastically to me from his seat in the balcony) and other rooms. We met in the actual Chapter room – about 50 pastors including the Bishop of Borgå – almost a double of Bp Perrin of Willesden. The Abp introduced me with generous warmth. Young Lehtonen interpreted me sentence by sentence. It went over fairly well. Coffee and cakes after. Hardly anyone knows English but I had some talk with 2 or 3 who did. I supped alone at the hotel off fried chicken, salad and beer – 200 mark or 6/8d. What a fine people the Finns are. The men finely built, manly, solemn dignity: the waitresses, un-made-up and ladylike in dark coats and skirts and white blouses. If only Mary could be here to enjoy it all too.

On the following day, 2 October, the Michael Agricola celebrations began:

Church festivals here are feasts also in the material sense. I have eaten more today than on any day I can remember. Bp Berggrav is here representing the Norwegian Church, Bp Jonzon of Luleå represents Sweden, the American Dr Michelfelder represents the Lutheran World Federation and a Swedish-American Dr Engstrom represents Lutheran World Action – a sort of relief society. No one from Denmark appears to have arrived though the Primate was expected. I sat next to Berggrav at lunch. He tells me he introduced George Bell to Churchill in 1945. When I said 'Do you like Churchill?' he turned to me in blank surprise and said 'of course'. A marvellous reception at the Archbishop's house with coffee and cream cakes – all most friendly. It does you good just to stand in the same room as a group of Finnish pastors – fine husky fellows, big in body, mind and spirit, open-hearted and courteous. We squashed our way into the Abp's oratory and sang two hymns – a Finnish one and The Church's One Foundation, young Michael Lehtonen playing the harmonium. The Abp said a few prayers.

Compline in the rugged old cathedral with an immense congregation and a sermon by Dr Salomies Bishop of St Michael (ex-Viipuri [a town now in Russia]) was an inspiring occasion. 'Christe qui lux est et dies' was sung in Finnish to an old plainsong tune. Though actually new to everyone you wouldn't have guessed it from the singing. At the end they sang a hymn to 'Les Commandements de Dieu' to which I firmly sang 'The Day Thou Gavest'. October has brought hot water to the hotel taps. The weather is what one would expect in England at this time of year – no colder. At dinner Bp Berggrav smoked a pipe at least 18 inches long. He was in very good form.

On Sunday, 3 October, there was a Solemn Service in the cathedral. The official programme for the Jamboree treated the day as the day of St Michael and All Angels, without comment on this change of date. Colin's record of the day is interesting in itself and also tells us a lot about his own cast of mind:

It is interesting to note the differences in more or less casual church customs. Nobody in Finland bows to the altar on entering a church but there is universal mutual bowing between persons. When a pastor enters the vestry of a church he stands for a moment in prayer, his face turned to the wall. In Åbo cathedral the Bishops attending a service do not robe or sit in prominent seats. The bishops occupy three rows of pews near the pulpit in the nave and sit in their suits and overcoats. The front of these three rows is reserved for the Archbishop and his family. During those parts of the service in which he was not officially occupied, the Abp mooched about the cathedral unattended and unobserved. There are no attendants, no pokers. Everyone sits for hymns unless they happen to be special acts of praise. Everyone stands when the Bible is read – even for a short text. They stand for the Epistle at Mass. At all services I attended in the Cathedral four lighted candles burned on the High Altar, two tall and two shorter. Altar frontals seem universal. The clergy at the altar – and services are only conducted from the altar, even Compline – face the people nearly all the time, e.g. for the Nicene creed. The collects were said at the altar (even declaimed) but the responding Amen was sung. At the High Mass (without Communion) three priests all in full Gothic white chasubles stood at the altar. After the sermon (which followed the Creed – there was no Gospel today) the Bishops and visiting representatives of other churches left their seats in the nave and robed in the sacristy. The Finnish bishops vested in albe and cope: they each held their crozier. Visiting priests and other Finnish priests in the procession wore chasubles – some wore very short albes revealing at least 18' of trousers. The two American (non-episcopal) Lutheran visitors wore albes and stoles (worn straight) of different colours. I wore rochet, stole and cope and carried my mitre. The Abp said his people were very like Ulster Protestants! The procession entered during the singing of 'For All the Saints' – translated into Swedish by Söderblom, and sung to a superb modern Finnish tune. We swung jauntily down the North aisle. I was paired with Jonzon, the Swedish Bp of Luleå. We grouped ourselves on the altar steps for the Prayer for the Church. A Blessing followed and during the singing of '*Ein feste Burg*' we all went out.

The service was marred by the unrestricted activities of press photographers who walked about taking shots with blinding flashes all through the service. They even came between altar and people, taking the priests or the congregation. President Paasikivi in his seat in the nave was photoed over and over again.

Nothing can describe adequately the magnificent congregational singing. It is in effect their sacrament. I was quite stunned with its majesty. Voices rose full-throated, passionate, ecstatic, wholly un-self-conscious in their superb modal melodies. I have always admired German congregational singing, but the Finnish singing knocks it right out of the running. The tones and overtones of it all are running in my head as I write. We disperse and evenly distribute our worship in every direction. They concentrate it all in their hymn singing. Bishops may converse during the prayers and nudge one another in sermon and collect, but in the singing everybody is all out in the act of praise. It seems an inseparable and indivisible element in Lutheranism. I always feel with Lutherans in the Nordic countries that their traditions are greater than they know. I have never felt it more than here. They cannot analyse their inheritance. If one judged them by their words and description of themselves one would very much misjudge and underrate the glory of their traditions and church ethos.

The service of Greetings in the afternoon was really too long – 2½ hours. It seemed extra long to me for only now and then did I understand what was being said. We had a long lecture on Michael Agricola from some professor and then came the series of greetings. We had to walk half the length of the cathedral – up to the entrance of the sanctuary (All Saints Chapel) – in solitary state, past the President and Mme Paasikivi, past all the doctors, professors, deans and so on. The Abp greeted each arrival, who then spoke for 5 minutes or so. He greeted my advent with the reminder that it was an Englishman from whom the Finns had first received their faith [St Henry]. Samuel Lehtonen stood by me and interpreted me sentence by sentence. I reminded them of the vision in Revelation – the true heavenly setting of the Church as lamps in heaven and pictured our mutual greeting on earth being confirmed by greetings between the angels of the churches above. The high church people liked it: I doubt if the rest did. Gulin seemed a trifle disappointed. You can't tell with the Abp: he would give you the same amused and affectionate regard whatever you said.

There were two great banquets. Lunch was given by the City Council. Each of the guests was presented to the President. He is astoundingly ugly, but in quite new and unusual ways you become aware of his quiet power and intelligence. It is said that Stalin has a personal regard for him which explains Russia's 'gentleness' with Finland (incidentally Stalin also has a respect for the Finnish army for while Finns often captured Russians in thousands, Russians never even captured so large a group at a time as a company (120 men)!). I sat between the Minister of Justice and the President of the Åbo bench of judges. The former spoke English moderately well and we talked a good deal. He had been one of the delegation to Russia this February. Both he and Enckell described Stalin as personally attractive, very well informed, and amusing.

Dinner in the evening at the Abp's was a blend between extreme stateliness and decorative formality on the one hand and an informal intimacy, wholly unthinkable in English dinner parties, on the other. Nearly all the guests wore decorations, of which they had many. Jonzon, the Swedish bishop, looked like some ancient portrait of royalty or a famous general. The Finnish bishops had gay collars and stars and medals to a man. The laymen on the whole seemed to have fewer decorations – all wore white waistcoats and tailcoats. I who up to now have felt almost overdressed, felt as if I had been dragged in from the highways and hedges. The President was there of course and the Speaker of the house of Parliament (only one chamber) called the President of Parliament, several members of the Government and all the local bigwigs of state, university and church. In the middle of the smorgås, a woman played some Chopin; suddenly the Abp would get up and say something or other, or a university professor would make a speech. Then while waiting for the meat course we all broke into heartfelt song – a song, Gulin told me, which spoke of the beauty of the world and of the far greater beauty of the world to come. Quite a long speech from the Abp came at one point with some very nice things said about England. The President, too, made a speech, quiet, unemotional but emphatic which ended by saying that as God has always upheld Finland in unimaginable dangers in the past so he could not be expected to desert Finland in the future, however dark. Then we sang a hymn corresponding to 'How Sweet the Name of Jesus Sounds'. Mrs Lehtonen always acted as precentor and led the singing in a clear ringing voice. Then there was some more piano music – Grieg. The meal began at 7.15. At 9.30 coffee appeared. Then we went to the Abp's private oratory where there was a hymn and some prayers. I must add that at one point in the dinner, the Professor of Greek came to each foreign guest and presented him with a medal commemorating Michael Agricola. The meal was: smorgås, soup with little meat tartlets put in, roast beef, vegetables, salad, a wonderful real cream ice with strawberries, coffee.

On Monday, 4 October:

the foreign guests were entertained by the Swedish Theological Faculty of the Åbo Academy at luncheon in this hotel. I had met them all before but I had some talk with Bp Jonzon and with Lindgröm, one of the Swedish professors. I felt it time to make a speech so shortly after our host (president of the faculty) had made his speech of welcome – after the smorgås – I got up and spoke for about 3 minutes. I don't think I was very intelligible and I may even have put my foot in it, for I spoke of an English difficulty in understanding Lutheranism – owing to our history – but mentioned that experience of Lutheran worship was a very considerable help in that direction. I added that we were determined to understand and that we valued our contacts with the Lutheran churches of the North and hoped for the enrichment of our own faith thereby.

After lunch I was taken to see the fine new church of St Martin with its striking wall painting above and around the altar and the even finer painting of Our Lord's entry into Jerusalem along the whole length of the Western gallery. The organist was present and played some music on the excellent organ, We then visited the very pleasantly placed City Cemetery, among the pine woods towards the East. The chapel is the work of a contemporary Finnish architect (Brügmann?) and on the whole it 'comes off'. The 'north' side of the chapel, right along, has plate glass windows through which the trees outside and the whole scene there are, so to speak, 'pressed' into the balance and decorative scheme of the chapel. To secure a response to this the chapel itself is not built symmetrically. The result is effective. A creeper grows all over the flat 'East' wall. On the whole I think it is good.

We then went to Samuel Lehtonen's home. He lives in a sort of 'church plant'. Under one roof is the mission church of the cathedral district which he serves, his own house, club rooms, a crêche, a kindergarten, and a Finnish bath house (sauna). It is excellently built and planned by the same architect as the cemetery. As usual in the North, efficiency and beauty are secured by the right and economic use of very simple materials. I heard a roomful – about 20 – of Finnish girls (9-12) sing a hymn. In England their sound would have been a self-conscious and gassy whisper, but here they fairly took the roof off. We had a pleasant tea and much talk. Later Marti Paavio came in and we went through a number of English and Finnish hymns. I copied out the fine tune to 'For All the Saints' which had so struck me in the Cathedral on Sunday. After a light supper we all said Compline in English, and then I went home.

Today [5 October] I lunched with the Abp and his family. I had some private talk with the Abp: he hopes that contact with the C of E will help them to deepen their liturgical movement which he says is gaining strength. Like ours in its earlier stages this movement seeks to make the Church true to its earlier, post-reformation traditions which have become obscured and neglected. Even reciting the Creed is a novelty with them, though it is part of their rite. He spoke of their own 'pietistic' movements (of more than one kind) with great pride. All these movements remain within the national churches, subject to its bishops. One of them insists on praying on the knees, instead of sitting, and is said to have some historical continuity with ancient Franciscan influence. Another, in the North, specialises in mutual confession of sin: it has no connection with Buchmanism [Moral Rearmament]! I find myself so charmed with the Abp as a person that I often miss a great deal that he says.

The church assembly, now sitting, is to discuss the remarriage of divorced persons, and relations with the Anglican church, among other things, during its month.

The Helsinki theological faculty is against the Liturgical movement.

Colin left Turku the same evening 'by good Swedish boat, the Ragne', where he had a cabin to himself. The Embassy had reserved him a room in Castle Hotel, Stockholm. After signing in, he 'walked about' the city in sunlight and had lunch with 'the British lunch club', tea with his old friends from Hove, Horace and Stanny Fort and dinner with Peggy Scholander at her flat: 'lobster, cold pork, schnapps, white wine'. Next day he shopped with the Forts and wrote an article on Finland for the *Church Times*, and also the 'official' report on his visit for the 'Foreign Relations Committee'. For tea he went to the house of his old Confirmation Candidate Britt Carter and her architect husband and two little children. Later he took Jones the Chaplain out to dinner and next day, the 8th, he flew back to London.

*

In his report on his visit to the Council for Foreign Relations, Colin summarised his main impressions as follows:

Throughout the visit I was struck with the spirit of hopeful fortitude & calm trust in God which animates the Finnish people. The enterprise & determination with which they are shouldering their reparations burden so successfully is responsible for this prevailing mood: when you see an assembly of Finnish pastors & laymen & note their magnificent physique and their intelligent, spiritual faces you are not surprised that the Church they represent is the soul of a truly virile nation.

He also added the following on the question of achieving intercommunion: I agree with the Bishop of Sheffield that steps for securing closer relations on an official basis with the Church of Finland should not be delayed. Upon sentence: but Abp Lehtonen will not live for ever & I cannot imagine which of the existing bishops could adequately carry on his pro-Anglican work. I don't think any of them are against us – far from it – but they have not the same eagerness which is necessary in the early stages.

A Finn, Mika Pajunen, in his book about Archbishop Lehtonen and his hopes for closer relations with the Church of England, specially commends Colin, firstly for his much more positive attitude to Finland and the Finns than that of The Rev H.M. Waddams, of the CFR, who had visited Finland in 1944 on the initiative of the Ministry of Information, and secondly for reinforcing Bishop Hunter of Sheffield's recommendation that, in the matter of closer relations, there should be no delay. In the event nothing was done until the Porvoo Conference in the late 80s. One reason was connected with the whole question of Finno–Soviet relations, about which Colin had been given such misleading warnings before his departure.

4. *Visit to units of the Royal Air Force in Germany, 21–31 January 1949*

26.1.49 Trinity House, Hamburg: I arrived in Germany on 21st Jan, touching down at Bückeburg at about 3 pm. Bückeburg is in the tiny Principality of Schaumburg-Lippe and is about 30 miles from Hannover. It is at the moment the HQ of RAF in Germany, telescopically called BAFO, which stands for British Air Forces in Occupation.

The first evening was purely social. Lord Tedder, the Chief of Air staff, was visiting, and there was a cocktail party in A mess and a small dinner party afterwards at the AOC in C's country house 10 miles away. For all his simplicity of manner and friendliness of address I did not really like either Lord T or his wife. She is beautiful like a hard-edged crystal and with a plentiful fund of surface friendliness but I did not feel at ease with her or her husband, even though the latter was very nice to me and always looked at me when he came to the climax of his stories or anecdotes. I disliked his criticism of Winston Churchill and his assumption of being one of the people and a rather heavy sarcasm about public schools, etc. The American visitors, General Cannon and his wife, were delightful. He is the Head of the American Air Force in Germany and both he and his wife are said to be Mormons. They certainly live in Salt Lake City, but in conversation I was terrified of pursuing the matter. The AOC in C and his wife were both kindly but not very interesting – name of Williams.

I had a very luxurious room and our food and drink was good, well cooked and exquisitely (Epicuraeanly) served. I drank more than was good for me and felt very liverish all Saturday.

Hugh Langford-Sainsbury is the chief padré and his brother T.A.L-S (who was at Radley with me) had me to dine on Sunday. He has turned out a boisterous but shrewd man, with some real charm and goodness lurking behind his tiny little eyes. He is an Air Vice Marshall.

On Saturday afternoon I preached in the early 17th century Rococo Lutheran church at Bückeburg – a place of some charm and beauty; the RAF uniform looked incongruous in such a period piece. I preached from the steps of the font which is placed in the middle of the church, dividing it into two. In the evening I confirmed about 24 men (including 3 WAAF) in the camp church at Bad Eilsen where the headquarters offices are.

On Monday we flew to Berlin and touched down at Gatow at about noon. The pleasant CO (Gp Capt Yard) showed me dutifully round and explained all the workings of the Air Lift. It was intensely interesting and I marvelled at the smoothness with which everything and everybody worked. Every 3 minutes a plane comes in and a plane takes off – right round the clock. There was no sense of haste or bustle or conscious carrying out of an unprecedented task – it all quietly happened – a synchronisation of minds and wills on a vast scale. How long Berlin can be kept going on the supplies thus brought I don't know. Only food and fuel are brought. What happens when clothes wear out? Boots are getting pretty bad now.

In the afternoon we drove into Berlin. A more melancholy sight I have never witnessed and it had an air of menace about it. Up by the Brandenburg Gate was like being in Ypres in the first War. You expected to be sniped. Yet the only Russian on view was the solitary brown-coated sentry guarding the Russian War Memorial which they precipitately erected in our zone. The ghastly isolated white statues in the Tiergarten were frightening. I cannot really analyse my feelings and impressions. It was all so different a colour and a tone from my expectations. We ran Mary Bailey to earth in a dismal office with a dreary view. She took us out to tea at the YWCA and we had a delicious meal in a beautiful room – somewhere in Charlottenburg.

Confirmation in the Gatow station church at 16.30.

Next morning we motored in to see Bishop Otto Dibelius who has just been elected president of the German Evangelical Synod. He looked far nicer and more humanised than what I remember of him in 1930 when he came to Chichester. He talked about confirmation and 'holding' young people in the Church. They are contemplating a period of separation between the confirmation classes at school and the actual confirmation. He asked if the British would give him a good, big, car to help him in his work.

30.1.49 Wahn (nr Siegburg): It has not been possible to be alone much on this visit or have time for reading or writing. The programme has been concentrated. The retreat for chaplains went well at Hamburg, I think. At any rate, I enjoyed it. I duly saw the damaged city and called on Paul D-J at the broadcasting house. Langford-Sainsbury stood me a fine dinner at the *Vier Jahreszeiten*, now a NAAFI hotel. On the way to Uetersen whence we flew to Gütersloh we had my first car accident in which no-one in either car was hurt. [He must have forgotten the accident in Iceland!] The roads were icy. It was not our fault but the German's. Flying over Hamburg and seeing the towers and steeples emerging from a ground fog was nice.

At Gütersloh I was driven about in a car preceded by a jeep in which a white hatted police escort sat.

Several Station Commanders have spoken about the lack of initiative of the young airman. Though sport of all kinds, including gliding and riding, are available absurdly cheaply a very large number never do anything except sit about in canteens drinking coffee. No wonder padrés find their work discouraging.

We had a lovely flight from Gütersloh to here and flew over the Möhne Dam which Gibson blew up with torpedoes in the war. This camp is in a large cantonment where the famous Afrika Korps was trained under Rommel. We had a confirmation this morning. This afternoon we drove through Cologne. It was sad to see so many magnificent churches in irretrievable ruin – the fine skyline of the city as it was is now a meagre affair. We visited the cathedral – only the choir and transept is yet opened for use. The glass is back and looks glorious. It all reminded me of old days.

31.1.49 Wahn: Waiting in the CO's house for the car to take us to Oberhausen where we join the train for Hook of Holland. Have just been to get some money from the Accountant Officer. The men here are not paid in Marks but in an ad hoc military currency with pound, ten shilling, five shilling, half crown, even 3d notes – all very nasty to touch. Most of my time here (apart from Hamburg) has been spent in purely social contacts. I have always stayed in the CO's house as his guest and seen very little of the rest of the station except at perhaps lunch. One MT unit gave me a formal lunch at which I said grace: there was a long elaborate menu. I was Guest of Honour at Gütersloh at a Dining-in night, all very festive with pukka RAF evening dress worn by many. They all got very merry and I was actually addressed as darling by a WAAF officer who seemed well away, though for the most part under control. The RAF are housed in old Luftwaffe Stations for the most part. Their design is very good, and they reflect a standard of living far higher than our own RAF had before the war. Some of the Officers' and even the NCOs' messes are really first class buildings of real interest and beauty. They usually stand among many trees and the whole atmosphere of the 'camp' is delightful. The lovely sunny weather we have had has of course heightened the impression. On the outside of the walls of the barrack buildings here at Wahn, near the ground floor windows, are painted silhouettes of a man listening, eavesdropping. It is an effective design, far more stimulating than 'Beware of Enemy Spies' and other legends. Each figure is life-size and is said to be an attempt to portray Churchill. One needs to be told that.

Except for Clarke (at Hamburg) and Stanger (at Bückeburg) the Station chaplains here are not really up to much. The quality is lower than in the War, I thought.

16

LINCOLN

COLIN'S LONG-CHERISHED ambition to be Dean of Lincoln may well have dated from his honeymoon tour with Mary in the summer of 1935. On that occasion he had written a short article entitled 'Worship in Cathedrals and Elsewhere: a traveller's observations', in which he had contrasted the liturgical atmospheres of Ely and Lincoln as follows. 'If Thaxted [also visited, and its worship described] errs too much in the free-and-easy direction, Ely errs too much in rigidity. Certainly we had the Church's rite, but the rite presented more correctly than sympathetically.' Although 'the sermon of the canon-in-residence suggested a desire to revolt from an imperfect ecclesiastical traditionalism... the rest of the service seemed to pull in the opposite direction'. However, although 'weekday Evensong in Lincoln Cathedral a few days later ... had its merely decorous moments, especially in the psalms and in the collects and prayers, ... it had something more':

> Something of the romantic spirit of the cathedral's builders lives on in the present-day worship. The *Magnificat* and *Nunc Dimittis* of Harold Darke had a yearning and passionate element, while the anthem of Palestrina, 'By the Waters of Babylon', faultlessly sung, brought to the service the *Maranatha* [O Lord, Come!] of early Christianity. It was not only the French blue of the choristers' cassocks or the comely cloaks of the corner-boys which lent such majesty to the entrance and exit of choir and chapter; there must be somewhere in the daily life of this corporation that divine spark which is able to transform routine into living worship.

All that, of course, reflected the Lincoln of 25 years before his appointment, when Dean Fry was in post. But Colin's Lincoln ministry was deeply coloured by his liturgical interests and concerns in the widest sense, in which not merely the atmosphere and details of the conduct of worship, but the surroundings in which that worship takes place are of very great importance.

The Cathedral itself, has much in common with Durham. Ruskin thought Lincoln Cathedral the finest building in England, and many other writers on architecture have thought much the same. The position of Durham Cathedral on the very edge of a cliff above the wooded banks of the River Wear is, perhaps, incomparable, but Lincoln's situation quite near the edge of a (much higher) scarp makes it visible almost all over the city, and for many miles around. Any journey by train up the Eastern region main line between Grantham and Doncaster, or by car along the western edge of the Lincolnshire Wolds on the way to the Humber Bridge, seems to me incomplete without a glimpse of the familiar outline of Lincoln Cathedral on its eminence. It is also one of the largest of English cathedrals, but it is not merely imposing and majestic – 'half church of God, half castle 'gainst the Scot', as Walter Scott once said of Durham – but one of the most beautiful as well. Pevsner's observation that Lincoln, like Durham, is essentially uniform as regards architectural style, helps us to understand this. But, for all the splendours of the Cathedral itself, there is no real Cathedral Close in Lincoln like those of, say, Durham or Salisbury, and, when Colin was Dean, much through traffic passed very near the cathedral building itself.

Colin's diary entry for 28/1/50 records some of his first impressions of the day he and Mary moved into the Deanery after their short stay with the Srawleys:

> We are about to pass our first night in the Deanery. All day we have been working to get things straight and between us we have got the study ship-shape and our bedroom. I attended evensong and heard with pleasure Whyte's 'O praise God in his holiness'. Of the residentiaries only Lamplugh [Archdeacon of Lincoln] was present, though Srawley, Chard and Coulton assisted and Bentley [one of the Priest Vicars] sang the office. I can hardly believe it is all true and that I am veritably Dean of this vast and magnificent cathedral. Mary and I supped by the study fire off Douglas Chandor's cold tongue [*sic*!], and we opened a bottle of Madeira.

Next day he wrote:

> My first Sunday. On the whole I am pleased with the services and with their sober 1662 prayerbook tradition. There is room for improvement but it is all very much on the right lines. Mattins was well attended and I preached on the Cathedral Foundation and its duty of worship [a sermon published under the title 'Function of a cathedral']. Mary approved. Lunched with the Lamplughs who broached the question of a play in the cathedral. I have written to Martin Browne for his opinion upon the play and the producer they propose. It seems that the Bp of Grimsby [the Precentor] may object. ... The Bishop [of Lincoln, Harland] is away and also Milford [Chancellor]. Both are at Oxford, the former preaching the University Sermon, the latter conducting a university Mission.

'Function of a Cathedral' tells us a good deal about how Colin saw his post as Dean of Lincoln. Much of it is devoted to the rationale of worship, a frequent theme of Colin's sermons and at the heart of his book *Anglican Public Worship*, about which I shall have something to say below. But one or two things need to be emphasised here. After explaining that a Cathedral is the 'seat' of a diocesan bishop, which gives him the right 'to exercise episcopal jurisdiction in the diocese', and makes a cathedral the mother-church of the diocese, he goes on:

Because the cathedral is the mother-church, the seat of a bishop's pastoral authority, it has always been the aim to make it preeminent as a place of worship. To secure this, colleges or foundations of clergy and others were established and endowed. ... We have such a foundation here. And it consists not only of the Dean and Chapter and Priest Vicars – not only of clergy, that is, but of laymen also, the Organist, the Chapter Clerk, the Surveyor, Vergers, the Lay Vicars and Choristers, and the band of men who keep the fabric in repair. We are together a society banded together for the worship of God in the Bishop's Church.

J.H. Srawley, the retired Chancellor of Lincoln and distinguished scholar, with whom Colin and Mary had stayed before their furniture arrived, also emphasised in a contribution to the Diocesan Magazine written before Colin's sermon was preached, that a recent act of Canon Law made it possible for deans and even bishops to hold (unendowed) prebends, and thus 'brings all dignitaries into the full fellowship of the one body' of the cathedral Chapter. This theme of the brotherhood of the cathedral foundation was very important to Colin.

His next diary entry, on 17/2/50, tells us that he has been since 6 Feb 'stricken with flu' and has been for the greater part of the time in bed:

I therefore missed the Assizes and the visit thereto of the Lord Chief Justice and Sir John Morris, much to my disappointment. Our Finnish maid [Monna] arrived on 9th Feb. Preparations for the General Election are proceeding which means that the papers are full of quarrelling, mud-slinging and ineptitude ... Yesterday the Bishop motored Mary and me to Grimsby (introducing us to Lord and Lady Yarborough en route). We looked at St James's church and then returned by a pleasant route over the wolds to Market Rasen... The house is getting ship-shape.

After a break of almost eight weeks he wrote: '10th April, Easter Monday':

Mattins at 7.30. I acted as Gospeller at 8am Mass. After 9.45 Sung Eucharist I interviewed one Hayman, a theological student who wanted to discuss a curacy. He was a 'Power' in the War Office, it seems, and has written part of its official history. I recommended Henfield as a title and he seemed interested. I have written to the vicar. After lunch I walked about the Minster talking to sight seers. I want to acquire the art of doing this evangelistically. The Srawleys came to tea, after which I visited the prison. I find the locking of the cells after visits a difficult art. We dined with Harry Crookshank at the White Hart and met the Lord Chancellor and his lady (Lord and Lady Jowitt) and Lord Robinson, the head of the Forestry Commission. We dined well and drank a lovely Mosel wine. Both Lord and Lady Jowitt were most friendly, but I can't say I liked either. They were kind enough to approve my Easter Sermon. She belongs to the Church of Scotland while he is I should say a nominal adherent of the C of E.

Colin's next diary entry was written a little over one year later and comes as a shock. It is dated 16 April 1951:

I wish I liked my colleagues but, with the exception of the Subdean [Canon Cook], I cannot say, after 15 months experience, that I do. Even with the Subdean it seems unlikely that our personal relations will ever grow closer. We are really foreigners to each other, though I think mutually conscious of some genuine spark of affinity. The Precentor, in spite of his benevolent manner, can barely conceal his hostility and has never shown any attempt at a friendliness which goes beyond correct behaviour. For my part I find his sentimental Anglo-Catholicism almost nauseating and his evident resolution to concede nothing presents a bleak front. The Chancellor, having become a Pacifist, makes almost any attempt to pass beyond conventional politeness all but impossible. He has no manners either on the superficial or a more profound plane. The Archdeacon presents nothing either to like or dislike: he is scarcely a person at all, but has chosen to conceal what there is of himself behind an almost comic mask of ecclesiastical urbanity.

And so I have come to the point when I wonder what I can do with myself here. I cannot work without friends and in the circle of the Chapter I have none. At the best, my work as Dean seems likely to consist in little more than an attempt to live on terms of courtesy with my associates, an attempt which will engage every ounce of spiritual strength that I have. I am haunted by the notion that this is my punishment for always having wanted to be a Dean. Perhaps God had other ideas and perhaps unconsciously I resisted them. Since I returned from the Middle East in March I have experienced misery greater than any I have ever known before.

Four months later we find this:

20/8/51 I wonder how long I shall be able to stand this place. I feel bound hand and foot. I do not believe that either Cook or the Bishop of Grimsby wishes to do other than retain for themselves complete freedom of initiative in their own spheres and that both are determined to ignore my presence completely whenever it suits them. The Bishop [of Lincoln] also now begins to be standoffish. This may be due to his tiredness and need of a holiday but he has the reputation of hating to be thwarted in any plan and it seems that he was determined that the Archdeacon's stall business should be settled in his own way. Now that the Chapter has decided otherwise he seems determined to count it for unrighteousness to me [The Chapter minutes record that only the Bishop of Grimsby voted for Bishop Harland's preference]. I feel myself in a wholly new situation surrounded by people who appear to be more interested in power than anything else. I do not know how to face it; it is so shocking and so unfamiliar that I find myself without resources. May God help me through it. The prospect is bleak.

One may be reminded here of the occasion during his curacy at St Mary's, Primrose Hill, when he wrote in the same almost despairing and hopeless way about his ministry. On both occasions these outbursts may be seen as reactions on returning to 'the daily round, the common task', in the former case after an invigorating holiday, and in the latter after a highly interesting mission (his Middle East tour with the RAF). But there was clearly more to it in the case of Lincoln. When Colin took up his post as Dean, he may have been too sanguine about the chances of being able to transform the Chapter into a body of men who all felt part of a 'brotherhood' in 'full fellowship', and agreed with his conception of how this should be worked out in practice. The Bishop of Grimsby, ordained deacon in 1897, had been a Canon of the Cathedral since 1933, Subdean between 1933 and 1937, and Precentor from 1937, as well as being Bishop of Grantham from 1935, and then transferred to Grimsby in 1937. Canon Cook, about ten years junior to the Bishop of Grimsby, had been even longer in Lincoln diocese, and, after serving his title at Grantham Parish Church and ministering at another church there and one at Boston, had been Vicar of St Faith's, Lincoln, from 1921 to 1924 and then of St Peter in Eastgate with St Margaret's, less than 100 yards from the west front of the Cathedral, and had then held the important living of Boston Parish Church from 1931 to 1946, before he came back to Lincoln as Canon and Subdean.

Both of these men, thoroughly steeped in Lincoln ways, no doubt found it hard to submit to a new and younger Dean who had never served in the diocese and yet felt so strongly about the changes he advocated. The Chancellor and the Archdeacon of Lincoln – neither of them, as far as I know, hostile to Colin's general approach to running a cathedral – had both come to Lincoln in 1947, the latter moving very soon after Colin's arrival to be Bishop of Southampton and Canon of Winchester, and the former moving away in 1958 to be Master of the Temple. Again, unlike Durham Cathedral, which had once been a Benedictine monastery ruled by its Abbot, Lincoln Cathedral began as a Minster church, one originally staffed by a community of Mission priests which lacked the hierarchical structure and customs of an abbey.

Colin's depression, as manifested in the diary passages transcribed above, was therefore partly the result of his new post, which gave him no special authority beyond that of any other of the five Residentiary Canons. It is interesting to contrast his situation with that of Dean Alington at Durham. After a year or so of Chapter meetings there, it had seemed increasingly to Colin that Alington, the direct successor of a line of powerful abbots (and, of course, former Headmaster of Eton), had tried hard to persuade his colleagues that they should see themselves and him as a body of equal friends trying to decide what they should jointly do, though making sure in practice that his own opinion would prevail.

There are no more such despairing diary entries about his deanery after the ones I have quoted, but as there are very few entries of any kind, he must have felt more and more strongly that he had no time or energy for keeping a record of his ministry in Lincoln. Apart from two and a half pages written while attending the Lambeth Conference in 1958, there are no more entries after the end of March 1954, except for his separate account of his journey to the USA for the Anglican Congress in Minneapolis in August of that year (see Chapter 17). We have also to remember that his health was gradually deteriorating during the Lincoln days, while the scope of his responsibilities continued to increase. However, my own memories of Lincoln tell me that Colin got on very well with the men who succeeded the chapter members in post when he arrived in 1950.

In 1952 he completed his book, *Anglican Public Worship,* and handed in the manuscript to SCM Press during a three-day visit to London in January. His diary entry for the 17th first mentions a meeting of the Standing Committee of the Central Council for the Care of Churches, during which the plans for the new Coventry Cathedral were discussed. 'At the afternoon session', he wrote, 'we had Hugh Easton on the map for a window and I was deputed to formulate our criticisms.' The same evening there was a:

> reception given by Mrs Wand [wife of the then Bishop of London] in Central Hall for the Week of Prayer for Unity. Mostly Anglo-Catholic clergy, tho' I met Fr Pilkington of Westminster Cathedral and had some talk with him. Then a meeting, not very well attended, at which Kirk (of Oxford) spoke; also the Presbyterian Dr W.D.Maxwell of Glasgow and a very pleasant R.C. priest George Dwyer with whom I had much good conversation at the subsequent dinner at St Ermyn's Hotel. Stayed night at Priory of S. Paul, Community of the Resurrection, in Holland Park.

Next day he writes:

> I declined the invitation to celebrate as I do not approve of the system of private masses in use at the priory. Went to SCM Press to take my MS of *Anglican Public Worship*, now complete, and had some talk with [Ronald] Gregor Smith [Managing Director of the Press]. It will not be published for 15 months. Then went to see John Jagoe at the RAF club, over for a few weeks from Bermuda [where he was now Bishop], after which I lunched sumptuously with Sibyl at the Empress Club, Dover St, where she is giving up her membership. She seemed well and in full command of herself, and wore an almost jaunty little coat of sheepskin, with red hat and skirt. Called on Walter at 5pm.

On the following day he:

> Preached at S. Matthew's Westminster in connection with the Week of Prayer for Xtn unity. Not a bad congregation for a Saturday morning. Frank Biggart, C.R., played the organ – an unexpected accomplishment – the ceremonial was 'Western'. I wore black chimere and fur scarf to emphasise the Anglican nature of our allegiance. Returned to Lincoln in afternoon. Dined at the White Hart with the Conservative Political Centre's conference; met the Duke of Rutland, Sir Gyles Isham, and Peter Bailey. A delightful evening with excellent speeches.

Anglican Public Worship duly appeared in early 1953, and was very well received. The first edition does not discuss liturgical change, but the work was republished in 1961 with a new chapter on the subject, and remained in print for a good many years, appearing also in paperback. It was re-issued in 2012 in a paperback edition by the American publisher Wipf & Stock, of Eugene, Oregon. Their blurb runs as follows:

'I know of no book which does precisely what Bishop Dunlop's book does,' the Archbishop of York has written. First published in 1953, *Anglican Public Worship* has been valued by Anglicans and non-Anglicans alike for 'the balance of its exposition, its sharp clarity, its felicity of illustration, its temper of sweet reasonableness' (*Church Quarterly Review*); 'such confidence and persuasiveness and religious concern' (*British Weekly*). It has become the standard introduction to its subject, and it is now republished with a new chapter on Prayer Book revision [the one written for the 1961 edition], based on Bishop Dunlop's experience as Chairman of the Liturgical Commission of the Church of England from its formation until 1960.

The *Lincolnshire Echo*'s reviewer emphasises that the main value of the work lies in its explanatory power: 'Anglican public worship *explained*. The Dean of Lincoln ... has done it, and done it well', since he is 'a master in the art of explanation', and deals both with its origin and its nature. Thomas Christie, who was Chancellor of Peterborough Cathedral in the late 1990s, describes it in his sermon for St Peter's Day, 1999, as Colin's distillation of his 'lifelong vision of what it was to stand in the (cathedral) tradition and hand it on enhanced for future generations'. Thomas Christie was ordained in Lincoln Cathedral, after training at the Theological College (The Bishop's Hostel) and recalls Colin as 'a tall nervous man who preached powerfully at Mattins, twisting his episcopal ring behind his back whilst he spoke'.

Colin's book is underlain by a favourite theme of his in sermons and informal talks to different groups of people: what it is like to be human. He was, of course, not a teacher of philosophy as an academic discipline, but as a highly intelligent and well-read person reflecting on human life. Thus in Chapter One, 'The Justification of Public Worship', Colin appeals to the human need to have *something* to worship, a need which, because man is also a social being who depends on others in all sorts of ways, can only be fully satisfied alongside others, and its object is a *perfect* being.

The brochure of the 8th annual Festival of Music within the Liturgy at Edington, Wiltshire, in 1963, quotes from the first chapter of Colin's book to set out the presuppositions of the festival. In the next chapter of the book Colin discusses 'The Background of Public Worship', that is, our consciousness of sin, and the need to break down the barrier between man and God which this brings about. The Christian message is that the perfect man Jesus Christ was able to do this, and that we, by making Christ's perfect worship of the Father our vehicle, can gradually improve our initially very imperfect worship. It follows from all this that 'worship is more than a mechanism for feeling good, more than an occasion for 'giving our vote for God', ... it is to be led into the Father's presence and to live the life of God'. In the next three chapters on 'The Materials of Worship', Colin argues successively that Words, Music and Ceremonial are all extremely important. Words, as in the Lord's Prayer, are necessary if worship is to be a social offering, Music 'enables people to worship *together* (to keep time with others) ... and enables one to go out of oneself (ecstasy)', and Ceremonial 'is the contribution of the body to the offering of the total man'.

Another Edington Festival created a whole service around processions, and Colin's little book on the subject was given a 2nd edition by Mowbrays. Colin then goes on in *Anglican Public Worship* to talk about the Book of Common Prayer, both from the point of view of its history and of its internal coherence. In Chapter Seven, 'Eucharist and Sacrifice', an extremely illuminating chapter, he begins with 'the instinct to worship God in a *costing* manner', and shows how we can understand the atoning death of Christ as prefigured in the imperfect sacrificial offerings of the Jewish temple. There follows a detailed analysis of the Order of Holy Communion, followed by a chapter on Morning and Evening Prayer. The book originally ended here, but, as already pointed out, the edition of 1961 included a chapter on 'Prayer Book Revision'.

Although Colin had met many bishops from the Protestant Episcopal Church of the United States at the 1948 Lambeth Conference (and no doubt before that), and was known to them as a liturgical scholar, it must have been the first appearance of his book which prompted the organisers of the Minneapolis Anglican Congress of 1954 to invite him to give one of the two conference addresses on the theme: 'Our Worship'. This congress was the first 'pan-Anglican' congress to be held outside the British Isles. It was attended by 657 church delegates – bishops, priests and lay men and women – and included members from every branch of the Anglican Communion except 'Chung Hua Sheng Kung Hui', as the Anglican Church in China was called until soon after the Communist Revolution of 1949, which made Chinese participation impossible. Colin was asked to speak on 'The Liturgical Life of the Anglican Communion in the Twentieth Century'. He began with a brief discussion of 'Liturgical Freedom and Responsibility', and summed it up thus:

> *Liturgical Freedom,* ... like our freedom as Christians, ... consists, *not* in being your own master, but in having the *right* master. It therefore implies the rejection of obedience to private fancies, and the acceptance of the Lordship of Christ mediated through the canons and discipline of your own Church.'

This theme had been developed in a paper Colin read to a joint meeting of the Alcuin Club and the Anglican Society, and crops up again in an address to members of the London Diocesan Clergy Convention when they met at Keble College in 1957. But the main theme of the Minneapolis paper is its survey of the development of Anglican Liturgy since the nineteenth-century Evangelical and Catholic revivals, which leads in the third section to a discussion of 'Criteria for future development'. Colin's address followed that of The Revd. Professor Massey H. Shepherd, Jr., Ph.D, of the Church Divinity School of the Pacific, on the theme of 'Our Anglican Understanding of Corporate Worship'. In his account of his visit to Minneapolis he writes of his satisfaction that both he and Dr Shepherd had kept to their briefs, so that their papers did not overlap at all. He also records what Archbishop Fisher, who attended the Congress and preached at the closing service, said later: 'The Abp told me ... that when Dr Shepherd finished, he (the Abp) felt sorry for me who had to follow as Dr S had been so good. He added that his sorrow was ill-timed for I had more than held my own.'

During the autumn months of 1954 the (English) Church Assembly voted in favour of setting up a Liturgical Commission, and Archbishop Fisher wrote to the Bishops of Lincoln (Harland) and of Winchester (Williams), who knew Colin well from Durham days, asking them whether they thought he would be a suitable chairman. They both approved this choice, and neither thought that his 'uncertain temper' or 'irritability' would prevent him from carrying out his task well. Cyril Garbett, Archbishop of York, also approved the choice, adding that Eric Milner-White, the Dean of York, who was himself an experienced liturgist, did so too. Early in 1955 Colin accepted the position, and did much to ensure that the members of the Commission were well versed in 'liturgical scholarship', as well as being experienced in parochial work and, as a body, representative of all the main streams of English churchmanship. Among others, Colin was keen to have Ronald Jasper, who, in the words of his biographer, Donald Gray, became 'the main architect of the greatest changes in the worship of the Church of England for 300 years' [see *Ronald Jasper, His Life, His Work and the ASB*]. Jasper later became Dean of York, and, in an article, 'My Development as a Liturgist', written for the 62nd Annual Report of the Friends of York Minster in 1991, called Colin his 'liturgical Godfather'. Colin had got to know him at Durham when he was a curate at St. Oswald's parish. Donald Gray enlarges on this as follows:

> Dunlop was a keen liturgist, lent books to Ronald, and stimulated his latent interest in the subject. The early contact with Colin Dunlop proved to be one of the greatest possible significance for Jasper. In 1949 Bishop Dunlop organized a clergy school at Durham to commemorate the 400th anniversary of the 1st Prayer Book. Jasper was invited by Bishop Dunlop to be among the 7 lecturers at this conference. The others, besides Bishop Dunlop himself, were Bishop Henry de Candole, D.E.W. Harrison, R.A. Beddoes, G.W.O. Addleshaw and A.S. Duncan-Jones. At the time Jasper's name must have seemed a surprising addition to such a distinguished team.

By the late autumn of 1955, the membership of the Liturgical Commission was settled. One of Colin's first tasks as Chairman, which gave him much trouble, was to find out the exact terms of reference for its work. Even after he had succeeded in getting from the Archbishop's Secretary in writing a list of three points, namely: '1. Do only what the Archbishops ask, 2. Make proposals for revised service(s) for Baptism, both of infants and of adults, 3. Propose possible amendments to other parts of the Book of Common Prayer, especially in the light of what other churches of the Anglican Communion have done', it seemed to him that this was not quite what he had earlier been led to

understand. On 7 January 1956, Colin wrote again to say he was still not really
sure he knew what the Archbishop wanted them to do, and he didn't think he'd
been successful in getting this across to some of the Commission. On the 20th
he wrote again to the Secretary pleading for an answer to his letter and
stressing that they badly needed to know what the Archbishop meant by
'alterations now ripe to be made in BCP', since two memoranda were now on
the table which suggested that 'this revision is to be far more revolutionary
than the Abp intends'.

The volume of letters at Lambeth Palace Library written and received by
the Archbishop and his successor dealing with the early days of the Liturgical
Commission does, for all its length, contain tantalising gaps, so that a
completely clear idea of Colin's part in it all is not easy to grasp. Apart from
the difficulty just described, he seems to have been handicapped by his not
being a diocesan bishop (thus not present at their meetings), and by an
uncertainty about the status of the findings of the Commission: who did they
'belong to'?, and what were the Commissioners themselves allowed to do with
them?, etc. – an uncertainty shared with other members of the Commission.
The fact is that Archbishop Fisher was primarily interested in Reforming
Canon Law, and was really not very interested in liturgy himself, though
realised that liturgical change was 'in the air', and that the lack of liturgical
discipline that had prevailed, especially in the London diocese, would be easier
to deal with after the Commission had finished its work.

At the next Lambeth Conference, in July 1958, non-diocesan bishops were
not included unless invited as advisers, as was the case with Colin.
Unfortunately he had had an operation for hernia on 13 May, which made him
for some time get tired very easily, so that he thought it best not to attend either
the opening service at Canterbury or the service at St Paul's. Even his remarks
on the conference discussions are very short. He and Mary drove down to
London on 2 July to take up temporary residence at 7 Elsworthy Road, which
was where the Vicar of St. Mary's Primrose Hill then lived. In the afternoon he
attended an English Hymnal meeting at Vaughan-Williams' house in Hanover
Terrace:

> We decided formally to issue a Shorter English Hymnal to contain about 300
> hymns together with the Psalms (pointed) and material for the Parish
> Communion. After supper Mary and I walked on Primrose Hill: all the trees
> have grown up again after their destruction in the War years. How strange it is
> to be here again after 10 years for another Lambeth Conference.

On 12 July he wrote:

> We have been in London ten days and the Lambeth Conference has been fully
> launched. Our first week was a series of full sessions at each of which one of the
> 5 main subjects was discussed. The Abp of Canterbury said the object of this
> series was that bishops not on a particular committee could ask the committee to
> consider this or that point. ... When I spoke on the Wednesday and presented the

report on the Recognition of Saints I confess I was more concerned to impress certain matters on the Conference than to ask certain questions. Michael Ebor [i.e. Michael Ramsey, Abp of York] approved my speech but the Abp of Quebec attacked it. ... The weather has been hot most of this week and the Abp's injunction to wear frock-coat and gaiters has been ignored by all save himself – even Ebor and Winton [Bp Williams, transferred from Durham] abstaining. ... Last Sunday I sang the High Mass at St Mary's and confirmed some 36 candidates after the Creed – one of them an African girl called Gloria. It was to me a moving occasion.

Ten years later, the vicar, George Timms, wrote as follows to Mary after Colin's death: 'I shall *never* forget that wonderful Confirmation which he conducted at St Mary's ten years ago, during the last Lambeth Conference when you were both at 7 Elsworthy Road. It was everything that a Confirmation should be – and Colin was so evidently an apostolic minister of Our Lord in all that he said and did. I found it a most moving experience.'

For all his personal interest in its object, Colin found his task as Chairman of the Liturgical Commission increasingly onerous, and, in 1960 felt he had to resign. Ronald Jasper, in his book *The Development of the Anglican Liturgy, 1662–1980*, refers (as Colin himself did in his letter of resignation) to his increasing deafness, which sometimes resulted in meetings of the Commission being transformed into a number of private conversations between individuals, so that Colin sometimes completely failed to know what was going on. Jasper also says that he was 'too gentle and sensitive' to stand up to Geoffrey Fisher's determination to control things while being fundamentally uninterested in liturgy. There was also what Jasper calls the 'rather ruthless opposition' of the Dean of York to the Commission's proposed new baptism services (though he was a member himself), which prompted him to send the Archbishop copies of his own much less radical revisions of the BCP services as though they constituted a Minority Report *before* the rest of the Commission had themselves had a chance to look at them.

If the Archbishop had accepted Colin's protest at this unconstitutional conduct, some kind of rapprochement might have taken place, but he dismissed it as 'a lot of fuss', and defended Milner-White's procedure. He also referred to Colin in rather scornful and derisory terms in letters to others interested in the proposed new services because Colin had once casually asked whether it might be possible to televise the dummy runs of the services so that as many of the Commission as possible could fully realise what was proposed. Geoffrey Fisher interpreted all this as illicit 'propaganda' for 'his' view, and as mere self-advertisement, as though Colin himself wanted praise and support for having 'produced the last word on baptism services'. However, after Colin's offer to resign, which he accepted, he did stress that no members of the commission had ever complained about his chairmanship, and that he 'had held their affection and loyalty'. He also thanked Colin for what he had done, and, though admitting that he had not agreed with all the Commission's findings, had the grace to write:

the way in which the Commission has taken up its tasks, and gone steadily on with profound dedication and skill, fills me with gratitude and admiration. And whatever your powers of chairmanship I know that the Commission must owe an immense amount to your own scholarship and imagination, and in these greater matters you certainly have not failed in any way.

As for the new services of initiation themselves, Jasper writes:

> They were destined to have a short, unsuccessful and rather stormy existence, but they were by no means a waste of time and energy. Much of the material was ultimately used; and the exercise in itself constituted an important element in the Commission's 'growing pains'.

Bishop Riches, who had replaced Harland as Bishop of Lincoln in 1956, got Colin to 'describe and explain the proposals for new rites of Baptism and Confirmation' which the Commission had produced under Colin's chairmanship. In his article in the Diocesan Magazine Colin explained the five principles on which their work was based:

> 1. To restore the active involvement of the whole congregation in the rites by including them, wherever possible, in the usual Sunday services.
> 2. To simplify the structure and language of the existing services, and do away with pointed references to the controversies of the sixteenth century.
> 3. To abolish the exhortation, which is decidedly unhelpful today.
> 4. To return to Early Church practice by making adult baptism the norm, deriving infant baptism from it, not vice versa.
> 5. To reunite Baptism and Confirmation according to ancient practice.

Jasper's biographer, Donald Gray, told me that the Series 3 services were in a direct line of descent from what was produced under Colin's chairmanship, but that the services in *Common Worship*, the forms in use today, are in his opinion 'a mess', and went in quite a different direction.

It is important to add here that, although Colin's Minneapolis address and his contributions to the 1958 Lambeth Conference had marked him as a cautious conservative in the matter of liturgical change, mainly on the grounds that too much change and too many alternatives confuse the ordinary worshipper (in one talk to clergy he couples some remarks on liturgical change with the OT text: 'Cursed is he who removeth his neighbour's landmark') his experience of the Commission in action together with further reflection led him to write the following passage [my translation] in an essay *'Bibel und Gebetbuch'* [Bible and Prayer Book], published in 1966 by the Stuttgart Evangelical Press and commissioned for a series on the different Christian denominations. It was probably written in 1964 or 1965 and came out with ten other papers in *Die Kirche von England*:

> In view of the evangelistic challenge of the present day, in which most even baptised people are strangers to their church, and find it difficult to understand

the language of bible and prayerbook, when all the pressures of modern life (passive forms of recreation, mass media with their hunger for the sensational, the monotony of daily labour, sordid environments) make this even harder, the Liturgical problem of the present day will not be solved by biblical studies or a new understanding of the worship of the early church. It must do for the 20th century what Cranmer did for the 16th. It must make it possible for Englishmen to take part in a divine service with understanding, one that embodies God's own revelation to men, and it must enable them to pray to God and to praise him in their own mother tongue.

Colin served for two more years on the Liturgical Commission under the chairmanship of Donald Coggan, Bishop of Bradford, during which time procedural matters were sorted out and Morning and Evening Prayer were given a fairly conservative revision. In 1962 Archbishop Fisher was succeeded by Michael Ramsey, and the Liturgical Commission ceased to be, in Jasper's words, 'a specialist group doing what the Archbishops asked, but a representative group working for the church at large'. It was also reconstituted, and many of the original members, including Colin, were not asked to serve again. Colin was deeply disappointed, but wrote to Ramsey that he would 'of course be ready from time to time to give any help that may be needed, if within my capacity'. In 1964, Donald Coggan, now Archbishop of York, stood down from the chairmanship and Ronald Jasper was appointed in his place.

I return now to another theme of Colin's installation sermon, 'Function of a Cathedral' – its emphasis on the fact that the Cathedral Foundation does not just consist of the residential canons, but includes 'the Organist, the Chapter Clerk, the Surveyor, Vergers, the Lay Vicars and Choristers, and the band of men who keep the fabric in repair.' Colin described them as the 'cathedral family' in the sermon, and always made it his business to know them well, and to show his appreciation of their work for the life and worship of the cathedral. When he became Dean, R.S. Godfrey, the Cathedral Surveyor and Clerk of Works, had already done a great deal to prevent some extremely serious damage to the east end and Chapter House of the cathedral. *The Catholic Herald* summed this up in the headline it attached to a short description of Godfrey's achievement in its issue of 5 August 1938: 'Lincoln Cathedral Saved from Collapse – 'Touch and Go' at the East End'. It may well have been for this that Godfrey was awarded the CBE. In one of Colin's first chapter meetings, in April 1950, he saw that his salary was increased from £600 to £650. Next month he wrote in the Diocesan magazine about the refurbishing of the Chapel of St Mary Magdalene and its dedication as a memorial to Bishop Hicks:

The fabric has been thoroughly cleaned by the ingenious process invented by Mr Godfrey, and the result is truly amazing ... The work has all the freshness of a new building ... The work is a wonderful tribute to the skill and genius of our cathedral Surveyor and one of which the whole diocese will be rightly proud.

Two years later he wrote in his diary:

> Went to see Godfrey on his bed of sickness. He started to tell me how he first came into Cathedral employment, but after 5 minutes he was well away, scurrying down reminiscent by-roads and we never got to the answer. I shall try again as I really want to know. [There is no record of any further attempt.]

Soon after, Godfrey was awarded a Lambeth MA as a result of Colin's petition. Not long before his death in 1953, he presented Colin with a handsomely bound Folio copy of *The History and Antiquities of the Cathedral Church of Lincoln*, London: H.G. Bohn, 1837, containing some fine engravings. It was accompanied by a letter, which ran:

> Right Reverend Sir, I should esteem it a great privilege if you would kindly accept the attached book of the Cathedral Church of Lincoln by John Britton, F.S.A., in some small recognition for your many kindnesses for which I shall ever be grateful, I have the honour to remain, Your obedient servant, Robert Godfrey.

After Godfrey's death, Colin appealed in 'Minster Notes' for subscriptions for a memorial of the man 'who served the cathedral with such skill and distinction'. A few months before that, on Good Friday, he made the following entry in his diary:

> Since I last wrote two notable people have died – Queen Mary, and then our own Mr Godfrey. He had an operation and it seemed to leave him in a state in which he no longer had the will to live. He kept saying 'I'm so tired. So tired' and could not really talk coherently. Yet physically the operation was not specially serious. It is impossible to foresee the ways in which his loss will be felt – at least by no means all the ways. What a remarkable life he has led and what great achievements, in however narrow a compass, he has had. He had not I think great or outstanding gifts, but all he had he disciplined and organised and developed for the task in hand – the preservation of the Minster and the efficient ordering of those parts of its life which came under his control. He had that eye for detail and that energy to care for detail which must characterise the successful engineer and the capable administrator. Though he loved the cathedral with ardour he had very little love of beauty. It was the sound craftsmanship of the building which held his admiration and stimulated to a high degree his powers in this direction. He was I think fond of me and being a truly humble man he rated my inevitable appreciation of him and his powers too highly. He was almost absurdly grateful for my work in getting his Lambeth Degree. I never felt quite at home with him for he was rather more sentimental than I thought comfortable. He never seemed to resent my obvious disbelief in him as an artist. I am deeply grateful for his loyalty and unfailing kindness.

Colin was also on very friendly terms with Mr Godfrey's successor as Surveyor and Clerk of Works, J.A. Higgins, whom he also respected and admired – and missed very much when he retired to Henfield, not only because he now lacked an easily accessible and cheerful helper to telephone if anything needed doing in the house! Colin made sure that he was one of those introduced to the Queen when she visited the cathedral in 1958. When he resigned the Deanery, he made a special point, in an interview with the *Lincolnshire Echo* reporter (22 October 1964), of praising the cathedral staff, 'from the choristers up to the Chapter' ... 'Above all the Cathedral owes a great debt to its surveyor, Mr J.A. Higgins, who is in charge of all the work on the cathedral fabric.'

In March 1952, Colin wrote in his diary: 'Spent most of the morning drafting an Agreement for the new verger Barrett, who arrives next week, and in composing a form of public admission and investment as Verger to be used before Mattins on his 1st Sunday.' This suggests that there had been no previous ceremony of admission. Barrett was later promoted to Dean's Verger, and retired in July 1964, when he wrote to the Dean and Chapter expressing his 'heartfelt thanks ... for all the kindnesses and considerations shown to me whilst I was with you'. After Colin's death he wrote as follows to Mary:

> I, personally, loved the Bishop sincerely – he was the best Master and friend that I ever had, and I know how dearly he loved you; so realize how much you will miss him – even more than his great loss means to all that knew him in Lincoln – there will never be another Dean to compare with him.

Although the Cathedral bell-ringers are not listed by Colin as members of the Cathedral Foundation, they surely have at least an Honorary place alongside members of the choir. Colin 's very handsome obituary of J.H. Freeman, Master of the Cathedral Company of Bell-Ringers since 1929, in the Diocesan magazine of 1961, shows this. He himself quite often went up to the ringing chamber during the ringers' practice night, and, though there is no record of his trying his own hand again at ringing, the obituary shows that he had learnt a lot about the 'ringing world'. He was, in fact, asked to be President of the Lincoln Diocesan Guild of Ringers, and, on Saturday, 31 October 1964, the Guild rang 'A peal of 5007 Stedman Cinques in 3 hours and 28 minutes (a 'Ringing World' record) as a compliment to (him) upon his retirement' (*Lincolnshire Echo*, 22/10/64). Before that the ringers had also rung a splendid peal on the occasion of my brother's wedding in the cathedral in 1962, though they had no personal knowledge of him or his wife-to-be, but wanted to show their appreciation of Colin.

I have left until last Colin's attitude to the music of the cathedral services and to his relations with Gordon Slater, who was organist and choir trainer throughout Colin's time at Lincoln, and had been in post since 1930. Colin's early impressions of the music were good, and I have already quoted diary extracts which show this. An extract from his entry of 22/2/52 suggests a gradual change of mind about this: 'At Evensong [we had] the lovely motet of Eccard, "When to the Temple Mary Went", sung rather roughly, though the choir [was] as usual at its best with Slater conducting it.' Colin's private notebook of comments on the services of the cathedral, later handed on to his successor, Dean Peck, contains much criticism of the organist's inappropriate choice of anthems and hymns for particular occasions – though Slater appears to have learnt from Colin's criticism and suggestions. The Chapter Minutes for 16/11/53 suggest that Colin had raised the question of how Slater could be got to accompany the carols in the Carol Service more softly so that the words could be heard. The Chapter agreed that, in place of a letter from the Chapter as a whole, it would be better if the Precentor (the Bishop of Grimsby) could talk to him, though it sounds as though he was reluctant to do this. However, in the event he did so, to some effect.

Colin also seems to have persuaded the Chapter to shorten the annual service in commemoration of St Hugh by getting the organist to use Merbecke's unison settings of the Communion service, rather than the usually much longer part- settings. He also suggested more appropriate anthems for Ember-days. Mary's own diary also reflects Colin's judgments of the choral music: 17/6/53 'Choir and Choral Society sang Coronation music in the Cathedral. Slater doesn't get enough contrast of volume, but some of it [was] quite exhilarating.' Despite one or two favourable comments, Colin's letter to me at Christmas 1956 expresses what he generally felt: 'the choir always seem on the verge of breaking down. ... The fact is our choir is not good enough either for the quantity or the quality of our repertory of music', and in his own diary he wrote: 'Slater has been so much used to deceiving himself about the choir, that he has got into the way of always thinking it is good, whatever the evidence. He probably can't afford to retire.'

In the late 1950s the Chapter minutes record the choir's poor discipline, and in February 1960, they agreed on a proposal to move the Deanery to the former Precentory (the Precentor, Bishop Greave, having in the mean time died) and to make the large old Victorian Deanery into part of a new Choir School, so that the practice of recruiting boys from Lincoln School, a state-run day grammar school (for which the cathedral paid £300 p.a., though this was stopped in 1957) could be brought to an end, especially as the supply of good choirboys from there seemed to be drying up. But despite Colin's feelings about the choir and organist, he seems to have remained on excellent terms with Gordon Slater, and invited him to the small wedding reception held at the new Deanery after my brother Philip's wedding to Anna-Maria Brazil in 1962. In a postcard from Scotland he sent Colin three weeks later, Slater's tone is warm and friendly, and full of gratitude. I was also told by Maurice Wilson, an amateur organist who used to visit Lincoln on holiday and talk to Gordon Slater there after evensong, that Slater 'had great respect for your late father'.

Although the Chapter Minutes contain little more than the resolutions of those present, it is not difficult to see Colin's influence on many of the decisions taken during his incumbency. Some very important changes in the cathedral, such as the decision to commission a new memorial to the great medieval Bishop of Lincoln, Robert Grosseteste, statesman, theologian and scientist (the original memorial was destroyed in the sixteenth century) are not even mentioned at all, and most of them deal with everyday matters. But, after about a year in post, Colin's concern for appropriate ornaments led to his offer of a new Lenten array for St John's Altar in the retrochoir, to be designed by Randoll Blacking, which was 'gratefully accepted'.

Then, in November 1953, the Abbey Memorial Trust, set up to promote the work of contemporary artists in churches and cathedrals, offered to pay for a set of murals in the Russell Chantry, and mentioned Duncan Grant, and four other names, as possible artists. Colin, who knew and liked the post-Impressionist murals of Duncan Grant in Berwick church in Sussex, would certainly have supported both the acceptance of the offer and the choice of Grant with genuine enthusiasm, and to have persuaded his colleagues to do the same. There are no other records in the Chapter Minutes, but after five years the murals were installed, Colin having meanwhile suggested that the main subject for them should be the wool trade – so important for the economy of the diocese in the Middle Ages. They show the patron saint of wool-combers, St Blaise, in a painted roundel over the doorway, and 'overseeing' the activities of shepherding (a beardless Christ as the Good Shepherd is prominent), sheep-shearing, and loading bales for export in Brayford Pool, the former inland port of Lincoln since Roman times.

A few years later, almost certainly after Colin's retirement in 1964, the chapel was kept locked, so that the murals could only be viewed on application to a verger. The reason given was that the space was now needed to store important or valuable items frequently used in the cathedral, but there is no doubt that the scandals arising from contemporary publicity about the Grant family's irregular life-style and the identity of the painter's models played a large part in this (see Edward Mayor's fully illustrated booklet *The Duncan Grant Murals in Lincoln Cathedral*).

Another important artistic addition to the Cathedral was the Treasury, opened in 1960, for the display of gold and silver plate from the cathedral and parish churches of the diocese, with striking display cases, fine gates of wrought iron and stained glass in the windows, largely paid for and originally proposed by the Goldsmith's Company. Lincoln was the first cathedral to have one. When the glass was inserted Colin wrote to me: 'The 'abstract' stained glass is going up in the Treasury windows and looks impressive to me. What Lord Crookshank & Co say of it I can guess!'

Other modern windows put in during Colin's time are the four large and impressive windows by Harry Stammers in the Air Force chapel. The Chapter Minutes for 28/7/52 record that he would help Sir Arthur Sims, who was paying for the first of these, 'to find an artist'. The choice of an archangel in the first window in Stammers' very un-Victorian but symbolic-naturalist style, led, very naturally, to the other three windows representing the three other archangels whose names are commonly known in the English Church, with appropriate symbols and bright colouring by Stammers.

I have already mentioned the Grosseteste Memorial, which is outside the former Chapel of SS Peter and Paul, in the south-east transept, which, after the dedication of the new ledger slab and fine votive candlesticks (by Randoll Blacking) in 1953, was called the Student's chapel because Bishop Grosseteste taught for a time at Oxford University, and combined work in theology with that in science and mathematics – a most unusual combination for the 13th century. The 1953 celebration included a lecture, which, with a memorial service, has become an annual event. The writer of Colin's obituary in *The Church Times* suggests that he was the prime mover in this Memorial, because he felt that Grosseteste had been unjustly overshadowed by the Bishop of Lincoln who was canonised: Hugh of Avalon. In a letter to Colin of 1960, a friend of his, the Jesuit priest J. Brodrick, told him: 'There are better hopes today of canonising Grosseteste, passed over because he spoke to them too straight!' He added that he was very glad to know that he had been and was still locally regarded as a Saint. If he *were* canonised, 'he would stand with St. Albert the Great, as a saint who was also a true scientist'.

There are in the South Choir Aisle of Lincoln Cathedral remains of what was called the shrine of Little Saint Hugh. On the wall near them a notice explains the name and origin of the shrine. After Colin became Dean he decided to put up a new explanatory notice because he felt that the existing one came nowhere near doing justice to the Jews of Lincoln. When the body of 'Little Saint Hugh' was discovered at the bottom of a well, he was said to have been 'ritually murdered' by the Jewish Community, though the old notice seemed to leave it open whether this really happened. So he produced a notice of his own, which began (and still begins):

> Trumped up stories of 'Ritual Murders' of Christian boys by the Jewish communities were common throughout Europe during the Middle ages ... These stories do not redound to the credit of Christendom, and so we pray: Lord, forgive what we have been, amend what we are, and direct what we shall be.

It is likely that Colin's notice did not include this particular prayer, which takes over some familiar words from the Communion Service in *Common Worship*, the latest Church of England Prayer Book, but it is very likely that he did include *some* prayer. The substitution of his own explanation, the first words of which leave no doubt about what most educated people people feel today, was very much in keeping with his liturgical changes in the worship of the cathedral, aiming always at openness, reasonableness, clarity and the beauty of holiness, at godliness and good order. A very down-to-earth example of this is recorded in the Chapter Minutes for 10 December 1956, where the Dean is recorded as having 'pointed out that the rows of seats in the nave were too close for kneeling.' It was therefore resolved 'to ask the Clerk of Works to provide trial rows of chairs to make this possible.'

Colin devised many special services while he was at Lincoln, and took great care about the details. I have noted in a previous chapter his insistence that liturgical processions should have some obvious and justifiable rationale, and not be carried out just for the sake of moving about, or for display. His private notes on 'services on special days' give a good idea of the practices he felt he had to abolish or improve at Lincoln. These begin as early as 1950. He commented thus on an ordination service in that year: 'The ordination was on the whole well done, though the goings and comings suffer from raggedness and bad walking.' He adds that the Deacon ought to have read the Gospel among the people and be escorted there by his fellow-deacons, and suggests that the Bishop should intone *Veni Creator* and that the candidates 'should not wear hoods'.

After the main service on All Saints Day he wrote: 'a long procession is surely out of proportion when so few people attend', and bewailed the fact that some of the clergy were disregarding the old practice of reserving the sedilia (stone seats near the altar) during the sermon at the Sung Eucharist for those who read the Gospel and Epistle. After the Solemn Eucharist on Christmas Day he records 'An aimless procession as on other days, without goal or meaning, and this time without lay participants'. If there are to be processions 'people should be told *beforehand* to join in'. After the Mothers' Union Triennial Service in 1957 he ended his account thus: 'at the beginning, the Diocesan Banner was preceded by the Cross and carried down the nave to meet the banners from the parishes – a poor, meaningless, ceremony.'

At the first service for the 'Solemn Commemoration of Robert Grosseteste' in 1953, the first rubrics on the service sheet (the service was begun in the nave) run as follows:

> At 2.15pm the Graduates of Universities will enter from the Chapter House.
> At 2.20pm the Lord Lieutenant, the Lord Privy Seal, the High Sheriff, and the Judges of the Lincolnshire County Courts, are met at the West door.
> At 2.25pm the Members of Parliament, the Mayors of Lincolnshire Boroughs and the Mayor and Sheriff of Lincoln enter from the West End, while the Lay Vicars and Choristers enter from the South Choir Aisle.
> At 2.30pm the Carol 'Sing all good people gathered' will be sung. As it begins, the Chairmen of County Councils (and) of Education Committees, the Directors of Education, the representatives of Universities and the Vice-Chancellor and Chancellor of Oxford University will come up the Nave from the West end, while at the same time the Bishops of Lincoln and London with the Dean and Chapter of Lincoln enter from the Choir.

The carol referred to, from the *Mainz Gesangbuch*, translated by Geoffrey Dearmer, was followed by a versicle and a response, short introductory prayers, and the announcement of an anthem (Parry's 'I was glad when they said unto me', from Psalm 122). The first lesson is preceded by this explanation: 'The First Lesson (Ecclesiasticus 51, vv 13–22), which speaks of that zeal for wisdom that burned in the heart of Robert Grosseteste, will then be read by the Chancellor of Oxford University.' There followed a hymn ('Bright the vision that delighted'), and then the second lesson, which 'tells of the spiritual warfare of the apostle which Grosseteste also knew. It will be read by a Friar of the Society of S. Francis.' Then followed another hymn: The Golden

Sequence. 'It may have been written by Stephen Langton, a Lincolnshire man, whom Grosseteste probably knew.' Bishop Wand, of London, then preached the sermon, after which came the 'Procession to the Tomb' and the Singing of the hymn 'St Patrick's Breastplate'. Then (I quote the rubric), 'when the procession has reached S.Peter's chapel and all are conveniently arranged, the Vice-Chancellor of Oxford University will briefly rehearse the titles and principle acts of Robert Grosseteste as follows'; the short c.v. ends: 'He was a man of learning and an inspiration to scholars, a wise administrator while a true shepherd of his flock; ever concerned to lead them to Christ in whose service he strove to temper justice with mercy: hating the sin while loving the sinner: not sparing the rod, though cherishing the weak.' The Dean then says: 'When the body of Bishop Robert was first laid here, the place was marked by "a goodly tomb of marble with an image of brass over it". But in the course of time men in whom zeal burned stronger than charity destroyed it.' '(Now, with financial help from many sources), a new memorial has been set up, and this, Reverend Father in God, we now invite you to bless and dedicate.' This prayer follows:

> Almighty Father, who didst endow thy servant Robert with notable gifts of heart and mind; of thy mercy forgive those who with unheeding fervour wrought violence in this sanctuary: Accept at our hands this offering of graven stone and gilded bronze, that in its turn it may recall to the minds of men the wisdom, fortitude, and godliness of him whose body still lies at rest beneath. Grant this for the sake of Jesus Christ our Lord, who with thee and the Holy Ghost livest and reignest one God world without end.

The choir then sang in Latin: 'The souls of the righteous are in the hand of God, and there shall no torment touch them. In the sight of the unwise they seemed to die, but they are in peace' and Bishop Wand 'made pronouncement' in a short dedicatory prayer, while with 'the tip of his pastoral staff' he 'traced the form of a cross'. The procession then returned in reverse order 'by way of the Choir back to the Nave' during the singing of Abelard's hymn (tr. J.M. Neale) 'O what their joy and their glory must be'. Intercessions, with versicles, and responses for the congregation, followed, and then the Blessing, and there were more directions about how and in what order the various groups should leave the nave. On the final page we read, among much else: 'Tea has been provided for 800 people at the Castle, where a marquee has been erected. On presenting your ticket at the gate, you will be able to buy a tea-ticket for 2/6.'

The collection of Colin's special services in the Cathedral Library includes another, undated, Service of 'Solemn Commemoration' of Bishop Grosseteste, rather shorter and simpler, to be used at the annual services after 1953. There is only one lesson, from a different chapter of Ecclesiasticus (43, vv 1–12 and 27–33) and some different prayers. The biggest change is 'A Praise of God in Honour of Bishop Grosseteste', which consists of a more detailed life of the Bishop divided into short passages spoken by the Dean, with the repeated congregational response 'Blessed be God'. Here are two passages, which account for Father Brodrick's remark above about Grosseteste's fearless plain-speaking, which, after his death stood in the way of his canonisation:

> Praise be to God that this good bishop so valued the unity and strength of Christ's Holy Church that, though he revered the Pope as a cardinal instrument in God's hands for man's salvation, yet with courage he demanded that his authority be exercised in accordance with God's laws.
>
> Praise be to God for this high prelate who taught both kings and priests their duties, who knew everyone and feared nobody, who was the friend of those who prized the independence and the welfare of this country.

On the day after the first Commemoration service, with the dedication of the new Memorial (28/6/53), Mary recorded her memories and impressions as follows:

> The great Grosseteste Commemoration now safely over!' It all went exceedingly well with a minor crisis when Maurice Bowra (Vice-Chancellor) arrived from Oxford without his reading glasses – essential as he has to read a part of the service. However Curry & Paxton produced a pair which fitted and lent them to him!
>
> The lunch with the Lord Lieutenant was delightful; *lashings* of smoked salmon, very good chicken, etc, and strawberries and cream put us all in a good temper. I had the Vice-Chancellor and Judge Shove, Lady Middleton opposite, with the Bishop – at the Lord Lieutenant's end. Colin had Mrs Shove and Mrs Harland, Lady Welby opposite. We enjoyed it very much and were sorry to have to leave so that he could see to arrangements and I get dressed up in my cap and gown. Mrs Eric Kemp arrived from Oxford with a cap for me, and I went over to the Chapter House with her, also with Mary Fenton and Mrs Riches who is also a graduate. There we found a seething mob of caps and gowns with the Sub-Dean (Cook) in charge. Having organised the procession with the Doctors in front, and Oxford MAs next, we proceeded into Church, Pat Kemp and I and Mrs Phillips finding ourselves in a good strategic position in the front row behind the Doctors. The various Processions came in slightly otherwise than was laid down in the Service sheet, but not so that anyone would notice and all got safely and with dignity to their proper seats.
>
> The service Colin had drawn up was most impressive and all the congregation sang the hymns *magnificently* in spite of Slater's worst efforts at the organ. The choir sang 'I was Glad' (Parry) really well. The Bishop of London preached a very good, interesting and even quite learned sermon, but too fast for the microphones I fear. All listened very quietly.
>
> Then came the procession to the tomb which was most moving. The singing of St Patrick's Breastplate got a little ragged but the choir singing the verse 'Christ be with me' unaccompanied at the transept was simply lovely. We heard the words of the dedication very well over the microphone, and then they came back singing '*O quanta qualia*' [the Abelard hymn]. All joined in and sang like anything. It was grand.
>
> Afterwards we all went over in our robes and there was tea in the castle grounds. I was a little anxious trying to get round and see that all the notables

were being cherished and getting tea, but everyone seemed cheerful and enjoying life. We got them all away in time to come home for rest and baths before going to the Oxford dinner ... at the Saracen's Head. We went down in the Vice-Chancellor's car in great comfort. The dinner was good. I sat between Sir Maurice Powicke [the Grosseteste Lecturer] and Mr Birkbeck. The Bishop made a careful speech with a good deal of mugged up history – Maurice Bowra made a superbly witty and ebullient reply. Then Colin spoke very nicely in proposing the guests' health and Sir Maurice Powicke replied rather long-windedly, but with great sincerity and charm. He is a sweet creature. We returned [to the deanery] and sat for a little while over the remains of our whisky while Maurice effervesced in talk and enjoyment. It was a good end to a wonderful day. This morning he drove off to Oxford after breakfast – but *found* his own spectacles in the seat of the car as he was driving off!

Some of Colin's special services are additions to or adaptations of Mattins or Evensong, others, like the Grosseteste Memorial and Dedication, are wholly new. There are many thanksgiving services, services to mark special occasions, such as anniversaries, some of them annual, as in harvest festivals, or ones to coincide with some special local or national celebration, or thanks for scouting and guiding for the young, services of dedication, such as one for teachers in 1960, or as preparation for the new monarch (as in the Preparation Service for the Coronation of Queen Elizabeth II). There is a Christmas Gift Service, with many carols and lines from traditional Nativity Plays, the acting out of the visits of the Shepherds and Wise men at Christ's Birth, with the giving of real gifts by members of the cathedral foundation and the congregation. There are also services for the Inauguration and Dedication of the Lincoln Cathedral Treasury, the Dedication of the Bomber Command Memorial Window, a Battle of Britain Remembrance and thanksgiving service, a Thanksgiving for an 'Act of Praise by Officers and Members of the National Health Service in Lincolnshire', thanks for 100 years of the County Constabulary, or for the Return of the First Batallion of the Royal Lincolnshire Regiment from service abroad and many others.

These services are intended both as acts of worship, and also as important instruments of the Cathedral's mission to the city and the county or diocese, to get people who might not otherwise acknowledge the religious dimension in their lives to see its importance in connection with their work or in some human institution that was in some other way part of their lives. Colin was of course fully aware that some aspects of worship in cathedrals might possibly have a contrary, even off-putting, effect on non-churchgoers. In a sermon he was asked to preach in Westminster Abbey to The National Federation of Cathedral Old Choristers Associations he distinguished between the three types of worship cathedrals provide: the basic services which are their *raison d'etre*, the Sunday worship of local congregations analogous to the worship in parish churches, and the special services provided for organisations and professionals who may be quite unfamiliar with Christian worship. Just as different kinds or styles of music needed to be chosen by the choirmasters, so the composers of special services had to find language and material appropriate to the task in hand.

When Colin retired in 1964 there was a widespread hope in the Diocese that the Alcuin Club would publish a volume of these services, presumably with an introduction about the principles of their composition, and their importance in the Church's mission. Colin had kept up his membership of the Club since serving his title at Primrose Hill (though its activities virtually ceased during the war), and in 1955 he was asked (possibly not for the first time) whether he would be Chairman, though felt he could not accept. However, he acted *as* chairman at several meetings during this period, and signed the Minutes. In 1956 he was asked to take over as President, as Dr Wand, the Bishop of London, had resigned, but again felt he had to refuse. Pressure of his work as Dean led even to his resigning from the Committee in 1959.

Two years later, when he was asked to write a 'textbook' on Liturgy, he replied that he would like to have done it, but for the next two years he would be absorbed in business cares, 'for nearly all the Chapter members have changed'. In 1962 he was back on the Committee again, and the minutes report that at the society's AGM he introduced an informal discussion on 'Ceremonial in the Church of England today', which provoked a lively debate. Two years later he wrote to the Chairman, Dr Lowther Clarke, saying: 'I am glad you think the AC might have some use for a booklet on Special Services. I have most of the material by me but I shall not be able to start until after Easter. I hope you will allow me to have one or more ground plans of Lincoln Cathedral, so that readers can tell how the processions go.' Later in 1964 he told the committee that, as his retirement was imminent 'the completion of the manuscript would be delayed'. He retired in October, and, though he was present at a Committee meetings in February and July 1965, the minutes make no mention of his projected book, and it is clear that he never did manage to finish it.

One reason why he could not find time for these new publications before retiring arose from the again urgent need to raise new funds for the Cathedral fabric. This occupied much of his time almost from the beginning of his work as Dean. I have already mentioned the restorative work of R.S. Godfrey on the east end of the cathedral, but the reasons for the damage repaired by him had not perhaps been fully established in his time, and in 1955 the Clerk of Works was authorised by the Dean and Chapter to buy an instrument to measure vibrations in the ground outside the east end caused by the growing problem of slow-moving heavy lorries and buses grinding up to the top of the hill in low gear on the road which passes about 30–50 yards from the very foundations of the building, and then perhaps having to stop with engine still throbbing to allow oncoming traffic to come through a narrow archway.

In 1956 Colin, who was Chapter representative on the Development and Publicity Committee of Lincoln City Council, managed to get the Council to share the costs of special vibratory tests, and a few years later announced that at least £200,000 would be needed to do 'urgent work' on the fabric. In 1963 he wrote a special report on it for the Diocesan magazine, explaining that 'until 1939', Lincoln was 'one of the best cared-for churches anywhere'. But during the war and for a few years after it, 'even routine maintenance was impossible'. At the time of his writing the permanent staff of the works office numbered 14, whereas before the war there were 25. I remember how Colin would write letter after letter in his own hand to people he felt might have access to funds which they might be willing to use in supporting the cathedral financially, like, for example, the mayors of all the places in the British Empire he could find called 'Lincoln', or had material or ancestral links with the city. One appeal, to a small town in the USA, produced a reply from the Chamber of Commerce, Weatherford, Texas, addressed to 'The Very Right, The Dean of Lincoln....', which caused much innocent mirth in the family. Colin, of course, did not do all the work of fund-raising himself, but he undoubtedly inspired others to take up the cause.

When his successor as Dean, Michael Peck, wrote in his introduction to the Pamphlet issued on the occasion of the Cathedral's Jubilee in 1966, thanking those who had already contributed to the 1963 appeal and giving an account of the funds that were still needed, he finished his piece: 'May I add one personal note? I have not yet been here two years; but I came in January 1965, to find a Treasurer of the Appeal, a Secretary of the Appeal, an Architect and a Clerk of Works, with his staff, such as would be the envy of any Dean in the world. I add my sincere word of personal gratitude.' Colin's fund-raising had also born fruit in another field. In the Chapter Meeting of March 1955 he was thanked for his work in raising £3570/14/2 from the sale of a Cathedral library book entitled *The Fifteen Capital Laws of New England*. 'His initiative and hard work in finding a buyer (in the U.S.A.) has provided a sum to be invested in a maintenance fund for books in the library.'

Bofore I go on to say something of Colin's work in the City and County of Lincoln, I shall return briefly to the topography of the City. One result of this is to make it seem almost as though the 'uphill' part, on the top of the scarp, is not only topographically but also socially and culturally quite distinct from the 'downhill' part in the valley of the River Witham below. This impression was more pronounced soon after the war, during Colin's time as Dean, since the downhill area still contained much heavy industry, two railway stations with their attendant sheds, marshalling yards and coaling stations, what remained of the 'Port' of Lincoln, and many streets of small terrace houses. This gave it a more 'working-class' appearance, whereas the uphill area, quite apart from being the oldest settled area (it began as a Roman 'colony') and containing the cathedral and castle, had nothing 'industrial' about it, and made a much more 'genteel' impression.

Closer examination could, of course, greatly, though not entirely, reduce the differences, but, as a young man growing up in the shadow of the cathedral, I often heard remarks that tended to strengthen the impression of an important difference. I think now that human beings are nearly always influenced to some extent by topography, and that the 'uphill/downhill' social and cultural differences at Lincoln could never be entirely done away. But there is in the Lambeth Palace archive a letter written by Bishop Riches which seems to challenge this. Dated 14 September 1964, it was written to the Archbishop's Patronage Secretary in response to an enquiry whether he thought that Eric Kemp, later Bishop of Chichester, would make a good successor to Colin as Dean. The Bishop advises against this suggestion, because he felt that Colin and Eric Kemp were too similar, whereas, he writes:

> you know from the enquiries you have made that there is a very general desire that the new Dean should be a man of very different outlook and temperament, able to move out easily amongst people, with a strong personal concern to make the Cathedral the mother church of both the diocese and the city. Such a man would be able to bring to life so much of the excellent liturgical work of the present Dean. ... The right Dean could finally destroy the old uphill/downhill traditions.

The Bishop also repeats what others had said to the Archbishops before, that Colin is 'shy and diffident and of a very uncertain temper', but immediately adds to this phrase another: 'lacking any real pastoral sense or concern'. He goes straight on: 'As a result the influence of the Cathedral, both in the diocese and county, has greatly suffered.' He ends his letter by saying that we need a dean:

> with warm and generous qualities, not too concerned with the pedantries of ecclesiastical life and affairs, which would enable the cathedral to be in the vanguard of the life of the Church in the diocese.

Perhaps the bishop was right, that the Cathedral did need a different kind of Dean, and that therefore he was right to deprecate the suggestion of the Patronage Secretary, but it is not in the least clear to me that Colin lacked 'real pastoral sense and concern'. Colin certainly was very shy in some social situations. This is apparent in some press photographs, for example one in the *Lincolnshire Echo* of 23 April 1953, where Colin is seen in gaiters, frock coat and pectoral cross in a group of guests at the 'Lincoln Red Shorthorn Society's dinner'. He doesn't look at his ease standing in a group of farmers and others interested in this particular breed of cattle (though his expression is partly due to a *general* dislike of being photograped by the Press). And he certainly wasn't 'able to move out easily among people' he didn't know or with whom he suspected he wouldn't have much in common. In May 1959 Mary told me in a letter:

> (Colin) and I were the Mayor's Guests at a reception and dance given for the Annual Meeting of the National Institute of Water Engineers. The Mayor insisted on our joining his supper party later. It was quite an ordeal. (Colin)

looked magnificent in his evening dress. But, as the only representatives of the Church, I daresay it did some good.

Mary omitted to say here that Colin hated dancing in clerical dress because it made him too conspicuous. In any case it seems unlikely that Colin would have continued to be asked by the Royal Air Force to visit stations abroad after 1943 if he had had no real pastoral sense. On his retirement, the writer of 'Minster Notes' (a regular contribution to the Diocesan magazine), made a point of calling attention to his 'great gifts as a pastor', as, indeed, others did in different ways. Colin was spiritual adviser to several clergy in the diocese, and what I have heard from some of them strongly reinforces this description. But it is also true that he *was* diffident, and that his 'warm and generous qualities' were not always apparent to others in unstructured social situations. During my National Service I had written about the problems I myself faced standing about in the Officers' Mess and talking to people I didn't know. Colin wrote in a reply to this:

> I do so agree with you on the misery of perpetual standing-talking on Mess dining-in evenings. Very wearisome, but you would do well not to dislike them too openly but to work at them a bit, otherwise people would, quite wrongly, put you down as unsociable.

It *is* also plausible to suggest that his concern to 'get everything right' in liturgical matters might sound pedantic, but most of the things Colin stood for in this sphere were, he believed, for the greater glory of God, and were not personal fads. Many of those who wrote to my mother on Colin's death in 1968 make a point of emphasising in various ways the cumulative effect of this concern, and would almost certainly have felt as did the Right Reverend and Mrs Michael Manktelow. The Bishop wrote to me: 'The dignity and devotion with which he inspired the worship of Lincoln Cathedral made a lasting impression on us both.'

Colin's cuttings book records something which might possibly be thought at first to have exacerbated uphill/downhill relations. The *Lincolnshire Chronicle* report of the 1953 Harvest Festival service in the Cathedral begins:

> At their November meeting members of the Lincoln and District Trades Council took exception to remarks made by the Dean of Lincoln in his sermon at the harvest thanksgiving service at Lincoln Cathedral. They protested against such passages as 'work was done only for wages and salaries, and they were regarded as a sort of compensation for the inconveniences of it', and his mention of a 'deepening disgust and shyness for work'. Members described such remarks as 'half-truths' and others declared that 'workers were not mercenary to this degree'.

So a letter was sent to Colin setting out the Trades Council's views, and, at their next meeting (on a Sunday, when he would not have been able to attend in person) Colin's reply was read aloud to those present. After declaring how pleased he had been to know that the Trades Council members had attended the service, the Dean declared that he had noted the resolution regarding his sermon and stated: 'the Council is not the first body to find me unsatisfactory'. He went on to say that it was unlikely he would again preach at the service for five or six years, and added:

> I hope that on future occasions you will find the sermons more helpful. The Dean again thanked the Trades Council for attending the service and said they were always glad to have the organisation represented. The reading of the letter was received with good-natured laughter.

Colin had in fact preached this sermon at the Liverpool Cathedral Harvest Festival the previous year. Although the headline of the *Liverpool Daily Post*'s account is 'Dean Hits Out at "Distaste for Work"', the text of the sermon suggests that Colin's more negative generalisations were put more in the form of a question ('is it not true that ...?'), and he also says that reluctance to work 'was observable at all levels in the social scale' – so not just a 'downhill' phenomenon.

> [The Dean] thought that the reasons for the current growing distaste for work were partly due to the teachings of a false belief that all the difficulties of life could be removed by political action. According to this theory the possibilities of an easy life for all lay just around the corner. Suggesting that a waning belief in God was responsible for the situation, the Dean said when religion disappeared from daily life disenchantment grew, the world became a grey place, and nothing was worth while. Worshipping filled life with zeal and meaning. Work well done is one of the principle ways to serve God. The work is cleansed of its sting and drudgery, and becomes a noble thing. However ordinary it may be on the surface, it can, by the grace of God, take on an inner quality of glory.

The eight hundred worshippers at Liverpool were advised not to leave their work behind when they came to church but to offer it in prayer.

I have already mentioned that Colin was the Cathedral Chapter representative of the City Development and Publicity Committee. This certainly brought him into frequent contact with the Mayor and Corporation of the city, whose headquarters were in the Stonebow, which is 'downhill'. Colin's diary entries for 6 and 7 February 1952, are interesting in this connection:

> 6/2/52 King George's death. Arrangements for passing bell made – one stroke a minute on Great Tom for one hour and then the Nine Tailors. At Evensong we prayed for our Sovereign Lady Queen Elizabeth but in the Prayer for the Royal Family we omitted all names pending instructions from the Lord Chamberlain. I have cancelled my visit to King's College, Cambridge on Sunday.

7/2/52 Queen Elizabeth and the Duke of Edinburgh arrived from Kenya. Soon we shall get details of the funeral and can make our plans for the memorial Service. Largely at my instigation one of the places from which the Queen will be proclaimed tomorrow will be the West door of the cathedral.

A *Lincolnshire Echo* photograph shows the Mayor, Councillor T.F. Taylor, right arm outstretched, leading schoolchildren 'in three hearty cheers for the Queen', while Colin and the Bishops of Lincoln and Grimsby cheer in more restrained fashion, one or two army officers salute, and two civic officials in the ancient garb of their office stand to attention below, 'presenting arms' with sword and mace.

I must now say a little more about Colin's work in the City and Diocese, which went beyond being present at various of social and symbolic occasions. As at Durham, he was keen to establish good relations with industry, and I well remember him taking my brother and me to visit the huge factory of Ruston Bucyrus in Lincoln, which made heavy building and landscaping equipment such as bulldozers and walking draglines. We were also taken to see the Appleby Frodingham steel rolling mills at Scunthorpe, felt the heat of furnaces being stoked and of molten metal being moved around on a little railway from one building to another, and watched in amazement, safe behind glass, as cuboids of red-hot steel were gradually pressed and rolled into the shape of girders.

Nearer to home, we were, as a family, regular patrons of the Theatre Royal (downhill), which had a good repertory company. The actors were always invited to the Deanery at Christmas for mulled wine, mince pies and carol singing, and Colin was fairly soon asked to become vice-president of the Theatre Club. He was clearly also known in the Usher Gallery, Lincoln's own Art Gallery, since somebody connected with it had discovered that he had been a friend of the once well-known tenor Gervase Elwes, and he was asked to give a talk about him in the Gallery. Joan Varley, who was in the audience, mentioned it in her letter of condolence to Mary after Colin's death, which included the following passage:

> I think of many things, how he seemed to say effortlessly, brilliantly yet from the heart just the right words on occasions such as the last night of Canon Cook's subdeanery meetings, the talk and records on Gervase Elwes at the Usher Gallery ... when it was good to see and hear him.

Colin was also sometimes much in demand as an assistant Bishop of Lincoln, especially during the interregnum between Bishops Harland and Riches, and when the latter was ill and convalescing from illness during 1959. During his time in the diocese he took at least 47 confirmations, about which I was told the following by the mother of a confirmand: when Colin had arrived to take the service, he was looking rather tense and stern, but as soon as he began to lay his hands on the heads of the candidates he began to relax, and to enthuse the confirmands with some of his own reverence for the occasion, communicating to them a sense of holiness. His addresses to the candidates were short and very much to the point. He also conducted at least 33 institutions, and assisted Bishop Riches at ordinations of priests and deacons in the Cathedral. On one highly unusual occasion Colin stood in for him at Louth and Keddington (three miles from Louth) in the dedication of memorials to one of the greatest of nineteenth-century Greek poets, Andreas Kalvos.

Kalvos, born on the island of Zakynthos, was a brilliant but strange man, who led a very disturbed life in Greece, France, Italy, Switzerland and England during the time leading up to the achievement of Greek independence from Turkey in 1832. Towards the end of his life he married an Englishwoman, Augusta Wadams, and the couple moved to Louth, a peaceful market town in Lincolnshire, where his wife ran a girls' boarding school, and where he may have met Tennyson. They both died there and were buried in the churchyard at Keddington, and soon almost completely forgotten, as their shared gravestone became overgrown and almost illegible. But eventually some of Kalvos's fellow-countrymen discovered its whereabouts and steps were taken to exhume the remains and return them to Greece. The exhumation took place in March 1960, and the new memorials at Keddington and the tablet at Louth were dedicated in the Summer of that year. Colin wrote a special prayer for the Keddington ceremony:

> O Father of all, we thank thee for thy servant Andreas Kalvos who lived in this region in days gone by, and whose earthly remains found rest in the cemetery of this church: We thank thee for the beauty of his poetry and for noble thoughts made noble still by his genius. And we pray that through the inspiration and work of poets and all kinds of artists the nations of men may be drawn closer together in sympathy and understanding: through Jesus Christ our Lord.

The Greek Ambassador, Andreas Seferiades, himself a poet, who was present to represent the Greek government, was much struck by Colin's prayer and wrote to ask him for a copy. Colin's reply runs as follows:

> Your Excellency, it was a great pleasure and privilege to meet you and Madame Seferiades both at Louth and at Lincoln. I thought the ceremony on Sunday in Keddington Church was most moving and I greatly look forward to reading your Address which I was too deaf to hear on Sunday. It was a great delight to show round the Cathedral one who showed such deep interest in and knowledge of the building. I enclose, as promised, the Dedicatory Prayer which you asked for.

As I have already implied above, Colin's sense of the Church's mission led him to attach much importance to the way he showed visitors around the Cathedral. Among the last people Colin showed round was Charlie Chaplin and his wife Oona, who had stayed the previous night in the White Hart Hotel. 'The Gossiper' (the pen-name of the writer of a regular column in the *Lincolnshire Echo*), had been informed about this:

It was in the North Transept (he wrote) that I spotted them. But how to intrude upon the privacy which I knew they had asked for? The Dean passed by, after morning service. A heaven-sent opportunity. 'Mr Chaplin', I said (as though we knew each other), 'may I introduce the Dean of Lincoln?' It was done. We – Mr and Mrs Chaplin, the Dean, a cameraman and myself – set off on what turned out to be a most diverting tour of the Minster. But first let Charlie say what he thinks about Lincoln cathedral: 'It is like one of the great symphonies', he said, as he looked up and around. 'It is music in stone.'

In another reference to this tour in next day's paper the Gossiper adds that Charlie and his wife had been on the point of leaving, after walking around by themselves for about twenty minutes, 'but with the Dean as guide, they extended their stay over another hour', and when Charlie shook hands on leaving, 'extended to Bishop Dunlop a warm invitation to visit them at their home at Vevey in Switzerland'.

In the Chapter House, when Charlie took his seat on the 'throne' and the Dean told him that King Edward I had occupied the same chair when he held his Parliament in that same building in 1301, my mind went back to a day in June six years ago when Queen Elizabeth II accepted a similar invitation from the Dean. The Dean explained to Mr Chaplin that Lincoln was Edward's 'advance GHQ' for 'getting at the Scots'. Commented Charlie: 'The Scots were always troublesome, weren't they?' The Dean replied: 'I take a poor view of that. I'm a Scot!'

The *Lincolnshire Chronicle*, in an article dated 4 September 1964, headed 'Ill health causes Lincoln Dean to retire', writes that though 'several hundreds of thousands of visitors have visited the cathedral' during his time, the Dean 'could only recall one critical query'. Another American, obviously of quite a different sensibility from Charlie Chaplin, had, after hearing about the magnificence of the pre-Reformation cathedral, 'asked if there had not been any protest about so much money being given to a religious building'. The Dean said he had replied 'that there had been no *record* of any protest.' While he was at Lincoln he was asked by Pitkin Pictorials Ltd, of 11 Wyfold Road, London SW6, to produce a 'Pictorial History' of Lincoln Cathedral. 'It will need much study', he wrote to me, 'as I must be sure of my facts. Nothing annoys me more than written statements which exaggerate ascertainable facts or which are patent generalisations which may mean anything or nothing.' It was published in 1959; the text and choice of photographs were all Colin's, and the 24-page booklet is still an excellent introduction to its subject, though it seems now to have gone out of print.

There is no clock face on the outside of Lincoln Cathedral, and the striking of the hour and each quarter is of considerable volume. This had always kept some people awake at night until they got used to it. Colin's sister Sibyl, when she visited us at Lincoln for the second time, refused to stay at the White Hart Hotel (at the west end of the Cathedral) as she had previously done, but actually booked a room in a nearby village to escape the noise! In February 1953, the Chapter had agreed to stop the chimes during the Assizes, quite possibly as a result of Colin's calling on the judges as he liked to do when they came to Lincoln.

At their July meeting the Chapter agreed to investigate the cost of stopping the chimes mechanically so as to switch them off at night every day, since the cost of having someone to climb up to the bell chamber and do it manually was considerable. But it was discovered that the cost of installing mechanism was also considerable, and it was not until 1957 that the White Hart, whose transient visitors suffered most from being woken up or kept awake, offered to pay for this. The Chapter accepted the offer and, at the same meeting, had to turn down a contrary offer from Mrs Bertha Kennedy to pay to have the chimes reinstated! This offer was in fact an early manifestation of what Mary described in a letter to me as a 'fearful row'. One person had actually telephoned anonymously to say that 'the Dean will be very unpopular in the city', and a well-known local supporter of the Cathedral went so far as to cancel his regular subscription to cathedral funds.

In his letter to me, Colin talked of much anger and fierce criticism. 'But', he went on 'I am sure we are right to study those who are kept awake by the chimes more than those who merely get pleasure in occasionally hearing them when they wake up in the night.' This 'row' caused him much distress and, as Mary said, 'adds to his dreadful tiredness'. As far as I know, the vociferous opposition to Colin (as standing for the Chapter – though one member had voted against stopping the chimes) gradually subsided. It was also about this time that Colin started a study-circle on the Prayer Book.

Perhaps the 'row' over the clock chimes is an example of bad 'uphill/downhill' relations. But Colin did well as regards local schools. One of the letters Mary received after his death was from Mr L.R. Middleton, the Headmaster of the City School, the 'downhill' grammar school, who wrote of him:

> He always was so interested in the school and its activities, and it was very rare for him to miss one of our plays or a speech day. Indeed the whole field of education interested him and he served this city well in this sphere as well as in the greater field of religion. Men of his calibre are few and far between.

Colin was also a Foundation Governor of Lincoln School – the uphill boys' grammar school, from where the cathedral choir trebles were recruited until 1960 – and also of the Girls' High School (on the slope of the scarp). I also discovered a *Lincolnshire Echo* photo of Colin sitting on the platform at the opening ceremony of a Roman Catholic secondary modern school – probably somewhere downhill – in 1957.

Colin also did some prison visiting at Lincoln, possibly as a result of getting to know the Governor of the prison, which is in fact 'uphill' and not far from the cathedral. I am here totally dependant on spasmodic Diary entries, and therefore do not know how long he kept this up. But what he wrote about his visits is, as usual, full of interest. His first entry is dated 10/4/50, where he records that he found the locking of cells 'a difficult art'. The other entries are as follows:

7/1/52 Visited the prison after tea. I went by chance into the cell of a young RC who has just been given 8 years for passing on 'secret' military instructions to Austrian spies while in Austria; I visited also a man of 50 (who seemed more like 65) whose speech was all but unintelligible and whose mind could not stick to any point.

17/3/52 I talked to one man in the prison tonight of whose speech I could not follow more than one quarter. He pronounced 'now' as though it were 'nigh'. His spate of eloquence was directed upon his self-justification in most respects. He seemed sub-normal and a bit uncanny.

5/4/52 I visited two men in the prison. I am not good at answering the questions of simple men about the mysteries of the faith. Lockwood asked me how Jesus could be God if he prayed to God.

2/2/53 Just back from the gaol where I have had a long talk with young Spicer. Ever since the age of 8 when he went to an Approved School he has been in and out of penal institutions. Now at 23 he is serving a 2-year sentence for, I think, burglary. He is vivacious and mentally alert; crime, he says, gives him the only satisfaction for that urge for excitement which he says he must satisfy. Dalby tells me he is a weekly communicant.

8/3/53 Preached at 10.15 in the prison on this cold sparkling morning. The first hymn was 'New every morning', but none of the prisoners batted an eyelid as they chanted: 'We need not bid, for cloistered cell, our neighbours and our work farewell'. It only shows how insensible of hymn words people are. They were singing lustily.

24/3/53 I visited the prison after confirming 6 Grammar School boys in the Morning Chapel. Saw Spicer, who said that when a man gets out of prison, he completely forgets it so that the prospect of another prison sentence cannot act as a deterrent from further crime. He said the judges ought to know this. He is a strange mixture of nobility and baseness, of wisdom and insensate folly.

Colin also regularly visited members of the Cathedral's non-clerical congregation. Among those who answered my appeal in *Crosslinks*, a diocesan paper, was Jill Wilson, who had been confirmed by Colin as a girl in 1955. Her Godfather, Dr George Summers, a founder member of the Cathedral Friends, and a man and physician 'of the old School', knew Colin well, and had 'an enormous respect for him as both friend and spiritual guide'. His wife had died suddenly in 1953, and, after that, Mary and Colin 'took him under their wing', and often invited him for supper. Dr Summers later wrote an amusing little article in the Diocesan Magazine entitled 'Jugurtha'. Before going to Rome on holiday, he had diligently read up the sights of that great city. Among the buildings that he especially noted was the Carcer Mamertinus, an underground prison with a Christian church on top.

The *Baedeker* guide, he wrote, mentioned by name only two of the many prisoners it had once housed, Vercingetorix and Jugurtha. 'I knew the latter name only as being a christian name of the father of Bishop Dunlop' (a fact he had gleaned from *Who's Who?*), and about which he had felt very curious. 'Could I discover why?' He was reluctant to ask straight out, as two of the Residential Canons had warned him 'that the Dean might be sensitive' about it. Then an opportunity presented itself with a knock on the door from Colin one evening. Dr Summers asked him in and the talk turned to his Roman holiday. He did not omit what *Baedeker* had said about the Carcer Mamertinus, including – not unduly stressed, of course – its temporary occupant Jugurtha.

Colin had at once said 'My father's name was Jugurtha', and that the prisoner had been 'a Numidian prince'. He explained that there were two or three David Dunlops in the Edinburgh street where his great grandfather lived, whose letters were always being mixed up. So his grandfather had decided to give his father a name no one else was likely to have, and settled on David Jugurtha. Feigning surprise, Dr Summers had then gone on to tell Colin, 'with feeling': 'it's a lovely name'. Colin had replied 'we children didn't think much of it', and that it had once led him to tell a bare-faced lie. Once at Radley, the headmaster had asked him what his father's christian names were. 'David', Colin replied; 'any other?', the HM went on. 'No'. Years later he had met the HM in Nottingham, where he was now a canon, and confessed that he had once told him a lie, which had 'always been on my conscience'. On learning what it was, the ex-HM had replied 'If you had told me he was called Jugurtha. you would have been my favourite boy!' So, the Dean said, *'that is what I lost!'*

Another answer to my *Crosslinks* request was from Joan Chester, of Boston, who, in 1953, had begun to take her six-year-old daughter every Monday for speech therapy at Lincoln Hospital. During one such journey she met 'an exceedingly kind lady, a Mrs Dunlop' in the train, who invited them for tea after the therapy session. Mrs Chester remembered that the house was 'in the Cathedral Precincts'. 'The lady became a very good friend to us,' and they regularly had tea with her after the therapy sessions. Once she also had her eight-year-old son with her, and 'a gentleman who I thought could have been Mr Dunlop' taught him to play draughts. But she was never certain who the 'kind' people had been until I thanked her for her letter, enclosing a scanned photo of Mary, whom she recognised.

Outside the Diocese Colin was again much in demand as preacher and lecturer and, with so much to fit in around his work in Lincoln, it is not surprising that both he and Mary kept telling me in their letters how tired he was. For example, from 24 to 26 June 1959, he had to be in Oxford on Liturgical Commission business, for dummy runs on the new Baptism and Confirmation Services. He then had engagements at Lichfield, Wolverhampton and Aberystwyth, before getting back to Lincoln on 1 July. Not long before the

Oxford meetings, he had been to London and Gloucester. I think, too, that most of these journeys were done by car – driven, of course, by himself. Not surprisingly, Colin was asked to deliver an address on preaching to the Lincoln Clergy School in June 1950.

He was mainly concerned to counter the 'tendency to discount the importance of sermons' in the church's worship, appealing to the Tractarian revival of preaching, and to those who saw in it a means of grace. He was also insistent that 'the revolt against the emotions in religion' had gone too far; and that to show how 'all man's emotional life may be directed upon God' may bear much fruit. Colin also made nine broadcasts during his time at Lincoln, most of them sermons, one of them, at the BBC's request, with a special mention of his forthcoming visit to Minneapolis. He was also asked to read an abbreviated version of John Donne's sermon *Quis homo?* in the Aldeburgh Festival Evensong for 1953 – in her diary record of this Mary commented that it was 'difficult stuff', but that the congregation had been 'enthralled'. This was the occasion of their meeting up again with Michael Howard and his Renaissance Singers.

In 1956 he delivered a University Sermon at Oxford on Cranmer, entitled 'The First Great Figure in Anglicanism'. This succinct account of the genesis of the BCP, whose wonderful use of the English language had had such an enduring influence on the hearts and minds of all who were brought up on it, culminates in a most moving account of Cranmer's death at the stake, which powerfully illustrates the importance of emotion in preaching. It was published by SPCK. Another close involvement with music came when he was asked to give the 1957 St Cecilia's Day sermon in St Michael's, Cornhill, before the Lord Mayor and Sherrifs of London. 'It dates back to the 17th century', he wrote to me, 'and musicians such as Purcell, Blow, Handel, Vaughan-Williams, Rubbra and Howells have written for it. This time it's Gordon Jacob, of whom I hadn't heard.' The singing was provided by the choirs of St Paul's and Westminster Abbey. Shortly after this he confirmed at Gainsborough and was then off to Blackpool to 'lecture', probably on some liturgical topic, 'to the conference of clergy of Blackburn Diocese (which I shall like)'.

Apart from preaching and lecturing away from Lincoln Diocese and his chairmanship of the Church of England Liturgical Commission, his service on other non-local committees and publications further increased the considerable demands on his time and energy. The Warham Guild had been founded in London in November 1912, to augment the studies of the Alcuin Club and the directives of *The Parson's Handbook* in the matter of vestments, church furniture and other ornaments. Colin was Vice-chairman of the Advisory Committee in 1961, and Chairman in 1963. We have looked at his Alcuin Club activities. But around 1956 Colin took over the editorship of the English Churchman's Kalendar, the nearest approach to an 'official' calendar the Church of England had, and published by Mowbrays.

Apart from listing festivals, saints' days, etc. for the year, it contains a great variety of short articles both purely informative and also illustrative of good and bad practice in liturgical matters, church ornaments and restoration, according to the principles of Dearmer and the Warham Guild. Colin enjoyed writing these, and selecting photographs (many of them 'before and after' pairs), but found it increasingly difficult to think of new things to illustrate or write about. The 1956 cover picture is of the Grosseteste Memorial in Lincoln Cathedral. The 1957 number shows that Colin would have strongly disapproved of the modern trend to make all bishops' mitres in the C of E tall, slightly bulbous and uniformly gold. He was also on the Advisory Committee of the Central Advisory Council for the Care of Churches. His involvement with the English Hymnal Company, Ltd, also went back a long way, and he had been on the Committee at least since June 1951. But in 1952 Sir Humphrey Milford, chairman of the Directors, died. Vaughan Williams proposed Colin to succeed him, seconded by Jack Arnold, and he was elected. He was still Chairman in 1966, two years after he retired from Lincoln.

There was also an English Hymnal Revision Committee, of which Colin was chairman from the mid 1950s, whose members were responsible for the Shorter English Hymnal and the English Hymnal Service Book. After his death, the members resolved to give something 'suitable and needed by' St Mary's, Primrose Hill, as a memorial of Colin (I have not been able to discover what this was). The English Hymnal Co. also had a charitable arm, the Ecclesiastical Music Trust, set up and richly endowed in 1950 or early '51 by Vaughan Williams. They awarded Scholarships and Bursaries, and contributed to memorials. The Lincoln Cathedral (Choir) School, started in 1960 in the large Victorian Deanery we had lived in since late 1950, received many grants from them, as did St Michael's College, Tenbury, before it had to close in 1985. Colin was involved in all this work.

As I have already stressed, all this took a heavy toll on him, and also on Mary. One may look at this in two ways. Here is Bishop Harland, writing to Mary after Colin's death: 'His love of Our Lord and zeal for his Church meant that Colin simply worked himself out. He always gave royally of his best.' But from Mary's point of view, and that of the family, it was hard not to see his time as Dean as, in Mary's words, 'a gradual squeezing out of all the non-church things he so much enjoyed'. In putting together the following outline of Colin's health and morale in the years 1957–62, I have to rely almost entirely on letters to me from Colin and Mary written during the time when I was away from Lincoln. Colin continued for some time to be worried over staffing. On 10/2/57 Mary wrote:

> The Precentor gets more and more doddery but insists on doing things whenever he is up. He then suddenly takes to bed on Doctor's orders leaving various engagements for other people to carry out. Then Lee the verger has been seriously ill and according to private opinion from Dr MacLure will probably not be fit for work again. He hasn't got a pension arrangement so it is all rather difficult. However on the whole in spite of these worries Daddy is well and a great deal happier with our present Bishop than he was with the last one.

In Colin's letter of 2/2/58 he told me: 'The Bp of Grimsby has been ill for a month and the Subdean for the past ten days: The Chancellor is as usual very much away so everything falls on the Archdeacon and me.' On top of that Mary had been 'slightly ill', though was now up again. It was lucky that neither of them had had engagements. Two months later Colin wrote that he was much occupied with 'the Queen's twenty-five minute visit' in three months time (her visit to Lincoln had been primarily arranged as an opening of the Pelham Bridge, which greatly alleviated the traffic problem in the City). He had had to go to Buckingham Palace, then to talk it over with Lord Ancaster (the Lord Lieutenant) at Grimsthorpe Castle in the extreme south of the county. 'In the end one almost asks "Is it worth it?"'

On 18/4/58 Colin told me that Mary and he were having a short holiday in 'a village near Horsham', since Mary badly needed a rest. On 2/11/58 he told me that he had just taken Martin Shaw's funeral. 'Will you forgive me if I don't write any more? I have had a frightfully busy week.' Five days later he wrote: 'Nothing much is happening here which bears writing about but I've seldom been so busy and occupied.' However, he had bought tickets for the Pantomime and for *Anthony and Cleopatra*. But 'Next week is Church Assembly – an unwelcome interruption in my work.' The night before he had talked to a Men's Church Society on the Lambeth Conference.

On 5/2/59 Colin wrote that Mary was still at Church Assembly. 'I have an unreasonable number of letters to deal with.' Canon Cook had a broken arm, but 'The great news is that the Precentor ... has publicly stated that he will retire at the end of March. I am deeply thankful.' Twelve days later: 'Nothing much to tell about, my time being absorbed by my correspondence and with routine Cathedral business and Liturgical Commission business' – 'absorbing enough'. 'Before Mary went sick I had had to spend a couple of days in bed.' On 14/6/59 he wrote that the day before, he had gone to RAF Scampton for the Trooping of the Colour – 'I almost enjoyed it.' He was also 'just back from confirming at Hibaldstow. They used incense which I always like – I got so used to it in my first parish, and it's a link with churches of the past.' On 21/10/59 he told me that he would be 'preaching at Lancing next Sunday'. His hearing aid had come; but it 'takes a lot of getting used to'. A month later he wrote:

> Life has been very full for me and I find that keeping up with my correspondence and dealing with duties which present themselves take me all my time and one can seldom launch out and initiate new things. It is largely not having a secretary which is responsible for this. Our Bishop is convalescing away somewhere.

On 18/1/60 Mary reported that Colin had been quite ill for a week or so. But 'he set off for Convocation in quite good spirits'. He's 'improved enough to enjoy the thought of getting away [to Spain]'. This they did in February, when they relaxed on the then relatively unspoilt Costa del Sol. Afterwards she wrote (24/2/60): 'Daddy is very much better and he has been so warmly welcomed home that he is feeling very much heartened and encouraged.' On 28/2/60 Colin wrote: 'The holiday has done me a lot of good ... I was more tired than I knew', but then on 3/6/60: 'Do forgive me for writing so very little. I have no real *excuse,* but the reason is tiredness.' He wrote from the President's house at Trinity College, Oxford, where he preached in the College Chapel on the very difficult topic of 'The Trinity'. In November 1960 he wrote:

> I have been asked to write a book of 120,000 words [this was probably the textbook on liturgy mentioned above] but don't see how I can accept as I have to re-edit the Parson's Handbook and everything is so uncertain with Canon Cook retiring next year, which is bound to put a lot of extra work onto me. [Colin never did edit Dearmer's classic, and the next edition of it was prepared by The Revd. Cyril Pocknee in 1965].

In February 1961 Mary wrote to say that 'Daddy seems fairly well since the teeth went' and actually did half an hour's gardening by himself while I was out.' During the Summer term of that year Colin had a long rest at St Stephen's House, Oxford. When he got there – my brother Philip and I were now undergraduates – he wrote to me to report his arrival, explaining that before I could visit him he would have to discover the 'daily Programme of the House', adding 'I feel like going to school again, which, I suppose, is part of the intended cure!' The three of us used to drive out into the country every week with a thermos and sandwiches for a 'church crawl', which he much enjoyed.
Mention of 'the intended cure' is, of course, an indicator that Colin was not without medical supervision during these years. But for a long time it seems that, apart from a few definite diagnoses, one of which led to his hernia operation (mentioned above), his problems were largely referred to by such words as 'tiredness' and 'overwork', for which a 'rest cure' was prescribed. However, he did have some X-rays in 1961, which I think revealed some hardening of the arteries.
At the same time, Mary's letters to me suggested that some kind of dementia was already manifesting itself. On 15/2/61 she wrote to me that she had had to come home early from the Church Assembly 'so as not to leave Daddy too long'. Then, on 13/5/61 she wrote à propos of Colin's stay at St Stephen's House that she wondered whether Colin would 'open up' to Anna (later my wife) and me. She was feeling extremely tired herself, 'with the accumulated strain of trying to keep Daddy "shored up" for the last six months or more'. Around the beginning of 1962 he started seeing a psychiatrist, Dr Falla, who prescribed pills which, Colin wrote, make him feel 'muzzy', and, as Mary put it, 'have unpleasant side-effects'. In late February she said: 'Daddy is improving slowly under Dr Falla,' but 'still needs a tremendous lot of support and hand-holding and hates me to be out of the house for long – this is very tiring'.

On 3 May Colin wrote: 'I am not feeling over-well just now and I have a busy summer before me. I hope I shall have strength to go through with it in a way which will please God.' But soon after, he could still write, like a man in his prime, that he had been 'deeply impressed by the Consecration [of the new Cathedral] at Coventry, and by the building itself. It has a true monumental character quite worthy of its purpose ... The great tapestry was a marvellous blend of strength and serenity', though he didn't care for the Choir Stalls, of 'poor colour wood.' But the stained glass is 'miraculous'. In December 1963 Colin replied to a letter from Eric Whittome thus: 'Thank you for warning me against tying myself with Cathedral responsibilities. They are minute in themselves, but enormous when felt collectively. It is not a job for me really, but I cannot turn back now for I hope to retire in 1967. Still, I may get kicked out!'

In 1957 Mary had had a bad attack of phlebitis (on 3/5 she was in bed with 'large poultices all up her leg'). She was ordered to bed at the end of April, but felt unable to see the doctor again until after my two youngest brothers had gone back to school. As a result it got worse, and she had to spend time in the Bromhead Nursing Home. Again, in January 1964 Colin wrote to me 'Mummy has been overdoing it and Dr Maclure has forbidden her to do any work for a week'. In addition to this there was during these years bad sinus trouble, a complaint she was no stranger to, and also neuritis in the arm, caused by mosquito bites. She, too, was much in demand in Church matters, as well as running the household with (during the school holidays), three children at home as Philip was by then teaching in a boarding school and came home in the holidays. She did have the help of a resident nanny at the beginning of our time in Lincoln, and also, for short periods, two Scandinavian helpers, Monna, a Finn, and then Lida, a Swede, but, when the youngest of my brothers went to boarding school, Nanny left to look after her own mother, and there was only a 'daily' five days a week, who also often had to stay at home to look after her mother.

Despite all this Mary was a Governor of the Cathedral School, from 1959 Permanent Chairman of the Executive Committee of the Diocesan Board of Women's Work, a member and regular attender of the Church Assembly (making occasional speeches), on the Council for the Deaf and the Moral Welfare Council, and an important member of the Mothers' Union. On 28/11/58 she wrote to me: 'I've been very busy – lots of committees. I am on too many really, but people keep asking me to help and I find it hard to refuse.' Later she wrote that she had been 'talking to Church Wardens at Butlin's' – a holiday camp at Skegness often hired for groups like today's conference centres. She also told me of two rather unusual triumphs. The first was in February 1961: 'I actually preached from a pulpit at Ruskington, at a service for "Women's World Day of Prayer".' Then, in early June 1961, she wrote about a visit to the Theological College:

Today I have been making history by being the first woman to be included among the guests at the luncheon party of the Bishop's Hostel Festival. They have never had a woman on the Council of the College before. The toastmaster began each time: 'Your Graces (Archbishops of Dublin & York), My Lords (2 or 3 bishops), Mr Mayor, Mrs Dunlop and gentlemen! I was quite embarrassed. A memorable day.

But on 24/10/61 she wrote to me that she 'was beginning to feel she might be driven out of the church (as Wesley was) by the attitude to women of some of the C of E hierarchy'. The occasion for this was the remarks to the press of Bishop Carpenter of Oxford when a Methodist deaconess was invited to preach at the United Nations service.

Colin's hope that he might retire in 1967 proved over-optimistic and, in the spring of 1964 it seemed clear to both him and Mary that his health was extremely unlikely to get much – if any – better while he was still Dean of Lincoln, and that he should immediately take the first steps towards retirement and write to the Archbishop of Canterbury. Michael Ramsey replied as follows on 21 April:

My dear Colin, I am so very sorry to have your letter telling me that you are asking to resign the Deanery and am the more sorry to know that considerations of health have caused this decision. I remember so well the sadness which I felt when you left Durham to go to Lincoln, but at the same time the delight that you were going to the charge of that wonderful Cathedral. I am sorry your Lincoln years are now ending because they have been such very good ones, and I recall with happiness the occasions when we have been able to visit you, and I am proud to have been for a short time one of your Prebendaries. I hope your plans for your new home will go happily. Yours ever, Michael Cantuar.

The following letter is a reminder of the importance of economic considerations and the problems of owning one's own house for the first time which many people in Holy orders experience when they retire. Mary's letter to Barbara Halpern of 24 January 1965 is very frank about the difficulties:

last Spring we decided that he would have to ask for a disability pension and retire as soon as we could get a house. We thought this might take a year or two, but actually we were extremely lucky and found this house in Henfield within a few months. We got it for just over £6,000, but it remains to be seen whether it is going to prove too expensive living here. Sussex is exceedingly highly rated of course and although the Church Pensions Board have been quite generous it is going to be rather a squeeze to get through the next few years, during which we still have two dependant sons and are carrying rather heavy life insurance premiums – too heavy really, I think, but it would be silly to give it up now when there are only two years to run. However we hope for the best.

The Lincoln Cathedral Chapter Minutes for 19/10/64 contain the following item:

The Precentor (Binnall) said that, as it was the Dean's last Chapter meeting as Dean, he wished to express on behalf of the rest of the Chapter their best wishes to him in his retirement, and their deep thanks and appreciation of his great work as Dean, of his inspired leadership, and devoted service of all that appertained to the Cathedral, and of his unfailing friendship, for which they would always be deeply grateful.

The Writer of 'Minster Notes' for *The Diocesan* Magazine wrote:

His period of office has been a very happy and fruitful one for the Cathedral, the Diocese and the Church at large. As a distinguished scholar, with great gifts as a pastor and as a preacher, he will long be remembered with affection and respect by all who have known him. He and Mrs Dunlop go to their new home in Sussex with the prayers and hearty good wishes of an immense circle of Lincolnshire friends.

The headline of the *Lincolnshire Echo*'s 'Goodbye' article is: 'Dean who made his mark on City says farewell.' Beneath it is a small photo of Colin, which clearly shows his tiredness. Some time after he had left the following prayer was found in the recesses of the book shelf of his stall:

I want to think of nothing but You and the Holy Church – I am weak, my mind often wanders, but it is my desire, my wish, to remain attentive, and prostrate with the Angels and saints.
I believe that by this official prayer, of which I am the minister, I can achieve much, in union with Thy Son Jesus, for the needs of the Church, to help those in suffering, in their death agony, who are about to appear before thee, to co-operate in the conversion of sinners and of the indifferent, to unite myself to the holy saints on earth, and to the Blessed in heaven.
May everything that is in me, Lord, confess and adore thee.

Photo 18: Being installed as provost of Edinburgh Cathedral, 1940.
Colin is kneeling near the bottom right of the picture.

Photo 19: Colin's consecration as Bishop of Jarrow, 1944.

Photo 20: Visiting RAF bases in Habbaniyah (Iraq), 1945.

Photo 21: At Bad Eilsen (Germany), 1949.

Photo 22: In cope and mitre at service in Lincoln Cathedral, c. 1960.

Photo 23: Colin accompanies HM the Queen and the Duke of Edinburgh out of Lincoln Cathedral, 1958.

Photo 24: Colin's home (1950–60) in the Deanery, Lincoln. Photo taken from cathedral tower in 2013 when the building had become the Cathedral School.

Photo 25: Colin in carved chair, 1960s.

Photo 26: Colin working at his desk, 1960s.

17

OFFICIAL TRIPS ABROAD FROM LINCOLN

ERE ARE THREE accounts of trips abroad on Church business which Colin made while he was Dean of Lincoln. I have simply copied them without any abbreviation. The first two are from his diaries, and the third, which is not mentioned in his diaries, was printed in the *Lincoln Diocesan Magazine*.

1. *Visit to Armed Service Bases in the Middle East, 23 January to 27 March 1951*

Khartoum, Wednesday, 24 January 1951. Our 'Constellation' touched down at the airport at 3.25 a.m. having left Rome at 8 p.m. the evening before, i.e. a flight of about 7½ hours (from London 11 hours all told in the air). I was taken off to a vast bedroom in the RAF station where I was soon asleep. To awake to brilliant sun and a summer temperature, with green trees and flowers, was a wonderul moment. The CO (Grp Capt Lowe) drove me up to the Gelsthorpes' where I breakfasted plentifully and am now marking time till my programme begins. I have had a glimpse of the cathedral. It is a fine building – original without being freakish. Inside the fittings are good except for the Choir Screen, which does not please me and seems out of scale with the rest. It is strange to be surrounded by soft-footed black servants ministering to all one's needs. One is so unused to be waited upon that at first one is embarrassed.

This is all, alas, that Colin's diary contains about his time in Khartoum, but what immediately follows is part of a paragraph from an article he wrote for the *Lincoln Diocesan Magazine* for April 1951:

During my week here I was guest of the Bishop and later of the Provost and the Archdeacon (the justly famous 'Uncle' Harper) though I was entertained by the R.A.F. officers and especially by the Station Commander whose wife comes from Heckington [near Sleaford]. In Khartoum, General Gordon's memory is a living force, and if men were still reckoned to be Saints by popular acclamation, Gordon's name would be in the Church Calendar in that diocese. His example still casts its spell over the British administration in the Sudan, and the Cathedral, built in his memory is, in a very practical and striking manner, the spiritual home of the British Community in Khartoum, to a degree I have never seen paralleled elsewhere. The honour fell to me to preach the annual Gordon sermon, preached on the nearest Sunday to the anniversary day of his death. One of my tasks in Khartoum was to talk to the Rotary Club which boasts a membership drawn from about fifteen nations. I spoke to them of our Cathedral, its history and its work, and after the talk the Sudanese Speaker of the Parliament, a Mohammedan, told me he had twice visited Lincoln and spoke enthusiastically of the glories of the Minster. My duties with the R.A.F. were slight, as it is a small station. I addressed the officers in their cool ante-room, the N.C.O.s in a pleasant garden, and the rank and file in a large lecture room. Each talk was followed by a discussion and questions.

Aden. Steamer Point. Thursday, 1 February. We arrived (from Khartoum), Ainsworth and I, at the Landing Ground at 1 p.m., a journey in a Valetta of 4 hrs 20 mins. Crossing Eritrea was full of interest and I shall not quickly forget the surprise of the great falling away of the land after Asmara, which stands on the plateau about 10,000 ft above sea level. Aden looks hot and bleak at 1 p.m. but the great rocks should look lovely in the evening. I have been assigned a lodging of which the tenant returns in 3 days. There is not a drawer, not a hook free. I can unpack nothing, but have to find my way among his numerous possessions spread out everywhere. Lunch in the mess was the worst I've struck in a RAF station for many years. I look straight out of my window at the glorious blue sea from which a stiff cool breeze comes on to my verandah.
I am most struck at the friendly, forthcoming temper of RAF officers these days; strikingly different from the war years when they seemed suspicious and remote for the greater part.

Aden, 2.ii.51 It seems impossible that the attractive blue sea in which a bathe appears so desirable conceals sharks and sting-rays. One can only bathe in the Pool at the Club. Started today by celebrating at the Garrison Church (Ch. Ch.). Only Ainsworth and Padré Payne present. A clamorous bell is situated in the cliffs far above the church and its sound pierces the remotest corners of Steamer Point. Gave a talk to NCOs at the Lido. The discussion afterwards really stuck to the point of the talk, an almost unique occurrence in my experience. A talk to Officers in the Ante-room preceded lunch. I do not find either Padré Payne or Padré Bennett (of Khormaksar) particularly simpatico.

Aden, 3.ii.51 A mild day of sunshine. A talk to Army NCOs in morning followed by one to Officers. It is tragic the way so many of these young men fight against the inward call by citing the failures of Christians and clergy. I met a man who had been knifed by an Arab on Christmas Eve. If the knife had gone in 1/100 inch further it would have pierced his heart. At 4 p.m. Padré Payne motored us to a lovely sandy bay. We scrambled over the volcanic rocks and walked along the sand. Little crabs scuttled away with incredible velocity. Returning, we had tea at a sort of bathing club where the sea is enclosed in a fence to prevent sharks and sting-rays from entering.

Aden, 5.ii.51 Yesterday, Sunday, was passed according to plan. I celebrated at 7.30 at Ch.Ch. (about 35 communicants) and then had breakfast at the Church Club opposite (called Crossways). Preached at a Family Service at 9.30, spoke a word to children and then talked to parents about family life. At 6.30 I preached to the general congregation at E'song – both military and civilians – about 150 people. The Acting Governor – one Goode – read the 2nd lesson extremely well. A reception after at Crossways.

This morning I visited the Officers' shop and bought 1 Bath Towel (7/9), 1 Khaki Shirt (6/5), 1 Thin Vest and 1 Cotton Pants (2/3), 1 Pair Blue Poplin Pyjamas (23/7) – Total £2, an immense saving on what I would have paid at home. The last item would have been at least 50/-.

I have a slight stye in my right eye today and have received some drops from a medical officer.

Aden, 6.ii.51 Dined at Government House last night. The Acting Governor and his lady (Mr and Mrs Goode) entertained us delightfully in the stately apartments of the residence – white walls and pillars and much space. He was at Worcester [College, Oxford] and was captured in Malay by the Japs and forced to work on the railway. He spoke of the number of quite young men who died just because they could not face the horror of living in such conditions. It was the young men and not the middle aged.

My bearer, Ahmed, comes into my room so quietly that I almost never hear him till I see him. He is an Arab.

In the mornings I have a cold shower and again before dinner. The weather is still pleasant and agreeable.

We visited the Garrison school, high up among the 'barren rocks'. The head teacher is a Mrs Pemberton (née Palmer) who was at Lincoln Training College.

Aden, 7.ii.51 Ash Wednesday: Celebration at 7 at Ch.Ch. It's a gaunt and unattractive building. Gothicky architecture does not suit these tropical climates. It's full of noise from the streets at both ends of it and from the shipyard at the west side. The furnishings and ornaments are inept and puerile in design. It's hard to realise Lent when the thermometer stands at 85 or so. I had to give a talk to 7 senior officers in a little room at the mess at 1.30 p.m. I talked badly, but the questions I dealt with fairly well and the atmosphere was definitely sympathetic. We went over the hospital in the morning and I had words with the sisters and with most of the patients. Though a RAF institution the hospital has to serve the needs of casualties of all kinds from the ships which arrive in the harbour; indeed, these usually form the major part of the inmates. Aden has the 3rd largest number of ships to cope with of all the world's harbours, London and Port Said alone surpassing it. The view of Aden and its harbour from the heights on which the hospital stands is superb. One could spend hours enjoyably with a telescope here.

Last night we had tea with Padré McGuffie. A sapper in the 1914 war, he stayed on in Aden after having decided that he must be a missionary to the Arabs here. A gentle, modest, shy, exterior conceals a will of steel and a heart of flaming love. His wife is Danish and they live in a poky little flat attached to his Arab boys' club which includes a little chapel. The whole plant stands cheek by jowl with a mosque. Though he has to go carefully he appears to have won the affection and respect not only of the Muslim crowd around him but even of their religious leaders. He is so careful to avoid controversy that he does not even know to what Islamic sect the inhabitants of Aden belong. But he preaches the Cross outspokenly and shows in every corner of his life the marks of the Lord Jesus. I was so moved that I could hardly speak to him and he must have thought me standoffish and unfriendly.

8.ii.51 Aden (Khormaksar) We moved here this morning to the Flying Station. It's outside Aden proper on a narrow neck of sand connecting Aden with the mainland. Gp Capt Macdonald (late of RAF Coningsby) showed me round the station with much thoroughness and formality. Then I went for a flip in a Brigand, the modern development of the old Beaufighter. Over my clothes I had to put on a flying suit, a Mae West and parachute harness. Inside the plane, the heat was intense. We flew North to Dhala and got an idea of the country. It is hilly there, with sparse trees. But we saw little, as dense white cloud hung low. The mess here is very up to date and comfortable; I have a large sitting room and bed-room, and there is in addition a bathroom and separate WC (the first since leaving home) and shower-bath. French windows and shutters give out on either side onto verandahs. Lunch was most un-Lenten – curried prawns. More effort seems being made here to treat me with formal consideration and respect.

10.ii.51 Aden (Khormaksar) The padré here, Bennett, a dapper little man with a long thin black moustache, is one of the best I have ever struck. His hold on all sections of the station is amazing. The Church, under his direction, runs a local magazine and organises some 60 men in a regular Palm Court variety show. He is determined to prevent the men becoming lazy and without initiative.

Today we had a Quiet Afternoon – from 3 to 6 – in the little chapel of the Church of Scotland Mission hospital at Sheikh Othman. About 30 airmen attended it and tea was arranged somehow. It went well and I believe did much good.

In the morning I visited the Aden Protectorate Levies and was deeply interested in the way they train young native tribesmen to be soldiers. Their officers seemed admirable. I was persuaded to mount a camel and go for a ride, a strange sensation. My camel behaved well, but trotting is far from comfortable though walking is comfortable. The trickiest moments are when the camel rises from the ground and when it squats down again. But it was all accomplished without mishap.

Last night a completely drunken naval Commander, one Beloe, dined with Wing Cmdr Jones with whom I also was dining. It was rather embarrassing but it was almost a pleasure to see a man who remained a gentleman even when drunk.

12.ii.51 Aden (Khormaksar) My work here is now done except for attending the Dining-in night held in my honour. I was given a special lunch by the levies officers after a long session of questions and answers following my talk to them this morning. At 8 a.m. I attended the CO's Conference and found it very like a chapter meeting. Like us they hotly discuss details like whether NCOs may wear bow ties for evening wear and whether officers may attend the cinema in lounge suits.

It has been a very arduous time but I have enjoyed it, though I still suffer from much shrinking before I give my talks. I have found it easier to trust in God and really to leave it to him to help me to do things as he wants them done.

Here is Colin's *Lincoln Diocesan Magazine* summary of his time in Aden:

From Khartoum I flew to Aden, passing over the picturesque but savage country of Eritrea. Here I spent a fortnight, at two separate Stations, and gave about twenty-five talks, addresses, etc., to many groups of officers and N.C.O.s, to smaller gatherings in the camp churches, and also to Army units. There was a Quiet Afternoon on a Saturday to which, in blazing sunshine, some thirty N.C.O.s and Airmen came for three hours, a bold venture on the part of the Chaplains which was much rewarded. A Confirmation and a Mission Service in the garrison church concluded my work here. Aden seemed hotter than Khartoum, because of the humid atmosphere, though the thermometer was actually lower. It was full of interest and deals annually with the largest number of ships in the world. Learning to ride a camel was one of my relaxations in this place, and experience not without its pleasures, as well as its humiliations.

13.ii.51 Masirah. All day we have flown along the south coast of Arabia seeing various displays of arid scenery, relieved very occasionally with patches of cultivated land at the mouths of rivers. We stopped first at Riyan, near Macullah – the only town we passed – and then at Salalah for a meagre lunch. Masirah is on an island at the SE corner of Arabia, and nearer to Karachi than to Aden. I have half a Nissen hut to myself with electric light and fan; it is much cooler than Aden. The officer in charge is delightful and we are to have a celebration of H.C. tomorrow at 7 a.m. Tonight we are to watch a display of Arab war-dancing by soldiers of the Protectorate Levies .... (Later) The display took place and was of great interest. But as they danced on the windward side of us, all the dust and sand churned up by their feet blew over the spectators, carried by a strong breeze. It was often difficult to keep one's eyes properly opened. The scene was illuminated by electric light and the background was the white walls of the low buildings of the camp. They all wore brilliant colours and garments and head-dresses of most assorted shapes. The dancing was not intricate either as to figures or steps. A couple of primitive drums kept up a monotonous, but quite stimulating, rhythm and the dances were always done to singing i.e. the majority of the dancers sang and two at a time would come out and dance. Vigorous hand-clapping and knee-bending on the part of the 'chorus' was another feature. They also gave a few 'charades' revealing a sense of humour shared by ourselves, e.g. they 'took off' the arrival of a general in a car to inspect troops and did it quite amusingly. One man dressed up as a turtle and had rigged up inside his over-all 'costume' a wonderful apparatus for snapping at food and at people's feet.

14.ii.51 Sharjah. We left Masirah at about 8.45 and came round the S.E. tip of the Arabian coast, and passing near Muscat came straight over to this place. I sat next to the pilot most of the way and had thus a wonderful view. Muscat is a seaport town in two halves backed by a high amphitheatre of high crags, but we did not get very near to it. Most of Arabia seems sterile and inhospitable and for the most part uninhabited and uninhabitable. Yet at one time mighty rains must have worn out the deep channels and clefts in the mountains which now look so desiccated, and with the rain may have gone cultivation. How old the world must be. I said Mattins in the plane, and the words 'the gold of Arabia' came in the psalms. It is strange to think of this country being famous for gold. As we came up the Persian Gulf long thin streamers of orange stretched out on the water's surface, looking at times like tongues of flame. It is apparently the oil seeping out in some way from the tankers on their way to and from Abadan.

The wireless operator on the plane was Charman, an inhabitant of Henfield, who is now married to Betty Fry. He is a Flt/Sgt and reputed to be an exceptionally good NCO. At the celebration this morning the CO of the station (a very nice youth), a member of the Works detachment, and two airmen were present. Gordon Bennett, the padré of the Khormaksah station, has now returned. He has been exceptionally kind and considerate to me.

15.ii.51 Bahrein. This morning we were driven in a lorry at 55 miles per hour into Dubai, a large Arab town near Sharjah. I have seldom felt more in danger as we skidded over sand and dodged palm trees and finally hurtled down a bazaar in which one would have felt uncomfortable even on a bicycle. Our driver was an Irish doctor called Macaulay whose son is at Radley, a nice creature with whom I had a really furious argument in the mess. Dubai exhibits an architectural feature of the Persian Gulf towns – namely the wind tower, which brings coolness into the houses. They make an Arab town quite impressive looking.

On dismounting we were surrounded by an excited crowd of Arab boatmen competing for our patronage, for the town proper is across the creek. We were rowed across in the bright sunshine over the extraordinarily clear blue water. We wandered about the bazaar and saw the Sheikh's palace, and admired the pleasant and ingenious ornament on the larger houses and the finely carved centre posts of the entrance doors. Finally we called on a British merchant who entertained us with tea and cigars and talked incessantly about his life. Evidently, a very lonely young man whose wife does not join him till September. Name of Hoffmann, for he is partly Swiss.

We flew up here after lunch and are lodged in the CO's nice cool house. Now I must be off to Evensong and then after dinner, talk to Officers in Mess.

16.ii.51 Shaibah (Basra). The weather and air here are lovely. The day started with wind and rain at Bahrein and the whole place was damp. Here it is dry and exhilarating and the sunshine is like that of an English April. It is of course much cooler now and there is no question of wearing shorts and open-necked shirt as at Aden or even Sharjah. Last night I had two thin blankets but drew a third over me towards dawn. At Khormaksar I once slept without even a sheet. But I am getting undeniably tired. The perpetual travel, meeting new people, doing the same thing in a new place, the endless standing about in bars and messes talking and the strain of the talks and addresses is getting perceptible. Three weeks is really enough of this kind of thing. My deafness also is a real disqualification. I find it hard to hear questions put to me at meetings and even the short clipped sentences of people conversing in crowded places with me. In addition to RAF things there has been so much civilian social life too and of course at Aden there was the Army and the missionaries as well. Only about 10 days more now but how glad I shall be when 27th February comes, or rather 1st March. I was here last in 1932, I believe, when I came through to Basra from Baghdad with Bp Graham Brown of Jerusalem. I cannot pretend to recognise it, however, though the Mess building, etc, is alleged to be the same now as then. After a sermon at Evensong, a Talk to Officers and dinner, we drove out to Basrah to sleep and there I celebrate tomorrow and talk to Officers before lunch. Then plane for Habbaniyah.

21.ii.51 Habbaniyah. I had a pleasant weekend in Baghdad with Archdeacon Roberts at St George's House. There are very few people now there who were there in my day and none whom I cared for specially. The city has been greatly enlarged and there is an increase of magnificence, but everywhere still is the prevailing squalor which the days of Turkish rule so deeply engendered. This impression was doubtless heightened by the fact that it rained incessantly all Monday, making a prevailing atmosphere of sordid gloom. I entered the shop of 'El Dorado', the Armenian photographer with whom I had many dealings in days gone by. Though I had not seen him since 1934 he recognised me almost instantaneously and enquired after Evelyn. Most of the time I lounged in an armchair over a book. That, and a late breakfast on Monday and Tuesday gave me a deeply needed rest and I feel ready for the last few days' work here. But I shall be glad when I have done, though nothing can exceed the kindness and helpfulness of everyone. The Station Commander here is Hobbler, the very nice Australian who commanded the station at Lossiemouth in 1943 during my visit. We dined with him and his wife on Saturday. He is a good man, and I should think an extremely able officer. The AOC, George Beamish, does not return till tonight. This afternoon I am going for a sail on Lake Habbaniyah and as it is a sparkling sunny day it should be nice. The weather here is like late October in England. I wear gaiters at night and a grey suit and waistcoat all day. No temperature here for shirt and shorts as at Aden and in the Gulf. Tom Ryder, the padré, is a most excellent man, of many gifts. He has a most delightful and easy manner and seems a good and pious priest. He has served curacies at St Martin's, Brighton, and All Sts Margaret St. He makes the church respected on the station and seems to have the affection and the regard of all ranks, though is probably better with the Officers than with the men. He has a real style about him. His Anglo Catholicism of Margaret St days is not obtrusive. He seems to have absorbed the best of things wherever he has been.

I have been more than once struck in my various corporate discussions with NCOs of the changed attitude of that rank towards the Socialist creed. In the war Socialist sympathy and sentiment were universal and emphatic; now the prevailing attitude is hostile. Yesterday I said something about 'the People' in a rather scathing manner which 8 years ago would have been the rankest blasphemy. Now it was received with delight. Hostility to strikers is very strong and to Trade Unions in general. A most marked change.

23.ii.51 Habbaniyah. We were taken out by the OC Iraq Levies to witness a military tactical exercise, with live ammunition, in some undulating but barren terrain about 8 miles from here. Armoured cars and carriers took part, while lorries brought up and disgorged infantry. Machine guns cackled and mortars exploded, smoke screens were released and only aeroplanes were missing. As the exercise was meant to be the repulse of a force attacking the airfield, this seemed odd. I was struck with the far more formidable sound made by high explosive than in the days of 1918 when I was familiar with it – a sound revealing a tighter concentration of destructive power. After the weekend's rain the arid ground was all but imperceptibly covered by a thin sheen of green and looked very beautiful.

I have given two talks to junior officers and tonight I address the seniors. With the help of God I have found myself in fairly good form, though last night we got bogged down after a very short discussion. I continue to experience a dull ache of miserable anticipation most of the hours preceding a talk. But I am learning to offer this to God and to trust him more completely.

24.ii.51 Habbaniyah. When I visited the Levies I was entertained by the Rab Khaila, i.e. the principal Assyrian officer, by name Zaia Gewargis. He gave us tea, bread and honey from the North and we sat as in a diwan with myself occupying the chief seat. We spoke of the Levies' officers of my day, Brigadier Browne, Colonel Back, Captain Bamfield and others – also of George Reed at whose name the Rab Khaila's face softened and brightened. Except for the colour of his eyes and the shape of his skull one would imagine one was talking to a Yorkshireman.

In the afternoon I visited the Civil Cantonment where about 12,000 Arabs, Kurds, Assyrians and Indians live, families of men employed at this station. It is a complete and large Oriental village with its bazaar, mosque and churches. It strained the imagination to recollect that all this was part of a RAF station. We drove to the Assyrian church where the archdeacon and his church council received me with solemn dignity. I passed though a double file of men and women and entered the building. All around were those well-remembered faces, lined with care and toil, with that look of eagerness and expectation which the presence of a British 'official' always awakens among them, a long-suffering patience which I can scarcely look in the face. In the church a choir of men in dingy suits chanted some queer uncouth greeting, clustered round the tattered Syriac service books. I advanced and kissed the cross on the desk in front of the curtain. The curtain was drawn then, revealing the tawdry finery of the altar and its pitiful ornaments. The archdeacon (in his purple faced cassock) took me within the sanctuary. Meanwhile the church filled and as I turned to go I felt I must say something to them. But my mind was confused and haunted and I could only produce a few banal sentences. I got out quickly feeling hot with shame and soon was driving away in the luxurious car placed at my disposal. The final word, from an Assyrian layman who pushed himself forward was: father, our church is orphaned, we have no head, send us someone ... What will happen to them when the Treaty expires and Habbaniyah is no more? What a strange thing it is that this great air station (the nearest point at which our armed forces can get to Soviet Russia), with its enormous organisation and magnificent plant, should nevertheless lack a striking force. There are literally no bomber or fighter squadrons on the station, and almost no aeroplane of any sort or kind. True, within a few hours, such a force could be transported here from the Canal Zone of Egypt, but after Pearl harbour, a few hours might be as bad as a few days away. Further, the site of the great camp is about as unsatisfactory as could well be imagined, being wholly at the mercy of any force which appears upon the high ground which overlooks it from the South West.

25.ii.51 Habbaniyah. I write about an hour before the final act of my visit to the Middle East – the sermon at a united Mission service. This morning I preached at a Church Parade. Officially Church Parades have been abandoned. But as everyone regrets this a new observance has been inaugurated. It is held four times a year and a little oftener and is called 'Church Service following Ceremonial Parade'! And then they call clergy jesuitical! I stood by the AOC (George Beamish) to take the Salute at the March-past. A glorious sunny morning – as good as English June. The service was held in the station church, RCs and ODs marching to their respective shrines. We sang 'Guide me O thou great redeemer' to Cwm Rhondda and 'Jesu lover of my soul' to Aberystwyth and 'City of God' to Richmond. It is so interesting to notice how the lead of St

Mary's Primrose Hill has 'gone out into all lands' and the ideals set up there are now taken for granted (some of them) even in Church Parades in the Forces. I preached on Thanksgiving, paying due respect to St David and the Welsh in whose honour the parade was held.

After the service I had a lime juice in the Mess and then walked out to see a meet of the Exodus hunt. Bill Bailey came vividly to mind for he was a zealous member of this hunt in old days. I mentioned this to one of the huntsmen in his pink coat and he said 'My name is Bill Bailey too'. Many people came to see the meet: sandwiches and cherry brandy were handed round by waiters and there was much pleasant chat. How amiable a creature a fox-hound looks – almost soft.

We lunched with the AOC – a party of about 12 – and were regaled by a really glorious curry. George Beamish is a remarkable officer. He is enormous in bulk and awkward in movement but his eyes glow with friendly fatherliness. He is like an old-fashioned country rector with all his virtues and few of his vices. For all his massive frame he speaks with a high, quiet voice, often hard to hear, and he has a charming manner which is almost bashful.

26.ii.51 Habbaniyah. After the Mission Service last night (which was not very well attended) I went to the Club as the guest of a charming young man who is the Adjutant of the station. His Christian name is Eric but I can't remember his surname. He lives at Blackpool and has an uncle (a Methodist pastor) called Owen who lives in Monks Road, Lincoln. We were tête à tête as he wanted to discuss religious and moral problems. I fell quite in love with this modest but acutely intelligent young man and he spoke so frankly and sensibly about everything. He called me Sir almost all the time and his friendly deference, so natural and unassumed, made an easy background to an evening. A half drunk young officer joined us for part of the time and there was something pleasant even about him in that state. How revealing of his time and character a man is when he is in his cups.

27.ii.51 Ismailia. I spent the last night at Habbaniyah at Air House with the AOC in great comfort. Before dinner we watched boxing in the station gymn; and after we watched some dances by the Assyrian Levies and their womenfolk. The Arab levies did not dance with their women but the Christian Assyrians do. They wore their rich and fanfaronading national dresses and were accompanied by a drum and a reed instrument rather like a powerful bag-pipe chanter. Lady Baker arrived at Habbaniyah in the afternoon in her husband's private Valetta and in it we came hither this morning. The Assyrian Metropolitan, Mar Yussuf, came down to see me off. I had not seen him since 1933 and he did not remember me. His beard is white, though he is only my age, and he has still that quality of inner quiet which struck me so much about him before. He spoke cheerfully about his people and their prospects. What a mistake Providence made in not arranging that he, rather than Mar Shimun, should have been Patriarch during the past 20 years.

After Mafraq, in Jordan, where we touched down, I sat with the pilot all the way. We came over the mountains of Moab on the East of the Dead Sea. The whole course of the River Jordan northwards could be seen and in the distance the shimmering white of the unearthly Mt Hermon. There was Jericho and the steep and rocky road up to Jerusalem. Southward over the haggard mountains we flew down to Aqaba. A few miles South we turned round to W.N.W., crossed the Gulf of Aqaba and then flew over the 'wasteful wilderness' of Sinai to the Bitter Lakes, touching down here at 12.20. The C in C was on the airfield to meet me – a man of great charm and simplicity. We went off at once to lunch with his Senior Air Staff Officer, AVM Long, where we ate a wonderful stuffed fish. After lunch Lady Baker brought me to the two house-boats (where she and the C in C live) on the edge of the Bitter Lake just at the entrance to the Canal going north. At 4 I drove to the church in Ismailia and baptised Mary Elizabeth (Shaw)'s baby Hugo Martin. Her husband Major Montgomery-Campbell is a pleasant man and we had a small tea-party in their 'married quarters' after. I can hardly take the baptism service without wanting to cry. Its beauty and sublimity – especially We receive this child, etc – is such that one can hardly utter it. Mary Elizabeth is like Joan in almost all respects except that no soul looks out of her eyes, or if it does it eludes me. This is horribly uncharitable.

I write this in my little room on the bank before dinner. After dinner I show the Lincoln Cathedral film which they are all dying to see after the enthusiastic account given of it to Lady Baker by George Beamish.

This has really been the richest of all my RAF tours and I feel I have got nearer the officers than ever before. And I certainly have never before been so signally treated – far better than ever I deserve. One more engagement awaits me – a talk to the assembled officers and men of the Lincolnshire Regiment tomorrow morning in Moasca.

2. Visit to the United States to attend and address the Anglican Congress in Minneapolis, 23 July to 18 August 1954

Colin's diary begins as a daily record, but a large part of it was written on 18 August, the first day of his return sea-journey, when he had leisure to write again.

23/7/54 R.M.S. Scythia. Walter got me my breakfast at 8am at Pembroke Gdns and I went off by Underground from Earl's Court to Waterloo. A 1st class carriage was reserved for Canon Macleod Campbell and myself. He seems a pleasant elderly Scotsman... Mr Taylor of the Cunard kept a fatherly watchful eye over us. We got on board by 11.45am. Lunch began at 1pm, just at the interesting moment when we began to steam off. The Abp and Mrs Fisher joined Mac-C and me at lunch (Hors d'oeuvre, Soup, Lobster salad, Caramel Pudding). It was a bit heavy going. The Abp expects a rather boisterous form of conversation. I met White-Thomson and his extremely pretty bride. We four have formed a table party for the rest of the voyage. We arrived at Le Havre just as we were in the middle of dinner, which was excellent, though the service is slow. I have a fine cabin to myself, right up in the front of the boat – no portholes but a vigorous supply of ozone is laid on. ... Watched the transfer of cars from the quay at Le Havre to the hold, an amusing and at times breathtaking diversion.

24/7/54 It has been mainly foggy and drizzly with just one brief interval of pale sunshine. We have seen nothing of the Cornish coast just south of which we have passed. But the sea is mercifully calm, though the breeze is stiff. At breakfast we had brioches and croissants as well as toast. The food is really superb but the service is slow. Last night at dinner nobody changed but tonight quite a number dressed: it is far from obligatory. The Abp and Mrs Fisher continue friendly and I like my table companions. There are two priests – M. Ridgeway and Tindall (Chelmsford Diocese) whom I have got to know. At 4.30 we had a cinema show – 'isn't life wonderful?'. Amusing in parts.

Sunday, 25 July. Still no sun but mercifully calm. We passed, out of sight, the southern coast of Ireland. At 8am the Abp celebrated in the lounge – c.35 present. At 11 the Captain presided at Divine Service in the lounge. Crowded out, with an overflow (also full) in the Garden Lounge (a room reminiscent, as to its 'Garden' quality of the famous *'jardin d'été'* of the Toulouse Hotel). The captain took the service (mainly Mattins) in an admirable manner, a junior officer reading the Lesson. In the congregation were the Abp, myself and four priests. After the service the Abp etc and I were invited to the Captain's cabin for drinks. At 6.30 I conducted Evensong, prefacing it with a brief liturgical sermon. About 75-100 present, including the Abp, who gave the blessing in his cassock. I was astonished at the good congregations especially as there are so many French Canadians on board who are RC (there are 5 RC priests). The authorities keep one supplied with fresh fruit in one's cabin, a pleasant ministration. I had a fine chicken curry at lunch and, after whitebait, a good *jambon sauce madère* for dinner. I feel well and rested and enjoy everything that goes on.

26/7/54. A gale sprang up about 2am which has lasted all day, producing a rough sea with a heavy swell. We pitch to and fro on a great scale. At first, when I got up, I thought I was going to be bad, but Kwells made it all right. I celebrated in the Lounge at 7.30 and realised the force of the verse in the psalms: 'They reel to and fro and stagger like a drunken man.' It was very hard to maintain a standing position. To the disgust of my companions who were definitely queezy I ordered kippers and pork sausages for breakfast which I found utterly delightful.

I had some talk with one of the Judges of the International Court at the Hague, a Canadian. He said they don't get enough business: all transactions are either in English or French. If a party want another language they must employ an interpreter. The Abp goes faithfully round talking to everyone, putting everyone at their ease, and being most acceptable to all from the stewards upwards. He has a great gift for sympathy and friendly approachableness.
Smoked salmon, Trout, and Roast Beef for dinner. It's still rough as I go to bed, but the continuous sunshine has been lovely. I went to a good film about a village protest concerning use of a bird sanctuary for a bombing range.

27/7 (Wedding day) Assisted White-Thomson at Mass in lounge. Sunny day and quite calm again, good fresh breeze. Spent morning reading *Jerusalem Journey* and walked up and down the boat deck. The ship's surgeon joined me. He is at the Children's Hospital in Great Ormonde St and has taken on two trips of the Scythia as a holiday. Nice fellow – was at Merton. Fond of cathedrals. Unmarried. Read again in the afternoon in my deck-chair. At 4 they bring tea to one's chair. Another talk with Judge Read and his wife. She is some relation of

Mrs Hale (of Lincoln). He, it appears, was a Rhodes scholar at Univ: and is still an Honorary Fellow. Knows John Wild.

Sent off a cable to Mary at 12 noon. At dinner I bought a bottle of Burgundy (Nuits St George 1949) price 14/- and we all drank Mary's health. White-Thomson proposed 'and the four boys' and we drank again. A very nice dinner indeed in every respect. I feel immensely rested and content.

30/7 As soon as I had sent off my letter to Mary, telling her of our fog-bound condition, the fog lifted and the sun shone out in its full strength. We are in the entrance to the St Lawrence and are due to berth at 4pm tomorrow. As far as I can see we shall be almost fully occupied with formalities between now and then. The last two days with its fog and (largely unseen) icebergs has been rather a trial. The business of tipping looms before us all, with the rest of the problems of disembarcation. It is so hard to realise that for most of the people on the boat the arrival at Quebec is a home-coming and not the threshold of an unknown world.

18/8 S.S. Caronia. It wasn't easy to keep a diary at Minneapolis so a few of the impressions and events of that delightful time must now be recorded on the return voyage.

At Quebec I got on to a train with McLeod Campbell and the Fishers on which we all had sleepers and it took us to Toronto. Waking up and seeing Canadian villages out of the window was exciting, and breakfast in the restaurant car was also most pleasant. The trains are much larger and heavier than anything in Europe and the coaches more commodious (though the gauge of the rails *seems* smaller than our standard gauge). The dining car could carry a double row of tables for four and leave a nice wide gang-way between. All the train stewards are Negroes even in Canada, at any rate they were on the two trains I travelled by. Breakfast in Canada and USA is quite a heavy meal. You begin with fruit juice or cereal and and then have bacon and eggs and some other fairly solid dish. Marmalade etc follows.

We arrived at Toronto at 11. I then left McLeod Campbell and the Fishers and after feeling quite lost in the vast station, where everyone looked and seemed so foreign, I went to the Cathedral which is quite near. The weather was hot and sunny. I arrived in the midst of a Sung Eucharist in the large and not very attractive late Victorian Gothic church. The celebrant wore surplice and stole (red in honour of St James, though it was August 1st) but the assisting clergy were to me out of sight in the sedilia. The server wore a short surplice and a red cassock. Many communicated. The church was by no means full; the choir was large and sang well some of a Mass by Oldroyd.

I had lunch at the York Hotel, opposite the station, a regular hive of activity that day as there was a rally of the Canadian Legion. Lunch was beautifully served but, owing to my ignorance of how to read the menu properly and my pride in not asking for enlightenment, not very satisfying – a nice consommé, a salad with cold ham and some sort of an ice. After lunch Campbell joined me in having a sight-seeing tour of the city in a glass-roofed charabanc – very hot. Toronto is not a very impressive place, though of course, being new, I found every detail interesting. We had tea in some popular restaurant (coffee and cake) where everyone else was seriously eating solid dishes, e.g. salmon, beef-steak, etc. Then we strolled down to the lake-front. On our return we met the Abp and

Mrs Fisher bound on the same errand. Eventually we had a good dinner at the York. Prices for food are pretty high. You can't get much to eat at a decent restaurant under about two dollars odd, i.e. about 17/6d, though it can of course be done when you know the ropes. At about 10pm we boarded the train and I entered my Duplex Roomette, a wonderful institution of little compartments dovetailed into one another, each complete with bed, lavatory seat, wash-basin, iced water to drink. At first you don't see the bed at all, only a nice window seat. When you are undressed you pull the bed out of the wall like a drawer and it comes out already made up. There is only about 1 sq ft to stand in when the bed is out. In the morning you get out into the sq ft and push the bed back and you have your little compartment to dress and wash in, and the window seat all ready for the day. Porters in Canada and USA expect 20-25 cents for each bag and the steward of a sleeper about 50 cents a night. It's a lot of money but they do their work well and reliably and courteously.

In the morning Campbell and I breakfasted on the train with the Fishers (breakfast costs about $1.75 i.e, 12/6d) and we arrived in Chicago about 8.30 am. Here several high officials of the railway met us and a nice young man called Zimmermann devoted himself to Campbell and me, got us porters, got (and paid for) a taxi and took us from the Dearborn station where we arrived to the Union station whence we went to Minneapolis. When you arrive at an American station you get down out of the coach on to a very low concrete platform (as in France) between two tracks. It is severely practical and very narrow. There are no seats and the public is not admitted. It is usually dark and grim at the great termini. After walking along the immense length of the train (some of them have about 25 enormous coaches all drawn by 2 or 3 huge Diesel haulers, though in Canada the locomotives are still steam-powered and vaguely reminiscent of the shape and outline of European locomotives, though far more massive, with great cow-catchers and a perpetually ringing bell. We sped through the streets of Chicago, where much town re-planning is in progress and where we saw our first glimpse of big sky-scrapers and dived into the Union station, a truly wonderful place. Red-caps seized our luggage and bore it off while we walked leisurely to the train. Timidly I bought a copy of the *New Yorker* and the *Chicago Tribune*. The latter is the local daily, but it consists of a *series* of English-sized newspapers and makes a formidable bundle. We got into our Drawing Room or Parlour car, the last in the train. This contains a double row of beautiful arm-chairs which you can swivel round and make face any direction, and you can let down the back like a dentist's chair. All air-conditioned and deliciously cool. The car tapers off into a sort of observation annexe at the back. Next to our coach was the Dining car, lovely, cool and efficient with Negro waiters in spotless white uniforms. The Head waiter is a white man who wears grey trousers and a blue blazer, like a guardsman officer on holiday, cool and informal. Beyond the diner was the dome-roof observation car, a two-decker coach. Underneath is a nice cozy bar with tables and comfortable seats: above is a double row of double-seats right on the roof level of the rest of the train with a domed glass roof. You can see all the scenery in one, so to speak, and get a very complete view of the scenery you pass. Anyone can repair to this car and sit for a while. Though air-conditioned the sun is apt to make it a little trying for a long sojourn. Beyond the dome-car are the ordinary coach-class coaches. At each end of these is a little room; one for men and one for women, with lavatory and wash basins attached. It is all very comfortable. Every seat faces the direction of the train.

I was intrigued by the Negro waiters and attendants. They behave with great courtesy and yet are not at all obsequious. They are quick and efficient, and have a curiously aloof manner which is, however, not at all offensive or self-conscious. Some have a rather philosophically cynical bearing which again was not insolent. The porters (red-caps) were firm and stern but not in my experience rude. They worked hard and seemed careful of one's property and handled it deftly and surely. But they were very insistent on being paid well and often claimed their tip before carrying out their service. Pre-payment did not result in the work being done badly.

The country between Minneapolis and Chicago is most romantic and beautiful after passing Milwaukee. You go through Wisconsin first and then into Minnesota. Much of the 'Milwaukee Road', as our track is called, runs along the Mississippi and wonderful views open out. It is thickly wooded and there are many hills and limestone crags of strange appearance. The very train we sat in was called 'The Morning Hiawatha'. I have seldom enjoyed a train journey so much as on the Milwaukee Road. The towns and villages we passed were all set among trees and their outskirts consisted in trim avenues of trees with smooth lawns, no walls or fences, and neat well designed houses of endlessly varying design. The excellent taste of nearly everything modern in USA surprised and delighted me. Campbell and I had a wondrous lunch of strong consommé, tenderloin steaks and mushrooms, apple-pie and cheese, and glorious coffee.

At Minneapolis my kind host Mr Harold Tearse met me. I liked him at once, though his obvious wealth seemed likely to be a barrier. Yet it was not so. He is of the type of rich man who though enjoying his riches and the position they give him retains an essential purity of heart and a simple sense of moral responsibility. Mrs Tearse, once evidently a great beauty, shared some of this, though she was less unworldly in some sense of that word. But both were very sympathetically kind and did not 'kill one with kindness' so that my stay was wholly unembarrassing. Their home stood along the West Lake of the Isles Boulevard, facing the lovely tree-bordered lake. It was of modest size, sparely but sumptuously furnished, in most admirable taste. My room had attached wash-place, lavatory and shower. I met one of their daughters and their son. The daughter, aged 25 and married, was extremely beautiful; the son very common-place looking but very pleasant – also married.

I was taken round for drinks at Mrs Tearse's father's house. He is a Mr Searle, aged 92 and I should say a millionaire, with a fine collection of pictures. Though 92 he goes to his office every day and has all his wits about him. He too is Episcopalian and was much impressed that I had 'come over with the Archbishop of Canterbury'. In his house I met the Deputy Director of the Art Institute, a forthcoming and enthusiastic young man who was eager to hear about the stalls and stained glass at Lincoln.

On most days I breakfasted at the Tearses. Mrs T did not appear. We started with Honeydew Canteloupe, surely the most exquisite fruit in the world, and orange juice and then (after cereal) eggs (in varying forms) with bacon and once or twice brook trout. The tendency is to put everything on one plate so that one has bacon and eggs and toast and maramalade all going at once on the same plate.

Within 24 hours of my arrival I got a touch of laryngitis. It seemed sad to have come 4000 miles or more purely to make a speech and then to be unable to utter. But I stayed 2 days in bed and recovered enough to read my paper on Saturday 7th August. I was looked after by the two servants, Ida (an ancient Norwegian) and a second whose name I forget but who is a school teacher on holiday. They were both 'on my side' from the start, and brought up glasses of glorious iced milk, or ginger ale and grape juice at all hours.

The Congress centred on the Cathedral of S. Mark and its adjacent premises, a very large assortment of halls and offices. The Dean of Minneapolis could not believe me when I told him that at Lincoln we have neither the place nor the resources even to prepare a cup of tea or write a letter on cathedral premises. A great yard was used as the parking place for the vast fleet of superb cars which were at our disposal for getting about. The main sessions of the Congress were held in the polygonal Methodist church (Hennepin) nearby, while meals were served in its basement to all comers free of charge (good meals too). Committees met in various places. Mine was in the Unitarian church, a very modern streamlined construction quite near. As the real chairman never turned up I was elected in his place. I had as secretary a Mr Baldwin, some-time governor of Connecticut and now a Federal Judge, a man of incredible efficiency, who could turn into a polished resolution any remarks made, however brokenly, by any of the large committee and produce it almost before he or she had finished speaking. My committee included about 5 or 6 bishops (none of English provinces), 3 Japanese, 2 Negroes, I Indian and so on. We had the most free discussions and almost everybody spoke quite 'uninhibitedly' and on the most acutely controversial questions such as the Atom Bomb (raised by the Japs) and race problems (raised by coal-black Bishop Howells of West Africa). It was hard work and I am glad to say I did it well, according to Ian White Thomson [Dean of Canterbury] and the exuberant Bishop of Eastern Oregon.

In the general sessions we all sat where we liked in the body of the church. On the platform, on a raised dais on its 'Eastern' end sat Bp Sherrill, Presiding Bp of USA Anglicans, on an oaken throne, with the Abp of Canterbury on his right. (They both interfered in proceedings much too much.) To one side sat the Bishop of Connecticut and on the other Bp Carruthers of S.Carolina. In the middle at the front of the platform was a desk with microphone from which the speakers addressed the Congress.

Owing to Laryngitis I missed the first Session of the Congress, and the Saturday one, at which I read my paper on Worship, was the first I had attended. While Dr Massey Shepherd, who preceded me, read his paper I listened with anxious attention but only to know whether he would say anything that I had to say. I therefore missed the main import of his words which, as I afterwards discovered, was good. It is much to his credit and mine in sticking to our official syllabus that we did not even overlap in our speeches on any single point. The Abp told me later that when Dr Shepherd finished, he (the Abp) felt sorry for me who had to follow as Dr S had been so good. He added that his sorrow was ill-timed for I had more than held my own.

I was amazed at the success of my paper, for no sooner had I got into the reading of it than I realised it was going down well and that my style and its contents were appealing to the audience. This gave me good heart in reading it and the *way* you read a paper matters much. I had feared that much of the content and all the manner in which it was presented might be too provincial and awaken no response in the many-coloured audience with its differing cultures and national traditions. The fact that my paper 'went down' is a singular proof that there is an 'Anglican tradition' of quite a real kind within the Christian tradition and that it includes a 'pattern' of thinking and even a 'pattern' of the humorous. For all the jokes told, and were applauded vociferously and long. It was a most pleasant and heartening experience.

We had several excursions and treats during the Congress. The first was a bus ride to Faribault, some 60 miles south of Minneapolis where the first cathedral of this region of USA was built. It was also the first church built to be a cathedral. The Bp Coadjutor of Toronto was my companion on this trip – Wilkinson by name, a big, pleasant, man. Though the cathedral was a poor thing ecclesiologically and architecturally I found it very moving to think of anyone daring to build an Anglican cathedral in the midst of this outlandish district and to present Prayer Book Services to the Indian inhabitants.

One night the Tearses took me to some friends of theirs (with whom the Rawlinsons are staying – also Lady Swabey and Mrs Coombes) who live at Wayzatta on the edge of the lovely Lake Minnetonka. We had a wonderful trip in a terrific motor launch (capable of doing 45 knots) plentifully supplied with drinks – highballs and lowballs – the while. The warm summer twilight and distant setting sun added to the beauty of the scenes through which we passed. Our hosts were Mr and Mrs Strong. Mrs Strong was perfectly delightful and I quite liked Mrs Cole, the wife of the editor of *The Minneapolis Tribune*, also of the party, a woman with a voice as deep as Mrs Alington's. She told me she had 12 grandchildren and was a pioneer in the promotion of Birth Control in Minnesota. We had a wonderful supper in the Strongs' magnificent house after, though I cannot remember what we had.

Another night all the Bishops were entertained by Bp Keeler (of Minneapolis) and his Coadjutor Bp Kellogg. The dinner was at the Minneapolis Club and I sat between the Bp of Jerusalem, whom of course I knew well, and Bp Oldham (late of Albany, N.Y.) whom I have met on and off ever since I was at Fulham. Opposite were the Bp of Ripon and the Bp of Carlisle. We had wonderful beefsteaks but poor wine – the only occasion I met wine in USA. It wasn't very good. I asked Jerusalem if he knew what it was and he replied 'No, and I don't believe I want to'. A number of speeches were made after – a mere orgy of funny stories, some of which seemed to me rather unsuitable on such an occasion. Bp Sherrill tried commendably, but rather heavily, to raise the tone of the speeches, but his efforts were unavailing and not followed by successors.

On one night we were all entertained in parties of about 12 in the homes of church-people dwelling in S. Paul, the 'twin city' of Minneapolis on the left bank of the Mississippi. We had 'supper' at about 5.30. In my party was Cockin, Noel Hudson of Newcastle, Nigel Cornwall of Borneo, dear Bishop and Mrs Quin of Texas, a layman from Lincoln (Nebraska), Brown of the Missions to Seamen and others. We first of all walked or stood about the garden drinking an innocuous cool punch and after about three quarters of an hour went in to supper, which, as at the Strongs' and nearly everywhere in USA, was served in the cafetaria manner. The *pièce de resistance* was a gigantic cold turkey. We took our spoils to different tables. I found myself seated next to a layman from Philadelphia, a man about 70, very nice. He told me his mother was born in the South and at her wedding had one present consisting of four slaves. It was a very near connection to circumstances which I imagined were far more remote in time. After supper we went in buses (as we had arrived) to the Auditorium for the mass missionary meeting. It was beautifully cool for the whole floor was ice. We sat round the edges. Below the platform sat in red robes all the Archbishops and Primates. On the platform was a large choir of young men and women who sang extremely well. Their repertory included Holst's 'Turn back o man'. It was grandly done. The young men all wore light grey trousers, white shirts open at the neck, and light fawn jackets. There were three speakers; coal-black Bp Howells, who was too prosey for such an occasion, an American Bp from Alaska (not bad) and my old friend Bp de Mel from Ceylon, almost as black as Howells. But, better than anyone so far at the Congress, he knew how to use the English language, how to manage his voice and hands and what to say! It was a fine performance. Afterwards we drove back to Minneapolis. If S. Paul and Minneapolis are 'twin cities' they are far from being Siamese twins.

' Dinners in Minneapolis homes' on Thursday 12th August saw me a guest of Bp Kellogg in his very beautiful house (1805 Logan Avenue) not far from W.L. of the Isles. The Bps of Exeter and Johannesburg, and Bp Quin of Texas and one or two Americans were fellow guests. There was an hour's drinking before dinner and pretty stiff the drinks were. Exeter and I had almost as much as was good for us – 'bourbon on the rocks' i.e. neat whisky poured into a 'lowball' glass full of bits of ice – but John Gregg, one of the prominent laymen of S Mark's Cathedral got quite drunk. Mrs Kellogg was on the stage before she married the Bishop and she looked it. She and her husband were very kind hosts but did not appear unduly concerned at John Gregg's abiding state of intoxication. We had a great ham for supper, accompanied by the most marvellous shelled shrimps I ever saw – larger and better flavoured. We fended as usual for ourselves, and returned to sit at tables laid for 4. Gregg came to my table and was a never ending cause of embarrassment to one the entire evening.

Another evening the whole congress (it seemed) went to the Minnikahta Club – a large 'frame' building, luxuriously furnished and set in a wonderful park with lovely distant views. After a grand dinner (roast beef and lobster Newburg was the centrepiece) we were entertained by bathing belles and expert divers in the illuminated swimming pool.

There were many opportunities of course for getting to know individuals and exchanging ideas. I had several talks with Philip Carrington (Abp of Quebec) and found in him much to approve and enjoy. Like me he is a fanatic for the Authorised Version. Even though he rules in Quebec where Romanism is so aggressive and strong, he has a deep affection for the Roman church. Missionary Bishops such as Nigel Cornwall of Borneo and Coote of Rio Pongas I much enjoyed meeting – also Dale of Jamaica and the Bp of Qu'Appelle who is a Lincolnshire man from Sutton Bridge. I found Pike, Dean of New York, delightful and also the Bp of Eastern Oregon and Peabody, Bp of Central New York, who rowed in the same boat as Judge Shove at Trinity, Cambridge. And many others.

I stopped a few hours in Chicago on the return journey. It was very hot, and raining. I was met by a great 'limousine' (by order of Harold Tearse) which drove me about the city; it looked inhuman and cheerless in the rain. I boarded the 6.30pm train for New York, had a very economical dinner on the train, but slept very comfortably in my Roomette. Running down beside the Hudson from Albany to New York on Sunday morning was delightful, though the sun failed to appear and a strange haze made visibility hard. The train entered New York through what I knew must be Harlem since no one but Negroes was to be seen in the streets. At 2pm promptly we stopped at the Grand Central Station and I got a taxi without difficulty, a huge yellow monster. With a screech and a roar it leapt away with me from the curb and up from the bowels of the earth (where American stations in big towns seem to be) to the streets and avenues of New York, all looking rather Sabbatarian.

The General Theological Seminary, a building greatly reminiscent within and without of Keble College, stands in a very down-at-heel part of the city. But it has its lawns and trees which make it a pleasant retreat. I reported to Mrs Rose, the wife of the absent Dean of the Seminary and she gave me full instructions how to get to S. John the Divine by bus. I was very proud of my bus journey! Once you get used to it New York must be a singularly easy place to move about in. The Cathedral was terrific, but the Choir and Apse a sort of Romanesque. The latter is, I believe, destined for demolition and rebuilding. Some of the stained glass was good. The lighting was well done. Choral Evensong (only 1 priest present, and girls as sopranos) was soon over and though the Psalms, or rather Psalm, was despatched far too quickly the service had dignity. I did not wait for the sermon.

After tea at the Seminary some American parson drove the Bp of Truro and his friend John, a black priest from W.Africa, and me, all round the notable parts of New York for two and a half hours. The sun was out and it was all deeply interesting. Very famous, much photographed, places always have an air of familiarity when one first sees them in the flesh and yet of unfamiliarity too for the *colour* is nearly always a surprise. So it was with New York. I had not realised that the great sky-scrapers are not of a uniform tint: their variety was most pleasing and indeed the total view of New York as one steams away is of surpassing beauty, especially as to colour and texture of the mighty towers.

The next day (after a very hot and sleepless night) after a nice breakfast at the Roses' we went on the subway to 5th Avenue and wandered about window-shopping, went up the 102 floors of the Empire State Building, and in the evening went to see Cinerama, the latest thing in the Movie world, at some beautiful theatre in Broadway. It was an amazing experience. The Bishop of Southwark was now added to our party. At 12 noon next day, 17th August, I boarded the Caronia, a queen among ships known as the Green Goddess or the Millionaires' Paradise (34,000 tons). I have a very large two-berth cabin to myself, including a lavatory and shower. It's a touring ship, one class normally, but on its cross-Atlantic trips it carries a Cabin class, but the accommodation is really First class throughout. At my table sit the White-Thomsons, the Archdeacon of Brisbane (Birch) and a Mr Bryony, one of the Directors of Mowbray's. I have seen a lot of a Mr Jack Haskell, a not un-amusing or un-interesting American ex-producer who gave me some of his to-be-published memoirs to read and says I remind him of George Grossmith! A wild Episcopalian couple from Kansas (name of Harper) completes my company. Usual invitations to cocktails with the Captain, and also the Purser; all the officers of the ship are young and mainly unmarried owing to the long absence from home of the ship on cruises round the world.

On the way out we put our watches back an hour each day and so had 25-hour days. These seemed unduly long. Returning, we have reversed the process and have 23-hour days. These are *much* too short. It is strange what difference an hour either way can make to a day. I have slept poorly on the return journey. Today we have passed the Scilly Isles and later the Cornish coast looking lovely in the sun. But it's much colder.

TIPS At the end of the voyage I tipped as follows: Cabin Steward £1, Table steward £1, Chief table steward 10/- (unnecessary but he put on, especially for me, curry one day and snails another), Deck steward 10/-, Page boy 5/- (also unnecessary, but he was such a nice smiling boy who always paid great attentions to me!)

On the Scythia I only paid the Cabin and Table Stewards, for I never saw the Deck Steward on departure.

3. *A visit to Uppsala as one of two representatives of the Church of England at the Consecration of a new Bishop of Stockholm*

The only reference to this I have seen is the following article, composed by Colin and published in the *Lincoln Diocesan Magazine* for January, 1955

A SWEDISH CHURCH SERVICE

Now that Canterbury Convocation has given formal approval for closer relations with the Church of Sweden, it may interest Anglicans to hear something about the recent Consecration of a new Bishop of Stockholm at which the Bishop of Fulham and the Dean of Lincoln represented the Church of England at the request of the Archbishop of Canterbury.

The Consecration took place in the Metropolitan cathedral – that of Uppsala – about thirty-five miles north of Stockholm. The Archbishop of Uppsala, Dr Yngve Brilioth, presided at the rite. The bestowal of holy orders is not with the Swedish Lutherans, as with us, an integral part of the Eucharistic rite. It is a separate office and on Advent Sunday 1954 it immediately followed the now usual form of Sunday morning worship which we would call the 'Ante-Communion'. But it is a sign of the times that at 8.30am the same morning the Holy Communion was celebrated in an ancient brick church next door to the Cathedral at which the Archbishop (and most of the other bishops who were to assist at the laying on of hands) made his Communion, along with the Bishop-elect Dr Ljungberg. Even though this was an 'early service' and no choir assisted, it was sung very heartily by the congregation.

The celebrant was the Dean of Stockholm cathedral, who has the ancient title of Pastor Primarius. He was assisted by three priests in albes and crossed stoles, he himself of course wearing the chasuble, etc., over his albe. Wafer-bread is used and each communicant receives the Holy Sacrament in his mouth from the priest's hand. The congregation approaches the altar, with its crucifix and (in this case) three lighted candles, in railfuls, and does not wait in two files as we do. Everyone at the rails waits till all of his railful are communicated before leaving.

The consecration of the Bishop (preceded as I have said by the Ante-Communion) began at 11am in the cathedral. It is an impressive building built in the xiv-xv centuries in the regular Baltic Gothic style of the time. The great piers of the nave are enormously high and the vault springs from them only just below roof level. There is no triforium, only a clerestory. It is apsidal at the East end and behind the high altar is the great gilt shrine of St. Erik. The nave and chancel were well lit by immense crystal chandeliers bearing electric candles. The organ is placed in a gallery at the W. end of the nave and the choir also occupies part of this gallery – a choir of men and women.

Shortly before 11 the Archbishop and Dean went in their ordinary outdoor clothes to meet the King and Queen at the West door and escorted their Majesties to seats near the altar at the front of the congregation. The ancient Introit for Advent Sunday was then superbly sung to plainsong by the choir during which two priests in chasubles went to the altar and began the Ante-Communion. The Bishops who were to assist at the Consecration, together with the Archbishop, took no part in this preliminary rite but clothed in their outdoor dress sat in pews beneath the pulpit. But after the sermon these bishops went to the sacristy and were there vested in albes and copes, mitres being on this occasion restricted to the Archbishop and his two assistant bishops. This was done to keep in countenance the bishops from Iceland and Finland who do not habitually use them. All the bishops carried their pastoral staves. Among them were bishops from Norway, Denmark, Finland and Iceland as well as from England, a total of 17. The episcopal procession then went up the Nave to the high altar while the congregation sang what we would call a hymn, but the Scandinavians a psalm. No one who has not heard a Scandinavian congregation sing can have any idea of the utter majesty of sound which is put forth.

The bishops formed a semi-circle facing the altar with the bishop-elect at the 'peak' of the semi-circle, furthest from the altar. The Archbishop and his two Assistant Bishops stood on the footpace. A second sermon was now preached (the first was preached by the Dean of Uppsala) by the Archbishop from the altar and then the brief rite of consecration followed. A feature of this was a sort of 'liturgical testimony' in which each bishop in turn recited towards the bishop-elect a verse or two from the Scriptures setting forth aspects of the pastoral office. While the *Veni, Sancte Spiritus* was sung (in Latin) the Bishop-elect was vested in cope, stole, cross and ring. After the laying on of hands, during which the Lord's Prayer was recited by the Archbishop, he was given staff and mitre. After some more prayers the rite was complete and the Archbishop led the new Bishop of Stockholm out of the cathedral followed by all the other bishops.

English visitors of course missed the culmination of the rite in the Holy Eucharist, but there could be little doubt that the 'intention' of the whole service was to send forth a new bishop in the traditional and Catholic sense. These bald words give no inkling of the solemnity and fervour and outward splendour of the whole rite.

A banquet followed in the Archbishop's house and the King and Queen were there. In his speech the Archbishop laid special stress on his pleasure at the presence of two English bishops, and the Bishop of Fulham replied in terms which appeared to give general satisfaction. The King also spoke briefly and after the meal he and the Queen moved about talking to all the guests in a most charming and intimate way.

18

THE LAST FORTY MONTHS

C OLIN AND MARY moved to Henfield at the very end of October 1964, sooner than they had originally expected, because they had had their offer for a suitable house very promptly accepted. Almost at once Colin wrote two encouraging-sounding letters to me: 'It is hard work here trying to recognise not too slowly people one used to know in 1940, some of whom were old then'; 'Changes I made 25 years ago in the services are still observed', and adding that the congregations were now much bigger. Also, 'the place is much cleaner than industrial Lincoln'. Ten days later he wrote to say 'we get more 'straight' and 'settled in' every day but it is a lengthy business. He had been clearing out an old garden shed, and hoped to become more skilful at 'working with his hands'.

Incidentally, his dressing room-cum-study reminded him of Archdeacon Grantly's room [in Trollope's Barchester novels] where he kept his 'boots and his sermons'. In two more letters written before Christmas he talks about his frequent walks around the village, and the stimulus of the unspoilt scenery and the country air. Mary herself wrote: 'Daddy is *very* much better. He has hardly talked about his health since being here, and sleeps 8 to 8 1/2 hours every night.' She had just returned from a few days away, and was able to say 'Daddy and Michael got on well without me'. On 31 January 1965, she again reports that Colin coped well 'with the stoves and getting his meals'. When she had returned from a committee meeting in London, 'he was calm and cheerful'. All these things were signs of 'how much better he is'. She added that, if they could weather the next six months, after which there would be no more life insurance premiums to pay, she would feel very hopeful. Charles would by then be self-supporting and they could live on their income.

On 9 February Colin wrote that, far from being bored, he had lots to do:

> To begin with one can think more than seemed possible when there was so much to organize, and administration was so continuously pressing. The virtual disappearance of that is an immense relief and enables one to enjoy life even when there is not much obvious cause for rejoicing.

Quite apart from occasional work in the house, Colin also reported that he was 'enjoying a little work with the Old People's Home' – writing letters for one inmate, and ferrying three arthritic ones by car to the 'Darby and Joan'

417

club, run by Mrs Whittome. He also assisted the vicar, Paul Peters, by conducting or assisting at services, and took occasional confirmations around the diocese. But Mary's catarrh and sinus trouble got worse, and she was sent by the local doctor to Brighton for an ENT specialist test, which pointed to thyroid deficiency. She was now feeling too weak to garden, though this had encouraged Colin to do a lot of gardening himself, even to enjoy it. But then, in August, Colin had two strokes, so that he found reading very difficult. However, Mary's own health started to improve and she was soon writing to me:

> Things are very good here considering. Daddy is now allowed to do more or less what he wants provided he does not accept any engagements for 'duty' – either taking services or preaching – for the present.

She added that he was very cheerful and had been out of the house without getting giddy. In October they went to Bures Vicarage in Suffolk, where Colin's nephew, Ian, was then vicar. Just before they went, Colin wrote to tell me:

> I have agreed to preach [that is, read, a sermon] and also hold a special confirmation. It will be my first sermon since my strokes and I hope I shall be able to stay the course and not suddenly fade out. It's so embarrassing for the worshippers. ... I'm beginning to be able to concentrate and read a bit now. Until recently, I had hardly done either for the past year, almost.

Just after Christmas, 1965, Mary wrote:

> Daddy celebrated the Parish Communion without any mishap. The Vicar, who really is a *good* man, stood by him like an efficient but unobtrusive nanny, prompting occasionally if he looked like forgetting what to do next.

In March 1966, Colin 'had another cerebral thrombosis' after he had seemed 'pretty well for two or three days'. Mary wrote that it affected only his balance. He had called out that 'he was very queer and the room seemed to be tilted up so that he thought he would fall out of bed.' Later he was very sick, but felt better when wedged in bed in the darkened room. 'We had to cancel two confirmations he was to take tomorrow and next week, and I strongly suspect he will have to give up the idea of doing them as a regular undertaking.' Six days later, Colin wrote that this thrombosis was 'rather stronger than its predecessors and I still feel very giddy, and progress is slower than I could wish'. Mary reported on 5 April that, although he was progressing, 'he was a bit depressed at having had to give up the idea of doing confirmations this month. He walks pretty well now though occasionally his gait is a bit erratic'. But, by May, Colin and Mary were able to go on the Adriatic cruise for which they had booked. On their return from this Mary wrote: 'Daddy is much less mentally confused now at home, though occasionally talks oddly about people who don't exist – then 'comes to' and stops.' On 2 July Colin wrote to me:

Life ridiculously *seems* more busy now than when I was at Durham or Lincoln. It must be a delusion. I wonder how it is to be explained. I also find a strange delusion in that I *nearly always* think there are more people in a room than there really are. Sometimes this is most distressing!

He then goes on to tell me that he took a confirmation at West Grinstead, where he had never been before, and that there were brasses in the church. Soon afterwards, Mary wrote that they had both been to Repton, where my brother Philip was teaching. Colin had been very well: 'He had never got confused about who people were, or talked about 'the other Mary', and in fact she has only made a brief reappearance since our return, which is good.' She then enlarges on the problems of Evelyn's 'nervous trouble', and the fact that there is really nobody else near at hand who can take responsibility for her. As she will be moving to Henfield shortly she will at any rate be useful in looking after Colin when she has to go up to London for a meeting:

Things haven't been too bad. The new drug the psychiatrist prescribed has definitely helped. But his mental grasp *is* deteriorating slowly, and he knows it. He's going to the English Hymnal Trustees meeting and I think has made up his mind to resign the Chairmanship, as he simply cannot grasp even the ordinary business of the meeting. I shall have to take him to Brighton, put him on the train, and meet him on return. I have to go over and over what he must do in London. But if he does give up everything he will only have his *immediate* situation to brood over. It's hard to advise him. ... Though it is very painful and distressing, I feel quite serene inside most of the time. I have got through the turmoil of doubt and so on which I was in and settled down to a way which I can manage.

Colin and Mary came to us in Rugby for a week in September, and enjoyed also seeing much of their grandchildren. Next month Evelyn had a tumour removed from her large intestine. Mary wrote to tell us, adding that Colin had been very anxious about her, 'and consequently even more difficult than usual.' After Christmas she wrote (15/1/67): 'Daddy seems none the worse for the various comings and goings over the Christmas holidays, though he has been pretty demanding since he got me all to himself again, which I rather expected.' In February, when she came to Rugby for a meeting, we agreed to have him by himself for the inside of two days:

In the last few days he's been better. This follows a long spell of getting confused and difficult every single evening ... till I began to feel dreadfully weary and impatient. His contribution to a radio programme on Percy Dearmer, broadcast on February 12 th, was drastically cut, though the producer had been satisfied. Daddy took it surprisingly well.

After a visit of Philip, Anna-Maria and their children in April, 'he was very tired (and so was I) and more confused than ever, with worse aphasia, but he's had a few good times'. Colin was much cheered by the visit of Bishop Riches (of Lincoln) and his wife Catherine, as, indeed, he nearly always was when visited by people he knew and liked. In June, Michael Bede, now up at Oxford, had an operation for a detached retina, and had to recuperate at home. She wrote that 'Daddy is very exacting at present, and less able to concentrate on anything for more than a very short time, and of course he is terribly jealous of the fuss about Michael, poor darling.' 'Evelyn still looks very ill and terribly thin', she went on, 'though more cheerful than she was. I am *hoping* to get a night away in the first week of July. I need it badly.' Among other new problems Mary faced was 'the difficulty of getting forms filled in by him'. In a letter she wrote in October late one evening, she says: 'Evelyn's stay in hospital has done her good. But I must stop now or Daddy will be coming down and getting dressed again. An hour ago he went to start getting undressed and emerged after twenty minutes fully clad in his best overcoat and hat and stick and preparing to go out somewhere.' However, the day before Anna's birthday, she wrote enclosing some sweets for her, saying: 'Colin bought these sweets *by himself* – quite an achievement', and in December, Mary and he 'quite enjoyed (her) birthday lunch in Brighton'.

But the crisis came at the very beginning of 1968, when, on 5 January, I received an SOS telephone call from Mary. Colin was now refusing to take his pills and could not be persuaded to go to the lavatory at all. I arrived next morning from Rugby to find that there had been no change, and was unable to improve the situation myself. Mary had no alternative but to ring the hospital. The ambulance arrived in the afternoon, and we followed it in my car to Graylingwell Mental Hospital, on the edge of Chichester. When we had seen Colin settled down in bed in a ward which seemed quiet enough despite the good number of beds in it, we returned to Henfield. The arterio-sclerosis was much too far advanced to hope for any reversal, as Mary already knew, and he died peacefully after just under seven weeks in Graylingwell, in the presence of Mary and my brother Philip. Mary had visited him several times, but Colin accepted her departures without plea or protest. He was cremated at Chichester, and his ashes were buried in the south-east transept of Lincoln Cathedral, at the north-west corner of the carved stone slab which covers the grave of Bishop Grosseteste.

Obituary

Here is the obituary of Colin in The Times *written by George Timms, who was then Vicar of St Mary's, Primrose Hill:*

The Right Reverend David Colin Dunlop, former Dean of Lincoln and Bishop Suffragan of Jarrow, died yesterday in hospital in Chichester at the age of 70. With the death of Colin Dunlop one of the few remaining links has been broken with that brilliant group of priests, musicians and artists who found a spiritual home and an exciting sphere of work at St. Mary's, Primrose Hill, in the early part of this century.

Born July 1897, and brought up in a Presbyterian family, it was while living in Hampstead as a young man that he was captivated by the life and worship at St. Mary's, where the late Dean of Chichester, A.S. Duncan-Jones, had just succeeded Percy Dearmer as incumbent.

After serving in the First World War from 1915 to 1919, he took his degree at New College Oxford, offered himself for ordination, and was invited by Duncan-Jones to a first curacy at Primrose Hill, where he stayed for five happy and fruitful years, from 1922 to 1927. Here he gained that love of liturgical worship and of fine church music which was to remain with him for the rest of his days and which later found expression in his chairmanship of the committee of the English Hymnal, in the publication of several works for the Alcuin Club, in his book, *Anglican Public Worship*, and in his chairmanship for a number of years of the Church of England Liturgical Commission.

After the short period as domestic chaplain to the then Bishop of London, Winnington-Ingram, he went to be chaplain at H.M. Legation at Stockholm, from where he was called by the late Bishop of Chichester, Dr Bell, to be his domestic chaplain for three years. After a chaplaincy at Baghdad and two incumbencies in Sussex, he became in 1940 Provost of St. Mary's Cathedral, Edinburgh. In 1944 he was consecrated Bishop Suffragan of Jarrow, and with it was also appointed Archdeacon of Auckland, resigning in 1949 to become Dean of Lincoln, where he remained until his retirement in 1964.

He was much in demand as an able and attractive preacher - though never a superficial one – and was Select Preacher to the U of Cambridge, 1947, to the U of Oxford 1950–1951 and 1960–1962.

As a young man he was extraordinarily handsome; but his appearance, his charm of manner and his refinement of taste were outward signs of an inward beauty of spirit and character which deeply endeared him to all who came to know him intimately. He was a good and Godly priest, a man of prayer, and there are many who will remember his ministry with gratitude to God.'

EPILOGUE

A T THE END of this attempt to give a true portrait of my father and his life, the question now remains: how is one to think of all this? What does it all mean? I shall end with two attempts at an answer:

The first is that of a priest who had known Colin well for much of his own ministry, and wrote to Mary one of the very many letters of condolence she received after his death:

He has been a friend and father to me, in ways and manner not to be forgotten. I am a younger disciple of that glorious and stately serving in the House of God that has tumbled from fashion these last years, but retains its rightness and but sleeps in the custody of the children of the Beloved's Father. What Colin did and became are wonderfully united. One watched him battle with a wound in temperament, emerge into a wonderful measure of peace and poise, and then a new form of the conflict with the coming of full years' disabilities.

Things happened at Lincoln that are part of its history now, and a lot of us he helped, opened up new insights, encouraged, led and taught us things that have been good knowing. Such which seem at the time so much more fragile and transitory than the solid things of obvious achievement, have in them, given to them, an abiding force beyond all the present muddled visibilities. In the mysterious mercy of our maker and perfecter may Colin taken to pieces come together again in the wondrous way intended for him, amidst relationships that are the very activity of the divine loving, and be it given you to sense the truth possessing him.

The second is that of Mary herself, written 22 years after Colin's death, years in which her faith had wavered greatly and almost disappeared at times:

Today as I washed up the breakfast things and listened to a Radio programme I had a sort of minor revelation. I was listening to an interview with the (black) athlete who won a Gold Medal in the recent athletic championships in sport.

He spoke very modestly and convincingly about his running and his Christian belief that his ability was a gift from God that he was bound to use in whatever way he perceived God's will for him was, with the unspoken corollary that if he failed that was also something that could be used as part of God's will for him. It all fitted in perfectly with the speaker on *Prayer for the Day* who chose as his own the words of Jesus in Gethsemane – 'Father all things are possible with thee. Remove this cup from me – nevertheless not my will, but yours be done.' One always thinks of the 'cup' as being some terrible suffering and disaster or overwhelming fear. Today it came to me that this cup might also be some quite gradual loss or curtailment – or even the withdrawal of one of

God's own gifts to us. Because it seemed to me that I couldn't with sincerity pray the prayer *from myself* about sufferings which the mercy of God hasn't allowed to befall me in my weakness.

I felt uneasy about this – but after hearing the young athlete it came to me that the will of God might be the gradual removal of gifts and powers which were his gift. I thought briefly of the loss of my voice (for singing) and the increasing difficulty I have with my legs in walking and my fingers in sewing. These losses are the inevitable results of aging and not to be compared with losing sight or hearing or becoming crippled, but they are real and a 'cup' however tiny which I don't want to drink. But God gives me the loss as he gave me the power, and as in the right time he will give me the gift of death as he gave me life.

I think I have known this before – the 'revelation' was not about myself, but about Colin. The loss of his reasoning and intellectual powers, as well as the physical deterioration of his body, the loss of the power of communication and mutual recognition between him and me – the loss as it seemed and still seems of a precious and unreplaceable relationship, this was indeed a 'cup' for both of us, and I have gone on thinking in my selfishness as though God was giving it to me only. But it was *his* 'cup', and he had to drink it and in him Christ was suffering and Christ has triumphed. I believe this now. I'll be sure to go on forgetting it and thinking self-centredly but one short flash has brought understanding. Deo Gratias! I'll try to be more grateful.

Mary herself died quietly on 13 December 1999, on her 88th birthday, in a care home in Oxford, round the corner from the house of my brother Bede and his wife, Carolyn.

Appendix I

THE ASSYRIAN MASSACRE

Report on the events of July and August 1933 by the Civil Chaplain in Baghdad, the Revd Colin Dunlop

The occasion which prompts the request by the Foreign Relations Committee of the Church Assembly for a full report on the Assyrian situation is presumably the recent massacre of a large number of the Assyrians, followed by the deportation of the Assyrian Patriarch, Mar Shimun, and of his family, and the appeal by Mar Shimun to the League of Nations. The writer of the report is in no sense an expert, and his opportunities of investigation are those of any ordinary British Resident in Baghdad. He has however availed himself of the privilege of several conversations with the British Ambassador, Sir Francis Humphrys, both before his departure from Iraq in June 1933 and after his return in August; with the British Chargé d'Affaires during Sir Francis's absence when the massacre took place, and with the senior Officer of the British Military Mission to the Iraq Army. He has in addition had many conversations with Mar Shimun both before and during his detention in Baghdad during the summer and during his exile in Cyprus; with the Patriarch's aunt, the Lady Surma; with the Revd J.B.Parfil, the American clergyman who for the last eight years has presided over the educational affairs of the Assyrians and who knows their circumstances intimately. The writer however has never visited that part of Iraq where the majority of Assyrians live [he did later], nor has he any acquaintance with many of the Iraqi administrators and politicians.

In order to present a coherent account it is necessary to call to mind as briefly as possible the events which have led up to the recent crisis. The events will be well known to many of the readers of this report and they are outlined merely to give a more or less finished picture of the whole and to put the recent happenings in their proper setting.

The Assyrians, except for a tiny minority, are not natives of the country now called Iraq. It was not by their own free choice that they came here. Having been for centuries desirous of living under a Christian regime, they readily responded to the invitation of the Allies to turn against their Moslem overlords, the Turks, during the Great War. The invitation, originally given by the Russians, was reiterated by the British later in the war and there can be no doubt that we benefited greatly by their gallant and steadfast resistance to Turks, Kurds and Persians, a resistance which cost them the sacrifice of countless lives. But their alliance with us cost them not only their lives but also territory and they were gradually forced out of their homes in the mountains of Kurdistan and the plains around Lake Urmi which they had occupied for centuries. Towards the end of the war they were assembled in Hamadan in Persia and it was the British who then brought them into Iraq and settled them in a vast refugee camp. Their assistance to us, though no doubt in Assyrian interests, was encouraged by us with promises that they would not suffer on account of their decision, and what they had lost would be made good. The promises were no doubt vague, of that I am not certain, but coming from the representatives of a powerful and Christian Empire, they were accepted by this small and desperate people as genuine and serious. There can be no doubt either that they were made by us because we really needed the help which the promises would encourage.

In the years which immediately followed the war, the British had many problems to solve in Iraq. The problem of what to do with the Assyrians was only one of many. The impartial observer reading the minutes of the Permanent Mandates Commission sessions and other documents, cannot avoid the impression that our efforts to find the Assyrians a new permanent home, though numerous, were not pursued with that vigour which the payment of a debt of honour demands. The matter seems continually to have been allowed to stand over; what are sometimes spoken of as 'larger issues' were allowed to take precedence; the requisite pressure was not brought to bear at crucial moments. Though the British seemed ready to pay a price for the honouring of their word, frequently repeated, they were not ready to pay a *high* price. But meanwhile we continued to make use of the Assyrians. We mobilised the pick of their men into the Assyrian levies, which were used on many occasions for the pacification of the country. We should have had to use more British troops in the country, for a longer period, had we not had the assistance of the Assyrians. They made our work in Iraq more easy and less costly.

During all this time efforts were being made to repatriate or at least find new permanent homes for the Assyrians. The great opportunity was lost when we agreed to the drawing of the frontier line between Turkey and Iraq in such a way that the Hakkiari Mountains, the old home of the mountain Assyrians, passed to Turkey and not to Iraq. It is still difficult to understand how, in spite of the strong recommendations of the League of Nations Frontier Commission this fatal blunder was allowed to occur. The Turks did not really want these mountains, for to this day they are uninhabited. It points to the fact alluded to above; namely that we have shown throughout a strange lack of resolution in the settlement of the Assyrian problem.

Settlement in Iraq became the next problem now that repatriation was deemed impossible. Scheme after scheme was mooted, toyed with, and abandoned. The original idea was that the Assyrians should be settled in a compact group and that they should continue to enjoy 'a certain measure of autonomy', that they should be granted the privilege which they had had from the Turks 'officially or unofficially' before the war. This seems to have been the condition envisaged both by the Covenant of the League of Nations and by President Wilson's 'Fourteen Points' in the cases of freed minorities of the old Ottoman Empire.

No doubt one reason for the dilatoriness shown by the British in settling the Assyrians was the expectation that we should hold the Mandate of Iraq for at least twenty-five years. When the decision to abandon the mandatory responsibility at a much earlier date and to propose Iraq for membership of the League of Nations was made, the whole position changed. British anxiety was largely shifted from considerations of the internal welfare of the people in Iraq, to the securing of a satisfactory treaty with the country so soon to obtain its independence. The relations of autonomous Iraq to Great Britain as a foreign power became far more urgent than the welfare of minorities in Iraq. The Assyrian question took a back seat, and the question of their future and that of the other minorities in Iraq was not even mentioned in the Treaty. This was left to the 'Guarantees' exacted from Iraq by the League in 1932. It is hard to believe that anyone at all conversant with the nature of Iraqi politicians could have really believed that these guarantees meant much. It is difficult also to understand, on the more general side, how our representatives at Geneva could have expressed such confidence in the fitness of Iraq to govern itself, let alone the minorities. The Permanent Mandates Commission was clearly sceptical. With all our imperial experience we had found it a difficult task to manage this turbulent country, faced as it is with problems and clashes of interest of even wider scope than is the case in India. How could the Iraqis, for centuries under the domination of an imperial power, hope to accomplish at this stage what we had found so difficult ourselves? Yet we did express our confidence in their ability and even staked our national moral credit on the result.

It may be said in passing that the writer has scarcely ever heard any of the British officials in Iraq speak of the Iraqis and their powers of government with anything but the most profound distrust and even contempt, *when speaking off their guard.*

Political situation of Iraq since entry into the League

When Iraq found itself an independent power in the autumn of 1932, its rulers discovered quickly, if they had not known it before, that it was far from being a united country. The Kurds in the North had been silenced, largely owing to the work of the British Air Force, but they had not been satisfied. In the Spring of this year there were ominous rumblings from the mountains which, as it happened, came to nothing. But the Iraqi politicians have few illusions as to any fundamental loyalty of the Kurds to the central Arab Government. The Bedouin tribesmen, a very powerful factor in the country, as we discovered in the 1920 rebellion, have little community of interest in or love for the semi-westernised Effendi of the towns in general, of the Baghdad politicians in particular. But the most serious danger, which became apparent during the early part of this year, was the growing cleavage between Sunni and Shiah. Nearly all the Government posts are occupied by Sunnis, though of the two sects they are the smaller. The Sunnis however have availed themselves of the opportunities of imbibing Western education to a far greater extent than the more conservative Shiahs, and are undoubtedly as a whole more capable of government and administration. A serious cleavage was narrowly averted in May this year, as the result of the publication of a booklet entitled 'Arab Nationalism in the scales', in which the author, a Sunni, made statements which the Shiah population found highly unpalatable. The affair, however, passed off peacefully, except for a minor demonstration, for the author was sentenced to a short term of imprisonment.

This brief excursion into general political matters has been made to show how desirable it must have been to the Government to divert the attention of these conflicting Moslem interests to a common enemy. It has been noticeable that, as the Shiah-Sunni clash became more open, the tone of the Arab Press became more and more hostile to the Assyrians and more and more hostile to the British. Whereas two newspapers were suspended by the Government for giving publicity to Sunni-Shiah hostility, no such action has been taken against papers publishing anti-British or anti-Assyrian propaganda, in spite of protests from the British Embassy.

Side by side with this Press propaganda, common to a greater or lesser extent to all Arab newspapers, occurred attacks or mere innuendoes in the speeches in the Chamber of Deputies in the same direction. The Government took no steps to disassociate itself from such views. The inference is that the Government had, at the least, no wish to discourage them.

Goverment Policy towards the Assyrians, 1933

The Iraqi Government was not, however, so foolish as to side openly with the more extreme of the anti-Assyrians. It had realised that some sort of a land settlement must be prepared. It engaged a British settlement officer to assist in the work. The engagement of Major Thompson, a stranger to Iraq, in this capacity, was the result of an undertaking Iraq had made to the League. The Government made it quite clear that this officer's function was purely advisory. A sum of £13,000 was voted to prepare a piece of land, and irrigation works were begun to make it more habitable. Unfortunately, this scheme only provided for 600 families. The total number of Assyrians, none of whom *owns* any land, is estimated at 37,000. Even reckoning eight to a family, it will be seen that the scheme would only accommodate a small fraction of the whole. In addition, the Government made it clear that their future plans for settlement would not provide for settlement in a homogeneous group, but that the Assyrians would be scattered about the country in small 'homogeneous units'. It announced that, in any case, no land was available for settlement of the Assyrians in a single group. It will be remembered that this fact was deliberately questioned by the Permanent Mandates Commission in their 1932 session when they declared it not proven. When the writer mentioned this fact in conversation with the British Ambassador the latter pronounced this to be a 'piece of impertinence'. It may be true that settlement in a homogeneous group is impracticable. But Mr Parfil, who knows the mountains intimately, tells me that settlement in three large groups would certainly be possible and that such an arrangement would have been accepted by Mar Shimun.

Simultaneously with the preparation of its settlement scheme, the Government engaged upon a campaign of undermining the unity of the Assyrian people by attacking the Patriarch, and attempting to destroy his authority. This began on his return from Geneva in January this year. His statements at Geneva regarding his non-confidence in the Iraqi government had, not unnaturally, annoyed the powers that be. The Government officials in the villages of the North started on an attempt to wean the village headmen from their allegiance to Mar Shimun and in many small ways persecuted those who refused to forswear his authority. It is stated that they actually paid certain Assyrians, who objected to Mar Shimun, to act as 'official' Assyrian leaders. It seems beyond doubt that, whatever happened in the villages, it became clear to the rank and file of the Assyrians that their existence as a nation and as a chuch was being systematically threatened by the Government. This was further illustrated by the detention of Mar Shimun in Baghdad. He had gone there as a free man on the invitation of the Minister of the Interior in May. When however he refused to abdicate his temporal authority, he was forbidden to leave Baghdad and remained a virtual prisoner, residing in the YMCA. It was announced by the Government that his detention was due to a refusal by Mar Shimun to be loyal to King Faisal and to refrain from interfering in the Government's settlement scheme. What he actually refused to do was to sign a single document on which he was asked, not only to promise allegiance to the King and to refrain from interference in the settlement scheme, but also, *on the same document*, to abdicate his temporal authority. He naturally refused to do this. Whatever one's views may be as to the rightness or wrongness of the combination of temporal and spiritual authority in a single individual, it is clearly unreasonable to expect the holder of this twofold office to abandon it upon the peremptory word of an external authority, especially when signs were not wanting that the demand was a part of a general scheme to abolish everything distinctive about Assyrian nationality and the coherence of the Assyrians as a Christian tribal group. The Government's policy was to reduce Mar Shimun's authority to that enjoyed, for instance, by the Chaldaean Patriarch, or by the Syrian Catholic Archbishop. But these two prelates rule over communities which have not in the past enjoyed anything like the 'separateness' enjoyed by the essentially tribal Assyrians, and it was this very separateness which the Assyrians have been led throughout to expect they would be granted, and without which a tribal people cannot easily exist. It is often said that the difficulties of the Assyrian people have been brought about by the 'obstinacy' of Mar Shimun and his willingness to sacrifice the welfare of his people in order to preserve his full prestige as Patriarch. The truth is that he has by consistent courage and patience refused to surrender what is really vital to the Assyrians as a coherent tribal group; he has guarded the keystone of the whole arch. As well expect the Muntafiq or Shammah tribes to exist without their Sheikh, as the Assyrians to continue without their Patriarch in possession of his temporal authority. If the sovereignty of the Iraqi state is not endangered by the existence of Bedouin Sheikhs wielding authority over their tribes, why is the authority of the Assyrian Sheikh such an obstacle to Iraqi unity?

It can be imagined what the effect of the detention of Mar Shimun must have had on the great mass of the Assyrian people. They regard his office with an even greater veneration than many devout Roman Catholics have for the Pope. The news of his detention came as a climax to all the other evidences that the existence of a people was being systematically attacked.

Finally occurred the Mosul meeting on July 10th, at which the Government plans for resettlement were put to an assembly of Assyrian representatives. The plan, outlined above, was proposed, the plan that meant settlement of six hundred families only, the rest to go on living as before in the conditions described by the Rapporteur of the Permanent Mandates Commission last year as 'precarious and miserable'. In addition, it meant living in small isolated groups among the Kurds, who, besides being their traditional enemies, were not likely to be more favourably disposed towards the Assyrians in view of their having been used by the British to quell many Kurdish insurrections since the war. The Government put its plans before the Assyrians at this meeting through the mouths of the Arab Mutasarriff of Mosul, a British Administrative Inspector (servant of the Iraqi Government) named Colonel Stafford, and Major Thompson, the Advisory Settlement Officer (also a servant of the Iraqi Government). The plan was outlined in the form of an ultimatum; the Assyrians were told what the plan was, and then that if they did not like it, they could leave the country. There seems no doubt that the alternative of leaving the country was quite definitely proposed by the Government's representatives. It was this alternative which many of the leaders, in their desperation, immediately and literally accepted.

Departure for Syria

It was doubtless an unwise action to leave Iraq so precipitately and without warning the Government. Technically, no doubt, the Assyrians were performing an illegal act, since it is stated that the Government had recently forbidden movements of armed men in groups of more than about a dozen strong. But it seems absurd to attach moral blame to an action commenced under stress of fear and despair. The charge of moral wrongdoing must rather rest on those who, however legally, brought about the circumstances which drove the Assyrians to this ill-advised course of action. Mar Shimun is, of course, blamed for it. I have never heard any proof that orders to go to Syria were issued by Mar Shimun from his quarters in Baghdad, watched as they were, day and night, by plain-clothes detectives. Mr Lampard, the British Superintendent of the YMCA, told me that, as far as he could tell, no such orders could have been given. The only relevant evidence I have ever heard of is an attempt by a Police Official to induce persons to give evidence of such a kind as would lead people to suppose that Mar Shimun had given the order. The attempt however was not successful.

Whatever their authority, large numbers of Assyrians began to cross over the frontier into Syria towards the end of July near Faish Khabur, a village on the Tigris in the extreme north-west corner of Iraq. They crossed in large and small parties, taking with them their rifles, of which they were legally in possession. It is not certain how many crossed. The Government estimate was 1300; Mr Parfil thinks there may have been as many as 2000. Only men went. At the frontier, Malek Yaku (I think) sent a message to the Government explaining the cause of their departure and asking that their wives and children might be protected until they were in a position to follow their men-folk to their hoped-for homes in Syria.

How this belief that the French would settle them in their mandated territories arose, I have no knowledge. Whether the French did make overtures, definite or indefinite, to the Assyrians at this time, I do not know. There are some who have no hestitation in saying that the whole business was engineered by the French in order to make trouble in Iraq, so as to have a good excuse for prolonging their own mandate in Syria. I have never heard any proof adduced that this was the case. It is however plain that the Assyrians had reason to expect a sympathetic reception by the French. They were not disappointed. Though they disarmed their visitors, the French fed them, and provided some shelter. Meanwhile, on the Iraqi side of the frontier, military forces began to assemble, who prevented other bands of Assyrians following the example of the earlier parties.

Return from Syria

After some ten days the Assyrians who had crossed the frontier were informed by the French authorities that they must return to Iraq. Their rifles were returned to them. The Iraqi Goverment says that the Assyrians were warned by them that they could only return to Iraq on condition of their surrendering their arms.

What happened next is still, for the ordinary observer, wrapped in mystery. The Government version is that the Assyrians, under plea of coming across to surrender their arms, came across and immediately surprised and attacked the Iraqi army under cover of twilight, in a systematic and scientific manner. The only evidence for this is the word of the Iraqi Military Command whose later behaviour toward the Assyrians makes it difficult to accept their word unreservedly. Though none of them were actually present when the clash occurred (or for twenty four hours previously) the officers of the British

Military Mission profess their belief in the accuracy of the Iraqi army version. I have patiently listened to a detailed account of the battle by a senior officer of the British Military Mission, but at the end I was still unable to understand how a well equipped military force, trained by British officers, could be surprised by a smaller body of irregular fighting men, whose intention to cross the river was known, and whose arrival was expected.

What may be called the Assyrian version is that the decision to cross the Tigris and surrender was not unanimous; that the party which had so decided was actually in the course of doing so, when the dissenting party appeared on the banks excitedly remonstrating with the surrender party (many of whom were in mid-stream); that during the resultant confusion a shot was inadvertently fired by an unknown person from an unknown quarter and that this had the effect of a battle signal upon all concerned.

I do not pretend to decide which is the correct version. What is certain is that a clash did take place, that many casualties occurred on either side, that many of the Assyrians retreated into Syria (where presumably they still are), that others pushed past the Iraqi army and scattered in the mountains. The latter were pursued by the army who claim that they forced many to surrender.

The Massacre

I deliberately refrain from emphasising alleged atrocities on either side at this point. It is beyond dispute that Bakir Sidky, the Iraqi Commander in the field, did order the shooting of fourteen Assyrian prisoners. Other similar acts may or may not have occurred on both sides. But in view of later events such acts pale into insignificance. I refer primarily to the massacre in Simel. A detailed account of this appears among the accompanying documents. If the evidence of women, even in a high state of excitement and indignation, is never to be taken as proof or indication, then of course there is no evidence that the massacre in Simel was in fact committed by the armed forces of the Iraqi crown. But the testimony of these women refugees from Simel is so persistent that the massacre of from 200 to 600 men in Simel was carried out by 'men in blue shirts' that it is impossible to set it aside. Blue shirts were worn by the soldiers of the Machine-Gun Corps of the Iraqi Army. I do not believe that the women who gave this evidence were in the least aware of the special gravity with which massacre by the regular Army would be regarded, as opposed to massacre by Kurdish irregular or Arab tribesmen. To them it is all one who killed their men-folk. The evidence is therefore all the more difficult to set aside. Kurds and Bedouin tribesmen accompanied the soldiers but again the evidence that they were not responsible for the systematic killing of the Assyrian men is quite persistent.

The massacre is all the more appalling in that unarmed men from surrounding villages were sent to Simel on the plea that they would be safe there; also that many of the men massacred were what the Iraqi Government calls 'loyal' Assyrians, men who had renounced the authority of Mar Shimun. Some of them were Presbyterians.

It is said by the Government that this massacre was the work of Kurdish irregulars; others say that, even if soldiers were responsible, Bakir Sidky was not cognisant, still less the Iraqi Government. But if this was so, why were all English and American people who either lived in the neighbourhood, or whose duties normally took them there, withdrawn from the neighbourhood or prohibited from entering it? Why was Mr Cumberland, the American missionary resident in Dohuk not far from Simel withdrawn? Why was Captain Sargon, a British police adviser, whose duties took him all over the area, brought back from Mosul to Baghdad? Why at a later stage were the officers of the British Air Force, who went up north to superintend the relief of the relations of soldiers of the Assyrian levies, prevented from going further north than Mosul? It cannot be doubted that things had happened and were perhaps still happening up in the mountain villages, which the Government were desperately anxious to conceal.

Deportation of Mar Shimun

Shortly after the massacre, and the victory of the Iraqi army over the Assyrian irregulars, the Government turned its attention to the punishment of such Assyrian leaders as were within its power. So great was the surprise and joy of the Government at the success of its military forces against the Assyrians, that certain sections were said to be in favour of very drastic treatment of the leaders. The arraignment of Mar Shimun for High Treason was suggested and it was a foregone conclusion that, were this to be done, the death sentence would follow. More moderate opinion was in favour of deportatation; but a country without colonies cannot deport anyone unless some foreign power is willing to receive the deportee. Probably moved by the possibility that physical violence would be done to the Patriarch were he to remain in Iraq, the British Government consented to receive Mar Shimun, if deported, on British soil. But a technical difficulty now appeared. The constitution lays down quite unconditionally that no Iraqi subject can be either deported or tortured. The Council of Ministers actually passed an Emergency Decree deciding that if an Iraqi subject who did not himself, or whose parents did not, normally reside in Iraq before the war behaved in a manner which was deemed prejudicial to the interests of law and public security, his or her nationality could be cancelled. On the strength of this, Mar Shimun's Iraqi nationality was at once cancelled and the deportation order issued. Whether the Council of Ministers has legal power to amend the constitution and act upon it before such amendment has been ratified by the Senate and Chamber of Deputies is a matter for the jurists to decide.

With Mar Shimun were deported his father and brother. A British aeroplane conveyed them to Cyprus. A week later Lady Surma and a number of other members of the Patriarchal family, mainly women and children, were similarly deported.

About seven Assyrian leaders, not connected with the Patriarchal family, were transferred from the mountains of the North to Nasiriyah, a town near the Euphrates marshes in the South of Iraq. No news of these had yet been made public when I left Baghdad in early September.

The triumphant Army

Everything possible has been done by the Government and other administrative powers in Iraq to make the army thoroughly proud of its actions in the North. The fulsome joy with which the Army was received in Mosul and Baghdad can only be understood when it is remembered that this is the first victory which has attended the unaided arms of the Arab soldiers. Their excursions against the Kurds had not been marked with success. The Assyrians were reckoned better fighters than the Kurds and an encounter with them (although the Assyrians have no machine-guns) was not expected to be a certain prelude to victory. Yet victory they actually achieved and great was the universal relief and joy. It might be thought that, in spite of this unlooked-for success, arrangements might have been made for a very quiet and unobtrusive return of the troops in view of the massacre. But such was not the case. No effort was spared to make the return of the victorious troops an affair of national and religious self-glorification. Triumphal arches were erected in Mosul. Baghdad was gay with flags and wreaths. In each place the populace turned out to greet the heroes, armed with swords, daggers, revolvers and clubs. Water-melons stained with red pigment and carved to represent Assyrian heads were carried and transfixed with bayonets and daggers in Mosul, though this dramatic improvisation was forbidden in Baghdad. The newspapers kept the people up to the correct pitch; the dead soldiers were 'martyrs' who had died to protect the 'sacred country'. The public were reminded that the slaughtered Assyrians were Christians. The expectation that the Government might repudiate the massacre was dampened by the promotion of Bakir Sidky and the granting of a year's seniority to all officers who had taken part in the expedition. Free coffee for three days, and free shaves for the same period, were decreed for the rank and file, and presumably paid for by the Government. This is the first answer of the Iraqi Government to those who criticise them for the massacre.

'Hushing up'

The gesture of defiance to the civilised world implied in the triumphant and victorious troops is not the only sign that the Iraqi Government intends to try and bluff the whole matter through. Unfortunately, its conscience is so guilty that it has lost all sense of proportion. The telegram to the League of Nations giving the Government's story of what had happened is worded with more enthusiasm than sense. Its exuberant professions of innocence and its puerile attempts to express moral indignation with the wicked Assyrians are so childish that they will deceive nobody. Similarly, the congratulations of the Government by the octogenarian Chaldaean Patriarch extorted by threats (so it is most credibly asserted), will carry no weight. It is significant that in this alleged chorus of approval from non-Assyrian Iraqi Christians, the voice of the French Apostolic delegate, resident in Mosul, is silent – even in Government reports.

In short, the government plainly intends to deny the massacre or at best attribute it to the lawless Kurds. It is much to be hoped that the British Government will not try to assist the Iraqi Government in smoothing over the deplorable events of the past few months. There are, however, many British residents in Baghdad who see signs that we may not have the courage to admit at Geneva that the statements made there last year were over-sanguine, and that we may try to obscure the seriousness of the situation for which we shouldered deliberately the moral responsibility.

The Future

It is difficult to see how the Assyrians can continue to live under the Iraqi crown, unless a very special regime is set up within the Mosul vilayet by the League of Nations. Paper guarantees, however fulsome, are plainly no use. But as it seems unlikely that Iraq would peacefully submit to any external interference in their concerns, and as a very strong military force would be necessary if the country were to be again occupied by a Mandatory Power, this possibility may be set aside as impracticable. The only alternative is for the Assyrians to leave Iraq and find homes elsewhere. This can only be done with the efficient assistance of a Great Power which is prepared to make some sacrifices to bring it about. It is surely the task of Great Britain to do this and to do it thoroughly, in fulfilment of its pledges.

Mar Shimun himself told me on September 17th, 1933, that he was in favour of a migration from Iraq should a special regime in Iraq with efficient guarantees prove impossible. Nothing is more touching than the continual faith of the Assyrian Patriarch (after many disappointments) that in the end the British will not fail his people. It is much to be hoped that he will not be disappointed.

D.C. Dunlop, Civil Chaplain, Baghdad
September 1933

Appendix II

LETTER FROM KURDISTAN

from Colin to Mary

Diana, Kurdistan, 25.xi.33

My lovely bride to be

Yesterday and today have been among the happiest in my time out here, and certainly the most interesting of all. I set off in a car from Kirkuk about 9 am yesterday with Yussuf and two woolly Kurds. The road was at first rocky and bumpy, very rough and primitive, and the distant hills looked dull at first. Gradually however the whole empty landscape became very subtly coloured. The distant mountains became a sort of misty sapphire, the nearer hills a creamy purple, and the flat ploughland on all sides a mass of browns and greens of infinite variety of subtle, pale, shades. We passed Altun Keupri (the Golden Bridge), a large Kurdish village, which before my later experiences seemed very picturesque. After two hours we got to Erbil which is built on a high rock in the middle of a big plain, walled all round. It is the oldest inhabited city in the world and was flourishing long before Rome and Athens were thought of. It is the modern Arbela where Alexander the Great distinguished himself. We changed passengers here, and while the car waited in the Khan for the new ones, I walked up the cliff to the town proper, entered its massive gate and strolled through a maze of the narrowest streets I have ever known. Kurds in their outlandish dress everywhere and little Turkish children with large ear-rings and old little faces and clothes down to their feet. Then we motored on, after taking as passengers three of the fiercest and most disreputable Kurds I have ever seen; yellow teeth, bloodshot eyes, big knives in sash, and rifles. To ingratiate myself I offered them cigarettes continually which they eagerly accepted. They laughed and talked away among themselves all the way; Yussuf, who talks Kurdish and every other language fluently, held forth to them; I munched sandwiches. Soon we entered the Kurdish foot-hills and imperceptibly the scenery got less and less like Iraq, and more green and beautiful. Lovely little slender poplars with bright yellow and green leaves appeared everywhere, nice fresh little valleys and streams. Near Shaqlawah the hills were all red, which, with the greens and browns and yellows of the trees and shrubs, made a lovely picture. All this time we got higher and higher up the 'garden path' road; in the distance snowy mountains appeared. Then we got to a lovely village in a big valley where Mar Yussuf, the Metropolitan of the

Assyrians (second in command to Mar Shimun) lives. They told me he had gone for a walk so I went to meet him and presently I saw a tall white figure coming towards me. He looked most apostolic and beautiful in his coarse white cassock and green Assyrian turban, with his tranquil expression, brown eyes and full black beard. He took me to his 'palace', a small neat little farmhouse, and we had coffee and a long talk. He gave me a bunch of flowers from his very English-looking garden when I left. He took me into his tiny church where a big crowd of children and men had assembled and showed me some of the old Syriac service books and one new MS one by his own hand. It was a delightful half hour and I am quite unable in words to convey the charm of it or of the Metropolitan. I shall never forget the sight of him as he walked back from my car to the church. I don't know why it moved me so, and I wanted to cry and laugh all at once.

Then we went on, getting higher and higher, and then down a bit to the famous Rowanduz gorge, a magnificent spectacle, finer than anything of its kind I have ever seen; great perpendicular rocks towering up with quite a narrow passage between and down below a rushing stream. Waterfalls, bridges, patches of autumn-tinted vegetation, Assyrians or Kurds in their picturesque dresses going home with their cows and goats. Suddenly we overtook a herd of about 20 camels, untended and unharnessed. They began to trot stupidly down the road ahead of us, then they began to canter and then to gallop. They looked unutterably stupid and I thought my Kurdish fellow travellers would die of laughter. Finally the camels got off the road and we passed, winding through the deep gorge. It was incredibly romantic and beautiful. Just as we got to the top of the gorge we met an immense tribe of Kurds on trek coming in the opposite direction. They were more picturesquely dressed than any I had yet seen, in bright colours; the men with their hawk-like faces, some of them smoking cigarettes in wooden holders over a foot long. The women were very handsome and walked with an exaggerated sway of the hips, all very haughty-looking and contemptuous and often smiling and laughing.They had with them all their flocks and herds – cows, donkeys, goats. All the animals had panniers filled with household goods and covered with brilliant coloured carpets. Even the bullocks carried panniers, which looked extremely comic. There was enormous confusion, the animals terrified at our car and herded towards the edge of the ravine; the men and women shouted and laid about them with their shepherd crooks; little boys shouted and yelled and struggled with refractory beasts. It was a wonderful burst of life, and life in the raw, with more beauty and colour than I have ever seen in ten short minutes.

Finally in the dusk we reached Diana. The Consulate is a rough long low building of mud and wood, rather attractive. It was very nice seeing Jack, very proud and happy in his little kingdom. Huge wood fires (one in my bedroom), oil lamps, a marvellous hot bath in a zinc tub and much pleasant talking and joking. Diana lies in a big open valley hedged in with large and friendly mountains. Being here is like 'being abroad' as compared with the Iraq I have hitherto known. This morning we motored to Rowanduz, the big Kurdish village nearby. Not a sign of Western civilization – all primitive and interesting. The shops most attractive. I have bought a little bright Kurdish jerkin for you. More tomorrow.

Mosul. 28.xi.33 My Sunday church-going in Diana is recorded in an article I have sent to the *Guardian* of which I will give you a copy[7]. On Monday morning I left Diana and came back through the Rowanduz gorge. The Kurdish nomads were *still* going through. In all, there were about 4,000. When we got into the sunlight on the other side of the gorge I took a number of photos of them which gave them much pleasure. I stopped again at Mar Yussuf's and then came on through Erbil to this place. On the way I visited a Syrian monastery of great age and much interest and beauty. I was given ceremonial coffee by the monks and we crawled along an underground passage, stooping, and saw the grave of the saint in whose honour the monastery is built. He is called Mar Behnam and he was a chieftain's son who was martyred under the Sassanian Kings. I wish I could tell you fully about it all, but I have written several reports and an article and my creative faculty is a little cramped. Since coming here I have seen some of the sufferings of our friends. It is pitiful and terrible. They are so good to each other. I am seriously thinking of giving no Christmas presents, but of devoting the money to the needs of the people here. Or at any rate, very small presents. I must try and persuade some Baghdad people ro give too.

Tomorrow I go up to the neighbourhood of Glencoe[8] where I am going to stay with one of the American missionaries. This morning I baptised a little baby after Mass and this evening we have evensong. I wish I were fit to preach to these people. How humbling it is to be brought face to face with poverty, destitution and the fear of persecution, 'We are like dogs running from Butcher's to Butcher's in search of scraps, driven away from each with a kick and a curse' – so one of the priests said to me. And my own extravagant selfishness means that directly or indirectly I am one of the butchers. I do need your help and wisdom and goodness to think out this money question. Is one entitled to *any* luxuries while neighbours are next door to destitution? Darling, I love you and want you. I will try and write more later this week.

Dohuk. 30.xi.33 I arrived here yesterday in pouring rain and a howling wind after a dull, damp journey in a car with 6 others (Kurds)! The Cumberlands – American Missionary and his wife – are most charming and wonderful people and I have enjoyed every moment of my 24-hour stay. Unfortunately it has been too wet to get out to Glencoe. We have walked round the village in the mud and rain and seen something of its life. A queer mixture of people make

---

[7] Colin decided to prevent the publication of this, since it might compromise Jack Finch. I have been unable to trace any ms copy.

[8] Colin used this name, site of a massacre, to refer to Simel, to avoid attracting the attention of the Iraq censor.

up its 3000 inhabitants: Kurds, Assyrians, Armenians, Jews, Turcomans. Little cottages of stone or mud brick. A mosque with one low minaret. All built on a series of abrupt hillocks, precipitous little streets, half cobbled, half mud. Looked very uncomfortable in the damp raw evening. We called on a weaver and watched him working on a flowered piece of blue cloth – the stuff they make the picturesque Kurdish trousers out of. Coffee was produced – a fearsome brew – other men dropped in and sat on their haunches talking to Roger Cumberland in Kurdish. We strolled on and the village butcher, a Turcoman, invited us into his house for a talk. A fine looking man with nice gay eyes and a generous expression. His unveiled wife moved silently about her domestic work in the background. He said he felt moved to ask C a question. He is a Moslem and he said he had been told that according to the Koran a butcher might kill two or three thousand sheep legally, but after that it became a sin. What did C's religion say? C said that according to Christianity if it was not a sin to do it once, no additional amount of times could make any difference. He thanked him. Then we called on an influential Kurdish Agha (sort of squire) we sat in a freezing semi-westernized house and talked. Good coffee and cigarettes.

Mosul. later Since writing the above I have motored back to Mosul. To go back to Dohuk – we returned from our stroll and spent the evening in the Cs' tiny but very cosy little house. We talked a lot and after dinner we had the gramophone – Stravinsky's 'Firebird', Dvorak's 'New World' Symphony and some Magic Flute. Although poor they insisted on buying a grand piano and bringing it up to their Highland home. After gramophone I did some songs: 'I attempt from Love's sickness to fly' (quite untrue) and I attempted Brahms' '*Du bist meine Königin*' (quite true) and some Negro Spirituals. After that I retired to bed in a little outhouse and slept warmly and comfortably. Mrs C has a vague look of you about her, though it is you with you left out, if you understand me. They are a dear couple. I wish it had been fine so that I could have seen the place properly and taken some photos. The country and hills seemed very beautiful through the mist, but even the beauty could not rob the scene of the sinister memory of August happenings.

In a few minutes I am going to see the Refugee camp here, and then I want to visit a number of Assyrian houses so as to see the conditions under which they are living. I have found an ally and friend in the British Consul here who fully shares my opinion and fears. He can't do much himself as he is hampered by his official position.

Tomorrow I leave Mosul in a car at 4 am and am going right through to Baghdad – a long and boring journey. When I get there I shall almost certainly find two letters from you which will fill me with joy. Goodbye my beloved dear. I am all yours.

Your undeserving and ardent lover
Colin

Photo 27: Colin's four sons: Francis and Charles (*upper*), Philip and Bede (*lower*), during a family holiday in Pembrokeshire, 1958.

Photo 28: Colin and Mary at Francis and Anna's wedding, 1962.

Photo 29: Colin and Mary with Francis and Philip and their families, 1966.

Photo 30: Post-retirement on beach with Mary, 1967.

Photo 31: Colin with Francis and his family, 1967.

INDEX

Page numbers in bold refer to photographs